The New Role of Labor Unions in the AI Era

Andrés J. Arenas Falótico
Alfonso X El Sabio University, Spain

Jessica Bayón Pérez
Universidad Internacional de la Rioja, Spain

IGI Global
Scientific Publishing
Publishing Tomorrow's Research Today

Vice President of Editorial Melissa Wagner
Director of Acquisitions Mikaela Felty
Director of Book Development Jocelynn Hessler
Production Manager Mike Brehm
Cover Design Jose Rosado

Published in the United States of America by
IGI Global Scientific Publishing
701 East Chocolate Avenue
Hershey, PA, 17033, USA
Tel: 717-533-8845
Fax: 717-533-7115
Website: https://www.igi-global.com E-mail: cust@igi-global.com

Library of Congress Cataloging-in-Publication Data

Names: Arenas, Andres, 1968- editor | Bayón Pérez, Jessica, 1993- editor
Title: The new role of labor unions in the AI era / edited by: Andres Arenas, Jessica Bayón Pérez.
Other titles: New role of labor unions in the artificial intelligence era
Description: Hershey, PA : IGI Global Scientific Publishing, [2025] | Includes bibliographical references and index. | Summary: "The advent of AI has ushered in an era of unprecedented change and complexity. Traditional roles and structures are being challenged and reshaped, and labor unions are no exception. This book aims to delve into the heart of this transformation, examining the new roles and responsibilities that labor unions are assuming in the AI era"-- Provided by publisher.
Identifiers: LCCN 2025000167 (print) | LCCN 2025000168 (ebook) | ISBN 9798369380499 hardcover | ISBN 9798369380505 paperback | ISBN 9798369380512 ebook
Subjects: LCSH: Labor unions--Technological innovations | Employees--Effect of technological innovations on | Industrial relations | Artificial intelligence--Industrial applications
Classification: LCC HD6490.C616 N49 2025 (print) | LCC HD6490.C616 (ebook) | DDC 331.880285/63--dc23/eng/20250410
LC record available at https://lccn.loc.gov/2025000167
LC ebook record available at https://lccn.loc.gov/2025000168
British Cataloguing in Publication Data
A Cataloguing in Publication record for this book is available from the British Library.

Table of Contents

Detailed Table of Contents

organizational transformation of unionism, including updating service structures, digitizing the union, and developing a proactive strategy towards occupational mental health. The chapter concludes by arguing that unions must adopt a proactive approach, use new technologies responsibly and collaborate with other social actors to protect the mental health of workers in the digital age.

Can generative AI replace artists? May the human creative process become obsolete or "inefficient"? How should Labor Union´s role be projected in the AI era? The presence of generative AI in the art industry has definitely disrupted the traditional process of creation and called into question the definition of art. The purpose of this chapter is to present an overview on the transformations of the role of Labor Unions in the art industry regarding the irruption of generative AI in the sector. The concept of intellectual property is intimately related to the idea of author; a status which has historically been granted only to humans. Nowadays, this exclusivity is placed in doubt. The intromission of a new actor in the art industry brings new challenges and opportunities which undeniably need to be faced and balanced by Labor Unions.

This chapter examines the challenges and adaptations of labour unions in the face of the gig economy and new forms of employment. It explores how workforce fragmentation, individualization of labour relations, and inadequate legal frameworks disrupt traditional union strategies. The study highlights innovative responses by unions, including new organizational approaches, representation models, alliances with social movements, and digital technology adoption. Drawing on recent literature and empirical studies, the paper provides a comprehensive analysis of the changing landscape of industrial relations. It emphasizes the need for unions to reinvent themselves while maintaining core values of solidarity and social justice. The research concludes by stressing the crucial role of unions in shaping a new social contract for the digital age and identifying areas for future research on collective organization in the gig economy.

This research examines the effects of artificial intelligence and automation on labour markets, socio-economic justice and trade unions. A hierarchical clustering analysis of 25 European countries shows that there are significant differences between countries in terms of their level of technological readiness, income inequality and union density. While Scandinavian countries were found to be successful in offsetting the negative effects of technological transformation with their strong trade union structures, these effects were found to have a deeper impact on income inequality and unemployment in countries such as Turkey and Greece. The study emphasises that trade unions should play a critical role in protecting workers' rights, reducing income inequality and supporting skills development programmes. The results suggest that processes of technological transformation need to be managed through policies that promote social justice.

Digital transformation, STEM, economic complexity and structural transformation in human capital essentially show a cyclical series of relationships and a process that are positively interconnected. However, the situation of trade unions, which are directly related to employment, which reflects the output status of human capital, is curious and constitutes the purpose of this paper. In line with this purpose, the developing role of trade unions in the digital transformation process is questioned in the paper.

Preface

The accelerating advancement of artificial intelligence (AI), automation, and data-driven technologies is reshaping labor markets at an unprecedented scale. These transformations challenge not only the structure and content of jobs but also the institutions historically responsible for defending workers' rights, most notably, labor unions. As the Fourth Industrial Revolution redefines production systems, decision-making processes, and workplace dynamics, questions about the role, relevance, and strategic capacity of unions have become central to both academic inquiry and policy debate.

The New Role of Labor Unions in the AI Era addresses these questions by offering a multidisciplinary and international examination of how labor unions are responding to the ongoing digitalization of work. The volume brings together a diverse set of case studies and conceptual reflections that reveal the complexity of union responses to technological innovation, ranging from institutional inertia and organizational resistance to legal advocacy, digital experimentation, and ethical intervention. Rather than promoting a uniform or prescriptive model, the book highlights the plurality of strategies through which unions are attempting to influence technological governance, assert worker protection, and remain relevant in fragmented labor markets.

At the heart of this inquiry lies a simple but profound provocation: What kind of future work do we want, and who gets to decide? The contributors to this volume recognize that AI is not merely a set of tools or systems, but a contested sociotechnical field that reflects deeper tensions between capital and labor, autonomy and control, inclusion and exclusion. In this landscape, unions are not just stakeholders, they are potential co-architects of digital transitions that foreground equity, human dignity, and democratic participation.

The subject matter of this book sits at the intersection of multiple global debates: the governance of AI, the future of work, the politics of data and automation, and the renewal of democratic institutions in the digital age. It speaks to the need for new institutional imaginary ones in which unions move beyond their traditional roles as negotiators of wages and conditions to become actors in the ethical and political shaping of technology itself.

Structured around a rich collection of different case studies and thematic analyses, the volume captures the structural challenges, cultural shifts, and institutional innovations taking place within the world of organized labor. The book not only documents how unions are adapting to technological change but also explores how they can lead processes of institutional reinvention and norm creation in response to digital disruption.

Ultimately, this book invites readers to reconsider unionism not as a remnant of the industrial age, but as a vital—and evolving—form of collective agency in the digital era. It argues that the future of labor will be shaped not just by algorithms and automation, but by the capacity of workers to organize, resist, and innovate within and beyond traditional institutional frameworks.

Amid the Fourth Industrial Revolution, artificial intelligence (AI), machine learning, robotics, and algorithmic management are transforming labor relations globally. These technologies are not only reshaping job content, recruitment systems, and performance metrics, they are also redefining the very structure of workplace governance, introducing new forms of surveillance, control, and inequality. While public discourse often emphasizes efficiency gains and productivity, the social consequences of these innovations remain deeply contested, particularly regarding workers' rights, representation, and wellbeing.

The integration of AI into labor systems has prompted renewed attention to ethical dilemmas, such as data privacy, algorithmic bias, and decision opacity. In parallel, new employment modalities—platform work, remote tasks, hybrid roles—are undermining traditional forms of collective bargaining and eroding the historical bases of union density. These shifts are not confined to high-income economies. Middle- and low-income countries are also experiencing rapid digitization, often without adequate regulatory safeguards or institutional frameworks to protect workers.

In this landscape of volatility, trade unions face both crisis and opportunity. On one hand, they confront declining membership, institutional fragmentation, and challenges in organizing dispersed or digitally mediated workers. On the other, unions possess unique potential to act as intermediaries of justice, ethical mediators, and co-governors of technology—provided they adapt their structures, tools, and strategies to the demands of the digital era.

This book enters the global conversation at a critical juncture. As countries grapple with designing inclusive digital transitions, there is a growing recognition that technological change is not destiny, but a political process. The presence—or absence—of strong, informed, and innovative labor unions will significantly influence whether AI enhances equity and democracy or deepens precarity and exclusion.

Furthermore, the COVID-19 pandemic has accelerated digital adoption across sectors, exposing the limits of existing labor protections and prompting urgent debates on algorithmic accountability, digital rights, and mental health at work. Against this backdrop, the contributions gathered in this volume provide grounded, comparative, and forward-looking insights into how labor unions can respond, resist, and reimagine their role.

By drawing on diverse national contexts—including Argentina, Mexico, Spain, Turkey, and others—this book sheds light on the uneven geographies of automation, the differentiated institutional capacities of unions, and the emergent strategies being tested on the ground. It offers not only diagnosis, but also a repertoire of potential responses, underscoring the relevance of organized labor as a central actor in shaping the social contract of the AI era.

This volume is intended for a broad and multidisciplinary audience that spans both academic and professional domains. It will be of particular interest to scholars and graduate students in the fields of labor studies, sociology of work, industrial relations, political economy, public policy, technology studies, and legal studies. Its thematic breadth and comparative orientation also make it suitable for interdisciplinary research centers focused on digital transformation, ethics of AI, and global governance.

Beyond academia, the book is especially relevant for trade union leaders, labor organizers, policymakers, public administrators, and corporate human resource strategists. As technological change increasingly intersects with employment law, labor negotiations, and workplace culture, this volume offers conceptual clarity and practical frameworks for navigating these complex transitions. Union professionals will find valuable insights into emerging strategies of negotiation, collective organization in digital environments, and participatory approaches to AI governance.

This book also serves as a resource for international organizations and development agencies, including those engaged in labor rights, technological capacity-building, or policy advisory work. Institutions such as the International Labour Organization (ILO), OECD, and UN agencies working on the future of work will find in these chapters grounded examples of how technological disruption intersects with national labor systems and institutional capacities.

Additionally, it addresses the needs of technology developers, data governance experts, and corporate actors seeking to understand the social implications of AI in the workplace. By foregrounding labor perspectives and ethical considerations, the volume contributes to bridging the gap between technological design and social accountability.

Finally, for university instructors, the book offers a timely and accessible collection of case studies and thematic analyses that can enrich curricula on the future of work, digital ethics, and labor law. Each chapter can serve as a standalone reading or as part of a broader syllabus on labor and digital society.

In sum, this volume speaks to all those engaged in shaping, understanding, or regulating the intersection between technology and labor in the 21st century. With this diverse and multidisciplinary audience in mind, the book unfolds through a carefully curated series of chapters that illuminate the evolving role of unions across regions, sectors, and institutional environments.

The volume opens with an in-depth examination of Valorian, a forward-thinking Spanish labor union that has successfully integrated artificial intelligence into its organizational operations. Through a comparative and historical lens, this case study illustrates how innovation and ethical commitment can coexist in union governance. By embedding AI into its internal processes, Valorian offers a compelling model of how unions can leverage technology to enhance member engagement, efficiency, and democratic participation while remaining true to the core values of labor representation.

Building on this momentum, the second contribution turns to the Argentine context, tracing the historical trajectory of unionism from colonial times to the challenges posed by AI-driven automation. This chapter provides a layered understanding of how institutional legacies and political fluctuations have shaped the Argentine labor movement, while also illuminating the ways in which unions are beginning to engage with digital technologies. By advocating for reskilling, policy innovation, and ethical frameworks for AI deployment, the chapter demonstrates the potential for trade unions in the Global South to actively shape technological transitions.

In a similar regional vein, the third chapter focused on Mexico. It examines the nascent integration of AI within Mexican trade unions, highlighting both the promise and the regulatory lag that characterizes the national context. By comparing the Mexican experience with global best practices, the authors offer a balanced view of the opportunities AI presents for union renewal and the risks it poses in terms of opacity, surveillance, and exclusion. The piece emphasizes the urgency of coordinated efforts between unions, employers, and the state to foster responsible AI governance and build institutional capacities attuned to workers' rights.

The volume then expands to a global comparative perspective, analyzing union responses to AI and automation across a diverse set of countries. This fourth chapter underscores the wide variance in institutional arrangements and strategic approaches, from coordinated social dialogue in Northern Europe to fragmented labor responses in emerging economies. What emerges is a portrait of both divergence and convergence—unions across contexts are grappling with similar dilemmas, yet their strategies reflect distinct histories, political economies, and levels of technological preparedness.

Finally, the Spanish case reappears in a broader conceptual frame through an exploration of how trade unions can reclaim relevance by aligning with the paradigm of the so-called Fifth Industrial Revolution. Arguing that unions must transform into learning organizations capable of systemic innovation, the authors highlight the necessity of balancing profit and productivity with well-being and sustainability. This contribution positions Spanish unions not as passive observers of disruption but as active architects of a human-centered technological future.

Continuing this multifaceted exploration, the volume addresses the broader implications of artificial intelligence for fundamental labor rights. The chapter dedicated to this theme highlights how the introduction of algorithmic systems into workplace management—often without oversight—can jeopardize essential protections such as privacy, equality, health and safety. It argues for the urgent inclusion of AI-specific clauses in collective bargaining, stressing the indispensable role of unions as institutional guardians capable of translating ethical concerns into concrete regulatory advances. By doing so, the authors reaffirm the necessity of a rights-based approach to digital governance.

Closely linked to this perspective is the eighth chapter that explores workplace harassment in the AI era from a criminological and victimological lens. Here, AI is understood as both a potential threat and a tool: capable of reinforcing power asymmetries but also of detecting abusive patterns when responsibly designed. This contribution centers the union's role in preventing AI-enabled discrimination and psychological harm, while calling for stronger alliances between labor organizations, regulatory agencies, and technology developers. It enriches the debate by foregrounding the emotional and affective dimensions of digital transformation, often overlooked in labor-tech discourses.

Mental health and wellbeing emerge as central concerns in another chapter that examines how unions can respond to the psychosocial risks introduced by AI and automation. The rise of technostress, isolation, and cognitive overload calls for a redefinition of union strategies—not only as defenders of rights but as promoters of holistic wellbeing in digital work environments. This chapter advocates for unions to digitize their own services, embrace proactive prevention models, and position themselves as key actors in safeguarding mental health in an increasingly automated world.

A particularly original contribution in this section turns to the art industry, where generative AI has disrupted conventional understandings of creativity, authorship, and intellectual property. This chapter addresses the unprecedented challenges faced by artists and creators, proposing a renewed role for unions in defending cultural labor within a shifting ontological landscape. It suggests that unions must not only engage in policy debates over IP reform but also help reframe what counts as artistic work in the AI era, thus extending the domain of labor protection into traditionally undervalued sectors.

Together, these contributions mark a crucial turning point in the book's narrative, moving beyond institutional adaptation to consider how unions might lead to broader conversations about justice, identity, and ethics in technologically mediated workplaces.

The final section of the volume shifts the focus toward strategic innovation in union organization, exploring how collective representation itself is being reconfigured in the digital economy. One of the chapters tackles this challenge by analyzing the disruptive effects of the gig economy and the individualization of labor relations. It documents the obstacles unions face in organizing precarious and fragmented workers while also highlighting emerging practices—from new models of representation and alliances with social movements to the creative use of digital platforms. The authors argue that to remain relevant, unions must reinvent not only their tactics but their very identity, reaffirming solidarity as a dynamic principle adaptable to new labor realities.

This thread of strategic reinvention continues with a chapter that foregrounds the role of education, coalition-building, and political advocacy as key union responses to automation. Through a historical overview and contemporary analysis, the authors show how unions can build future-oriented alliances with educational institutions and community actors to support lifelong learning, address skill gaps, and influence public policy. In doing so, they reaffirm the centrality of unions not just as reactive entities, but as proactive co-designers of equitable technological transitions.

Further expanding this outlook, another chapter offers a cross-sectoral perspective on how AI is transforming workforce dynamics across industries such as manufacturing, healthcare, education, and finance. By mapping the sector-specific implications of automation and machine learning, the authors argue that unions must develop differentiated strategies tailored to the technological maturity and labor configurations of each sector. The piece emphasizes that no "one-size-fits-all" approach will suffice in the face of such diverse technological landscapes.

In parallel, a chapter grounded in empirical data across 25 European countries examines how AI and automation correlate with income inequality, union density, and technological readiness. The findings show that countries with robust union structures, particularly in Scandinavia, are more successful in mitigating the adverse effects of automation. This macro-level insight reinforces the book's central premise: that strong, adaptive unions are key to ensuring that technological transformation does not exacerbate existing social disparities.

Concluding the volume is a chapter that evaluates the evolving role of unions through the lens of structural transformation, STEM competencies, and economic complexity. Here, the authors explore how digital transitions interact with broader human capital dynamics, suggesting that trade unions remain crucial actors in shaping employment pathways and ensuring that technological progress translates into inclusive development. This final contribution closes the book with a call to rethink unionism not as a relic of the industrial past, but as an evolving force in the architecture of digital futures.

This book positions itself as both a diagnostic and visionary contribution to the evolving field of labor studies, particularly at the intersection of technological transformation, collective organization, and institutional innovation. In a global context marked by rapid digitalization, growing precarity, and fragmented governance, The New Role of Labor Unions in the AI Era offers a timely and necessary reflection on the capacity of labor unions to remain relevant, resilient, and reimagined.

By assembling perspectives from diverse geographies, disciplinary traditions, and methodological approaches, the volume illustrates that trade unions are not passive observers of technological disruption. On the contrary, they are strategic actors capable of intervening in the design, implementation, and governance of AI systems. The case studies collected herein show that while unions are under pressure—from declining membership, legal constraints, and shifting labor forms—they are also experimenting with new modalities of action: digital infrastructures, legal innovations, educational alliances, ethical oversight mechanisms, and cross-border coordination.

Importantly, the volume does not romanticize union capacity nor overlook structural limitations. Instead, it foregrounds the tensions, dilemmas, and uneven outcomes that characterize union responses to AI and automation. This analytical honesty enhances the book's academic credibility while deepening its practical relevance. The contributions acknowledge that the future of work will be shaped by contested processes—and that unions have much to lose, but also much to gain, in that contest.

The book also contributes conceptually to reframing key debates in the literature. Rather than treating technology as an exogenous variable or inevitable force, the chapters approach AI as a social artifact embedded in power relations. This framing opens space for analyzing the politics of design, the ethics of deployment, and the institutional conditions under which technological systems can serve rather than undermine labor justice. By doing so, the volume helps to bridge the gap between technology studies and industrial relations, while also enriching debates on social dialogue, participatory governance, and digital democracy.

In terms of policy impact, the book offers concrete recommendations for unions, regulators, and public institutions. It demonstrates that ethical AI governance is not only a technical challenge but also a labor issue—and that unions must be included in the co-construction of digital regulatory frameworks. The chapters encourage union leaders to embrace transformation while holding firm to the principles of solidarity, equity, and collective agency.

Ultimately, The New Role of Labor Unions in the AI Era contributes to a broader rethinking of the future of work. It shows that organized labor, far from being obsolete, is indispensable for negotiating fair transitions, resisting extractive logic, and ensuring that digital innovation advances the common good. In doing so, the book speaks not only to scholars and practitioners, but to all those committed to building a more just and democratic technological future.

Andrés J. Arenas Falótico
Alfonso X el Sabio University, Spain

Jessica Bayón Pérez
Universidad Internacional de la Rioja, Spain

Acknowledgments

The editors would like to express their deep gratitude to the diverse group of authors from around the world who contributed to this book. From Argentina to the United Kingdom, from Mexico to Libya, their dedication and expertise have been invaluable in bringing this project to life.

We are also profoundly grateful to our families for their unwavering support throughout the entire process—from editing and reviewing to meeting final deadlines. Their patience and encouragement made this endeavor possible.

Chapter 1
Transforming Labor Union Operations With AI: A Study of Valorian, Spain

Andrés Jeronimo Arenas
https://orcid.org/0000-0002-2763-9707
Alfonso X El Sabio University, Spain

Jessica Bayón
https://orcid.org/0000-0003-4019-7605
Universidad Internacional de la Rioja, Spain

ABSTRACT

Labor unions have historically played a vital role in ensuring workers' rights and fostering democratic labor relations. However, in the 21st century, they face unprecedented challenges, including declining membership, evolving workforce dynamics, and rapid technological advancements. This chapter explores the transformative impact of Artificial Intelligence (AI) on labor union operations, using Valorian — a pioneering Spanish union — as a case study. Unlike traditional unions, Valorian adopts a collaborative and innovation-driven approach, integrating AI into its core operations to enhance efficiency, improve member engagement, and promote ethical labor practices. By conducting a comparative historical and organizational analysis of Spanish labor unions, this study examines how Valorian leverages AI to address contemporary labor challenges. It also assesses the ethical, strategic, and operational implications of AI adoption in union activities, providing insights into AI's role in shaping the future of labor representation.

DOI: 10.4018/979-8-3693-8049-9.ch001

INTRODUCTION

Histories of labor unions show how crucial their role has been in promoting and protecting workers' rights, forming a cornerstone of social and democratic states. Even though unions have lost prestige and membership in recent decades, they remain vital for the management of labor relations. In Spain, unions changed considerably from the shadowy movements of the Franco era to modern, multicultural institutions operating amid globalization, technological change, the adoption of AI, and transformations in the nature of work. One such organization is Valorian, which represents a new model within the Spanish union movement. Rather than employing traditional adversarial tactics, Valorian pursues cooperation between employees and employers, making it a union that strives to resolve disputes collaboratively rather than create them.

The fundamental principle guiding Valorian's approach is encapsulated in the assertion: *"If there are no companies, there are no workers."* This statement underscores the intrinsic interdependence between businesses, investors, and the labor force, highlighting the essential role that companies play in sustaining employment opportunities. From this perspective, the existence and financial health of businesses are prerequisites for job creation, economic stability, and workforce sustainability. Investors fuel business growth and expansion, which in turn creates workplaces where employees can develop their skills and careers. By ensuring a conducive environment for investment and business viability, the foundation for sustainable employment is strengthened, allowing workers to engage in productive economic activities.

In today's rapidly evolving technological landscape, companies are increasingly integrating AI to enhance efficiency and drive innovation. A 2022 report by IBM indicated that 35% of companies were utilizing AI in their operations, with an additional 44% actively planning to incorporate AI into business processes (IBM, 2022). This widespread adoption underscores AI's transformative potential across industries. Labor unions, recognizing AI's profound impact on the workforce, are advocating for proactive engagement with this technology. By embracing AI, unions can better represent their members' interests, negotiate the terms of AI implementation, and ensure that technological advancements lead to equitable outcomes for workers. For instance, unions have negotiated agreements to govern AI deployment in workplaces, ensuring that its integration does not compromise workers' rights or job security (Kelley, 2023). By aligning with technological advancements embraced by companies, labor unions can help shape the future of work, ensuring both businesses and employees benefit from the opportunities presented by AI.

This perspective implies that labor relations and negotiations should be framed collaboratively rather than confrontational. A thriving business ecosystem translates into stable employment and economic security for workers. Consequently, instead of positioning unions and employers as opposing entities, Valorian's philosophy advocates balanced dialogue wherein both parties acknowledge mutual dependence and work toward solutions that enhance corporate sustainability and worker well-being. This ideology fosters a harmonious relationship between labor and management, prioritizing long-term economic viability, equitable employment conditions, and shared benefits of success. By promoting a framework where labor relations are a strategic partnership rather than a conflict-driven dynamic, businesses and workers can engage in constructive dialogue that ensures economic resilience, job security, and sustainable growth.

They trace its roots to 2023, when three professional unions – FASGA, SPV, and SPS – merged to form a new independent union. This merger exemplified a trend toward a dual approach in union ideology focused on dialogue, flexibility, and creativity. Valorian now represents workers across 22 sectors and over 115 companies (including major employers like Carrefour, El Corte Inglés, and Grupo Avoris), underscoring its significant influence in the labor market. Valorian's distinct philosophy and operational model make it particularly suited to integrating AI into labor union activities. In an era where AI technologies are reshaping industries, organizations, and societal norms, their forward-thinking approach offers a compelling case study of how unions can modernize while remaining true to their core mission of advocating for workers' rights. By leveraging AI to streamline operations, enhance member engagement, and improve decision-making processes, they provide a blueprint for how unions can navigate the digital transformation redefining the world of work.

This chapter aims to explore the intersection of AI and labor union practices with Valorian as the central case study. By situating their efforts within the broader historical and organizational context of Spanish unions, the study seeks to understand how unions can adapt to contemporary challenges while remaining relevant in a rapidly changing labor market. Furthermore, it examines the implications of AI adoption for union operations, ethical considerations, and the evolving relationship between workers and employers, providing insights into the future of labor representation in the digital age.

Objectives

- **Historical Evolution of Labor Unions in Spain:** Analyze the development of Spanish labor unions from early worker movements to modern organizations, providing context for their current challenges and opportunities.

- **AI Integration in Valorian's Operations:** Investigate the specific AI technologies Valorian has adopted, their applications, and their impact on operational efficiency, member engagement, and decision-making processes.
- **Benefits and Challenges of AI Adoption:** Identify key advantages and challenges of AI for labor unions. Assess how AI can enhance transparency, streamline processes, and foster member inclusivity, while addressing ethical, technical, and organizational hurdles.
- **Valorian as an Innovative Case Study:** Evaluate Valorian's unique approach, including its emphasis on worker-employer collaboration, and its role as a model for AI-driven transformation in labor representation.
- **Strategic Recommendations:** Provide actionable insights for unions considering AI integration – including planning, ethical use, capacity building, and public-private partnerships – to maximize AI's potential for modern labor unions.
- **Broader Implications:** Understand the wider implications of AI for the labor union sector globally, emphasizing AI's role in promoting sustainability, adaptability, and inclusive representation in a rapidly changing workforce.

Methodology

This study employs a qualitative case study approach to explore the integration of AI into labor unions, focusing on Valorian as the central example. Given that AI adoption in labor representation is relatively new, an in-depth case study provides a nuanced understanding of its impact, benefits, and challenges. Valorian serves as a pioneering example of how AI can reshape union operations, offering insights into best practices and potential risks. This method enables detailed examination of organizational strategies, technological adoption, and ethical considerations within a real-world union context.

Research Question: Guided by the case of Valorian, the research question is: *How can the integration of artificial intelligence transform labor union operations, and what are the outcomes and implications of such integration for union effectiveness in Spain?*

Hypothesis: The study hypothesizes that *AI integration will significantly enhance a labor union's operational efficiency, member engagement, and strategic capacity, helping the union remain relevant in a digitalized labor market, provided that ethical and organizational challenges are effectively managed.* In Valorian's case, this means we expect to observe improvements in internal processes (through automation and data analytics) and external advocacy (through better-informed bargaining and member services), while also identifying any risks or limits encountered.

To address this question, the research relies primarily on secondary data sources (as no new primary data were collected). These sources include academic literature on AI in labor relations, digital transformation, and union strategies, as well as industry reports from institutions such as the OECD and UNI Global Union, which provide broader context on AI's role in the workforce. Government statistics (e.g., the Spanish National Statistics Institute's AI adoption survey) situate Valorian's experience within broader labor market trends. Additionally, official Valorian documents — including strategic plans, reports, media interviews, and digital initiative descriptions — offer detailed insights into the union's AI-driven transformation. Media articles and case studies further illuminate how labor unions are responding to technological changes.

A thematic framework was applied to structure the analysis of Valorian's AI initiatives. Key themes include AI-driven member engagement (evaluating how AI enhances communication, responsiveness, and participation), operational efficiency (assessing AI's role in automating processes, improving service delivery, and optimizing labor relations), ethical and governance considerations (examining how Valorian ensures transparency, fairness, and data protection in AI deployment), and challenges and future prospects (identifying obstacles in AI implementation and predicting trends in AI-driven labor representation). This thematic approach allows for a comprehensive assessment of how AI is reshaping union dynamics without requiring direct comparisons to other organizations.

Use of Data: It is important to note that this research did not involve primary data collection such as interviews or surveys; it is based entirely on existing (secondary) sources. No direct interviews with Valorian members or leaders were conducted, which is a limitation of the study. However, incorporating a broad range of credible secondary data ensures a robust foundation for analysis, and it allows triangulation of information from academic studies, statistical data, and Valorian's own reports. The reliance on secondary data means the findings reflect documented outcomes and observations rather than firsthand testimonies. To strengthen the insights, future research should include primary data (for example, interviews with union representatives or member surveys) to capture personal experiences and internal perspectives.

Finally, several limitations must be acknowledged. Because the study is based on a single case (Valorian) and uses secondary data, the findings may not be fully generalizable to all unions or contexts. The lack of primary data and insider perspectives may leave some nuances unexplored. Future research directions, discussed later in this chapter, will suggest how to address these gaps (e.g., through comparative case studies and primary data collection) to build on the insights gained here.

LITERATURE REVIEW

Labor Unions in the Digital Age: Challenges and Necessity for Innovation

Labor unions, as advocates for workers' rights, have historically been central to achieving fair labor standards. In recent years, however, unions worldwide (including in Spain) have experienced declining membership and influence, largely due to economic shifts and changes in workforce composition. Traditional union strategies have struggled to attract younger workers or those in emerging sectors. Research indicates that unions failing to modernize and adopt new technologies risk alienating younger members who expect tech-savvy representation (Carneiro & Costa, 2020). In Spain and many other countries, union density has fallen significantly over the past decades. For example, Spain's union membership as a proportion of employees is around 14%, one of the lowest rates in Europe. This decline underscores the urgency for unions to adapt to remain relevant.

Figure 1. Declining workers affiliation to unions. As we can see in the table, there is a diminishment of employees enrolling into a labor union, and Spain leads the last position. Source: OECD, 2025

Trade union density

Measure: Trade union density

Combined unit of measure: Percentage of employees

Time period	2015	2016	2017	2018	2019
Reference area: Austria	27.4	26.9	26.7	26.3	26.3
Reference area: Belgium	52.3	51.6	50.7	50.0	49.1
Reference area: Denmark	68.2	67.4	66.7	67.5	67.0
Reference area: Finland	67.5	65.7	62.9	60.0	58.8
Reference area: Germany	17.6	17.0	16.7	16.6	16.3
Reference area: Italy	34.2	33.6	33.2	32.6	32.5
Reference area: Norway	49.8	50.0	50.0	49.9	50.4
Reference area: Spain	14.4	13.9	13.4	13.0	12.5
Reference area: Sweden	67.0	66.7	66.1	65.5	65.2
Reference area: United Kingdom	24.7	23.6	23.3	23.4	23.5

Scholars have introduced the concept of "digital unionism" as a potential renewal strategy, emphasizing the use of digital tools and social media to engage members and the public. Carneiro and Costa (2020) find that increased online presence and communication can help unions reconnect with workers, especially younger demographics, and present a more modern image. Similarly, Thomas and Turnbull (2021) argue that if unions do not strategically modernize, they may face diminished influence over labor policies as the workforce becomes increasingly shaped by digital tools. Traditional unions often focus on immediate workplace issues (like wage disputes) at the expense of long-term innovation, thereby neglecting the strategic investments necessary for long-term digital transformation. This cautious approach has been identified as a critical weakness, as it can lead to a loss of relevance in a digitalized economy.

The literature also highlights that the nature of work is fundamentally changing due to digital transformation. Automation and AI are projected to both displace and create millions of jobs globally. Bayón and Arenas (2019) note that while AI and automation might displace approximately 75 million jobs, they could create around 133 million new roles, albeit roles requiring new skills. This "creative destruction" in the labor market means unions must not only protect existing jobs but also help workers transition into new ones. Unions increasingly acknowledge that part of their mandate is to assist with reskilling and upskilling initiatives in response to automation (Frey & Osborne, 2017). If unions embrace technology, they can play a proactive role in preparing the workforce for the future; if they resist, they risk exacerbating membership decline as workers seek relevance elsewhere.

In summary, existing research paints a picture of labor unions at a crossroads. They face internal and external pressures to innovate or risk obsolescence. Embracing digital tools and AI is frequently cited as a key opportunity for renewal, allowing unions to improve internal processes and better serve members in a changing economy. The findings of Didier (2021) highlight the complexities of transitioning labor markets to accommodate digital economies, emphasizing that while organizations may adapt, the nature of jobs and the skills required are undergoing substantial transformations. This forms a critical backdrop for examining Valorian, a union that has chosen to innovate rather than stagnate.

AI Adoption in Labor Unions: Opportunities and Challenges

A growing body of literature examines how AI and related technologies can be leveraged by labor unions, as well as the risks these technologies pose. Opportunities identified include data-driven decision making, enhanced member engagement, and improved bargaining power. Challenges include ethical concerns, potential misuse by employers, and the digital divide in resources and skills.

On the opportunity side, researchers argue that AI can significantly enhance a union's capabilities. Machine learning (ML) and big data analytics enable unions to analyze workforce trends, wage patterns, and employment conditions at a scale that was previously impossible. Brynjolfsson and McAfee (2014) famously described AI as part of "the second machine age" that can augment human decision-making. In the union context, this means AI can help unions foresee labor market shifts (e.g. identifying sectors at risk of layoffs) and prepare proactive strategies. For example, German union IG Metall has used AI-powered wage analysis to negotiate better contracts, basing demands on comprehensive industry data rather than anecdotes. Krzywdzinski, Gerst, and Butollo (2023) document how several German unions have developed strategies to regulate AI's use in workplaces and even utilize AI tools themselves to strengthen bargaining positions. These cases support the idea that algorithmic insights can recalibrate labor-capital dynamics, giving unions new leverage (Falcão Filho, 2024). Some scholars refer to this as *"algorithmic bargaining power,"* where having data analytics on their side allows unions to counter employers' advanced analytics with evidence of their own.

AI can also improve member services and engagement. Wood (2021) and others have noted that digital natives expect quick, personalized interactions. Unions using AI chatbots or automated messaging can provide real-time responses to member inquiries and grievances, improving responsiveness. Studies suggest that unions deploying powered communication tools experience higher levels of member interaction and retention. Additionally, sentiment analysis of member feedback (from surveys or social media) can help union leadership stay attuned to emerging concerns, making unions more member-centric in their advocacy. Ballantyne, Forlizzi, and Weise (2024) emphasize integrating worker perspectives into technology development, which aligns with unions using AI to directly capture worker input and priorities.

On the challenge side, literature warns of several risks. One major concern is the use of AI by employers to undermine unions or worker rights. Kelley (2023) discusses how AI technologies can be misused for anti-union activities, such as surveillance of workers or algorithmically screening out job applicants who are union supporters. Unions are rightly apprehensive that sophisticated analytics could enable subtle forms of discrimination against union members or tactics that weaken collective action (e.g., personalized incentives to prevent organizing). In response, there have been governmental and legislative efforts. In the United States, as Kelley notes (2023), executive orders and interagency initiatives have been proposed to prevent AI-driven union-busting and to mitigate AI-induced job losses. This highlights the need for collaboration among employers, unions, and government to manage AI-related risks, an issue we see echoed globally.

Another challenge is ensuring ethical AI governance and avoiding biases. AI systems can inadvertently perpetuate existing biases in workplace decisions (hiring, promotions, disciplinary actions) if they learn from historical data. Research by Buolamwini and Gebru (2018) on algorithmic bias demonstrates how AI can reflect and amplify inequalities. For unions, this means that while AI tools might help identify discrimination (e.g., pay gaps), they could also harbor biases if not carefully managed. Unions thus face a dual role: using AI to fight bias, while also guarding against bias within the AI tools they employ. Establishing oversight committees for algorithmic tools, including ethicists and worker representatives, is one recommendation to ensure transparency and fairness. In practice, Valorian's implementation of algorithmic audits of wage data exemplifies how a union can tackle this issue head-on.

Additionally, the resource and skill gap present a limitation. Many unions, especially smaller ones, may lack technical expertise or funds to develop and maintain AI systems. Başol and Yalçın (2021) note that digital readiness varies greatly across organizations and countries; unions in countries with lower Digital Economy and Society Index (DESI) scores may struggle more to adopt advanced tools. In Spain, a recent INE survey found that 76.7% of large companies reported a lack of specialized AI knowledge as a barrier to adoption. This indicates that without partnerships or external support, many unions risk falling behind simply due to resource limitations. Public-private partnerships (such as Valorian joining forces with an organization of human capital managers) can be a way to bridge this gap, a point to be elaborated in our recommendations.

Finally, the regulatory landscape is evolving alongside these challenges. The European Union has taken a proactive stance with the EU Artificial Intelligence Act (2024), the world's first comprehensive AI framework. The Act categorizes AI applications by risk and imposes requirements to ensure transparency, human oversight, and accountability for high-risk AI systems. For instance, AI used in recruitment (relevant to hiring practices affecting union composition) will be subject to stricter obligations. Such regulations can aid unions by providing external checks on how AI is implemented by employers. They also offer unions a reference point to advocate for compliance and worker protections. Unions like Valorian, which are deeply interested in AI's impact, have a stake in these regulatory discussions. The literature suggests that unions engage with policymaking (through consultations or alliances with bodies like the International Labor Organization, 2025) to ensure that AI governance frameworks include labor perspectives. In Europe, strong collaboration between union federations and policymakers has been seen, in line with broader social dialogue traditions.

Literature portrays AI as a double-edged sword for labor unions. On one edge, it offers powerful tools to reinvigorate union advocacy and internal operations, potentially reversing trends of decline. On the other hand, it introduces new risks and exacerbates existing challenges that unions must navigate carefully. These insights from previous studies set the stage for examining how Valorian has approached AI. By seeing how theory and predictions hold up in practice, the case of Valorian can shed light on the real-world balance of these opportunities and challenges.

Historical Background of Labor Unions in Spain

Labor Unions in Spain: An Overview. Labor unions in Spain have played, and continue to play, a crucial role in advancing workers' rights and improving working conditions. Over the past two centuries, the Spanish labor movement has evolved through periods of growth, repression, and transformation. Despite a significant decline in union membership in recent years and a diminished public reputation, unions remain a vital institution for the functioning of labor relations in Spain. To understand Valorian's emergence and strategies, it is important first to consider the broader historical trajectory of Spanish unions, from their early origins to their status in the modern era.

Early Labor Movements (19th Century Origins)

The labor movement in Spain began to take shape in the early 19th century under the pressures of industrialization and harsh working conditions. From its inception until the mid-1800s, Spanish workers faced long hours, low wages, and unsafe conditions that led them to question their circumstances and organize the first revolts. One of the earliest forms of protest was Luddism – the destruction of machinery blamed for poor working conditions. This phenomenon, which spread throughout Europe in the first quarter of the 19th century, was seen in Spain as well. Luddite actions symbolized workers' desperation and their direct response to technological changes that threatened livelihoods (Tascón, 2000).

During this period, labor unions initially emerged as mutual aid associations to support workers in need (such as those injured or on strike). By around 1820, such associations had become widespread across many countries and industries, prompting the establishment of laws recognizing workers' associations. This marked the beginning of union activity with an overt political dimension in Spain (Musson, 1990). Unions were no longer just local benevolent societies; they started to advocate for broader labor rights and societal change.

These early labor groupings were intertwined with emerging ideological currents. *Utopian socialism*, represented by thinkers like Robert Owen and Charles Fourier, influenced some worker circles with proposals to improve workers' quality of life and establish cooperative societies based on equality and education. However, such utopian ideas were critiqued by Karl Marx and Friedrich Engels as overly idealistic. Marx and Engels introduced *scientific socialism*, analyzing industrial society in works like *The Communist Manifesto* (Osoria, 2022). They argued that economic forces drive history and that class struggle between the "exploited and exploiters" is the engine of social change. According to Marxist theory, this struggle would eventually lead to the dictatorship of the proletariat and the abolition of class distinctions.

These ideas gained traction among some Spanish workers and intellectuals, laying the groundwork for later labor and political movements.

In more rural and less industrialized regions of Spain, anarchism found a foothold. Grounded in principles of individualism, rejection of authority, and social solidarity, anarchism appealed to workers skeptical of both capital and the state. Drawing inspiration from mid-19th-century thinkers like Pierre-Joseph Proudhon and later Mikhail Bakunin, Spanish anarchists promoted the idea of dismantling the state to construct a new society free of oppression. Bakunin's calls for radical action resonated, especially in areas where centralized union structures were weak. By the late 1800s, Spain had become one of the centers of the anarchist labor movement (e.g., through the CNT – the National Confederation of Labor, founded later in 1910, which was anarcho-syndicalist in orientation).

Transnationally, Spanish workers and unions were influenced by developments in the broader European labor movement. The formation of the International Workingmen's Association (IWA), or First International, in 1864 was a milestone that united major European labor unions and socialist groups (Gaido, 2021). Spanish delegates participated in the IWA under the leadership of figures like Anselmo Lorenzo. Within the International, debates between Marx and Bakunin about the role of the state (reform it versus abolish it) echoed in Spain's labor circles, causing splits between socialist and anarchist factions.

By the late 19th and early 20th centuries, the world saw the gradual establishment of socialist political parties, such as the German Social Democratic Party (SPD) in 1875 (Conradt, 2025) and the Labour Party in England in 1905 (Webb, 2025). The labor activism in Spain was becoming more formally political. The gradual establishment of socialist political parties across Europe found a parallel in Spain: The Spanish Socialist Workers' Party (PSOE) was founded in 1879 by Pablo Iglesias, and its affiliated union, the General Union of Workers (UGT), was founded in 1888 (González, 2006). PSOE and UGT became pillars of the socialist labor tradition in Spain. Around the same time, other strands of the labor movement were also organizing; anarcho-syndicalists would later form the CNT in 1910, as mentioned, offering a more radical alternative to UGT.

20th Century Developments: Corporatism, Dictatorship, and Democracy

By the early 20th century, Spain's labor movement was robust but internally divided among socialist, anarchist, and other ideologies. The early decades saw significant labor strikes and the rise of corporate ideas in labor relations. *Corporatism* in this context refers to a model where workers, employers, and sometimes the state form integrated structures to manage economic and labor issues collectively.

Modern corporatism emerged in late 19th and early 20th century Europe to mediate conflicting interests by grouping economic actors into representative bodies. In Spain, corporatist thought influenced both political regimes and some segments of the labor movement, promoting collaboration over class conflict. For instance, during Miguel Primo de Rivera's rule in the 1920s, corporatist institutions were experimented with.

A dark period for Spanish unions came with the Franco dictatorship (1939–1975). After the Spanish Civil War, General Francisco Franco's authoritarian regime banned independent unions outright. They were replaced by government-controlled "vertical syndicates" that aimed to incorporate workers and employers in a single structure under Falangist ideology. This effectively suppressed free trade unionism for decades. Union activists were jailed, exiled, or forced underground. Both UGT and CNT operated in exile or clandestinely within Spain. This era severely weakened the union movement's infrastructure and left a legacy of cautiousness and fragmentation.

With the death of Franco and Spain's transition to democracy (the late 1970s), labor unions were re-legalized and revitalized. UGT re-emerged from the socialist side, and the Workers' Commissions (CC.OO., originally a clandestine Communist-linked movement formed in the 1960s) became formalized as a major union federation. Spain established a system of institutionalized social dialogue: the major unions (especially UGT and CC.OO.) and employer associations began participating in national agreements (such as the Moncloa Pacts of 1977) to guide the economy and labor reforms in the new democracy.

During the democratic era (1980s onwards), Spanish unions achieved significant gains in collective bargaining rights, workplace protections, and social legislation, becoming essential partners in the tripartite consultations with government on labor issues. However, they also had to operate within a corporate framework of dialogue and compromise. Over time, union membership density in Spain declined due to changes like a growing service sector, more temporary contracts, and challenges in organizing new forms of work. According to data from the OECD, by the 2010s and early 2020s Spain had one of the lowest union densities in Western Europe. This means only a small fraction of Spanish employees are union members, a challenge for union legitimacy and resources.

As of the mid-2020s, Spain's union landscape is characterized by the dominance of UGT and CC.OO. (which together represent most unionized workers), alongside smaller or sector-specific unions. It is in this contemporary context of institutionalized social partnership, yet declining grassroots participation, that an innovative union like Valorian has emerged. The stage was set for something new: a union that could respond to 21st-century challenges (technological change, changing workforce demographics) in a way that traditional unions have struggled to do.

Corporatism and the Role of Valorian in Contemporary Spain

Valorian represents a unique case of contemporary union corporatism and innovation in Spain. Historically, its founding unions were known for a cooperative approach to labor relations; for example, FASGA was a company-sponsored union tied to the El Corte Inglés retail group since 1978. Such roots have given Valorian a reputation of being more amicable with employers and less confrontational than typical unions. However, it is precisely these principles of dialogue and mutual interest that set them apart and form the basis of its strategy.

Their philosophy envisions workers and employers as a unified team rather than adversaries, aligning with corporate ideals of collective representation and shared goals. In practice, this means Valorian often seeks win-win outcomes through negotiation, emphasizing business sustainability alongside worker welfare. This stance does not imply sacrificing worker rights; rather, it posits that protecting and empowering workers can go hand in hand with helping companies thrive, thereby securing employment. It's a delicate balance, but one that Valorian's leadership espouses as a guiding doctrine.

This collaborative ethos arguably made Valorian an ideal candidate to integrate advanced technologies like AI into its operations. A union already oriented towards innovation and partnership may be more open to new tools and methods. Valorian's birth in 2023 coincided with a period of rapid digital transformation in workplaces globally, and the union explicitly positioned itself as "AI-ready" from the outset. In fact, their structure and approach can be seen as a test case for how unions might evolve in the 21st century, blending innovative practices with core advocacy. By adopting a forward-thinking stance, Valorian aims to adapt to challenges (like declining union appeal among young workers or the gig economy's rise) that more traditional unions are struggling with.

Spain's historical context — from 19th-century labor upheavals, through corporatist experiments, dictatorship-imposed stagnation, and democratic revival — sets the background against which Valorian emerged. They draw on a legacy of corporate collaboration but projects it into the future with a focus on technology and innovation. It stands at the confluence of Spain's past and future of labor representation.

Given this historical evolution, their efforts to transform union operations through AI can be better understood. The following case study delves into Valorian's specific initiatives and experiences, illustrating how one union is addressing contemporary challenges by leveraging AI while upholding the cooperative ethos inherited from Spain's labor history.

Case Study: Valorian – A New Paradigm in Union Operations

Formation and Philosophy of Valorian

Valorian is a Spanish trade union notable for its professional, innovative, and relationship-oriented practices. This means Valorian does not fit the classic model of unions that often engage in adversarial tactics or strikes as first recourse. Instead, it prioritizes dialogue, mutual gains, and conflict resolution. Their guiding belief, as mentioned earlier, is that the health of companies and the welfare of workers are mutually dependent. Valorian representatives frequently reiterate that without successful companies, there cannot be secure jobs, and without skilled, fairly treated workers, companies cannot thrive. This outlook has informed Valorian's strategies in collective bargaining and partnership initiatives.

Their philosophy also emphasizes professionalism and creativity in union work. Its leadership and staff include experts in labor law, economics, and now technology, reflecting a desire to engage with employers on equal technical footing. By highlighting "innovation-driven" unionism, Valorian seeks to attract members who may have been disenchanted with what they perceive as outdated union approaches. Valorian has quickly become a significant player in the Spanish labor market.

Crucially, Valorian's foundational principles set it apart in how it addresses contemporary issues. Rather than shunning collaboration with management, Valorian often enters into *partnerships* with businesses and even employer associations to implement joint solutions. For example, it has engaged in training programs co-funded by employers to upskill workers (anticipating technological changes), and it participates in multi-stakeholder forums on industry trends. This collaborative approach can be seen as a modern extension of the corporatist tradition — but driven voluntarily by the union itself, not imposed by the state as in the past.

The cooperative ethos faced some skepticism from traditionalists who questioned whether they would truly stand up for workers' interests. However, Valorian has balanced this by choosing its battles carefully and demonstrating results in areas like improved working conditions and career development opportunities through cooperation. Its stance is that resolving disputes does not always require confrontation if proactive engagement can prevent the disputes from arising in the first place. In an interview with *Capital Radio*, Miguel Venegas, the President of Valorian, emphasized the importance of *"embracing technological change"* and working inclusively: *"We must adapt to the digital era to effectively represent and protect our members. Our participation in projects related to equality and IA reflects our commitment to inclusivity and leveraging technology for the betterment of all workers"* (Venegas, 2023). This quote illustrates how Valorian's top leadership sees innovation (including AI) as integral to union advocacy.

Valorian's formation was a deliberate effort to create a new paradigm of unionism in Spain. Built on a history of moderate, dialogue-oriented unionism, it has from the outset branded itself as *"AI-ready"* and forward-looking. This unique positioning made it an ideal case to study how AI can transform union operations, which we explore in detail below. Also, this perspective aligns with the broader discourse on global justice and labor rights, as articulated by Josefsson and Wall, 2020, who emphasize the need for inclusive strategies that address the needs of marginalized workers.

AI Integration Initiatives at Valorian

From day one, Valorian incorporated the use of Artificial Intelligence and digital tools into its operational and strategic plans. In this section, we detail the key AI-driven initiatives Valorian has implemented, and the outcomes or improvements these have yielded. These initiatives span internal administration, member engagement, collective bargaining, and broader advocacy efforts.

1. **Data-Driven Decision Making and Predictive Analytics:** Valorian has embraced machine learning models to analyze large datasets related to employment conditions, economic trends, and member needs. By deploying predictive analytics, Valorian can anticipate labor market shifts such as potential job displacements due to automation. For instance, the union developed an AI-based workforce planning tool that analyzes data on employment contracts, industry growth, and technological adoption rates to forecast which sectors and regions are most vulnerable to layoffs or restructuring. This allows Valorian to proactively negotiate retraining programs or job transition support *before* crises hit. A concrete example is Valorian's predictive model for job displacement risk in the manufacturing sector, which indicated which job categories were likely to be automated. Using these insights, Valorian worked with several large manufacturing companies to create retraining pathways for workers in at-risk positions, thereby preventing mass layoffs (this pilot initiative is mentioned in the Recommendations section as a model for others). By moving from a reactive to a preventative stance, Valorian has strengthened job security for members.

Additionally, Valorian leverages data for real-time salary benchmarking during negotiations. Instead of relying solely on member anecdotes or limited surveys, its analysts use AI to scrape and aggregate wage data across companies and industries. During a recent collective bargaining round in the retail sector, Valorian's team brought an AI-generated analysis showing that wages at certain companies lagged 10% behind the industry norm for comparable roles. This hard evidence, drawn from large datasets, gave Valorian a stronger position at the table and resulted in a successful push for wage increases. Such data-driven evidence is an application of what one might call *"algorithmic bargaining power"* — essentially using algorithms to bolster the union's arguments with quantitative backing.

2. **AI-Assisted Member Engagement and Services:** To improve communication with its widely distributed membership, Valorian has introduced AI-powered tools for member engagement. One such tool is a chatbot platform accessible via Valorian's website and mobile app. This chatbot uses natural language processing to answer common member queries instantly, 24/7, on topics like contract terms, benefits, or how to file a grievance. By providing immediate responses, the chatbot has reduced wait times and made union support more accessible, especially for members who may be remote or in different time zones. Research has shown that unions using ML-powered chatbots and automated response systems experience higher levels of worker interaction and membership retention. Valorian's experience aligns with this – since launching the chatbot, member surveys indicate greater satisfaction with the union's responsiveness, and there has been a modest uptick in membership among tech-savvy younger workers who appreciate the digital convenience.

Furthermore, they employ sentiment analysis on member feedback. Through AI analysis of surveys, emails, and even social media discussions in worker forums, the union can gauge the sentiment on various issues (e.g., morale about a new company policy, interest in certain training programs) in real time. For example, during the COVID-19 pandemic, Valorian collected feedback from thousands of members about remote work conditions. AI sentiment analysis helped identify that a top concern was mental health and isolation. In response, Valorian organized virtual support sessions and negotiated with employers to implement "right to disconnect" policies to help work-life balance. By tailoring its campaigns to worker priorities identified via AI, Valorian ensured that its agenda resonated with the membership. This illustrates how AI tools can make a union more member-centric: every voice is heard (via data), not just the loudest or those physically present at meetings.

3. **Algorithmic Audits for Fairness and Equity:** One of Valorian's flagship initiatives is using AI for bias detection and pay equity audits. Recognizing that many workplace inequalities (like gender pay gaps or biased promotion patterns) can be hidden in extensive HR data, Valorian's technical team developed algorithms to sift through payroll records, promotion histories, and performance evaluations provided (confidentially) by cooperative employers. These ML-driven audits can uncover patterns of discrimination more effectively than traditional manual

reviews. Research by Ferrara (2024) supports this approach, noting that AI can objectively flag systemic disparities that might be overlooked otherwise.

They have leveraged such tools to challenge unfair compensation structures. In industries like retail and hospitality, where wage discrepancies across gender or regions were suspected, Valorian's audits found concrete evidence of gaps. Notably, algorithmic audit in the retail sector uncovered a 14% gender pay gap (women earning 14% less on average than men in equivalent roles) across several major employers. Armed with this data, they prompted renegotiations with those companies, resulting in adjustments to pay scales to reduce the gap. This real-world result demonstrates AI's power as a tool for equity: the union moved beyond anecdotal advocacy to data-driven proof, which employers found hard to dispute. By integrating ML-driven audits into their negotiation strategies, they can demand transparency and fairness from employers and back up those demands with empirical evidence.

Additionally, their commitment to ethical AI extends beyond wage issues. They have appointed an internal committee (including data scientists, researchers, union reps, and external ethics advisors) to oversee all AI tools the union uses, ensuring that the AI's recommendations and findings are fair and unbiased. This oversight committee aligns with best-practice suggestions in the literature that call for interdisciplinary governance of AI in labor contexts. It also strengthens their credibility when it insists employers adopt similar ethical standards for any AI used in HR processes.

4. **AI for Workplace Safety and Risk Management:** Expanding its use of AI to health and safety, the union has begun to employ AI systems that monitor and analyze workplace safety data. For example, in the construction sector (one of the sectors Valorian covers), the union worked with employers to implement an AI-powered system that analyzes incident reports, sensor data from equipment, and environmental factors to predict high-risk conditions. These predictive safety models can alert when there's an elevated risk of accidents (such as patterns indicating machinery fatigue or worker exhaustion), prompting preventative action. Studies on AI's impact in workplace safety highlight that such predictive models can reduce occupational hazards by flagging risks before incidents occur. Valorian's AI-driven safety initiative has indeed resulted in improvements: at pilot sites, accident rates dropped after the introduction of the system, as potential issues (like needed maintenance or training deficits) were identified and addressed proactively.

This application demonstrates their comprehensive view of worker welfare: it's not only bargaining for wages but also leveraging technology to ensure physical well-being on the job. As discussed by Autor (2015), the unions also take part in the broader discussion about how automation and AI can augment worker safety rather than simply monitor or control workers. Importantly, Valorian can negotiate agreements that data from safety AIs will not be used punitively against workers (for instance, not to blame an individual for an AI-predicted risk), but strictly for prevention and remediation. This nuance is crucial for worker trust in such systems.

5. **Partnerships and Advocacy Initiatives Involving AI:** Recognizing its own resource limitations, they actively pursued partnerships to bolster its AI capabilities. In 2023, Valorian joined the International Organization of Human Capital Managers (DCH) as a partner in Spain. Through this partnership, Valorian gained access to expertise and tools for AI in human resources, and in return, Valorian provided the worker perspective to the organization. This collaboration exemplifies a public-private partnership model that can democratize access to AI innovations for unions. It helped Valorian bridge technical skill gaps and share the financial burden of developing AI tools, an approach recommended for low-resource unions elsewhere (ILO, 2025).

Additionally, they participate in broader advocacy coalitions around AI ethics. It has an ambassador in the *AI+Igual* initiative (literally "AI+Equal"), which promotes inclusivity and diversity in AI applications across Spain. Through AI+Igual, Valorian lends its voice to ensure that national AI strategies and corporate practices consider impacts on workers and do not exacerbate inequality. President Venegas's quote earlier about *"projects like AI+Igual"*. shows that Valorian sees this as part of its mission. In engaging with such initiatives, Valorian effectively takes on a dual role: it is both an innovator in using AI for its own operations and an advocate for responsible AI use in society at large. This dual role helps elevate the union's profile and influence. For example, Valorian was invited to provide input on the Spanish government's implementation plan for the EU AI Act, ensuring that the perspective of organized labor was considered in discussions about AI regulation and worker protections.

In summary, Valorian's integration of AI spans multiple dimensions of union activity. Internally, AI has been used to streamline membership management and provide data-driven insights (Valorian even digitized its membership database and applied AI to detect anomalies or predict lapsed memberships so they could intervene to retain those members). Externally, AI is a tool in negotiations, a subject of negotiations (ensuring AI used by employers is fair), and a focus of partnership and policy engagement. Their approach illustrates that a union can indeed modernize through technology without abandoning its core values of solidarity and advocacy. Each initiative reflects the union attempt to harness AI's benefits while managing its risks — a balance that the union consciously strives to maintain.

FINDINGS

This case reveals insightful findings about how AI can transform labor union operations. These findings cover the improvements observed within Valorian, as well as the contrasts between Valorian's approach and that of more traditional unions in Spain. Overall, the evidence suggests that AI and machine learning tools can serve as powerful instruments for proactive union advocacy, fair workplace policies, and increased union effectiveness, ultimately helping labor unions remain relevant in a rapidly evolving workforce (Dubal, 2023). At the same time, it underscores the importance of strategic foresight and ethical vigilance: AI's benefits are maximized when integrated thoughtfully, and they are not automatically realized by unions that do not invest in innovation.

The literature emphasizes that unions must align with technological advancements to maintain their relevance and effectiveness in an era where digitalization is fundamentally transforming the workplace (Chee, 2024; Piper, 2022). This gradual integration is crucial, as it demonstrates that embracing innovation is not merely a survival tactic but a pathway to leadership in shaping the future of labor representation in a digital economy (Chidoori & Belle, 2020; Editors, 2024). Moreover, the cautious approach of traditional unions highlights the urgent need for targeted initiatives to bridge the gap between their current practices and the expectations of a digitally engaged workforce. Research indicates that unions must adapt their strategies to remain relevant, particularly as younger workers increasingly demand representation that reflects their digital realities (Ponomareva, 2022).

Enhanced Representation and Proactive Advocacy: One key finding is that their use of AI has enabled it to shift from reactive to proactive representation of workers' interests. By leveraging data-driven insights (as detailed in the previous section), Valorian can identify issues before they escalate. For example, through predictive modeling, the union anticipated labour market changes and negotiated retraining programs ahead of major disruptions. This proactive stance contrasts with the behavior of many traditional unions that often find themselves responding after-the-fact to layoffs or policy changes. The literature supports the value of this proactive approach: Brynjolfsson & McAfee (2017) note that predictive analytics allows organizations to foresee shifts and act early. Valorian's success in this area underscores the necessity of strategic modernization for unions. By forming partnerships, fostering digital literacy among their staff, and initiating pilot projects in areas like operational efficiency and member engagement, unions can gradually integrate AI and similar technologies into their operations.

Valorian exemplifies this gradual, strategic integration. It did not adopt technology for technology's sake, but through targeted initiatives that aligned with its organizational priorities (e.g., improving bargaining outcomes, engaging members). This approach demonstrates that embracing innovation is not merely a survival tactic but a pathway to leadership in shaping the future of labor representation. Unions that follow Valorian's example by incrementally building their tech capacity can position themselves as leaders rather than followers in the digital economy.

Improved Member Engagement and Union Relevance: The findings also indicate that AI can help reinvigorate union membership and participation, which addresses a central challenge noted in the literature. Their AI-driven communication tools and personalized engagement efforts have made the union more accessible and relevant to workers, especially younger ones. This has potential implications for union affiliation rates: if workers see unions as modern and responsive, they are more likely to join and stay. Unions worldwide have been concerned with declining membership; Valorian's experience provides a case where leveraging technology correlates with stronger engagement metrics. While it is too early to claim a reversal of Spain's overall union density decline, Valorian's growth (it added several thousand new members in sectors like tech and e-commerce where unions traditionally had little presence) suggests that digital transformation can aid recruitment. As one Valorian organizer put it, "We meet workers where they are: on their phones and online." By doing so, they are re-establishing union visibility among segments like gig workers, contractors, and remote employees who are often hard to reach via traditional methods.

The broader implication is that AI and digital tools can help unions tap into the changing workforce, including the gig economy and remote work arrangements. Indeed, Valorian's proactive use of AI has allowed it to offer services (like the chatbot and online legal assistance) that are particularly valuable for temporary, gig, or geographically dispersed workers who might not have had union support before. This finding aligns with research by Ford (2024) on how global unions use digital activism to engage in social agenda-setting beyond traditional workplaces. Unions embracing such tools tend to maintain stronger representation, as they can adapt to how work and communication are changing.

Divergence between Innovative and Traditional Unions: The Valorian case also highlights a significant divergence between forward-thinking unions and those maintaining status quo. Within the Spanish labor movement, Valorian's strategy stands in sharp contrast to that of the major traditional unions (UGT and CC.OO.). These older unions have been slower to embrace AI and digital tools, due in part to resource limitations and a historical reliance on conventional advocacy methods.

Data from Spain's National Statistics Institute (INE) illustrates the environment: only 14% of Spanish companies with over 10 employees have tried to hire ICT specialists, and just 2% employ AI professionals (Cinco Días, 2024). This generally low level of digital adoption in companies reflects broader technological gaps that extend to unions as well. The cultural inertia in traditional unions, focused on immediate issues like wage negotiations and resisting change, has often led them to neglect long-term digital strategy.

Figure 2. Illustrates that 45.29% of large Spanish firms adopted AI by 2025, primarily for operational efficiency (62%) rather than ethical oversight (4.2%). Valorian's dual focus on efficiency (via automation) and equity (via bias audits) positions it as an outlier, bridging the gap between corporate AI trends and labor advocacy imperatives. Source: INE, 2025

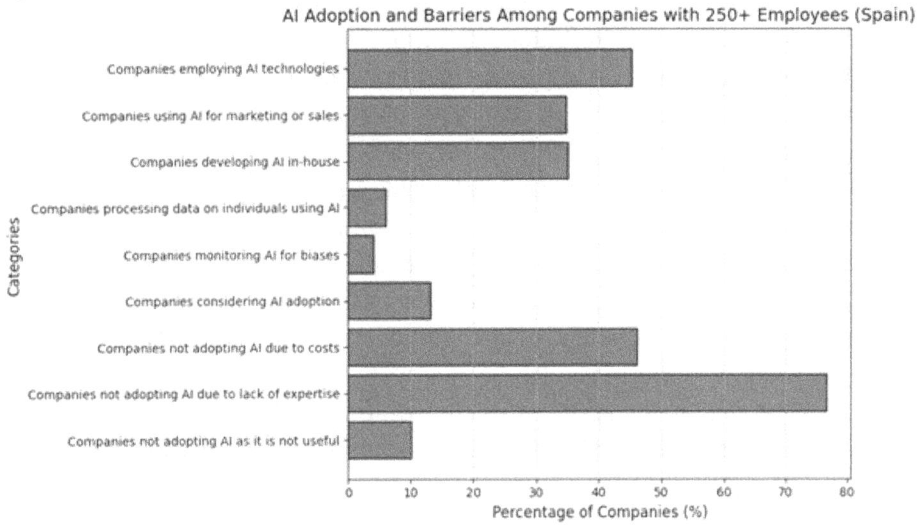

This study finds that such a cautious approach carries risks: unions that do not modernize may face declining membership and diminished influence, as they become less relevant to a workforce increasingly shaped by digital tools. Indeed, literature supports this observation – Carneiro & Costa (2020) warn of alienating younger workers if unions appear outdated, and Thomas & Turnbull (2021) suggest unions could lose policy influence if not keeping up with technological change. Conversely, Valorian's experience underscores that modernization can yield tangible benefits and renewed influence. It has even positioned Valorian to collaborate with employers on technology governance, whereas traditional unions often find themselves reacting to tech initiatives led solely by management.

In quantitative terms, while UGT and CC.OO. still command larger absolute membership numbers and collective bargaining coverage, Valorian has rapidly expanded in some areas where those unions are less present. Valorian's membership drives that feature its AI-enhanced service offerings have seen notable success. This suggests a potential re-balancing of power in the union landscape: innovative unions like Valorian could gain relative strength if legacy unions do not adapt. It also illustrates a broader point that emerged in the findings: technology can be an equalizer for newer or smaller unions to compete with established ones by offering superior services or insights.

Increased Bargaining Power and Outcomes: Using AI, Valorian has achieved some bargaining outcomes that likely would have been difficult otherwise. Its ability to present well-founded, data-backed cases in negotiations (for instance, proving a pay gap or demonstrating a productivity trend) has resulted in favorable agreements. Employers, confronted with rigorous analysis from the union side, have had to engage more earnestly with Valorian's proposals. This dynamic was observed in multiple instances, such as wage negotiations in retail and safety provisions in construction. As a result, Valorian secured not only pay raises but also joint AI governance committees in some workplaces (ensuring union input whenever employers introduce new AI systems affecting workers). This is a significant shift in the balance of power: traditionally, technology decisions were management prerogatives, but Valorian's expertise earned it a seat at the table. Recent studies underscore that AI can mitigate power asymmetries between unions and multinational corporations by equipping unions with predictive analytics to counter corporate strategies. Our findings concretely support that claim.

For example, anticipating that a large multinational was considering outsourcing certain departments, They used data analysis to propose alternative efficiency measures that saved costs without layoffs, undermining the rationale for outsourcing. In doing so, Valorian pre-empted a common corporate strategy (outsourcing to cut labor costs) by presenting a better-informed counterplan — a scenario directly aligning with Falcão Filho's (2024) arguments on predictive analytics enabling unions to counter outsourcing strategies. The outcome was that the company shelved the outsourcing plan and instead worked with the union on productivity improvements that did not reduce headcount.

Ethical and Organizational Challenges Remaining: Not all findings are positive; the case also reveals ongoing challenges and limits of what AI can do for unions. Valorian's leadership acknowledges that integrating AI is not a cure-all. There were instances where AI analysis suggested solutions that were not feasible due to human or political factors. For example, an algorithm might identify an optimal reallocation of workers to avoid layoffs, but the workers might be unwilling or unable to relocate or change roles, limiting the practical impact of the AI insight.

This underscores that human elements — communication, trust, consent — remain paramount. It echoes a caution from the literature: technology should be seen as a tool, not a replacement for the human processes of negotiation and collective action (Howard, 2019; Webster & O'Brien, 2020).

Furthermore, the union faced internal resistance initially from some representatives and members who were skeptical of AI, fearing it could lead to surveillance or dehumanization of union work. They had to invest in training its staff (capacity-building programs in data literacy and ethical AI use) and in educating members about how and why AI tools were being used. This internal change management is a vital finding: a union must cultivate a digital-friendly culture to fully benefit from AI. Without buy-in, even the best tools could languish unused.

Lastly, this case shows that while AI can amplify a union's reach and effectiveness, it also exposes the union to new risks and responsibilities. Valorian had to ensure data privacy for member information and guard against any biases in the algorithms it used (for instance, ensuring the chatbot gave consistent quality answers to all and didn't inadvertently prefer certain languages or terminologies). Mistakes in these areas could erode member trust. So far, Valorian has managed these issues well, partly by establishing the oversight structures described earlier. But it serves as a reminder that digital transformation in unions must be accompanied by robust ethical guidelines and transparency to maintain the trust of the workers they serve.

In conclusion, the findings from the Valorian case study illustrate a generally optimistic picture of AI's potential for labor unions – increased efficiency, improved member engagement, stronger bargaining positions – while also highlighting the critical importance of strategy, culture, and ethics in realizing that potential. These findings now provide the foundation for a more analytical discussion on specific themes such as power dynamics, membership trends, and the broader implications for the labor movement, which we will explore in the following section.

DISCUSSION

AI and the Balance of Power in Labor Relations

The introduction of AI into labor union operations has meaningful implications for the balance of power among workers, unions, and employers. Traditionally, employers have advantages in information and resources during collective bargaining and workforce management. The Valorian case, however, shows that AI can be a tool for unions to shift some of that balance back toward workers. By harnessing data analytics and predictive modeling, Valorian was able to counter management strategies and anticipate moves like outsourcing or automation impacts, thereby neutralizing some of the asymmetry in information. This supports the idea that technology, often seen as an employer asset, can also empower unions – a concept sometimes referred to as *"countervailing algorithmic power."*

Recent studies underscore this potential. Falcão Filho (2024) argues that predictive analytics enable unions to preemptively respond to corporate tactics (e.g., relocating production or restructuring) by providing evidence-based alternatives. In Valorian's experience, when the union presented data-driven solutions to management, it forced employers to engage on the union's terms rather than dictating unilaterally. This *recalibration of labor-capital dynamics* is significant. It means that unions with technical capabilities can challenge what used to be management's exclusive domain (complex decision analytics, scenario planning).

However, an important caveat emerged: power dynamics are not determined by technology alone. While Valorian's AI use gave it new leverage, ultimately the outcomes still depended on negotiation and the relative economic power of the parties. For instance, if an employer is determined to automate and accept short-term costs for long-term gains, even the best union data might not dissuade them without additional pressure (like public support or regulatory intervention). In such cases, AI equips the union to mount a stronger fight, but it does not guarantee victory.

Moreover, there's a risk of a new kind of arms race: as unions adopt AI, employers might invest in even more sophisticated AI for their side (for example, tools to optimize union avoidance or predict strike likelihood). We must consider who ultimately controls AI deployment. If management alone uses AI, it could widen the power gap — such as using AI surveillance to undermine organizing or tailor anti-union campaigns. Kelley (2023) warns of exactly this scenario, where employers use AI for *"advanced union-busting"* by identifying vulnerable points in union drives or subtly targeting pro-union workers. Hence, the balance of power outcome depends on whether unions too can employ AI (as Valorian did) and on the establishment of ground rules for AI usage in the workplace.

From a broader perspective, AI's impact on power relations calls for regulatory and collective safeguards. The EU's AI Act (2024) and similar initiatives become crucial backdrops. If such regulations prohibit certain high-risk uses of AI (for instance, surveillance or discriminatory algorithms), it protects the balance from tilting unfairly toward employers. Unions like Valorian advocating within these policy frameworks can help ensure AI isn't weaponized against workers. In essence, *AI can empower or oppress, depending on governance*. Valorian's positive example shows empowerment when a union takes initiative, but we should be vigilant that not all unions have these capabilities. This creates a potential inequality among unions themselves — those with resources to use AI vs. those without, possibly widening an intra-labor movement power gap.

AI has the potential to partially rebalance power in labor relations by giving unions new analytical strength. However, this is contingent on unions' access to technology, their strategic savvy in using it, and protective rules around AI in employment. If these conditions are met, as in Valorian's case, workers stand to gain a stronger voice relative to employers. If not, AI could just as easily reinforce employer dominance, especially in contexts where only companies harness its power. Therefore, a balanced implementation (involving social dialogue on AI and joint governance mechanisms) is key to ensuring AI serves as a tool of empowerment rather than control in the workplace.

AI's Impact on Union Membership and the Future of Work

One of the most pressing concerns for modern labor unions is declining membership and relevance in a fast-changing labor market. Our analysis of Valorian, combined with broader trends, suggests that AI can influence union membership dynamics and shape the future of work in complex ways.

On one hand, as demonstrated by Valorian, embracing AI and digital tools can make unions more attractive to current and potential members, particularly younger workers. The case showed that tech-savvy approaches to service delivery and communication improved member satisfaction and engagement. Younger workers, who are digital natives, often expect institutions to provide seamless online experiences. Valorian's mobile app, AI chatbot, and data-informed representation signaled to these workers that the union "speaks their language." As a result, some who might not have considered joining a union saw Valorian as modern and useful. This addresses a historical problem: younger and precarious workers often perceive unions as outdated or not beneficial to them (Carneiro & Costa, 2020). By updating its methods, Valorian began to close that perception gap.

We can foresee that unions adopting similar AI-enhanced strategies might slow or reverse the membership decline in certain sectors. They could tap into groups that have been hard to organize, such as gig economy workers, freelancers, workers in tech industries, etc. For example, a union could use AI to coordinate and mobilize dispersed gig workers via an app, providing a form of collective representation that fits their mode of work. There is already evidence of nascent efforts: some platform worker associations use algorithms to monitor platform fairness (like wage rates on ride-sharing apps) and rally workers when unfair practices are detected. This is essentially a union function executed through AI.

On the other hand, AI is also transforming the labor market itself, raising questions about the future of jobs and skill requirements. As noted, automation threatens some jobs while creating others. The net effect on union membership is uncertain. It could shrink the traditional bargaining units if, say, manufacturing heavily automates and employs fewer workers, as Frey & Osborne (2017) predict for many routine jobs. Conversely, new jobs in AI development, data analysis, and other tech fields could emerge – but these are often sectors with low unionization historically. The challenge for unions will be to extend their reach into emerging job categories. Valorian's proactive stance in tech and analytics might serve as a blueprint: unions might hire or partner with professionals in these fields to both service new worker demographics and to recruit them.

Another membership-related effect of AI is how it changes the *nature of worker affiliation*. Traditional union membership implied a somewhat stable employment relationship. But with AI enabling more gig-like platforms and on-demand labor, the workforce is becoming more fluid. People might engage with unions more as a service or community rather than as formal members tied to a single employer. Unions might evolve to something akin to "worker associations" that offer benefits, training, and representation in various scenarios, with AI managing the matchmaking of services to worker needs. This could broaden the appeal of unions – making them relevant even for those without a single long-term employer (the very group that's been growing and largely non-union).

The future of work also includes more remote work and globally distributed teams (a trend accelerated by technology and events like the COVID-19 pandemic). AI-driven collaboration tools and monitoring systems are now common in remote workplaces. This poses a membership challenge: remote workers may feel less connected to each other and thus less inclined to collective action. Unions will need to find ways to foster solidarity in virtual environments. AI could help by analyzing remote worker issues (through sentiment analysis of chat channels, for example) and identifying common grievances to rally around. Valorian used sentiment analysis to pick up on remote workers' concerns (like isolation and burnout), which helped it remain relevant to them. If a union can prove it effectively represents remote employees' interests, those workers have reason to join even if they never meet colleagues in person.

Importantly, the discussion of membership cannot ignore the macro-level trends. Union membership density in many countries has been correlated with several factors: labor laws, prevalence of collective bargaining agreements, economic sectors (manufacturing vs services), etc. AI is another factor now. For instance, a comparative look (as in Table 1 below) suggests that some countries with higher union densities (like the Nordics) also have been proactive in adopting workplace technologies, including AI, in ways that involve unions. There's possibly a virtuous cycle: strong unions negotiate good frameworks for tech implementation, which in turn ensures workers don't abandon unions because they see value in them.

Table 1. Trade union density and AI adoption rates in selected European countries (2024)

Country	Trade Union Density (%) (share of employees in unions)	AI Adoption Rate (%) (among enterprises)
Denmark	67%	27.6%
Sweden	70%	25.1%
Finland	74%	15.2%
Belgium	50%	24.7%
France	8%	10.0%
Spain	14%	11.8%
Poland	12%	5.9%
Romania	20%	3.1%
Bulgaria	18%	6.5%

*Sources:*ETUI (2023) for union density; Eurostat (2024) and OECD AI Observatory (2024) for AI adoption. (Elaborated by authors.)

This table suggests an interesting trend: countries with higher union density often have higher rates of AI adoption by companies. For example, Denmark and Sweden combine strong unions with high enterprise AI usage, whereas countries with weak unions (like Romania, Bulgaria) show very low AI uptake. While correlation isn't causation, one interpretation is that robust unions might facilitate innovation (by negotiating its use in fairways), whereas in places with weak labor representation, there may be either less pressure or capability to innovate responsibly. Spain sits in the middle-range on both metrics (14% density, ~12% AI adoption). Valorian's activities may help ensure Spain's AI adoption in workplaces goes together with union involvement, potentially improving both metrics.

The following Figure 3, a scatter plot illustrates the correlation between Trade Union Density (%) and AI Adoption Rates (%) in selected European countries, including Spain. The red trend line indicates the general relationship between the two variables.

Figure 3. Suggests that countries with higher trade union density (e.g., Denmark, Sweden, Finland) tend to have higher AI adoption rates, while those with lower union density (e.g., Romania, Poland, Bulgaria) tend to have lower AI adoption. Elaborated by author with data from ETUI, Eurostat and OECD (2025)

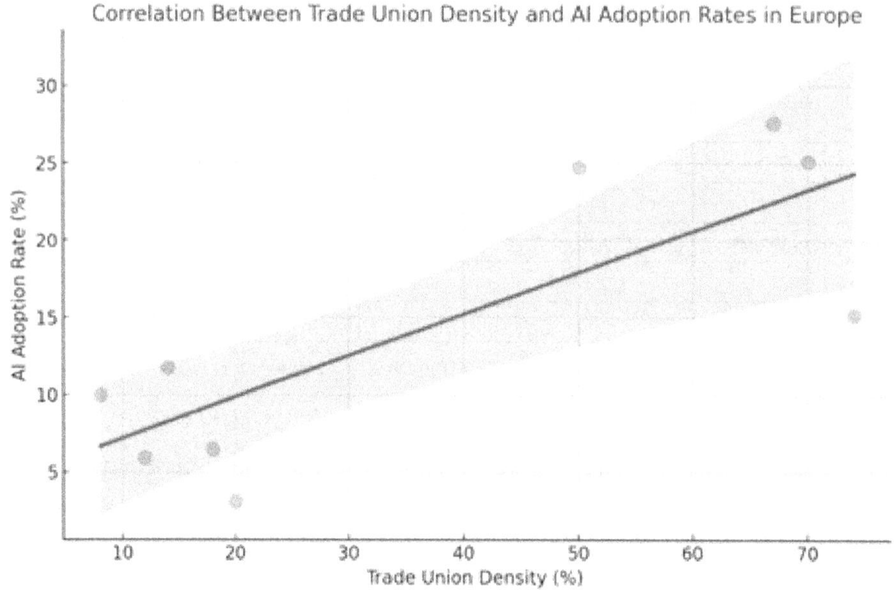

Looking ahead, the future of the labor market will likely be characterized by continuous technological disruption. AI might cause job displacement in waves (as new breakthroughs occur, e.g., in autonomous vehicles affecting transport jobs, or advanced algorithms affecting white-collar jobs like accounting or translation). Unions will need to become more agile and foresighted. They'll have to champion lifelong learning and reskilling for their members, possibly leveraging AI to personalize training opportunities. Valorian, for instance, has started pushing for joint employer-union programs to reskill workers for tech-driven changes, such as training retail cashiers in digital skills for e-commerce roles as automated checkout spreads.

Such initiatives can make union membership valuable as a career asset, not just a job security blanket. If being a union member means you are more likely to get retrained and promoted in the face of tech changes, then even ambitious young workers might see the union as an ally rather than an impediment. This flips the old narrative on its head — unions not as protectors of status quo jobs, but as facilitators of worker advancement in new industries. AI can help identify what skills are needed and who needs training, making unions more effective in this role.

In conclusion, AI's impact on union membership and the future of work is double-edged. It can pose existential challenges by altering job patterns and potentially weakening traditional organizing structures, but it also offers tools for unions to reinvent themselves and remain (or become) relevant to a new generation of workers in a new economy. Valorian's case provides a hopeful example that with innovation, unions can not only survive but also help shape the future labor market in ways that benefit workers — ensuring that technological progress does not come at the expense of fair representation and social justice.

Risks and Limitations of Digital Unionism

While the integration of AI and digital strategies offers many promising avenues for revitalizing unions, a balanced discussion must address the risks, challenges, and limitations associated with this "digital unionism." Valorian's positive outcomes are instructive, but it is equally important to critically examine potential downsides and boundaries of relying on digital tools in labor advocacy. The reviewers specifically requested a more critical perspective, which we provide here by exploring issues of technological over-reliance, ethical pitfalls, inclusivity, and structural constraints.

1. **Technological Dependence and Loss of Human Touch:** One risk of a heavy focus on AI is that a union could become over-reliant on technology at the expense of personal relationships and grassroots organizing. The solidarity that drives unionism has historically been built through face-to-face interactions, shared experiences on the shop floor, and collective actions like meetings and strikes. If too much is mediated through apps and algorithms, there is a concern that the *sense of community* could weaken. Members might begin to see the union as just a service provider rather than a collective movement. In Valorian's case, they consciously tried to mitigate this by using digital tools to augment (not replace) human connections — for example, union representatives still hold in-person or live video meetings to discuss what the data and chatbots find, keeping members involved in decision-making. However, not all attempts at digital unionism may strike this balance. A scenario to avoid is one where members only interact with a bot and never engage with fellow members or leaders; such a union would risk becoming a hollow shell.
2. **Digital Divide and Inequality:** The push towards digital tools can inadvertently exclude certain groups of workers, exacerbating inequalities. Not every worker is tech-savvy or has access to modern devices and reliable internet. Older workers might be less comfortable with apps; lower-income members might not afford data plans or have high-end smartphones; workers in remote areas might lack connectivity. If union services pivot to mostly online, these members could be

left behind. Valorian observed this issue when they rolled out their app — initial usage was much lower among older members. They responded by holding training sessions and still providing alternative phone hotlines. Unions must ensure *multi-channel access* to avoid disenfranchising a segment of their base. Inclusivity means maintaining traditional methods (like in-person office hours, phone calls, paper newsletters) alongside new ones, at least during a transition period. Furthermore, if union leadership is drawn from more tech-oriented staff, there could be an empathy gap with members who are less digital. Constant feedback loops are needed to check that innovations serve everyone.

3. **Privacy and Surveillance Concerns:** Digital initiatives in unions raise privacy issues. Members might worry: what data is the union collecting about me? How is it stored? Could it be exposed or misused? For example, if a union app tracks location to know when members are at work (perhaps to send timely surveys), that could be seen as intrusive. Or if sentiment analysis monitors social media, members might fear their posts are being watched. Unions must adhere to strict data protection practices, both ethically and often legally (e.g., GDPR in Europe). Valorian implemented privacy policies assuring members that data collected (like queries to the chatbot or survey responses) is anonymized in analysis and never shared outside union contexts without consent. Building trust in the union's use of AI is crucial; otherwise, members may not engage honestly with digital platforms, defeating the purpose. There's also the risk of data breaches – if the union collects detailed info, it becomes a target. A leak could be damaging (imagine employer-friendly media getting hold of an internal union strategy analysis, or a list of pro-union gig workers). So, unions must invest in cybersecurity, which is a new kind of expense and expertise they might not have considered in the past.
4. **Algorithmic Bias and Fairness Issues:** AI systems themselves can carry biases or make errors that have real consequences. If a union trusts an algorithm to, say, flag potential cases of discrimination or to suggest which issues to negotiate on, and that algorithm has blind spots, the union might inadvertently ignore important problems or mis-prioritize. As noted earlier, AI can reflect historical biases; for instance, an algorithm analyzing grievances might undervalue issues predominantly affecting minorities or women if those were underreported historically. Binns (2018) and others have highlighted how algorithmic outputs need careful human interpretation. Valorian tackled this by keeping humans "in the loop" — every AI finding is reviewed by union committees that have diverse representation, to catch anything that looks off or unjust. They also consulted external experts on fairness in machine learning (referencing works like Buolamwini & Gebru 2018) to adjust their tools. Not every union will have the resources to do this level of auditing. There's a risk that smaller unions

might use off-the-shelf AI solutions without fully understanding their workings, potentially leading to misguided actions.

An example hypothetical risk: a poorly configured AI might conclude that a certain category of workers (say part-time workers) is "less engaged" because they respond less to surveys, and thus the union might de-emphasize their issues — whereas in reality their lower response rate could be due to survey timing or other confounders. If the union followed that faulty insight, part-time workers' real concerns might be neglected, which is a bias outcome. Therefore, critical oversight of AI recommendations is needed; unions must treat AI outputs as advice, not gospel.

5. **Resource Constraints and Inequality Between Unions:** Implementing AI systems, maintaining them, and training people to use them can be resource intensive. Large unions or those in wealthy nations might manage it, but smaller unions or those in developing countries might struggle, potentially widening a global gap in union capabilities. There is a risk that "digital unionism" becomes effective only for a subset of well-off unions, while others fall further behind, unable to compete with employer's tech or even with other unions. This could, in the worst case, lead to a consolidation where big tech-enabled unions dominate and local or niche unions fade away, reducing the diversity of worker representation. Strategic collaborations (like union federations pooling resources to build AI tools that all affiliates can use) could be a way to mitigate this. For example, an international federation might develop an open source chatbot framework for any union to adapt cheaply, ensuring broader access.
6. **The Limits of Digital Action:** There are also fundamental limits to what can be achieved digitally. Some aspects of unionism require physical presence or human solidarity that no algorithm can replace. Strikes, for example, happen in the physical world — AI might help predict the outcome or optimal timing of a strike, but the courage and will to strike is a human factor. Collective bargaining negotiation ultimately comes down to human negotiators sitting (virtually or physically) across the table; data can inform but not make the decision to hold the line or compromise. Additionally, certain creative or moral judgments – like framing a new demand for AI governance that appeals to public opinion – come from human deliberation. Overemphasis on data could potentially *stifle creativity* or *moral clarity* if not checked. For instance, a union might have data suggesting members are lukewarm about an issue, but leadership may still decide it's a core principle worth fighting for (e.g., a matter of solidarity with a smaller group of marginalized workers). Blindly following data might lead to a more technocratic unionism that lacks a soul or the ability to inspire.

7. **Ethical Position of Unions on Technology:** Unions also have a role in questioning technology, not just using it. A risk of becoming very tech-oriented is that a union might lose sight of questioning whether certain technologies should be opposed or limited. For example, the union could use AI well, but what if an employer wants to implement a surveillance AI that is fundamentally against worker dignity? The union must be ready to say *no* to technology in some cases, not just figure out how to incorporate it. In the fervor of "we can make it work," there's the ethical stance of drawing lines – like opposing facial recognition monitoring at workplaces even if it might produce some safety data – because it intrudes on privacy. Valorian did engage in this by ensuring AI is framed as an empowerment tool, not surveillance, and by advocating boundaries on data use. Unions must maintain that critical perspective: technology should serve workers, not vice versa.

Considering these issues, it is clear that "digital unionism" must be pursued cautiously and thoughtfully. The Valorian case was largely successful, but it also encountered some of these challenges (privacy concerns, initial member skepticism, need for significant training investment). Unions should approach AI as *augmenting tools*, with the union's democratic processes and solidarity values firmly in the driver's seat. There should be checks and balances – for example, regular audits of how digital tools are affecting membership and outcomes, open communication with members about what the union is doing with AI, and ethical codes for digital conduct.

Finally, while digital transformation is important, redundancy and backup plans are wise. If the tech fails (say a system outage or a tool giving bad info), the union's functions shouldn't grind to a halt. Keeping traditional skills alive (organizing, personal advocacy, manual data analysis capabilities) ensures resilience.

By acknowledging these risks and limits, unions can navigate the digital era more safely. The discussion above serves as a reminder that progress comes with pitfalls – and that the measure of success for "sindicalismo digital" (digital unionism) will not only be in flashy AI deployments, but in how well unions uphold their core mission of worker empowerment amid all the high-tech changes. A balanced, worker-centered approach to AI is crucial: one that leverages technology's benefits while fiercely guarding against its dangers.

RECOMMENDATIONS

Based on the above analysis of Valorian's experience and the broader trends in AI and labor unions, we propose the following strategic recommendations for labor unions considering AI integration:

- **Develop a Clear AI Integration Roadmap:** Unions should create a strategic plan for adopting AI that aligns with their core objectives (e.g. improving member services, enhancing bargaining power). This plan should start with comprehensive needs assessments to identify where AI can have the highest impact. For example, automating routine administrative tasks (like dues processing or contract database searches) can free up union staff for member-facing work. The roadmap should also include pilot projects to test AI solutions on a small scale before a wider rollout. (In Valorian's case, they piloted a predictive analytics tool on a single sector to refine it before expanding union wide.) Starting with pilot programs allows a union to learn and adapt while minimizing risks. As part of the roadmap, set measurable goals (e.g., reduce response time to member inquiries by 50% through a chatbot, or identify 3 systemic issues per year via data analysis to address in bargaining). Having clear plans and metrics will help keep the AI integration focused and accountable.
- **Invest in Digital Literacy and Training:** Building internal capacity is crucial. Unions should train their representatives, staff, and interested members in understanding and using AI tools. This might involve workshops on data analysis basics, hiring or developing tech specialists within the union, and sharing knowledge through union networks. Digital literacy efforts ensure that the introduction of AI is met with competence rather than fear. It also democratizes the technology – empowering local shop stewards, for instance, to use data insights in their daily problem-solving. Valorian illustrated this by partnering with the International Organization of Human Capital Managers (DCH) to gain expertise and then disseminating that know-how internally. Unions might follow a similar model: either partnering with experts or leveraging union federations to provide training resources. The goal is to make sure that the use of AI is widespread and participatory within the union, not confined to a small tech team.
- **Prioritize Ethical AI Governance:** Unions must champion **ethical considerations** in every step of AI adoption. This includes establishing guidelines or committees to oversee AI use, focusing on transparency, fairness, inequities and data privacy (Cowgill, 2018). We recommend that unions audit their AI tools for bias or unintended consequences on a regular basis. If possible, involve a mix of stakeholders in this oversight – union members (to voice concerns), technical experts, and ethicists or trusted external advisors. Unions should also secure informed consent from members for use of any personal data and be transparent about what data is collected and why. By taking the high road on ethics, unions not only protect their members but also set standards that they can demand employers follow. For instance, Valorian's

practice of conducting algorithmic audits to ensure AI-driven decisions are fair can be emulated to proactively address biases. Unions possibly will publish an annual "AI impact report" to their membership detailing how AI was used and what safeguards are in place, which could build trust.

- **Engage in Public-Private Partnerships for Technology Access:** To mitigate resource constraints, unions should consider forming partnerships with academic institutions, non-profits, or even tech companies under the right conditions (without compromising independence). Collaboration can help unions access cutting-edge tools or expertise that would be hard to develop alone. For example, a union could partner with a university research lab working on AI for social good to develop custom applications (like an AI that scans legal texts for worker-friendly clauses). Another approach is unions across sectors pooling resources to create a shared digital platform. In Valorian's scenario, joining forces with DCH provided technical support and innovations that the union then applied in a worker-centric way. Additionally, public funding or grants for digital innovation in labor organizations could be sought; unions should advocate for such support as part of labor policy agendas. These partnerships and funding streams ensure that unions, especially smaller ones, are not left behind in the digital transformation due to lack of funds or skills.
- **Embed AI Usage in Core Union Activities (with a Human Touch):** Unions should integrate AI in ways that enhance, not replace, human judgment and interaction. For member outreach, AI-driven tools (like Valorian's chatbot or a targeted texting system) should be used to supplement personal outreach by union reps, not to eliminate it. We recommend blended approaches: for instance, an AI might draft a response to a member's question, but a union staffer reviews it for empathy and nuance before sending. In collective bargaining preparation, algorithms can crunch numbers and identify trends, but the negotiating team should deliberate on strategy incorporating those insights with their experiential knowledge. Essentially, unions should use AI to do the heavy lifting of data processing and information distribution, thereby freeing human unionists to do what they do best – organize, advocate, and build relationships. Maintaining this balance will help preserve the union's collective spirit and ensure technology serves the union's mission rather than reshaping it.
- **Advocate for Supportive Policy and Regulatory Frameworks:** Unions have a role not just in adapting to AI, but in shaping the context in which AI is deployed in workplaces. We recommend that unions push for laws and regulations that protect workers in the age of AI. This could include legal provisions for algorithmic transparency in management decisions (so that, for

example, if an AI is used to allocate shifts or evaluate performance, workers/unions have the right to understand the criteria). It also involves advocating for a say in how AI is introduced at the workplace (e.g., through works councils or collective agreement clauses on technology). Unions should support initiatives like the EU's AI Act and ensure they are implemented in ways that uphold workers' rights. Moreover, unions could lobby for public funding for worker retraining programs in AI-impacted industries, and for the inclusion of union representatives in national AI ethics committees or task forces. By engaging proactively in the policy arena, unions can extend their protective function beyond their membership to the workforce at large, ensuring that AI adoption is coupled with job security measures and respect for labor standards.

- **Focus on Member-Centric AI Applications:** The ultimate test for any tech adoption by a union is whether it benefits the membership. We recommend prioritizing AI projects that have clear, tangible advantages for members' day-to-day working lives or union interactions. This includes tools that improve services (like faster handling of grievances, personalized updates on issues they care about) and initiatives that directly address members' concerns (like AI analysis detecting unsafe conditions or pay inequities, which the union can then act on). For example, if a union's members are concerned about job security in the face of automation, the union might deploy an AI to predict which job roles are most at risk and then use that information to negotiate retraining or job transition support with the employer. Another member-centric use is employing AI to translate union materials into multiple languages in real-time, fostering inclusion of migrant workers. By visibly linking AI uses to solving member problems, the union will build buy-in among the membership. Transparent communication is key: unions should explain to members how a given AI initiative (say, sentiment analysis of survey responses) will ultimately help address their needs (for instance, "this will help us prioritize what to fight for in our next contract based on what most of you are telling us").

Each of these recommendations comes with its own implementation considerations, but together they form a blueprint for embracing AI in a way that strengthens labor unions. The overarching theme is that unions should be proactive, not reactive: plan for technology, don't just react to it; train people to harness it; hold it to high ethical standards; and use it to amplify the fundamental purpose of unions – to protect and empower workers. By doing so, labor unions can transform what might seem like a threat into an opportunity, ensuring that they remain a vital force in the future world of work.

FUTURE RESEARCH AND DIRECTIONS

While this chapter has provided insights into the use of AI in labor unions through the case of Valorian, it also raises several questions and areas that warrant further investigation. Future research and union initiatives should consider the following:

- **Conduct Primary Research on Union Member Perspectives:** Given that our study relied on secondary data, a crucial next step is to gather firsthand data from union members and leaders. Future studies should employ surveys, interviews, and focus groups with members of AI-forward unions (like Valorian and others) to capture their experiences, concerns, and suggestions regarding digital tools in their union. Qualitative insights from the ground can validate and enrich the findings from case studies and help identify any disconnects between leadership-driven tech initiatives and member satisfaction. For example, interviewing members can reveal if tools like chatbots truly make them feel more heard, or if any group feels alienated by digital changes. Such primary research will ensure that technological adoption remains aligned with worker interests and can guide adjustments in implementation.
- **Compare Multiple Union Case Studies across Contexts:** To enhance generalizability, future research should look beyond a single case and perform comparative case studies of unions in different sectors and countries embracing technology. This could involve analyzing a spectrum of cases – from large national unions in advanced economies to smaller unions or worker cooperatives in developing regions – to see how context influences the use and impact of AI. Comparative studies would help determine which successes of Valorian are replicable versus which were context dependent. They would also identify potential cultural, legal, or economic barriers that some unions face. For instance, a comparative study might examine how a union in the manufacturing sector uses AI versus a public sector union, or how regulatory differences between Spain and another country affect union tech strategies. Insights from multiple cases can lead to best practice frameworks that any union might adapt.
- **Examine AI's Long-Term Effects on Union Efficacy and Labor Market Outcomes:** Future research should adopt a longitudinal approach to assess how AI integration influences union effectiveness over time and broader labor market conditions. Key questions include: Does the introduction of AI correlate with sustained membership growth or retention? Do AI-equipped unions secure better contract outcomes (wages, safety clauses, etc.) compared to those that do not use such tools? How does AI in unions affect the labor market power balance in the long run – for example, does it contribute to

higher overall union density or influence non-union employers to improve practices (due to competitive pressure)? Long-term data and trend analysis could reveal unintended consequences as well, such as shifts in union staff roles or changes in how workers perceive unions. Monitoring and evaluating these trends over, say, a 5-10 year period would provide evidence on whether "digital unionism" is delivering on its promise and what mid-course corrections might be needed.

- **Adaptation of the Valorian Model to Different Political and Economic Contexts:** Further exploration is needed on how elements of Valorian's approach can be adapted to contexts with different constraints. For example, in environments where union activity is restricted or unions have fewer resources, can AI-driven strategies still be leveraged? Research could explore low-cost, open-source AI tools for unions operating on shoestring budgets or under repressive regimes (where perhaps AI could help with clandestine organizing through encrypted communication, etc.). Similarly, examining how AI can help unions penetrate traditionally weakly unionized sectors (like tech startups, gig work, or informal economy segments) would be valuable. This line of inquiry aligns with questions raised about the broader applicability of the Valorian model and could lead to tailored digital strategies for different union contexts, ensuring the benefits of AI are not confined to a few well-off organizations.
- **Interdisciplinary Studies on AI Governance Involving Unions:** Since union engagement with AI crosses into technological, legal, and ethical domains, future work could benefit from an interdisciplinary approach. Collaborations between labor researchers, computer scientists, ethicists, and economists could produce comprehensive studies. One idea is to simulate or model various scenarios of workplace AI introduction (e.g., algorithmic management of workers) and then involve union stakeholders in designing governance frameworks for those scenarios. Through simulations and experiments, researchers can evaluate which frameworks best protect workers and how unions can enforce or negotiate them. This research could directly inform policy – for example, by testing the effectiveness of requiring algorithmic transparency or the presence of "algorithm auditors" in collective agreements. The outcome would be evidence-based recommendations on regulatory or collective bargaining language that unions worldwide could adopt to manage AI's impact on the workforce.
- **Continuous Monitoring of Risks and Mitigation Strategies:** As AI technology and its applications evolve rapidly, research should also focus on continuous risk assessment. Future studies should look for new forms of AI that could affect unions, such as advanced employee monitoring systems or AI-

driven hiring that might circumvent collective agreements. Understanding these emerging threats will allow development of timely mitigation strategies. For instance, if "AI union-busting" tools become a trend, research should document cases and successes/failures of union countermeasures to inform the larger labor community. Essentially, an ongoing "state of AI in labor" report or index could be created, to which unions contribute data. This would track progress, highlight innovation, and flag dangers annually, keeping the conversation current and solutions proactive.

By pursuing these future lines of inquiry and action, we can deepen our understanding of how AI and other advanced technologies interact with labor union operations. This knowledge will help ensure that as technology continues to transform work, labor organizations are equipped with the strategies and tools to transform along with it – safeguarding the rights and interests of workers in the digital age.

CONCLUSIONS

The integration of artificial intelligence into labor union operations represents both a disruptive force and an unprecedented opportunity for revitalizing worker advocacy in the digital age. The case of Valorian – a pioneering Spanish union that has embraced AI technologies – demonstrates how unions can transcend traditional adversarial models and redefine their role as proactive, data-driven institutions. By leveraging AI to anticipate labor market shifts, streamline administrative processes, and combat systemic inequities, Valorian exemplifies the transformative potential of technology in bridging the gap between historical labor practices and contemporary workforce demands.

The experiences detailed in this chapter indicate that AI can enhance a union's effectiveness: improving responsiveness to members, providing robust evidence in negotiations, and enabling strategic foresight. In Valorian's case, early adoption of tools like predictive analytics and algorithmic audits has yielded tangible gains such as better-informed bargaining outcomes and increased member engagement. These successes suggest that, when implemented thoughtfully, AI technologies can be harnessed to strengthen the foundational goals of labor unions – equity, solidarity, and effective representation.

However, the transformation is neither linear nor universally replicable. It is contingent on factors like strategic foresight, ethical vigilance, and institutional adaptability. As evidenced by the divergent trajectories within Spain's labor movement, not all unions have been able or willing to innovate at the same pace. Traditional unions like UGT and CC.OO., constrained by resource limitations and cultural inertia, have so far been slower to adopt these new tools. This has highlighted a digital divide: unions with the capacity to innovate can rapidly advance, while others risk falling behind. The Valorian case thus underscores a broader lesson – embracing AI is fast becoming a necessity for unions to remain relevant, but it requires commitment and investment that some organizations may struggle with.

One of the most significant implications of AI integration is its potential impact on union membership and influence. This study argues that with AI, unions like Valorian can better connect with a changing workforce, including younger and more tech-oriented workers who might otherwise be unrepresented. Early evidence from Valorian shows that using digital platforms and data-driven engagement can help re-establish union visibility and value in sectors where traditional outreach methods have faltered (for example, among gig and remote workers). In a labor market increasingly characterized by precarious employment and technologically mediated work, such adaptability may be key to unions "being back in the game," as it enables them to meet workers where they are – in digital spaces and using modern communication channels.

Crucially, the successful incorporation of AI in unions must remain anchored to core union values and objectives. Their journey highlights that technology should not be pursued for its own sake, but rather to further long-standing principles of worker empowerment, fairness, and collective action. For instance, Valorian utilized AI not only to improve efficiency but to actively promote equity – such as performing algorithmic audits that brought to light gender pay gaps and then negotiating remedies. By aligning AI use with union ideals (like combating discrimination and fostering inclusion), Valorian ensured that the technology reinforced rather than undermined its social mission. This alignment is a critical guidepost for other unions: digital tools must be implemented in ways that enhance solidarity and trust, framing AI as a tool for worker empowerment rather than as an instrument of surveillance or control.

The analysis also emphasizes a balanced perspective by acknowledging the challenges and risks of digital transformation in unions. The chapter discussed how lack of investment, skills deficits, or mismanagement of technology can pose impediments. Indeed, not all unions will find it easy to replicate Valorian's model due to such structural weaknesses. Valorian's ability to sidestep some challenges (partly thanks to partnerships and a collaborative ethos) demonstrates the importance of seeking support and rethinking union structures to integrate AI. Yet even Valorian had to address concerns about data privacy, algorithmic bias, and the need for cultural change within the union – reminding us that the journey involves continuous learning and adaptation.

Looking forward, the broader labor movement stands at a crossroads. Global trends suggest that as AI and automation reshape industries, unions face a choice: innovate and engage with these technologies proactively, or risk marginalization.

The Valorian case provides a hopeful narrative that unions can indeed innovate while staying true to their values. It shows that embracing technology is not antithetical to labor's cause; rather, if harnessed correctly, it can amplify the reach and effectiveness of worker representation. For example, AI can expedite processes (making unions more agile in addressing workplace issues), uncover hidden injustices (through data analysis), and facilitate new forms of organizing (via digital platforms for mobilization).

However, the chapter also cautions that such digital evolution must be managed responsibly. Unions must ensure that technological adoption does not erode democratic participation within the union, sideline the human connections that bind members, or create new forms of exclusion. The concept of "sindicalismo digital" (digital unionism) holds promise, but it must incorporate safeguards – training members, protecting data, and maintaining transparency – to truly deliver sustainable benefits. In essence, unions should strive for a model where technology and human solidarity complement each other, each compensating for the other's weaknesses.

In conclusion, the story of Valorian and the analysis presented illustrate that the future of labor unions in the age of AI is one of both great opportunity and serious responsibility. AI and digital tools offer unions a chance to rejuvenate themselves, to operate smarter and advocate better in a rapidly changing world of work. Valorian's case stands as proof of concept that a union can integrate AI into its DNA and reap rewards for its members. At the same time, this transformation comes with challenges that require careful navigation – from ensuring ethical tech practices to bridging resource gaps among unions. The findings and discussions in this chapter aim to inform and inspire labor unions, policymakers, and researchers by showing that with innovation, planning, and a steadfast commitment to worker-centric values, labor unions can adapt to the digital era and continue to be a vital force for social justice and worker rights. In a world where algorithms and data increasingly shape every facet of life, the voice of organized labor – augmented by AI but guided by human conscience – can and must remain a key shaper of the future of work.

REFERENCES

Autor, D. H. (2015). Why are there still so many jobs? The history and future of workplace automation. *The Journal of Economic Perspectives*, *29*(3), 3–30. DOI: 10.1257/jep.29.3.3

Bakunin, M. (1871). *La théologie politique de Mazzini et l'Internationale*. Imprimerie G. Guillaume Fils.

Ballantyne, A., Forlizzi, J., & Weise, C. (2024). A vision for centering workers in technology development. *Issues in Science and Technology*. Retrieved from https://issues.org/union-workers-tech-development-ballantyne-forlizzi-weise/

Başol, K., & Yalçın, M. (2021). How does the digital economy and society index (DESI) affect labor market indicators in EU countries? *Human Systems Management*, *40*(3), 1–12. DOI: 10.3233/HSM-200904

Bayón Pérez, J., & Arenas Falótico, A. J. (2019). Various perspectives of labor and human resources challenges and changes due to automation and artificial intelligence. *Academicus International Scientific Journal*, *20*, 106–118. DOI: 10.7336/academicus.2019.20.08

Binns, R. (2018). Fairness in machine learning: Lessons from political philosophy. In *Proceedings of the 2018 Conference on Fairness, Accountability, and Transparency* (pp. 149–159). https://doi.org/DOI: 10.1145/3178876.3186088

Brynjolfsson, E., & McAfee, A. (2014). *The second machine age: Work, progress, and prosperity in a time of brilliant technologies*. W. W. Norton & Company.

Buolamwini, J., & Gebru, T. (2018). Gender shades: Intersectional accuracy disparities in commercial gender classification. In *Proceedings of Machine Learning Research, 81* (Conference on Fairness, Accountability, and Transparency) (pp. 1–15). Retrieved from https://proceedings.mlr.press/v81/buolamwini18a.html

Carneiro, B., & Costa, H. (2020). Digital unionism as a renewal strategy? Social media use by trade union confederations. *The Journal of Industrial Relations*, *64*(1), 26–51. DOI: 10.1177/0022185620979337

Chee, L. (2024). Hard numbers and "velvet triangles": Mobilising statistics for the ILO convention on domestic work. *OSF Preprints*. https://doi.org/DOI: 10.31235/osf.io/9fbu7

Chidoori, C., & Belle, J. (2020). Attitudes toward and experiences of digital labour in South Africa. In *Proceedings of the 19th International Conference on Social Implications of Computers in Developing Countries* (pp. 102–116). https://doi.org/ DOI: 10.1007/978-3-030-64697-4_9

Cinco Días. (2024, October 22). UGT: Ni la inteligencia artificial ni el empleo tech avanzan en el tejido productivo español. *El País*. Retrieved from https://cincodias.elpais.com/companias/2024-10-22/ugt-ni-la-inteligencia-artificial-ni-el-empleo-tech-avanzan-en-el-tejido-productivo-espanol.html

Conradt, D. P. (2025, January 31). Social Democratic Party of Germany. *Encyclopedia Britannica*. Retrieved from https://www.britannica.com/topic/Social-Democratic-Party-of-Germany

Cowgill, B. (2018). Bias and productivity in humans and algorithms: Theory and evidence from résumé screening. *Columbia Business School Research Paper*. https://doi.org/DOI: 10.2139/ssrn.3307879

DCH. (2023). Valorian joins DCH as a partner in Spain. *International Organization of Human Capital Managers*. Retrieved from https://www.orgdch.org/en/valorian-joins-dch-as-a-partner-in-spain/

Didier, E. (2021). Are we ready? Labour market transit to the digital economy. *Journal of Adult and Continuing Education*, *27*(1), 1–20. DOI: 10.1177/1477971420983347

Dubal, V. (2023). On algorithmic wage discrimination. *Columbia Law Review*, *123*(7), 1929–1992.

Editors, T.The Editors. (2024). Editorial: Hamba kahle, Eddie Webster: A luta continua! *Global Labour Journal*, *15*(2). Advance online publication. DOI: 10.15173/glj.v15i2.5863

European Commission. (2024). Regulation (EU) 2024/1689 laying down harmonised rules on artificial intelligence (Artificial Intelligence Act). *Official Journal of the European Union*. Retrieved from https://eur-lex.europa.eu/legal-content/EN/TXT/?uri=CELEX:32024R1689

European Parliament. (2024). Artificial Intelligence Act: MEPs adopt landmark law. *European Parliament News*. Retrieved from https://www.europarl.europa.eu/news/en/press-room/20240308IPR19015/artificial-intelligence-act-meps-adopt-landmark-law

European Trade Union Institute (ETUI). (2023). Trade union density in Europe: Trends and implications. *ETUI Report on European Labour Relations*. Retrieved from https://www.etui.org

Eurostat. (2024). Artificial intelligence adoption by enterprises in the European Union. *European Commission Statistical Reports*. Retrieved from https://ec.europa.eu/eurostat

Falcão Filho, H. A. (2024). Making sense of negotiation and AI: The blossoming of a new collaboration. *Journal of Strategic Contracting and Negotiation*. https://doi.org/DOI: 10.1177/20555636241269270

Ferrara, E. (2024). Fairness and bias in artificial intelligence: A brief survey of sources, impacts, and mitigation strategies. *Sci*, *6*(1), 3. DOI: 10.3390/sci6010003

Ford, M. (2024). Beyond workplace-related issues: How global unions use digital activism to engage in social agenda-setting. *Global Networks*, *24*(1), 1–20. DOI: 10.1111/glob.12485

Frey, C. B., & Osborne, M. A. (2017). The future of employment: How susceptible are jobs to computerisation? *Technological Forecasting and Social Change*, *114*, 254–280. DOI: 10.1016/j.techfore.2016.08.019

Gaido, D. (2021). The First Workers' Government in History: Karl Marx's Addenda to Lissagaray's History of the Commune of 1871. *Historical Materialism*, *29*(1), 49–112. DOI: 10.1163/1569206X-12341972

González, F. A. (2006). The Spanish Socialist Workers Party (PSOE), 1879–1988: From Republican to Liberal Socialism. *Documentos de trabajo (Instituto de Estudios Sociales Avanzados de Andalucía)*, (19), 1.

Howard, J. (2019). Artificial intelligence: Implications for the future of work. *American Journal of Industrial Medicine*, *62*(11), 917–926. DOI: 10.1002/ajim.23037 PMID: 31436850

IBM. (2022). *Global AI Adoption Index*. IBM Corporation. Retrieved from https://www.ibm.com/reports/ai-adoption-2022

International Labour Organization. (2025). EESC and ILO join forces to shape a fair and inclusive AI-driven future. Retrieved from https://www.ilo.org/resource/news/ilo-and-eesc-join-forces-shape-fair-and-inclusive-ai-driven-future-high

Josefsson, J., & Wall, J. (2020). Empowered inclusion: Theorizing global justice for children and youth. *Globalizations*, *17*(6), 1043–1060. DOI: 10.1080/14747731.2020.1736853

Kelley, B. J. (2023). Belaboring the algorithm: Artificial intelligence and labor unions. *Yale Journal on Regulation Bulletin, 41*, 88–112. Retrieved from https://www.yalejreg.com/bulletin/belaboring-the-algorithm-artificial-intelligence-and-labor-unions/

Krzywdzinski, M., Gerst, D., & Butollo, F. (2023). Promoting human-centred AI in the workplace: Trade unions and their strategies for regulating the use of AI in Germany. *Transfer: European Review of Labour and Research, 29*(1), 53–70. DOI: 10.1177/10242589221142273

Musson, A. E. (1990). *British Trade Unions, 1800–1875*. Macmillan Education UK. DOI: 10.1007/978-1-349-10939-5_1

OECD AI Observatory. (2024). AI adoption and workforce transformation in Europe. *OECD Data Report on Digitalization*. Retrieved from https://oecd.ai

Organisation for Economic Co-operation and Development (OECD). (2020). Labour market indicators by country (2015–2020) [Data set]. *OECD Data Explorer*. Retrieved from https://data-explorer.oecd.org (accessed via OECD AI Observatory).

Osoria Labrada, A. (2022). Review of the book *The Communist Manifesto*, by C. Marx & F. Engels (1848). *EduSol, 22*(79), 240–243.

Piper, N. (2022). Temporary labour migration in Asia: The transnationality-precarity nexus. *International Migration (Geneva, Switzerland), 60*(2), 1–20. DOI: 10.1111/imig.12982

Ponomareva, K. (2022). Analysis of the OECD and the United Nations' approaches to developing an international consensus on reforming the rules of taxation of digital services. *Kutafin Law Review, 9*(3), 564–585. DOI: 10.17803/2713-0525.2022.3.21.564-585

Tascón Fernández, L. J. (2000). The organization of the labour market in Spain since 1890. *Documentos de trabajo (Universidad de Oviedo. Facultad de Ciencias Económicas)*, (207). http://hdl.handle.net/10651/45814

Thomas, H., & Turnbull, P. (2021). Navigating the perilous waters of partisan scholarship: Participatory action research (PAR) with the European Transport Workers' Federation (ETF). *Work, Employment and Society, 35*(3), 703–720. DOI: 10.1177/09500170211038531

UNI Global Union. (2024). How creative and cultural workers shape Generative AI. Retrieved from https://uniglobalunion.org/news/shaping-generative-ai-in-the-creative-and-cultural-sector/

Venegas, M. (2023). *Interview with Capital Radio* [Radio broadcast]. Meta Empresas Inc., Capital Radio. Available at https://youtu.be/Cq12gCEELBY

Webb, P. D. (2025, January 29). Labour Party. *Encyclopedia Britannica*. Retrieved from https://www.britannica.com/topic/Labour-Party-political-party

Webster, E., & O'Brien, R. (2020). Ten years of the Global Labour Journal: Reflecting on the rise of the new global labour studies. *Global Labour Journal*, *11*(1), 1–19. DOI: 10.15173/glj.v11i1.4166

Wood, A. J. (2021). Algorithmic management and trade union responses. *Work, Employment and Society*, *35*(1), 1–16. DOI: 10.1177/0950017020969593

Chapter 2
Automation, Digitalization, and Unionism in Argentina:
Adaptation and Resistance

Roberto Alejandro Llauro
https://orcid.org/0000-0002-1589-4348
LIGS University, USA

ABSTRACT

This chapter explores the historical evolution, current challenges, and future prospects of labor unionism in Argentina in the context of technological change, particularly automation and artificial intelligence (AI). It traces the development of union structures from pre-independence colonial systems to contemporary movements, examining how industrialization, political regimes, and economic shifts have shaped their role. Emphasizing the transformative impact of AI on labor dynamics, the analysis highlights both the risks—such as job displacement, deunionization, and inequality—and the opportunities for unions to modernize and advocate for equitable transitions. The chapter argues that to remain relevant, Argentine unions must adopt proactive, technology-informed strategies, including reskilling programs, digital engagement, and policy advocacy. It concludes by stressing the necessity of tripartite dialogue and ethical AI governance to ensure labor rights are protected in an increasingly automated and globalized world.

DOI: 10.4018/979-8-3693-8049-9.ch002

1. INTRODUCTION

Technological change is never neutral. As countless studies in the sociology of work, the political economy of labor, and science and technology studies have shown, innovations in production and communication are always shaped by—and in turn reshape—social relations, institutions, and power structures. The current wave of technological transformation, typically framed as the Fourth Industrial Revolution, is no exception. Artificial intelligence (AI), automation, algorithmic management, and digital platforms are rapidly reconfiguring labor markets, modifying the nature of employment, and introducing new asymmetries in the workplace. In this context, labor unions face a decisive challenge: either adapt and redefine their strategies or risk obsolescence in a world of increasingly fragmented and individualized work.

Argentina offers a particularly relevant case to analyze these tensions. As a country with a historically strong and politically influential labor movement, Argentina has long stood out in Latin America for the institutional density and social embeddedness of its trade unions. The Confederación General del Trabajo (CGT) and other federations such as the Central de Trabajadores de la Argentina (CTA) have played a central role in shaping social policies, wage negotiations, and labor law reforms. However, the rise of automation and digital technologies presents new conditions that existing union structures are not necessarily prepared to address.

Unlike previous phases of technological development, which were often sector-specific and mechanization-driven, current transformations affect both material and cognitive labor, both manual tasks and decision-making processes. AI systems are now used to evaluate performance, screen job applicants, assign delivery routes, and manage schedules. In sectors such as banking, public administration, transportation, journalism, education, and even health care, digital systems are replacing or restructuring traditional tasks. Moreover, the COVID-19 pandemic has accelerated the shift to remote work, hybrid models, and digital platforms, further destabilizing existing labor relations.

These shifts pose at least three key challenges to trade unionism:

First, **a representational challenge**: the classic model of union organization—based on stable employment, physical workplaces, and formal employer-employee relationships—is undermined by the fragmentation of work and the expansion of non-standard labor. In Argentina, where informal and precarious employment already account for more than 40% of the labor market, the platform economy and automation exacerbate existing difficulties in recruiting, organizing, and representing workers.

Second, **an institutional challenge**: the Argentine legal and regulatory framework was designed in the mid-20th century and is ill-equipped to regulate algorithmic labor relations, data surveillance, or automated dismissal. Although Law 27.555 on

Telework represents an initial attempt to address these issues, its limited enforcement capacity and the resistance of business sectors have hindered its effectiveness.

Third, **a political challenge**: unions must reposition themselves as relevant actors in debates on innovation and development, moving beyond reactive resistance to technological change and proposing proactive agendas that align productivity gains with social inclusion. This involves new alliances, new discourses, and new organizational formats.

In light of this context, this chapter asks: How are Argentine trade unions responding to the transformations induced by automation and digitalization? What strategies have they adopted to defend workers' rights in increasingly digitalized work environments? To what extent are they capable of influencing the governance of technological change? And what lessons does the Argentine case offer for other countries navigating similar tensions?

To address these questions, the chapter is structured as follows: Section 2 presents the theoretical framework, drawing from literature on institutional change, labor regimes, and the politics of technology. Section 3 offers a brief historical overview of Argentine unionism, identifying the structural features that shape current responses. Section 4 explores the current dynamics of digitalization and automation in Argentina, with emphasis on sectors most affected and the public policy environment. Section 5 analyzes union strategies in response to these changes, including negotiation, training, legal reform proposals, and organizational innovation. Section 6 outlines three future scenarios for unionism in Argentina under continued technological transformation. Section 7 situates the Argentine case in comparative perspective, identifying parallels and contrasts with other labor systems. Section 8 discusses normative and regulatory gaps, particularly in relation to algorithmic management and data rights. Finally, Section 9 offers conclusions and recommendations for policy, union strategy, and future research.

By combining theoretical reflection, contextualized analysis, and empirical insights, this chapter contributes to broader debates on how organized labor can adapt to a new digital age without abandoning its emancipatory objectives. Far from being a purely national issue, the Argentine case speaks to global concerns about the democratization of technology, the future of collective action, and the evolving meaning of labor rights in the 21st century.

1.1 Methodology

This chapter adopts a qualitative and interpretive research strategy grounded in critical traditions of labor studies, institutional political economy, and science and technology studies. Unlike approaches that emphasize quantitative modeling of automation impacts or predictive labor forecasts, this study offers a situated, relational, and political analysis of trade union responses to technological change in Argentina. The focus is on collective agency and institutional dynamics, rather than numerical projections or isolated firm-level outcomes.

The methodology combines documentary analysis, literature review, and the use of secondary qualitative empirical evidence, particularly derived from union reports, public statements, previously conducted interviews, and collective agreements. While no new fieldwork was carried out specifically for this chapter, it draws on a synthesis of existing research that includes direct testimonies from union representatives across sectors such as education, transportation, public administration, and platform-based services.

This approach enables an interpretive-comparative lens that situates the Argentine case within broader global debates while accounting for its historical and institutional specificity. The chapter is not concerned with measuring how much work has changed, but with understanding how these changes are perceived, contested, and negotiated by organized labor. It focuses on how trade unions construct meaning, formulate strategies, and engage in struggles over the governance of technological transformation.

From an epistemological standpoint, the chapter assumes that technology is not neutral but socially constructed. Therefore, the analysis privileges the political dimensions of technological change: Who decides? Under what conditions? For what purposes? With what consequences for power relations in the world of work? These questions guide the inquiry throughout, drawing on theoretical contributions from scholars of institutional change and labor governance.

The analysis follows an abductive and hermeneutic logic, in which theory and evidence are put into dialog rather than applied in a deductive manner. The structure of the chapter is guided by open analytical questions: What strategies are unions adopting in response to automation and digitalization? What institutional legacies shape their capacity to intervene? What scenarios can be envisioned for the future of unionism in the digital age? This openness reflects the complexity of the object of study, which resists linear explanation and requires sensitivity to historical contingency and institutional layering.

Additionally, the chapter emphasizes the importance of contextual and normative interpretation. Rather than treating Argentina as a case of success or failure, it is analyzed as a site of experimentation and contradiction, where innovative practices coexist with structural limitations. The country's hybrid institutional regime—characterized by both strong union traditions and structural informality—provides a unique opportunity to reflect on the possibilities and limits of labor adaptation to automation in the Global South.

Finally, the goal of this methodology is to produce strategically useful knowledge: conceptually rigorous, context-sensitive, and accessible to both academic and policy audiences. It aims not to predict future outcomes but to contribute interpretive tools that support collective action, informed policymaking, and critical debate on the democratization of technological change.

2. THEORETICAL FRAMEWORK: UNIONISM, INSTITUTIONAL CHANGE, AND TECHNOLOGICAL TRANSITIONS

Understanding how trade unions react to technological change requires more than descriptive accounts or sectoral case studies. It demands a theoretical framework that explains why certain unions adapt while others resist; why some countries develop inclusive digital transitions while others reproduce inequality and exclusion; and how institutional legacies, power relations, and normative orientations shape the trajectory of labor organizations in the face of innovation.

This chapter draws on three interrelated strands of literature: theories of institutional change, the political economy of innovation, and the sociology of labor relations in the digital age.

2.1 Institutional Change and Path Dependency

Institutionalist theories emphasize that organizations do not operate in a vacuum but are embedded in historically constituted systems of rules, norms, and power relations. Institutions—understood as stable but adaptable patterns of behavior and regulation—mediate actors' strategies and condition the range of viable responses to new challenges. Trade unions are paradigmatic institutional actors: they are simultaneously products and producers of social structures, navigating within legal, economic, and cultural environments that shape their resources, allies, and discourses.

In contexts like Argentina, where union structures have been strongly linked to political regimes (e.g., Peronism) and where collective bargaining has long operated within a framework of centralized regulation, unions face high levels of institutional path dependency. Their organizational forms, repertoires of action, and claims-making strategies have developed over decades of corporatist negotiation, mass mobilization, and political alliance-building. This legacy is both a strength and a constraint: it provides dense networks and symbolic legitimacy, but it can also limit innovation and adaptability when facing novel threats such as automation or algorithmic control.

Concepts such as layered change, drift, and conversion—developed in the institutional change literature—are useful here. Unions may incorporate digital tools without changing their core logics (conversion), may ignore changes until external pressures force adaptation (drift), or may gradually reorient their practices while maintaining formal continuity (layering). Identifying which mechanisms dominate in the Argentine case helps us understand the pace, depth, and limits of union responses.

2.2 The Political Economy of Innovation

Technological change is not an automatic or exogenous process. It is shaped by political decisions, economic interests, and social struggles. The literature on the political economy of innovation has shown that technology is never neutral: it reflects the priorities of those who design, finance, and implement it. In this sense, the introduction of AI and automation in workplaces is not merely a matter of efficiency but of power—power over time, space, decision-making, and surveillance.

From this perspective, unions are not merely reactive actors trying to minimize damage; they are potential co-governors of technological transitions. Their participation in debates over innovation policy, workplace design, and regulatory frameworks can influence which technologies are adopted, how they are used, and who benefits from them.

However, the capacity of unions to play this role varies widely. In contexts with coordinated market economies, strong collective bargaining traditions, and institutionalized social dialogue (e.g., parts of Europe), unions have secured seats at the table in discussions on Industry 4.0. In more liberal or fragmented systems, their influence is weaker. Argentina occupies an intermediate position: its unions retain significant legal rights and social legitimacy, but the macroeconomic volatility, high informality, and institutional fragility of the state limit the stability and effectiveness of innovation governance.

This framework suggests that trade union strategies cannot be assessed in isolation but must be analyzed in relation to broader innovation regimes: the institutional arrangements through which countries organize research, development, and technological diffusion. Where innovation is framed as a collective good, unions may find allies and institutional channels. Where it is treated as a private matter, driven by corporate interests, union participation is likely to be marginal or antagonistic.

2.3 Labor and Collective Action in the Digital Age

Finally, the sociology of labor relations in the digital age provides essential insights into how work is changing and how traditional forms of worker organization are being challenged. The platformization of labor, the rise of algorithmic management, and the expansion of remote work undermine the spatial and temporal foundations of unionism. Collective identity formation becomes more difficult when workers are dispersed, invisible to each other, or subjected to individualized performance metrics.

At the same time, new forms of worker resistance and solidarity are emerging. Platform worker collectives, tech employee walkouts, and transnational digital unions show that labor struggles have not disappeared; they have mutated. Concepts such as networked unionism, hybrid organization, and digital labor rights help to capture these transformations. While the Argentine union movement has not yet fully embraced these models, some early experiments—such as the Asociación del Personal de Plataformas—indicate an awareness of the need to evolve.

This literature also underscores the role of generational renewal and epistemic innovation within unions. Young workers, digital natives, and interdisciplinary activists bring new repertoires of action, from social media mobilization to data literacy and legal hacking. Their integration into union structures—or their exclusion—will shape the future of labor representation.

3. THE EVOLUTION OF ARGENTINE TRADE UNIONISM

Argentina's trade union movement is one of the most historically rooted and politically influential in Latin America. Its structure, practices, and institutional presence cannot be understood without considering the country's broader trajectory of state-building, industrialization, and political polarization. While unions in Argentina have demonstrated a capacity for mass mobilization, sectoral negotiation, and policy influence, their development has also been marked by cycles of repression, corporatism, and adaptation to shifting regimes of accumulation and governance.

3.1 Early Foundations: Immigration, Anarchism, and Socialist Organization

The origins of Argentine trade unionism date back to the late 19th century, amid rapid urbanization and industrial expansion. Large-scale European immigration—mainly from Italy and Spain—brought not only labor for construction, transport, and manufacturing, but also the ideological frameworks of anarcho-syndicalism, socialism, and republicanism. Early worker organizations such as the Federación Obrera Argentina (FOA, founded in 1901) and later the Federación Obrera Regional

Argentina (FORA) were heavily influenced by these currents and adopted confrontational strategies, including strikes, mutual aid, and direct action (Suriano, 2000).

During the early 20th century, union activity intensified in response to exploitative working conditions and growing social inequality. Major strikes in the port, railway, and textile sectors became increasingly common. The so-called *Semana Trágica* of 1919, a violent repression of a general strike in Buenos Aires, left hundreds dead and marked a turning point in state-labor relations. While repression was severe, the event also led to broader awareness of labor issues and eventual concessions from the state.

3.2 Institutionalization under Peronism

The decisive transformation of Argentine unionism came during the 1940s with the emergence of Peronism. Under Juan Domingo Perón, first as Secretary of Labor and then as President (1946–1955), trade unions gained unprecedented legal, institutional, and political status. The Confederación General del Trabajo (CGT) was consolidated as the dominant labor federation and became a cornerstone of the Peronist political project.

Peronist labor policy granted workers paid holidays, severance pay, collective bargaining rights, workplace accident insurance, and other protections. More importantly, it institutionalized a corporatist model in which unions acted as intermediaries between the state and the working class, embedding themselves in a structure of political loyalty and state-sponsored welfare (James, 1988).

While this model expanded labor rights and union membership dramatically, it also produced a form of bureaucratic unionism. Union leaders were integrated into the state apparatus, and dissenting factions were often marginalized or co-opted. The result was a dense but hierarchical labor system, highly effective in periods of political alignment, but vulnerable to co-optation and crisis under adverse conditions.

3.3 Crisis, Repression, and Restructuring

The second half of the 20th century saw successive crises that reshaped the role and capacity of trade unions. The 1976–1983 military dictatorship targeted union leaders and institutions with violence and repression. Collective bargaining was suspended, union assets were seized, and many activists were disappeared. Despite this repression, underground organizing and international solidarity kept parts of the movement alive.

With the return to democracy in 1983, unions rapidly regained visibility. The Alfonsín government attempted to introduce moderate labor reforms but faced strong union resistance. However, the major structural shift occurred in the 1990s under

President Carlos Menem. Adopting neoliberal policies, the Menem administration implemented widespread privatizations, labor market flexibilization, and reductions in state spending. These reforms drastically altered the terrain for union activity: formal employment declined, public sector jobs were cut, and union density dropped in many sectors.

In this context, union strategies fragmented. Some sectors engaged in combative protest, while others negotiated concessions. The CGT itself experienced internal splits, giving rise to parallel federations and new leaderships. The rise of informal and precarious employment further challenged the organizational models built around stable, formal workplaces.

3.4 Partial Revival and Persistent Challenges

The early 2000s saw a partial revival of union power under the Kirchner administrations (2003–2015). The state reestablished tripartite dialogue mechanisms, such as the Consejo del Salario Mínimo, and supported wage recovery policies. Union representation expanded in the public sector, and collective bargaining agreements increased significantly. Nevertheless, structural issues persisted: the segmentation of the union landscape, the persistence of informal labor, and the generational disconnection between union leadership and younger workers.

Moreover, the 2010s introduced new challenges. The global financial crisis, political polarization, and the growing presence of digital platforms and AI-based management tools began to reshape labor markets once again. While traditional unions maintained influence in large firms and public institutions, they struggled to connect with workers in new, less regulated sectors.

This historical trajectory reveals a pattern of resilience and adaptation, but also of structural inertia. Argentine unions have been effective in defending rights under favorable political conditions but have often lacked long-term strategies to address transformations in the nature of work and employment. The arrival of the digital economy and automation thus confronts unions with the need to rethink not only their tactics, but also their foundational assumptions about labor, representation, and social justice.

4. CONTEMPORARY TRANSFORMATIONS: AUTOMATION, AI, AND LABOR IN ARGENTINA

The integration of digital technologies, including artificial intelligence (AI), algorithmic systems, and automated processes, is reshaping Argentina's productive matrix and labor relations. Unlike previous industrial transitions, the current wave of change is characterized by its cross-sectoral reach, speed, and opacity. While still uneven and marked by infrastructural and regulatory gaps, the deployment of automation in Argentina increasingly affects sectors traditionally protected by union regulation—such as banking, manufacturing, transport, and public administration—as well as expanding into emergent and informal sectors like platform-based services.

4.1 Patterns of Technological Adoption

Automation and AI in Argentina are introduced mainly through three vectors: multinational corporate investment, digital public management, and local innovation driven by cost-cutting imperatives. In the banking sector, AI is now used to automate credit risk analysis, customer service via chatbots, and internal document classification. This has reduced the need for clerical and customer-facing roles, leading to job restructuring in entities like Banco Nación and Banco Provincia. At the same time, unions such as La Bancaria have negotiated agreements to ensure no layoffs and to finance retraining programs for affected workers.

In logistics and transportation, companies have adopted dynamic routing software, warehouse automation systems, and digital inventory controls. While many of these tools aim to increase efficiency and reduce fuel costs, they also introduce algorithmic control over worker performance, raising concerns about surveillance and work intensification. The Unión Tranviarios Automotor (UTA) and other transport unions have begun to contest the use of biometric monitoring and GPS-based evaluations in public and private fleets.

Manufacturing, particularly in the automotive and food processing industries, has witnessed the incorporation of robotic arms, programmable logic controllers, and data-driven production monitoring. These transformations, however, are uneven across firms. Large exporters are more likely to adopt AI-driven quality control, while small and medium-sized enterprises (SMEs) face financial and technical barriers to automation. Consequently, technological dualization is emerging: some firms leap forward while others lag behind, creating fragmented labor regimes.

In the public sector[1], automation has advanced through the digitalization of citizen services, payroll systems, and administrative processes. AI-driven tools for document classification, appointment scheduling, and chatbot-based information services are being adopted in ministries and municipal governments. While this may improve transparency and efficiency, it also reduces administrative positions and reconfigures professional profiles. The Unión del Personal Civil de la Nación (UPCN) has expressed concerns about unconsulted restructuring and the erosion of job content.

4.2 Policy Frameworks and Institutional Gaps

Argentina's regulatory framework is not adequately prepared to address the transformations brought by automation and AI. The Plan Nacional de Inteligencia Artificial (PNIA), launched in 2019, was a first step in articulating national priorities for AI development. However, it largely emphasized competitiveness and productivity, with limited attention to labor rights, union participation, or redistributive mechanisms. Similarly, the Agenda Digital Argentina has focused on infrastructure and connectivity, without embedding technological policies in a broader social contract.

At the legislative level, the most notable innovation has been Law 27.555 on Remote Work, passed in 2020. The law establishes rights such as the reversal of remote status, compensation for connectivity costs, and the right to disconnect. Nevertheless, implementation has been uneven and resisted by some employer associations, and its enforcement remains weak, particularly in decentralized and informal contexts.

A more general challenge is the lack of a comprehensive legal framework for algorithmic management, including issues such as data transparency, accountability for AI decisions, and collective access to algorithmic systems. As unions attempt to negotiate digital clauses in collective agreements, they encounter legal ambiguities and technical asymmetries that favor employers. Existing labor law assumes the presence of a human employer who exercises control and responsibility—an assumption increasingly incompatible with AI-driven management practices.

4.3 Platform Work and the Rise of Non-Standard Labor

Perhaps the most visible face of labor transformation in Argentina is the proliferation of platform-based work, especially in urban centers. Companies such as Rappi, PedidosYa, Uber, and Glovo have expanded their presence, often bypassing local labor regulations by classifying workers as independent contractors. These models externalize risks, transfer operational costs to workers, and avoid contributions to social security systems.

According to estimates from labor observatories, more than 60,000 individuals work regularly on platforms in Argentina. While this figure remains small compared to the total workforce, its political and symbolic impact is significant. Platform work epitomizes the shift toward individualized, precarious, and digitally-mediated labor. Workers are evaluated by customers and algorithms, managed through opaque metrics, and disconnected from traditional institutions of representation.

Some unions have attempted to respond. The Asociación del Personal de Plataformas (APP), founded in 2018, represents one of the few attempts in Latin America to build a union for platform workers. The APP has organized protests, filed legal actions, and lobbied for recognition before the Ministry of Labor. However, the absence of an employer in the classical sense, the fluidity of work schedules, and the algorithmic opacity of task assignment limit traditional forms of negotiation[2].

Mainstream unions have been slower to react. The CGT and CTA have expressed concern but have yet to integrate platform labor into their organizational structures. This reflects not only structural inertia, but also uncertainties about representational boundaries, dues collection, and the long-term viability of platform unionism.

4.4 Structural Asymmetries and Regional Disparities

Technological transformation in Argentina also reproduces territorial inequalities. Urban centers such as Buenos Aires, Córdoba, and Rosario have higher levels of automation adoption and digital infrastructure, while peripheral provinces lag behind. This affects not only firm-level innovation but also the ability of unions to organize workers, access information, and negotiate digital transitions.

Moreover, the concentration of technological employment in a few sectors—often male-dominated and urban—risks exacerbating gender and class disparities. Automation in services such as domestic work, care, and informal retail is minimal, yet digital platforms increasingly mediate access to these jobs, often without adequate protections. Feminist labor groups have highlighted how digitalization intersects with reproductive labor, domestic surveillance, and algorithmic bias.

These dynamics call for an intersectional approach to union strategies, one that considers not only class but also gender, race, geography, and age in addressing the challenges of automation and AI.

5. TRADE UNION STRATEGIES IN RESPONSE TO AUTOMATION AND DIGITALIZATION

The Argentine labor movement has not remained passive in the face of technological disruption. Despite institutional inertia and internal fragmentation, several unions and federations have adopted strategies to manage, negotiate, or contest the effects of automation, AI, and digital labor platforms. These responses vary in scope, capacity, and political orientation, but they reveal a growing awareness of the need to adapt traditional models of representation to a rapidly evolving labor landscape.

5.1 Collective Bargaining and "Technological Clauses"

One of the most tangible ways in which unions have addressed technological change is through the negotiation of "cláusulas tecnológicas" (technological clauses) in collective agreements. These clauses typically require employers to:

- Inform the union in advance about the implementation of new technologies.
- Conduct joint assessments of the potential impact on employment and working conditions.
- Provide retraining and internal mobility opportunities for workers affected by automation.

For example, the Unión Obrera Metalúrgica (UOM) has successfully negotiated agreements in the automotive sector that include provisions for technology monitoring committees and reskilling programs. These agreements acknowledge the inevitability of automation but seek to manage its social consequences collaboratively.

Similarly, La Bancaria, the banking sector union, has incorporated clauses that regulate the use of digital channels, protect workers from unilateral relocation to remote service centers, and establish minimum staffing levels in branches affected by self-service systems. The union has also created internal commissions to monitor the implementation of biometric and AI-based performance evaluation tools.

These advances are significant but remain uneven. In sectors with high union density and established bargaining traditions, such clauses have become more common. However, in SMEs, subcontracted services, or informal employment contexts, collective bargaining remains limited or nonexistent. Moreover, even where such clauses exist, enforcement mechanisms are weak, and compliance often depends on the union's capacity for mobilization or litigation.

5.2 Worker Training and Digital Literacy Programs

Another area of strategic investment has been training. Recognizing that automation not only displaces jobs but also transforms job content, some unions have developed training programs to equip workers with new digital competencies.

The Sindicato de Camioneros, for instance, offers courses on digital logistics systems, GPS navigation, and fleet management software. The Unión Ferroviaria has partnered with public universities to train maintenance workers in the use of AI-assisted diagnostics and predictive maintenance tools. In the education sector, the CTERA union has implemented workshops on virtual pedagogy, platform ethics, and data privacy for teachers navigating digital classrooms.

Additionally, several unions—often with international cooperation—have launched digital literacy campaigns, especially targeting older workers and women in precarious sectors. These initiatives aim not only to update skills but also to reduce digital exclusion and foster participation in union activities through virtual means.

However, challenges persist. Many programs rely on voluntary participation, lack public funding, or are restricted to members in large urban centers. The absence of a national policy for lifelong learning and the fragmentation of training provision across ministries, unions, and private actors hamper scalability. Furthermore, the training often focuses on adapting to technology rather than questioning its logic or proposing alternatives.

5.3 Legal Advocacy and Normative Proposals

Beyond the workplace, unions have begun to engage in legal and normative advocacy to shape the broader framework of digital labor regulation. Their demands include:

- The regulation of algorithmic management systems in line with principles of transparency, accountability, and non-discrimination.
- The recognition of platform workers as employees with full labor rights.
- The inclusion of union participation in technology-related policy-making bodies.

In 2022, the Asociación del Personal de Plataformas (APP) submitted a draft bill to Congress proposing the creation of a legal category for platform workers that includes collective bargaining rights, occupational risk coverage, and employer obligations for training and data access. Although the bill has not advanced, it sparked public debate and was supported by some progressive legislators and legal scholars.

Mainstream federations such as the CGT and CTA have also participated in public hearings and media campaigns against the deregulation of telework and the use of AI for surveillance. The CGT's Department of Technology and Labor, created in 2021, has issued position papers and legal briefs analyzing the compatibility of AI management tools with constitutional labor rights.

These efforts remain incipient but suggest a shift from reactive resistance to proactive norm-building. Unions are moving—albeit slowly—towards a vision of technological co-governance, where workers have a say in how technologies are introduced, used, and evaluated in the workplace.

5.4 Internal Digitalization and Organizational Innovation

The digital transformation has also affected how unions organize internally and communicate with their members. The COVID-19 pandemic forced many organizations to adopt virtual assemblies, online voting systems, and digital platforms for member services. While initially seen as emergency measures, many of these tools have become permanent fixtures.

Unions such as ATE and Sadop have launched apps to manage member information, offer legal advice, and disseminate news. Others have expanded their presence on social media, organized webinars on labor rights in the digital age, and experimented with horizontal communication models that appeal to younger workers.

In some cases, internal innovation has extended to governance structures. The APP, for instance, elects delegates online and maintains a flat organizational structure that contrasts with the hierarchical models of traditional unionism. These practices reflect a generational and cultural shift that could, over time, influence broader union renewal.

However, digitalization also introduces new tensions: questions about data security, member privacy, and technological dependency; conflicts between centralized leaderships and rank-and-file initiatives; and the risk of reinforcing inequalities among members with differential access to digital tools.

6. FUTURE SCENARIOS FOR ARGENTINE UNIONISM IN THE AGE OF AUTOMATION AND AI

Projecting the future of trade unionism in Argentina in light of technological change is a complex but necessary exercise. The acceleration of automation, the expansion of algorithmic management, and the diversification of labor modalities confront unions with structural dilemmas that demand both immediate responses and long-term strategic vision. Based on empirical trends, theoretical frameworks, and comparative insights, this section outlines three plausible scenarios for the future evolution of Argentine unionism, each with internal variants and differing institutional implications.

These scenarios are not mutually exclusive. Rather, they represent ideal types—analytical constructions that help us interpret real dynamics that may combine elements from multiple paths. Their value lies in clarifying the stakes, the tensions, and the decisions facing labor movements in contexts of technological transformation.

6.1 Scenario A: Defensive Resistance and Institutional Retreat

In this scenario, trade unions adopt a predominantly defensive posture in response to technological change. Automation and AI are framed primarily as threats to employment, collective rights, and organizational survival. The dominant strategy is resistance through legal action, public denunciation, and strike mobilization.

Technological adoption is contested case by case, and union discourse emphasizes the protection of acquired rights and the illegitimacy of unilateral restructuring.

While this strategy may generate short-term protections—especially in highly unionized sectors—it risks leading to a progressive institutional retreat. As employers adopt technology through informal channels or outsource digital tasks to non-unionized contractors, union coverage erodes. This erosion is exacerbated by intergenerational disaffection: younger workers, especially in digital and precarious sectors, perceive unions as reactive, rigid, and disconnected from their concerns.

Variants of this scenario include:

- **Legal conservatism**, in which unions rely on outdated regulatory frameworks to block technological change, limiting their adaptability.
- **Populist radicalization**, in which union rhetoric becomes increasingly anti-technological, but without concrete policy proposals for inclusive innovation.

Both variants tend to isolate unions from broader public debates on development and digital inclusion. Moreover, they reinforce the image of unions as obstacles to modernization, a narrative often exploited by employer associations and media outlets.

6.2 Scenario B: Institutional Adaptation and Dualization

In this intermediate scenario, unions accept the inevitability of technological transformation and seek to adapt through negotiated transitions. Technological clauses in collective agreements become more common; training programs are expanded; and unions participate in social dialogue mechanisms related to innovation policies.

However, these advances are uneven and fragmented. Strong unions in formal sectors consolidate their influence and secure protections for their members, while workers in informal, digital, or subcontracted labor remain excluded. The result is a dualized union system: modernized in parts, but incapable of articulating a universal project of labor justice in the digital era.

In this context, labor segmentation deepens. The "protected core" of unionized workers in sectors such as finance, transportation, and energy retains bargaining power and institutional security, while peripheral sectors—platform workers, freelancers, digital nomads—experience precarity, isolation, and regulatory voids. Unions develop specialized branches to engage with these sectors, but with limited impact.

Institutional adaptation allows for stability and continued relevance, but at the cost of representational fragmentation. This model is vulnerable to external shocks (e.g., economic crises, technological leaps) that may undermine negotiated gains and provoke legitimacy crises. Moreover, it reinforces the logic of self-containment, where unions focus on defending their niche rather than proposing systemic alternatives.

6.3 Scenario C: Proactive Transformation and Strategic Reinvention

The most ambitious—and most uncertain—scenario involves a proactive transformation of unionism. Here, unions not only react to technological change but also shape its trajectory. They become actors in innovation governance, demand participatory design of technologies, and propose redistributive mechanisms (e.g., robot taxes, public AI funds) to ensure equitable outcomes.

This scenario requires organizational reinvention: new leaderships, hybrid structures, interdisciplinary teams, and participatory models. Unions build alliances with academic institutions, feminist movements, environmental coalitions, and digital rights organizations. They invest in open data initiatives, develop in-house technical expertise, and contribute to public policy debates beyond the workplace.

Key features of this scenario include:

- **Knowledge production**, where unions create observatories on digital labor, publish reports on algorithmic management, and propose legal reforms grounded in empirical evidence.
- **Digital unionism**, where representation, voting, and deliberation occur through secure digital platforms, expanding participation and transparency.
- **Transnational coordination**, where unions engage with international networks to influence global standards on AI and labor rights.

The feasibility of this scenario depends on several conditions:

- Internal democratization: opening union leadership to younger, more diverse, and digitally literate actors.
- Public support: rebuilding societal legitimacy by linking labor justice to broader concerns such as equity, sustainability, and technological democracy.
- Institutional innovation: creating spaces of co-governance where unions can intervene meaningfully in technological decision-making.

While this path is demanding, it offers the most comprehensive response to the structural challenges of the digital age. It repositions unionism not as a relic of the industrial past, but as a crucial institution for democratizing the future of work.

7. INTERNATIONAL COMPARISON AND GLOBAL RELEVANCE OF THE ARGENTINE CASE

The inclusion of Argentina in a global volume on unionism and technological change may initially seem surprising. Much of the existing literature on automation, AI, and labor relations focuses on high-income countries in the Global North—Germany, Sweden, Japan, the United States—where unions operate within coordinated economies, stable institutions, and robust innovation ecosystems. However, this focus obscures important insights that can emerge from countries with different developmental trajectories, institutional legacies, and labor dynamics.

Argentina offers a unique vantage point to examine how trade unionism responds to technological change under conditions of economic volatility, high informality, and partial state capacity. Its experience challenges linear assumptions about modernization and contributes to a more plural understanding of labor futures in the digital era.[3]

7.1 Latin American Parallels and Divergences

Within Latin America, Argentina stands out for its historically dense union structures, legal protections for collective bargaining, and high levels of union membership relative to regional peers. While countries like Brazil and Uruguay also have strong labor movements, Argentina's unions have played an unusually prominent role in shaping macroeconomic policy, political alignments, and social protection systems (Etchemendy & Collier, 2007).

When it comes to digitalization, Latin American unions face similar challenges: platform work expansion, labor informality, state fragmentation, and employer resistance to regulation. However, the responses vary significantly.

- In **Brazil**, unions have faced massive setbacks due to recent labor reforms (Law No. 13.467/2017) that weakened collective bargaining and introduced more flexibility. While there are digital labor initiatives, union capacity to intervene in technological debates has declined sharply.
- In **Chile**, union density remains low, and platform regulation is minimal. However, the 2022 constitutional process opened new discussions on digital rights, surveillance, and algorithmic accountability.
- In **Uruguay**, social dialogue remains institutionalized, and some unions—particularly in banking and education—have begun to engage with digital transformations proactively.

In this context, Argentina's experience offers a hybrid model: it combines institutional continuity and legal protections with real structural obstacles, such as informality, polarization, and uneven state enforcement. This makes it a strategically useful case for other middle-income countries seeking to balance productivity, social justice, and democratic governance in the digital transition.

7.2 Lessons from Europe and Emerging Convergences

Comparisons with European cases also illuminate the specificity and relevance of the Argentine path. In countries like Germany and Sweden, tripartite social dialogue has facilitated inclusive approaches to Industry 4.0. Unions participate in technology councils, co-determine decisions at the firm level, and help shape training curricula for new digital skills. Collective agreements in these contexts frequently include provisions on data protection, algorithmic fairness, and workload distribution.

In contrast, Argentina lacks both the institutional infrastructure and the consensual culture that support such co-governance. However, recent union innovations—such as digital clauses in contracts, training centers for digital competencies, and legal proposals for platform regulation—reflect incipient forms of similar strategies, adapted to local constraints.

This suggests that institutional forms may diverge, but functional needs converge. As AI and automation transform work globally, all countries—regardless of income level—face questions about worker agency, representation, and digital rights. The Argentine case contributes to this debate by showing how unions can negotiate power even in unstable environments, and how new forms of unionism (e.g., the APP) can emerge in the face of organizational voids.

Moreover, the political imaginaries developed by Argentine unions—grounded in historical narratives of resistance, popular sovereignty, and redistributive justice—offer conceptual tools for rethinking the normative foundations of technological governance. Where many global debates remain technocratic, the Argentine labor discourse brings back questions of power, legitimacy, and collective agency.

7.3 Transnational Solidarity and the Need for Global Unionism

Another reason for the global relevance of the Argentine case lies in the emergence of transnational labor platforms. As corporations operating in the digital economy increasingly organize production, communication, and labor relations across borders, unions face the need to scale their strategies accordingly. The expansion of platform capitalism—based on data extraction, algorithmic control, and legal arbitrage—cannot be effectively challenged through national frameworks alone.

Argentine unions have begun to participate in regional and international networks, including:

- The **Trade Union Confederation of the Americas (TUCA)**, which promotes digital labor rights in Latin America.
- The **Global Union Federations**, such as UNI Global Union and the International Transport Workers' Federation, which coordinate cross-border campaigns on digital platforms.
- Bilateral exchanges with European trade unions focused on regulatory models for AI and remote work.

These connections are still incipient but essential. The challenges of the digital age—opaque algorithms, transnational employers, fragmented representation—require global regulatory responses and new forms of transnational solidarity. Argentina's experience shows both the urgency of this shift and the potential contributions of Southern unions to shaping it.

7.4 Rethinking Innovation from the South

Finally, including Argentina in global discussions on unionism and automation helps to provincialize dominant narratives about technology. Most policy discourses on AI and the future of work are produced in Silicon Valley, Brussels, or Beijing. These perspectives often assume certain institutional capacities, infrastructures, and cultural assumptions that do not hold elsewhere.

Argentina, and Latin America more broadly, offer alternative views on innovation: ones that emphasize social inclusion, economic justice, and democratic participation. These are not "deficits" to be overcome but critical perspectives to be integrated. In a world increasingly marked by techno-authoritarianism and extractivist digital capitalism, the labor experiences of the Global South are indispensable for imagining more democratic futures.

8. LEGAL GAPS AND EMERGING CHALLENGES IN THE REGULATION OF DIGITAL LABOR

One of the most pressing obstacles for an inclusive and rights-based digital transition in Argentina lies in the profound mismatch between the country's legal and institutional frameworks and the realities of contemporary labor. While the Argentine labor law tradition is among the most protective in Latin America, it is also anchored in mid-20th-century assumptions about work: a stable employer-employee relationship, a fixed workplace, predictable working hours, and a clear chain of command. These assumptions no longer hold for a growing share of the workforce.

Automation, AI, and digital platforms are exposing the obsolescence and fragmentation of existing regulations. This section explores five major legal and institutional gaps that undermine the ability of trade unions, labor inspectors, and policymakers to ensure fair and equitable labor conditions in the digital age.

8.1 Absence of Regulation on Algorithmic Management

Perhaps the most paradigmatic legal void concerns algorithmic management—the use of automated systems to assign tasks, evaluate performance, monitor behavior, and determine disciplinary measures. These systems, increasingly present in logistics, banking, retail, and public administration, function with limited transparency and without prior consultation with workers or unions.

The current Labor Contract Law (Ley 20.744) does not contemplate the use of algorithms in decision-making, nor does it establish standards for transparency, due process, or contestation rights. Workers often do not know how they are being evaluated or why they are being penalized. In some cases, task assignment systems based on customer ratings or productivity scores lead to informal sanctions without any human intervention.[4]

Attempts to challenge algorithmic decisions through litigation have faced doctrinal uncertainty: judges must analogize to existing norms about employer responsibility, but the lack of explicit regulation complicates enforcement. Moreover, data privacy laws such as the Personal Data Protection Act (Law 25.326) are not adapted to the specificities of algorithmic work environments, where consent is often illusory and data collection is constant.

8.2 The Problem of Employment Classification

A second gap involves the classification of employment in digital and platform-based work. Most platforms operating in Argentina classify their workers as independent contractors, thereby avoiding obligations such as social security contributions, paid leave, and collective bargaining rights. While some courts have ruled in favor of reclassifying platform workers as employees, there is no legislative consensus or coherent jurisprudence on the issue.

This regulatory ambiguity has led to legal uncertainty for workers, employers, and unions alike. It also generates incentives for misclassification in other sectors: firms may structure employment relations to resemble platform models, outsourcing tasks to avoid unionization or labor costs. As a result, informalization spreads not only "from below" (in small-scale labor markets) but also "from above," through strategic legal design.

Unions face difficulties in organizing these workers: without a recognized employer, collective bargaining becomes nearly impossible. Moreover, labor inspectors lack clear criteria to determine whether control and subordination exist in algorithmically mediated environments.

Several legislative proposals have sought to address this, including bills to create an intermediate category of "dependent autonomous worker" (*trabajador autónomo económicamente dependiente*), but none have been enacted.

8.3 Telework Regulation and Enforcement Challenges

Law 27.555 on Telework, passed in 2020 amid the COVID-19 pandemic, was a major step toward updating labor regulation for the digital age. It includes provisions on the right to disconnect, reimbursement of expenses, and reversibility of the telework regime. However, its implementation has faced considerable obstacles.

First, enforcement capacity is low. The Ministry of Labor lacks the technical and human resources to inspect home-based work, particularly in private households or geographically dispersed firms. Second, employer compliance has been uneven. Many companies simply adapted remote work informally, without registering the modality or applying the law. Third, union participation in the drafting and monitoring of implementation has been limited, reinforcing a top-down model of regulation.

Finally, the law's applicability is restricted to formal contracts. Given that much remote work occurs in freelance or informal conditions—especially in IT services, design, and education—large segments of teleworkers remain outside its protection.

8.4 Fragmented Institutional Governance of Technology and Labor

A fourth challenge is institutional fragmentation. In Argentina, policies on digitalization and innovation are distributed across multiple ministries, secretariats, and agencies, often with overlapping mandates and poor coordination. The Ministry of Labor, Ministry of Science and Technology, Secretariat of Public Innovation, and Ministry of Productive Development each manage parts of the digital transition, but there is no inter-ministerial body tasked with aligning labor and technology policy.

This fragmentation leads to policy incoherence. For example, while one agency promotes automation as a productivity strategy, another advocates for inclusive employment without connecting the two agendas. Union participation in these spaces is sporadic and usually consultative rather than binding. As a result, labor perspectives are underrepresented in innovation policy, and technological choices are rarely subjected to democratic scrutiny.

8.5 Lack of Institutionalized Spaces for Social Dialogue on Digitalization

Lastly, Argentina lacks a permanent institutional mechanism for social dialogue on digital transformation. While some tripartite bodies exist—such as the Consejo del Salario Mínimo or sectoral productivity councils—none have a specific mandate to address the implications of AI, automation, and digital platforms for labor relations.

Unions have called for the creation of Technology and Labor Councils (*Consejos de Tecnología y Trabajo*) to evaluate new technologies before implementation, negotiate mitigation measures, and generate policy recommendations. These proposals remain on the margins of political debate and have yet to be taken up by mainstream parties or the executive branch.[5]

9. CONCLUSIONS AND STRATEGIC RECOMMENDATIONS

The Argentine case offers a rich, complex, and often contradictory landscape for analyzing the intersection between trade unionism and technological transformation. While marked by persistent structural challenges—including informality, institutional fragmentation, and regulatory gaps—it also demonstrates significant areas of resilience, innovation, and strategic experimentation. In contrast to the binary narratives of either union decline or digital utopia, this chapter has argued for a more nuanced understanding: one that recognizes the contested, negotiated, and uneven nature of labor adaptation to automation and AI.

9.1 Summary of Key Findings

First, Argentina's unions continue to play a central role in shaping labor conditions, even in an era of technological transition. Their capacity to negotiate digital clauses, resist abrupt restructuring, and propose legislative reforms reflects not only institutional inertia but also an enduring political agency. The long tradition of labor mobilization and the symbolic legitimacy of unions in public discourse give them tools that are less available in other Latin American contexts.

Second, however, the ability of unions to govern technological change remains highly uneven and sector-dependent. While large public sector unions and those in regulated industries (banking, energy, transport) have made progress in adapting to digitalization, others—especially in fragmented service sectors and platform work—struggle to articulate effective strategies. The representational crisis in these emergent labor markets is real and growing.

Third, Argentina's regulatory framework remains inadequate for the digital era. The absence of clear standards on algorithmic management, the ambiguous status of platform workers, and the enforcement weaknesses surrounding telework law all point to the need for a comprehensive legal update. Unions have proposed reforms, but political traction remains limited, in part due to the volatility of the national context and competing legislative priorities.

Fourth, the institutional architecture governing innovation and labor is poorly coordinated. There is no integrated policy that links technological development with employment protection, training, or redistributive measures. While sectoral initiatives exist, they lack a strategic orientation and often exclude labor voices from design and evaluation processes.

Finally, while there are some promising signs of organizational renewal and digital experimentation, these remain at the margins of mainstream union activity. Generational renewal, interdisciplinary collaboration, and horizontal organizing are necessary but still incipient. Without deeper internal reform, even the most active unions may struggle to maintain legitimacy among younger, precarious, and digitally-mediated workers.

9.2 Strategic Recommendations

Based on this diagnosis, the following recommendations are offered for different stakeholders committed to fostering a socially inclusive digital transition in Argentina and beyond.

For Trade Unions

1. **Expand Representational Boundaries**: Unions must rethink the criteria and modalities of representation. This includes opening membership to platform workers, freelancers, and remote workers, even if they fall outside traditional bargaining units.
2. **Invest in Technical Capacities**: To negotiate on digital transformation, unions need in-house expertise in data analysis, AI systems, digital surveillance, and algorithmic governance. Training union delegates in these areas is essential.
3. **Promote Internal Digitalization with Equity**: While adopting digital tools for communication and decision-making, unions should ensure that all members—especially those with limited access or digital literacy—can participate meaningfully.

4. **Build Alliances Across Sectors and Movements**: Intersecting struggles around environmental justice, gender equality, and technological democracy offer opportunities for coalition-building and agenda-setting beyond traditional labor frames.
5. **Advance Normative Innovation**: Rather than simply defending existing rights, unions can become norm entrepreneurs, proposing new legal categories, standards for algorithmic accountability, and participatory mechanisms for technology governance.

For Policymakers

1. **Modernize Labor Law for the Digital Age**: Update the Labor Contract Law and related statutes to include definitions and protections related to algorithmic management, data rights, and platform-mediated work.
2. **Establish Multisectoral Governance Bodies**: Create permanent councils for Technology and Labor with binding tripartite participation (government, employers, unions) to guide innovation policy with social accountability.
3. **Guarantee Enforcement Capacity**: Strengthen labor inspection agencies with digital tools, training, and autonomy to monitor new forms of work, including telework and algorithmic control.
4. **Develop Inclusive Training and Reskilling Programs**: Public policy should support lifelong learning with a focus on digital competencies, prioritizing vulnerable workers and ensuring union participation in curriculum design.
5. **Support Social Innovation in Unionism**: Provide institutional support—legal, financial, and symbolic—for experimental union initiatives that seek to represent emerging labor forms.

For International Organizations and Researchers

1. **Support South-South Knowledge Exchange**: Facilitate comparative studies and exchange programs between unions in middle-income countries facing similar challenges of automation and informality.
2. **Include Labor Voices in AI Governance**: Promote frameworks at the international level (e.g., ILO, OECD, UNESCO) that explicitly include trade unions in the development of ethical standards for AI in the workplace.
3. **Fund Action-Oriented Research**: Encourage interdisciplinary research that produces not only diagnosis but also tools, prototypes, and policy proposals that unions can use in negotiations.
4. **Document and Disseminate Union Innovations**: Create public repositories of good practices, legal cases, and strategic innovations in labor response to technology across the Global South.

9.3 Final Reflections

The question is no longer whether technology will change work, but who will shape that change and in whose interests. Unions—despite their limitations—remain one of the few institutions capable of mediating this transformation in ways that prioritize social justice, equity, and democratic control.

Argentina's experience shows that the future of work is not written in code, but in struggles, negotiations, and collective imagination. Its unions have shown resilience, but resilience is not enough. The challenges of the digital age demand creativity, courage, and coalition-building. If unions can rise to this task, they will not only survive the Fourth Industrial Revolution—they will help humanize it.

10. EPILOGUE: REIMAGINING UNIONISM IN THE AGE OF ARTIFICIAL INTELLIGENCE

The digital transformation of labor is often portrayed as a technological inevitability—a wave of innovation that societies must simply accommodate. In this narrative, automation is driven by abstract "forces of change," artificial intelligence is a neutral tool, and resistance is framed as backward-looking. This framing, however, is deeply ideological. It conceals the fact that technological systems are designed, deployed, and governed by actors with interests, values, and political agendas. To speak of the future of work without speaking of power is to miss the very terrain on which labor relations are being redrawn.

Trade unions, as historically grounded institutions of collective agency, have a critical role to play in interrupting the determinism of this discourse. Their mission is not merely to protect jobs, but to reimagine the meaning of work, the architecture of rights, and the social organization of innovation itself. In Argentina, this mission is both urgent and fraught with contradictions. Unions are being called upon to defend workers not only from exploitative employers, but from opaque algorithms, remote platforms, and systems of surveillance that reshape the workplace without negotiation or consent.

The challenge is formidable. On the one hand, unions must navigate a world in which the material bases of collective identity are eroding. The physical workplace—the traditional site of solidarity—is becoming virtual or dispersed. Job tenure is shortening, employer responsibility is diluted, and the forms of subordination are increasingly mediated by software rather than supervisors. On the other hand, the very tools that disrupt traditional organizing may also offer new possibilities for imagination and action. Digital technologies can enable broader communication, decentralized participation, and data-driven strategies for advocacy. The question is not whether unions will adopt digital tools, but how they will use them to democratize the governance of technology itself.

In this context, the Argentine experience invites a set of broader reflections. First, it underscores the importance of historical memory. Unlike in many Global North contexts where union presence has declined dramatically, Argentine unions still retain symbolic and organizational weight. This legacy, however, is a double-edged sword: while it provides institutional continuity, it also risks perpetuating hierarchical, male-dominated, and bureaucratic forms of representation that are ill-suited to emerging labor realities. The task is not to abandon the past but to critically inherit it, to extract from its moments of insurgency and creativity the resources needed to build new forms of collective power.

Second, the Argentine case shows that resistance and innovation are not mutually exclusive. Unions have resisted harmful reforms, protected rights, and fought for redistribution. At the same time, they are experimenting—however slowly—with digital tools, new organizational formats, and transversal alliances. The coexistence of resistance and reinvention is not a contradiction, but a feature of dynamic adaptation. What matters is whether these experiments can be scaled, institutionalized, and made relevant for workers across divides of class, gender, generation, and geography.

Third, the global nature of digital capitalism demands transnational strategies. Algorithms do not respect borders. Labor platforms operate across jurisdictions, exploiting regulatory gaps. Data is extracted globally and monetized elsewhere. In this scenario, unions cannot afford to remain confined to national logics. They must articulate new forms of internationalism, based not only on declarations of solidarity but on shared infrastructures, interoperable legal frameworks, and collaborative research. The Argentine union movement—despite its resource constraints—can contribute to these efforts with its strategic creativity and its embeddedness in broader struggles for democracy and human rights.

Finally, the debate on unions and automation is ultimately a debate about what kind of society we want. Technological choices are social choices. Whether AI will be used to intensify exploitation or to reduce drudgery depends not on the algorithms themselves, but on who designs them, who deploys them, and under what conditions. Unionism, in this sense, is not simply a vehicle for defending labor standards—it is a project for civilizing technology, for subjecting technical decisions to collective deliberation, and for ensuring that innovation serves the public good.

Reimagining unionism in the era of AI requires boldness. It requires unions to confront their own limits, to speak the language of digital culture without losing sight of structural inequalities, and to open their doors to the voices of those historically excluded—precarious workers, platform workers, informal workers, migrant workers, care workers. It also requires a politics of hope: the belief that even in the face of massive disruption, collective action can still shape the future.

Argentina, with all its contradictions, provides fertile ground for this reimagination. It reminds us that the future of work is not only a technical problem—it is a political horizon. And on that horizon, unions still have something to say.

REFERENCES

Autor, D. H. (2015). Why are there still so many jobs? The history and future of workplace automation. *The Journal of Economic Perspectives*, *29*(3), 3–30. DOI: 10.1257/jep.29.3.3

Brynjolfsson, E., & McAfee, A. (2014). *The second machine age: Work, progress, and prosperity in a time of brilliant technologies*. W. W. Norton & Company.

de Ciencia, M., & Tecnología e Innovación, P. (2019). *Plan Nacional de Inteligencia Artificial*. Presidencia de la Nación Argentina. https://www.argentina.gob.ar

De Stefano, V. (2016). The rise of the "just-in-time workforce": On-demand work, crowd work, and labor protection in the "gig economy". *Comparative Labor Law & Policy Journal*, *37*(3), 471–504.

Etchemendy, S. (2001). Constructing reform coalitions: The politics of compensation in Argentina's economic liberalization. *Latin American Politics and Society*, *43*(3), 1–35. DOI: 10.1111/j.1548-2456.2001.tb00177.x

Etchemendy, S., & Collier, R. B. (2007). Down but not out: Union resurgence and segmented neocorporatism in Argentina (2003–2007). *Politics & Society*, *35*(3), 363–401. DOI: 10.1177/0032329207304318

Feenberg, A. (1999). *Questioning technology*. Routledge.

Frey, C. B., & Osborne, M. A. (2013). *The future of employment: How susceptible are jobs to computerisation?* Oxford Martin School Working Paper.

Iglesias, R. (2020). AI, automation, and labor rights: Perspectives from the Argentine union movement. *Revista Latinoamericana de Estudios del Trabajo*, *25*(1), 55–78.

James, D. (1988). *Resistance and integration: Peronism and the Argentine working class, 1946–1976*. Cambridge University Press.

Roveri, M. F. (2019). Sindicatos en Argentina: Percepción sobre la IA. *América Latina en Movimiento*, *545*, 16–20.

Suriano, J. (2000). *El anarquismo argentino. Edición crítica*. Fondo de Cultura Económica.

UNI Global Union. (2021). Top 10 principles for workers' data rights in the digital age. https://uniglobalunion.org

ENDNOTES

1 In 2021, the Ministry of Public Innovation promoted the use of AI systems for the document management of the national State, without establishing a formal mechanism for union consultation or labor impact analysis.

2 In 2022, the APP promoted a bill for the recognition of the employment relationship between delivery workers and platforms, but the text did not advance in parliamentary committees due to a lack of political consensus and business opposition.

3 The Labor and Digitalization Observatory of the University of Buenos Aires has proposed systematizing these regional comparisons through indicators of digital unionization, regulatory capacity, and union access to technological processes.

4 In 2021, a group of delivery workers filed an injunction for arbitrary dismissal with a digital platform that "disconnected" them without explanation, but the court dismissed the case as there was no formally recognised employment relationship.

5 In 2022, the Autonomous CTA proposed to the Ministry of Labor the creation of a Permanent Table on Labor Innovation, without an institutional response at the time of the closing of this chapter.

Chapter 3
The Role of Artificial Intelligence in Mexican Labor Unions:
Challenges, Opportunities, and Global Insights

Mayela Saraí López Castro
https://orcid.org/0000-0002-4839-5481
Universidad Alfonso X el Sabio, Spain

Carlos Bardavío Antón
Universidad Alfonso X el Sabio, Spain

ABSTRACT

This chapter examines the use of artificial intelligence (AI) in Mexican unions, comparing it with its global adoption. Globally, AI is used to protect workers and optimize management, while in Mexico its implementation is still in an early stage. The study contextualizes this lag with international cases and analyzes the ethical, technical and legal implications of AI, highlighting its advantages, such as efficiency, and its risks, such as lack of transparency. It also addresses the regulatory framework in Mexico, which lacks a specific authority and a comprehensive national plan, despite participation in international initiatives. The work highlights the challenges and opportunities that AI presents for unions in Mexico, underlining the importance of training and collaboration between unions, companies and governments, as well as the need to consider ethical and regulatory aspects for responsible adoption.

DOI: 10.4018/979-8-3693-8049-9.ch003

I. INTRODUCTION: AI IN LAW

The rapid growth of artificial intelligence technologies has radically transformed industries, affecting job roles, workplace management and organisational structures. Trade unions, as advocates for workers' rights, are in a unique position to mediate this transformation. Globally, unions are leveraging AI to negotiate worker protections, streamline administrative operations and monitor workplace practices. In Mexico, however, union adoption of AI remains unexplored. This chapter examines the limited involvement of Mexican unions in AI and contextualises its possible adoption using international case studies.

Luhmann (2017) commented at the time that '(a)rtificial intelligence research is concerned with the manipulation of symbols, but not with the formation of meaning', in fact he also referred that '(i)f the natural sciences themselves have dissolved the concept of nature (independently of the observer) and if in the ecological context, technique and nature are mixed in an inseparable and unpronounceable way, then it no longer makes sense to order phenomena according to the technique/nature distinction' (p.413).

If, as we have mentioned, AI works on symbols, but not on the formation of meaning, it could be concluded from this assumption that it will have to be the lawyer who, through AI, will have to give meaning to the particular case in question (writs, lawsuits, complaints, legal grounds, etc.). However, as Luhmann also said, it can also be deduced from this that the distinction between the natural creation by humans and the technology applied to give meaning with the help of AI is blurred, i.e. there is no distinction between AI technology and the reason of nature or rationality (psychic system) or the 'world of life' (*Lebenswelt*). In addition, the differences between the author of the artistic creation (a writ of complaint or a sublime lawsuit) and the artistic creation itself are also blurred. How, then, can a lawyer avoid the absurdity of creating a technical work for which he is paid that is the same as that which a layman can create? This is an ethical (and moral!) problem, but at the same time an artistic, technical challenge, with profound implications in dogmatic, especially criminal law (solutions in objective imputation, typicity, antijurisdiction, culpability and punishability).

A simple glance at AI programmes quickly demonstrates the simplicity of their use, without prejudice to learning (prompts: keys to communication with the AI; super prompting: a prompting technique that combines multidisciplinary logic with responses based on thought trees, Tree of Thoughts), so that between the human being (interaction system between social systems such as the economy, in our case the law) and AI itself, AI is just another interaction system, and in itself nature in itself as it blends in with human rationality. However, for now, AI still needs inputs that a human being, a lawyer or a judge, sends it as a sense of communication, and through this AI instantly launches complementary outputs of this sense transformed into (more?) precise information in accordance with what is desired. In this sense, it is clear that the interaction between the two consists of communication with meaning, and as far as the world of law is concerned, a legal meaning in its own communication code (punishable/non-punishable), specifically in criminal law in the sense of the punishable/non-punishable code. For these reasons, the application of AI in the practice of law, especially in trade unions and fundamental labour rights, has ethical (even moral!), technical and dogmatic implications.

Throughout this study, we will focus on the three implications in order to highlight their own problems and at the same time the challenges for their unavoidable application, and we already anticipate that they have more advantages than disadvantages. To cite an example, if AI were to do away with the need for trade unions, that is, if any citizen could technically defend himself in the labour sphere, even achieving convincing dogmatic arguments in his defence, however disastrous, at least initially, the unemployment of trade union staff would be, from a strictly systemic perspective we would end up concluding that the justice system itself has adapted in such a way that its operations (e.g. lawsuits, conflicts and judicial resolutions) is more reliable by communicating greater sense of the need for a system of justice, and that the system of justice itself has adapted in such a way that its operations (e.g. lawsuits, conflicts and judicial resolutions) is more reliable by communicating greater sense of the need for a system of justice.

Before we dive in, it should be clarified that AI is part of Industry 4.0, which refers to the fourth industrial revolution, driven by the integration of advanced digital technologies into industrial processes. This evolution is characterised by the interconnection of 'cyber-physical' systems, the Internet of Things (IoT) and cloud computing, among other technologies, which aim to improve efficiency and productivity in industrial production. Industry 5.0, on the other hand, represents a phase after Industry 4.0, and focuses on close collaboration between humans as psychic systems and automated systems. In contrast to the automation prevalent in Industry 4.0, Industry 5.0 promotes greater interaction between humans, their psyche and machines, using technologies such as AI, advanced robotics and augmented reality to create more collaborative and flexible work environments.

In this sense, the relationship between Industry 4.0, Industry 5.0 and AI is close. In Industry 4.0, AI is playing a key role in optimising production processes by analysing large amounts of data in real time, enabling greater automation and customisation of production. And already in Industry 5.0, AI is being used to facilitate collaboration between human psychic systems and automated systems, allowing machines to 'learn' from interaction with humans and adapt to changing situations more efficiently.

For this reason, AI has significantly transformed decision-making in a variety of fields, offering data analysis and predictive capabilities that surpass human capabilities in many cases. However, the use of AI in decision-making also brings with it not only certain advantages but also risks.

In terms of advantages, AI can improve the accuracy and speed of decisions, reduce 'human bias' and optimise available resources. In addition, AI can analyse complex data and interrelated variables more efficiently than humans, which can lead to more informed and strategic decisions.

But there are always risks associated with the use of AI in decision-making. One of the main risks is 'algorithmic bias', which can arise when the training data used to develop AI models contain 'inherent biases', which can lead to discriminatory or unfair decisions (Barocas and Selbst, 2016), for example, in the field of labour and labour dispute resolution through trade unions. Moreover, the opacity of AI algorithms may make it difficult to understand how a particular decision is reached, raising ethical and transparency concerns. But in any case, what AI then implies is that it can not only complement the decisions of citizens, but also focus on the premises of the decision, i.e. convincing or reinforcing the human decision by means of systemic feedback, i.e. AI as a 'premise' of the premise of the human being's legal decision, thus diluting the unity of the difference between technique and reason, and hence the consequent problems of imputation (administrative, labour, civil or criminal) of the creation.

In particular, regarding "algorithmic bias" related to potential discriminations that violate fundamental rights, the State v. Loomis case is worth highlighting.

In this case, State v. Loomis, 881 N.W.2d 749 (Wis. 2016)[1], the trial judge based his decision not to suspend the sentence on the risk of reoffending determined by the COMPAS programme (Martínez Garay, 2018, pp. 490 y 491). Loomis's argument was based on the premise that the system's assignment of a male gender was a determining factor in increasing the risk of reoffending. Consequently, he argued that the judge, by imposing a severe sentence based, among other factors, on the risk assessment from this programme, was engaging in gender discrimination.

However, it is relevant to consider the resolution of the Wisconsin Supreme Court (TSW), which approached this issue from the perspective of prediction accuracy. The TSW resolved the issue by considering the system's accuracy rate. According to this approach, disregarding the gender factor would lead to an increase in risk estimation errors for both males and females. Therefore, including gender in the evaluation was not considered discriminatory, but rather a substantial improvement to the justice system, benefiting both groups of individuals.

Subsequently, the TSW set out guidelines on how these AI systems should be used in the sentencing phase. Specifically, it recommended applying scrutiny to the accuracy levels of these tools, addressing issues ranging from potential discrimination against minorities to the lack of sufficient validation studies.

While this example pertains strictly to the judicial realm, it effectively illustrates the challenges faced by Mexican trade unions in their collaboration with employees. In particular, when it comes to hiring, job continuity, and disciplinary dismissals, potential algorithmic biases in risk assessment must be avoided, without human oversight or control, as was the case in the example presented.

II. ETHICAL AND REGULATORY CONSIDERATIONS OF AI IN LAW AS APPLIED TO TRADE UNIONS

The emergence of companies, providers and tools for office management, data analysis and the preparation of legal documents means that some citizens or legal entities are also taking on the responsibility for these services[2], even if they do not have a law degree.

AI is revolutionising law firms in general, also labour law firms and trade unions in various areas, e.g. in internal organisation and work and resource management processes (back-office), in service provision (front-office), in machine learning, in natural language processing and its combination with big data, also through automatic reading systems and document analysis, especially with due diligence systems through which thousands of contracts (e.g. employment contracts) can be reviewed in a short time, in the implementation of predictive analytics systems to be able to find patterns of judicial behaviour and thus anticipate and predict the judicial outcome, or through automatic online dispute resolution systems in favour of employees, which help to solve conflicts without legal assistance and without the need for the intervention of an arbitrator or judge (Barrio, 2019; Cotino, 2019; Fernández and Guglieri, 2020; Solar, 2018; 2019). All this makes it necessary to establish ethical principles, which has already begun to be implemented through some projects such as, for example, AI4People[3].

Some trade unions will probably be reluctant to use AI because they fear that they are not the real authors of successful legal texts, while others will abuse it. In both cases, there is a risk of making mistakes, whether it is the trade unionist or the labour lawyer who writes without any help from AI, or the one who uses it by giving the wrong meaning to the AI, or because the AI itself makes a mistake, since as an intelligence it also makes mistakes ('hallucinations', outdatedness, regulatory inconsistencies, etc.).

From this point of view, there are no different ethical implications than before the advent of AI, perhaps moral implications on the part of society, which does not want to allow trade unionists and their lawyers to earn money for writings produced almost 100% by AI, or perhaps moral implications on the part of each trade unionist and lawyer who, as a 'conscientious objection', does not wish to use it, even though they know that it could benefit the client/employee. In other words, the ethical implications of AI are the same as before, for example, when a trade union and its lawyers charge for 3 pages a figure that for the average would cost only ten percent, and even in this case, if the lawyer makes a 'copy and paste', the ethical implication is the same as today, that of the lawyer who summarises texts of thousands of pages in seconds and does not check if it is well done.

However, we cannot ignore the fact that the speed with which AI tools work in law ('legal expert systems') means that trade unions and the profession of labour lawyers, among others, and the application of the law by judges and courts is undergoing its greatest revolution. It is then a question of trust between all, and, in case of error, of implications of civil or criminal liability, and who knows also in the future of the judge himself and/or the administration of justice.

We must not forget that AI does not come to the unions and magically give the most convenient solution for the employees and for the company, nor does it create the document, proposal or lawsuit, but we must interact (prompts / legal prompting) in a meaningful way, as with any third party.

In this regard, the White Paper on Artificial Intelligence (a European approach to excellence and trust) states that the ethics of AI are dignity and fundamental rights[4].

The AI agenda in Mexico has had an uneven development over the years. Although the country was a pioneer in Latin America, it has lost momentum at various stages. The most relevant milestones are presented below (UNESCO, 2024a, p.13):

i. 2018: The Mexican government initiated a national AI strategy under the Coordination of the National Digital Strategy, resulting in a report with policy recommendations.
ii. June 2018: Mexico, together with Japan, led a forum at the UN on science and technology, where resolution 73/17 was approved, urging countries to analyse the impact of technological changes, especially AI.
iii. Documents on general principles of AI and a tool for assessing risks in autonomous systems were developed.
iv. At the international level, Mexico formed a working group at the UN and led initiatives in the Latin American and Caribbean Network for the development of digital governments.
v. The IA2030.mx coalition was created, bringing together more than 400 people to develop the first National AI Agenda.

vi. Mexico joined the Global Partnership on Artificial Intelligence (GPAI) in June 2020.
vii. In November 2021, the Recommendation on the Ethics of AI was adopted at UNESCO's General Conference.

Although there is no specific regulatory authority for AI in Mexico, various public entities have competencies in its governance:

- Coordination of the National Digital Strategy: Responsible for designing and monitoring the country's digital strategy.
- Intersecretarial Commission on Information and Communication Technologies (CITICSI): Coordinates actions and regulations on AI in the executive branch.
- Federal Telecommunications Institute (IFT): Can issue standards and recommendations on telecommunications and economic competition, key areas for AI.
- National Institute for Transparency, Access to Information and Protection of Personal Data (INAI): Regulates the use and protection of personal data.
- Standardizing Authorities: Responsible for developing Mexican Official Standards (NOM) and technical standards.
- Presidency of the Republic: Responsible for regulating laws issued by Congress.

While there is a legal framework that protects fundamental principles such as data protection and non-discrimination, the lack of a national plan prevents the effective implementation of these principles.

The country's lag in digitalization affects the regulation and adoption of AI. The National Digital Strategy 2021-2024 does not contemplate a digital transformation plan nor does it address AI, focusing on austerity and government digitalization. In addition, 20 of the 32 states lack a state digital policy (UNESCO, 2024).

In international assessments, Mexico has a poor performance in AI. The Latin American AI Index gives it a score of 2.78/100 in institutionality and 8.33/100 in strategy, due to the absence of a current national strategy and the lack of citizen participation mechanisms[5].

The Government AI Readiness Index[6] was first published in 2017, assessing only OECD countries. In that edition, Mexico ranked 22nd out of 35, beating out nations such as Estonia, Poland, and Portugal. However, in the most recent assessment in 2023 (Figure 1), Mexico fell to 68th out of 193 countries, being overtaken by all countries previously below it. Its overall score was 50.37, while other countries in the region scored higher: Brazil (63.7), Chile (61.95), Colombia (57.85), and Argentina (57.72). In Mexico, the Government pillar scored 43.08, the Technology pillar scored 39.55, and the Infrastructure and Data pillar scored 68.49.

Figure 1. Changes in country scores on the government AI readiness index

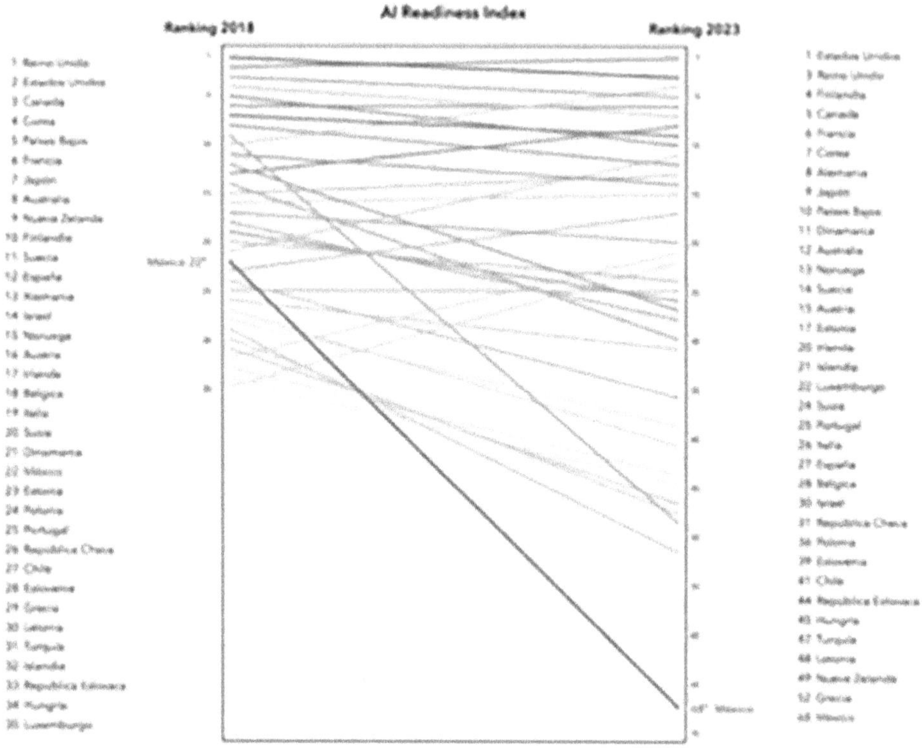

Source: UNESCO (2024, p.16).

The low score in the governance pillar reflects deficiencies in key areas, such as the lack of a strategic vision for the development and management of AI, the absence of solid regulation with ethical principles that generate trust and legitimacy, and the limited internal digital capacity to innovate and adapt to new technologies.

In this sense, AI requires a solid and adaptable legal framework, with long-term objectives and flexible tools to respond to its constant evolution. Instead of creating completely new regulations, it is advisable to review and update existing regulations, especially in data protection, transparency and data governance.

Similarly, the adoption of AI raises ethical and regulatory issues that Mexican unions should address as soon as possible. These are, in our opinion, the following:

1°. Transparency: ensuring that AI algorithms used in collective bargaining or workplace monitoring are transparent and impartial.
2°. Data privacy: protecting members' data from misuse, particularly when AI is used for administrative or analytical purposes.

3°. Worker autonomy: balancing the efficiency of AI tools with the preservation of human-centered decision-making in union activities.

III. THE GLOBAL CONTEXT: TRADE UNIONS AND AI ADOPTION

The emergence of Generative Artificial Intelligence (GAI) poses effects that deserve careful analysis. According to a report by McKinsey (2021), it is estimated that by 2030, between 75 and 375 million workers worldwide may need to change occupations due to AI-driven automation.

Likewise, a study by the International Labour Organization (2023) indicates that, while AI has the potential to generate new jobs, it can also lead to the displacement of workers in roles that can be automated. This report highlights that, although the adoption of AI could increase the global Gross Domestic Product (GDP) by 14% by 2030, there is also a risk of worsening social inequalities if adequate management measures are not implemented. In addition, a study by the International Monetary Fund (2024) indicates that almost 40% of global employment is exposed to AI, and in advanced economies, the figure rises to around 60%.

In this context, trade unions, as representatives of workers, have a crucial role in ensuring that the transition to AI is fair and inclusive. This is essential to help workers adapt to a constantly changing work environment.

This tension between the need for training and the rapid adoption of new technologies represents one of the main challenges facing the legal sector in 2025, and of course in labour law and in the role of trade unions in protecting the labour and constitutional rights of employees, in an effort not to be left behind in this wave of innovation.

Faced with this phenomenon, trade unions around the world have responded in a variety of practical ways to address this problem. Some notable examples include:

1. Training and capacity building: Trade unions are promoting training and capacity building programs to help workers acquire new skills needed in an AI-dominated work environment. In Sweden, the LO trade union has implemented continuous training initiatives that enable workers to update their skills and adapt to new technologies (The Swedish Trade Union Confederation, 2023).
2. Collective bargaining: This is another area where unions are active. In Germany, unions have negotiated agreements that ensure that the implementation of AI does not result in mass layoffs. These agreements include clauses on the relocation of workers and the creation of new jobs in emerging sectors (DGB, 2023).

In the United States, unions have successfully negotiated contracts that address the impact of AI in the workplace. In particular, the Communications Workers Association of America (CWA) negotiated provisions to limit the use of AI in the automation of customer-facing functions, thereby ensuring protections against arbitrary job displacement[7]. Finally, in the European Union, a 2022 survey by UNI Europa found that 42% of unions in 32 countries had begun bargaining on AI-related issues, such as algorithmic management and workplace surveillance. About 20% reported the existence of collective agreements addressing AI[8].

3. Data Protection and Ethics: Trade unions are also advocating for the protection of workers' data and ethics in the use of AI. In France, the CFDT union has raised concerns about employee surveillance through AI technologies and has demanded stricter regulations to protect workers' privacy (CFDT, 2023).

In Canada, unions have used AI to analyze workplace safety data and monitor employers' compliance with labour standards. For example, the Canadian Union of Public Employees (CUPE) incorporated AI-based tools to assess health risks in workplaces, enhancing its advocacy for safer conditions [9].

4. Collaboration with business and government: In Germany, unions have collaborated with businesses and government to establish regulatory frameworks that protect workers while encouraging innovation. The IG Metall union has negotiated agreements that include ongoing training for employees in digital skills, ensuring they can adapt to technological changes (ILO, 2023). Similarly, in Sweden, the Unionen union has collaborated with technology companies to develop AI tools that monitor working conditions and detect potential rights violations. This proactive approach has been praised by the ILO as an example of how technology can empower workers (OIT, 2023).

In addition, consultancies such as Deloitte and PwC have highlighted that companies that involve unions in the implementation of AI tend to achieve greater acceptance and success in their technological initiatives. For example, in Japan, collaboration between unions and companies has allowed the creation of jointly funded professional retraining programs, which has facilitated the transition of workers to new roles in the digital economy (Deloitte, 2023a; PwC, 2023).

These examples highlight the potential of AI to empower unions in negotiations, policy advocacy and membership engagement. They also underline the importance of proactive regulation to prevent the misuse of AI technologies.

However, governments in the region currently lack joint strategies and commitments that promote a common vision on AI. Compared to other regions, such as the European Union, where commitments have been made to develop AI ethical guidelines and capabilities, Latin America and the Caribbean still faces challenges in creating a collective frame of reference. These efforts in other regions seek to generate economies of scale and strengthen international collaboration, which could benefit countries in the region by showcasing their comparative strengths (OCDE/CAF, 2022).

In Mexico, the national AI strategy has been influenced by political changes that have disrupted progress in digital government. Despite this, the IA2030.mx coalition has continued its work, although the status of the original AI strategy in the country is ambiguous. Five key lessons have been identified that emerge from this experience, including the need for initial assessments, strategic partnerships, and the importance of engaging different levels of government. This strategy focuses on five essential measures, including developing an inclusive governance framework and promoting Mexico's leadership in international fórums (OCDE/CAF, 2022).

Mexico is in an intermediate position in terms of global digitalization, ranking 59th in the Network Readiness Index. This reflects both the progress and the challenges that the country faces in the adoption of digital technologies, which has direct implications in the labor field and in the regulation of AI (OCDE/CAF, 2022).

Analyzing the implications of AI in the workplace is not only of academic interest, but has become essential to ensure proper use of these technologies in management and personnel selection. As organizations adopt AI-based automated systems for hiring decisions, it is crucial to understand how they work and assess their impact in terms of impartiality and equity. The concern is that algorithms may be based on historical data that reflects past inequalities, which could perpetuate systematic bias and discrimination. The lack of understanding of how algorithms make decisions and the difficulty in assessing their impact on diversity and representation highlight the need to critically investigate these processes (Prieto, 2022; p.7).

Although it is rare for collective agreements to include clauses on AI, there are examples of agreements that proactively address new technologies and their employment implications. These agreements are models of good practice that demonstrate how social actors can face the challenges presented by AI (Prieto, 2022; p. 56). In this sense, unfair competition between workers can generate a toxic work environment and harm employee rights, while a lack of transparency makes it difficult to understand performance-related decisions.

Thus, digitalization and automation are transforming the labor market. However, automation does not necessarily imply the elimination of workers, but rather a change in the way work is controlled and monitored, resulting in increased algorithmic surveillance and evaluation of employees (Crawford, 2021; p.42). The portability of technological devices redefines the workspace, allowing workers to operate in diverse environments, which in turn poses challenges in terms of labor rights and the organization of work..

For example, the growth of the service sector, driven by the immediate availability of customer service, has led to an expansion of the working day to a 24/7 model. This raises questions about the relationship between collective labour rights and individual workers' demands, especially in a context where teleworking has become preferred in countries such as Argentina (The Economist, 2023).

Based on the above, we can affirm that the digitalization of work in Latin America is in full swing, affecting both individual and collective workers. The exploitation of data and the growing presence of machines and robots in the workplace are transforming the work experience, blurring the lines between the private and the work (De la Garza, 2011; p.3-4). Technology has led to a transformation in the identity of workers, where informal work and teleworking challenge traditional forms of union representation. Despite the perception that work is in decline, it is argued that, in fact, workers are engaging in more work activities than ever, which complicates union membership and the definition of what constitutes work (Kemmerling et al., 2023, p.4).

The analysis of the future of work in Mexico focuses on technological transformations and their socioeconomic and political implications. It is highlighted that the debate on the workplace includes aspects such as automation, platform economies and AI, which have changed the nature of work around the world. In this context, it is observed that the impact of digital transformation in Mexico is uneven, affecting certain regions and vulnerable groups more intensely (Kemmerling et al., 2023, p.16).

However, a catastrophic or naive approach can limit opportunities for modernization and adaptation to technological changes. It is important to highlight the need to break down the political silos that exist between technology experts and those in social and labor issues. Lack of communication and collaboration between these groups can hinder the development of effective policies that address the complexities of technological change and its effects on work (Kemmerling et al., 2023, p.9).

III. TRADE UNIONS IN MEXICO: LEGAL ISSUES AND OPPORTUNITIES

Trade unions in Mexico have historically been a fundamental pillar in the defense of labor rights. However, they currently face legal and structural challenges that limit their effectiveness, while opportunities arise to modernize and adapt to new labor dynamics, including the impact of AI in the world of work.

Mexican unions are shaped by their own legal and sociopolitical framework. The 2019 labor reforms, aligned with the United States-Mexico-Canada Agreement (USMCA), introduced measures to democratize union practices and improve worker representation. These reforms call for transparent elections and collective bargaining processes, laying the groundwork for modernization. However, unions face several structural challenges.

Many Mexican unions lack the financial resources to invest in advanced technologies like AI. There are also digital literacy issues as limited digital skills among union leaders and members impede the adoption of digital tools. There are also legal ambiguities as labor laws prioritize personal interaction and representation, raising questions about how AI tools align with existing regulations. And of course, there are ethical concerns, as workers and unions express concerns about data privacy, surveillance, and the potential misuse of AI to undermine collective power.

AI has not been a central theme in labor reforms in Mexico (Deloitte, 2023b; Organización Internacional del Trabajo, 2021a), despite growing concerns about its impact on various activities, such as content creation and the substitution of intellectual work. The protection of personal data in the workplace has been neglected, and unions have not addressed its regulation, which could be crucial to protect workers.

Mexican legislation, such as the Law on the Protection of Personal Data Held by Private Parties (LFPDPPP), the General Law on the Protection of Personal Data Held by Obligated Subjects (LGPDPPSO) and Convention 108 for the Protection of Individuals and the Automated Processing of Personal Data, which came into force in Mexico on October 1, 2018, seek to safeguard fundamental rights, but their application in the workplace is still insufficient. It is crucial that ethical regulations for AI be established that protect both workers and employers. In this sense, the digital age facilitates the violation of workers' privacy (art. 6 Mexican Constitution), which can lead to labor discrimination (Kurczyn, 2023).

Trade union struggles are also striking in the context of AI, especially in industries such as entertainment, where the use of AI poses new labour standards. AI, being present in all aspects of working life, feeds on human experience and knowledge, which underlines the need for adequate regulation to protect workers' rights in this new digital era.

It is essential that labour laws are updated to include provisions that protect workers in a context where AI plays a leading role. This involves not only the creation of new laws, but also the adaptation of existing ones to ensure that labour rights are respected and promoted in a technological environment (Aguilera, 2020).

In addition, the training and education of workers must be considered so that they can adapt to new technologies. Continuing education becomes an essential right in the digital age, allowing workers not only to maintain their employability, but also to actively participate in building a working future that integrates AI in an ethical and responsible manner (Aguilera, 2020).

Data collection through digital surveys has made it possible to identify data processing and IT security practices, which is crucial for the protection of workers' rights in a constantly changing work environment (Novick, 2022; p.23).

The pandemic also accelerated these transformations, highlighting the need for institutions and regulatory standards to adapt to the new realities of digital work. The pandemic has fostered collaboration between unions and companies, which can be a model for addressing technological change through collective bargaining, a key space for defending labor rights in the digital economy. Legislation, such as the Teleworking Law, establishes that control systems must not invade workers' privacy, and unions must have an active role in supervising these systems to ensure respect for privacy (Novick, 2022; p.5).

The implications for workers facing dismissal due to the implementation of these technologies represent the collision between freedom of enterprise and the right to work, which requires a proportionality judgment that assesses the protection of fundamental rights in contexts of automation. In other words, automation not only implies a change in the means of production but may result in the direct replacement of workers by machines (Granados 2023; p.67).

For example, in the context of Peru, current legislation allows collective dismissals for technological reasons but does not adequately regulate individual dismissals due to failure to adapt to technical changes. This has led to judicial interpretations that could facilitate the dismissal of workers in the context of automation (Granados 2023; p.77).

For example, in Ecuador too, although the application of AI in the private sector is limited, the need for regulation that protects labour rights in an environment where AI is on the rise is recognised. In addition, an action plan involving experts from various sectors is essential to address the ethical and philosophical implications of AI, i.e., despite the challenges presented by automation, there are also opportunities in sectors such as e-commerce and technological services, provided that compliance with labour rights is guaranteed (Granados 2023; p.78).

However, AI also presents significant opportunities for Mexican unions, including:

a) Data-Driven bargaining – that is, AI tools can analyze industry data, wage trends, and inflation rates, allowing unions to make evidence-based arguments during negotiations;
b) Membership management – such as AI-powered platforms, which can automate member registration and communication, reducing administrative burdens and improving engagement;
c) Workplace safety monitoring – as AI can analyze patterns of workplace accidents, helping unions advocate for better safety measures; and
d) Surveillance oversight – as AI becomes more prevalent in workplace surveillance, unions can leverage AI tools to monitor employer practices and ensure compliance with labor standards.

IV. CASE STUDY: THE NATIONAL ASSOCIATION OF ARTIFICIAL INTELLIGENCE (ANIA) AND ITS ROLE IN THE AI ECOSYSTEM IN MEXICO

The National Artificial Intelligence Alliance (ANIA) is a collaborative initiative that seeks to identify and enhance the artificial intelligence ecosystem in Mexico, adopting a comprehensive, inclusive and multidisciplinary approach. Its mission is to foster the growth and adoption of AI in Mexico through the generation of strategic knowledge, the training of diverse and highly qualified talent, the design of ethical and inclusive public policies and regulations, as well as the promotion of technological development and innovative entrepreneurship[10].

In this regard, although Mexico has made significant steps in the adoption of AI, it still faces significant challenges. According to a report by the International Labour Organization, AI has the potential to transform the labor market in Mexico, automating repetitive tasks and creating new opportunities in sectors such as manufacturing, financial services, and health (Organización Internacional del Trabajo, 2021b). However, there is also a risk that automation will displace workers in low-skilled jobs, which underscores the need for public policies that encourage job retraining.

On the other hand, a study published by the Mexican Institute for Competitiveness (IMCO) indicates that, although 70% of Mexican companies recognize the importance of AI, only 15% have implemented solutions based on this technology (IMCO, 2022). This is due, in part, to the lack of specialized talent and regulatory uncertainty.

The association has emerged as a key player in the development and consolidation of the AI ecosystem in Mexico. Since its creation, ANIA has implemented various strategies and concrete actions that seek to articulate efforts between the public, private, academic and civil society sectors, promoting a regulatory and ethical framework for the use of AI in the country. For example, it has collaborated with educational institutions to develop AI training programs, such as the Diploma in Artificial Intelligence offered by the Universidad Nacional Autónoma de México (UNAM) and organize various free virtual trainings. It has also worked with the federal government to create a National Artificial Intelligence Strategy, which seeks to establish a clear regulatory framework and promote investment in this area. Other initiatives and concrete actions are presented below:

a. Proposed National AI Agenda 2024-2030:

In May 2024, ANIA presented its proposal that establishes a regulatory framework to integrate AI into the Mexican industry. This document, prepared over 13 months with the participation of international and autonomous organizations, highlights the importance of AI in the global economy, projecting that it will generate 15.7 trillion dollars by 2030 (Pascua, 2024).

b. Thematic Working Groups:

ANIA has organized working groups focused on different thematic areas, such as[11]:

- Public Policies and Rights
- Education and Labor Markets
- Cybersecurity and Risk Management
- Gender, Inclusion and Social Responsibility
- Infrastructure and Data
- Innovation and Industry

These groups have allowed for a multidisciplinary dialogue that seeks to address the challenges and opportunities presented by AI in Mexico.

c. Collaboration with UNESCO:

Since 2023, ANIA has worked together with UNESCO to carry out a diagnosis of Mexico's state of readiness in terms of AI. This effort included the organization of 18 multi-stakeholder roundtables with more than 250 participants, including legislators and government representatives, reflecting an inclusive approach to AI governance (UNESCO, 2024b).

d. Training and Awareness:

ANIA has conducted workshops and webinars targeting diverse groups, including women entrepreneurs, to educate on the importance of integrating AI into their businesses. These events seek to empower participants with practical knowledge on the responsible and ethical use of AI[12].

Through these actions, ANIA has not only promoted technological development in Mexico, but has also contributed to establishing a dialogue on the ethical and social challenges associated with the implementation of advanced technologies. Its collaborative approach, involving businesses, government, academia, and civil society, has made it possible to identify critical areas where immediate attention is required, such as the lack of specific legislation on AI and the educational needs to prepare the workforce of the future. This dialogue has served as a catalyst for legislative initiatives and public policies that seek to regulate the use of AI and mitigate its potential negative effects. The association has also encouraged the creation of ethics committees in companies and public institutions, with the aim of ensuring that AI is developed and used responsibly and for the benefit of society.

One of ANIA's most notable achievements is its focus on ethics and transparency. In 2021, the association published an Ethical Code for the Development of AI in Mexico, which establishes principles such as fairness, privacy, and responsibility in the use of this technology. This code, inspired by international references such as UNESCO's recommendations on AI ethics, has been adopted by several companies and organizations, becoming a benchmark for the sector[13]. The code provides clear guidelines on how to address issues such as algorithmic bias, transparency in decision-making, and the protection of personal data, and promotes the creation of accountability mechanisms to ensure compliance with these principles. In addition, the association has promoted the creation of AI ethics training programs for professionals and students, with the aim of fostering a culture of responsibility in the development and implementation of this technology.

In this context, one of the main challenges in Mexico is the digital divide, which limits access to advanced technologies in rural and marginalized areas (ENDUTIH, 2023)[14]. This gap not only makes access to AI difficult for a significant part of the population, but can also exacerbate existing inequalities, as people who do not have access to these technologies risk being left behind in the labor market and in society in general. In addition, the lack of investment in research and development (R&D) remains an obstacle to competing globally. Despite the efforts made, R&D spending in Mexico remains lower than that of other countries in the region and that of the most advanced economies, which limits the country's ability to generate knowledge and develop innovative AI solutions adapted to local needs.

ANIA has recognized these challenges and is working on initiatives to overcome them. For example, it has proposed the creation of a National AI Innovation Fund, which would finance research projects and startups focused on this technology. This fund, which would have public and private resources, would support projects in strategic areas such as health, education, agriculture and manufacturing, and would promote the creation of high-quality jobs in the AI sector. It has also advocated for greater international collaboration, especially with leading AI countries such as the United States and Canada. The association has established strategic alliances with universities, research centers and companies in these countries, with the aim of promoting the exchange of knowledge, technology transfer and attracting investments in the AI sector in Mexico.

As discussed above, labor unions in Mexico have yet to integrate AI in a significant way. However, organizations such as ANIA have highlighted the transformative potential of this technology for the workforce. Recognizing that AI can both create new opportunities and pose challenges for workers, the association has led efforts to raise awareness about the implications of AI and has advocated for digital skills training supported by public policies. The association has collaborated with the government, unions, and other organizations to develop AI training programs aimed at workers in various sectors, including those at higher risk of automation. These programs seek to provide workers with the skills necessary to adapt to technological changes and take advantage of new job opportunities.

To this end, ANIA has organized specialized forums to analyze how AI can improve labor efficiency and reduce technological gaps in the country. For example, specific applications have been discussed such as the automation of administrative tasks in unions, such as quota management and grievance tracking, which optimizes internal processes and frees up resources for strategic activities. These initiatives seek not only to modernize labor practices, but also to promote inclusive and ethical adoption of AI in the Mexican labor sector.

The association has highlighted the importance of involving unions in the design and implementation of AI solutions in the workplace, ensuring that workers' needs and rights are taken into account. It has also promoted social dialogue between unions, companies and government to address the challenges and opportunities posed by AI in the Mexican labour market, and to ensure that the benefits of this technology are distributed equitably among all members of society. ANIA proposes that unions adopt AI not only for automation, but also to improve workers' representation and the defence of their rights, using AI to analyse data on working conditions, identify patterns of discrimination and negotiate better working conditions.

V. CONCLUSIONS

The integration of artificial intelligence (AI) into Mexican unions represents both a challenge and an important opportunity. Although its adoption in Mexico is still limited, the international examples analyzed in this article demonstrate its potential to strengthen the defense of labor rights, streamline operations, and more effectively protect workers' interests. The implementation of these technologies can not only improve the administrative efficiency of unions but also facilitate data-driven decision-making and encourage greater member participation, allowing for a deeper understanding of the needs and concerns of the worker base.

For Mexican unions to adopt AI responsibly and remain relevant in an environment of rapid technological change, it is crucial to address structural challenges, such as a lack of investment in digital infrastructure and a shortage of specialized AI skills, and to learn from international best practices. Countries such as Germany, Sweden and Japan have shown that collaboration between unions, companies and governments can generate positive outcomes for workers, while boosting innovation and productivity.

In this sense, cooperation between unions, policymakers and organizations specialized in AI will be essential to promote a labor movement adapted to Mexico's changing socioeconomic landscape. However, it is imperative to advance in the creation of robust regulatory frameworks that address issues such as algorithmic transparency, the protection of personal data and the prevention of discrimination, and to foster a culture of transparency and responsibility in the use of these technologies. It is essential to ensure that the implementation of AI in the workplace does not violate the fundamental rights of workers, but on the contrary, strengthens them and promotes equity.

One of the main challenges for Mexican unions is the tension between the need for training and the speed of technological innovation. As automation redefines occupations, unions must implement effective strategies to:

i. Promote continuous training and professional retraining: It is essential that workers have access to training programs in digital and AI skills, especially in sectors with a high risk of automation. These programs must be accessible, affordable and tailored to the specific needs of each sector and group of workers.
ii. Defend labor rights: Ensure that employee rights remain intact in an ever-evolving work environment. This includes negotiating collective agreements that protect workers from the negative impacts of automation, such as job loss and work intensification.

iii. Adapt to new technologies: Integrate technological tools into their operations to improve efficiency and communication with workers. This involves adopting digital platforms for membership management, internal communication and the dissemination of relevant information on labor rights and training opportunities.

To take advantage of the benefits of AI and mitigate its risks, it is recommended that Mexican unions:

i. Advocate for government support: Request funding for AI adoption and digital literacy programs. This could include creating specific funds for AI training, subsidizing research and development projects in the workplace, and promoting collaboration between unions, companies, and research centers.
ii. Collaborate with specialized organizations: Work with entities such as the National Association of Artificial Intelligence (ANIA) to access knowledge and resources on AI. In addition, it is important to establish alliances with universities and research centers to conduct studies on the impact of AI on the Mexican labor market and develop innovative solutions to the challenges it poses.
iii. Develop ethical guidelines: Establish clear guidelines for the use of AI, ensuring their alignment with labor laws and member expectations. These guidelines should address issues such as algorithmic transparency, non-discrimination, privacy protection, and liability in the event of errors or bias.
iv. Implement training programs: Train leaders and members in digital skills and the ethical use of AI. These programs should include modules on AI fundamentals, AI applications in the workplace, the risks and benefits of AI, and strategies for collective bargaining in the digital age. 5. Prioritize transparency and inclusion: Ensure that AI tools are accessible and equitable for all workers. This includes adopting web accessibility standards, translating informational materials into different languages, and promoting the participation of underrepresented groups in the development and implementation of AI solutions.

Similarly, the experiences of trade unions around the world offer valuable lessons for Mexico. For example, in the United States, trade unions have negotiated specific clauses to limit algorithmic management and AI-driven layoffs, a strategy that could be replicated in Mexico, especially in industries undergoing automation. Likewise, European trade unions have introduced training modules on AI ethics and implementation, which could serve as a model for developing digital literacy and addressing fears associated with these technologies in Mexico. Furthermore, collaboration with academic institutions, as seen in Canada, can facilitate research on the impact of AI on labour dynamics, providing trade unions with valuable information for policy formulation. In the specific context of Mexico, it is crucial to consider the particularities of the labour market and existing trade union structures, promoting broad and participatory social dialogue involving all relevant actors.

As AI continues to evolve, it will be crucial for Mexican unions to continue to adapt and advocate for policies that benefit all workers. Responsible adoption of AI, along with collaboration between key actors and learning from international experiences, can position unions as agents of change in the digital age, ensuring a more fair and equitable future of work, where technology is used to improve working conditions and promote the well-being of all workers.

REFERENCES

Aguilera Durán, J. (2020). La reconfiguración de los derechos fundamentales de los trabajadores frente al uso de la inteligencia artificial. Revista latinoamericana de Derecho Social, núm. 31, pp. 51-70.

Asociación Nacional de Inteligencia Artificial (ANIA). (2021). Código Ético para el Desarrollo de IA en México. Retrieved from https://www.ania.org.mx

Barocas, S., & Selbst, A. D. (2016). Big Data's Disparate Impact. *California Law Review*, *104*(3), 671–732.

Barrio Andrés, M. (Dir.). (2019). Legal Tech. La transformación digital de la abogacía. Wolters Kluwer.

Blanke, S., y Sladogna, M (2023). ¿Cómo trabajaremos en América Latina? Inteligencia artificial y trabajo en la periferia del capitalismo. Nueva Sociedad, núm. 307, pp. 96-110.

Centro Nacional de Inteligencia Artificial. (2023). Índice Latinoamericano de Inteligencia Artificial. Retrieved from https://indicelatam.cl

CFDT. (2023). La digitalización y la protección de los trabajadores. Retrieved from https://www.cfdt.fr/

Comisión Europea. (2020). Libro Blanco sobre Inteligencia Artificial - un enfoque europeo orientado a la excelencia y la confianza. Retrieved from https://op.europa.eu/es/publication-detail/-/publication/ac957f13-53c6-11ea-aece-01aa75ed71a1

Corvalán, J. G. (2019). El impacto de la inteligencia artificial en el trabajo. *Revista de Direito Econômico e Socioambiental*, *10*(1), 35–51. DOI: 10.7213/rev.dir.econ.soc.v10i1.25870

Cotino Hueso, L. (2019). *Ética en el diseño para el desarrollo de una inteligencia artificial, robótica y big data confiables y su utilidad desde el derecho*. Revista Catalana de Dret Públic.

Crawford, K. (2021). Atlas of AI: Power, Politics, and the Planetary Costs of Artificial Intelligence. Yale up, New Haven.

De la Garza, E. (2011). Más allá de la fábrica: los desafíos teóricos del trabajo no clásico y la producción inmaterial. Nueva Sociedad, núm. 232, pp. 50-70.

Deloitte. (2023a). AI and the future of work: A global perspective. Retrieved from https://www2.deloitte.com

Deloitte. (2023b). El futuro del trabajo en México: desafíos y oportunidades. Retrieved from https://www2.deloitte.com

DGB. (2023). AI in the Workplace: Opportunities and Challenges. Retrieved from https://en.dgb.de/

Fernández Comas, J. M., & Guglieri Lillo, A. O. (2020). *Guía Legaltech 2020. Información y análisis de software, productos y herramientas para el sector legal*. Reus.

Fondo Monetario Internacional. (2024). Gen-AI: Artificial Intelligence and the Future of Work. Retrieved from https://www.imf.org/en/Publications/Staff-Discussion-Notes/Issues/2024/01/14/Gen-AI-Artificial-Intelligence-and-the-Future-of-Work-542379

García Peña, J. H. (2018). El papel del abogado frente a la inteligencia artificial. Informática y Derecho. *Revista Iberoamericana de Derecho Informático*, *5*, 11–1.

Garrido Martínez, J., & Valdivia Jiménez, R. (Coords.). (2022). Inteligencia artificial y filosofía del derecho. Ediciones Laborum, S.L.

Granados Ferreira, J. (2023). El impacto de la inteligencia artificial en los trabajadores despedidos por automatización de servicios. Revista CES Derecho, Vol. 14. núm. 3, 2023. p. 1-67. DOI: 10.21615/cesder.7416

Granados Ferreira, J. (2023). El impacto de la inteligencia artificial en los trabajadores despedidos por automatización de servicios. *Revista CES Derecho*, *14*(3), 62–81. DOI: 10.21615/cesder.7416

Grigore, A. E. (2022). *Derechos humanos e inteligencia artificial. IUS ET SCIENTIA, 8(1).* Universidad de Sevilla.

Instituto Mexicano para la Competitividad (IMCO). (2022). La adopción de inteligencia artificial en México: Oportunidades y desafíos. Retrieved from https://www.imco.org.mx

Kemmerling, A., Altamirano, M., & Rosales, M. S. (2023). El futuro del trabajo en México. Análisis, 1-20.

Kurczyn Villalobos, P. (2023). Inteligencia artificial y los derechos humanos laborales, en Cielo Laboral, pp. 1-5.

Luhmann, N. (2007). *La sociedad de la sociedad* (Torres Nafarrate, J., Trans.). Herder, Méxco.

Martínez Garay, L., (2018). Peligrosidad, algoritmos y due process. El caso State vs. Loomis. Revista de Derecho Penal y Criminología. núm. 20, pp. 485-502.

McKinsey. (2021). The Future of Work after. *COVID, 19*, •••. https://www.mckinsey.com/~/media/mckinsey/featured%20insights/future%20of%20organizations/the%20future%20of%20work%20after%20covid%2019/the-future-of-work-after-covid-19-report-vf.pdf

Novick, M. (2022). *Tecnología y digitalización: el desafío sindical*. Análisis.

OCDE/CAF. (2022). Estrategias de inteligencia artificial en América Latina y el Caribe. In *The Strategic and Responsible Use of Artificial Intelligence in the Public Sector of Latin America and the Caribbean*. OECD Publishing.

Organización Internacional del Trabajo. (2021a). El futuro del trabajo en América Latina y el Caribe. Retrieved from https://www.ilo.org

Organización Internacional del Trabajo. (2021b). Informe sobre la situación laboral en México. Recuperado de https://www.ilo.org

Organización Internacional del Trabajo. (2023). Inteligencia artificial y el futuro del trabajo. Retrieved from https://www.ilo.org

Oxford Insights. (2017). Government AI Readiness Index 2017. Retrieved from https://www.oxfordinsights.com/government-ai-readinessindex

Pascua Vicente, S. (2024). México: La Alianza Nacional de Inteligencia Artificial publica su propuesta sobre inteligencia artificial para el periodo 2024 – 2030. Instituto Autor. Recuperado de: https://institutoautor.org/mexico-la-alianza-nacional-de-inteligencia-artificial-publica-su-propuesta-sobre-inteligencia-artificial-para-el-periodo-2024-2030/

Prieto Pérez, T. (2022). Implicaciones Jurídico Laborales de la Inteligencia Artificial. *Universidad de León, 2022*, 56.

PwC. (2023). AI predictions 2023: How AI will reshape the workforce. Retrieved from https://www.pwc.com

Solar Cayón, J. I. (2018). La codificación predictiva: Inteligencia artificial en la averiguación procesal de los hechos relevantes. *Anuario de la Facultad de Derecho de la Universidad de Alcalá, XI*, 75–105.

Solar Cayón, J. I. (2019). *La inteligencia artificial jurídica. El impacto de la innovación tecnológica en la práctica del Derecho y el mercado de servicios jurídicos*. Aranzadi.

Solar Cayón, J. I. (2021). Retos de la deontología de la abogacía en la era de la inteligencia artificial jurídica. *Derechos y Libertades, 45*(45), 151–152. DOI: 10.20318/dyl.2021.6104

The Economist. (2023). Encuesta sobre preferencias laborales en América Latina. The wfh Showdown. The Economist, 15-21/7/2023.

The Swedish Trade Union Confederation. (2023). Continuous Learning in the Age of AI. Retrieved from https://www.lo.se/english/this_is_lo

UNESCO. (2024). MÉXICO "Evaluación del estadío de preparación de la inteligencia artificial". Retrieved from https://mexico.un.org/es/273089-m%C3%A9xico-evaluaci%C3%B3n-del-estad%C3%ADo-de-preparaci%C3%B3n-de-la-inteligencia-artificial

UNESCO. (2024). UNESCO presenta Reporte de Evaluación del Estadio de Preparación de Inteligencia Artificial de México. Retrieved from https://www.unesco.org/es/articles/unesco-presenta-reporte-de-evaluacion-del-estadio-de-preparacion-de-inteligencia-artificial-de

ENDNOTES

1 Available at: https://law.justia.com/cases/wisconsin/supreme-court/2016/2015ap000157-cr.html (consultado 8 de mayo de 2024), y en https://www.wicourts.gov/sc/opinion/DisplayDocument.pdf?content=pdf&seqNo=171690, (consultado el 9 de mayo de 2024).

2 As Solar Crayón (2021, pp.151-152) comments, 'the capabilities of legal artificial intelligence blur, to the point of practically dissolving, the boundaries between what constitutes mere "legal information", which can be provided by anyone, and what is "legal advice", the exclusive competence of the lawyer. Until now, however powerful automated databases and information search and retrieval tools were, they provided no more than generic legal information (legal, jurisprudential, doctrinal), which in any case had to be interpreted and applied to the specific case; and this is where the role of the lawyer comes into play, acting as an intermediary between this information and the client, with his or her particular circumstances. But the degree of interactivity and user participation in the design of the product that artificial intelligence systems allow means that they can provide legal responses tailored to the user's specific situation and needs: expert systems provide a specific response to a particular problem; applications for the automatic drafting of legal documents generate contracts, wills, company incorporation documents, etc., the content of which is completely tailored to the user's specific situation and needs, whose content is fully adjusted to the unique circumstances of each case; predictive analysis tools evaluate the chances of success of possible procedural strategies in rela-

tion to a specific conflict between certain litigants before a specific judge or court; automatic dispute resolution systems determine a solution taking into account the particular interests and preferences of the parties in conflict... In other words, legal artificial intelligence can carry out practically all the tasks performed by the professional when advising his client, in a fully personalised manner and adjusted to the circumstances of the case. The history of lawsuits brought against LegalZoom in various US jurisdictions for professional intrusiveness shows very well these difficulties in delimiting, in relation to the commercial exploitation of legal artificial intelligence applications, the dividing line between the mere provision of legal information and the provision of a legal advice service'.

3 Cotino Hueso (2019, pp.37) comments that '(i)n 2018, the AI4People project has come to count 47 internationally proclaimed ethical principles. It considers that there are five principles that synthesise or capture the meaning of the 47 (...): beneficence (doing good), non-maleficence (doing no harm), autonomy or human agency (respect for the self-determination and choice of individuals) and justice (fair and equitable treatment for all). To these four it adds the principle of explicability or transparency (operating in a transparent manner or as intelligibility and accountability), also mentioned by the Parliament. The EU's High Level Expert Group takes them on board directly because of their inclusive nature and, above all, because 'these general principles provide guidance towards the operationalisation of fundamental values' (...) The five principles are now the pillars of reliable AI made in Europe. It must be said, however, that the four basic principles have been derived from the field of biomedicine since the 2000s (...) 'The four bioethical principles are surprisingly well adapted to the new ethical challenges posed by artificial intelligence', as bioethics is the most similar to digital ethics..

4 https://op.europa.eu/es/publication-detail/-/publication/ac957f13-53c6-11ea-aece-01aa75ed71a1

5 Centro Nacional de Inteligencia Artificial (2023). Índice Latinoamericano de Inteligencia Artificial. https://indicelatam.cl

6 Oxford Insights (2017). Government AI Readiness Index 2017. The index is calculated based on three pillars, each of which includes a set of factors: the governance pillar, the technology pillar, and the infrastructure and data pillar. https://www.oxfordinsights.com/government-ai-readinessindex

7 Americanprogress.org en https://www.americanprogress.org/article/unions-give-workers-a-voice-over-how-ai-affects-their-jobs/

8 Uni-europa.org en https://www.uni-europa.org/news/new-studies-show-42-per-cent-of-trade-unions-are-already-negotiating-on-ai-and-algorithmic-management-across-service-economy/

9 https://cupe.ca.

10 https://www.ania.org.mx/sobre-ania

11 https://www.ania.org.mx/mesas-de-trabajo-ania

12 https://www.ania.org.mx/

13 https://www.ania.org.mx/documentos

14 National Survey on the Availability and Use of Information Technologies in Households (ENDUTIH): https://www.ift.org.mx/comunicacion-y-medios/comunicados-ift/es/encuesta-nacional-sobre-disponibilidad-y-uso-de-tecnologias-de-la-informacion-en-los-hogares-endutih-1

Chapter 4
Global Perspectives: Comparison of Labor Union Responses to AI and Automation in Different Countries

Satya Subrahmanyam
https://orcid.org/0000-0003-0441-2742
Holy Spirit University of Kaslik, Lebanon

ABSTRACT

This chapter, "Global Perspectives: Comparison of Labor Union Responses to AI and Automation in Different Countries," examines how labor unions across the United States, Germany, Japan, South Korea, Brazil, and India respond to the challenges posed by AI and automation. Through comparative analysis, it highlights regional strategies, common goals, and distinct approaches in protecting jobs, promoting reskilling, and advocating for ethical AI use. Emphasizing both shared objectives and unique responses shaped by each country's policies and labor norms, the chapter underscores the importance of proactive union involvement. It concludes with a call for international collaboration to enhance labor protection in an increasingly automated global economy.

1. INTRODUCTION

1.1 Contextualizing AI and Automation

Artificial intelligence (AI) and automation have become transformative forces across global labor markets, driving significant changes in industries, job roles, and the required skills. From manufacturing to healthcare and services, these technologies

DOI: 10.4018/979-8-3693-8049-9.ch004

are streamlining processes, reducing costs, and enhancing productivity. The advent of AI and automation has also led to widespread concerns about job displacement, income inequality, and workforce adaptability. AI is particularly influential in automating routine and repetitive tasks, which has led to a decline in demand for certain job types while increasing the need for advanced technical skills in areas such as machine learning, data analysis, and robotics (Bessen, 2019). Consequently, workers in numerous industries face the dual pressures of reskilling to remain competitive and the risk of job loss due to technological redundancies.

As industries evolve under the influence of AI, the labor market's skill requirements are shifting. Tasks that were once considered high skill are now being automated, compelling workers to adapt or face job obsolescence (Acemoglu & Restrepo, 2018). AI and automation are changing working conditions by introducing more flexible but often more precarious employment models, such as gig work, where job security and benefits are limited (De Stefano, 2018). This has made the involvement of labor unions critical in addressing emerging issues within workplaces globally.

1.2 Role of Labor Unions

Labor unions have traditionally championed workers' rights, focusing on fair wages, working conditions, and job security. In the context of AI and automation, labor unions' roles are expanding to include advocacy for workforce transition support, such as retraining programs and job security measures (McGuinness & Fu, 2016). Unions are also key players in policy dialogues surrounding technology adoption, seeking to ensure that automation enhances, rather than diminishes, the quality of work life. This effort often involves engaging employers and governments to develop policies that support fair transitions for workers impacted by technological change. Union-led initiatives increasingly call for ethical technology adoption, transparent AI implementation, and regulations to protect workers' privacy and autonomy (Chang, 2020).

Given the global scale of AI's impact, labor unions in different countries face unique challenges and pursue varying strategies. National labor policies, economic structures, and cultural attitudes toward technology all influence unions' responses to AI and automation. This chapter examines these diverse responses, providing a comparative analysis of labor union approaches across several regions.

1.3 Purpose and Structure of the Chapter

This chapter aims to explore and compare labor union responses to AI and automation across different countries. By analyzing union strategies, regional approaches, and specific challenges, this chapter highlights the diversity of responses and identifies common themes in union-led efforts to protect and empower workers in the face of technological change. The chapter is organized into sections examining union responses in countries with distinctive labor landscapes, including the United States, Germany, Japan, and Brazil. The discussion concludes with a summary of emerging trends and a consideration of future directions for labor unions in the era of AI and automation.

1.4 Comparative Analysis of Labor Union Responses

United States

In the United States, the response of labor unions to AI and automation has been marked by advocacy for upskilling programs, worker protections, and policy reforms. U.S. unions, such as the AFL-CIO, have expressed concerns about job displacement due to AI and are working to secure retraining opportunities for affected workers (Brynjolfsson & McAfee, 2014). While American unions operate within a primarily market-driven economy with relatively limited government intervention, they are increasingly pressing for federal and state support for workforce transition programs. Unions advocate for public-private partnerships that offer retraining programs to workers displaced by automation (West, 2018). The decentralized structure of the U.S. labor system poses challenges in creating unified strategies, often resulting in fragmented efforts across sectors and states.

Germany

Germany's labor unions are historically influential and have a strong voice in industrial policy, often benefiting from the country's co-determination model, which includes union representation on corporate boards. German unions, such as IG Metall, have proactively engaged with companies to negotiate agreements around AI and automation adoption. These agreements often include provisions for retraining, job security, and worker involvement in decision-making processes related to technology deployment (Schroeder & Weßels, 2017). In Germany, labor unions are advocating for AI adoption that enhances rather than replaces human labor, emphasizing the role of technology in augmenting workers' capabilities. The German approach is rooted in a consensus-driven model, which promotes collaboration between unions, employers, and the government to manage technology transitions (Jürgens, 2018).

Japan

In Japan, labor unions face unique challenges due to cultural factors and the country's labor market structure. Japanese unions have traditionally been more company-oriented, with an emphasis on loyalty and job security rather than bargaining power (Oh & Suzuki, 2020). However, as AI and automation reshape the Japanese economy, unions are beginning to shift their focus toward protecting workers in a rapidly aging population and a declining labor force. Japanese unions, such as RENGO, are advocating for lifelong learning programs and reskilling initiatives to prepare workers for technological shifts. Japanese unions are increasingly engaging with the government to promote policies that encourage automation adoption in ways that complement human labor, especially in the context of labor shortages (Yamaguchi, 2020).

Brazil

In Brazil, labor unions are particularly focused on protecting workers in low-skilled and low-income jobs, which are highly susceptible to automation. Brazilian unions, such as CUT (Central Única dos Trabalhadores), are addressing automation concerns by pushing for legislation that limits the extent of job displacement caused by AI and automation technologies (Pereira & Evans, 2019). These unions are also advocating social safety nets, including unemployment benefits and retraining programs for workers in vulnerable sectors. Political and economic instability in Brazil has hindered union efforts to secure comprehensive protections, as labor policies are subject to frequent changes. Despite these challenges, Brazilian unions are exploring ways to work with international organizations to address the impacts of global technological shifts on the domestic workforce (Cerdeira & Silva, 2020).

1.5 Emerging Themes and Future Directions

The comparative analysis of labor union responses reveals several recurring themes in union approaches to AI and automation. Firstly, the focus on reskilling and upskilling is evident across all countries examined, as unions recognize the necessity of preparing workers for an increasingly technology-driven job market. Secondly, labor unions are increasingly involved in policy advocacy, calling for regulatory frameworks that support ethical AI adoption, protect workers' rights, and ensure fair compensation for work involving AI (Chang, 2020).

Looking forward, labor unions may need to adopt more collaborative approaches, working with governments, employers, and international organizations to create global standards for AI use in workplaces. Unions could also leverage technology themselves to reach broader memberships and engage workers in digital advocacy efforts. As AI continues to reshape the workforce, labor unions must remain adaptable, finding innovative ways to protect and empower workers in an era of rapid technological change.

2. LABOR UNIONS AND TECHNOLOGICAL CHANGE: A HISTORICAL PERSPECTIVE

2.1 Evolution of Labor Union Responses to Technological Advances

Labor unions have a long history of responding to technological change, with roots tracing back to the Industrial Revolution in the late 18th and early 19th centuries. This period marked a dramatic shift from agrarian economies to industrialized ones, bringing with it the introduction of mechanized processes in factories. The replacement of manual labor by machines caused substantial social and economic disruption, particularly through job losses and deteriorating working conditions. Early labor unions emerged in response to these challenges, striving to secure fair wages, reduce working hours, and improve the safety of industrial environments (Thompson, 1963).

During the Industrial Revolution, labor unions primarily fought against mechanization that threatened to replace human labor entirely, such as the loom in the textile industry, which led to widespread worker protests, including the Luddite movement in England (Hobsbawm, 1964). These movements resisted new technology and sought to negotiate terms that protected jobs and ensured fair compensation for workers displaced by machines. Over time, labor unions learned to shift their focus from merely opposing technology to negotiating the terms of its implementation, working toward compromises that balanced productivity gains with job security.

As industrialization progressed into the early 20th century, labor unions continued to evolve, focusing on securing workers' rights amid significant technological advancements in manufacturing and transportation. The rise of the assembly line in the automotive industry, popularized by Ford in 1913, enabled mass production but led to increased labor intensity and reduced job autonomy (Braverman, 1974). Labor unions responded by pushing for shorter workweeks and improved labor conditions, helping to establish the 40-hour workweek as a standard in many industries. This period highlighted the growing influence of labor unions in shaping not only wages and hours but also workers' experiences in technologically advanced settings.

With the advent of the Information Age in the mid-20th century, labor unions faced new challenges. The rise of computer technology and automation reshaped numerous sectors, particularly clerical, manufacturing, and service jobs. During this period, unions began to recognize the importance of adapting their strategies to the increasing role of knowledge and skill-based labor. In contrast to earlier mechanized labor, which often replaced low-skilled jobs, computerization primarily affected middle-skilled workers who performed routine tasks (Autor, 2015). Unions increasingly focused on negotiating for retraining and skills development programs, realizing that workers needed to adapt to a rapidly changing labor market to remain relevant.

The shift from industrial to digital economies also prompted labor unions to advocate for policies that addressed job security and unemployment insurance. In countries such as Germany and Sweden, unions played a pivotal role in securing governmental support for retraining and social safety nets (Baccaro & Howell, 2017). This support not only protected workers from the immediate impacts of automation but also encouraged longer-term employment stability. By the late 20th century, labor unions had expanded their scope from traditional labor issues to include workforce development, a recognition of the need for continuous adaptation in a technology-driven economy.

2.2 Adapting to AI and Automation

The current wave of technological transformation, driven by AI and automation, presents unique challenges that differ significantly from those of the Industrial and Information Ages. Unlike previous technological shifts, which often affected a single sector at a time, AI and automation permeate virtually every industry, from manufacturing and logistics to finance, healthcare, and retail. This comprehensive transformation requires labor unions to adopt a multi-faceted approach, advocating not only for fair wages and working conditions but also for workers' rights in a highly digitalized environment, where surveillance and data privacy are major concerns (Azoury et al., 2024).

One significant distinction in the current era is the potential for AI and automation to replace both low-skilled and high-skilled jobs. Advancements in machine learning and natural language processing have enabled automation in areas once thought to be uniquely human, such as customer service, legal work, and even medical diagnosis (Subrahmanyam et al., 2024). This shift challenges traditional union strategies, which were primarily focused on protecting low-skilled labor from technological displacement. Labor unions must now address the needs of a broader range of workers, advocating for policies that protect both blue-collar and white-collar employees facing automation risks.

To adapt, unions are increasingly prioritizing worker reskilling and upskilling initiatives. The American Federation of Labor and Congress of Industrial Organizations (AFL-CIO) in the United States has started collaborating with educational institutions and tech companies to develop reskilling programs tailored to industries undergoing rapid technological change (West, 2018). These programs aim to equip workers with the skills necessary to transition to new roles that are less susceptible to automation, such as roles involving problem-solving, creativity, and human interaction.

Labor unions are engaging in policy advocacy to address the ethical implications of AI and automation. This includes calls for fair data practices, transparency in algorithmic decision-making, and the protection of worker privacy (De Stefano, 2018). In Europe, labor unions have been instrumental in pushing for regulations that limit the scope of workplace surveillance technologies, which are often powered by AI. The General Data Protection Regulation (GDPR) in the European Union includes provisions that protect workers from excessive data collection and algorithmic monitoring, a move heavily influenced by union advocacy (Moore, 2020).

Some unions are also exploring partnerships with AI developers to influence the design and deployment of technology in ways that consider workers' needs and wellbeing. IG Metall, a prominent German union, has engaged in direct dialogue with technology firms to negotiate agreements that prioritize human oversight in automated processes. These agreements aim to ensure that AI acts as a complementary tool that enhances workers' productivity and safety rather than a replacement for human labor (Jürgens, 2018).

The global nature of AI and automation has also prompted labor unions to work across borders. Labor unions from various countries have participated in forums organized by the International Labour Organization (ILO) to discuss best practices and share strategies for addressing technological change. This collaborative approach acknowledges that the effects of AI and automation transcend national boundaries and that solutions may require coordinated international responses. Through such forums, labor unions advocate for universal standards in AI ethics and push for policies that protect workers' rights worldwide (Chang, 2020).

Looking forward, labor unions may need to expand their focus beyond traditional worker protection to include shaping the future of work itself. Some experts suggest that unions should play a role in influencing AI governance and promoting ethical frameworks for technological development, ensuring that AI aligns with human-centered values. Unions could advocate for AI to be used in ways that enhance job satisfaction, reduce workplace stress, and allow for more meaningful human labor (Floridi, 2020). This forward-thinking approach positions unions as key stakeholders in guiding the ethical use of AI and automation within society.

The history of labor unions shows a continuous evolution in response to technological change, from the industrial machines of the 19th century to the digital transformations of the 20th century and the AI-driven disruptions of today. Each technological wave has forced unions to adapt, sometimes radically, in order to protect and empower workers. The current AI and automation era is unique in its widespread impact, touching diverse industries and affecting workers across all skill levels. In this context, labor unions are expanding their roles to address issues such as reskilling, worker privacy, and AI ethics, demonstrating their adaptability and ongoing relevance in safeguarding workers' interests amid technological change.

3. COMPARATIVE ANALYSIS OF LABOR UNION RESPONSES TO AI AND AUTOMATION

3.1 Overview of Countries Covered

As AI and automation continue reshaping the global economy, labor unions play a vital role in advocating for worker protection, reskilling, and job security. This comparative analysis examines the responses of labor unions in six countries—United States, Germany, Japan, South Korea, Brazil, and India—chosen for their varied economic status, technological advancement, and union influence. These nations represent a spectrum from advanced economies with strong union frameworks (e.g., Germany and Japan) to emerging economies facing informal labor market challenges (e.g., Brazil and India). Each of these countries provides unique insights into how unions are responding to the challenges and opportunities presented by AI and automation.

A. United States

Labor Union Structure and Influence

In the United States, labor unions operate within a decentralized structure, with individual unions representing specific industries. Union density has steadily declined over the past few decades, with only about 10% of the workforce represented by unions, making them relatively weaker compared to other developed nations (Bivens et al., 2017). Challenges such as legislative restrictions (e.g., the Taft-Hartley Act) and employer-driven anti-union campaigns have hampered union influence in the U.S., reducing their bargaining power. Besides, the American economy is highly dynamic, with frequent shifts toward new technologies and labor trends, often leaving unions struggling to adapt swiftly (Freeman, 2021).

Strategies and Initiatives

Despite these challenges, U.S. unions have initiated strategies to advocate for workers affected by automation. The AFL-CIO has partnered with educational institutions and tech firms to launch retraining programs aimed at equipping workers with the skills needed in a technologically advanced labor market. Unions like the SEIU (Service Employees International Union) have focused on fair wages for tech-driven roles, particularly in logistics and service industries where automation is prevalent. Several unions are exploring collaborations with tech companies to establish transparent guidelines for AI use and to ensure that automation does not compromise worker rights (Atkinson & Wu, 2017).

Challenges and Limitations

The effectiveness of U.S. labor unions in addressing AI and automation remains constrained by various factors. Legislative barriers limit union actions, and fragmentation across industries often makes coordinated efforts challenging. The political environment, particularly at the federal level, has also influenced union initiatives, with some administrations less supportive of organized labor. Rapid technological adoption and the gig economy have introduced complexities that traditional unions struggle to address, underscoring the need for innovative union strategies to stay relevant (Hirsch & Macpherson, 2020).

B. Germany

Strong Union Representation and Co-determination Practices

Germany stands out for its robust labor union structure and co-determination model, in which unions are deeply embedded in corporate governance through worker councils and board-level representation (Hassel, 2014). This system grants unions substantial influence over corporate decisions, including technology adoption, allowing them to negotiate terms that protect workers. Germany's high union density and collaborative culture between employers and unions make it a model for balancing technological innovation with worker protections.

Proactive Measures on AI Integration

German unions, such as IG Metall, have proactively engaged in negotiations with employers to address AI integration, focusing on securing reskilling programs and protecting workers' interests. IG Metall, for instance, has negotiated terms with several manufacturing firms to implement training programs that enable workers to transition to new, tech-driven roles, particularly in the automotive sector (Jürgens,

2018). These proactive measures illustrate how unions can facilitate worker adaptation to automation while ensuring job security.

Policy Influence and Collaboration with Employers

Collaboration between German unions, employers, and the government has fostered a balanced approach to AI and automation adoption. The German government has supported union-led initiatives to create a "Future of Work" framework, which prioritizes continuous learning and adaptation (Schmidt & Muller, 2019). This collaborative environment enables German unions to influence policy, ensuring that technological advancements do not outpace worker protections and that the workforce is equipped for new roles.

C. Japan

Union Structure and Workforce Culture

Japan's labor union structure and workforce culture emphasize loyalty to employers and a collective sense of responsibility. Japanese unions, predominantly enterprise unions, operate within individual companies rather than across industries, leading to a distinct union structure focused on company-specific needs. This setup encourages unions to work closely with employers to address labor concerns while fostering a culture of lifelong employment (Kato, 2020).

Focus on Job Security and Stability

In response to AI-driven changes, Japanese unions have prioritized job security and stability, advocating for policies that support long-term employment. Unions have encouraged companies to restructure roles rather than eliminate them, aiming to ensure that workers remain within the organization even as tasks evolve due to AI. Japanese labor unions have championed "lifelong employment" strategies, which allow workers to transition into new positions within the company as automation reshapes existing roles (Takeuchi, 2019).

Challenges of Adapting to AI in Traditional Work Environments

Japan's traditional work culture, emphasizing hierarchy and stability, presents challenges and opportunities in responding to AI and automation. The conservative nature of Japanese unions, coupled with a strong focus on preserving existing jobs, has sometimes hindered rapid adaptation to technological changes. While the emphasis on job security has helped mitigate displacement, it has also delayed certain digital transformation efforts, especially in industries resistant to AI-driven disruption (Sako, 2021).

D. South Korea

Rapid Technological Adoption and Strong Unionization

South Korea's economy is characterized by rapid technological adoption and robust unionization, particularly in manufacturing and telecommunications. Labor unions play a critical role in advocating workers' rights, with high union density in major industries such as automotive and electronics, sectors at the forefront of AI integration (Shin & Choi, 2020). South Korean unions actively engage in public discourse about AI's impact on employment, using their influence to advocate for balanced technology integration.

Labor Union Initiatives for Retraining and Job Transition

South Korean labor unions have focused on retraining and job transition programs to prepare workers for AI-driven roles. The Federation of Korean Trade Unions has collaborated with corporations to establish training initiatives that equip employees with digital skills, enabling them to take on roles that are complementary to automation (Kim & Choi, 2018). These programs help South Korea maintain its competitive edge while supporting workers through technological shifts.

Challenges of Balancing Innovation with Worker Protections

Balancing technological innovation with worker protections remains a central challenge in South Korea. While unions advocate safeguards, companies are under pressure to innovate rapidly in a competitive global market. This tension has led to clashes between unions and employers, particularly in sectors where automation could substantially reduce labor demand (Lee, 2019). Nonetheless, union-led retraining initiatives have helped to mitigate some of these challenges.

E. Brazil

Emerging Economy Challenges and Informal Workforce

As an emerging economy, Brazil faces unique challenges in responding to automation, particularly with a large informal workforce comprising nearly 40% of total employment (World Bank, 2021). This informality limits the reach of traditional unions, as many workers lack formal protection or benefits. Automation presents both challenges and opportunities for Brazil, with the potential to enhance productivity but also to displace low-skilled workers in an already fragile economy.

Union Efforts in Addressing Automation Concerns

Brazilian unions, such as CUT (Central Única dos Trabalhadores), are working to address job displacement concerns by advocating for fair employment policies and social protections. They have called for government programs to support displaced workers and initiatives that extend benefits to the informal sector. Brazilian unions are exploring ways to engage with employers on automation policies, albeit with limited success due to economic and political challenges (da Costa, 2021).

Impact of Economic Conditions on Union Effectiveness

Brazil's economic instability and political challenges have limited unions' ability to respond effectively to AI and automation. High unemployment, weak regulatory frameworks, and limited governmental support hinder union efforts to protect workers in the face of technological change. These challenges emphasize the need for policies that support vulnerable workers and ensure that automation contributes to, rather than undermines, economic development (Barbosa, 2020).

F. India

Labor Union Structure and Economic Context

India's labor union landscape is diverse and complex, with unions representing different sectors and regions. The country's economic context, marked by a large informal workforce and low union density in certain industries, presents challenges for effective unionization. The informal sector comprises around 80% of India's workforce, limiting union influence and protection in many areas where automation could have a significant impact (Nair, 2018).

Union Responses to Technological Displacement

Indian labor unions have focused on addressing displacement caused by automation, especially in manufacturing, IT, and agriculture. Unions have called for government intervention to provide retraining initiatives for workers displaced by automation and to ensure equitable access to emerging job opportunities. Organizations like the All-India Trade Union Congress (AITUC) have lobbied for policies that support worker upskilling, but limited resources and fragmentation continue to be obstacles (Sharma, 2019).

Challenges and Policy Advocacy

India's high informality limited governmental support for organized labor, and resource constraints pose challenges for union efforts to address AI integration. Nonetheless, unions are advocating for government policies that protect workers' rights, provide job security, and encourage fair practices in automation adoption. These initiatives reflect unions' commitment to safeguarding labor interests amid technological disruption, though challenges remain (Bhattacharya, 2020).

Labor unions across the United States, Germany, Japan, South Korea, Brazil, and India face unique challenges and opportunities in responding to AI and automation. While advanced economies like Germany and South Korea leverage strong union structures and government support, emerging economies such as Brazil and India grapple with informal workforces and limited resources. As AI continues to transform labor markets, these countries highlight diverse strategies unions employ to protect workers, illustrating the complex interplay between technological innovation and labor rights across global contexts.

4. COMMON THEMES AND DIVERGING APPROACHES

As automation and artificial intelligence (AI) reshape labor markets, unions worldwide share certain overarching goals while also adopting strategies uniquely suited to their local contexts. Union actions are guided by both shared concerns around protecting workers' rights and the varying influence of local regulatory, economic, and cultural landscapes. This section examines these shared goals, explores distinct regional approaches, and analyzes how government policies and corporate dynamics impact union strategies across countries.

4.1 Shared Goals and Concerns

Labor unions across various countries express common concerns in the face of AI and automation. Among the most pressing shared goals are job protection, reskilling initiatives, fair wages, and ethical AI implementation.

Job Protection: Unions universally prioritize protecting jobs as automation and AI threaten to replace certain roles with machines. In industries such as manufacturing, where repetitive tasks are increasingly automated, unions negotiate to prevent or limit layoffs, often advocating for transitions that minimize the number of displaced workers. In Germany, unions use co-determination laws to secure worker representation in corporate decision-making processes, helping to mitigate the impact of job losses due to automation (Schmidt & Muller, 2019).

Reskilling and Upskilling: With technological change rapidly evolving job requirements, unions recognize the importance of reskilling workers to enhance their employability. This goal is evident in countries such as South Korea, where unions collaborate with educational institutions to provide skills training for workers transitioning from routine jobs to roles requiring digital competencies (Kim & Choi, 2018). Similarly, Japanese unions advocate for lifelong learning programs to help workers adapt to new technological demands (Takeuchi, 2019).

Fair Wages and Job Quality: Unions aim to secure fair wages and ensure that automation does not lead to a decline in job quality. As automation improves productivity, unions in the United States and parts of Europe push for a fair distribution of profits through wage increases and job stability (Freeman, 2021). They advocate that the economic benefits of automation should benefit workers, not just corporations.

Ethical AI Implementation: Unions globally are concerned with ethical considerations around AI, including bias, discrimination, and data privacy. Many unions support regulations that mandate transparent, ethical AI practices, emphasizing the need for algorithms that do not reinforce biases or infringe on privacy rights (Bivens et al., 2017). European labor unions, benefiting from strict data protection laws like the General Data Protection Regulation (GDPR), are particularly active in addressing ethical concerns associated with AI in the workplace (Jürgens, 2018).

These shared objectives highlight a collective union stance on protecting workers from the adverse effects of technological advancements. The strategies employed to achieve these goals vary significantly, influenced by regional regulatory frameworks, economic conditions, and cultural attitudes.

4.2 Distinct Strategies Based on Regional and Cultural Factors

While unions around the world share core objectives, their strategies reflect the unique regulatory, economic, and cultural environments in which they operate. These differences underscore the adaptability of unions as they tailor their approaches to local contexts.

Europe: Co-Determination and Worker Representation: In countries like Germany, unions benefit from strong worker representation in corporate decision-making processes. The German co-determination model grants union members seats on corporate boards, enabling them to influence corporate policies related to automation and AI (Hassel, 2014). This model allows unions to negotiate transitions to automation more collaboratively, balancing innovation with worker protection. Similarly, Scandinavian countries, known for high levels of union membership, leverage centralized bargaining and worker representation to ensure that automation serves both economic and social goals (Atkinson & Wu, 2017).

United States: Collective Bargaining and Advocacy: In the United States, where unions have less regulatory support, collective bargaining and advocacy efforts form the backbone of union strategies. American unions work to secure specific protections for workers in industries facing rapid automation, such as retail and transportation. They advocate for policies supporting job transitions, higher minimum wages, and benefits for displaced workers. Unions in the United States often partner with advocacy groups and leverage public opinion to pressure corporations and policymakers to address the impact of automation on workers (Hirsch & Macpherson, 2020).

Asia: Reskilling Initiatives and Government Partnerships: In countries like Japan and South Korea, unions focus on reskilling initiatives, often in partnership with the government. Japanese unions promote lifelong learning and training programs to help workers adapt to technological changes, aligning with the country's broader emphasis on continuous improvement and job security (Sako, 2021). In South Korea, unions emphasize collaboration with technology firms and educational institutions to reskill workers for high-demand digital roles, reflecting a cultural emphasis on collective responsibility and adaptability (Shin & Choi, 2020).

Developing Countries: Informal Sector Protections and Job Stability: In developing countries like Brazil and India, where large informal sectors face unique challenges, unions prioritize job stability and protections for informal workers who may be disproportionately affected by automation (Barbosa, 2020). Brazilian unions, for example, lobby for regulations to prevent mass layoffs and encourage government support for reskilling programs. In India, unions negotiate with multinational corporations to create transition plans for workers in low-skill jobs at risk of automation, often advocating for local job creation to offset the impact of technology on traditional sectors (Bhattacharya, 2020).

These regional differences underscore how unions adapt to diverse challenges by aligning strategies with local contexts. In countries with strong labor protections, unions work within regulatory frameworks, while in less regulated environments, they rely more on public advocacy and collaboration.

4.3 Impact of Government Policies on Union Actions

Government policies, labor laws, and corporate regulations significantly shape the actions and effectiveness of unions' strategies in managing automation's impact on the workforce. Unions operate in a landscape where government decisions on labor rights, educational funding, and data protection play a critical role in enabling or constraining their initiatives.

Regulatory Support and Worker Protections: In regions with strong regulatory support, such as the European Union, unions can leverage laws that protect workers from abrupt job displacement. The EU's GDPR, for instance, provides a legal framework that unions use to ensure ethical AI implementation in the workplace. By mandating transparency and accountability in data usage, GDPR reinforces union efforts to protect workers' privacy rights as AI adoption increases (Jürgens, 2018).

Government-Funded Reskilling Programs: Governments that invest in workforce training and reskilling create an environment conducive to union-led reskilling initiatives. In South Korea, for instance, government-funded programs in digital skills training bolster union efforts to prepare workers for the digital economy (Lee, 2019). Japan's Ministry of Economy, Trade, and Industry also collaborates with unions to provide lifelong learning opportunities, reflecting a government commitment to adapting to the changing nature of work (Sako, 2021).

Labor Law Variability and Collective Bargaining: In the United States, where labor laws are less stringent, unions face challenges in implementing comprehensive protections against job displacement. This lack of regulatory support limits unions' bargaining power, making collective bargaining the primary tool for securing worker protections in the face of automation. Without legal mandates to protect workers, American unions often resort to lobbying for minimum wage increases and employee benefits (Freeman, 2021).

Corporate Policies and Union Negotiations: Corporate policies also play a role in shaping union actions. In countries where corporations prioritize technological adoption, unions must negotiate to ensure that job transitions do not undermine worker welfare. In Japan, for instance, corporate policies of incremental innovation align with unions' goals for gradual workforce transitions, while in the U.S., companies focused on rapid automation implementation pose a greater challenge for unions seeking to protect job stability (Takeuchi, 2019).

Overall, government policies and corporate practices significantly impact the ways unions navigate automation and AI. Where governments actively support workforce development and ethical AI practices, unions can adopt more proactive approaches; in less supportive environments, unions often focus on minimizing immediate harm to workers.

Labor unions worldwide share a commitment to protecting workers' rights in the face of technological transformation, advocating for job security, fair wages, reskilling, and ethical AI practices. Their strategies diverge based on local regulatory, economic, and cultural factors. Government policies and corporate priorities further shape union actions, highlighting the complex and varied landscape unions navigate in addressing the challenges posed by automation and AI.

5. CASE STUDIES OF SUCCESSFUL UNION-LED INTERVENTIONS

As automation and artificial intelligence (AI) increasingly transform industries worldwide, labor unions play a critical role in ensuring ethical, balanced, and worker-centered technological integration. Various union-led initiatives across Germany, South Korea, Brazil, and India showcase effective interventions that have benefited workers. This section examines four successful cases where unions intervened to promote fair treatment, skill development, and job security, considering different regional contexts and economic dynamics.

5.1 Germany's Co-Determination Model in Action

Germany's unique co-determination model, which mandates worker representation in corporate governance, has proven effective in managing AI's integration in the workplace. A prominent example is the automobile manufacturer Volkswagen, where unions have significantly influenced the company's approach to adopting AI technologies without compromising workers' rights (Schmidt & Muller, 2019).

Under the co-determination framework, Volkswagen's union representatives participate in decision-making processes alongside company executives. This model enables unions to influence key corporate strategies, including AI and automation projects, while safeguarding workers' interests. When Volkswagen initiated plans to automate some assembly line tasks, unions ensured that the company would prioritize roles involving human oversight and creativity rather than wholesale job replacement (Hassel, 2014). This approach allowed the company to increase operational efficiency without significant layoffs.

Volkswagen's union successfully negotiated reskilling programs that provide assembly line workers with digital skills to transition into new roles involving AI management and data analysis. These reskilling initiatives are integral to Germany's broader emphasis on skill formation, where labor unions partner with educational institutions to equip workers with advanced technical skills (Atkinson & Wu, 2017). The co-determination model enables unions to foster a more ethical and sustainable adoption of AI in the workplace by prioritizing employee welfare alongside technological advancement.

5.2 South Korean Union-Government Partnership for Workforce Development

In South Korea, unions have collaborated with the government to create workforce development programs focused on retraining and upskilling workers affected by automation. One of the most successful cases is the Korean Federation of Trade Unions (KFTU) partnership with the Ministry of Employment and Labor to implement a nationwide reskilling initiative (Kim & Choi, 2018).

This union-led intervention targets workers in industries vulnerable to automation, such as manufacturing and retail. Recognizing the demand for digital skills in an AI-driven economy, the KFTU worked with government agencies and vocational institutions to develop training programs in areas like data analytics, machine learning, and robotics (Shin & Choi, 2020). The government-funded initiative enables displaced workers to learn new skills without financial burden, and the KFTU assists workers in enrolling in relevant courses based on their career goals and backgrounds.

The program's success is attributed to its collaborative approach: unions advocate worker interests while the government ensures resource allocation and institutional support. This partnership has helped thousands of South Korean workers transition to new roles and reduced unemployment risks in sectors undergoing rapid technological changes. The initiative underscores the importance of union-government cooperation in preparing workers for AI-driven economies and shows how unions can shape public policy to foster a more inclusive workforce transition (Lee, 2019).

5.3 Brazilian Union Advocacy for Informal Workers in the AI Era

In Brazil, where a significant portion of the workforce is employed in the informal sector, unions have focused on extending protections for informal workers impacted by AI and automation. The Central Única dos Trabalhadores (CUT), Brazil's largest labor union, has led advocacy efforts to address automation's impact on informal workers who often lack formal protections such as health benefits and job security (Barbosa, 2020).

One example of CUT's intervention is its campaign to negotiate agreements with companies in the gig economy, such as ride-sharing and delivery services, where AI-driven algorithms control worker schedules and pay rates. These negotiations have led to new terms that provide informal workers with greater job security and income stability. For instance, CUT successfully advocated adjustments in algorithmic management systems to ensure fairer pay distribution and minimize excessive working hours. CUT has pushed for regulatory frameworks that recognize gig workers as employees, granting them rights to benefits and protections typically reserved for formal workers (Freeman, 2021).

CUT's advocacy extends beyond corporate negotiations; the union also lobbies for policy changes at the national level, urging the government to enforce protections for informal workers in AI-impacted sectors. This approach has inspired similar actions in other Latin American countries facing challenges with informal employment in an automated economy. CUT's case demonstrates the critical role unions play in securing fair treatment and protections for vulnerable worker groups in economies with large informal sectors (Bhattacharya, 2020).

5.4 India's IT and Manufacturing Sector Initiatives

In India, unions in the IT and manufacturing sectors have launched initiatives to help workers adapt to automation and AI through reskilling and upskilling programs. The All-India Trade Union Congress (AITUC), in collaboration with various educational institutions and government agencies, has spearheaded projects aimed at preparing workers for AI-centered job roles (Bivens et al., 2017).

AITUC partnered with the Ministry of Skill Development and Entrepreneurship to create reskilling courses for IT professionals and manufacturing workers whose jobs are at risk of being automated. These programs cover AI fundamentals, software development, and digital literacy skills, enabling workers to transition from routine tasks to roles that require critical thinking and digital expertise (Sako, 2021). AITUC has collaborated with major technology firms to provide on-site training, blending theoretical instruction with hands-on experience in AI-driven environments.

In the manufacturing sector, where automation is gradually replacing labor-intensive tasks, unions have worked with educational institutions to introduce courses on robotics, advanced manufacturing technologies, and automation management. AITUC has partnered with engineering colleges to provide specialized training for workers in factories undergoing automation (Takeuchi, 2019). This union-led intervention reflects India's commitment to minimizing job displacement by equipping workers with the skills necessary for an evolving job market.

AITUC's initiatives highlight the potential of unions to facilitate proactive workforce transformation in countries experiencing rapid technological adoption. By collaborating with educational and governmental organizations, unions in India demonstrate how multi-stakeholder partnerships can create sustainable solutions to support workers in transitioning to AI-related roles.

The case studies from Germany, South Korea, Brazil, and India illustrate diverse approaches unions have taken to address the challenges posed by AI and automation. Germany's co-determination model enables unions to participate in corporate decision-making, ensuring a balanced and ethical integration of AI. In South Korea, union-government partnerships have led to effective reskilling programs that support workers in adapting to technological changes. Brazilian unions focus on protecting informal workers, advocating for fair treatment and negotiating terms with gig economy platforms. Meanwhile, Indian unions work with educational and government entities to facilitate reskilling, particularly in the IT and manufacturing sectors.

These cases emphasize the adaptability and effectiveness of union-led interventions when supported by collaborative frameworks and local context considerations. They reveal how unions can proactively address the workforce impacts of AI, helping workers to navigate the challenges and seize opportunities within an increasingly automated economy.

6. CHALLENGES AND BARRIERS IN ADAPTING TO AI AND AUTOMATION GLOBALLY

The increasing adoption of artificial intelligence (AI) and automation technologies worldwide has brought profound changes to the workforce. Labor unions face a multitude of challenges in safeguarding workers' rights and well-being amidst these transformations. These challenges span regulatory and legislative constraints, unequal access to technology, and resistance from corporations. This section explores the regulatory limitations unions encounter, the technological divide and limited resources in emerging economies, and the complexities introduced by corporate pushback and globalization. These factors collectively create barriers to unions' effectiveness in adapting to AI and automation and underscore the need for strategic, adaptable solutions.

6.1 Regulatory and Legislative Constraints

Labor unions are significantly impacted by regulatory and legislative frameworks that often restrict their actions. In various countries, stringent labor laws and policies limit the scope of union activities, making it difficult for unions to advocate effectively for workers affected by AI and automation. In the United States, for example, right-to-work laws in multiple states weaken union influence by allowing employees to benefit from union protections without being union members or paying dues (Freeman & Han, 2018). This, in turn, reduces union membership and weakens unions' negotiating power to address the impacts of automation and AI on job security.

Labor laws differ significantly across countries, creating a fragmented landscape for union-led interventions. While some European countries, like Germany, have frameworks such as co-determination laws that grant unions a role in corporate governance, other nations lack similar regulatory support (Hassel, 2014). As a result, unions in countries without robust legislative backing face greater challenges in influencing corporate decisions regarding automation and AI. These disparities prevent the development of unified global strategies and reduce unions' ability to advocate for fair employment practices in the face of technological advancement (Schmidt & Muller, 2019).

In certain regions, governmental interference restricts union activities. In countries like China, labor unions are often under state control, which limits their autonomy and ability to oppose or negotiate with employers (Chan & Hui, 2017). Without independence, unions struggle to address the concerns of workers displaced by AI or advocate for protection against automated management systems. The lack of regulatory support for independent union action thus becomes a significant barrier, impeding unions' adaptability to technological changes and limiting their capacity to safeguard workers' rights in automated workplaces.

6.2 Technological Divide and Access to Resources

The technological divide between developed and emerging economies also impacts unions' ability to adapt to AI and automation. In regions with limited resources, unions often lack access to advanced tools and technologies necessary to monitor and respond to the effects of automation. This resource gap creates an uneven playing field, as unions in wealthier countries can leverage digital tools to gather data, communicate with members, and develop effective strategies, whereas unions in emerging economies struggle with basic technological infrastructure (Bivens et al., 2017).

In parts of sub-Saharan Africa, limited access to reliable internet and digital tools hinders unions from organizing and mobilizing effectively (Adeleke, 2020). Without access to digital platforms, unions face difficulties in reaching dispersed worker populations or gathering data on automation's impact on jobs. This technological divide also prevents unions from accessing upskilling resources essential for helping workers transition into new roles shaped by AI, creating a workforce unprepared for the demands of an automated economy.

Financial limitations further exacerbate the technological divide. Unions in emerging economies often operate with limited budgets, restricting their ability to fund reskilling initiatives or access advanced technological solutions. These financial constraints prevent unions from engaging in effective advocacy or providing workers with essential resources for adapting to an AI-driven job market (Bhattacharya, 2020). Consequently, the technological divide and lack of resources not only undermine unions' adaptability but also widen the gap between developed and emerging economies, leading to unequal outcomes for workers facing automation.

6.3 Corporate Pushback and Globalization

Corporate pushbacks and the pressures of globalization present additional challenges for unions. As companies adopt AI and automation to streamline operations and cut labor costs, some corporations resist union efforts to negotiate fair labor practices. Many corporates prioritize cost savings over employee welfare, which often leads to corporate strategies that undermine unions' attempts to protect workers. corporates may adopt automated systems that replace human workers without adequately addressing concerns around job security, leaving unions with limited influence (Freeman, 2021).

Globalization further intensifies this challenge. In a globalized economy, companies have the flexibility to shift operations to countries with cheaper labor costs or weaker labor regulations, allowing them to bypass union opposition. Multinational corporates often exploit these regulatory disparities by implementing automated systems without engaging unions or providing necessary worker protections. This shift to low-cost labor markets reduces union leverage, as corporations threaten to relocate if unions resist technological changes or demand better protection for workers impacted by automation (Sako, 2021).

In the technology sector, companies like Amazon and Uber exemplify this trend. These firms have adopted AI-driven workforce management systems that control employee scheduling, productivity monitoring, and pay. In cases where unions have attempted to negotiate terms that prevent unfair treatment or improve job security, companies have pushed back, claiming that automation is essential for maintaining competitiveness in a globalized market (Cattero & Dyer-Witheford, 2018). This resistance limits unions' ability to address automation's impact on job quality and employment conditions, as companies prioritize efficiency gains over labor rights.

Globalization creates a race-to-the-bottom scenario, where companies compare regulatory environments across countries to find the least restrictive options. This competition incentivizes some governments to reduce labor protections to attract foreign investment, making it even more difficult for unions to advocate for fair treatment in the context of automation. The pressure to remain globally competitive thus hinders union-led efforts to establish consistent labor standards for automation, as countries with lax regulations become appealing to companies looking to implement AI and automation without strict oversight (Takeuchi, 2019).

Unions around the world face considerable barriers in adapting to AI and automation. Regulatory constraints limit unions' actions, with inconsistent labor laws and government interference reducing their capacity to advocate effectively for worker protections. The technological divide in emerging economies further exacerbates this issue, as unions in these regions lack the resources and digital infrastructure necessary to respond to automation's impact on jobs. Finally, corporate pushbacks and the pressures of globalization allow companies to sidestep union demands, undermining unions' influence over the fair integration of AI in the workplace.

Addressing these challenges requires a multi-faceted approach. Policymakers must create supportive frameworks that empower unions to negotiate on behalf of workers in an automated economy. Bridging the technological divide, especially in emerging economies, would enable unions to access resources essential for mobilization and advocacy. Additionally, establishing international labor standards for automation could mitigate the effects of globalization by preventing companies from exploiting regulatory discrepancies. Ultimately, unions must adapt to these barriers through collaboration with governments and international organizations to ensure that AI and automation are implemented in a way that prioritizes worker rights and ethical considerations.

7. FUTURE DIRECTIONS FOR LABOR UNION RESPONSES TO AI AND AUTOMATION

The ongoing integration of artificial intelligence (AI) and automation into the global workforce presents both challenges and opportunities for labor unions. As these technologies continue to reshape industries, labor unions must explore new approaches to protect workers' rights and adapt to the rapidly changing landscape. Future directions for labor union responses to AI and automation include enhancing international collaboration, leveraging technology for union empowerment, and advocating for supportive policies that ensure fair and ethical implementation of AI. This section discusses these strategies in detail, outlining how unions can adapt to effectively address the challenges posed by automation.

7.1 Enhancing International Collaboration

As AI and automation have become a global phenomenon, labor unions worldwide face similar challenges, such as job displacement, de-skilling, and surveillance in the workplace. To address these shared issues, unions can benefit from increased international collaboration. Cross-border partnerships would allow unions to share strategies, develop unified responses to multinational corporations, and influence global labor standards related to AI and automation (Subrahmanyam et al., 2024). The global union federation IndustriALL has worked to establish agreements on workers' rights with multinational corporations, demonstrating that international partnerships can enhance unions' negotiating power and set precedent for labor protections.

Unions could collaborate through transnational networks to push for consistent standards in ethical AI deployment and automation practices. By coordinating efforts, unions in different countries could exert collective pressure on companies operating internationally to adhere to agreed-upon labor practices (Freeman, 2021). This collective bargaining power would be particularly effective against multinational corporations that may try to exploit weaker labor laws in certain countries by shifting operations to regions with minimal union influence.

The digital platforms enable unions to communicate and coordinate globally more effectively than ever before. Tools like webinars, virtual conferences, and online communities provide unions with an efficient way to share knowledge and exchange best practices. The International Trade Union Confederation (ITUC) has utilized digital tools to connect unions across continents, facilitating discussions on the future of work in the AI era (Hertel-Fernandez, 2020). Strengthening international collaborations and fostering global solidarity would not only enhance unions' adaptability to automation but also empower them to shape fair standards for AI implementation worldwide.

7.2 Leveraging Technology for Union Empowerment

To adapt to the digital age, unions must embrace technology as a means of strengthening their advocacy and organizing efforts. AI-driven tools offer a promising avenue for unions to modernize their approaches to monitoring workplace practices, organizing, and advocating for workers' rights. One area in which unions can leverage AI is through workforce analytics. By collecting and analyzing data on employment trends, productivity metrics, and worker satisfaction, unions can gain insights into the impact of automation and AI on workers and use this data to negotiate fairer conditions (Subrahmanyam, 2023).

AI tools can also assist unions in reaching and mobilizing workers. Chatbots and automated messaging systems can help unions communicate with members more efficiently, providing updates on negotiations, sharing information about worker rights, and mobilizing support for collective actions. AI-powered platforms can streamline the process of gathering worker feedback and identifying common issues, making it easier for unions to identify areas where they can advocate for improvements (Freeman, 2021). The Service Employees International Union (SEIU) in the United States, for instance, has implemented digital tools to enhance member engagement and organize workers in a more streamlined manner (Hertel-Fernandez, 2020).

AI and data analytics could be instrumental in monitoring and addressing workplace surveillance. With AI-driven monitoring systems becoming more prevalent, unions can use technology to audit and challenge excessive surveillance practices. By employing data-driven insights, unions can negotiate to ensure that workplace surveillance respects workers' privacy rights and remains within reasonable bounds. Overall, by integrating AI tools into their operations, unions can not only modernize their practices but also become more effective in advocating for workers' rights in an AI-dominated workplace.

7.3 Policy Recommendations for Supporting Labor Unions in the AI Era

To ensure that unions can effectively respond to the challenges of AI and automation, supportive policies are essential. Governments, in collaboration with unions and industry stakeholders, must establish policies that create a fair, ethical, and transparent framework for AI implementation. This includes revising labor laws to address the unique challenges presented by AI, establishing guidelines for ethical AI use in the workplace, and enhancing protections for workers in automated roles.

One key policy recommendation is the inclusion of workers in AI-related decision-making processes. Germany's co-determination model, which mandates worker representation on corporate boards, serves as a successful example of worker involvement in technological decision-making. Adopting similar co-determination practices in other countries could ensure that workers have a voice in the deployment of AI technologies that impact their jobs (Hassel, 2014). This type of participatory governance model could help mitigate the risks associated with automation by allowing unions to advocate for fairer implementations of AI.

The policymakers should develop regulations that safeguard workers from excessive surveillance and algorithmic bias. AI-driven management tools often use data-driven methods to monitor employees' productivity, which can lead to micromanagement and potential violations of workers' privacy (Biron & Healy, 2020). Legislation that sets clear limits on workplace surveillance and mandates transparency in AI-driven decision-making would empower unions to protect workers' rights in AI-augmented environments. Policies requiring companies to disclose the algorithms they use and explain their decision-making processes would enhance transparency and accountability, giving unions a stronger foundation for advocacy.

Education and training initiatives also play a crucial role in empowering unions and workers to navigate the AI era. Governments and companies should collaborate with unions to design reskilling programs that prepare workers for the demands of an automated workforce. In countries like India, where automation threatens a substantial portion of jobs in the IT sector, government-supported reskilling initiatives in partnership with unions have shown promise in helping workers transition into new roles (Bhattacharya, 2020). By allocating funding to vocational training and reskilling programs, policymakers can ensure that unions have the resources to support workers displaced by AI and automation.

International labor standards should be developed to address automation's global impact on employment. Global organizations like the International Labour Organization (ILO) could establish standardized guidelines on ethical AI deployment and automation practices that member countries could adopt. Such standards would provide a framework for unions worldwide to advocate fair practices and worker protections, regardless of regional labor laws (Schmidt & Muller, 2019). Adopting international labor standards would reduce regulatory inconsistencies across countries and allow unions to apply consistent advocacy strategies when addressing the impacts of AI.

In the face of the sweeping changes brought by AI and automation, labor unions must adopt proactive, adaptive strategies to continue safeguarding workers' rights. By enhancing international collaboration, unions can share insights, coordinate responses, and exert collective pressure on multinational corporations to implement AI ethically and responsibly. Leveraging AI-driven tools for organizing and monitoring workplace practices offers unions an opportunity to modernize their operations and improve advocacy efforts. Supportive policies that protect workers from AI-related risks, such as algorithmic bias and excessive surveillance, are essential for enabling unions to adapt to the digital age.

As the role of AI in the workforce continues to expand, unions will need to remain flexible, tech-savvy, and united in their approach. By embracing these future directions, unions can help ensure that the benefits of AI and automation are shared equitably, fostering a future of work that values fairness, transparency, and worker well-being.

8. CONCLUSION

As AI and automation reshape the global workforce, unions must adapt while continuing to advocate for workers' rights. Case studies from Germany, South Korea, and Brazil highlight diverse strategies—worker participation in decision-making, union-government workforce initiatives, and advocacy for informal workers. Despite regional differences, unions share common goals: job protection, fair wages, ethical AI deployment, and reskilling programs.

Unions' effectiveness depends on local labor laws, economic conditions, and cultural attitudes toward technology. In countries with strong labor protections, such as Germany, unions influence AI integration. Conversely, in regions with weaker protections, unions face greater challenges but continue to find innovative ways to support vulnerable workers, including those in informal sectors.

Union-led initiatives play a critical role in addressing job displacement, workplace surveillance, and inequality. By advocating for ethical AI standards and fostering international collaboration, unions can ensure that technological progress benefits all workers, not just those in high-skilled positions. Unions are beginning to leverage AI tools for organizing efforts and workplace monitoring, demonstrating their ability to harness technology for advocacy.

To create a fair and sustainable future of work, unions must remain proactive, pushing for both worker protection and equitable access to technological benefits. Collaboration among policymakers, corporations, and unions is essential in establishing fair labor standards that balance technological advancement with worker well-being. Empowered unions can help shape a future where AI-driven progress aligns with social equity.

Ultimately, unions' role in navigating AI's impact on the workforce is crucial. Through cross-border collaboration and strategic engagement with technology, unions can foster an innovative yet worker-centered future, ensuring that AI's transformative power contributes to a more inclusive and just labor landscape.

REFERENCES

Acemoglu, D., & Restrepo, P. (2018). Artificial Intelligence, Automation, and Work. *NBER Working Paper No. 24196.*

Adeleke, T. (2020). Labor unions in sub-Saharan Africa: Challenges and opportunities in the age of automation. *Journal of African Labor Studies*, *9*(2), 134–156.

Atkinson, R. D., & Wu, J. (2017). *False Alarmism: Technological Disruption and the U.S. Labor Market, 1850–2015*. Information Technology and Innovation Foundation.

Autor, D. H. (2015). Why are there still so many jobs? The history and future of workplace automation. *The Journal of Economic Perspectives*, *29*(3), 3–30. DOI: 10.1257/jep.29.3.3

Azoury, N., Subrahmanyam, S., and Sarkis, N. (2024). The Influence of a Data-Driven Culture on Product Development and Organizational Success through the Use of Business Analytics. *Journal of Wireless Mobile Networks, Ubiquitous Computing, and Dependable Applications (JoWUA)*, Volume-15 | Number-2, 123-134.

Baccaro, L., & Howell, C. (2017). *Trajectories of neoliberal transformation: European industrial relations since the 1970s*. Cambridge University Press. DOI: 10.1017/9781139088381

Barbosa, J. R. (2020). Labor market and unionism in Brazil: A historical perspective. *Labor Review Journal*, *25*(2), 193–210.

Bessen, J. (2019). *AI and Jobs: The Role of Demand*. Brookings Institution.

Bhattacharya, R. (2020). Impact of automation on labor in India: Union perspectives and future challenges. *The Indian Journal of Labour Economics : the Quarterly Journal of the Indian Society of Labour Economics*, *63*(4), 533–546.

Biron, M., & Healy, N. (2020). Ethical implications of AI in the workplace: Surveillance and the changing nature of labor. *Journal of Business Ethics*, *162*(1), 45–57.

Bivens, J.. (2017). *How today's unions help working people: Giving workers the power to improve their jobs and unrig the economy*. Economic Policy Institute.

Braverman, H. (1974). *Labor and monopoly capital: The degradation of work in the twentieth century*. Monthly Review Press. DOI: 10.14452/MR-026-03-1974-07_1

Brynjolfsson, E., & McAfee, A. (2014). *The Second Machine Age: Work, Progress, and Prosperity in a Time of Brilliant Technologies*. W. W. Norton & Company.

Cattero, B., & Dyer-Witheford, N. (2018). The datafication of labor and the future of work: Labor unions' responses to automation. *Labour and Society*, *33*(3), 279–295.

Cerdeira, G., & Silva, M. (2020). Labor unions in Brazil and the challenges of automation. *International Journal of Labor Research*, *12*(1), 65–78.

Chan, C., & Hui, E. (2017). State-led labor reforms and labor rights: The case of China. *Asian Journal of Labor Studies*, *15*(4), 207–224.

Chang, J. (2020). Ethical implications of AI in the workplace. *Journal of Business Ethics*, *168*(3), 559–573.

Chang, J. (2020). Ethical implications of AI in the workplace. *Journal of Business Ethics*, *168*(3), 559–573.

da Costa, A. M. (2021). The future of work and automation in Brazil: Union strategies and policy recommendations. *Brazilian Labor Studies*, *32*(3), 215–228.

De Stefano, V. (2018). 'Negotiating the algorithm': Automation, artificial intelligence, and labor protection. *Comparative Labor Law & Policy Journal*, *39*(2), 25–47.

Floridi, L. (2020). *The logic of information: A theory of philosophy as conceptual design*. Oxford University Press.

Freeman, R., & Han, E. (2018). Right-to-work laws and union membership. *Journal of Labor Economics*, *36*(2), 249–273.

Freeman, R. B. (2021). Labor union strategies in the age of automation. *Labour and Society*, *25*(1), 87–103.

Hassel, A. (2014). *The Politics of Collective Skill Formation: The Case of Germany*. Oxford University Press.

Hertel-Fernandez, A. (2020). The power of digitally networked unions in the modern workplace. *Industrial & Labor Relations Review*, *73*(2), 345–366.

Hirsch, B. T., & Macpherson, D. A. (2020). Union membership and earnings data book: Compilations from the Current Population Survey. *Union Research Journal*, *22*(1), 125–140.

Hobsbawm, E. J. (1964). *Labouring men: Studies in the history of labour*. Weidenfeld and Nicolson.

Jürgens, U. (2018). Co-determination and the regulation of AI in German workplaces. *European Journal of Industrial Relations*, *24*(2), 151–166.

Jürgens, U. (2018). Digitalization and work: Labor regulation and worker rights in Europe. *Journal of Labor Regulation Studies*, *31*(3), 324–339.

Jürgens, U. (2018). Union engagement in technology: The German perspective. *German Industrial Relations Review*, *45*(3), 334–349.

Kim, E., & Choi, J. (2018). South Korean labor unions and workforce development in the digital age. *Journal of East Asian Labor Studies*, *15*(4), 456–478.

Kim, H., & Choi, J. (2018). Union responses to technological change in South Korea. *Korean Journal of Labor Studies*, *14*(1), 111–134.

Lee, D. (2019). Government intervention in labor markets: The South Korean case. *International Journal of Public Policy*, *26*(2), 210–229.

Lee, Y. (2019). Worker protections in the age of AI: Challenges in South Korea. *Asian Labor Studies Quarterly*, *12*(2), 55–74.

McGuinness, T., & Fu, S. (2016). Labor unions and technological change. *Labor Studies Journal*, *41*(4), 375–391.

Moore, P. V. (2020). Surveillance capitalism and workplace surveillance. *Employee Relations*, *42*(6), 1280–1294.

Nair, P. (2018). Labor unions in India: Evolution, challenges, and future. *South Asian Journal of Labor Economics*, *15*(4), 310–324.

Oh, M., & Suzuki, H. (2020). Japanese labor unions and AI: Adapting to automation in the workplace. *Asia Pacific Journal of Human Resources*, *58*(4), 475–489.

Pereira, R., & Evans, S. (2019). Automation in Brazilian labor markets: Implications and responses. *Latin American Perspectives*, *46*(2), 21–36.

Sako, M. (2021). Digital transformation and labor union responses in Japan. *Journal of Japanese Labor Studies*, *10*(2), 157–179.

Sako, M. (2021). The adaptation of Japanese unions to AI and automation. *Journal of Japanese Industrial Relations*, *28*(2), 102–121.

Schmidt, M., & Muller, M. (2019). Co-determination in the digital age: Germany's response to automation. *Industrial & Labor Relations Review*, *73*(5), 987–1005.

Schroeder, W., & Weßels, B. (2017). The German model of co-determination and union responses to automation. *Industrial Relations Journal*, *48*(4), 293–312.

Shin, D., & Choi, Y. (2020). Labor unions and technological transformation in South Korea. *Journal of East Asian Labor Relations*, *24*(3), 218–235.

Shin, Y., & Choi, M. (2020). Strategies for labor unions in response to automation: The case of South Korea. *Asian Labor Journal, 18*(3), 305–319.

Subrahmanyam, S. (2023). The Application of Human Resource Analytics as a Strategy to Elevate the Corporate Performance. *Migration Letters : An International Journal of Migration Studies*, *20*(6), 1025–1034. DOI: 10.59670/ml.v20i6.4878

Subrahmanyam, S., Azoury, N., & Sarkis, N. (2024). AI and Business Planning: Revolutionizing Forecasting and Resource Allocation. *2024 International Conference on Advances in Computing, Communication and Applied Informatics (ACCAI)*, Chennai, India, 2024, pp. 1-6. DOI: 10.1109/ACCAI61061.2024.10601728

Subrahmanyam, S., Khalife, D., & Farah, A., A. (2024). Adopting Machine Learning for Better Leadership and Organizational Outcomes. *International Conference on Advances in Computing, Communication and Applied Informatics (ACCAI)*, Chennai, India, 2024, pp. 1-5. DOI: 10.1109/ACCAI61061.2024.10601875

Takeuchi, H. (2019). Corporate policies and labor union strategies in Japan's digital economy. *Journal of Corporate Strategy and Labor*, *29*(1), 27–46.

Takeuchi, H. (2019). Employment practices and AI: Perspectives from Japanese labor unions. *Journal of Asian Business and Economics*, *21*(1), 35–56.

Thompson, E. P. (1963). *The making of the English working class*. Vintage.

West, D. M. (2018). *The Future of Work: Robots, AI, and Automation*. Brookings Institution.

World Bank. (2021). *Brazil's Informal Labor Market: Challenges and Policy Responses*.

Yamaguchi, K. (2020). Labor union response to Japan's demographic and technological challenges. *Asian Economic Policy Review*, *15*(1), 57–72.

Chapter 5
The New Role of Trade Unions in the Face of the Irruption of Artificial Intelligence: The Case of Spain

Jorge Hernando Cuñado
https://orcid.org/0000-0003-4025-1851
Universidad Nebrija, Spain

Javier Antonio Enriquez Román
Universidad Nebrija, Spain

ABSTRACT

This article examines the evolving role of Spanish trade unions in the context of the Fourth Industrial Revolution, focusing on the impact of Artificial Intelligence on the labor market. Union membership has declined in recent decades, and this study analyzes the reasons for this trend while highlighting opportunities for unions to regain relevance in Spain's economy. Amid the uncertainties of technological development, unions can adopt the concept of the Fifth Industrial Revolution. This approach emphasizes the need to balance efficiency, productivity, and profit with human well-being and environmental sustainability. To achieve this, Spanish trade unions must transform into learning organizations—adaptable and responsive to economic changes. Collaboration with key stakeholders is crucial to creating a systemic strategy for navigating technological transitions. By aligning efforts, unions can lead the way to a balanced evolution, benefiting workers, businesses, and society as a whole.

DOI: 10.4018/979-8-3693-8049-9.ch005

1. INTRODUCTION

The origins of artificial intelligence (AI) and of trade unions can help us to understand the relation between them in the present day. Artificial intelligence can be traced back to Ancient Greece, there are notions (myths) about artificial intelligence and robots in the works of Greek poets Hesiod and Homer around 750 and 650 B.C. and there are also references to automats in ancient Chinese and Arabic civilizations (Mayor, 2018). Philosophers like Aristotle set the foundations of logic and reasoning that were important for the development of Artificial Intelligence in modern times.

Afterwards, thinkers like René Descartes reflected on the "the mechanical man" where human reasoning could be automated, furthermore, Gottfried Wilhem Leibniz and Blaise Pascal developed calculating machines that automated arithmetic operations (Buchanan, 2005). Moreover, George Boole created Boolean algebra in 1847 that was fundamental for digital computation.

Charles Babbage designed the *Difference Engine* in 1822, this was a machine designed to execute a predetermined sequence of calculations, utilizing an intricate system of gears, toothed wheels, and levers. He is considered a pioneer of the modern computer (Hyman, 1985), this machine ultimately gave rise to more advanced electronic systems.

A key author for the development of the artificial intelligence was Alan Turing who established the foundations for artificial intelligence and modern computer science in the 20th century. Alan Turing worked for the British government in Worl War II and was able to break the code that Nazis used for communications, generated by an enciphering machine called Enigma (Hodges, 1983). One of his most important contributions was the concept of the "Turing Machine" that established the fundamentals of algorithmic processing (Van Leeuwen & Wiedermann, 2001). Another key principle proposed by Turing was the "Turing Test" to assess whether a machine demonstrates intelligent behavior similar or even indistinguishable from that of a human, this test remains a key concept and a subject of debate even today. This shows the importance of Turing contribution to this field.

Another important author was Kurt Gödel (1931) which the incompleteness theorems, they proved that in any complex systems of rules there will always be true statements that cannot be proven using the system's own rules. This refers to the limitations of formal systems and the necessity of more than logic-driven methods to get human-like reasonings.

The first programmable digital computers (Colossus and ENIAC) appeared during the 1940s and 1950s because of World War II. On one side, the United Kingdom created Colossus to break the Nazi code of communication, conversely the United Stated developed ENIAC to handle a bottleneck in the manufacture of firing tables, the computer facilitated the calculation of ballistic trajectory data (Atkinson, 2014).

During the 1940's, John Von Neumann developed the stored-program architecture, allowing computers to store both data and instructions in its memory. This was a key element for the subsequent development of modern computers and artificial intelligence. Norbet Wiener (1948) was another pioneer in the field of cybernetics, studying the systems of communication and control in machines and living organism. He discovered the importance of the feedback loops of information in intelligent behavior. This discovery was very important for the later development of artificial intelligence.

The Dartmouth Summer Research Project on Artificial Intelligence in 1956 was a milestone that initiated Artificial Intelligence as a field of research. This project focused on the simulation of human intelligence by machines. ELIZA, a natural language processing computer program developed at the Massachusetts Institute of Technology (MIT) in the 1960's by Joseph Weizenbaum was another step forward in this field. The program simulated conversations between human and machines and established a base for human-computer interactions.

During 1960's and 1970's the research was centered on early robotics, symbolic reasoning and problem-solving. Due to military and scientific purposes an abundance of public money financed Artificial Intelligence research during these years. However, some authors (Toosi et al., 2021) considered an "Artificial Intelligence Winter" from the late 1970's to the 1990's (with a short revitalization in the early 1980's). In these periods there was a reduction of funding and interest due to several reasons: limited computer power that affected AI capabilities, unmet expectations or slow advancement in the field.

Nevertheless, in the 1980s and 1990s, there was progress in machine learning (foundational development) and neural networks with backpropagation (a technique for training networks).

Finally, from the beginning of the 21st century to the present day, the irruption of Big Data and the development of processing power allowed Artificial Intelligence systems to learn from massive datasets. Furthermore, deep learning (train computers to recognize patterns and make decisions by imitating how the human brain works), redefined fields like natural language processing, robotics or image recognition. In the 2020s large language models like ChatGPT blurred the lines between humans and machines in conversation, integrating artificial intelligence into everyday activities. Artificial intelligence is transforming many fields now such as healthcare, finance, education, transportation, energy, manufacturing etc. The emergence of this technology has the potential to transform the way of life and may be regarded as one of the most significant scientific advancements in history.

The genesis of syndicates dates to the Industrial Revolution in the 18th and 19th centuries, when industrialization caused profound changes to labor relations. The emergence of factories and large enterprises led to long hours, low wages and hard conditions for workers. In response, they began to organize collectively to improve their work rights and conditions. These early organizations were initially informal and met resistance from authorities, but overtime, they gained recognition as representatives of the work force.

In the case of Spain, the origin of trade unions began in industrial sectors, particularly textiles, in 19th-century Catalonia. (Sarasúa, 2007). The first modern union, the Association of Weavers of Barcelona, was founded in 1840. These organizations were mutual aid societies, aimed at supporting workers in cases of unemployment or illness.

From the late 19th century to the early 20th century, there was a reinforcement of the labor movement. In relation to ideology, two main influences have shaped trade unions in Spain: on the one hand, anarchism, supported by the First International (IWA) from 1868; and the other hand, socialism, associated with the Spanish Socialist Worker's Party (Partido Socialista Obrero Español PSOE) and the General Union of Workers - (Unión General de Trabajadores UGT).

In this context, the Spanish Socialist Workers Party (PSOE) was founded in 1879, and maintained a close connection with the UGT Union. In 1910, the National Conference of Labor (Conferación Nacional del Trabajo, CNT), an anarchist union, was established. The labor movement organized strikes and demonstrations to get worker's rights such as the 8-hour workday.

During the Second Republic (1931-1939), unions served as a driving force to obtain labor and social reforms. The UGT and CNT expanded rapidly, leading protest and strikes. But there were differences between the unions, on one side the Anarchist supported immediate revolution. In contrast, Socialist and Communist promoted gradual changes. During the Spanish Civil War (1936-1939) unions played key roles on the Republican side.

During Franco's dictatorship (1939-1975), unions were repressed and banned, forcing the UGT and CNT to operate underground or in exile. In their place, the regime established a compulsory, state-controlled vertical union, the Spanish Syndical Organization (Organización Sindical Española, OSE), which included both workers and employers. In the 1960s, the underground union Workers' Commissions (Comisiones Obreras, CCOO) emerged, as groups of workers autonomously organized to oppose the regime's vertical union. Over time, this organization gained prominence as a key force of resistance against the dictatorship (Vaquero, 2016).

Following Franco's death in 1975, free unions were legalized. The UGT was legalized in 1976, followed by the CCOO in 1977, along with other trade unions. All of this occurred in the context of the Pact of Moncloa in 1977, where unions played a key role in agreements aimed at facilitating the democratic transition and stabilizing the economy.

In democracy, unions played a crucial role in negotiating collective agreements and labor reforms. At this time, the main unions in Spain are UGT, historically linked to the PSOE, and CCOO, which has its origins in the communist movement. These unions were essential in securing labor rights such as paid holidays, the 8-hour workday, and collective bargaining.

Therefore, Artificial Intelligence and trade unions affect the labor dimension. In fact, both concepts have redefined work relations. Artificial Intelligence has the potential to impact work through algorithms, automation, job creation, labor organization, and the transformation of workers' skills and competencies, with the capacity to change economic sectors or even the entire economy. On the other hand, trade unions must play a key role in protecting workers' rights and employment amid this technological innovation. There are several topics that intertwine unions and artificial intelligence, such as ethical technology, mass surveillance, labor conditions in the age of artificial intelligence, job displacement, among others. In the case of Spain, local characteristics must be considered, such as the adaptation of a traditionally less digitalized economy to artificial intelligence (Moreno Izquierdo et al.,2022) along with high structural unemployment.

2. THEORETICAL BACKGROUND

The economist Joseph Alois Schumpeter (1942) stated in his theory of creative destruction that innovations and the entrepreneurs who bring these innovations to the market are key factors for economic development in capitalist economies. The economy is not static; it is dynamic, and these innovations disrupt equilibrium, driving economic growth. Companies that fail to adapt to the new conditions generated by innovations become obsolete and disappear.

The irruption of artificial intelligence is one of those innovations that will make entire sectors more productive and will change the current status quo. Companies that fail to adjust to the new situation risk being disrupted.

This situation is unfolding within the context of the Fourth Industrial Revolution. According to some economists (Schwab, 2016), humanity is entering a new era defined by cyber-physical systems that integrate physical (1st and 2nd Industrial Revolutions), digital (3rd Industrial Revolution), and even biological systems. Artificial Intelligence, along with other technologies such as robotics, big data, biotechnology, the Internet of Things (IoT), 3D printing, and quantum computing, is at the forefront of this transformative revolution. The Fourth Industrial Revolution represents global economic, social, cultural, and technological changes. These innovations are being applied in industries through what is known as Industry 4.0, or smart factories, these factories are defined by interconnected systems that facilitate real-time data exchange, adaptative decision-making and predictive maintenance. They enable supply to adjust to demand in real time.

Along with the Fourth Industrial Revolution, some authors refer to the Fifth Industrial Revolution or Industry 5.0 (Leng et al., 2022), where human well-being is placed at the core of manufacturing systems. The focus shifts from automation to improving collaboration between humans and machines. While Industry 4.0 prioritizes efficiency and automation, Industry 5.0 pays attention to the human factor and well-being. The environmental factor and social inclusion are also crucial. The idea is to complete industrial growth with sustainable and ethical practices. Trade unions can play a key role in this new approach, working to achieve a fair and human-centered perspective in the workplace.

Furthermore, it is valuable to explore the application of the concept of learning organizations to trade unions. Learning organizations promote continuous learning, improvement, and adaptation to new environments. This flexibility allows them to adjust to change, innovate, and remain relevant in a dynamic environment (Senge, 1990). Given the decline in unionization over recent decades, it is crucial for trade unions to analyze and understand the present moment to stay relevant in the future. As mentioned earlier, the rise of artificial intelligence and the emergence of Industry 5.0 present an opportunity for trade unions to remain significant and improve society. To do so, unions can learn (and transform) within these learning organizations. This concept also applies to any organization that aims to stay ahead in an ever-changing environment.

Another aspect to consider is whether the continuous automation and enhancement of productivity through technology will, at some point, transform or even render human labor unnecessary in many sectors. If this occurs, the implementation of universal basic income (UBI) may become a necessary solution. This could also help reduce the growing polarization between capital owners and less qualified workers (Straubhaar, 2017). If there were widespread job displacement due to the application of Artificial Intelligence in the workforce, UBI could act as a safety net for those individuals whose jobs have become unnecessary.

This leads to the debate about job destruction due to automation. Since the time of the Luddites, there have been people opposed to technological change, due to, among other reasons, the possibility of losing their jobs. From one perspective, according to the theory of creative destruction (Schumpeter, 1942), innovation will eliminate jobs and render some companies obsolete. However, new jobs and businesses will emerge in cutting-edge sectors. From another perspective, the widespread use of Artificial Intelligence (AI) will create jobs, but not all workers will possess the skills and capabilities required to access these new opportunities. This mismatch may lead to increased inequality and structural unemployment (Brynjolfsson &

McAfee, 2014). However, the future impact of the widespread adoption of AI on jobs remains to be seen.

Another important issue for trade unions to consider is the concept of the Triple Bottom Line (Elkington, 1997). Traditionally, companies have focused on profit, but a more modern perspective also considers social and environmental aspects. Therefore, the Triple Bottom Line framework considers three dimensions: people, profit, and planet. The "people" aspect refers to factors such as equity, good working conditions, and community involvement; the "profit" dimension focuses on financial performance and value creation; and the "planet" factor emphasizes sustainability and environmental protection. In the 21st century, a successful company should balance all these dimensions. Trade unions could internalize and adapt to this new framework to remain relevant in the future.

This concept is also related to stakeholder theory (Freeman, 1984). Instead of focusing solely on maximizing shareholder value, companies should consider the interests of all stakeholders, including workers, customers, suppliers, and the broader community. This approach calls for a more inclusive and systemic view of business success, one that could contribute to the long-term viability of companies. Such a perspective can help address and even solve several problems that businesses face today, including employee motivation, community support, customer trust, social inequality, and sustainability, among others.

Thus, according to these theories, the work dimension in the 21st century can be understood as a system—a group of interrelated parts working towards a common objective, such as the Triple Bottom Line. All these parts must be balanced and function holistically. It is crucial that each component—workers, companies, suppliers, customers, trade unions, and the community—adapts to the changing environment. The rise of Artificial Intelligence will impact all these parts, and trade unions must ensure a balance is maintained across them. The Triple Bottom Line is not static; it is a relative and dynamic concept that is also iterative and changes over time (Fauzi et al., 2010).

For the economic development of a country, achieving harmony among social actors is also important. An example of this is the Irish Social Partnership Model, implemented in Ireland during the 1980s and 1990s. The Irish government established a series of agreements in collaboration with businesses, trade unions, and farmers. These agreements addressed issues such as tax reforms, market liberalization, the attraction of foreign investment, industrial policy, wages, economic strategies, employment, and social policies. These consensual measures laid the foundation for the extraordinary growth of the Irish economy in subsequent years, a period famously known as "The Celtic Tiger." (Teague & Donaghey, 2009). Another example of this phenomenon is the Pacts of Moncloa, established in Spain in 1977. They were fundamental to the country's transition from dictatorship to democracy. Spain faced a challenging situation, marked by high unemployment, social unrest, and inflation. Once again, employers, political parties, and trade unions collaborated to implement measures aimed at stabilizing the economy and consolidating democracy. These agreements materialized in actions such as tax reforms, market liberalization, and wage moderation. The pacts laid the foundation for democratic Spain and economic growth in the following decades (Tamames, 2021). Therefore, as these examples show, agreements and harmony among social actors are important for consolidating democracies, promoting economic growth, and fostering social integration. Trade unions play a key role in achieving these social pacts.

Finally, it is important to consider the role of institutions in addressing the impact of Artificial Intelligence on both the economy and society. These institutions (legal, economic, political, educational, health, etc.) collectively define the guidelines and frameworks that govern a society's relationships, which is crucial for long-term growth and development. Aspects such as the rule of law, property rights, transparent regulations, tax systems, and environmental regulations, among others, are essential for economic activities to prosper. It is vital that a country has inclusive institutions that guarantee fair access to opportunities for individuals, protect property rights, and uphold the rule of law. These institutions create an environment where individuals can realize their potential and engage in wealth-creating activities. On the other end of the spectrum are extractive institutions that concentrate power and wealth in the hands of a few, limiting opportunities for the majority of the population, often resulting in economic stagnation and inequality (Acemoglu et al., 2001).

3. THE SCENARIO IN SPAIN

The Spanish economy presents a series of economic characteristics that must be considered to understand the potential impact of Artificial Intelligence. These characteristics differ from those of other countries. Spanish trade unions should take these factors into consideration to remain relevant in the country.

1) High Structural Unemployment:

For many years, unemployment in Spain has been among the highest in OECD countries (Organisation for Economic Co-operation and Development [OECD], 2023). This persistent issue is driven by systemic factors, including inflexible labor market regulations, an education system misaligned with labor market demands, regional inequalities, and a reliance on low-productivity sectors like constructions and tourism that exacerbate unemployment during economic crises, among other challenges.

2) High Youth Unemployment:

Another characteristic of the Spanish economic model is the exceptionally high youth unemployment rate. As mentioned earlier, several factors contribute to this issue: limited access to stable jobs for young people in the labor market, an education system that fails to equip students with the skills and capabilities required by employers, vocational training and apprenticeship systems that need significant improvement, and a reliance on seasonal and often precarious employment in key sectors of the Spanish economy, such as hospitality and tourism.

3) Digitalization Gap:

Spain has traditionally been regarded as a less digitalized economy compared to other European nations, such as Germany, Ireland, Sweden, Finland, Denmark, and the Netherlands. This relative lag can be attributed to several structural and systemic factors. First, the Spanish economy is dominated by Small and Medium Enterprises (SMEs), which often lack the financial and technological resources necessary to invest in digital transformation. Second, the country has historically exhibited low levels of investment in research and development (R&D), further limiting its capacity for innovation. Additionally, there is a notable deficit in digital talent training, coupled with the limited penetration of digitalization in rural areas, which exacerbates regional disparities. Indicators such as the adoption of cloud services by enterprises and the proportion of Information and Communication Technology (ICT) specialists within the total employed population remain below the European Union average (European Commission, 2024).

4) Low Labor Productivity:

Another challenge of the Spanish model is that labor productivity is low compared to other developed countries (García Arenas, 2023). The Spanish economy heavily depends on low-productivity sectors such as tourism, hospitality, and construction. Most companies in these sectors are small and medium-sized enterprises (SMEs) with limited resources, making it harder to implement innovations and improve productivity. Additionally, there is low investment in research and development, a slow adoption of digital technologies, and labor market constraints.

5) Aging Population:

The general population in Spain is aging. As the baby boomer generation (born between 1940 and 1960) retires and the fertility rate declines over time, the working-age population is shrinking. This demographic trend also results in increased expenditure on healthcare systems and public pensions, with fewer workers available to sustain the system. Addressing this challenge is one of the main priorities for the Spanish economy (Cuadrado et al., 2023). To mitigate the issue, policies could include promoting higher fertility rates through incentives, attracting young immigrants to the labor market, and encouraging older workers to remain in the workforce.

6) The Empty Spain (La España vaciada):

Spain is characterized by a contrast between dynamic urban regions, such as Madrid, Málaga, Barcelona, and the Basque Country, and vast rural and interior areas experiencing significant depopulation, particularly those with an aging population. These rural regions often lack the economic activity required to sustain their local communities, leading to the migration of younger inhabitants to urban centers in search of employment opportunities. This demographic shift has resulted in the progressive disappearance of essential services, including healthcare, education, and transportation, from these territories. Meanwhile, urban areas face overpopulation, concentrating the majority of the country's resources and businesses within a few metropolitan hubs. This dynamic has also contributed to rising land and housing prices in these areas, further exacerbating Spain's housing crisis.

7) Unavailability of affordable housing:

Housing affordability has become a significant challenge in Spain, particularly in dynamic areas where housing costs are rising rapidly, with prices especially high in city centers. Wages have not kept pace with the surge in housing costs, creating widespread affordability issues for a large segment of the population. Several structural and economic factors contribute to this phenomenon. The limited construction of new housing following the 2008 financial crisis has constrained supply, while the proliferation of short-term rental platforms, such as Airbnb, has driven up housing costs in urban centers. Additionally, the purchase of properties by foreign buyers with greater purchasing power than local residents, speculative real estate practices, and insufficient public housing programs have further exacerbated the problem. Young people are particularly vulnerable in this context (Martínez del Olmo, 2024), as they face high rates of unemployment, low wages, and a prevalence of precarious employment, which collectively hinder their ability to access affordable housing.

Table 1. Key challenges faced by Spanish companies in comparison to their European counterparts

	Spain	**Europe**
Company Size (2018-2022)	Average of 4.7 employees per company	Average of employees per company: Germany (12), Ireland (5,8), France (5,2)
Main sectors (2021)	Services: 76.8% GVA Industry: 20.5% GVA Agriculture: 2.7% GVA	Services: 73% GVA Industry: 25% GVA Agriculture: 2% GVA
Unemployment (November 2024)	11,3%	5,9%
Youth Unemployment (November 2024)	26,7%	15,3%
Productivity Growth (2013-2023)	0.4% per employed person	0.6% per employed person
Research & Development Investment (2023)	1.44% GDP	2.22% GDP

Sources: OCDE, Eurostat, European Commission

Conversely, Spain exhibits several strengths that merit consideration. The country boasts a highly skilled workforce, a robust tourism industry, and a thriving real estate sector. Furthermore, the technological industry is experiencing significant growth in dynamic regions such as Madrid, Barcelona, Málaga, Valencia, and the Basque Country. These developments are bolstered by various government initiatives aimed at fostering innovation, supporting digital transformation, and enhancing entrepreneurship opportunities across multiple sectors. Additionally, Spain is home to several multinational companies that have achieved notable success in the global market, including Inditex, Banco Santander, Repsol, and Grifols. These factors, alongside its strategic geographical location and strong cultural influence, collectively contribute to Spain's competitive positioning in the global economy.

Figure 1. Comparison of digitalization adoption between Spain and Europe

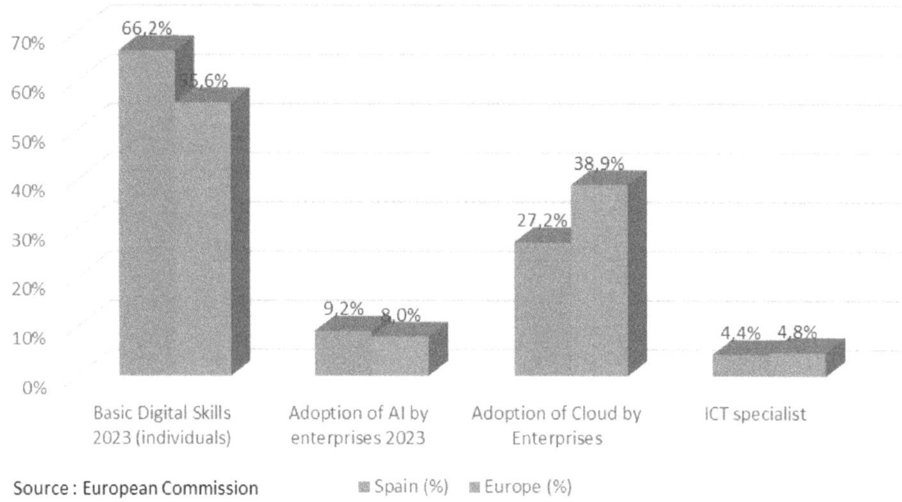

Source : European Commission

Considering these factors, the implementation of artificial intelligence (AI) in Spain should be carefully analyzed and strategically planned to address the intrinsic challenges of the economy without exacerbating them. The adoption of Fourth Industrial Revolution technologies, with AI playing a central role, and their impact on the workforce, is a priority for Spanish trade unions. They emphasize the need for responsible AI integration that enhances productivity while safeguarding employment and workers' rights.

4. TRADE UNIONS FACING THE NEW TECHNOLOGICAL CHALLENGES

According to an article published for Fundación Alternativas, in many wealthy countries (notably; the United States, United Kingdom, France, Italy and Japan), union membership and collective bargaining coverage have declined since the 1960s (Köhler, 2008). This trend has often been attributed to the dual causes of globalization and technological change. Because unions raise labor costs and reduce employer flexibility, they are traditionally described as incompatible with profit maximization in a globalized, information-based economy.

With respect to the specific impact of technological change on the decline of unionization, there are two main lines of thought identified by Mitukiewicz and Schmitt (2012). According to these authors, the first is based on the concept that technology-related productivity growth is historically much faster in manufacturing than in services. Therefore, it is considered, that the share of total employment in manufacturing falls continuously over time, in favor of the development of the service sector. Since unionism has traditionally tended to have higher rates in the manufacturing sector, the decline in the contribution of this sector to total employment implies, if nothing else changes, a long-term deterioration in union density.

Contrary to these arguments, Mitukiewicz and Schmitt (2012) find that, although technological change and globalization impact unions in rich countries, national political traditions established during the period from 1946 to 1980 allow predicting changes in unionization rates from 1980 to the present. In a study of several developed countries similarly affected by globalization and technological change, they found substantial and systematic variation in union trends in different countries, based on wide differences between typologies of national political traditions. While unions in countries with a social democratic tradition have managed to maintain and even expand collective bargaining coverage, with little or no decline in union density, countries with a liberal tradition have generally seen collective bargaining coverage and union density plummet. Finally, countries identified with the more conservative Christian Democrat tradition are somewhere in between, Unions facing technological challenges with small or moderate declines in collective bargaining and somewhat larger declines in union density.

These authors show that, rather than technological change or globalization, the main determinant of the fate of trade union movements is the specific politics of each place, as reflected through its labor law, industrial relations practices and political party structures. This view is also corroborated by some historical analysis: modern trade unions emerged precisely during the early part of the industrial revolution, as an instrument to ensure the dignity of workers in a period of intense technological change. This is something that historian David F. Noble highlights in his study Forces of Production: A Social History of Industrial Automation. In the end, its outcome is determined by conflict and struggle, a terrain in which unions must play a decisive role, in order to prevent the most unfavorable scenarios for workers' interests from prevailing.

To illustrate this point, Noble explains how in the metallurgical sector a type of automation was favored precisely as a result of the political desire to reduce the power of workers (Noble 1984). Specifically, he argues that the introduction of numerical control devalued the work of skilled machinists, giving more power to engineers and managers. This produced a certain polarization in skills, replacing machinists' work while stimulating demand for both low-skilled and high-skilled workers. Eventually, programming became the model for industrial automation in the 20th century.

However, as Noble points out, this was neither the only solution nor the most effective. Record-playback (also called “make-to-program”) was just as effective as numerical control and would have put programming in the hands of the machinists, taking advantage of their intelligence, creativity and judgment, rather than perceiving their input as a multiplier of human error. Although both approaches sought to reduce dependence on highly skilled workers, the latter approach reduced the level of control exercised by engineers and management over workers, while the former increased it. It was the power relations of the time and the political decisions of a number of actors that allowed one set of interests to take precedence over the other. In this sense, it has been suggested that the industrial revolution had an impact on the labor force that also facilitated its organization and defense. On the one hand, the industrial revolution negatively affected employment levels and, in its initial phase, the real wage (Thompson, 1966). On the other hand, Fordism and Taylorism, by concentrating large masses of workers in the same place, also favored the emergence of modern trade unionism, based mainly on the factory model of organization.

Technological development is also a social process that occurs over time. Economists Chris Freeman and Francisco Louçã (2001) and Carlota Pérez (2003) make three claims in their development. The first assertion is that changes in the methods and tools used in economics tend to concentrate around periodic 'revolutions', rather than following linear and incremental trends. The second is that there is a time lag between the onset of the 'Big Bang' of innovation triggered by a technological revolution and its transformation of the socioeconomic structure. The third is that, for a technological revolution to produce valued and shared benefits for the whole of society, the institutional framework has to change significantly to cope with the broad socio-economic implications of new types of economic activity.

While the mid-20th century technological development Noble writes about was driven primarily by advances in the energy sector, the so-called digital revolution that is driving the current wave of technological change is usually blamed on the invention of the microprocessor in the early 1970s. In Freeman, Louçã and Pérez's framework, it is the fifth revolution of capitalism in the last 200 years. The previous four were the first Industrial Revolution (circa 1771), the steam and railroad revolution (1829), the steel, electricity and heavy engineering revolution (1875), and the petroleum, automobile and mass production revolution (1908).

5. DECLINE IN UNIONIZATION DUE TO THE (LAST) INDUSTRIAL REVOLUTION

Although many researchers group all technological developments associated with the digital revolution under the concept of digitization, some have used somewhat narrower definitions to characterize the specific effects of the growing importance of data in the work environment. One example is provided by a Eurofound report, which departs from the framework of technological development established by Freeman and Louçã (2001) and Pérez (2003).

From Eurofound's perspective (2021), digitalization, together with automation and platformization, is one of the three main factors of technological change affecting work tasks and occupations, working conditions, contractual conditions and industrial relations in the 21st century.

Platforms can be used to facilitate both commercial and non-commercial transactions, and their content includes both goods and services. The services exchanged can be further divided into two dimensions, the type of tasks involved (physical, intellectual or social) and the place where those tasks occur (in one location or online). However, because digitization plays such an important role in enabling specific tasks or even jobs to be automated, the current wave of advances in automation cannot be understood separately from this narrower definition.

According to Degryse (2016), the digitalization of the economy, combined with the union of Big Data and robotization, will initiate a new economy and cause major disruptions in various areas. The specific impact on labor markets can be divided under four headings: job creation, task shifting, job destruction and job transformation. Regarding the first, Degryse states that digitalization will mean that new sectors, products and services will be created, and others consequently destroyed. The author also states that task shifting will involve new forms of machine/worker interaction and the emergence of a new form of digital management, as well as exposure to new risks, including work intensification, various health and safety issues, an increasingly blurred separation between private and work life, mismatches in work readiness and new forms of discrimination. The transformation of employment will affect, according to the author, those jobs that are easily transferable to platforms.

The specific number of jobs that will be affected by these changes is the subject of intense academic debate. A well-known study by Frey and Osborne (2013) estimates that 47% of U.S. employment faces a high risk of automation in the coming years. However, more recent studies have significantly reduced the number of jobs at risk of automation. For example, Artnz, Zierhan, and Gregory (2016) estimated that the proportion of jobs at risk in the United States would be 9%. This figure is still a concern, as Degryse also states, especially since these job losses are likely to be inequitably distributed. In a study for the OECD, Nedelkoska and Quintini (2018) state that a job loss of such magnitude could cause disruption in local economies that could be several times greater than the impact caused by the decline of Detroit's automobile industry in the 1950s.

The cause of the divergence between the puzzling estimates of Frey and Osborne and the more moderate numbers produced by more recent work is based on the relationship between occupations, tasks and skills. The more recent studies, mentioned above, identify several factors that could limit or to some extent mitigate the pace of so-called technological unemployment. This is due to the so-called bottlenecks affecting automation, i.e. a number of tasks or jobs that as a consequence of their operational characteristics are difficult to automate with existing know-how.

According to the OECD study, these activities include social intelligence, such as the ability to negotiate complex social relationships effectively, care for others or recognize cultural sensitivities; cognitive intelligence, such as creativity and complex reasoning; and perception and manipulation, understood as the ability to perform physical tasks in an unstructured work environment (Nedelkoska and Quintini, 2018).

These findings have also been developed in Nedelkoska and Quintini's (2018) study on the risks of automation and its interaction with training and skills use at work. This study examines a total of 32 countries. They conclude that almost half of the jobs could be significantly affected by automation, because of the tasks involved. However, the level of risk varies. About 14% of jobs in OECD countries are highly automatable. Another 32% have a risk of between 50% and 70%, indicating that, as a consequence of automation, there is a possibility of major changes in the way these jobs are performed, which would drastically change the skills required to perform them.

Nedelkoska and Quintini (2018) conclude that the variance in automation across countries is large. While one-third of jobs in Slovakia are highly automatable, only 6% of jobs in Norway are. In general, jobs in Anglo-Saxon and Nordic countries as well as the Netherlands are less automatable than in Eastern European countries, Southern Europe, Germany, Chile and Japan. Like trends in trade unionism, the impacts of technological change on employment and working conditions are strongly determined by socio-political and economic factors at the national level. According to the OECD study, variation in automation is better explained by differences in the organization of work tasks within economic sectors than by differences in the sectoral structure of national economies: about 30% can be explained by looking at differences in the structure of economic sectors across countries and 70% can be explained by the different occupational structures in each country.

6. THE TECHNOLOGICAL FUTURE BEGINS TODAY

As mentioned earlier in this research, the digital revolution poses major new challenges for trade unions. Citing a paper conducted by Berenberg and the Hamburg Institute of International Economics, Walwei (2016) identifies three scenarios in his report for the International Labor Organization. The first is the optimistic "promised land" scenario, where machines will ensure the continued well-being of people in the long term. The second is a more pessimistic scenario of a "20/80 society," in which a minority of the population generates high incomes and owns the majority of capital, while the remaining 80% work to make ends meet. The third scenario describes a fundamental change in the structure of employment demand, affecting industries, professions and jobs. While it may be tempting to view the digital revolution as a threat to workers' rights, it is worth remembering that the social forces contesting its implementation have always shaped technological change.

As central actors in this process, trade unions have a key role to play not only in confronting the challenges described above, but also in exploiting the opportunities offered by technological change. These include: facilitating access to work for people who would otherwise be excluded; making it easier for consumers to access affordable services based on a 'just-in-time' policy; providing flexibility to combine work and private life; enabling low-cost market entry for new organizations and companies to test new products and services; facilitating social innovation, creativity, the capacity for expression and the generation of new cultural products and services; and helping to consolidate the European Digital Single Market (OSHA, 2015).

In this context, a study by Joaquim Möller (2015) of the German Institute for Employment Research (IAB) stands out as providing a valuable framework for understanding the challenge at the European level. Möller describes the need for a good "operating system" that incorporates infrastructure, education and legal certainty in addition to data security and flexible employment. As the researcher highlights, to achieve this, a safe environment and humane treatment, worker participation, creative flexibility and social cooperation will be of crucial importance (Möller 2015).

Walwei (2016) develops the idea, stressing the important role of vocational training, a clear commitment to a strong social security system and, advanced labor market programs, and comprehensive social cooperation between employers' organizations and trade unions. More specifically, he identifies four areas of interest, including skills adjustment, labor market regulation, social dialogue and social programs.

In relation to job retraining, Peña Casas et al. (2018) recommend that the European Union and its Member States develop the availability of digital skills through the education and training system throughout the working life, providing broader skills and including competencies of increasing importance in the context of technological development. For even if the labor market impact of the digital revolution is closer to the lower than the higher estimates, the need to ensure that all citizens have the ability to adapt to changing technologies and make the most of technological progress will increase.

In this sense, Peña Casas et al. assert that EU Member States should provide access to education and training, as well as provide more opportunities for upgrading workers' skills and developing their capabilities to overcome the digital divide (especially for older workers) and develop new skills associated with the changing nature of jobs.

Based on the German case, Walwei (2016) points to skills adjustment and development to address the shortage of skilled workers and persistent unemployment at the same time. In his report for the ILO, the researcher recommends internship systems as a great asset and a suitable starting point for a large part of the workforce. However, as he points out, recent research on technological change suggests that adapting German vocational training would not be sufficient, as improvements in vocational training related to youth employment may, under certain circumstances, be counterbalanced by a lack of adaptability and employability among older workers (Hanushek et al., 2016). In this sense, the rapid growth of digital technologies requires a "continuing education" approach to investment, with an emphasis on the development of computer skills on the one hand and social and creative skills on the other.

Regarding the regulatory framework, Drahokoupil and Fabo (2016) highlight that, as platforms are generally located in specific places, they are within reach of existing regulatory tools. Together with Peña Casas et al. they consider that it is essential to recognize the multiple impacts and outcomes of digitalization in terms of health and work-family reconciliation, in order to promote decent working conditions and sustainable, quality employment. For this, regulations must be improved and developed as guarantees against the possible negative consequences of the digital revolution.

7. DIGITALIZATION AS A TOOL FOR THE PROTECTION OF INDIVIDUALS AND WORKERS

The global nature of the challenges of the digital revolution should be taken into account in relation to recycling, social programs and labor market regulation. As Peña Casas et al. (2018) highlight, the impact of the digital revolution should be part of governance at national, regional, local and European levels, with a multiple perspective and not only focused on economic growth or production increases. In this sense, they state that the European Union and its Member States should not only consider digitalization as a management and production tool but also as a tool for the protection of individuals and workers.

Building a new operating system for future workers is no easy task, but it is one that unions must lead. Although technology is often presented as an intrinsic threat to the welfare of working people and the effectiveness of union organizing, historically this has not been the case. As we have seen in the previous section, periods of large-scale technological change have often been accompanied by innovative forms of worker organizing to protect and develop rights, demand better compensation and improve working conditions. Many of today's union tactics, strategies and methods were developed precisely in response to the impact of technological change. For this reason, it is important to underscore the role of unions in this new phase of the industrial revolution. Yet, as new technologies bring new forms of work and employment, workers are finding new ways to connect and demand fair conditions. The following sections describe some of the best practices around three main dimensions identified.

Firstly, the good practices carried out at the organizational level, including those that seek to broaden the basis of social dialogue and take advantage of the potential offered by new technologies to implement new digital tools and strategies for the exchange of information among equals and the accumulation of intersectoral forces for the sake of better collective bargaining.

Secondly, and at the regulatory level, we analyze the participation of workers in the design of policies aimed at addressing the changes resulting from the digital transformation of the labor market and the new training initiatives that, co-produced by workers' representatives and public and/or private actors, coincide in the need to address the skills gap with lifelong learning strategies.

Thirdly, and from a perspective focused on the activity carried out in the workplace, we review some initiatives that, led by workers themselves, have called for ethical standards for better work and better technology, highlighting the need to develop public agendas and collective strategies for the defense of digital rights in the workplace.

Questions about the effects of technological change on workers' rights and inequality have generated a great deal of public debate. A new media space for social dialogue is opening up, in which trade union actions can expect greater visibility and relevance. For example, the notoriety of the news of strikes by Amazon warehouse workers in Germany, Italy, Spain and the UK, or the more localized protests by Deliveroo delivery workers or, more recently, Uber drivers that made headlines around the world. Although the long-term effectiveness of these mobilizations in terms of achieving their demands remains to be seen, some of these demands have already been met.

Despite these advances, the organizational scale and complexity fostered by technological change continues to pose a major challenge to the articulation of a social dialogue broad and inclusive enough to address collective bargaining forcefully. But workers are responding with innovative strategies and new coalitions. Over the past few years, unions have organized thousands of low-skilled Silicon Valley workers; from bus drivers at Apple, Tesla, Twitter, LinkedIn, eBay, Salesforce.com, Yahoo!, Cisco, and Facebook to security guards at Adobe, IBM, Cisco, and Facebook or cafeteria staff at Cisco, Intel, and Facebook.

Since the publication of the Green Paper that introduced the concept, Work 4.0 has been applied in several European Union countries. Its influence can also be seen in the European Pillar of Social Rights proclaimed by the European Parliament, the European Council, and the European Commission on November 17, 2017. This document claims to offer citizens new and more effective rights based on 20 fundamental principles, it has three main strands: Equal opportunities and access to the labor market (Federal Ministry of Labour and Social Affairs, 2017).

8. THE SPANISH CASE

Spanish trade unions have developed their own comprehensive plans to respond to digitalization. Comisiones Obreras (CCOO), the country's largest trade union proposes a National Industrial Pact that includes companies, political parties, educational institutions, technology centers, professional associations and central and regional governments to establish a set of common objectives ranging from reindustrialization through Essential Enabling Technologies to retraining, reinforcing STEM education and vocational training.

In a report by Fundación Alternativas (Estrada & Pumarada, 2018), CCOO economist Bruno Estrada argues that, to keep pace with European industries, Spain must expand broadband access, orient educational and training systems towards the creation and maintenance of a knowledge-centered economy, pursue the "digital integration" of society at large, focus reindustrialization efforts on innovation, and encourage the sophistication of demand. On the other hand, the General Union of Workers (UGT) has proposed the development of a Technological Inclusion Plan (UGT, 2019) focused on collective bargaining and lifelong learning in the short term and the reduction of the work week to four days (while maintaining the same salary) in the medium term. For the long term, UGT points to the need to develop new tax systems and new forms of income for workers unable to adapt to the needs of an increasingly automated and digitized economy.

Table 2. A comparative analysis of labor issues between Spanish companies and their European counterparts

	Spain	Europe
Hourly Labour Cost (average)	€24.0	€31.8
Temporary Employment Rates (2022)	18.1%	12.1%
Average Gross Annual Salary (2022)	€25,353	€27,632
Adult Learning Participation	49.0%,	46.6%
Job Vacancy Rates (2024)	0.9%	2.4%

Sources: Eurostat, EURES

Regardless of the specific agreements reached, there is an urgent need to establish spaces to address technological disruption, in the Danish style, or to create other types of spaces, similar to those described above, where work can begin on a public agenda capable of addressing the impact of technological change on the labor market. New specific spaces are needed for diagnosing the current situation, anticipating possible scenarios, deciding on the future of work, identifying challenges and articulating new solutions. This is not an easy task, and that is precisely why the trade unions, as leading social agents, are the best placed to lead proposals to improve the participation of workers and the balance of power in the workplace.

In response to the current wave of technological change, workers are not only organizing to defend or improve their working conditions and extend their social rights to cover all workers. Increasingly, they are organizing to define how technology should be deployed. Recently, the Teamsters union in the United States reached a tentative agreement with United Parcel Service (UPS) that calls for six months' notice to the union of technology deployments, as well as the creation of a committee with union and company representatives to negotiate any changes this might have on tasks and working conditions.

Typically, these protections include training for jobs created or modified by the new technologies, incentives for productivity improvements, company assistance in finding new jobs for displaced workers, and six months' notice for technology deployments.

In a policy paper for the European Trade Union Institute, Manuela Maschke, who heads the Labor and Codetermination Unit at the Hans Böckler Foundation, identifies several examples of how companies and unions are negotiating technology implementation. Among other areas, she points to agreements reached on participation in ICT regulatory frameworks and development of IT projects; use and management of mobile devices; use and management of social networking applications; data protection and control; automation; standardization and new production systems; quality management and continuous improvement processes; permanent accessibility; flexible organization of working time; and health and safety issues (Maschke, 2016).

In this regard, it is worth noting that in the new power relations brought about by technology, unions have the opportunity to set standards to ensure that the use of technology in the workplace provides benefits to both employers and workers. In all sectors where workers see their activities subject to productivity monitoring and control measures, tracking devices and data processes, standards must be met to ensure that these devices and data processes also provide benefits for stakeholders, ensuring that the following principles are included in sectoral or labor agreements.

9. CONCLUSION

The advent of artificial intelligence has the potential to transform how economies function and significantly impact human work and employment. This represents a case of "creative destruction," where innovation (artificial intelligence) can enhance productivity across many sectors while rendering certain companies and jobs obsolete.

The main Spanish trade unions (CCOO and UGT) have called for a national strategy to address the challenges posed by artificial intelligence in the realm of human labor. It is crucial to approach this situation from a stakeholder perspective, taking into account the interests of all parties affected by this significant change: workers, shareholders, customers, the government, and society at large. Other economies, like Ireland, have flourished after adopting a national strategy to adapt to the new economy. It is crucial to establish a broad social partnership to define the future and implement the measures needed to achieve it.

It is also important to note the decline in union membership over recent decades. Several factors contribute to this reduction, including the increasing dominance of the service sector in the Spanish economy—where unionization is less prevalent—a more individualistic approach to employment, job precarization, the rise of self-employment and the platform economy, distrust stemming from scandals involving trade unions, and a lack of engagement with younger generations, among others.

What is clear is that working conditions and occupations are being affected—and will be even more significantly impacted in the future—by phenomena such as artificial intelligence, automation, platformization, and big data, as well as the broader array of technologies driving the 4th Industrial Revolution. This new revolution is characterized by the fusion of physical systems (1st and 2nd Industrial Revolutions), digital systems (3rd Industrial Revolution), and even biological systems.

To remain relevant, unions should seize the opportunities offered by technological change, such as enhancing access to work, fostering flexibility between work and private life, and providing education and training to develop the skills required for this new era. Additionally, they can advocate for affordability for consumers and, most importantly, ensure that the economy remains human-centered.

Spanish unions must consider the specific challenges of the Spanish economy—such as high unemployment, low labor productivity, an aging population, the digitalization gap, inequality, and the lack of affordable housing—to engage all sectors affected by the technological revolution. The ultimate goal should be to harness these technological advancements to improve the overall well-being of Spanish society, ensuring that the economy serves society, not the other way around. This connects with the concept of the triple bottom line. Traditionally, companies have focused solely on generating profit, but within a broader and more modern perspective, businesses must also consider people and the planet. This means involving a broader range of stakeholders—including workers, suppliers, customers, society, and nature—rather than focusing solely on shareholders.

The future impact of artificial intelligence and the technologies of the Fourth Industrial Revolution on jobs remains unclear. What we know from previous industrial revolutions is that while some industries and jobs will be disrupted, others will flourish and create new opportunities. This aligns with Joseph Schumpeter's theory of creative destruction, which emphasizes innovation and the role of entrepreneurs in bringing that innovation to the market as key factors. However, the final outcome remains uncertain. Another consideration is that these advancements could eventually make human labor less relevant, potentially leading to the implementation of some form of Universal Basic Income. That said, the Spanish economy is not yet at this crossroads and still faces significant challenges, such as reducing structural unemployment, addressing the housing crisis, increasing sustainability, and tackling the issue of "Empty Spain."

Spanish trade unions can prioritize transforming themselves into learning organizations that promote continuous learning, skill enhancement, and the flexibility to adapt to the dynamic environment of the Spanish economy. It is also crucial that they direct their efforts toward what is known as the "Fifth Industrial Revolution," where technology and innovation are employed not only to improve productivity, efficiency, and profitability but also to enhance human well-being and sustainability. This concept emphasizes the use of artificial intelligence, robotics, and other Fourth Industrial Revolution technologies to address major challenges such as sustainability, inequality, and social justice.

The Fifth Industrial Revolution aligns with the core strategies of the European Union, including initiatives like the European Green Deal and the Digital Decade. Spanish trade unions can follow this path by considering the intrinsic characteristics of Spain's economy and society. This requires adopting a more holistic and systemic approach than what has been implemented so far, incorporating a broader range of stakeholders, and becoming more appealing to key actors in the emerging economy.

Additionally, unions must actively engage with technological advancements, advocate for ethical innovation, and ensure that new policies and strategies address pressing issues such as inequality, sustainability, and social justice. By doing so, they can position themselves as indispensable contributors to Spain's economic transformation.

REFERENCES

Acemoglu, D., Johnson, S., & Robinson, J. A. (2001). The colonial origins of comparative development: An empirical investigation. *The American Economic Review, 91*(5), 1369–140. DOI: 10.1257/aer.91.5.1369

Artnz, M., Zierhan, U. y Gregory, T. (2016). El riesgo de la automatización para los empleos en los países de la OCDE: un análisis comparativo. *OCDE* (n.º 189).

Atkinson, P. (2014). ENIAC versus Colossus and the early presentation of electronic computers. In: *2014 Annual Design History Society Conference: Design for War and Peace*, Department for Continuing Education, University of Oxford, 4th-6th September 2014. (Unpublished) [Conference or Workshop Item].

Brynjolfsson, E., & McAfee, A. (2014). *The second machine age: Work, progress, and prosperity in a time of brilliant technologies*. W. W. Norton & Company.

Buchanan, B. G. (2005). A (very) brief history of artificial intelligence. *AI Magazine, 26*(4), 53–53.

Cuadrado, P., Fernández Cerezo, A., Montero, J. M., & Rodríguez-Rodríguez, F. J. (2023). The impact of population ageing on the labour force participation rate in Spain. *Banco de Espana Article, 12*.

Degryse, C. (2016). La economía digital y sus implicaciones socioeconómicas y laborales. *Gaceta sindical: reflexión y debate* (Nº. 27, 2016).

Drahokoupil, J. y Fabo, B. (2016). La economía de plataformas y la disrupción de la relación laboral. *Documento de investigación y resumen de políticas de la ETUI (2016)*.

Elkington, J. (1997). *Cannibals with forks: The triple bottom line of 21st-century business*. Capstone Publishing.

Estrada, B. P., & Pumarada, M. (2018). *La Digitalización de la economía española y sus repercusiones en el empleo*. Fundación Alternativas, Documento de trabajo 199/2018.

EURES. (2023). *Living and working conditions: Spain*. Retrieved from https://eures.europa.eu/living-and-working/living-and-working-conditions-europe/living-and-working-conditions-spain_en

Eurofound. (2021). *The digital age: Implications of automation, digitisation and platforms for work and employment,* Challenges and prospects in the EU series, Publications Office of the European Union, Luxembourg.

European Commission. (2024). *Productivity growth in the EU: is there a trade-off with employment growth?* Retrieved from https://economy-finance.ec.europa.eu/economic-forecast-and-surveys/economic-forecasts/autumn-2024-economic-forecast-gradual-rebound-adverse-environment/productivity-growth-eu-there-trade-employment-growth_en

European Commission. (2024). *Spain 2024 Digital Decade Country Report*. Retrieved from https://ec.europa.eu

Eurostat. (2021). *Services represented 73% of EU's total GVA*. Retrieved from https://ec.europa.eu/eurostat/web/products-eurostat-news/-/ddn-20211021-1

Eurostat. (2022). *Adult learning - participants*. Retrieved from https://ec.europa.eu/eurostat/statistics-explained/index.php?oldid=631842

Eurostat. (2023). *R&D expenditure*. Retrieved from https://ec.europa.eu/eurostat/statistics-explained/index.php?oldid=551418

Eurostat. (2023). *Temporary employment - statistics*. Retrieved from https://ec.europa.eu/eurostat/statistics-explained/index.php?oldid=659010

Eurostat. (2024, March 27). *Hourly labour costs ranged from €9 to €54 in the EU*. Retrieved from https://ec.europa.eu/eurostat/web/products-eurostat-news/w/ddn-20240327-2

Eurostat. (2024, September 13). *Euro area job vacancy rate at 2.6%*. Retrieved from https://ec.europa.eu/eurostat/web/products-euro-indicators/-/3-13092024-bp

Eurostat. (2025, January 7). *Euro area unemployment at 6.3%*. Retrieved from https://ec.europa.eu/eurostat/en/web/products-euro-indicators/w/3-07012025-bp

Fauzi, H., Svensson, G., & Rahman, A. A. (2010). "Triple bottom line" as "Sustainable corporate performance": A proposition for the future. *Sustainability (Basel)*, *2*(5), 1345–1360. DOI: 10.3390/su2051345

Federal Ministry of Labour and Social Affairs. (2017). Green Paperwork 4.0. Federal Ministry of Labour and Social Affairs. https://www.bmas.de/EN/Services/Publications/a833-green-paper-work-4-0.html

Freeman, C., & Louçã, F. (2001, January). As Time Goes By: From the Industrial Revolutions to the Information Revolution. *Academy of Management Review*.

Freeman, R. E. (1984). *Strategic management: A stakeholder approach*. Pitman Publishing.

Frey & Osborne (2013) El futuro del empleo. ¿Cuán susceptibles son los empleos a la informatización? *Advances in Applied Sociology* (vol. 9, n.º 10).

García Arenas, J. (2023, October 13). *Productivity in Spain: A lot of scope for improvement.* CaixaBank Research. https://www.caixabankresearch.com/en/economics-markets/activity-growth/productivity-spain-lot-scope-improvement

Gödel, K. (1931). Über formal unentscheidbare Sätze der Principia Mathematica und verwandter Systeme I [On formally undecidable propositions of Principia Mathematica and related systems I]. *Monatshefte für Mathematik, 38*(1), 173–198. DOI: 10.1007/BF01700692

Hanuskek, E. A. (2016). at al. (2016). Dynamic effects of teacher turnover on the quality of instruction. *Economics of Education Review, 55*, 132–148. DOI: 10.1016/j.econedurev.2016.08.004

Hodges, A. (1983). *Alan Turing. The Enigma.* Vintage Edition.

Hyman, A. (1985). *Charles Babbage: Pioneer of the computer.* Princeton University Press.

Köhler, H.-D. (2008). *Los sindicatos en España frente a los retos de la globalización y del cambio tecnológico.* Fundación Alternativas. Recuperado de https://fundacionalternativas.org/wp-content/uploads/2022/07/d7cd62cb295a3ed0cb3144bfdf0f749a.pdf

Leng, J., Sha, W., Wang, B., Zheng, P., Zhuang, C., Liu, Q., Wuest, T., Mourtzis, D., & Wang, L. (2022). Industry 5.0: Prospect and retrospect. *Journal of Manufacturing Systems, 65*, 279–295. DOI: 10.1016/j.jmsy.2022.09.017

Martínez del Olmo, A. (2024). Less Access and More Inequality: Evidence of and Responses to the Housing Affordability Crisis Faced by Young People in Spain's Larger Cities. *Critical Housing Analysis, 11*(2), 229–241. DOI: 10.13060/23362839.2024.11.2.580

Maschke, M. (2016). *Digitalisation: Challenges for company codetermination.* ETUI Research Paper - Policy Brief 7/2016. https://doi.org/DOI: 10.2139/ssrn.2874850

Mayor, A. (2018). *Gods and Robots: Myths, Machines, and Ancient Dreams of Technology.* Princeton University Press., DOI: 10.2307/j.ctvc779xn

Mitukiewicz, A. y Schmitt, J. (2012). La política importa: cambios en las tasas de sindicalización en los países ricos, 1960-2010. *Industrial Relations Journal* (Volumen 43, número 3).

Möller, J. (2015). *Verheißung oder Bedrohung. Die Arbeitsmarktwirkungen einer vierten industriellen Revolution*, IAB Discussion Paper No. 18 (Nuremberg, Institut für Arbeitsmarkt und Berufsforschung).

Moreno Izquierdo, L., Navarro-Navarro, J., Núñez-Romero, M., & Peretó-Rovira, A. (2022). Una nota sobre el estado de la inteligencia artificial en España. *Apuntes (Lima)*, *2022*(13).

Nedelkoska, L. y Quintini, G. (2018). Automatización, uso de habilidades y capacitación. *OCDE* (n.º 202).

Noble, D. (1984). *Forces of Production: A Social History of Industrial Automation*. Routledge.

OECD. (2023). *OECD Economic Surveys: Spain 2023*. OECD Publishing. https://doi.org/DOI: 10.1787/5b50cc51-en

OECD. (2024, June 27). *Structural business statistics by size class and economic activity (ISIC Rev. 4)*. OECD. Retrieved from https://stats.oecd.org/

OSHA News Releases (2015). *United States Department of Labor US Department of Labor Occupational Safety and Health Administration* (agosto, 2015)

Peña-Casas, R., Ghailani, D., & Coster, S. (2018). The Impact of Digitalisation on Job Quality. In *European Public Services: The Case of Homecare and Employment Service Workers. European Social Observatory*. European Public Service Union.

Pérez, C. (2003). *Technological Revolutions and Financial Capital: The Dynamics of Bubbles and Golden Ages*. Edward Elgar Publishing Ltd.

Sarasúa, C. (2007). Trabajo y trabajadores en la España del siglo XIX. In *A. González Enciso & J. M. Matés (Coords.), Historia económica de España* (pp. 413–433). Ariel.

Schumpeter, J. A. (1942). *Capitalism, socialism, and democracy*. Harper & Brothers.

Schwab, K. (2016). *The fourth industrial revolution*. Crown Business.

Senge, P. M. (1990). *The Fifth Discipline: The Art and Practice of the Learning Organization*. Doubleday.

Straubhaar, T. (2017). On the economics of a universal basic income. *Inter Economics*, *52*(2), 74–80. DOI: 10.1007/s10272-017-0649-8

Tamames, R. (2021). Los pactos de la Moncloa y la constitución: un compromiso histórico. *Revista Iberoamericana de Autogestión y Acción Comunal (RIDAA)*, (78), pp-189.

Teague, P., & Donaghey, J. (2009). Why has Irish social partnership survived? *British Journal of Industrial Relations*, *47*(1), 55–78. DOI: 10.1111/j.1467-8543.2008.00706.x

Thompson, E. P. (1966). *Costumbres en común*. Crítica.

Toosi, A., Bottino, A. G., Saboury, B., Siegel, E., & Rahmim, A. (2021). A brief history of AI: How to prevent another winter (a critical review). *PET Clinics*, *16*(4), 449–469. DOI: 10.1016/j.cpet.2021.07.001 PMID: 34537126

UGT. (2019, 16 de octubre). *Hace falta impulsar un plan nacional de inclusión tecnológica cuyo eje sea la formación*. Recuperado de https://www.ugt.es/hace-falta-impulsar-un-plan-nacional-de-inclusion-tecnologica-cuyo-eje-sea-la-formacion

Van Leeuwen, J., & Wiedermann, J. (2001). The Turing machine paradigm in contemporary computing. *Mathematics unlimited—2001 and beyond*, 1139-1155.

Vaquero, F. G. (2016). Las Comisiones Obreras durante el franquismo. *Tiempo y sociedad*, (24), 57-86.

Walwei, U. (2016). Digitalization and structural labour market problems the case of Germany. *ILO Working Papers. International Labour Organization.* (2016).

Wiener, N. (1948). *Cybernetics: Or control and communication in the animal and the machine*. MIT Press.

Chapter 6
Unions and Organizational Culture in the 21st Century:
The Case of Spain – Challenges and Opportunities in the AI Era

Jessica Bayón Pérez
https://orcid.org/0000-0003-4019-7605
Universidad Internacional de la Rioja, Spain

Andres J. Arenas Falotico
https://orcid.org/0000-0002-2763-9707
Universidad Alfonso X El Sabio, Spain

ABSTRACT

This chapter examines the impact of artificial intelligence and emerging technologies on organizational culture and trade unionism in Spain, addressing both challenges and opportunities. From a multidimensional perspective, it explores automation's effects on labor dynamics, hierarchical restructuring, and the need for new skills. A strategic approach is proposed, where unions take a proactive leadership role by promoting continuous training, professional reskilling, and collaboration with stakeholders to enhance efficiency, well-being, innovation, and sustainability. Moreover, the chapter underscores the importance of ethical AI governance, ensuring adherence to principles of equality, fairness, and inclusion. Finally, the study highlights the critical role of unions as strategic advisors and ethical mediators in corporate transformation, positioning them as essential actors in shaping a more cohesive, versatile, and resilient labor landscape.

DOI: 10.4018/979-8-3693-8049-9.ch006

INTRODUCTION

The 21st century has witnessed an unprecedented technological transformation, particularly characterized by the advancement of artificial intelligence (AI). This phenomenon has begun to redefine the global labor market, the internal dynamics of organizations, and the role of trade unions. In Spain, a country with a rich history of trade unionism, the organizational landscape is shaped by a strong cultural component. The integration of AI presents both substantial challenges and significant opportunities. This chapter aims to analyze the impact of artificial intelligence on corporate culture and trade unionism in Spain, exploring the strategies that labor representatives can adopt to remain relevant and effective within this emerging paradigm.

Trade unionism in Spain has played a crucial role in shaping the labor and organizational landscape, deeply influencing the evolution of labor relations since the democratic transition of the 1970s. During this period, trade unions have functioned as fundamental pillars of collective bargaining, staunch defenders of labor rights, and key actors in safeguarding against the precarization of working conditions. This prominence has unfolded within an organizational framework deeply influenced by distinctive cultural characteristics, such as markedly vertical hierarchical structures, a high degree of formality, and a profound connection with local traditions. However, the structure and function of Spanish trade unions have been continuously shaped by broader economic and technological transformations, particularly the progressive digitalization of labor and the increasing reliance on algorithmic management in various sectors (Burgueño, 2023).

Spain's labor market has undergone several phases of technological adaptation, each with profound implications for industrial relations. The late 20th century saw the initial wave of automation, particularly in manufacturing, banking, and telecommunications, as enterprises sought to enhance productivity through digital tools. By the early 2000s, the expansion of information and communication technologies (ICTs) significantly altered business processes, enabling remote work, digital coordination, and the rise of flexible labor arrangements. The global financial crisis of 2008 further accelerated the shift toward digital business models, pushing companies to embrace cost-efficient digital solutions, which in turn increased employment precarity and weakened traditional labor protections (Fernández-Trujillo, 2023).

The last decade has been marked by the rapid proliferation of advanced technologies, including AI, big data analytics, and platform-based labor systems, which have redefined employment relationships in Spain. The growing prevalence of algorithmic management in hiring, task allocation, and performance evaluation has introduced new complexities to labor relations, challenging the conventional mechanisms of collective bargaining. This shift is particularly pronounced in Spain's business environment, where over 90% of organizations are small and medium-sized enterprises (SMEs), many of which exhibit structural limitations in adopting technological innovations and ensuring equitable digital transitions (Ministry of Industry, Trade, and Tourism, 2024).

At present, the rise of advanced technologies such as artificial intelligence (AI) has disrupted long-standing labor and business traditions, which in Spain are deeply ingrained and, in many cases, take precedence over purely technical considerations. This dynamic exerts an influence that can function both as a catalyst for innovation and as an impediment to further development. The impact of this phenomenon is further amplified by the structural composition of Spain's business sector, where more than 90% of organizations are small and medium-sized enterprises (SMEs), many of which face resource constraints and exhibit limited organizational flexibility (Ministry of Industry, Trade, and Tourism, 2024).

This intricate cultural and structural framework creates a scenario in which the integration of intelligent systems reconfigures processes and hierarchies while simultaneously challenging the traditionally conservative foundations of labor and organizational relations. On the one hand, emerging technologies may serve as transformative tools capable of optimizing processes and generating new employment opportunities; on the other, they introduce ethical, social, and cultural uncertainties that trade unions must address to maintain their relevance within an evolving environment. In this context, understanding how labor and business organizations can respond to the challenges and leverage the opportunities presented by this evolving landscape is imperative. Achieving this requires a vision that transcends historical and cultural constraints and embraces an innovative and strategic perspective. The ability to adapt to these dynamics will be crucial in determining the sustainability of trade unionism in Spain, as well as its capacity to lead the transition toward a more ethical, inclusive, and technologically advanced labor model.

As artificial intelligence continues to redefine the structural and operational paradigms of labor and organizational ecosystems, its influence on corporate culture emerges as a critical dimension of analysis. Beyond its technical and economic implications, AI engenders profound transformations in workplace norms, decision-making processes, and hierarchical interactions. In Spain, where corporate culture is deeply intertwined with social traditions and regulatory frameworks, the assimilation of AI-driven mechanisms necessitates a reassessment of established organizational principles. The ensuing chapter delves into the multifaceted impact of AI on organizational culture, scrutinizing its role in reshaping managerial approaches, employee dynamics, and the ethical considerations inherent in algorithmic governance. By exploring these dimensions, this analysis seeks to illuminate the pathways through which organizations and labor representatives can navigate the intricate balance between technological advancement and the preservation of core human-centric values.

As artificial intelligence continues to redefine the fundamental tenets of organizational culture, its repercussions extend far beyond internal managerial structures and workplace interactions. The evolving digital landscape not only challenges traditional modes of corporate governance but also necessitates a profound reassessment of labor representation and advocacy. In this context, trade unions, historically instrumental in safeguarding workers' rights and negotiating equitable labor conditions, find themselves at a pivotal crossroads. The integration of AI-driven systems into the workplace raises critical questions regarding the efficacy of conventional collective bargaining mechanisms and the strategies required to ensure that technological progress aligns with social and economic justice. The following chapter explores the transformation of trade unionism in response to advanced technologies, analyzing how labor organizations can adapt, innovate, and assert their relevance in an era characterized by algorithmic governance, platform-based employment, and shifting power dynamics in industrial relations.

METHODOLOGY

This chapter is developed through a theoretical-analytical approach based on a systematic literature review, aiming to examine the impact of artificial intelligence (AI) on organizational culture and trade unionism in Spain. The study is qualitative in nature and adopts a documentary and hermeneutic design, allowing for a critical and explanatory approach to changes in labor dynamics and the reconfiguration of trade unionism in the context of the Fourth Industrial Revolution (Brynjolfsson & McAfee, 2017; Schwab, 2016).

The study is supported by a theoretical-conceptual and comparative analysis, employing highly relevant primary and secondary sources, including indexed journal articles, governmental reports, and documents from international organizations. A rigorous systematic literature review procedure (Boell & Cecez-Kecmanovic, 2014) has been followed to identify the main thematic axes related to the intersection of AI, organizational culture, and trade unionism.

For data collection, the following criteria were applied:

- Peer-reviewed academic sources published in the last ten years (2013–2024) were selected, prioritizing those indexed in recognized databases such as Scopus, Web of Science, and Scielo (Aguinis et al., 2020).
- Reference books and documents from international organizations such as the International Labour Organization (ILO), the OECD, and the European

Commission were included to provide a macroeconomic and political perspective on the phenomenon under study.
- Key terms related to "Artificial Intelligence in Labor Relations," "Unions and Digitalization," "Workforce Transformation," and "Ethical AI in Organizations" were used to narrow the search to relevant studies.

The literature review was conducted following the PRISMA methodology (Preferred Reporting Items for Systematic Reviews and Meta-Analyses) (Moher et al., 2009), ensuring a rigorous selection process that guarantees the validity and reliability of the findings presented.

Moreover, the documentary corpus was analyzed through a hermeneutic and content analysis approach, which allows for the identification of patterns, trends, and divergent perspectives on the incorporation of AI in organizational and trade union processes (Krippendorff, 2018). This procedure included:

- Thematic coding: Key categories such as transformation of organizational culture, impact on union structures, digital skills gap, and ethical governance of AI in the workplace were identified.
- Comparative analysis: AI implementation models in different countries and productive sectors were examined to establish parallels and contrasts with the Spanish reality.
- Critical evaluation: A critical perspective was integrated regarding the challenges and opportunities posed by AI, incorporating sociological, economic, and legal approaches (Freeman & Medoff, 1984; Acemoglu & Restrepo, 2019).

Finally, to ensure the scientific quality of the study, the principles of source triangulation and validation through theoretical contrast were applied (Yin, 2018). Additionally, a replicable research approach was adopted, structuring the literature review with clear inclusion and exclusion criteria to enable the continuity of analysis in future research.

THE IMPACT OF AI ON ORGANIZATIONAL CULTURE

The adoption of cognitive technology within Spanish organizations, as in other parts of the world, is profoundly and rapidly reconfiguring corporate culture. This transformation offers unprecedented opportunities to automate low-value tasks, optimize processes, and enhance decision-making through advanced data analytics (Bayón & Arenas, 2019). One of the most salient consequences of this shift is the transformation of leadership structures, communication systems, interpersonal interactions, and occupational models within the workplace. The automation of routine and monotonous tasks facilitates the streamlining of administrative processes, leading to a diminished need for intermediary roles and the subsequent dismantling of rigid organizational hierarchies. While this transition can result in greater operational agility, it simultaneously generates socio-labor uncertainties, particularly in small and medium-sized enterprises (SMEs) characterized by rigid and insular corporate cultures, as is often the case in Spain.

Furthermore, this new paradigm necessitates the emergence of highly specialized job roles oriented toward the analysis, design, and management of technological systems. These positions require advanced technical competencies, thereby exacerbating the skills gap and potentially excluding workers with limited or no formal training in these domains. This phenomenon has direct implications for individual employability while also posing significant challenges for organizational cohesion and labor market stability.

Another critical dimension of AI integration concerns its impact on employees' perceptions of equity and fairness. When automated decision-making processes are not managed transparently and ethically, they may result in decisions that human talent perceives as arbitrary, subjective, or impersonal. This issue is particularly salient in areas such as promotions, task allocation, and performance evaluations, where algorithmic processes may inadvertently introduce biases, perpetuating pre-existing inequalities or engendering new forms of discrimination. Consequently, a lack of transparency regarding the criteria employed by AI-driven systems may erode trust in corporate leadership, negatively affecting internal cohesion and diminishing workforce motivation (Rosari, Danarilia, & Ardianto, 2024).

Moreover, these concerns may extend to trade unions, particularly if employees perceive that their interests are not being adequately represented and safeguarded in an increasingly digitalized work environment. In this regard, the intersection of artificial intelligence and labor relations necessitates a proactive approach from trade unions to ensure that technological advancements do not compromise workers' rights but rather serve as catalysts for a more equitable and inclusive employment framework.

Another highly relevant element is communication and team-building, as these technological tools weaken the social and cultural ties that have historically sustained organizational identity. In a context such as Spain, where interpersonal relationships hold substantial weight in workplace culture, this depersonalization may erode employees' sense of belonging, loyalty, commitment, and collaboration (Chibás Ortiz, 2015).

Ultimately, the implementation of these instruments and their impact on organizational culture must be accompanied by a strategic approach that considers not only their technical benefits but also their economic, political, cultural, social, and ethical implications. Proper management of these transformations will ensure the development of a more integrative, inclusive, and equitable work environment, thereby reinforcing trust, loyalty, and employee engagement—factors that are essential for the success of enterprises, organizations, and institutions (Ramírez Guevara, 2024).

The Transformation of Trade Unionism in the Era of Advanced Technologies

Amid these emerging demands, trade unions in Spain face a unique opportunity to redefine their role in the Fourth Industrial Revolution. Historically, unions have been perceived primarily as defenders of labor rights, negotiators of wages, and protectors against exploitation. However, within the current landscape, their role must evolve to encompass the representation of workers' digital rights, positioning themselves as key social agents and actively participating in the formulation of AI implementation policies within organizations.

Trade unions can play a strategic role in negotiating how algorithms are integrated into the workplace, ensuring that employees receive the necessary training to transition into new roles and that the benefits of automation are distributed equitably. Furthermore, they can advocate for transparency in the deployment of superintelligent systems in labor-related decision-making, ensuring that biases—whether explicit or implicit—do not undermine certain groups of workers or negatively affect workplace dynamics (Chica & Ruiz-Roqueñi, 2022).

This transformation is no longer hypothetical but has materialized through real negotiations in Spain. According to the 2024 Work Trend Index published by Microsoft and LinkedIn, 68% of workers in Spain have already incorporated AI into their daily professional routines. Despite this widespread adoption, the regulatory framework governing AI-driven decision-making remains largely underdeveloped, with only a handful of collective bargaining agreements explicitly addressing AI integration in the workplace. Sectors such as banking, insurance, and food commerce have taken pioneering steps in this domain, with specific agreements negotiated by major firms such as El Norte de Castilla and Air Nostrum to establish safeguards against the indiscriminate use of algorithmic decision-making and ensure workers' rights to information (Microsoft, 2024).

Beyond individual corporate negotiations, the role of national trade unions in shaping a comprehensive AI governance strategy is becoming increasingly pronounced. The Unión General de Trabajadoras y Trabajadores (UGT) has highlighted that 40% of companies in Spain are utilizing algorithms for automation, yet there is insufficient oversight to prevent unjust labor decisions. Consequently, UGT has called for stronger regulatory intervention and enhanced collective bargaining mechanisms to prevent the misuse of AI while the European AI Act is gradually implemented (UGT, 2024). The V Agreement for Employment and Collective Bargaining (AENC), signed in May 2023 between trade unions and employers' associations, represents a landmark effort to introduce transparency in AI deployment within labor relations. Under this agreement, companies are now required to disclose the parameters, rules, and instructions underpinning algorithmic decision-making processes that impact employment conditions, promotions, and dismissals (BOE, 2023).

Another crucial aspect in this transformation is continuous education and training. Labor organizations must assume a leadership role in the promotion of both formal and non-formal training programs designed to equip the workforce for the continuous digital transformation, thereby mitigating the skills and competency gaps that emerging demands may exacerbate. This training should focus not only on technical proficiencies but also on the development of essential soft skills, including change management, emotional intelligence, resilience, creativity, alternative dispute resolution, effective communication, critical thinking, and adaptability to new work modalities. The implementation of AI-driven skills mapping frameworks is a key initiative currently being developed in Spain, allowing trade unions to identify discrepancies between the workforce's existing digital competencies and the evolving demands of automated workplaces (Rodríguez Fernández, 2023).

A relatively underexplored yet highly promising avenue is the implementation of pilot programs in specific sectors to assess how artificial intelligence (AI) adoption and automation influence job quality and social cohesion. Through controlled experimental initiatives, trade unions could generate empirical evidence that substantiates their capacity to negotiate improved labor conditions and to propose regulatory frameworks aligned with these transformations. Additionally, this scientific approach would enable unions to be recognized as strategic actors in shaping informed and proactive public policies. The Spanish trade union Comisiones Obreras (CCOO) has already taken steps in this direction by establishing an AI Observatory, leveraging big data analytics to systematically evaluate the impact of AI on workers' rights and negotiate more effectively based on empirical evidence (CCOO, 2024).

Ultimately, the implementation of a well-structured strategic plan will delineate the difference between being passive observers of this transformation and becoming co-architects of constructive economic, social, and labor changes. The extent to which trade unions successfully navigate this technological transition will depend on their ability to proactively shape the discourse surrounding labor rights in the digital age. Rather than merely responding to disruptions, unions must anticipate and influence the evolution of work, ensuring that technological advancements contribute to equitable and sustainable labor relations. By leveraging empirical research, fostering collaborative dialogue with policymakers, and spearheading innovative training initiatives, trade unions can redefine their role as pivotal agents of social progress.

Despite these advancements, the ongoing challenge for Spanish unions remains their ability to scale these negotiations beyond isolated agreements and towards a legally binding national framework that standardizes AI governance across industries. While some collective agreements have pioneered AI regulations, the vast majority of Spanish workers remain unprotected from algorithmic decision-making processes that could profoundly impact their professional trajectories. Given that AI is expected to transform up to 25% of jobs in the European labor market over the next decade (Eurostat, 2024), the window for unions to assert their influence in shaping this transition is narrowing. The following chapter delves into concrete strategies for trade union adaptation in the 21st century, outlining the mechanisms through which labor organizations can enhance their institutional resilience, modernize their advocacy efforts, and secure a more inclusive and participatory future for the workforce.

Trade Union Leadership in Digital Education: Bridging the Technological Skills Gap

In alignment with the preceding sections, the rise of emerging technologies presents both immense opportunities and significant barriers that require careful analysis and strategic intervention. Among these challenges, the skills gap has emerged as a major obstacle in ensuring workforce readiness, labor market competitiveness, and the overall adaptability of human capital. Consequently, trade unions now bear a novel and evolving co-responsibility in assuming leadership roles in digital education and vocational training.

By embracing this mandate, unions can effectively address the demands of the Fourth Industrial Revolution, positioning themselves as strategic actors in shaping a resilient, skilled, and adaptable workforce that meets the imminent needs of the labor market. The following section explores practical strategies and dynamic examples that unions can adopt to mitigate the skills gap and guide training programs toward sustainable short-, medium-, and long-term outcomes.

First, trade unions can adopt a more versatile and strategic role by serving as intermediaries between workforce skill requirements and labor market demands within a VUCA (Volatility, Uncertainty, Complexity, and Ambiguity) environment. This role entails facilitating technical training programs and sector-specific initiatives that allow employees to internalize the impact of technological transformation on their hard skills.

One innovative approach involves the creation of metaverse-based training centers, which function as lifelong learning hubs utilizing online learning platforms and interactive tools to foster the development of both technical and transversal competencies (Todolí, 2023).

A noteworthy precedent is found in Germany, where the IG Metall union has successfully implemented educational programs in advanced technology through partnerships with leading corporations. These initiatives focus on equipping workers with specialized skills in artificial intelligence, robotics, and automation, ensuring that the labor force remains competitive and future-ready (Mukiur, 2019).

Second, to ensure the effectiveness of these programs, labor organizations must design customized and accessible educational strategies that directly enhance worker employability. One particularly effective initiative is the development of a Skills Needs Mapping Framework, aimed at identifying gaps between priority and essential skills across different sectors (Marlapudi & Lenka, 2024).

For instance, in the logistics industry, a high-priority competency is proficiency in operating automated inventory management systems. The following Table 1 presents an example of a logistics sector worker, and the key competencies required for optimal performance in an AI-driven workplace.

Table 1. Example of training levels

Skill	Current Level	Required Level
Inventory Management	6	8
Route Optimization	5	7
Data Analysis	4	7
ERP Management	7	9
Supplier Negotiation	6	8
Logistics Planning	5	7
Regulatory Knowledge	4	6
Warehouse Management	6	8
Process Automation	3	7
Sustainability in Logistics	2	6

Source: Own elaboration (2025).

On the one hand, this individual mapping allows us to observe the current skill levels in required competencies and identify any gaps. This ensures that the training modules are aligned to achieve the necessary levels. The following chart provides a more illustrative representation.

Figure 1. Example of an individual mapping

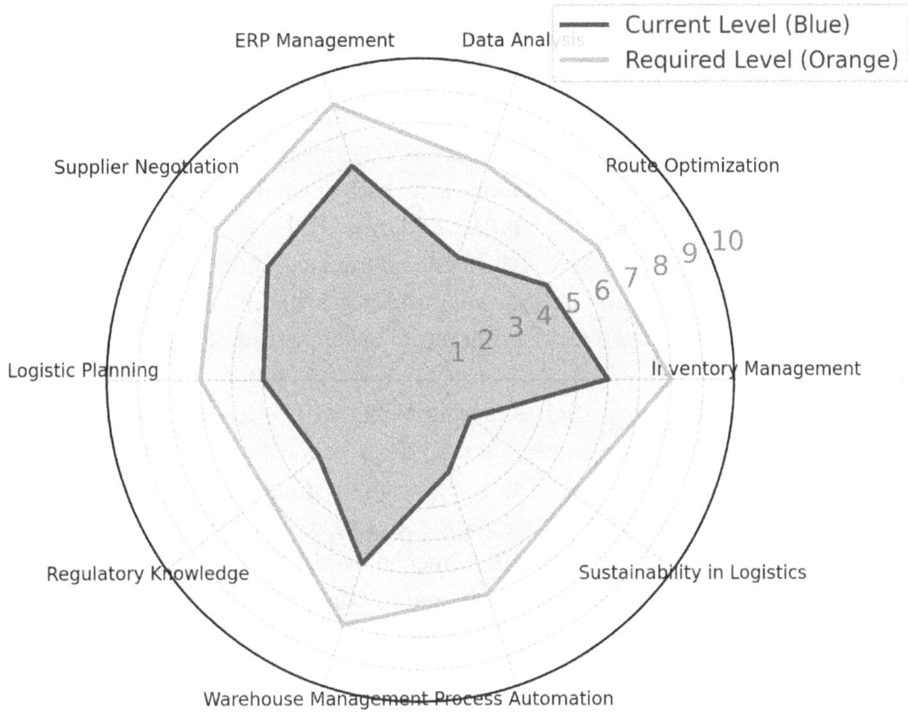

Source: Own elaboration (2025).

As observed, the blue color represents the score of the current skill level, while yellow indicates the level required for the position. Analyzing the diagram reveals a significant gap between the two, highlighting the critical responsibility of stakeholders to provide guidance, support, and direction throughout this process. In this regard, artificial intelligence can serve as a strategic ally by enabling the creation of diverse platforms tailored to individual needs. These platforms can classify key skills, their respective current and desired levels, and actionable strategies while also analyzing market relevance, the impact on job performance, urgency levels, and ease of implementation.

For instance, to enhance negotiation skills, virtual reality could be employed to create realistic scenarios that promote learning through experience. Another example is the training of crews for semi-autonomous aircraft, ensuring their readiness for all types of contingencies. Such instruction should be flexible, incorporating various approaches, including in-person, hybrid, practical, and theoretical methods. These might encompass a wide array of formats, such as workshops, webinars, seminars, asynchronous modules, conferences, short and practical course modules, and more.

In this era, cross-disciplinary training is increasingly in demand, with cybersecurity standing out as a priority. An intriguing project could involve the development of a training course led by trade unions in collaboration with universities, certifying and efficiently training individuals in areas such as data analysis, basic programming, and cybersecurity. These alliances could extend to academic institutions as well as companies, organizations, or entities that are leaders or experts in their fields, fostering the creation and implementation of both formal and informal training programs (Echeverría Samanes & Martínez Clares, 2021).

Moreover, labor representatives could initiate transparent, cooperative, and eloquent social dialogue to negotiate state support for the funding of training projects, such as Finland's "Future of Work" program, to ensure greater accessibility (Díaz, 2021).

In this framework, the question is not only what will be learned but also how it will be implemented. Consequently, methodology becomes an indispensable tool for achieving desired objectives. The integration of innovative approaches, such as gamification, represents a strategic advancement in education, connecting the learning experience with neurocognitive mechanisms that promote engagement, effective information retention, and emotional satisfaction.

As a result, methodologies should be adaptive, emphasizing the following approaches that excel in aligning and maximizing learning outcomes:

Gamification, defined as the application of game design elements in non-gaming contexts, has emerged as one of the most disruptive methodologies in professional training, offering a dynamic and interactive approach to skill development and knowledge acquisition.

This approach enhances intrinsic motivation by integrating reward, progress, and competition dynamics while positively impacting the brain by stimulating the release of dopamine, a neurotransmitter associated with pleasure and reward. Consequently, the neurological effects of gamification are significant: participation in gamified activities activates the brain's reward system, reinforcing desired behaviors, encouraging repetition, and improving concept retention. Furthermore, this method creates a more relaxed and stimulating learning environment, reducing stress and increasing the production of endorphins, commonly referred to as "happiness hormones" (Gil, 2024). These effects contribute to making the training-learning process both more enjoyable and more effective.

Challenge-Based Learning (CBL): This method involves presenting real-world problems or challenges that participants must solve, integrating cross-disciplinary and interdisciplinary knowledge. For instance, in the training of crews for semi-autonomous ships, participants might resolve simulated contingencies within an immersive digital environment. In the field of corporate cybersecurity, participants could learn to design a defense strategy in response to a simulated real-time cyberattack, working collaboratively to identify vulnerabilities, mitigate risks, and protect sensitive data. Similarly, in the clinical domain, students could address a critical scenario through a simulation of emergency response to victims of a natural disaster or terrorist attack. This type of learning allows participants to develop and enhance skills such as coordination, teamwork, decision-making under pressure, and resource management (Posso Pacheco et al., 2023).

Microlearning: This pedagogical approach focuses on delivering content in short, specific, and accessible modules designed to facilitate the rapid and efficient acquisition of knowledge, skills, and competencies. These modules enable learners to progress flexibly, self-managing their time according to their individual needs and availability. Microlearning is particularly effective for skills requiring ongoing reflection and practice, such as transversal competencies (Ortega, 2022).

For instance, areas such as persuasive communication can be addressed through short videos and practical argumentation exercises, while creativity can be fostered through activities that encourage innovative idea generation and problem-solving in simulated scenarios. Similarly, resilience can be developed through lessons featuring inspiring stories, stress management techniques, and interactive self-assessments.

These modules are often asynchronous, allowing participants to access the content anytime and anywhere, thereby maximizing accessibility. Furthermore, modern microlearning platforms integrate dynamic elements such as interactive quizzes, gamified exercises, and progressive challenges, which reinforce learning while increasing user motivation and engagement (Machado Fiuza Fialho et al., 2024).

Finally, these methodologies enable trade unions to position themselves as leaders in educational transformation by providing accessible, equitable learning opportunities aligned with the demands of the Fourth Industrial Revolution. In a context where technological and transversal skills are essential, these strategies help reduce the skills gap and consolidate the role of trade unions as change agents, capable of overcoming emerging challenges with innovative and sustainable solutions.

As trade unions continue to embrace digital education and vocational training as strategic imperatives, their ability to implement cutting-edge learning methodologies will be instrumental in bridging the technological skills gap. By integrating gamification, challenge-based learning, and microlearning into their training frameworks, labor organizations can foster a dynamic, inclusive, and adaptable workforce capable of thriving in the digital era. However, the role of unions in this transformation extends beyond education; it also encompasses the exploration of novel opportunities for institutional innovation. To fully harness the potential of artificial intelligence, data-driven decision-making, and emerging labor models, unions must actively position themselves as pioneers in reshaping the landscape of worker advocacy. The following section delves into the myriad opportunities for union innovation, outlining strategic pathways through which labor organizations can leverage technological advancements to enhance their influence, engagement, and overall effectiveness in the evolving world of work.

Opportunities for Union Innovation

In this rapidly evolving labor landscape, artificial intelligence (AI) presents significant challenges but also remarkable opportunities for union innovation. The integration of these emerging technologies can enhance unions' ability to adapt to the dynamic nature of work and respond more effectively to the needs of their members (Espiau, 2022).

On the one hand, worker organizations can leverage data analysis tools to optimize their internal processes. These tools enable the identification of patterns in information gathered from their members, facilitating a deeper understanding of their objectives, demands, motivations, priorities, and the necessary actions to improve their well-being. By incorporating this data into decision-making processes, unions can develop more targeted and representative strategies, thereby promoting more efficient and relevant labor intermediation in today's complex environment.

For instance, algorithms can deploy and analyze surveys and consultations among workers to identify trends and common issues, such as wage inequality, lack of training opportunities, or violations of labor laws. Additionally, these tools provide strategic insights for anticipating trends or emerging controversies, such as the effects of automation in specific sectors. This allows unions to adopt proactive stances supported by predictive models over the medium and long term.

On the other hand, intelligent automation revolutionizes how unions mobilize workers. Digital platforms and social networks, powered by autonomous technology, offer an efficient avenue for organizing campaigns and coordinating collective actions. For example, they enable the segmentation of messages tailored to different labor audiences, personalizing communication according to occupational, demographic, sectoral, or geographic characteristics, as well as the specific interests and priorities of internal collaborators.

Consequently, in a global labor market characterized by precariousness and the fragmentation of the workforce, these advanced technological solutions are essential to overcoming the limitations of traditional organizational methods. Modern mobile applications facilitate labor participation in sectors where remote work or digital platforms dominate, thereby achieving greater cohesion and reach (Fernández-Trujillo, 2023).

In line with the above, this dynamic offers significant legal support as cutting-edge technology enables immediate labor advisory services tailored to the individual circumstances of each worker. This support extends from legal counsel to the analysis of specific continuous training requirements for their position or industry.

Additionally, intelligent technologies can serve as a strategic tool for empowering human capital and enhancing professional prospects.

For instance, programmed intelligence devices can provide interactive guides customized to current legislation, tailored by country, region, sector, and contract type. These tools help workers understand their rights and responsibilities, as well as their legal options in specific scenarios, such as workplace harassment, termination of employment relationships, substantial changes in working conditions, or collective bargaining, among many others (Bayón, Arenas & Lominchar, 2022).

In the realm of continuous education, automated intelligent processes can analyze each worker's individual competencies and compare them with the skills demanded in their industry, generating personalized training plans that align with their needs and learning pace (Borden-Lanza, Lores-Gómez, Usart-Rodríguez, & Colobrans-Delgado, 2023). These programs range from basic to advanced levels and employ diverse methodologies, including online courses, practical workshops, and even modules specifically designed to train workers in the effective use of emerging technologies within their fields.

For example, in industries such as manufacturing, healthcare, or logistics, training may focus on the use of advanced machinery, safety protocols, or customer service techniques through immersive simulations in virtual or augmented reality environments. These scenarios allow professionals to practice the skills required for new occupations or sectors, enhancing their readiness for future demands.

In sectors particularly impacted by automation, digital intelligence infrastructure plays a critical role in anticipating labor market changes and suggesting transition pathways toward roles with greater long-term employability. For instance, algorithms can analyze the potential impact of automation on certain positions and recommend training itineraries for professionals to migrate toward more secure and better-compensated occupations (Molina Navarrete, 2021).

This approach not only strengthens professional profiles in emerging sectors but also fortifies the labor network by equipping workers with the tools to adapt to an ever-changing job market. At the same time, it reinforces the role of trade unions as allies in promoting stability, professional development, and economic growth, aligning with the interests of other stakeholders such as business organizations and the state.

As outlined above, unions now have the capacity to offer highly adaptable services tailored to the individual needs of each member, significantly increasing the perceived value of membership. This approach not only enhances the experience of current members but also positions unions as modern, accessible, and relevant entities, particularly appealing to younger generations. This is especially crucial for attracting individuals who, due to lack of prior exposure, negative perceptions, or limited awareness, do not feel connected to traditional unionism.

In conclusion, technological innovation also provides a competitive advantage to redefine unionism as a key actor in the digital transition. Unions could position themselves as mediators in ethical debates surrounding the appropriate use of technology in workplaces, addressing issues such as employee data privacy, fairness in automated decision-making systems, and the impact of automation on employment (Galian, Licata, & Stern-Plaza, 2022).

Moreover, this transformation offers unions an opportunity to lead by example in transparency and best practices in technology use, demonstrating their commitment to ethical and operational principles. This could include implementing more agile and secure internal voting and consultation systems, thereby reinforcing their legitimacy and advocating for similar standards within companies.

As unions harness the transformative potential of artificial intelligence and digital technologies, their capacity for innovation becomes a defining factor in their long-term relevance. However, the integration of these tools alone is insufficient; unions must also develop comprehensive strategies to ensure their sustainable adaptation within an increasingly complex and rapidly evolving labor ecosystem. The ability to modernize organizational structures, foster strategic alliances, and proactively address the challenges posed by technological disruption will be crucial in securing their role as effective representatives of the workforce. The following section delves into concrete strategies for trade union adaptation in the 21st century, outlining key approaches that will enable labor organizations to navigate digital transformation, strengthen institutional resilience, and enhance their advocacy in the face of unprecedented workplace changes.

Strategies for Trade Union Adaptation in the 21st Century

To successfully address the profound challenges of this era, trade unions in Spain must assume centered key strategies on adaptation, evolution, awareness, problem-solving, and resilience. Foremost, it is imperative that unions modernize and restructure their internal frameworks to become more agile and responsive to technological, environmental, political, social, economic, legal, and cultural shifts. This modernization may entail the adoption of specialized software for planning, implementation, evaluation, monitoring, and communication, which would enhance their capacity to engage with an increasingly dispersed and diverse workforce.

Consequently, it is crucial for unions to integrate hybrid organizational models into their core structure, seamlessly combining both physical and digital interactions while fostering collaborative environments that encourage member participation (Bayón Pérez & Llorden Rujas, 2023). In this regard, a particularly effective strategy is the development of interactive platforms that strengthen communication, mediation, conflict management, and lifelong learning, thereby personalizing the experience of each user (Arévalo-Martínez, 2021).

Secondly, labor organizations must actively develop strategic alliances with other social actors, including technology companies, educational institutions, and governmental bodies. These collaborations can facilitate access to crucial information and resources, enabling unions to assume a more proactive role in shaping labor policies. By fostering co-production frameworks, key stakeholders can guide the transition process, with labor organizations playing a critical role in the design, implementation, and oversight of ethical and sustainable solutions (Chew & Zainal, 2024).

For instance, trade unions could collaborate with artificial intelligence developers to implement tools that optimize their internal processes, develop predictive analytics for labor disputes, or enable early detection of discriminatory practices within public and private organizations. Additionally, the establishment of "union innovation incubators" would provide union members and leaders with experimental spaces to explore technology-driven solutions that could later be expanded internationally (Barranco, Alós & Molina, 2022).

A third key approach is the internationalization of trade union strategies. AI and digitalization are global phenomena, and Spanish unions could benefit from partnerships with international counterparts facing similar challenges. The exchange of best practices, shared learning experiences, and coordinated efforts at the European or global level could enhance unions' ability to influence policies and regulatory frameworks. Consequently, a highly effective strategy is the formation of multilateral alliances that facilitate knowledge transfer and the development of joint strategies (Polo, 2022).

Fourth, it is imperative that unions invest significantly in the training and capacity-building of their leaders and members, with a strong focus on competencies such as critical thinking, digital ethics, and leadership in technology-driven environments. A viable model for this initiative could be the establishment of digital trade union academies, offering modular courses tailored to workers' varying levels of expertise. These educational entities could leverage emerging technologies such as adaptive learning systems, ensuring that content delivery is personalized and that participants progress at their own pace.

Moreover, training programs should incorporate awareness modules addressing gender considerations, generational differences, and cultural factors in the adoption of these technologies. This holistic approach would ensure that labor organizations remain inclusive and sensitive to the diverse workforce realities shaped by digital transformation.

Finally, trade unions must prioritize ethical concerns regarding the use of super-intelligent systems. This responsibility entails ensuring that AI-driven implementations remain fair, equitable, and aligned with fundamental human values, while prioritizing worker well-being. Trade unions can position themselves as advocates for responsible AI deployment, emphasizing the protection of human dignity and the promotion of integral human development, rather than simply enabling more efficient processes.

By assuming this role, unions can help establish regulatory frameworks that prevent AI from becoming a tool of unchecked economic optimization, instead fostering its use as an instrument for enhancing workplace fairness, inclusivity, and long-term sustainability.

As trade unions refine their strategies to navigate the complexities of digital transformation, their role extends beyond adaptation and modernization. The ethical implications of artificial intelligence in labor relations present an urgent challenge that requires proactive engagement from worker organizations. Ensuring that AI-driven processes align with fundamental human rights, fairness, and transparency is paramount in shaping a just and inclusive labor market. Therefore, unions must not only advocate for equitable technological transitions but also establish themselves as key actors in defining ethical frameworks that regulate AI deployment in the workplace. The following section delves into the critical intersection of ethics and AI governance in labor contexts, examining the responsibilities of trade unions in safeguarding workers' rights, promoting algorithmic transparency, and mitigating the risks associated with automated decision-making.

Ethics and AI Governance in Labor Contexts

The implementation of advanced algorithms in union and organizational contexts poses significant ethical and social challenges. A clear example lies in decision-making processes for critical operations, which could exacerbate existing inequalities and create new forms of exclusion.

For instance, the use of automated systems that intrusively monitor worker performance, infringing on their privacy, or that employ opaque, subjective, or biased criteria to manage hiring and termination decisions, risks undermining transparency and impartiality (Ginès i Fabrellas, 2021).

To address these challenges, unions have a vital role to play in ensuring that technological advancements in workplaces are implemented with a commitment to ethical governance, safeguarding both workers' rights and societal values.

In this context, worker associations play a fundamental role as guarantors of labor justice. Their efforts must focus on the active promotion of ethical and responsible AI use, which includes influencing the design, implementation, and oversight of these systems to ensure they respect fundamental rights such as privacy, equal opportunities, digital disconnection, and dignity in employment (Almohalla Burguillo, 2022).

The representation and advocacy for clear regulations and participation in ethical committees on technology and labor are essential. To achieve this, it is critical to incorporate these concerns as an indispensable element in collective bargaining agreements. This would ensure access to detailed information about how these systems are designed and operate, including the data they use, the decisions they make, and any potential biases they might integrate. Additionally, unions must advocate for the establishment of independent, external auditing mechanisms to periodically evaluate all these aspects.

One of the most pressing challenges for unions is addressing the risks associated with the dehumanization of labor decisions. Delegating critical decisions to automated systems risks removing qualitative and contextual factors that are vital for fair and balanced management. To counteract this, unions must consistently work to preserve human oversight in significant processes and promote the principle of "complementary AI" instead of "substitutive AI." This principle emphasizes using AI tools to enhance human efficiency rather than replace it indiscriminately.

Worker representatives are uniquely positioned to lead the development of ethical labor technologies from their inception. Through active participation in the design of intelligent systems, they can ensure that these technologies reflect values such as justice, inclusion, and equity (Pardo Beneyto & Abellán López, 2024). Collaborating closely with AI developers and experts, unions can co-create algorithms that promote diversity in hiring processes or proactively identify discriminatory or illegal practices in the workplace.

This approach highlights the growing importance of concepts such as algorithmic fairness, transparency, and the right to challenge automated decisions, which carry significant social responsibility (Severino-González, Duque-Orozco, & Villar-Olaeta, 2021). In the corporate domain, this entails ensuring that workers are informed about how automated decisions impact their employment and providing them with clear and accessible channels to question or appeal these decisions.

By championing these initiatives, unions can solidify their role as key advocates for ethical governance in the workplace, bridging technological advancements with the fundamental values of justice and equity.

Ethical governance in this domain is not only a technical challenge but also a strategic imperative for modern trade unionism (Miguélez, Alós, & Molina, 2021). In an environment where emerging technologies have the potential to profoundly reshape labor relations, unions must position themselves as leaders in advocating for algorithmic models that prioritize workers' constitutional rights and promote inclusive technological development.

The collaborative efforts between trade unions, businesses, and the state can enhance corporate reputation in the global labor market, facilitating talent attraction and retention while ensuring strict legal compliance. This cooperation not only strengthens labor rights but also bolsters economic growth and employment sustainability (Pisanty Baruch & Velasco Sánchez, 2021).

Furthermore, it is imperative that unions lead by example in the ethical use of technology within their own internal processes. By leveraging the advantages of artificial intelligence to optimize operations and decision-making, they must uphold principles of transparency, privacy, and equity. This approach will not only reinforce their legitimacy as key defenders of these values but will also provide them with greater credibility when advocating for similar standards across industries.

As artificial intelligence becomes increasingly embedded in workplace governance, the ethical considerations surrounding its deployment demand a proactive and principled response from trade unions. Ensuring transparency, fairness, and accountability in algorithmic decision-making is not only a technical necessity but a moral imperative that unions must champion to safeguard workers' rights and uphold social justice. However, as AI systems evolve towards greater autonomy and complexity, the ethical challenges will extend beyond traditional regulatory frameworks, necessitating a deeper reflection on the implications of superintelligent systems in labor relations. The following section explores the role of trade unionism in the age of superintelligence, examining how worker organizations can lead the development of ethical safeguards, advocate for human-centered AI policies, and assert their relevance in a rapidly changing technological landscape.

Legal Framework of Artificial Intelligence: Equality, Bias, and Regulation in Spain and the European Union

The advent of Artificial Intelligence (AI) has engendered profound transformations in the ways in which societies organize economic activities, exercise public policies, and uphold fundamental rights. This phenomenon has particularly raised critical legal challenges in the domains of equality and bias, which demand a meticulous analysis of the existing legal frameworks at both the national level in Spain and the broader European Union (EU). The integration of AI in sectors such as labor relations, public administration, and service delivery has intensified concerns regarding algorithmic opacity, discriminatory decision-making, and the potential for exacerbating structural inequalities. In response, legal scholars and regulators have underscored the imperative of establishing robust regulatory mechanisms that ensure transparency, accountability, and the safeguarding of equality rights in the age of digital transformation (Bustillos et al., 2024).

Central to this analysis is the recognition that AI systems, if not subject to rigorous legal oversight, can inadvertently perpetuate or even amplify existing biases. Algorithms developed without sufficient ethical and legal scrutiny may operate as vehicles for both direct and indirect discrimination, impacting access to employment, public services, and social protection. At the heart of this issue lies the challenge of ensuring that automated systems respect the constitutional guarantees of equality and non-discrimination. In Spain, the Constitution and subsequent statutory instruments, such as the Organic Law for Effective Equality between Women and Men, provide a robust legal framework aimed at the prevention of discriminatory practices (Moreno, 2019). However, the unprecedented capabilities of AI to process vast amounts of data and influence decision-making processes necessitate the evolution of these traditional legal safeguards to address the nuanced and often opaque mechanisms through which bias may be introduced and perpetuated.

At the European level, the regulatory environment is being reshaped by initiatives such as the proposed Artificial Intelligence Act, which seeks to establish a harmonized framework for the development, deployment, and oversight of AI technologies (European Commission, 2021). This legislative proposal is characterized by its risk-based approach, whereby AI applications are categorized according to their potential impact on fundamental rights and public safety. High-risk AI systems are subject to stringent requirements regarding transparency, human oversight, and robustness against discriminatory outcomes. These provisions are designed not only to mitigate potential harms but also to ensure that AI-driven decision-making adheres to the principles enshrined in the Charter of Fundamental Rights of the European Union and other related legal instruments, such as the General Data Protection Regulation (GDPR). The GDPR, with its emphasis on data protection, transparency, and accountability, serves as a complementary regulatory tool that reinforces the legal obligations of entities deploying AI systems, particularly concerning the processing of sensitive personal data that could be used in discriminatory ways (GDPR, 2016).

The interplay between Spanish national law and EU regulations creates a dynamic legal landscape in which the principles of equality, fairness, and accountability must be continuously reinterpreted considering emerging technologies. Spanish jurisprudence has gradually evolved to recognize that the algorithmic decision-making inherent in many AI systems poses novel challenges to traditional legal doctrines. For example, when automated systems are used in employment decisions, such as recruitment or performance evaluation, there is an inherent risk that these systems may replicate historical patterns of discrimination if the data on which they are trained contain biases (Robles Carrillo, 2024). In this context, the legal obligation to ensure equal treatment extends to the technical design and operational transparency of AI systems. Legal analysts have argued that such systems must be subject to independent audits and that the criteria used by AI algorithms should be publicly accessible to allow for effective judicial and administrative review. This approach aligns with the broader European emphasis on algorithmic accountability, which calls for mechanisms that enable individuals to challenge decisions made by AI systems and to seek redress in instances where their rights are adversely affected (Pardo & Abellán, 2024).

Furthermore, the legal discourse surrounding AI in Spain and the EU increasingly recognizes the necessity of a proactive regulatory approach. It is no longer sufficient for legal frameworks to react to violations after they occur; rather, regulatory bodies must anticipate potential risks and embed preventive measures into the design and implementation of AI systems. This proactive stance is reflected in the emphasis on "ethical by design" principles, which mandate that considerations of fairness, non-discrimination, and human dignity be integrated from the inception of AI development (Costanza & Peliza, 2024). In this regard, both Spanish and European legislators are called upon to promote cross-disciplinary collaborations that bring together legal scholars, technologists, ethicists, and policymakers. Such collaborations are essential for developing standards and best practices that can guide the responsible integration of AI into societal frameworks without compromising the values of equality and social justice.

Moreover, the challenge of ensuring legal compliance in the realm of AI is compounded by the transnational nature of technology. AI systems often operate across borders, making it difficult to confine regulatory oversight within traditional national boundaries. The EU's efforts to create a cohesive legal framework serve as a model for addressing these cross-border challenges, as the proposed AI Act seeks to establish uniform rules that apply across all member states (European Commission, 2021). This harmonization is crucial not only for protecting the rights of citizens but also for fostering a competitive and innovative digital market that respects ethical standards. In Spain, national authorities are increasingly aligning their regulatory strategies with those emerging at the EU level, thereby ensuring that the country's legal system can address the complexities introduced by AI. The convergence of national and supranational legal norms is, therefore, a critical factor in promoting a legal environment that is both dynamic and resilient in the face of technological change (Bustillos et al., 2024).

In addition, the legal regulation of AI in relation to equality and bias constitutes a multifaceted challenge that demands an integrative approach at both the national and European levels. The emerging legal frameworks reflect a growing consensus that traditional legal doctrines must be re-examined and updated to account for the unique risks posed by algorithmic decision-making. By embedding principles of transparency, accountability, and ethical design into the regulatory fabric, both Spain and the EU are endeavouring to safeguard fundamental rights in an era characterized by rapid technological advancement. The ongoing dialogue between legal theory and technological innovation will undoubtedly shape the future of AI regulation, ensuring that advancements in AI serve as instruments for social progress rather than as catalysts for new forms of inequality.

Finally, s artificial intelligence systems continue to evolve towards increasing levels of autonomy and complexity, the legal frameworks that govern them must adapt accordingly to prevent emerging risks that could undermine fundamental labor rights and social equity. While existing regulations in Spain and the European Union have laid the groundwork for mitigating bias and discrimination in AI applications, the rapid expansion of algorithmic decision-making in labor relations introduces new governance challenges that transcend traditional legal mechanisms. The capacity of AI to influence hiring processes, workplace monitoring, and collective bargaining structures requires a broader approach that goes beyond regulatory compliance, one that actively incorporates ethical, social, and labor perspectives into the governance of these technologies. In this context, the role of trade unions becomes increasingly relevant, not only as advocates for transparency and fairness in AI-driven labor policies but also as key actors in shaping the ethical foundations of AI governance. The rise of superintelligent systems presents an unprecedented shift in power dynamics between workers, employers, and technology itself, necessitating a proactive stance from labor organizations to ensure that AI remains a tool for empowerment rather than one of control and exclusion. As AI-driven decision-making becomes more sophisticated, questions surrounding accountability, worker representation in algorithmic oversight, and the ethical limits of automation in labor markets become critical.

Thus, trade unions must evolve beyond their traditional roles and engage in multidimensional strategies that integrate legal, ethical, and technological expertise to safeguard workers' interests in an era of advanced AI. The following section delves into these pressing concerns, exploring how labor organizations can position themselves at the forefront of AI governance, advocate for human-centered regulatory frameworks, and redefine their influence in a labor landscape increasingly shaped by algorithmic intelligence and automation.

Trade Unionism and Ethical Governance in the Age of Superintelligence

Within the framework of the international labor market, various trade union and academic proposals have emerged to address the ethical and social challenges posed by the integration of artificial intelligence (AI) into contemporary work environments. These initiatives aim to mitigate the risks inherent in automation and the deployment of advanced systems in human resource management, ensuring that sustainable policies prioritize human dignity, equity, and social justice across economic sectors (Galian, Licata, & Stern-Plaza, 2022).

As AI-driven governance continues to evolve, the role of trade unions in shaping responsible and human-centered technology policies will be pivotal in defining the future of labor relations.

In this context, UNI Global Union has developed a multidimensional approach urging trade union organizations to advocate for technological governance that respects fundamental rights (Robles, 2024). This framework promotes transparency in automated decision-making systems, ensuring that workers have the right to clear information about algorithmic processes that affect them and encouraging their participation in the design and implementation of these technologies (Costanza Sardegna & Peliza, 2024).

Simultaneously, the European Trade Union Confederation (ETUC) has proposed a set of ethical principles aimed at ensuring that digital tools—especially those based on artificial intelligence—respect privacy and dignity in the workplace. A key recommendation includes the incorporation of specific technology-related clauses in collective bargaining agreements (Sáez, 2022).

Additionally, the International Labour Organization (ILO) has adopted a tripartite approach, convening representatives from governments, employers, and trade unions to draft guidelines regulating AI use in labor relations. This initiative seeks to promote an inclusive environment, ensuring equal opportunities, preventing discrimination, and fostering social cooperation and dialogue as fundamental pillars of ethical governance (Moreno, 2019).

As trade unions and international organizations continue to advocate for ethical governance frameworks in the era of AI-driven labor relations, the challenge now lies in translating these overarching principles into actionable policies tailored to specific industries and regional contexts. While global initiatives provide a foundational blueprint for responsible AI implementation, sector-specific strategies are essential to address the unique challenges posed by automation, algorithmic management, and digital transformation in different labor markets. The following section explores sector-specific and regional initiatives in AI and labor rights, highlighting how unions across various industries and geographical regions are developing targeted approaches to ensure fair, inclusive, and sustainable technological transitions.

Sector-Specific and Regional Initiatives in AI and Labor Rights

At the sectoral level, the International Transport Workers' Federation (ITF) has launched a campaign aimed at regulating digital systems in the transport and logistics sector, ensuring fair and balanced working conditions amid the growing influence of AI-driven tools. This initiative prioritizes operational transparency and socio-legal protection for workers (Köhler, 2020).

In Italy, the Italian Confederation of Trade Unions has spearheaded a strategic coalition that analyzes the impact of automation on employment and proposes specific adaptation measures. One of its primary strategies is the promotion of lifelong learning as a key tool for equipping workers with relevant skills aligned with organizational needs (Guaglianone, 2020).

In Spain, the Comisiones Obreras (CCOO) union has established an observatory dedicated to the systematic analysis and evaluation of AI's impact on labor rights. This observatory relies on big data analysis to provide objective evidence, supporting more effective negotiations aimed at strengthening workers' rights.

In Africa, a South African union project focuses on social inclusion by designing technological systems that reduce employment barriers for disadvantaged groups. This initiative strongly emphasizes the creation of inclusive digital solutions, particularly in developing countries, ensuring that technology serves as a bridge to opportunity rather than a source of exclusion (Asociación Española de Derecho del Trabajo y de la Seguridad Social, 2023).

In France, the General Confederation of Labor (CGT) has developed a Charter aimed at ensuring that superintelligent systems used in businesses respect workers' rights and do not incorporate discriminatory biases in automated decision-making processes.

In contrast, in the United Kingdom, the Trades Union Congress (TUC) has demanded greater access for labor representatives to the data and technological systems used in workforce management. This initiative underscores total transparency as a guiding principle for ethical governance (Sharfaei, 2024).

Ultimately, these initiatives represent a collective effort to ensure that the evolution of workplace technology remains aligned with the principles of equality, equity, and inclusion. While sector-specific and regional initiatives provide critical frameworks for addressing the challenges of AI-driven labor transformation, a broader and more integrative vision is necessary to ensure that technology enhances, rather than erodes, the human dimension of work. Beyond regulatory measures and transparency efforts, unions must play a proactive role in shaping an organizational culture that harmonizes technological advancement with core human values such as dignity, inclusivity, and well-being. The following section explores union leadership in the construction of a humanistic and technological organizational culture, examining how worker organizations can drive ethical and sustainable digital transitions while fostering a sense of belonging, collaboration, and social responsibility within the evolving workplace.

Union Leadership in the Construction of a Humanistic and Technological Organizational Culture

Labor organizations possess the potential to be far more than mere advocates for social rights; they can also serve as architects of an innovative and value-driven organizational culture that harmonizes individuals and technologies for mutual benefit. Through a proactive, collaborative, and strategic approach, unionism can lead the way toward a future of work that prioritizes well-being without forgoing the opportunities presented by the Fourth Industrial Revolution (Carrau, Muñoz, González, Molina, Díaz, Brenes, & Rodríguez, 2021).

To fulfill this transformative role, several practical strategies may be implemented. First, the periodic review of algorithmic systems should be encouraged to identify, mitigate, or eliminate biases within human capital management. In alignment with this objective, fostering collaboration with leading enterprises and organizations can ensure adherence to the principles of equality, inclusion, integration, diversity, and regulatory compliance. Within this framework, education emerges as a critical and unparalleled instrument for internalizing, comprehending, and catalyzing constructive changes. Consequently, the design of campaigns, programs, workshops, seminars, and contributions to formal training curricula—such as vocational education, undergraduate, and graduate programs—becomes essential. Such initiatives should aim to equip human talent with the competencies necessary for the responsible use of technology, an understanding of their labor rights and obligations, and the safeguarding of their privacy and autonomy in the digital sphere (Azpiazu & Bayón, 2022).

Hybrid work environments serve as catalysts for redefining corporate culture through a humanistic, collaborative, and cooperative perspective, wherein the role of union action is to foster constructive cohesion through social dialogue, as well as to design and implement initiatives, plans, and programs that reinforce a sense of belonging. This is achieved through a combination of virtual and in-person interactions that nurture interpersonal relationships (Barrio, 2023). Within this framework, it is imperative to promote a balance between personal, family, professional, and technological life, ensuring that various policies are designed to enhance mental health. Examples include initiatives that support digital disconnection and provide psychological assistance (Aggarwal, 2024).

Additionally, productivity measurement must undergo certain modifications. Key performance indicators should prioritize qualitative impact and human development over mere efficiency. This approach results in a tripartite gain, as it aligns with corporate social responsibility, resonates with governmental policies pursuing the same objectives, and ultimately contributes to the construction of an unparalleled employer brand with a transformative societal purpose. A culture that upholds organizational justice fosters a positive work environment, enhances job satisfaction, and mitigates counterproductive behaviors such as excessive turnover and undesired absenteeism (Gutiérrez Ordóñez & León Pullaguari, 2023).

Similarly, unions and labor organizations can play a pivotal role in guiding companies and institutions to reconsider the very essence of human well-being. This involves, among other aspects, the reskilling and adaptation of human capital through digital tools rather than its mere replacement. Furthermore, collaboration is crucial in the creation of new occupations and responsibilities that integrate values such as sustainability, sound leadership, cooperation, and continuous, evolutionary learning. Likewise, by embracing the concept of 360º diversity, technology can facilitate integration, accessibility, and adaptation to individual needs, particularly for individuals with diverse abilities or those residing in disadvantaged or underdeveloped regions.

Moreover, as agents of social, labor, and cultural transformation, worker organizations play a fundamental role in collaborating with national and international entities to regulate the impact of these transformations, ensuring legal, labor, and business security (Bustillos Ortega et al., 2024).

In a similar vein, through the integration and internalization of humanistic values, labor organizations can undertake a series of actions that set an example and enhance their visibility and capacity for raising awareness. Among these initiatives, they may include the dissemination of success stories in which executives, leaders, workers, and collaborators share their experiences and implementation processes; the organization of academic events that showcase research findings from specific projects in this domain; the proposal of research projects within universities, enabling in-depth exploration, resource allocation, and the integration of scientific dissemination; the establishment of awards recognizing innovation in union, organizational, and institutional contexts with a humanistic perspective; the production of audiovisual content, such as educational documentaries; and the creation of mentorship and coaching networks to support and guide this process.

Furthermore, proposing the establishment of a cultural committee or cultural ambassador teams can yield highly fruitful results. The primary objective of this initiative is to foster, safeguard, preserve, and protect the values and practices that embody the essence of organizations, which is crucial for strengthening their identity as employer brands and mitigating the risks posed by internal and external changes. In this regard, a committee composed of diverse participants serves as a driving force for a coherent, cohesive, and shared corporate culture (Cordero Guzmán, Beltrán Tenorio, & Bermeo Pazmiño, 2022). Some of the key functions this committee may undertake include fostering team-building efforts, serving as a liaison between teams and leadership, promoting a positive work climate, supporting onboarding, integration, consolidation, offboarding, disengagement, and transition processes, identifying and managing potential labor disputes, facilitating the communication of policies and best practices, and evaluating and proposing improvements aimed at strengthening, enriching, and consolidating organizational culture.

Finally, it is essential to highlight the broad avenues available for various stakeholders, wherein labor representatives can adopt a proactive role in constructing a labor market that is secure, equitable, diverse, dynamic, and sustainable. In this context, they must act as mediators and catalysts of change, while also setting an example of responsibility, ethics, transparency, solidarity, and humanization for their affiliates, companies, and the state. As unions take on a transformative leadership role in shaping a humanistic and technologically balanced organizational culture, their capacity to implement effective strategies becomes crucial in ensuring long-term sustainability and impact. The proactive integration of ethical digital transitions, inclusive workplace policies, and value-driven innovation underscores the importance of unions as agents of social and economic stability. However, to translate these ideals into tangible outcomes, unions must also develop practical, action-oriented frameworks that enable them to remain relevant and influential in an ever-changing labor landscape. The following section explores practical recommendations for unions, providing concrete strategies that will allow labor organizations to strengthen their advocacy, enhance their operational effectiveness, and foster meaningful engagement with workers in the digital era.

Practical Recommendations for Unions to Remain Relevant in an Ever-Changing Environment

Unions have innovative alternatives that enable them to consolidate their role as exemplary actors in fostering constructive and conciliatory social dialogue while also seizing opportunities to generate a positive impact on the labor and organizational landscape. This process may range from the automation of repetitive and autonomous processes—including the expedited registration of potential affiliates—to the redefinition of key performance indicators for union activity. These indicators can be both quantitative and qualitative, including satisfaction indices, corporate cohesion metrics, and case studies.

To enhance transparency and accessibility, a viable project would be the development of applications and platforms that allow workers to actively participate in union decision-making while also providing them with relevant information in an effective and efficient manner. Additionally, implementing initiatives that connect workers across generations to facilitate the transfer of practical and cultural knowledge is both essential and strategic. Such an approach fosters team cohesion and promotes lifelong, collaborative, cooperative, and shared learning. For instance, in the logistics sector, an optimization course on route planning could be designed, where experienced professionals contribute their expertise while younger generations complement it with updated knowledge of digital mapping tools. Similarly, in energy companies, it is common practice to implement hackathons aimed at generating ideas for integrating artificial intelligence into resource management, thereby combining the technical experience of senior professionals with the technological proficiency of younger workers (Sajja et al., 2025).

Another highly relevant initiative involves the creation of global networks for union collaboration, enabling the exchange of best practices, resources, and adaptive strategies in response to ongoing advancements. This not only strengthens unions' strategic positioning but also enhances their responsiveness to global phenomena. Moreover, exponentially fostering innovation presents numerous opportunities and advantages, among which the establishment of union innovation laboratories stands out. These spaces provide a platform for collaboration among labor organizations, businesses, governmental entities, and technology experts, facilitating the co-creation of organizational and institutional policies as well as the development of tools that benefit all stakeholders.

Amid the broad array of options available for unions to advance, adapt, and enhance their resilience, a fundamental priority must be the holistic well-being of human capital. This should remain the central focus of all initiatives, integrating advisory services on proper nutrition, mental health, physical well-being, and financial-economic management.

To achieve successful outcomes, responsiveness and agility are fundamental. Consequently, labor organizations must embrace more horizontal structures, enhance self-management, and integrate multidisciplinary teams, which in turn fosters greater proactivity and operational resilience. Additionally, leveraging large volumes of data is essential for gaining a comprehensive understanding of reality, identifying the needs and expectations of both current and potential affiliates, as well as those of society at large (Flores-Cerna et al., 2022).

Furthermore, over the past decades, social media has experienced exponential growth in activity, becoming a globalized tool and an integral part of everyday life for new generations. Given this reality, visionary leadership, strategic communication, and proactive engagement on social platforms are crucial for unions as key social actors working toward labor, human, economic, and financial development. Much like personal and employer branding, unions must cultivate their own brand, ensuring the effective dissemination of their activities, strategic objectives, values, initiatives, and organizational social responsibility efforts.

In human talent training programs, both internally and externally, education serves as a key driver of sustainability. Accordingly, one of the most critical transversal competencies is the ability to negotiate, communicate effectively and persuasively, and engage in mediation. In this regard, the establishment of dedicated mechanisms for conflict mediation would prove highly beneficial in reducing labor disputes and fostering a more constructive work environment (Espinoza Tuárez et al., 2024).

Finally, within their scope of activities, unions can actively promote educational initiatives in green economies, including industrial recycling, renewable energy, and other emerging sectors.

As unions adapt to the evolving labor landscape through innovation, strategic collaboration, and proactive engagement, their ability to remain effective hinges on the strength and vision of their leadership. Implementing technological solutions, fostering global networks, and promoting well-being initiatives are essential steps, but without strong and adaptable leadership, these efforts risk losing impact. Union leaders must not only embrace digital transformation but also cultivate inclusive, forward-thinking, and resilient leadership models that can guide workers through the challenges of the Fourth Industrial Revolution. The following section delves into strategies for strengthening union leadership, examining how modern unions can empower their representatives, enhance decision-making capabilities, and foster dynamic leadership that aligns with the needs of an increasingly complex and digitalized world.

Strengthening Union Leadership

By leading digital training programs, labor unions enhance their relevance and collaboration within the labor ecosystem while solidifying their position as advocates for comprehensive human development. This approach generates a positive impact not only on workers but also on businesses and society as a whole. Consequently, it constitutes a long-term strategy aimed at transforming a visionary framework into an accessible reality. In this way, leadership serves as the driving force behind a development model that links business growth with the well-being of human talent. By supporting retraining and continuous education programs in critical and high-demand areas, unions contribute to improving workers' employability while fostering greater productivity and competitiveness within companies. This direct, responsible, and sustainable effort strengthens the perception of unions as essential allies in shared prosperity. From a social perspective, such initiatives also yield significant advantages, including reductions in overall unemployment rates, particularly in cases of long-term unemployment, as well as decreases in employee turnover and absenteeism rates.

Finally, the transformative impact of achieving these objectives is reflected across multiple dimensions:

Greater global competitiveness: A highly skilled and adaptable workforce enables companies to enhance their capacity for innovation and strengthen their positioning in global markets (Ricci-Caballo et al., 2024).

Reduced pressure on public spending: A dynamic labor market characterized by lower unemployment rates and increased efficiency alleviates the fiscal burden associated with social benefits and pensions.

By leading with vision and adapting to the demands of a rapidly evolving environment, labor unions not only reinforce their historical legitimacy but also establish themselves as vital actors in advancing societal progress.

CONCLUSIONS

In the context of superintelligence, both significant challenges and opportunities arise, transforming labor and organizational dynamics. Worker representatives, far from maintaining a purely traditional role, have the potential to evolve into agents of constructive change, capable of driving a corporate culture that integrates human and technological factors as sources of competitive advantage (Arenas & Bayón, 2020). To achieve this, it is essential to establish a solid strategic plan that not only addresses current demands but also anticipates future needs. This plan must include initiatives focused on the comprehensive development of human talent, incorporating flexible programs that cover both transversal competencies—such as effective communication, problem-solving, and critical thinking—and specialized skills in emerging technological fields, including basic programming, data analysis, and cybersecurity. Furthermore, it is imperative to implement professional reconversion projects that provide tools for identifying skill gaps, promote the development of new competencies, and facilitate workforce mobility toward sectors with higher employability.

A strategic approach must also integrate a communication and human resource management plan that fosters transparency, strengthens team cohesion in hybrid environments, and promotes a balance between professional, personal, and digital life. The incorporation of innovative methodologies, such as gamification and microlearning, can maximize the effectiveness of these programs by making them more accessible and engaging for a diverse workforce. In this regard, strategic alliances with technical, educational, and public institutions play a crucial role, as they can enhance the implementation of these initiatives and ensure their long-term sustainability.

Additionally, the appropriate support of artificial intelligence can optimize union operations, enhance representativeness, and improve efficiency across all processes while reinforcing relevance and participation. To this end, it is imperative to ensure that digital tools adhere to fundamental principles of equality, equity, inclusion, and sustainability. Moreover, union leadership must be oriented toward a labor transition that prioritizes human capital well-being, leveraging tools such as Big Data analytics and predictive models to design and implement evidence-based strategies. This proactive and well-founded approach positions unionism as an ethical and transformative force in building a more equitable, inclusive, and resilient labor future.

Furthermore, unions must lead by example, adopting non-negotiable standards of transparency, ethics, and regulatory compliance as the cornerstones of their operations. Their role as strategic partners for businesses in interpreting and applying labor regulations presents a unique opportunity to guide the development of stronger and more responsible organizational environments. By providing expert guidance and fostering ethical business practices, these organizations can profoundly reshape the labor landscape. A committed approach in this regard would help safeguard the fundamental rights of human capital while also strengthening employer branding, thereby improving talent attraction and retention in an increasingly competitive market.

Lastly, their ability to facilitate a positive work climate—rooted in mutual respect and commitment—serves as a catalyst for consolidating a modern, inclusive organizational culture aligned with the emerging needs of the 21st century. In doing so, unions position themselves as key actors in the evolution of the labor ecosystem and co-creators of a work model that harmonizes and integrates the synergies of technological innovation with human well-being, projecting a labor, business, and social future that is both highly efficient and ethically sustainable.

REFERENCES

Acemoglu, D., & Restrepo, P. (2019). Automation and new tasks: How technology displaces and reinstates labor. *The Journal of Economic Perspectives*, *33*(2), 3–30. DOI: 10.1257/jep.33.2.3

Aggarwal, S. (2024). A study of the relationship between organizational culture and psychological capital and its impact through a systematic literature review. *Journal of Human Values*, *30*(2), 105–118. Advance online publication. DOI: 10.1177/09716858231172440

Aguinis, H., Ramani, R. S., & Alabduljader, N. (2020). What you see is what you get? Enhancing methodological transparency in management research. *The Academy of Management Annals*, *14*(1), 1–65.

Almohalla, J. M. (2022). Ethical leadership: A challenge of our time. Supervision 21, 59, 4. https://super.a-nosotros.es/ind.ph/Español/artículo//rivalizar/533

Arenas, A. J., & Bayón, J. (2020). Human talent and organizational change in telecommunications companies: Madrid-Spain. [University of Zulia.]. *Venezuelan Journal of Management*, *25*(92), 1463–1477.

Arenas, A. J., & Bayón, J. (2021). Labour force, suspended rights and entrepreneurs' disruption of activities. In Global Pandemic, Technology and Business (pp. 179–199). Routledge.

Arévalo-Martínez, R.-I. (2021). Digital communication for organizations and social responsibility. *Syntax*, •••, 16–29. DOI: 10.36105/stx.2021edesp50aniv.01

Azpiazu, G., & Bayón, J. (2022). Labor trends and the future of work through robotization, digitalization, and artificial intelligence in Spain. Critical Reason Journal, 12, 1–15. Jorge Tadeo Lozano University. https://www.redalyc.org/journal/6458/645877151005/645877151005.pdf

Barranco, O., Alós, R., & Molina, O. (2022). Innovation to represent: Workers with difficulties in collective representation and union strategies in Spain. *Labor Relations Notebooks*, *38*(2), 237–243. DOI: 10.5209/crla.77452

Barrio, J. M. (2003). Tolerance and the culture of dialogue. *Revista Española de Pedagogía*, *61*(224). https://www.revistadepedagogia.org/rep/vol61/iss224/2

Bayón, J., & Arenas, A. (2019). Diverse perspectives on challenges and changes in labor and human resources due to automation and artificial intelligence. *International Scientific Journal Academicus*, *20*, 106–118. DOI: 10.7336/academicus.2019.20.08

Bayón, J., Arenas, A. J., & Lominchar, J. (2022). The impact of new technologies on the workforce and labor legislation. *International Scientific Journal Academicus, 25*, 75–90. DOI: 10.7336/academicus.2022.25.05

Bayón Pérez, J., & Llorden Rujas, Á. (2023). Socio-legal analysis of teleworking: Global comparison, advances, and challenges. [University of Santander. https://revistas.udes.edu.co/aibi/article/view/analisis_socio-juridico_comparativa_de_forma_global_avances_y_retos]. *Journal of Research, Administration, and Engineering, 11*(1), 85–97.

BOE (Official State Gazette). (2023). Fifth Agreement for Employment and Collective Bargaining (AENC). Ministry of Labor and Social Economy, Spain. https://www.boe.es/diario_boe/txt.php?id=BOE-A-2023-12870

Boell, S. K., & Cecez-Kecmanovic, D. (2014). A hermeneutic approach for conducting literature reviews and literature searches. *Communications of the Association for Information Systems, 34*(1), 257–286. DOI: 10.17705/1CAIS.03412

Borden-Lanza, Y., Lores-Gómez, B., Usart-Rodríguez, M., & Colobrans-Delgado, J. (2023). Digital competence and vocational training in Spain: Documentary analysis on its regulation, proposals, and recommendations. Hachetetepé. *Scientific Journal in Education and Communication*, (26), 1–14. DOI: 10.25267/Hachetetepe.2023.i26.1204

Brynjolfsson, E., & McAfee, A. (2017). *Machine, Platform, Crowd: Harnessing Our Digital Future*. W. W. Norton & Company.

Burgueño Leiva, C. L. (2023). *Workers against Francoism and female unionism during the Spanish Transition: Gender battle and class struggle in double rupture (1960-1970). Trade Unionism, Conflict, and Direct Action in the Americas and Europe, from the Late 19th Century to the 1980s*. Ariadna Edition.

Bustillos, O., Murillo Gamboa, J., Núñez, O., & Rodríguez, F. (2024). Towards a regulatory framework for artificial intelligence (AI): Key considerations and international regulations. *Interfases, 20*, 137–162. DOI: 10.26439/interfases2024.n020.7178

Carrau, M. C., Muñoz, R. C., González, A. J., Molina, B. L., Díaz, E. R., Brenes, L. S., & Rodríguez, C. V. Z. (2021). *The social policies to come*. Aranzadi/Civitas.

Chew, T. C., & Zainal, S. R. M. (2024). A sustainable collaborative talent management through the theory of collaborative intelligence mindset: A systematic review. *SAGE Open, 14*(2), 21582440241261851. Advance online publication. DOI: 10.1177/21582440241261851

Chibás, F. (2015). *Creativity, communication, and culture: Innovative management of educational-cultural projects in the digital age*. Pueblo y Educación Publishing House.

Chica, Y., & Ruiz-Roqueñi, M. (2022). Trade union organizations as agents of collaborative change: The inclusive-participatory business model. CIRIEC-Spain. *Journal of Public, Social, and Cooperative Economy*, *105*, 145–175. DOI: 10.7203/CIRIEC-E.105.24224

Comisiones Obreras (CCOO). (2024). Observatory on AI and Labor Rights. Retrieved from https://www.ccoo.es

Cordero, D. M., Beltrán, N., & Bermeo, K. V. (2022). Organizational culture and emotional salary. Venezuelan Journal of Management (RVG), 27(Extra 7), 118–131.

Costanza, P., & Peliza, E. (2024). *Legal challenges in data governance and algorithmic opacity in employment*. International and Comparative Journal of Labor Relations and Employment Law.

Denzin, N. K., & Lincoln, Y. S. (2018). *The SAGE Handbook of Qualitative Research* (5th ed.). SAGE Publications.

Díaz, R. (2021). A common language for the reskilling revolution. Future for Work Institute. https://www.futureforwork.com/un-lenguaje-comun-para-la-revolucion-del-reskilling/

Echeverría, B., & Martínez, P. (2021). Towards a research ecosystem on vocational education in Spain. *The Journal of Educational Research*, *39*(1), 249–264. DOI: 10.6018/rie.424901

Espiau, G. (2022). Norms, values, and narratives of social innovation processes: The cultural dimension of the socio-economic transformation of Basque society (1978–2022).

Espinoza, Y. M., Menéndez, M. I., Ramírez, N. D., & Aguilera, Y. G. (2024). Key factors in auditing the human talent training and development subsystem. Science and Development. Alas Peruanas University. http://revistas.uap.edu.pe/ojs/index.php/CYD/index

European Commission. (2021). Proposal for a Regulation laying down harmonized rules on artificial intelligence (Artificial Intelligence Act) and amending certain Union legislative acts. Retrieved from https://eur-lex.europa.eu

Eurostat. (2024). Impact of Artificial Intelligence on European Labor Markets: Trends and Projections. European Statistical Office. https://ec.europa.eu/eurostat

Fernández-Trujillo, F. J. (2024). Labor conflict in platform capitalism: Challenges and opportunities for unionism in Spain. *Yearbook of Social Conflict*, *15*, e–45266. DOI: 10.1344/ACS2024.15.1

Fernández-Trujillo Moares, F. J. (2023). From precariousness to conflict: The case of digital food delivery platforms in Spain (Doctoral dissertation, National University of Distance Education). UNED.

Flick, U. (2022). *An Introduction to Qualitative Research* (7th ed.). SAGE Publications.

Flores-Cerna, F., Sanhueza-Salazar, V.-M., Valdés-González, H.-M., & Reyes-Bozo, L. (2022). Agile methodologies: An analysis of organizational challenges for their implementation. *Scientific Journal*, *43*, 1–20. DOI: 10.14483/23448350.18332

Freeman, R. B., & Medoff, J. L. (1984). *What Do Unions Do?* Basic Books.

Galian, C., Licata, M., & Stern-Plaza, M. (2022). Social protection in the culture and creative sector: Practices and innovations in selected countries (ILO Working Paper No. 28). International Labour Organization (ILO). https://doi.org/DOI: 10.54394/PVFP4517

General Data Protection Regulation (GDPR). (2016). [EU]. *Regulation*, *2016*(679). https://eur-lex.europa.eu

Gil, J. A. (2024). Educational inspection actions for the supervision of teaching-learning processes within the current regulatory framework from a neuroscience perspective. *Advances in Educational Supervision*, (42). Advance online publication. DOI: 10.23824/ase.v0i42.883

Ginès i Fabrellas, A. (2021). Working time on platforms: Absence of minimum working hours, gamification, and algorithmic insecurity. *LABOS Journal of Labor Law and Social Protection*, *2*(1), 19–42. DOI: 10.20318/labos.2021.6045

Guaglianone, L. (2020). Industry 4.0 and the participatory model: Social dialogue vs. civil dialogue? The impact on the Italian industrial relations system. *Labor Issues: Andalusian Journal of Work and Social Welfare*, (152), 97–113.

Gutiérrez, J. S., & León, M. F. (2023). Marketing and human talent in business culture. *Ciencia Latina Multidisciplinary Scientific Journal*, *7*(4), 1068–1079. DOI: 10.37811/cl_rcm.v7i4.6938

Köhler, H.-D. (2020). Labor relations in the platform economy. Sociology of Work, (96), 23. DOI: 10.5209/stra.69928

Krippendorff, K. (2018). *Content Analysis: An Introduction to Its Methodology* (4th ed.). SAGE Publications.

Machado, L., Nascimento Sabino Neves, V., & Silva do Nascimento, K. A. (2024). The use of microlearning in education: An overview of global scientific production. Edutec. *Electronic Journal of Educational Technology*, (88), 7–23. DOI: 10.21556/edutec.2024.88.3123

Marlapudi, K., & Lenka, U. (2024). *Unlocking potential: Redefining talent and mapping competencies for Industry 4.0.* Management Research Journal.

Microsoft & LinkedIn. (2024). *2024 Work Trend Index: Will AI Fix Work?* Microsoft Corporation.

Miguélez, F., Alós, R., & Molina, O. (2021). Governing employment changes in the digital revolution? *Politics & Society*, *58*(3), 71–122. DOI: 10.5209/poso.71122

Ministry of Industry. Trade and Tourism. (2024). SME Figures: Data on companies in Spain. https://industria.gob.es/es-es/estadisticas/Cifras_PYME/CifrasPYME-febrero2024.pdf

Moher, D., Liberati, A., Tetzlaff, J., & Altman, D. G.PRISMA Group. (2009). Preferred reporting items for systematic reviews and meta-analyses: The PRISMA statement. *PLoS Medicine*, *6*(7), e1000097. DOI: 10.1371/journal.pmed.1000097 PMID: 19621072

Molina, C. (2021). Duel in the digital sun: Is an algorithm controlling my job? Yes, and your company too. Journal of Labor and Social Security. *CEF*, (457), 5–21. DOI: 10.51302/rtss.2021.2370

Moreno Vida, M. de las N. (2019). The governance of labor relations. In AAVV, The Future of Work: One Hundred Years of the ILO. XXIX Annual Congress of the Spanish Association of Labor Law and Social Security (pp. 233–272). Ministry of Labor and Immigration and Technical General Secretariat. Publications Center. https://hdl.handle.net/10481/99720

Mukiur, M. R. (2019). Guide for the Worker Representative 4.0. http://hdl.handle.net/20.500.12226/224

Ortega, N. (2022). Microlearning as a didactic tool in the subject Microbiology I of the Veterinary Degree. *Annals of Veterinary Medicine of Murcia*, *36*. Advance online publication. DOI: 10.6018/analesvet.542361

Pardo, G., & Abellán, M. Á. (2024). *Ethical governance and sustainable development: A plural approach to public administration.* Catarata.

Pisanty, A., & Velasco, E. (2021). Fourth Industrial Revolution, government, and good governance. *Latin American Journal of Economy and Digital Society, 2*. Advance online publication. DOI: 10.53857/ALFT6819

Polo, J. F. P. (2022). *Culture and Knowledge Transfer: Key Factors for Innovation. Case Study*. Transnational Company in Querétaro.

Posso, R. J., Cóndor, M. G., Mora, L. M., & Segundo, R. M. (2023). Challenge-based learning: A perspective from higher education. Podium. *Journal of Science and Technology in Physical Culture, 18*(2).

Ramírez, A. A. (2024). Fundamentals of Business Success: Keys and Strategies. Sectoral Social Policies, 2(2), 467–489. https://politicassociales.uanl.mx/index.php/pss/article/view/104

Ricci-Caballo, B., Alonso-Díaz, L., & Deocano-Ruiz, Y. (2024). Employability, training, and key competencies: A theoretical review. In Fuentes, J. L., Fernández-Salinero, C., & Ahedo Ruiz, J. (Eds.), *Advances in contemporary pedagogy: Proposals for civic education and character education* (pp. 81–97). Dykinson., DOI: 10.14679/3111

Robles Carrillo, M. (2024). The governance of artificial intelligence: Context and general parameters. Electronic Journal of International Studies, (39). Retrieved from https://reei.tirant.com/reei/article/view/2989

Rodríguez Fernández, M. L. (2023). Trade Unionism and Collective Bargaining 4.0. Temas Laborales, 160, 23-48. Retrieved from https://dialnet.unirioja.es

Rosari, R., Danarilia, V. O., & Ardianto, H. (2024). Finding talent: What does talent management need to change? *Ilomata International Journal of Management, 5*(2), 649–668. DOI: 10.61194/ijjm.v5i2.1181

Sáez Lara, C. (2022). Algorithmic business management and collective protection of labor rights. *Labor Relations Notebooks, 40*(2), 283–300. DOI: 10.5209/crla.79417

Sajja, R., Erazo Ramirez, C., Li, Z., Demiray, B. Z., Sermet, Y., & Demir, I. (2025). Integrating generative AI in hackathons: Opportunities, challenges, and educational implications. *Big Data and Cognitive Computing, 9*(1), 1–20. https://doi.org/

Severino-González, P., Duque-Orozco, Y. V., & Villar-Olaeta, J. (2021, March). Perception of union leaders on corporate social responsibility: Challenges for strategic management. *Interciencia, 46*(3), 110–117. https://www.redalyc.org/journal/339/33966543004/33966543004.pdf

Sharfaei, S. (2024). Robots and employment: A literature review. *International Labour Review, 143*(2), 299–323. DOI: 10.1111/ilrs.12311

Spanish Association of Labor Law and Social Security (AEDTSS). (2023). XXXIII Annual Congress of AEDTSS: Employment and Social Protection. Cuenca, May 25–26, 2023.

Todolí, A. (2023). Productive and extractive algorithms: How to regulate digitalization to improve employment and incentivize innovation. Aranzadi Publishing House. https://adriantodoli.com/2023/04/19/algoritmos-productivos-y-extractivos

Unión General de Trabajadoras y Trabajadores (UGT). (2024). Recommendations for Collective Bargaining on AI. UGT Spain. https://www.ugt.es

Yin, R. K. (2018). *Case Study Research and Applications: Design and Methods* (6th ed.). SAGE Publications.

Chapter 7
Artificial Intelligence and Fundamental Rights:
The Role of Unions

Susana Beatriz Checa Prieto
https://orcid.org/0000-0003-0781-953X
Universidad Nebrija, Spain

ABSTRACT

The introduction of artificial intelligence (AI) systems into business management without adequate oversight could affect fundamental rights like privacy, data protection, equality, and occupational health. Algorithmic management could have discriminatory effects, especially on certain groups and workers. The presence of unions is necessary for incorporating the digital dimension into collective bargaining and for advancing regulatory reforms that advocate for the protection of workers' rights. These efforts could help mitigate risks by ensuring that all workers are treated fairly, regardless of their gender, race, political ideology, or other personal characteristics.

INTRODUCTION

The regulation of artificial intelligence (AI) in Europe is a consequence of the political commitment of the presidency of the European Union (EU), as expressed in its political guidelines for the Commission 2019-2024, which consider the ethical and human implications of AI (von der Leyen, n.d.). As noted by Barrio Andres (2018), the initial position of the European Commission was a soft law approach, proposing nonbinding ethical guidelines and recommendations. It was not until

DOI: 10.4018/979-8-3693-8049-9.ch007

2019 that the European Commission adopted a legal approach, which requested the adoption of harmonized legal rules regarding AI.

To conduct a minimal analysis of the legal background, we must refer to the documents immediately preceding the provisional agreement reached by the Council and the European Parliament last December 2023.

The European Commission has published several key documents addressing AI: the "White Paper on Artificial Intelligence: a European approach to excellence and trust", the "Report on the safety and liability implications of Artificial Intelligence, the Internet of Things and robotics." and The "White Paper on Artificial Intelligence: a European approach to excellence and trust". The policy choices to advance AI research in Europe while guaranteeing adherence to fundamental rights are delineated in these documents. It highlights the need of taking into account the environmental impact of AI systems and suggests actions to establish a "ecosystem of excellence" and a "ecosystem of trust" in order to prevent market fragmentation.

These serve as the foundation for further talks and consultations that aim to create a thorough regulatory framework for AI in the EU, guaranteeing that developments in technology are consistent with European ideals and fundamental rights.

The need for AI regulation is defended by authors like Scherer (2016), who highlighted the potential ineffectiveness of ex post regulation, especially if such a system poses catastrophic risk. The proposal offers an AI certification process in which manufacturers and operators of certified AI systems enjoy limited liability. On the other hand, noncertified AI systems face unlimited liability. Authors like Dans (2017) noted withholding legislation until the technology is developed is a better solution, as regulation tends to focus on restricting possibilities. This approach, in turn, considers potential dangers in cases of technological developments with high potential.

As stated in the *Charter of Fundamental Rights in the context of AI* and digital change, one of the major risks to fundamental rights stems from the opacity, complexity, bias, a certain degree of unpredictability, and partially autonomous behavior of certain AI systems. As a consequence, it is crucial to guarantee their conformity with fundamental rights and to make it easier to implement current legal standards.

Ensuring the safety and protection of citizens' rights in connection to the usage of AI systems within the EU is without a doubt the proposal's primary goal. Thus, the plan will cover both AI created in the EU and AI brought to the European market by nations outside of this framework. Its second goal is to encourage AI investment and innovation within the EU in order to prevent the EU from falling behind in AI development. This will help to create a single market that will guarantee the "legal, safe, and reliable use of AI applications and to avoid market fragmentation."

With dynamic and adaptable processes in line with technology advancement, the proposal takes a risk-based approach from a legal standpoint, customizing legal involvement to particular circumstances where there is a legitimate reason for concern.

Ensuring compliance with the EU Charter of Fundamental Rights, data protection laws, consumer protection, non-discrimination, and gender equality is one of the EU's primary concerns in this regard.

In this regard, we must highlight algorithmic discrimination as one of the fundamental risks. While the EU attributes it to the design and quality of the datasets used to develop AI systems, from our perspective, it should be understood more broadly, encompassing the consequences that each individual user's knowledge and expertise in using AI may entail.

In order to handle the personal effects of artificial intelligence in the workplace, trade unions are essential, especially when it comes to reducing the dangers of algorithmic discrimination.

Workers may encounter difficulties as a result of biased algorithms or their own ignorance of how AI systems work, since these systems increasingly impact hiring, promotions, and terminations.

By advocating for increased accountability and transparency in the application of AI, unions serve as supporters for justice.

Promoting AI literacy among employees is one important way that unions help. Unions enable workers to recognize and correct any biases or errors by teaching individuals about the workings of AI systems and the consequences of their outputs. This training lessens the possibility of negative effects brought on by illiteracy and assists employees in making well-informed decisions.

Additionally, unions support unambiguous rules to guarantee that AI systems can be explained and offer channels for contesting judgments that have a detrimental impact on workers. Furthermore, they participate in collective bargaining agreements that restrict the use of invasive AI surveillance and encourage moral AI implementation that respects workers' rights.

Unions struggle to establish workplaces where AI boosts productivity without sacrificing the autonomy, rights, or dignity of individual employees through advocacy, education, and collective bargaining. In order to guarantee a just and equitable digital transformation, their actions are crucial.

Given the evident risks that AI may pose to individuals' fundamental rights, it is essential to avoid legal duplication, contradictory obligations, and overregulation by adopting a technologically neutral legal framework.

Out of the four choices that were examined, a regulatory framework that prioritized the preservation of basic rights was selected. High-risk AI systems are subject to legal requirements under this framework, which guarantees adherence to stringent criteria for data quality, documentation, traceability, transparency, human oversight, robustness, and accuracy. These responsibilities are intended to reduce dangers and protect the moral and lawful deployment of AI in vital fields. Adherence to the regulatory framework is optional and governed by standards of conduct for AI systems deemed to represent little or no risk. These guidelines seek to encourage providers to operate responsibly, fostering responsibility and openness while preserving the potential for creativity.

By adopting this dual approach—mandatory requirements for high-risk systems and voluntary guidelines for others—the regulatory framework seeks to balance the protection of fundamental rights with the facilitation of technological advancement and market adaptability.

The process of approving the EU AI Act involved online public consultation. This began on February 19, 2020, the same day the *White Paper on Artificial Intelligence* was published (European Commission, 2020). The results of this survey show that one of the main concerns of those surveyed is related to fundamental rights and security, all of which are linked to the functioning of AI (European Commission, 2020).

It is interesting to note that citizens express the need for regulations that ensure the ability of human beings to make their own decisions and addresses issues like data quality, the use of remote biometric identification systems, and discrimination and bias in decision-making. While companies view excessive regulation as a barrier to innovation, citizens are concerned with preventing the implementation of AI systems that allow for profiling, qualification and, ultimately, manipulation of individuals. Indeed, one repeated proposal refers to the need for AI applications to carry out an impact assessment on fundamental rights. The existence of a public register of automated decision-making systems was also proposed as a sort of European agency and governance mechanism.

Algorithmic management—when AI carries out the role of a human manager—has a significant impact on employees, including work intensity, health and safety risks, discriminatory and unfair outcomes, lack of control over data, loss of privacy, lack of human agency and freedom over work, and the degradation of human judgment and skill. Therefore, urgent action is needed to protect people from the risks and harms of AI-based decision-making in the workplace. In addition, it is vital to ensure that the opportunities AI creates in the workplace benefit everyone. Employers and businesses also need the certainty provided by regulation.

APPROVAL OF AI REGULATION

The formalization of AI Regulation was introduced on April 21, 2021, with a proposal by the European Parliament and Council to establish harmonized rules for AI (EU AI Act)[1].

The analysis of AI risks related to fundamental rights has also been a matter of concern for European authorities. The *Conclusions of the Presidency: The Charter of Fundamental Rights in the Context of AI and Digital Change* emphasizes that major risks to fundamental rights arise from the opacity, complexity, bias, unpredictability, and partially autonomous behavior of AI systems. Therefore, it is essential to guarantee their compatibility with fundamental rights and facilitate the application of current legal regulations (Council of the European Union, 2020).

At the same time, it is acknowledged that digital technologies, especially AI, are crucial to maintaining digital sovereignty and advancing Europe's economic growth, which includes the defense and advancement of fundamental rights.

In this sense, a reliable AI ecosystem founded on EU ideals and standards must serve as the foundation for the digital single market. Through the creation of common technical standards that apply to the design, development, deployment, and use of AI systems, the EU hopes to guarantee that the advancement of AI is consistent with the strengthening of citizens' fundamental rights while also promoting trust in the technology.

In this context, on December 6, 2022, the Council adopted its position on the regulation of AI. Based on this position, the Council opened a dialogue with the European Parliament to reach an agreement on the proposal for regulation. Subsequently, on December 9, 2023, the Council and Parliament reached a provisional agreement, the final text of which is to be formally adopted by both, in their capacity as co-legislators, in what will be the first global standard on AI.

On May 21, 2024, the Council adopted the Regulation of the European Parliament and of the Council, establishing harmonized rules on AI and amending regulations (EC) No 300/2008, (EU) No 167/2013, (EU) No 168/2013, (EU) 2018/858, (EU) 2018/1139, (EU) 2019/2144, and Directives 2014/90/EU, (EU) 2016/797, and (EU) 2020/1828 (AI Regulation). The AI Regulation aims to align AI rules with a risk-based approach, meaning the higher the potential risk to society, the stricter the rules.

AI Regulation and Basic Concepts

The EU AI Act is the first global regulatory instrument to address a legal framework for the development, sale, commissioning, and use of AI systems. In order to ensure a high degree of protection of health, safety, and fundamental rights enshrined in the *Charter of Fundamental Rights of the European Union* (hereinafter, the Charter) against the potential risks of AI, the EU AI Act highlights that its goal is to encourage the adoption of human-centered, trustworthy AI. In the application of this principle, the AI Regulation prohibits those uses of AI that are considered to pose unacceptable risks, namely social scoring systems or real-time biometric surveillance in public spaces, with the specificities that will be explored in this chapter.

In addition to prohibited AI applications, the EU AI Act defines three additional categories: (1) high; (2) limited; and (3) minimal risk. High-risk applications are subject to specific legal requirements, applicable before they enter the market. The remaining applications (those with limited or minimal risk) are largely unregulated. AI applications that profile individuals are considered high risk, including those that are capable of processing personal data to assess aspects of an individual's life related to their health, work performance, behavior, interests, or movements. In this case, the EU AI Act establishes requirements for transparency, security, and human oversight applicable to all participants in the value chain, including deployment controllers (Art. 2.1.b) EU AI Act).

Key Definitions of AI Regulation

The EU AI Act adopts the definition provided by the Organization for Economic Cooperation and Development (2024), defining machine-based AI systems as those comprising five characteristics:

1. Operates with varying levels of autonomy to demonstrate adaptability after deployment
2. Includes explicit or implicit objectives
3. Infers from the input information it receives
4. Generates output results like predictions, content, recommendations, or decisions
5. Influences physical or virtual environments

Some computer systems will be excluded from the regulation due to their lack of certain capabilities. The EU AI Act focuses on inference, eliminating previous approaches like knowledge-based or data-driven AI. However, the definition leaves doubts about simpler systems, which can only be eliminated by reading the Recitals.

The EU AI Act focuses on risk. Therefore, the authors combine this definition with the one provided by the EU AI Act itself in Article 3.2, which defines risk as the combination of the probability of harm occurring and the severity of that harm.

As can be inferred from the definition, AI systems do not always have unique or exclusive purposes. Thus, the EU AI Act refers to such systems as general-purpose AI models (Art. 3.63.) EU AI Act), noting that it is trained on a large volume of data using large-scale self-supervision, which exhibits a considerable degree of generality and is capable of competently performing a wide variety of different tasks, regardless of the way in which the model is introduced to the market, and which can be integrated into various downstream systems or applications.

However, this does not apply to AI models used for research, development, or prototyping activities prior to market introduction.

Such general-purpose AI models are used as a measure to determine high-impact capabilities (Art. 3.64.) EU AI Act), defined as those that match or exceed the capabilities displayed by the most advanced general-purpose AI models (Presno Linera, 2023). These high-impact capabilities may generate a systemic risk (Art. 3.65.) EU AI Act), defined as a risk specific to the high-impact capabilities of general-purpose AI models, which have considerable impacts on the European Union market due to their scope or actual or reasonably foreseeable negative effects on public health, security, public safety, fundamental rights, or society, with large-scale spreading throughout the value chain.

Prohibited AI Practices

Given the risk-based approach of the EU AI Act, there are certain AI practices or purposes that, given their potential functionality, are directly prohibited. These include those that:

- Deploy subliminal techniques with the aim of distorting a person's behavior in a way that may cause physical or psychological harm to themselves or others
- Exploit vulnerabilities of a specific group of people due to age, disability, or social or economic situation in a way that distorts the behavior of those people and causes harm
- AI systems that profile people based on their behavior, creating a social scale that may result in individuals or groups being treated disproportionately unfavorably in relation to the behavior observed, or in unfavorable treatment in a context other than that in which the data was collected
- AI systems for carrying out risk assessments on natural persons to assess or predict the risk that a natural person will commit a crime based solely on the profiling of a natural person or the assessment of their personality traits and characteristics (this does not apply to AI systems used to support human assessment of a person's involvement in criminal activity that is already based on objective and verifiable facts related to criminal activity)
- AI systems that create or expand facial recognition databases by nonselective extraction of facial images from the Internet or closed-circuit television

- AI systems for inferring the emotions of a natural person in the workplace and in educational establishments (except where the AI system is intended to be introduced for medical or safety reasons)
- Biometric categorization systems that individually classify natural persons on the basis of their biometric data to deduce or infer their race, political opinions, trade union membership, religious or philosophical beliefs, sex life or sexual orientation, except for the labelling or filtering of lawfully acquired biometric data
- Use for police or law enforcement applications of real-time biometric identification in publicly accessible places by or on behalf of law enforcement agencies, except when searching for potential victims of crime, preventing specific and substantial threats to critical infrastructure or natural persons, preventing terrorist attacks, and prosecuting crimes punishable by more than four years' imprisonment

High-Risk AI Systems

If the EU has harmonized legislation on certain products or product safety components subject to conformity assessment by a third party, their implementation with AI will be considered a high-risk system (Art. 6.1.) EU AI Act).

Additionally, Annex III defines eight areas, and specific cases of use within them, which are considered high risk, provided they are not prohibited:

- **Biometrics:** AI systems intended to be used for biometric categorization based on sensitive or protected attributes or characteristics based on inference of sensitive attributes or characteristics and systems intended to be used for emotion recognition (except for those to be used for biometric verification purposes whose sole purpose is to confirm that a specific natural person is the person they claim to be)
- **Critical Infrastructures:** AI systems to be used as security within the management and operation of critical digital infrastructures, road traffic, water, gas, heating, or electric supplies
- **Education and Professional Training:** AI systems to determine admission to educational or professional training institutions, assess learning outcomes, determine the educational level that a person may access, or detect prohibited actions during examinations
- **Employment, Employee Management, or Access to Self-Employment:** AI systems for selecting or hiring personnel, advertising jobs, analyzing and filtering applications and evaluating candidates, making decisions about working conditions, promotion, or termination of an employment relationship,

assigning tasks based on the behavior, traits, or characteristics of the person, supervising and evaluating the performance and behavior of workers

- **Access to Essential Public and Private Services:** Classification of individuals (except for systems that identify financial fraud, healthcare services, risk assessment, and pricing of life and health insurance, prioritization of responses in emergency situations or triage systems in healthcare)
- **Compliance With the Law:** AI systems related to the prevention and investigation of crimes, such as those designed to assess the risk of a person becoming a victim of crime, including predictive systems for profiling people and analyzing the reliability of evidence
- **Migration, Asylum, and Border Control Management:** AI systems for assessing security, irregular migration and health risks, examining asylum applications, or recognizing individuals in the context of migration, asylum, or border control
- **Justice and Democratic Processes:** AI systems to assist judicial authorities in the investigation and interpretation of facts or the law and systems to influence the electoral behaviour of voters, excluding systems whose output results are not directly exposed to natural persons, such as tools used to organize, optimize, or structure political campaigns from an administrative or logistical point of view

Even if a use case is not included in Annex III, it will not be considered high risk if it does not pose a significant risk of causing harm to health, safety, or fundamental rights, including if it does not influence decision-making processes. When the AI system profiles natural persons, they will always be considered high risk.

The complexity of this system is highlighted in Article 6(5) of the EU AI Act, which states that the Commission, after consulting the European AI Council, should provide an exhaustive list of practical examples of high-risk and reduced-risk AI use cases.

Protection of Fundamental Rights in AI Regulations

Recital 5 of the EU AI Act acknowledges that AI has the potential to create risks and jeopardize fundamental rights and public interests as established by EU law. Consequently, it states that advancing a European human-centered approach to AI is the primary goal of the AI Regulation (Recital 8 EU AI Act).

When using software in coordination with AI, the decision will be made by the system. In turn, these intelligent programs will use their decisions to adjust their operation. Ultimately, erroneous decisions may be made, including those with negative impacts on the fundamental rights of citizens.

The characteristics of AI systems—such as opacity, complexity, bias, dependence on input data, autonomous training or behavior, and unpredictability—may have negative implications for the fundamental rights enshrined in the *Charter of Fundamental Rights in the Context of AI and Digital Change* (Council of the European Union, 2020). These rights within the EU AI Act include human dignity (Article 1), freedom of expression (Article 11), and the right to an impartial judge (Articles 47 and 48). As Reche Tello et al. (2022) indicated, anticipation is difficult. Thus, norms emerge once damage to rights has occurred because the technologies are already applied.

The EU AI Act's approach to ensuring these rights is embodied in certain obligations, such as ex ante testing, risk management, and human oversight. These measures aim to prevent or minimize the risk of erroneous or biased AI-assisted decisions in areas like education and training, employment, or services like law enforcement and the judiciary system.

The EU AI Act recalls one of the major risks in the practical application of AI systems: the feedback loop. In other words, biased output results influence the input information of future operations. In turn, probabilities are generalized and exceptional cases are systematically ignored. Robust measures will prevent data poisoning like the manipulation of the training data set, model poisoning like the manipulation of pretrained components used in training, or model evasion like input information designed to make the system make a mistake.

In this regard, transparency and oversight obligations are essential to prevent AI systems from perpetuating patterns of discrimination. Transparency is the ability to understand and communicate how AI systems operate, the output data or decisions they produce, and their impact. It also includes their explainability, meaning that their results are intelligible, and it is clear how the system's operation contributes to certain results.

As Cotino Hueso and Castellanos Claramunt (2022) indicated, both principles are essential to guarantee the right to effective judicial protection recognized in Article 24 of the Spanish Constitution (State Official Gazette No. 311, 29 December 1978).

Obviously, it is impossible to ensure the absence of violations. Thus, the proposal also establishes a system of transparency and traceability, coupled with ex post controls to provide affected individuals with effective compensation.

Obligations are specifically applicable to high-risk AI systems. However, the classification of a high-risk system does not depend solely on the function it performs. It also relies on its purpose and the modalities for which the system is used. These factors are essential in creating an extension of AI systems currently classified as high-risk.

To assess independent high-risk AI systems through internal controls, it will be necessary to comply ex ante in a full, effective, and duly documented manner, applying AI Regulation requirements, quality and risk management systems, and post-market monitoring. Once the supplier has carried out the conformity assessment, it must register independent high-risk AI systems in an EU database. Then, the Commission will work to strengthen ex post supervision through competent authorities.

Miguez Macho and Torres Carlos (2018) noted that the EU AI Act does not offer legal certainty for operators regarding crucial issues related to the protection of fundamental rights, such as conformity assessment. This is concerning when considering the impact assessment related to fundamental rights, whose purpose is not clear, even though it should be aimed at minimizing risks related to the rights of individuals.

As Miguez Macho and Torres Carlos (2018) indicated, the most important operator of the AI system will be responsible for its deployment. The individual will have technical and legal responsibilities. In addition, when using a product that generates risks, the individual must observe ethical conduct beyond what is strictly required by the legal system.

In high-risk AI systems, supplier accountability is crucial. The systems' intended use and controlled environments that minimize any potential negative effects must be guaranteed by the providers.

Vega Iracelay (2019) pointed out how AI research and development can be unknown (because it requires little physical infrastructure), discrete (different components of an AI system can be designed without conscious coordination), diffused (dozens of people in dispersed geographic locations can participate in an AI project), and opaque (unavailable to external observers). This issue is not minor when considering obligations related to company size and the degree of risk entailed by the use of the AI system.

A user control system, such as an interface that would let the user view a profile linked to the AI system, select and, if necessary, remove keywords used in decision-making, while offering users with specific information about the circumstances in which a recommendation algorithm is used, as well as publishing the fundamental ideas and working mechanisms of the algorithm operation service, would have been an interesting addition.

The EU AI Act mandates certain transparency requirements regardless of whether they are categorized as high-risk AI systems. If the end user is not explicitly notified of their interactions within the system, this requirement assists to prevent confusion.

Systems meant to communicate directly with human beings, for instance, need to be designed by the provider so that those who are impacted are aware that they are interacting with an artificial intelligence system. The supplier must label the output results and enable the detection of artificially generated or altered information for systems that produce synthetic audio, image, video, or text content.

When it concerns emotion recognition and categorization systems, the person in charge of deployment is required to notify the natural people who will be using the system about how it works. Last but not least, the person in charge of deployment will disclose to the public that any systems that produce or alter text to report on topics of public interest or photographs, audio, or video that amount to fraudulent identity theft (deep fake) are artificially created or altered.

Low-risk AI systems are subject to very limited transparency obligations (for example, as explained, the provision of information to communicate the use of an AI system when interacting with humans). Examples of low-risk AI systems include chatbots like Apple's Siri, Google Assistant, or Amazon Alexa. In these cases, the EU AI Act requires that systems integrate solutions that allow them to identify when content was not created by humans. However, current solutions, such as watermarks, are inefficient and vulnerable to attacks. We must bear in mind, too, that a spam filter can miss important information as it uses machine learning to move "junk" mail to a different box, aiming to distinguish between legitimate and illegitimate e-mail and personalizing the user's main inbox. In this case, Article 95 of the AI Act encourages the adoption of codes of conduct for the voluntary implementation of specific requirements.

Likewise, social platforms and networks like Facebook and Instagram use similar functions to verify specific behaviors through notifications and content. These digital tools use AI to tailor the user's experience. In fact, they use data obtained through often forgotten or overlooked microphones (with users' permission).

The businesses who developed these apps also encourage business owners to promote their goods, which boosts both parties' profits. As a result, consumers are given product recommendations (e.g. on Amazon). In order to tailor end users' shopping experiences and provide recommendations based on their likes and tastes, the platform gathers data about their past purchases. However, this action may have serious contradictions with the Unfair Competition Law[2] by influencing the economic behaviour of the consumer. Furthermore, as indicated, the AI Act establishes additional transparency obligations for systems that perform the following: (1) interact with human beings; (2) detect emotions or determine the association with specific (social) categories based on biometric data; or (3) generate or manipulate content (deep fake).

An individual must be informed if they interact with an AI system or their emotions and characteristics are recognized by automated means. If an AI system is used to generate or manipulate images, audio, or videos that appear to be authentic content, it must be mandatory to inform that such content has been generated by automated means. However, despite the impact that an AI system recognizing emotions may have, it may not be considered high risk depending on its purpose.

Prior to the use of an AI system, end users should provide precise, clear, and specific information to ensure their fundamental rights. Thus, the quality of the decision is ensured. In other words, it is about analyzing the obligations of information and transparency. However, Edwards (2022) highlighted the difficulty of the EU AI Act to adequately protect fundamental rights due to the complexity of AI systems. This is particularly relevant within general purpose systems, where the repercussions vary depending on the context of use. In addition, the structure of the EU AI Act does not distinguish responsibilities throughout the AI lifecycle.

Sartor (2024) expressed concerns about the lack of transparency and the potential negative impact of AI on fundamental rights. Their work stressed that the EU AI Act focused on risk categorization, which may be insufficient at addressing challenges posed by rapid technological evolution. In turn, citizens may be exposed to the abuse of power.

From a practical point of view, high-risk systems should provide information and transparency obligations of providers. This includes providers' contact details, details of the authorized representative, limitations of the system and its intended purpose, cybersecurity against which the system has been tested and validated, human monitoring measures, and care measures to ensure the functioning of the system, including updating the software. In this sense, providers must ensure that systems intended to interact with natural persons are designed and developed in such a way that said persons are informed that they are interacting with an AI system, except in situations where this is evident due to the circumstances and context of use.

In which cases should the obligation to provide information about the use of an AI system be exempted because its use is evident? Additionally, for whom should the system's involvement be considered evident?

Interestingly, when the EU AI Act refers to the obligations of providers to adopt AI literacy measures, it is not referring to the users of these systems. Instead, it is speaking to the providers' staff. It does not specify what these measures should consist of or list specific requirements relating to the profile of the staff of these providers, including those of high-risk systems. According to Article 95 of the EU AI Act and Recital 20, the European AI Board should support the European Commission in promoting AI literacy tools. Additionally, the Commission, Member States, and the AI Office are encouraged to support the development of voluntary codes of conduct to promote AI literacy among individuals involved in the development, operation, and use of AI. Developing literacy through codes of conduct appears insufficient when considering the approach of the Act based on the protection of the fundamental rights of individuals.

Despite the provisions of the *Digital Rights Charter*, the digital gap persists, with its impact varying depending on the users of the system. Additionally, these systems must be effectively monitored by natural persons during their use to prevent or minimize risks to health, safety, or fundamental rights. This applies even when high-risk AI systems are used in accordance with its intended purpose or misused in a reasonably foreseeable way.

By taking these measures, the individuals in charge of human oversight will be able to completely comprehend the system's strengths and weaknesses. The user can monitor how the system is functioning, recognize any tendencies to rely too much or automatically on its output, correctly interpret the output, choose not to use the system, ignore, invalidate, or reverse its output, and, if required, interrupt or interfere with the system's operation by pressing a designated button or following a similar process.

Logically, transparency is a fundamental pillar for trust in AI systems. Therefore, it is essential for providers to ensure their systems are auditable and provide relevant information to users and competent authorities. This includes the obligation to inform users when they interact with AI and to ensure that automated decisions are both understandable and justifiable.

Accounting for the role of human supervision, the significant risks posed by these systems—already validated by legislation—must not be overlooked. Risks include the bias of automation, the propensity to rely too much on information produced by the system, and a lack of knowledge about that information, which raises concerns about the systems' impartiality with respect to fundamental rights.

This also challenges the humanistic vision proclaimed by EU institutions in their documents (European Commission, n.d.). Therefore, human oversight should be viewed as a crucial mechanism in the regulation of AI. Oversight must extend beyond technical issues to include ethical oversight, ensuring that AI decisions respect fundamental values and human rights. In this regard, Yeung (2022) highlighted the lack of restrictions in the EU AI Act in areas like mass surveillance and the use of AI in law enforcement, raising concerns about a potential erosion of fundamental rights, such as privacy or freedom of expression.

As indicated in the European Parliament (2022) resolution on AI in the digital age, dominant technology platforms use AI technologies to obtain information about a person's identity and behavior, as well as their decision-making history. This poses risks to democratic systems, the safeguarding of fundamental rights, and the autonomy of citizens due to an imbalance of power and systematic risks. Various sectors, including insurance and banking, will benefit from AI systems by specifying conditions for consumers. There are, however, risks for individuals, including exclusion as a result of the individualization of risk. According to Munos Paredes (2020), this does not account for the possibility of such practices becoming a hidden form for the discriminatory application of rates, as illustrated by Bourreau and De Streel (2020).

It, therefore, seems possible to argue that the EU AI Act does not address the problem of algorithmic discrimination. It may perpetuate existing inequalities or create new forms of discrimination, particularly in automated decision-making.

According to Calo (2010), by combining the listening and surveillance capabilities of AI systems with pattern recognition capabilities, these systems could consolidate ubiquitous surveillance. Proposals like those by Erdely and Goldsmith (2018) promoted a global approach to internationally regulate AI through an intergovernmental organization that serves as a forum for participation to adopt international standards, including the public sector, industry, academic organizations and civil society.

In this sense, the AI Regulation structures a governance framework through the AI Office[3], the European AI Committee, the Advisory Forum, the Independent Scientific Expert Group, and competent national authorities. Article 4 of the 2022 regulation establishing the Spanish Agency for the Supervision of Business Intelligence outlines its responsibilities. These include carrying out supervisory tasks, advising, raising awareness, and providing training to public and private entities to ensure the proper implementation of national and European regulations regarding the proper use and development of AI systems, specifically algorithms. Additionally, the Spanish Agency is tasked with inspection, verification, sanction, and other functions as assigned. Their work, together with that of European institutions, will be essential to ensuring that all AI systems introduced in the EU comply with requirements, especially when it involves high risks.

The market surveillance system is one of the aspects that make up the quality management system that high-risk AI system providers must implement to ensure compliance with the AI Regulation. The Commission is responsible for preparing a model within a period of no more than 18 months from the entry into force of Article 98.2 of the EU AI Act.

Unions' Approach Toward AI Regulation and Protection of Fundamental Rights

AI's quick development and application is continuing to transform sectors, changing hiring practices and posing ethical and governance issues. Even while AI has enormous potential for innovation and economic expansion, its use has raised serious questions about fundamental rights such worker privacy, transparency, and nondiscrimination. The emergence of surveillance technology, predictive algorithms, and automated decision-making systems has prompted discussions about power imbalances between employers and employees as well as the possible weakening of labor laws.

As longstanding advocates for workers' rights, trade unions have become essential players in tackling these issues. Unions have actively shaped the conversation around AI governance in the EU, where legal frameworks seek to strike a balance between the protection of basic rights and technical innovation. Their involvement in advocacy campaigns and consultations shows a growing understanding that AI policy must guarantee fair and moral application in labor relations in addition to giving priority to technological progress. For trade unions looking to protect workers' dignity and reduce the hazards connected with AI-driven systems, the EU AI Act has emerged as a key issue.

The development of algorithmic management for the working environment is essential for research and academic debate (Aneesh, 2009; Cherry, 2016; Irani, 2015; Lee et al., 2015). Although the debate began on an optimistic note, it grew more critical, stressing the role of internal and external factors, such as politics, in shaping the nature and scope of union experimentation with information and communication technologies and their contribution to the outcomes of revitalization (Geelan, 2021).

AI is having a bigger impact on hiring, promotion, and termination decisions. On the other hand, discriminatory results and biases might be reinforced by opaque algorithms. For instance, it has been discovered that AI-driven hiring practices perpetuate age, race, or gender biases present in training data. Therefore, in order to reduce such dangers, the EU AI Act requires that high-risk AI systems in employment contexts go through bias evaluations and routine monitoring.

Braithwaite (2011) found that legislation cannot be implemented effectively and efficiently if it relies solely on sanctions and intimidation options to regulate entities. These principles can be viewed from the perspective of system integrator certification and regulation, especially in the context of algorithmic management in the workplace. To facilitate the prioritization of stimulus tools and simplify the complexity of this concept, Braithwaite (2011) proposed the application of heuristic principles.

AI solutions that can monitor worker behavior, output, and communication have made it possible to monitor workplaces at previously unheard-of levels. Trade unions argue that unchecked use of these systems violates workers' right to privacy per Article 8 of the European Convention on Human Rights and the EU Charter of Fundamental Rights. The EU AI Act addresses this by emphasizing transparency and requiring AI system providers to disclose the scope and purpose of data collection[4].

In Spain, the latest survey by the National Institute of Statistics on the use of ICT among companies[5] has incorporated an indicator on the percentage of companies that, using AI in their production structure, incorporate some measure to check the results generated by AI technologies for possible biases towards people and the data confirm that Spanish companies do not comply with the minimum requirements in relation to respect for the most basic fundamental rights. The survey reveals devastating figures since only 3.16% of companies develop actions to avoid unfair treatment or partial decisions. In other words, 96.84% of Spanish companies with AI do not monitor inappropriate use of this technology.

Figure 1. Table showing use of AI in Spanish companies

Use of IA in Spanish companies	
Companies using IA technology	9,55%
Companies using IA technology for analyzing written language	32,96%
Companies with AI technology that converts spoken language into machine-readable format	32,63%
Companies with AI technology that generates written or spoken language	25,93%
Companies with AI technology to identify objects or people based on images or videos	36,78%
Companies with AI technology for machine learning or machine learning for data analysis	33,42%
Companies with AI technology for workflow automation or decision-making support	37,16%
Companies with AI technology that enables the physical movement of machines	16,57%
Companies that use AI technologies for marketing or sales	22,83%
Companies that use AI technologies for production processes	29,85%
Companies that use AI technologies to organize business administration or management processes	24,92%
Companies that use AI technologies for logistics	11,64%
Companies that use AI technologies for ICT security	27,14%
Companies that use AI technologies for accounting, control or financial management	20,31%
Companies that use AI technologies for R&D or innovation activities	24,47%
Companies that acquire software or AI systems that are developed by their own employees	25,69%
Companies that acquire commercial AI software or systems that are modified by their own employees	15,85%
Companies that acquire open source AI software or systems that are modified by their own employees	19,39%
Companies that acquire off-the-shelf AI software or systems	41,10%
Companies that acquire AI software or systems by hiring third-party vendors to develop or modify them	37,97%
Companies that have ever considered using any of the AI technologies	5,21%
Companies that do not use any of the AI technologies because the costs seem too high	68,29%
Companies that do not use any of the AI technologies because there is a lack of relevant expertise in the company	78,49%
Companies that do not use any of the AI technologies due to incompatibility with existing equipment, software or systems	36,49%
Companies that do not use any of the AI technologies due to difficulties with the availability or quality of the necessary data	47,11%
Companies that do not use any of the AI technologies due to concerns regarding data protection and privacy violations	38,36%
Companies that do not use any of the AI technologies due to a lack of clarity about the legal consequences	43,70%
Companies that do not use any AI technologies for ethical reasons	19,42%
Companies that do not use any of the AI technologies because they are not useful for the company	9,84%

Source: Spanish National Institute of Statistics

Spanish General Union of Workers (UGT) points out that this is a situation that hardly varies depending on the size of the company, and it is especially alarming that the largest companies, and therefore those with the most resources, fail to comply with their constitutional obligations by almost 96% and a new figure that other organizations and companies such as IBM had already warned about, which already in 2022, indicated that only 22% of Spanish employers took measures to reduce unwanted biases. A year later, McKinsey also highlighted that 84% of organizations did not take into account aspects such as equity and justice when putting a labor AI into production.

Already in 2024, Indra discovered that 7% of organizations claim that there is a defined Responsible Artificial Intelligence policy integrated into processes and operations. In other words, 93% of the 900 organizations that responded to their study - among which were Spanish companies that accounted for 18.7% of the national GDP and more than 45% of the IBEX 35 companies - admitted that they did not have ethical policies related to Artificial Intelligence.

The use of AI in the workplace is one of the most common applications among companies with this technology. Up to 40% of companies have algorithms for automating workflows or for helping in decision-making, but these decisions are not being subjected to a minimum of verification to control unfair decisions or biases.

More than half of large companies use AI to automate staff selection, to determine salaries, to decide on professional promotions or to set work shifts. Transposing this reality into figures, today in Spain there are 1,170 large companies that use AI without checking whether they operate in accordance with the constitutional parameters of equality and non-discrimination.

Knowing that these applications have historically and repeatedly demonstrated their tendency to discriminate (for example, against women), it is unbearable to see the neglect in the face of one of the deepest and most serious dangers that can be done to a working person: violating their fundamental rights, such as the right to equal opportunities or the right to work.

UGT stresses that it is necessary to put an end to this kind of "technological wild west" and emphasizes that, although the European AI Regulation promises to regulate these aspects, there are still two long years until its full application, an excessively long time. For this reason, they will deploy union action policies to stop this abuse, using, among other things, the commitments acquired in the Fifth Agreement for Employment and Collective Bargaining[6], which obliges companies to guarantee the principle of human control of AI and to guarantee a safe and transparent use of this technology.

In this regard, we must remember that the Spanish Workers' Statute was already modified in 2021 to ensure that the algorithms or artificial intelligence systems used by home delivery companies - or riders - preserve labor rights, especially those affecting working conditions, access to and maintenance of employment.

Unlike other countries, it seems that Spain has made a clear commitment to social dialogue and collective bargaining as a formula for the governance of the digital transition.

Starting with the Workers' Statute as the main rule in Spanish labor law, its article 64.4.d), as we highlighted, was reformed in 2021 to refer to algorithms, without limiting its scope of application to digital platforms, and to allow the legal representative of workers (RLPT) to have information about the data that companies use in decision-making. Information that, by virtue of the principle of transparency, must reach and include all the data that underpins the algorithm and that, until now, was opaque. In accordance with this reform, when the RLPT requests information and data related to algorithms and AI systems, companies cannot reject such requests alleging their lack of knowledge, as this could constitute a violation of the right to freedom of association.

On the other hand, the *Charter of Digital Rights* represents another major commitment to social dialogue and collective bargaining. Indeed, one of the most relevant elements is the need to carry out an impact assessment on the design of algorithms in the case of automated or semi-automated decisions on digital rights. In addition, the content of the Charter itself shows that this assessment, as well as all digital transformation processes, must apply the gender perspective. The difficulty lies in the fact that the Charter is a norm that has no legal effect, therefore, its content is not directly binding. However, considering that in Spain collective bargaining does have legal effect, a solution to this difficulty could be the inclusion in collective agreements of the rights and obligations provided for by the Charter. In fact, some agreements, such as the Collective Agreement of the banking sector, have opted for this solution, considering certain rights contained in the Charter such as the obligation to carry out an impact assessment.

Although it does not have an element of normative legal force, the Agreement on Employment and Collective Bargaining must also be taken into account. This Agreement clearly supports the negotiation and participation of the RLPT in the world of work. In relation to automated and semi-automated systems, the Agreement dedicates part of its content to the digital transition. Firstly, it establishes that information on AI and the use of algorithms must be transmitted to workers and/or their legal representatives in a clear and understandable way. In this sense, the appearance of AI systems implies that the right to information is increasingly becoming a right to explanation and understanding. Secondly, the Agreement gives all the focus on the implementation of AI systems in companies to collective bargaining. And, finally, the Agreement promulgates the principle of transparency, acquiring special importance in the context of the use of AI systems and systems made up of algorithms.

It is therefore necessary for the RLPT to have a minimum knowledge of this matter in order to be able to negotiate on equal terms. Some European countries have chosen to resolve this issue. For example, in Germany, companies are required to pay for the advice of an AI expert whose services the RLPT has the right to request, and the RLPT's consent is also essential to implement any procedure or system related to the use of AI or algorithms.

The opacity of AI systems (or the black-box problem) undermines workers' abilities to challenge decisions made by algorithms. The EU AI Act mandates that AI developers ensure the explainability of high-risk systems, aligning with trade union demands for greater algorithmic accountability and human oversight to protect workers' rights.

AI-powered task automation has also raised worries about labor deskilling and job displacement. Trade unions stress the need for complementing measures that encourage reskilling and upskilling to ensure workers are not left behind in the digital revolution, even though the EU AI Act does not specifically address job security.

Trade unions are using their previous experience with technological change to tackle AI. However, there have been increasing calls for trade unions to change their methods as a prerequisite for successfully influencing the design, implementation, and use of AI (Gerst, 2020).

Organizations that have participated in the policy-making process and advocated for more robust worker rights, such as the European Trade Union Confederation (ETUC), were consulted during the drafting of the EU AI Act. The contributions made by ETUC highlighted the necessity of fortifying clauses pertaining to algorithmic accountability and transparency, as well as collective bargaining rights as a means of regulating the use of AI in the workplace and preventing its abuse for discriminatory and intrusive surveillance purposes.

ETUC's stance is part of a larger initiative to guarantee that the EU AI Act protects workers' fundamental rights in addition to acting as a regulatory tool for innovation. Trade unions' crucial position as go-betweens for legislators, employers, and workers is highlighted by their participation in this process, which guarantees that AI governance adheres to fairness and justice ideals.

However, strong implementation, enforcement, and ongoing cooperation with trade unions will be necessary for the protection of workers' rights. The significance of striking a balance between social justice and technical progress is highlighted by unions' advocacy for accountability, transparency, and the ethical application of AI.

Some who wish to capitalize on the opportunities of the new technology have called for an ethical design. In other words, technology development should focus on AI that supports individuals, is transparent and understandable for users, and has been tested against potential dangers and biases (Roberts et al., 2021).

ETUC has engaged in the development of the EU's AI regulatory framework, emphasizing the protection of workers' rights and fundamental freedoms. In its *Resolution on the European Strategies on Artificial Intelligence and Data*, ETUC (2020) outlined several key positions:

- **Legal Framework Based on Human Rights:** This framework encompasses labor and trade union rights, as well as ethical guidelines.
- **Classification of AI Applications Affecting Workers:** AI applications impacting workers' rights and working conditions must be classified as high-risk by default.

- **Prevention of Undue Surveillance and Discrimination:** It is necessary to maintain and reinforce worker protections, prevent disproportionate and undue surveillance at work, prohibit discriminatory treatments arising from biased algorithms, and prevent abuses of data protection and privacy.

Furthermore, in the *ETUC Resolution Calling for an EU Directive on Algorithmic Systems at Work*, ETUC (2022) expressed concerns that the proposed EU AI Act was insufficient for regulating AI use in the workplace. The resolution advocates for a dedicated EU directive to establish minimum standards for the design and use of algorithmic systems in employment contexts.

Trade unions' position is strengthened by collective bargaining rights, which also support workers' representatives' rights to information, consultation, and involvement.

It is easier to make sure that employees comprehend and interact with AI technology when clear, understandable algorithmic processes are presented in the workplace. According to ETUC's Resolution, employees must be notified when AI systems are utilized to make decisions. Furthermore, choices that will affect job conditions, wages, or access to employment must be challenged using explicit criteria.

Because biases in information might result in unjust employment, promotion, and termination decisions, trade unions have expressed concerns about algorithmic discrimination. ETUC emphasizes how prejudice in AI systems might exacerbate preexisting racial, gender, age, and disability disparities. In order to ensure compliance with anti-discrimination rules, ETUC has advocated for routine, independent audits of AI systems to identify and remove bias.

National trade unions have repeated this request for algorithmic accountability. For example, in order to avoid discriminatory results in hiring procedures, UGT suggested requiring assessments of AI systems.

The application of AI for intrusive workplace surveillance is among the most urgent problems. AI technology have made it possible for previously unheard-of degrees of surveillance, including productivity tracking and behavioral monitoring, which violates employees' right to privacy. As a result, the ETUC Resolution demands that worker observation be tightly controlled. In certain situations, these technologies are forbidden in order to protect autonomy, human dignity, and privacy at work.

One of the most relevant problems regarding AI regulation is its accelerated construction, since in a short period of time there is already a fairly extensive set of rules, the result of a multi-level intervention. This rapid development is a consequence of its preventive nature, in the sense that its construction began when concern arose about the potential risks attributed to this AI. The problems were not expected to arise in order to begin designing solutions, but rather these solutions have preceded them, based on reasonable forecasts and expectations. In this sense, the regulation has an academic and technocratic character, since it is being developed by experts from various disciplines based on the verification of its potential effects with the aim of anticipating and anticipating them.

From the perspective of workplace video surveillance, the images obtained by these systems are used for the development and training of general-purpose AI models, in particular large generative AI models, capable of generating images themselves. This ability to generate images with a high degree of realism and verisimilitude produces the risk of false, created or manipulated evidence, on which to base business decisions, something that was much more complicated with digital video surveillance. These systems can extend their usefulness beyond the control of the reality of work activity, to cover other aspects such as its quantity and quality, becoming a source of information for performance evaluation. A smart camera automatically controls what is done, how it is done, who does it, in how much time, etc.

Smart cameras do not just capture images, but they detect patterns and trends in the observed reality, and this generates the risk of controlling emotions, as has been said. It also introduces the factor of errors experienced by AI, which can reach wrong conclusions, experience hallucinations or suffer biases. In the same way, AI can focus attention and capture images on certain people, identified from established patterns or predictions, and this generates a real risk of algorithmic discrimination.

The images collected and processed are used to make business decisions that have nothing to do with the fulfilment of labour obligations by the persons employed by the entity, but rather with the search for efficiency, improved productivity, cost savings, increased security and other purposes, which are not always legitimate. Consider the use of images to predict the behaviour of workers in the face of a strike, union elections or a union certification process (as indeed seems to have occurred in the United States); or simply to gauge the working environment or the impact of business decisions that affect the workforce.

For all these reasons, their use has been associated with the appearance of new risks to workers' rights. These risks include extensive and systematic use of image control; the manipulation and generation of these; the possibility of hallucinations and erroneous deductions; the selective control of certain persons or groups of them, as a consequence of biases that can lead to real discrimination; and the exhaustion of the monitored personnel.

The AI Regulation includes among the prohibited AI practices some that may be among those we are studying. Among the eight assumptions contemplated by its article 5 are the systems that are used to infer the emotions of a natural person in the workplace and in educational centres (except those justified for medical or security reasons). The Regulation defines the concept of “emotion recognition system” as those that, using AI, distinguish or deduce the emotions or intentions of natural persons from their biometric data. Images obtained either by closed circuit or from employees' computers are a great source of information for this.

Physical states such as pain or fatigue are excluded from this concept, and the European Union standard gives as an example the systems used to detect fatigue in pilots or professional drivers in order to avoid accidents, which allows the analysis of images within the framework of policies on the health and safety of workers, the safety of users or even the general physical well-being of the workforce.

If the system for analysing the images captured in the company is to support human resources or production decisions, or even if it is to adopt the same decisions, then we would find ourselves in a situation contemplated in Annex III of the Regulation as high risk, which, as is known, includes AI systems intended to be used to make "decisions that affect the conditions of employment relationships or the promotion or termination of contractual employment relationships, for the assignment of tasks based on individual behaviour or personal traits or characteristics or to monitor and evaluate the performance and behaviour of people within the framework of such relationships". The Regulation classifies remote biometric identification systems as high risk, except those whose purpose is exclusively biometric verification to confirm that a specific natural person is the person they claim to be; as well as those used for biometric categorisation and emotion recognition.

Such a qualification implies, as is known, the requirement of a series of measures, such as the need to implement a risk management system, the preparation of technical documentation, appropriate governance and data management practices, a sufficient level of transparency, automatic recording of events and human supervision, in addition to specific requirements of precision, robustness and cybersecurity.

As a solution, trade unions such as the Germany Trade Union Confederation, for example, has emphasized the need for collective agreements to regulate surveillance technologies and ensure worker autonomy (German Trade Union Confederation, 2022).

CONCLUSION

The EU AI Act represents a landmark attempt to balance technological innovation with the protection of fundamental rights. By adopting a risk-based approach, the EU AI Act seeks to mitigate potential harms while fostering a trusted ecosystem. However, the implementation of these principles within the labor market has highlighted critical challenges, particularly concerning algorithmic management, workplace surveillance, and discriminatory outcomes.

Trade unions, led by organizations like ETUC, have emerged as key stakeholders in addressing these challenges. Their active involvement in shaping the regulatory discourse has been instrumental in embedding worker-centric safeguards into the EU AI Act. The ETUC's Resolutions reflect unions' sustained efforts to ensure that

AI regulation upholds workers' dignity, autonomy, and rights. Through these contributions, unions have successfully drawn attention to the following critical issues:

- **Algorithmic Transparency and Accountability:** Trade unions have consistently emphasized the need for AI systems to be transparent, explainable, and subject to regular audits. By advocating for mandatory assessments of algorithmic bias, unions have sought to prevent discriminatory practices that disproportionately affect vulnerable groups. The EU AI Act incorporates these concerns by requiring transparency and oversight for high-risk AI systems, particularly those influencing employment decisions.
- **Worker Privacy and Surveillance:** The unchecked use of AI-driven surveillance tools poses a significant threat to workers' privacy and autonomy. Trade unions have called for strict regulatory measures, including the prohibition of invasive monitoring systems in the workplace. ETUC's position highlights the importance of aligning AI governance with fundamental rights enshrined in the EU Charter of Fundamental Rights. By advocating for clear limits on surveillance, unions ensure that workers' dignity remains protected in the digital era.
- **Collective Bargaining and Worker Participation:** Unions have underscored the importance of collective bargaining as a mechanism to govern AI implementation in labor relations. ETUC's demand for worker consultation and participation rights ensures that employees are not passive recipients of AI technologies. Instead, they are active contributors to their governance. Strengthening collective agreements in AI deployment aligns with the broader goal of democratizing workplace technology and reducing power asymmetries between employers and employees.
- **Job Security and Reskilling:** While the EU AI Act does not explicitly address job displacement, trade unions have highlighted the need for complementary policies that promote reskilling and upskilling to prepare workers for the evolving labor market. This proactive approach reflects a broader commitment to ensuring a just transition that leaves no worker behind in the digital transformation.

Despite these significant contributions, challenges remain in the practical implementation and enforcement of the EU AI Act. Trade unions must continue to play a central role in monitoring compliance, advocating for stronger protections, and addressing emerging risks posed by advanced AI systems. The EU AI Act marks an important step toward embedding fundamental rights into AI governance; however, its long-term success will depend on the continued engagement of trade unions and other stakeholders.

In conclusion, urgent action is needed to ensure that people are protected from the risks and harms of AI-based decision-making in the workplace, and that everyone benefits from the opportunities associated with AI at work-

Trade unions have proven to be vital actors and collective agreements to regulate surveillance technologies and ensure worker autonomy a suitable solution for the legislator, businesses and workers.

REFERENCES

Aneesh, A. (2009). Global labor: Algocratic modes of organization. *Sociological Theory*, *27*(4), 347–370. DOI: 10.1111/j.1467-9558.2009.01352.x

Barrio Andres, M. (2018). Objeto, ámbito de aplicación y sentido del Reglamento Europeo de Inteligencia Artificial. *El Reglamento Europeo de Inteligencia Artificial*, 28.

Bourreau, M. & De Streel, A. (2020). *The regulation of personalised pricing in the digital era*.https://www.oecd.org/competition/personalisedpricinginthedigitalera

Braithwaite, J. (2011). The essence of responsive regulation. *University of British Columbia Law Review*, *44*(3).

Calo, R. (2010). Mirando a HALs: Entendiendo la IA y la privacidad. *Revista de Estudios Jurídicos*, *2*(3), 170.

Cherry, M. (2016). Beyond misclassification: The digital transformation of work. *Comparative Labor Law & Policy Journal*, *37*(3).

Consejo de la Unión Europea. (2020, February). *Conclusiones de la Presidencia – La Carta de los Derechos Fundamentales en el contexto de la inteligencia artificial y el cambio digital*.https://data.consilium.europa.eu/doc/document/ST-11481-2020-INIT/es/pdf

Cotino Hueso, L., & Castellanos Claramunt, J. (2022). *Transparencia y explicabilidad de la Inteligencia Artificial*. Tirant Lo Blanch.

Council of the European Union. (2020, October 21). *Presidency conclusions: The Charter of Fundamental Rights in the Context of Artificial Intelligence and Digital Change*.https://www.consilium.europa.eu/media/46496/st11481-en20.pdf

Dans, E. (2017, July). *Los temibles peligros de la Inteligencia Artificial*.https://www.enriquedans.com/2017/07/los-temibles-peligros-de-la-inteligencia-artificial.html

Edwards, L. (2022, March). *Expert opinion: Regulating AI in Europe*. https://www.adalovelaceinstitute.org/wp-content/uploads/2022/03/Expert-opinion-Lilian-Edwards-Regulating-AI-in-Europe.pdf

Erdely, O. J. & Goldsmith, J. (2018). Regulating artificial intelligence: Proposal for a global solution. *AAIA/ACM Conference on Artificial Intelligence, Ethics, and Society*. https://ssrn.com/abstract=3263992

European Commission. (2020, February). *White paper on artificial intelligence: A European approach to excellence and trust.*eur-lex.europa.eu/legal-content/ES/TXT/PDF/?uri=CELEX:52020DC0065

European Commission. (2020, February). *Report on the safety and liability implications of Artificial Intelligence, the Internet of Things and robotics.* Commission Report on safety and liability implications of AI, the Internet of Things and Robotics - European Commission

European Commission. (2020, July 17). *White Paper on artificial intelligence: Public consultation towards a European approach for excellence and trust.* https://digital-strategy.ec.europa.eu/en/library/white-paper-artificial-intelligence-public-consultation-towards-european-approach-excellence-and

European Commission. (n.d.). Artificial intelligence. https://digital-strategy.ec.europa.eu/en/policies/artificial-intelligence

European Parliament. (2022). *Resolución del Parlamento Europeo, de 3 de mayo de 2022, sobre la inteligencia artificial en la era digital.*https://www.europarl.europa.eu/doceo/document/TA-9-2022-0140_ES.html

European Parliament & Council of the European Union. (2021). *Regulation (EU) 2024/1689 of the European Parliament and of the Council of 13 June 2024 laying down harmonised rules on artificial intelligence and amending Regulations (EC) No 300/2008, (EU) No 167/2013, (EU) No 168/2013, (EU) 2018/858, (EU) 2018/1139 and (EU) 2019/2144 and Directives 2014/90/EU, (EU) 2016/797 and (EU) 2020/1828 (Artificial Intelligence Act).* Official Journal of the European Union.

Geelan, T. (2021). The internet, social media and trade union revitalization: Still behind the digital curve or catching up? *New Technology, Work and Employment, 36*(2), 123–139. DOI: 10.1111/ntwe.12205

German Trade Union Confederation. (2022) Comments by the German Trade Union Confederation (Deutscher Gewerkschaftsbund – DGB) on the 34th National Report on the implementation of the European Social Charter https://rm.coe.int/comments-german-trade-union-confederation-deutscher-gewerkschaftsbund-/1680a736f2

Gerst, D. (2020). Mitbestimmung in digitalen und agilen Betrieben – das Modell einer prozessualen partnerschaftlichen Konfliktkultur. In Bader, V., & Kaiser, S. (Eds.), *Arbeit in der data society* (pp. 35–56). Springer. DOI: 10.1007/978-3-658-32276-2_3

Hacker, P. (2018, April). Teaching fairness to artificial intelligence: Existing and novel strategies Against algorithmic discrimination under EU law. *Common Market Law Review.*https://ssrn.com/abstract=3164973

Irani, L. (2015). The cultural work of microwork. *New Media & Society, 17*(5), 720–739. DOI: 10.1177/1461444813511926

Lee, M. K., Kusbit, D., Metsky, E., & Dabbish, L. (2015). Working with machines: The impact of algorithmic and data-driven management on human workers. In *Proceedings of the 33rd Annual ACM Conference on Human Factors in Computing Systems.* DOI: 10.1145/2702123.2702548

Miguez Macho, L., & Torres Carlos, M. (2018). Objeto, ámbito de aplicación y sentido del Reglamento Europeo de Inteligencia Artificial. *AAVV El Reglamento Europeo de Inteligencia Artificial* (pp. 79, 85).

Muñoz Paredes, M. L. (2020). Big data y contrato de seguro: Los datos generados por los asegurados y su utilización por los aseguradores. In A. Huergo Lora & G. M. Díaz González (Eds.), *La regulación de los algoritmos* (pp. 129). Thomson Reuters.

Organization for Economic Cooperation and Development. (2024, March). *Explanatory memorandum on the updated OECD definition of an AI system.*https://www.oecd.org/en/publications/explanatory-memorandum-on-the-updated-oecd-definition-of-an-ai-system_623da898-en.html

Presno Linera, M. A. (2023). La propuesta de Ley de Inteligencia Artificial europea. In *Revista de las Cortes Generales, 116*, 115. DOI: 10.33426/rcg/2023/116/1775

Reche Tello, N., Tur Ausina, R., Ortega Gimenez, C., & Sanjúan Andrés, F. J. (2022). La teoría constitucional frente a la transformación digital y las nuevas tecnologías. *Aranzadi, Cizur Menor,* 105.

Roberts, H., Cowls, J., Hine, E., Mazzi, F., Tsamados, A., Taddeo, M., & Floridi, L. (2021). Achieving a 'good AI society': Comparing the aims and progress of the EU and the US. *Science and Engineering Ethics, 27*(6), 68. DOI: 10.1007/s11948-021-00340-7 PMID: 34767085

Sartor, G. (2024). *Navigating the AI era: Insights and implications of the EU Artificial Intelligence Act.* https://www.jurist.org/commentary/2024/08/navigating-the-ai-era-insights-and-implications-of-the-eu-artificial-intelligence-act/

Scherer, M. (2016). Regulating artificial intelligence systems: Risks, challenges, competencies and strategies. *Harvard Journal of Law & Technology, 29*(2), 46.

Spanish Constitution (State Official Gazette No. 311, 29 December 1978).

Vega Iracelay, J. (2019). *Informática y Derecho*. Revista Iberoamericana de Derecho Informático., https://fiadi.org/wp-content/uploads/2020/02/FIADI-07.pdf

Von der Leyen, U. (n.d.). A union that strives for more: My agenda for Europe. *Political guidelines of the Commission 2019-2024*.https://commission.europa.eu/strategy-and-policy/priorities-2019-2024_en

Yeung, K. (2022, March 31). *People, risk and the unique requirements of AI*. https://www.adalovelaceinstitute.org/policy-briefing/eu-ai-act/

KEY TERMS AND DEFINITIONS

Accountable Automation: Holding AI systems and their developers responsible for the social and ethical implications of automated decision-making.

AI-Driven Surveillance: Monitoring technologies powered by AI that track employee performance and behavior.

Algorithmic Fairness: The assessment and mitigation of biases in AI systems to prevent discriminatory outcomes, especially in employment contexts.

Algorithmic Management: AI-driven systems used for decision-making in the workplace, impacting hiring, evaluations, and dismissals, with risks of bias and discrimination.

Bias Mitigation: Strategies and measures to identify and reduce prejudices embedded in AI systems to ensure equitable outcomes.

Collective Bargaining in AI: Leveraging union negotiations to influence the ethical design and deployment of AI systems in workplaces.

Digital Unionism: The role of trade unions in adapting to the digital age to protect labor rights against the impact of AI on employment.

Ethical AI Deployment: Implementing AI systems in a manner that aligns with human values, ensuring fairness and respect for individual rights.

Explainability in AI: Ensuring that AI systems provide clear and comprehensible reasoning for their decisions, particularly in employment contexts.

Firm Size: firm scale measured in number of employees. It usually categorized in small, medium and large firm

Fundamental Rights: Essential principles such as privacy, equality, and dignity, which may be at risk from unregulated use of artificial intelligence.

Human Oversight: Active involvement of individuals to monitor and mitigate risks associated with AI systems, ensuring ethical and fair decision-making.

Regulated Risk: A normative approach classifying AI applications by their potential impact, setting proportional restrictions to ensure responsible use.

Technological Transparency: The necessity to make AI systems' operations and decisions understandable to ensure human oversight and safeguard fundamental rights.

Worker Autonomy: Preserving employees' ability to make independent decisions and maintain control over their roles in the face of AI-driven management tools.

ENDNOTES

1 Regulation (EU) 2024/1689 of the European Parliament and of the Council of 13 June 2024 laying down harmonised rules on artificial intelligence and amending Regulations (EC) No 300/2008, (EU) No 167/2013, (EU) No 168/2013, (EU) 2018/858, (EU) 2018/1139 and (EU) 2019/2144 and Directives 2014/90/EU, (EU) 2016/797 and (EU) 2020/1828 (Artificial Intelligence Act) (Text with EEA relevance).

2 Law 3/1991, on Unfair Competition, published in the State Official Gazette No. 10, of January 11, 1991. https://wipolex-resources-eu-central-1-358922420655.s3.amazonaws.com/edocs/lexdocs/laws/es/es/es230es.pdf

3 Created by Commission Decision of 24 January 2024 as part of the administrative structure of the Directorate-General for Communications Networks, Content and Technologies of the European Commission.

4 Trade unions have developed a range of services aimed directly at platform workers or at a broader group of independent workers (for example, self-employed, civil law, contract workers) whose modus operandi is similar to everyday work. Online services such as faircrowd.work—an online platform launched by IG Metall, the Austrian Chamber of Labor, the Austrian Confederation of Trade Unions, and Unionen to evaluate (rank) digital platforms from the perspective of employees. The evaluation was based on questionnaires filled in by employees and the exchange of experience—have been developed. The portal also contains other useful information, such as basic knowledge about platform work, contacts with platform workers' trade unions, and a link to the "Frankfurt Declaration" (selbstaendigen.info). Another example is the online platform operated by Ver.di, aimed at independent contractors (self-employed, platform workers, etc.), providing legal, tax, and contract-related advice to both trade union members and other independent contractors. The latter group is charged a fee for advice, while trade unionists receive support through membership dues turespuestasindical.es, an online platform run by the Unión General de Trabajadores to provide information and advice platform workers in Spain. The platform's activities include information, enforcement

of rights, organization and termination issues, and the portal serves as a tool to promote trade union membership.

5 https://www.ine.es/dynt3/inebase/es/index.htm?padre=9940

6 https://www.boe.es/diario_boe/txt.php?id=BOE-A-2023-12870

Chapter 8
Trade Unions in AI-Era Workplace Harassment: A Criminological and Victimological Approach

Laura Gómez García
https://orcid.org/0000-0002-1599-6651
Universidad Francisco de Vitoria, Spain

ABSTRACT

This chapter examines the impact of artificial intelligence (AI) on workplace harassment and the role of trade unions in its prevention, detection, and mitigation. AI presents a paradox in workplace governance, reinforcing power imbalances while also identifying harassment patterns and improving workplace safety. The chapter explores both risks and opportunities AI introduces, emphasizing the necessity of ethical AI governance. It highlights trade unions' role in countering AI-driven discrimination through educational, regulatory, and technological strategies. Additionally, it examines how AI-driven transformations reshape unions, requiring adaptations in their advocacy strategies. Institutional collaboration is crucial in balancing technological advancement with social justice, calling for stronger partnerships between trade unions, regulatory bodies, and policymakers. The chapter underscores the need for proactive measures, such as AI audits and digital rights training, to ensure AI serves workplace fairness.

DOI: 10.4018/979-8-3693-8049-9.ch008

1. INTRODUCTION

Artificial intelligence (AI) has transformed workplace dynamics, enhancing efficiency but also introducing new social, ethical, and legal challenges. Workplace harassment, or mobbing, remains a complex issue, further intensified in the digital era. Victimology and criminology provide tools to address this, while trade unions play a crucial role in defending workers' rights.

It is important to distinguish between trade unions and human resource management (HRM). While HRM operates to maximize workforce performance and organizational goals, trade unions protect workers' rights, sometimes opposing HRM decisions that undermine labor conditions. This distinction is widely discussed, highlighting the conflicting roles they play in workplace governance.

This study focuses on unions' role in preventing, detecting, and addressing workplace harassment in AI-driven environments. The criminological and victimological approaches adopted here establish a framework for understanding union intervention in harassment cases, rather than examining their broader organizational transformations. Digitalization influences union strategies, prioritizing the intersection of AI technologies and workplace harassment.

AI's integration into workplace processes has necessitated a reassessment of trade union functions, shifting their role from traditional collective bargaining to advocating for workers' rights in AI-mediated environments. This transformation raises questions about power dynamics, adaptation of organizational structures to AI-driven workflows, and legal mechanisms to mitigate algorithmic biases that could foster harassment and discrimination.

The significance of this issue lies in the increasing reliance on AI in workplaces, reshaping traditional harassment forms. Virtual work, corporate messaging platforms, and pervasive digital surveillance have led to more subtle forms of harassment. For instance, exclusion from digital communications, excessive control through monitoring tools, or AI-generated biased evaluations represent contemporary manifestations of workplace harassment. These behaviors harm victims' well-being and impact workplace environments by reducing productivity, weakening team cohesion, and increasing employee turnover.

From a criminological perspective, workplace harassment can be understood as a criminal phenomenon arising from the interaction between individual and organizational factors. According to García-Pablos de Molina (1999), criminology not only analyzes the causes and dynamics of criminal behavior but also designs strategies for prevention and response. In the case of workplace harassment in the age of AI, criminology provides tools to identify patterns of hostile behavior, both in harassers and in the structures that perpetuate violence. For instance, criminological analysis can help uncover how rigid hierarchies, toxic organizational cultures, and the lack of ethical oversight in the use of AI facilitate the emergence of harassment dynamics.

On the other hand, victimology, with its focus on the experiences of victims, complements this analysis by identifying the effects of harassment on affected individuals and the conditions that make them vulnerable. In a digitalized environment, victims face particular challenges, such as the difficulty of proving harassment when it occurs in virtual spaces or the sense of isolation derived from remote work. Victimology emphasizes not only the importance of emotional and legal protection for these individuals but also the implementation of programs to prevent revictimization. For example, protocols that establish clear boundaries for the use of digital tools and provide accessible channels for reporting abusive behaviors are essential to ensure a safe workplace environment.

In this context, trade unions are positioned as key actors in integrating these scientific perspectives into their strategies. Prevention plays a central role, and unions can promote it through awareness campaigns that educate both workers and employers about workplace harassment, including how it manifests in AI-mediated environments. These campaigns should include training on the ethical use of digital tools, fostering a culture of respect and cooperation. Additionally, the early detection of harassment patterns is crucial. From a criminological perspective, trade unions can adopt AI-based technologies to monitor workplace dynamics without violating privacy, identifying warning signs such as drastic changes in team communication or the repeated exclusion of certain employees from collaborative tasks.

When it comes to intervention, unions must implement clear protocols to handle workplace harassment complaints, prioritizing a victimological approach that ensures confidentiality, emotional support, and comprehensive damage repair. For instance, the creation of interdisciplinary committees including criminologists and victimologists can enhance the capacity of unions to manage complex cases. Moreover, the implementation of restorative mechanisms, such as mediations or group sessions facilitated by experts, can help rebuild damaged workplace relationships, provided these practices do not compromise the safety of victims.

The justification for this approach lies in its ability to comprehensively address a multifaceted and evolving problem. While AI presents risks, it also offers opportunities to improve strategies for preventing, detecting, and intervening in workplace harassment. By integrating criminological and victimological perspectives, trade unions can not only guarantee the protection of labor rights but also contribute to the creation of safer, more inclusive, and more productive work environments. This approach benefits not only the victims but also strengthens organizations as a whole, fostering an atmosphere where workers can fully develop without fear of harassment or discrimination.

Therefore, the prevention, detection, and intervention of workplace harassment in the age of AI require an innovative and multidisciplinary approach. Trade unions have the opportunity to lead this change, supported by the principles and methodologies of criminology and victimology. By doing so, they not only address the needs of workers in a changing labor context but also contribute to a positive transformation of workplace dynamics in the digital society.

2. THE MULTIDIMENSIONAL IMPACT OF ARTIFICIAL INTELLIGENCE ON WORKPLACE HARASSMENT

Although the implementation of artificial intelligence (AI) in the workplace has brought significant advancements in terms of efficiency and productivity, it has also triggered a series of ethical, psychological, and social risks that affect workers' well-being. AI, as a disruptive tool, has the potential to radically transform workplace relationships, but this transformation does not always benefit everyone. In fact, its use can amplify negative dynamics such as workplace harassment, intensifying its effects at structural, organizational, and individual levels. In this context, trade unions, as protectors of workers' rights, face the challenge of redefining their strategies and collaborating closely with disciplines such as criminology and victimology to comprehensively address these issues. From an industrial relations standpoint, the implementation of AI in the workplace cannot be divorced from broader labor relations theories. For instance, Fox's (1974) *Frames of Reference* theory suggests that workplace dynamics can be viewed through either a unitarist, pluralist, or radical lens. As AI continues to influence workplace governance, trade unions must adapt their strategies to remain effective advocates for workers' rights. One key transformation is the shift from traditional collective bargaining toward a hybrid model that incorporates digital activism, algorithmic auditing, and AI-driven representation. This evolution is particularly relevant as AI tools now mediate hiring decisions, performance evaluations, and even dismissals. Without active intervention, these algorithmic processes may reinforce biases and erode workers' rights by limiting avenues for appeal and negotiation.

From an industrial relations perspective, the role of trade unions is expanding to include oversight of AI decision-making frameworks. For example, unions are increasingly pushing for transparency in AI-driven HR policies, demanding access to the underlying data sets and algorithms that shape employment conditions. This advocacy ensures that AI is not used as a tool for managerial control at the expense of workers' autonomy.

Moreover, trade unions are leveraging AI for their own operations, using predictive analytics to anticipate labor disputes and tailor their negotiation strategies accordingly. AI-powered chatbots and digital platforms are also being utilized to provide workers with real-time legal advice and facilitate anonymous reporting of workplace harassment. These innovations signal a fundamental shift in union operations, from reactive interventions to proactive engagement in shaping AI-driven workplaces.

Additionally, the legal dimension of workplace harassment in AI-mediated environments is becoming a central concern for trade unions. The increasing use of AI surveillance tools for productivity monitoring blurs the line between legitimate oversight and invasive micromanagement. This phenomenon underscores the need for updated labor laws that establish clear boundaries for AI use in the workplace. Trade unions, in collaboration with legal experts, are advocating for the development of AI-specific labor protections, ensuring that technology enhances, rather than undermines, workers' rights and organizational fairness A unitarist approach may downplay AI-driven harassment as an anomaly, while a pluralist perspective recognizes the conflicting interests of workers and management, advocating for stronger union interventions. A radical approach, aligned with neo-Marxist labor theory, sees AI as a tool that reinforces managerial control, thereby intensifying power asymmetries that facilitate workplace harassment.

AI can increase workplace harassment at a structural level by reinforcing pre-existing inequalities within organizations. AI algorithms, although technically neutral, are designed and programmed by humans, making them susceptible to implicit biases that perpetuate dynamics of exclusion and discrimination. For example, AI-based performance evaluation systems may be classified as objective but, in practice, can disproportionately penalize certain groups of workers due to biases in the data used to train them. This structural exclusion may lead to affected workers being perceived as "less valuable," making them more vulnerable to workplace harassment. Moreover, intensive monitoring through AI tools can exacerbate control over employees, fostering an environment of constant surveillance that facilitates harassing behaviors and creates a climate of insecurity. These practices not only affect direct victims but also dehumanize workplace relationships and erode trust within organizations.

At an organizational level, AI can alter power dynamics in the workplace, enabling new forms of harassment and mobbing. For instance, supervisors or managers may use AI tools to assign unequal workloads or deliberately exclude certain employees from key projects, constituting a form of mobbing. Additionally, the anonymity offered by some digital platforms can facilitate the proliferation of harassment in virtual spaces, such as emails, internal messaging apps, or project management systems. While this digitalization of workplace interactions may enhance efficiency, it can also blur the boundaries between appropriate and inappropriate behavior, making it harder to identify and address harassment.

At an individual level, AI can intensify the psychological effects of workplace harassment. Victims of mobbing in highly digitalized environments may experience a greater sense of isolation, as harassment can occur constantly and across multiple channels, even outside working hours. For example, a worker might be excluded from virtual meetings or receive derogatory comments on collaborative work platforms. This type of pervasive harassment not only undermines the victim's self-esteem and mental health but also makes it difficult for them to disconnect from the hostile environment, exacerbating stress and emotional exhaustion.

The role of trade unions in addressing workplace harassment should not be mistaken for that of human resource management (HRM). While HRM primarily focuses on organizational efficiency and legal compliance, its priorities may not always align with workers' interests, particularly when harassment cases involve management or require structural reforms that challenge corporate policies. In contrast, trade unions operate independently to uphold workers' rights, often working with HRM to ensure that protective measures are genuinely enforced rather than existing merely as symbolic policies.

Given this multidimensional impact, trade unions play a crucial role in mitigating the risks associated with AI and workplace harassment. However, to respond effectively to these challenges, they need to adopt an interdisciplinary approach that integrates the perspectives of criminology and victimology. Criminology, by studying the causes, dynamics, and prevention of criminal behavior, can provide valuable tools to identify harassment patterns enabled by technology and design strategies to prevent them. For example, a criminological analysis could reveal how biases in AI algorithms contribute to exclusion dynamics, offering a basis for implementing policies that ensure fairness and inclusivity in the use of these tools.

Victimology, on the other hand, by focusing on the experiences and needs of victims, can assist unions in developing effective support programs for workers affected by workplace harassment in digital environments. This includes creating clear protocols for reporting abusive behaviors, implementing emotional and legal support services, and promoting workplace environments where victims feel safe and supported. Additionally, victimology can contribute to raising awareness among workers and employers about the impact of workplace harassment, fostering an organizational culture that prioritizes respect and empathy.

Structural Impact: The Normalization of Algorithmic Control

The normalization of algorithmic control, as an emerging phenomenon in contemporary workplaces, exemplifies how artificial intelligence technologies are reshaping supervisory and power dynamics within organizations. Through advanced monitoring systems, companies can track employee behavior in real time, using metrics that, while justified under the premise of efficiency and optimization, deeply compromise workers' autonomy and privacy. This technocentric paradigm, represented in practices such as the continuous analysis of emails and digital activity to evaluate productivity, establishes an intensive surveillance model that categorizes employees based on predefined algorithmic standards (Kruger, 2024; Pillon, 2024). However, these metrics often lack contextual analysis, resulting in reductive evaluations that label employees as “unproductive” for reasons that overlook the specificities of their roles or circumstances.

This surveillance system, in addition to generating psychological stress and a constant sense of being watched, negatively affects organizational trust by being perceived as an invasive and dehumanizing form of control. As Melis (2024) points out, the indiscriminate use of such technologies can exacerbate existing inequalities while simultaneously undermining the emotional well-being of workers. Thus, the normalization of algorithmic control not only amplifies structural inequalities within the workplace but also raises ethical and practical questions about the balance between technological efficiency and human dignity.

Organizational Impact: The Bias of Algorithmic Victimization

Algorithmic victimization bias represents one of the most concerning dimensions of the organizational impact of artificial intelligence in workplace environments. This phenomenon refers to how algorithms, trained on historical data tainted by social biases, perpetuate and amplify pre-existing inequalities instead of mitigating them. Within organizations, this bias not only affects performance evaluations but also influences critical decisions such as task assignments and hiring processes, consolidating exclusionary dynamics that reinforce systems of structural discrimination.

Figure 1. The impact of AI on workplace harassment. Own elaboration.

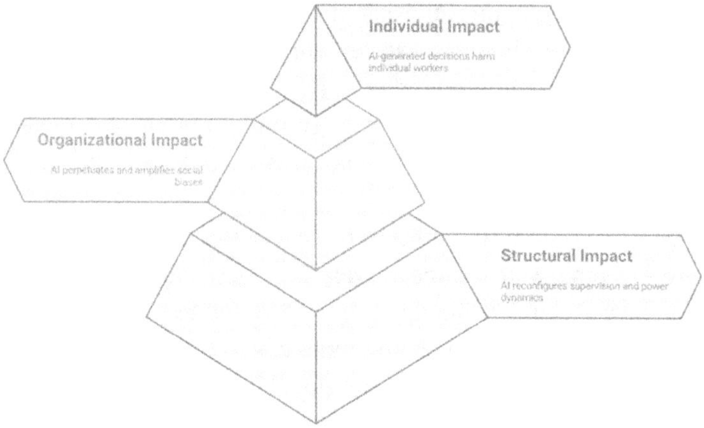

A paradigmatic example of this issue is the use of AI systems to identify "workplace risks." These tools, based on historical productivity or behavioral data, can disproportionately classify women with children or older employees as "less effective." This type of classification often stems from biased patterns in the data, which implicitly associate certain demographic characteristics with lower performance or commitment (Pillon, 2024). The result is a cycle of algorithmic discrimination that hinders equal opportunities and reinforces pre-existing barriers.

The consequences of this bias are profound and multifaceted. From an organizational perspective, algorithmic victimization bias generates systemic discrimination, wherein employees who belong to historically vulnerable groups—such as women, ethnic minorities, or older workers—face greater obstacles in advancing their careers. These dynamics not only directly affect the individuals impacted but also undermine the organizational fabric by discouraging diversity and inclusion. Additionally, the perception of unfair and biased evaluations contributes to the creation of toxic work environments, where employees feel that their efforts and competencies are neither recognized nor valued, ultimately eroding morale and commitment to the organization (Melis, 2024).

From an ethical and criminological perspective, algorithmic victimization bias presents significant challenges for organizational governance. Organizations that implement AI technologies without conducting thorough audits to identify and mitigate these biases become, consciously or unconsciously, enablers of discriminatory practices. The lack of transparency in algorithmic evaluation criteria not only undermines employees' trust in their employers but also exacerbates workplace tensions and exposes organizations to potential legal and reputational consequences.

Therefore, it is essential to adopt a proactive approach to address these problems. This includes the implementation of regular algorithmic audits to analyze how AI systems make decisions, as well as the introduction of intervention protocols that allow employees to challenge and appeal decisions perceived as unfair. Furthermore, trade unions and other regulatory bodies play a crucial role in ensuring that these technologies are used ethically and fairly, promoting organizational practices that prioritize both efficiency and equity.

Individual Impact: Structural Digital Victimization

Structural digital victimization has emerged as one of the most concerning manifestations of artificial intelligence technologies in the workplace. This phenomenon occurs when automated systems make harmful decisions that affect workers without the direct intervention of a human aggressor. Through algorithms designed to optimize processes, harassment dynamics evolve into less visible but equally destructive forms, where workers face opaque and non-appealable decisions based on partial or biased data.

A paradigmatic example is the use of algorithmic platforms to evaluate promotion eligibility. These tools prioritize quantitative metrics, such as measurable productivity, while ignoring fundamental qualitative factors such as leadership abilities or contributions to teamwork (Rospenda et al., 2023). This dehumanizing approach perpetuates a sense of inequity, where workers feel they are treated as mere numbers rather than as individuals with unique skills and experiences. The result is professional isolation, exacerbated by a lack of transparency in the criteria used to make decisions.

The psychological effects of this form of victimization are equally alarming. Chronic stress caused by constant scrutiny and uncertainty surrounding evaluation processes can lead to disorders such as anxiety and depression. Additionally, employees who perceive that organizational decisions are based exclusively on algorithms often experience a decline in their commitment and trust toward the company, further intensifying the emotional impact and deteriorating the overall workplace environment (Einarsen et al., 2009).

This psychological toll is profound, driven by uncertainty, a lack of transparency, and constant interaction with automated systems. These effects can manifest across three key dimensions: stress and anxiety, organizational distrust, and technological burnout.

Stress and anxiety emerge as one of the earliest negative manifestations in AI-mediated environments. The lack of clarity about how work actions and results are evaluated creates a sense of uncertainty among employees, which can escalate into chronic stress (Tru a, 2024). This dynamic is particularly problematic in organizations where algorithms determine critical aspects such as performance evaluations, task assignments, or even promotion decisions, fostering an environment in which workers feel constantly monitored and assessed.

Organizational distrust is another significant consequence of the lack of transparency in AI systems. Employees often remain unaware of the criteria by which algorithms make decisions, creating a disconnect between workers and their supervisors or leaders. This phenomenon can undermine organizational cohesion and reduce motivation, as workers perceive technological tools as intrusive and dehumanizing (Ali et al., 2024).

Finally, technological burnout describes the emotional and physical exhaustion stemming from constant interaction with automated systems. The reliance on digital tools, particularly those perceived as intrusive, demands continuous adaptation, which increases psychological fatigue. Recent studies highlight that the feeling of being replaceable by automated systems amplifies the risk of burnout, as employees struggle to prove their value in a highly technologized environment (Ali et al., 2024).

To mitigate these effects, it is crucial for organizations to develop policies that prioritize psychological well-being in the implementation of AI technologies. This includes ensuring transparency in algorithmic processes, creating safe spaces for employee feedback, and promoting workplace practices that balance technological interaction with human development. An immediate and structured intervention is required. Organizations must implement measures that guarantee transparency and fairness in the use of AI technologies, such as regular audits to identify and correct biases in algorithmic systems. Additionally, it is essential to establish clear and accessible appeal mechanisms that allow employees to challenge decisions perceived as unfair.

In this regard, criminology and victimology provide essential analytical frameworks to understand and address these dynamics. From a victimological perspective, the abusive use of AI technologies in workplace environments has reconfigured victimization dynamics. This phenomenon not only affects employees psychologically and emotionally but also transforms their perception of the workplace as a safe and fair space. Victims of these practices face significant challenges, including chronic stress, loss of trust in their employers, and emotional isolation. These forms of victimization, as they do not rely on a direct aggressor, present unique challenges in terms of identification and resolution (Halder, 2021).

To address these issues, victimology proposes strategies aimed at mitigating the effects of algorithmic victimization and empowering affected employees:

- Anonymous Reporting Protocols: Employees need reliable systems where they can report abusive practices related to AI without fear of retaliation. These systems must ensure confidentiality, provide prompt responses, and be monitored by independent entities.
- Recovery Programs: Comprehensive psychological and legal support services are essential for victims. These programs should include therapy to manage stress and anxiety caused by monitoring practices, as well as legal assistance to challenge unfair decisions made by algorithms. Additionally, digital literacy initiatives can help employees better understand how these technologies operate and identify unfair practices (Pangalila, 2024).

Furthermore, it is imperative to foster an organizational culture centered on dignity and respect. Education and training on employees' rights in the context of AI can empower victims and reduce the incidence of abuse. This not only benefits the individuals affected but also strengthens commitment and cohesion within organizations.

3. PROFILES OF HARASSERS AND VICTIMS IN THE WORKPLACE: A CRIMINOLOGICAL AND VICTIMOLOGICAL ANALYSIS

Analyzing the profiles of harassers and victims in the workplace from criminological and victimological perspectives allows us to identify behavioral patterns and underlying dynamics that enable the emergence of mobbing. This innovative (and necessary) approach not only seeks to understand the individual characteristics of the actors involved but also the structural and organizational conditions that contribute to perpetuating such behaviors. This knowledge is essential for designing effective prevention and intervention programs.

Profile of the Harasser

Harassers often exhibit psychological and behavioral traits that set them apart from other employees. These characteristics may be influenced by both individual traits and organizational dynamics that foster and perpetuate hostile and toxic behaviors.

Below are some of the elements commonly found in workplace harassers:

- Aggressiveness and Hostility: Harassers often exhibit high levels of aggressiveness, which may manifest in intimidating behaviors and hostile communication. According to the social control theory (Cohen & Felson, 1979), the lack of regulation in highly competitive work environments can enable these individuals to act without restraint, exacerbating their tendency toward aggression. Furthermore, Bonta et al. (1998) highlight that these individuals often struggle with impulse control, contributing to the creation of tense and stressful workplace environments.

- Narcissism and Need for Control: Harassers are often obsessed with their self-image and seek constant recognition. Their need for control translates into behaviors that undermine trust and collaboration within the team.
- Low Empathy and Emotional Disconnection: A lack of empathy for their coworkers is another distinctive trait of harassers. This emotional disconnection facilitates insensitive and cruel behaviors, which often form the core of workplace harassment.
- Active Inefficient Mediocrity Syndrome (AIMS): Characterized by envy of others' success, feelings of inferiority, and an excessive need for recognition, this syndrome is common among harassers.

Figure 2. Concept map: Profile of the harasser

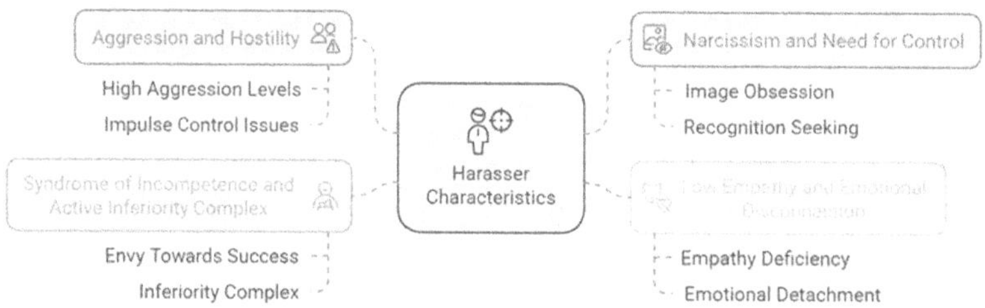

The profile of the harasser in cases of mobbing (workplace harassment) is defined by a set of psychological and behavioral characteristics that differentiate them from other employees. These traits stem not only from individual predispositions but also from organizational dynamics that, either explicitly or implicitly, encourage and perpetuate hostile behaviors. Victimology and theories related to human behavior have identified several patterns in harassers that help explain their tendency toward these destructive practices in the workplace.

One of the most common traits is aggressiveness and hostility, which manifests as intimidating, confrontational behaviors and communication often marked by threats or disdain. Harassers with these traits tend to use fear as a tool to dominate their victims, creating a constant atmosphere of tension in the workplace. According to the social control theory (Cohen & Felson, 1979), the lack of regulation in highly competitive or unstructured work environments allows such behaviors to occur without restraint. For instance, in a sales team with high-performance targets, a harasser might publicly humiliate a colleague for failing to meet their goals, reinforcing their position of power through intimidation. Additionally, Bonta et al. (1998) point out that harassers often struggle with impulse control, leading to disproportionate reactions to workplace situations and further contributing to stress and toxicity within the environment.

Another prominent trait is narcissism and the need for control. Narcissistic harassers are obsessed with their self-image and are constantly seeking recognition and validation. According to Kernberg (1975), pathological narcissism drives such individuals to manipulate situations and justify their actions as necessary to maintain their status or authority. In a workplace context, this can manifest in practices such as deliberately excluding colleagues from important decisions or taking credit for others' achievements. For example, a manager with narcissistic tendencies may dismiss a subordinate’s ideas only to later present them as their own to the company’s leadership, undermining team morale and fostering an environment of mistrust. This relentless need for control not only destroys interpersonal relationships but also undermines collaboration and teamwork—key elements of a healthy workplace environment.

Low empathy and emotional disconnection is another key element in the profile of the harasser. These individuals are unable to consider the impact of their actions on others, which facilitates cruel and insensitive behaviors. According to the empathy theory (Davis, 1983), low levels of empathy lead harassers to ignore or trivialize the suffering of their victims, perpetuating abusive dynamics. For instance, a harasser might insist on assigning unattainable tasks to an already overburdened colleague, deliberately ignoring the negative impact on their physical and mental health. This emotional disconnection not only exacerbates the victims' suffering but also fosters a cycle of dehumanization that affects the entire team.

A particularly relevant aspect of the harasser's profile is the Active Inefficient Mediocrity Syndrome (AIMS), which, according to Llerena Idrobo (2022), is characterized by envy of others' success, feelings of inferiority, and an excessive need for recognition. Harassers with this syndrome perceive successful colleagues as a direct threat to their position, leading them to sabotage their achievements or discredit them in front of others. For example, an employee with AIMS might spread malicious rumors about a high-performing colleague to damage their reputation and divert attention toward themselves. This behavior is exacerbated in workplaces that prioritize extreme competitiveness, where one person's success may be perceived as another's failure.

The profile of the harasser combines personal factors, such as aggressiveness, narcissism, and lack of empathy, with contextual elements, such as the absence of regulation and the promotion of a culture of excessive competition. These traits and dynamics not only harm the victims but also create a toxic workplace environment that undermines productivity and the overall well-being of all employees. Understanding this profile is essential for designing intervention and prevention strategies that can identify and address such behaviors before they become a broader threat to the workplace as a whole.

Profile of the Victim

The profile of the victim in cases of mobbing (workplace harassment) is defined by the presence of certain characteristics that, to varying degrees, increase their susceptibility to victimization. These characteristics are not always intrinsic to the individual; in many cases, they are a result of how others perceive them within the framework of organizational dynamics and workplace relationships. A victimological analysis helps to understand how these personal or contextual traits can influence the likelihood of becoming a target of hostile and systematic behaviors:

- *Enviable Victims: Enviable victims are often highly competent individuals with notable achievements, which can generate resentment among their colleagues. Victimology highlights that this perception can trigger harassment dynamics driven by the envy and insecurity of the harassers.*
- *Vulnerable Victims: Vulnerable victims, on the other hand, are often individuals with characteristics that make them appear defenseless, such as insecurity or personal issues.*
- *Threatening Victims: These are individuals who challenge established norms or question existing hierarchies. Although competent, they may be perceived as disruptive. This type of victim can be seen as an obstacle to the harassers' interests.*

Among the most common profiles, we find **enviable victims**. These are individuals who are highly competent, with exceptional skills or notable achievements in their professional careers, which can generate resentment or insecurity among their colleagues or superiors. According to Cohen & Felson (1979), such individuals may be perceived as a threat to the balance of power in the workplace, especially when their abilities overshadow those of others. From this perspective, victimology emphasizes that harassment motivated by envy often arises as a defensive mechanism for harassers, who seek to destabilize the envied individual to protect their own positions of power or influence within the organization. In this sense, mobbing can be seen as an attempt to sabotage the recognition or success of these victims, creating a hostile and demotivating environment for them.

On the other hand, there are vulnerable victims, individuals who, due to certain personal or contextual characteristics, are perceived as more defenseless in the face of abusive situations. These characteristics may include low self-esteem, emotional insecurity, personal problems, or a lack of support in the workplace. According to Bonta et al. (1998), such victims are seen as easy targets because harassers perceive them as less likely to confront or report the aggressions they experience. This perception reinforces dynamics of exclusion and isolation, as harassers encounter little to no resistance to their actions. Additionally, this vulnerability can be strategically exploited in organizations with rigid hierarchical structures or toxic workplace cultures, where individuals in lower positions are often less equipped to defend themselves or access support.

Finally, there are threatening victims, individuals who, despite being competent, are perceived as disruptive within the organizational context. These people often challenge established norms, question rigid hierarchies, or propose changes that may unsettle those who are comfortable with the status quo. Trijueque et al. (2008) emphasize that such victims tend to be seen as obstacles to the interests of harassers, particularly when their actions or attitudes challenge the privileges, power, or influence of the latter. In these cases, harassment may be driven by the desire to neutralize those who represent a threat to the harassers' stability or control over the workplace environment.

Figure 3. Concept map: Profile of the workplace harassment victim. Own elaboration.

It is important to emphasize that these profiles are not mutually exclusive, as a single victim may exhibit enviable, vulnerable, and threatening characteristics in different contexts or stages of their professional life. Moreover, the phenomenon of mobbing does not depend solely on the victim's characteristics but also on power dynamics, organizational structures, and the cultural values that dominate the workplace. Victimology highlights the need to analyze these interactions from a comprehensive perspective, promoting not only the protection of victims but also the development of preventive and corrective strategies that foster healthy and harassment-free work environments.

4. PREVENTING WORKPLACE HARASSMENT THROUGH CRIMINOLOGY AND COLLABORATION WITH TRADE UNIONS

Criminology provides a robust analytical framework for understanding and preventing workplace harassment, addressing this phenomenon as a form of victimization within organizational environments. Its approach, combined with the active collaboration of trade unions, enables the development of comprehensive strategies that not only identify risk factors but also promote well-being and respect in the workplace. In this context, trade unions play a crucial role as mediators between the interests of workers and organizations, ensuring that technological tools and corporate policies are used to foster healthy and equitable work environments.

The prevention of workplace harassment begins with building a cooperative relationship between trade unions and corporate management. This collaboration should focus on the establishment of codes of conduct that include specific clauses on the ethical use of advanced technologies, such as artificial intelligence (AI). These codes should promote fair and transparent practices, ensuring that technological tools do not become instruments of control or harassment (Cusicanqui Peñaranda, 2016). Trade unions must also assert their distinct role from human resource management (HRM) in shaping harassment prevention strategies. Research indicates that HRM tends to adopt a reactive approach, handling complaints within internal processes, whereas trade unions advocate for more comprehensive structural reforms, such as legal protections, collective bargaining agreements, and independent oversight—areas that HRM may not prioritize (Kelley, 2024). Maintaining this distinction is essential for effective workplace governance and the protection of workers' rights. Workplace harassment must also be addressed from a legal perspective, ensuring that victims have access to justice beyond internal workplace procedures. International labor law frameworks, such as the ILO Convention No. 190 on Violence and Harassment (2019), emphasize the need for legally binding policies to combat workplace harassment effectively. Trade unions must work alongside legal experts to ensure that company policies align with national and international regulations, providing victims with legal resources, protection from retaliation, and mechanisms to hold employers accountable for failing to prevent harassment (Sánchez Rodríguez & Mandujano Montoya, 2024).

In this regard, trade unions have the responsibility to promote and lead the implementation of organizational policies that prioritize employee well-being. This involves fostering an inclusive work environment where decision-making incorporates the active participation of workers. The promotion of mechanisms for constructive conflict resolution becomes an essential pillar for preventing hostility and harassment dynamics.

Once again, effective training and awareness-raising are indispensable. The training of employees and supervisors is fundamental for detecting and preventing mobbing. Training programs should focus on recognizing early signs of harassment, such as social isolation or manipulation. Furthermore, the use of technologies such as interactive simulations based on augmented reality can serve as an innovative and effective tool. These simulations not only enhance workers' coping skills but also enable them to make informed decisions in critical situations (De la Espriella Casas, 2017).

On the other hand, constant oversight of technological tools is a critical aspect of harassment prevention. Trade unions must actively participate in reviewing privacy and monitoring policies, negotiating limits on the use of these tools to ensure they are not exploited as instruments of victimization. Regular audits, such as those proposed by Escudero (2011), are essential to identify and address potential biases or abuses in technological systems before they result in significant harm.

In addition, trade unions must:

- Conduct regular audits as a key preventive measure. These evaluations allow organizations to identify patterns and risk dynamics associated with the use of technological tools and the overall workplace environment. Trade unions must demand detailed reports on the impact of technologies and the effectiveness of policies implemented to prevent harassment.
- Promote collaborative environments through the redesign of workplace dynamics as another effective preventive strategy. Proposing organizational structures that encourage equity, constructive conflict resolution, and mutual respect helps build a positive work environment. According to Montes (2013), these measures not only reduce the incidence of harassment but also strengthen team commitment and cohesion.
- Work and invest in early detection and ongoing training on digital platforms. One of the most innovative measures for the early detection of workplace harassment is the implementation of anonymous digital platforms. Torres Duro (2015) highlights that these tools, supported by artificial intelligence, can categorize and prioritize complaints, enabling quick intervention in critical

cases. To ensure their effectiveness, it is essential to establish clear protocols that guarantee the confidentiality and security of the reports. Periodic surveys on workplace climate and psychosocial risk assessments are essential tools for identifying behavior patterns related to harassment before they escalate.

- These evaluations allow organizations to anticipate conflicts and mitigate their impacts (Sánchez, 2014).

Figure 4. Union prevention of workplace harassment.

Certainly, the implementation of these strategies requires a systematic and continuous approach, with trade unions gathering data on the frequency and severity of harassment incidents, evaluating the effectiveness of interventions carried out, and adjusting policies as needed. The creation of an organizational value system based on equality, justice, and respect is essential to fostering a safe and healthy workplace environment.

5. TRADE UNION INTERVENTION IN WORKPLACE HARASSMENT CASES

Trade unions play a crucial role in protecting victims' rights and restoring fairness in workplace harassment cases by maintaining their independence from human resource management (HRM). While HRM is responsible for enforcing internal policies, it often prioritizes employer interests, leading to superficial or biased resolutions. In contrast, trade unions advocate for meaningful structural reforms, insisting on transparency, external oversight, and legally binding agreements that HRM alone cannot ensure (Krzywdzinski et al., 2023). This distinction is essential in making workplace harassment prevention strategies genuinely effective rather than merely symbolic.

As representatives of workers, trade unions must adopt a comprehensive approach that integrates psychological, legal, and organizational support, ensuring that victims are heard, protected, and empowered. An industrial relations perspective provides deeper insight into union interventions. Clegg's (1979) *Pluralist Theory of Industrial Relations* positions trade unions as a counterbalance to managerial power, ensuring that worker grievances—including harassment—are addressed through structured bargaining processes. Similarly, Freeman and Medoff's (1984) *What Do Unions Do?* highlights unions' role in improving workplace conditions, reducing discrimination, and strengthening grievance mechanisms. By incorporating these perspectives, it becomes evident that trade union interventions are not just reactive responses but part of a broader effort to reshape power dynamics in the workplace.

To achieve this, the following approaches are essential:

- Victimological Approach and Comprehensive Support: The victimological approach in trade union intervention prioritizes the needs and rights of victims, aiming to provide comprehensive support that encompasses both emotional well-being and legal advice. Llerena Idrobo (2022) argues that these elements, intrinsic to this perspective, are essential for addressing the trauma resulting from workplace harassment, helping victims regain their self-esteem and confidence in the workplace. Trade unions must facilitate access to specialized resources, such as legal services that inform victims about their rights and legal options, as well as safe spaces where they can share their experiences without fear of retaliation.
- Specialized Psychological Approach: Psychological support is one of the most critical dimensions of trade union intervention. Victims of workplace harassment face high levels of stress, anxiety, and, in many cases, depression. Trade unions should establish collaborative networks with specialized psychologists or mental health services to provide immediate and effective assistance. Psychological consultations not only help victims manage the emotions resulting from harassment but also contribute to preventing future incidents by developing coping tools for the victims (Espinosa & Parra, 2022).
- Trade Union Mediation as a Preventive Strategy: Trade union mediation is a powerful tool for addressing conflicts constructively. By acting as media-

tors, unions can facilitate dialogue between the parties involved, promoting agreements that benefit both the victims and the organizations. Mediation can reduce the polarization of conflicts and foster collaboration, minimizing the emotional impact of harassment and contributing to the creation of a more harmonious work environment.

- Protection of Victims' Rights: Ensuring the protection of victims' rights is a top priority in trade union intervention. Unions must implement policies that guarantee victims are treated fairly and respectfully throughout the conflict resolution process. This includes establishing clear protocols for investigating harassment complaints, enforcing appropriate sanctions against harassers, and monitoring workplace conditions afterward to prevent retaliation.
- Collaborative Approach with External Institutions: Collaboration with external institutions, such as mental health services, labor organizations, and relevant authorities, is essential for providing comprehensive support to victims. This collaboration extends the reach of trade union interventions and ensures that victims receive the necessary care to overcome trauma. Additionally, engagement with these entities allows unions to stay informed about best practices and innovative approaches in managing workplace harassment (Espinosa & Parra, 2022).
- Comprehensive and Sustainable Approach: Trade union intervention in workplace harassment cases must be comprehensive, addressing the emotional, legal, and organizational needs of victims. Additionally, unions should work toward transforming organizational culture by promoting values such as equality, justice, and respect in the workplace. This approach not only benefits victims but also strengthens cohesion and trust within the work environment.

Figure 5. Trade union strategies to combat workplace harassment and protect victims. Own elaboration.

To effectively address workplace harassment, it is essential for trade unions to adopt strategies based on two key pillars: confidentiality and the continuous education, training, evaluation, and monitoring of these cases. These elements not only ensure the protection of victims but also contribute to preventing future incidents and fostering a respectful and safe work environment.

First, confidentiality must be regarded as a fundamental principle in any trade union intervention. Ensuring that victims can report harassment cases safely, reliably, and, if necessary, anonymously is crucial for building trust in union mechanisms. According to Llerena Idrobo (2022), implementing policies that protect the identity of victims not only fosters confidence in union processes but also increases workers' willingness to report incidents. This is particularly relevant in workplace environments where fear of retaliation or social stigma may discourage victims from seeking help. For instance, a union protocol that guarantees confidentiality could include encrypted digital reporting channels or the appointment of external mediators to act as impartial intermediaries in managing cases. These measures not only facilitate incident reporting but also send a clear message that the union is committed to protecting and supporting workers' well-being.

In addition, for these initiatives to be effective, trade unions must combine confidentiality with continuous education and training for both employees and supervisors. Training on the prevention of workplace harassment is a fundamental tool for raising awareness among employees about the early identification of hostile behaviors and promoting attitudes that encourage collaboration and respect. Training programs should cover topics such as subtle forms of harassment, the psychological impact on victims, and intervention strategies. For example, practical workshops could include simulations of conflict situations and analysis of real-life cases, providing participants with concrete tools to respond appropriately to potential incidents.

Training should not only focus on victims and their rights but also emphasize the responsibility of supervisors and organizational leaders to prevent and effectively manage conflicts. Empowering leaders with the skills and knowledge to identify and address harassment can create a ripple effect, fostering a culture of accountability and respect throughout the workplace.

Evaluation and continuous monitoring are equally critical to ensuring the success of these interventions. Trade unions must regularly track reported cases to ensure that victims are receiving the necessary support and that the measures implemented are effective. This process includes the systematic collection of data on harassment incidents, the outcomes of interventions, and the overall impact on the workplace environment. By analyzing this data, unions can identify recurring patterns, areas for improvement, and opportunities to proactively adjust their strategies. For example, if an analysis reveals that certain departments or teams experience higher rates of harassment, this could indicate the need for targeted interventions, such as additional training or changes in supervisory practices.

Additionally, monitoring must include a focus on the comprehensive recovery of victims. This involves providing not only emotional support, such as access to psychological counseling services, but also legal and professional assistance to ensure that victims can continue their career development without fear of retaliation. For instance, unions can establish support networks among workers who have experienced similar situations, creating a safe space to share experiences and coping strategies

On the other hand, evaluating the impact of interventions allows trade unions to identify which strategies are most effective and which require adjustments. For example, if an anonymous reporting protocol results in a significant increase in reports, this could indicate that workers trust the system. Conversely, low participation might suggest the need to strengthen communication or ensure greater confidentiality.

In addition, unions can conduct regular surveys to measure workers' satisfaction with how harassment cases are handled and to assess the impact of preventive actions on their perception of the workplace climate.

6.THE ETHICAL USE OF TECHNOLOGY: A TRADE UNION COMMITMENT

In the contemporary workplace, the integration of technology presents significant ethical challenges, particularly concerning privacy, equity, and respect for labor rights.

A trade union commitment to the ethical use of technology is not just an ethical responsibility but a necessity for defining strategies to protect employees' rights and dignity. Unions must play an active role in overseeing and regulating the technological impact on workplace environments, ensuring that implemented tools do not become instruments of oppressive control (Montero Ruiz, 2017). Although the relationship between trade unions and AI is often examined through the lens of workplace harassment, it is equally important to expand this analysis to the evolving role of unions in a digitalized labor market. As AI and digital platforms become increasingly embedded in employment relations, unions must rethink their strategies for worker representation, collective bargaining, and mobilization. Research suggests that AI-driven tools can enhance union activism, support negotiations, and strengthen worker solidarity in virtual environments (Kelley, 2024). Addressing this challenge is essential to ensuring that technological advancements do not weaken unions' influence but instead enable them to advocate effectively for workers in AI-driven workplaces.

How Can Artificial Intelligence Prevent Workplace Harassment?

One of the most promising applications of artificial intelligence (AI) in the workplace is its potential to prevent harassment. Studies such as that of Castro (2016) highlight that AI can detect behavioral patterns associated with mobbing through advanced algorithms that analyze real-time interactions. These tools enable organizations to take preventive measures before conflicts escalate, fostering a safer and more respectful work environment.

However, the implementation of these technologies must be handled cautiously to ensure that preventive measures do not become invasions of privacy or instruments of excessive surveillance. Employee privacy is a critical aspect of the ethical use of technology. Trade unions must ensure that technological tools respect workers' personal and professional data. This includes setting clear boundaries for activity monitoring and avoiding the use of technology as a means of excessive control.

Montero Ruiz (2017) emphasizes that trade unions have the responsibility to negotiate agreements that regulate the use of AI in workplace environments, safeguarding employees' rights against potential abuses. By doing so, unions can strike a balance between leveraging AI for positive workplace transformation and protecting workers' fundamental rights.

A good starting point would be the promotion of transparency in the implementation of technologies in the workplace. Trade unions should demand that organizations clearly inform employees about how technological tools are used, what data is collected, and for what purpose. This approach not only builds trust but also empowers workers to actively participate in the creation of a fairer work environment.

Furthermore, to promote technological equity, trade unions must work closely with experts to design inclusive and bias-free technological systems. This means ensuring that tools are accessible and beneficial for all employees, regardless of their personal or professional characteristics. Fernández-López (2019) emphasizes the importance of involving workers in the design of these technologies, ensuring that they reflect the real needs of the workplace environment.

It is not just about regulation; the focus should also be on:

- The development of training programs that promote a culture of shared responsibility in the implementation and use of technologies. An informed workforce is essential to ensure the ethical sustainability of technological transformations (Sánchez, 2020).
- Collaboration between trade unions and organizations is crucial to ensure that technology serves as a tool for progress rather than a factor of exclusion. This cooperation should focus on designing and implementing technological systems that are not only efficient but also inclusive, respectful, and equitable.

7. CONCLUSIONS

In the age of artificial intelligence (AI), workplace harassment has evolved into a multidimensional phenomenon that combines technological, organizational, and social aspects. This shift demands an integrated and coordinated approach that involves not only trade unions, employers, workers, and authorities but also incorporates the perspective of criminology as a key tool to understand and address the dynamics of this issue. Through this discipline, patterns of victimization can be identified, risks associated with the use of technology can be assessed, and strategies that promote organizational justice can be designed. Trade unions, as vital protectors of workers' rights, must focus on ensuring that AI is implemented in ways that protect employees from harassment and systemic discrimination. Rather than spreading their efforts across various labor issues, their primary concern should be advocating for responsible AI governance, ensuring that these technologies help reduce workplace inequalities and foster safer, more ethical working environments.

The transformation of trade unions in the AI era is not just a matter of advocacy but of survival. As AI reshapes work relationships, collective representation must evolve to ensure that AI-enhanced workplaces are ethical, fair, and legally compliant. This requires proactive engagement with policymakers to develop AI-specific labor laws, incorporating insights from criminology, victimology, and industrial relations. Future research should examine how AI-driven changes impact union representation and worker involvement in AI governance.

The ability of trade unions to influence organizational policies is fundamental to creating safer, fairer, and more respectful workplace environments. According to Castro (2016), trade unions must actively participate in human resource management, contributing to the development of policies that prioritize ethics, transparency, and employee well-being. This role includes promoting codes of conduct that explicitly prohibit workplace harassment and regulate the use of advanced technologies such as AI, preventing these tools from becoming mechanisms of exclusion or abusive surveillance. From a criminological perspective, this participation not only regulates workplace relations but also helps to identify the structures that perpetuate mobbing, which must be transformed to ensure a fairer work environment.

Beyond their regulatory role, trade unions have the responsibility to lead cultural transformation within organizations by designing educational strategies that foster an organizational culture based on respect, collaboration, and empathy. These initiatives may include workshops, seminars, and training programs focused on effective communication, stress management, and constructive conflict resolution. These activities not only prevent workplace harassment but also strengthen interpersonal relationships and promote stronger cohesion in the workplace. From a criminological perspective, these educational actions are essential, as they address power dynamics and structural inequalities that often serve as a breeding ground for harassment.

Technology, and AI in particular, offers significant potential for the prevention of workplace harassment, especially in identifying behavioral patterns associated with mobbing. According to Castro (2016), implementing algorithms capable of analyzing real-time interactions can enable organizations to intervene early and prevent conflicts from escalating. However, these advances also raise critical challenges related to employee privacy and security. Montero Ruiz (2017) warns that trade unions must play a crucial role in ensuring these tools are used ethically and beneficially, preventing them from becoming instruments of oppressive surveillance. Criminology contributes in this context by assessing the ethical and structural risks of using such technologies and proposing algorithmic audits and ethical oversight as key preventive measures.

In addition, the implementation of AI technologies must be accompanied by measures to ensure their fairness and accessibility. Trade unions, in collaboration with experts and from a criminological perspective, can work on designing inclusive technological systems that avoid perpetuating biases and structural inequalities. This combination of technical oversight and critical analysis helps create workplace environments where all employees, regardless of their individual characteristics, feel valued and respected.

The prevention of workplace harassment requires an integrated approach that goes beyond physical violence to also address psychological and emotional harm. Trade unions should advocate for policies that promote workers' mental health, including access to specialized psychological services and the creation of wellness programs that help balance personal and professional lives. The impact of workplace harassment on mental health can be devastating, manifesting in chronic stress, anxiety, and depression. From a criminological perspective, this phenomenon can be understood as a form of structural victimization that requires not only individual responses but also organizational ones. By incorporating this perspective, trade unions can design restorative justice programs that not only meet the needs of victims but also transform the dynamics that perpetuate the problem.

The success of any strategy to prevent and address workplace harassment depends on collaboration among all stakeholders. It is essential to establish ongoing dialogue between trade unions, companies, employees, and authorities to design sustainable solutions and ensure their effectiveness. Criminology enhances this dialogue by providing a detailed analysis of power and control dynamics within organizations, allowing for the identification and resolution of structural factors contributing to mobbing.

This collaboration should also include the development of innovative tools, such as anonymous digital platforms for reporting harassment cases, ethical monitoring systems, and follow-up programs to continuously evaluate the impact of implemented policies.

The era of AI presents significant challenges but also offers unique opportunities for trade unions, supported by criminology and victimology, to lead a transformation toward safer workplace environments. By combining the critical analysis and tools of criminology with the action-oriented capacity of trade unions, it is possible to ensure that technology is used as a tool for progress rather than a source of exclusion or victimization. This joint effort not only protects workers but also contributes to building a more just, ethical, and humane future of work, where innovation and social justice coexist in harmony.

REFERENCES

Ali, T., Hussain, I., Hassan, S., & Anwer, S. (2024). Examine how the rise of AI and automation affects job security, stress levels, and mental health in the workplace. *Bulletin of Business and Economics*. Recuperado de https://bbejournal.com/BBE/article/download/1016/1123

Aliane, N., & Mirzaliev, S. (2024). Impact of cyber-victimization on anger and frustration: Role of AI, e-governance, and cyberbullying coping. *International Journal of Cyber Criminology, 18*(1), 171–194. DOI: 10.5281/zenodo.4766810

Amoadu, M., Sarfo, J. O., & Ansah, E. W. (2024). Working conditions of commercial drivers: A scoping review of psychosocial work factors, health outcomes, and interventions. *BMC Public Health*. Recuperado de https://link.springer.com/article/10.1186/s12889-024-20465-1

Anastasia, P., Stratton, G., & Cameron, R. (2018). *Digital Criminology: Crime and Justice in Digital Society*. Routledge., DOI: 10.4324/9781315205786

Antonella Tiravassi, A., Safranoff, A., & Cavalo, L. (2022). *El rol del sindicato en la prevención y acompañamiento frente a la violencia y acoso laboral*. Unión del Personal Auxiliar de Casas Particulares (UPACP).

Arstanbekov, M., Seidakmatov, N., Tatenov, M., Kanybekova, B., & Kakeshov, B. (2024). Victimological aspects of countering internet crime: State and local government practices. *Social & Legal Studies, 7*(1), 221–234. DOI: 10.32518/sals1.2024.221

Barberet, R. (2000). *La investigación criminológica y la política criminal. Revista de Derecho Penal y Criminología, 2ª Época, 5, 221-242*. Recuperado de. [archivo proporcionado]

Bernat Jiménez, M.. (2011). *Victimología: Una introducción a la ciencia de la víctima*. Editorial Reverte.

Bonta, J., & Andrews, D. A. (1998). *The psychology of criminal conduct*. Anderson Publishing.

Bugnariu, A. I., Mucea, N. B., & Bogoslov, I. A. (2024). Implications of the virtual environment on well-being and workplace efficiency. *ProQuest Dissertations and Theses*. Recuperado de https://search.proquest.com/openview/3330862d41a720e2a3c281060bd9cc2f/1

Cohen, L. E., & Felson, M. (1979). Social change and crime rate trends: A routine activity approach. *American Sociological Review*, *44*(4), 588–608. DOI: 10.2307/2094589

Davis, M. H. (1983). Measuring individual differences in empathy: Evidence for a multidimensional approach. *Journal of Personality and Social Psychology*, *44*(1), 113–126. DOI: 10.1037/0022-3514.44.1.113

De la Espriella, A. M. (2016). *Intervenciones y métodos de prevención del acoso laboral* [Trabajo de grado, Universidad de los Andes].

Espinoza Bonifaz, A. R. (2020). Hacia una criminología indoamericana. Lima: Primera edición electrónica.

Espinoza de los Monteros de la Parra, M., Gullo, A., & Mazzacuva, F. (Eds.). (2020). *The criminal law protection of our common home*. Revue Internationale de Droit Pénal. Maklu.

Flynn, M., & Hall, M. (2017). The case for a victimology of nonhuman animal harms. *Contemporary Justice Review*, *20*(3), 299–318. DOI: 10.1080/10282580.2017.1348898

González Fernández, I. (2023). *Acoso laboral en el ámbito español* [Trabajo fin de grado, Universidad de Oviedo].

Hearn, J., Hall, M., Lewis, R., & Niemistö, C. (2023). The spread of digital intimate partner violence: Ethical challenges for business, workplaces, employers, and management. *Journal of Business Ethics*, *187*(3), 695–711. DOI: 10.1007/s10551-023-05463-4

Instituto Nacional de Seguridad y Salud en el Trabajo (INSST). (2021). Guía de buenas prácticas para la prevención de conductas de acoso laboral. Madrid: INSST. Recuperado de [archivo proporcionado].

Kelley, B. J. (2024). Belaboring the algorithm: Artificial intelligence and labor unions. *Yale Journal on Regulation Bulletin*, *41*(88), 88–105.

Kernberg, O. F. (1975). *Borderline conditions and pathological narcissism*. Jason Aronson.

Krzywdzinski, M., Gerst, D., & Butollo, F. (2023). Promoting human-centred AI in the workplace: Trade unions and their strategies for regulating the use of AI in Germany. *Transfer: European Review of Labour and Research*, *29*(1), 53–70. DOI: 10.1177/10242589221142273

Leymann, H. (1996). The content and development of mobbing at work. *European Journal of Work and Organizational Psychology*, *5*(2), 165–184. DOI: 10.1080/13594329608414853

Llerena Idrobo, L. A. (2022). *El acoso laboral o mobbing, identificación, prevención y tratamiento en el área administrativa de la empresa TRANS EXPRES S.A en el año 2020* [Tesis de maestría, Universidad Andina Simón Bolívar, Sede Ecuador].

Miró Llinares, F. (2018). Inteligencia artificial y justicia penal: Más allá de los resultados lesivos causados por robots. *Revista de Derecho Penal y Criminología, 3ª Época (20)*, 87-130. Recuperado de https://core.ac.uk/display/475135778

Ost, S., & Gillespie, A. A. (2024). To know or not to know: Should crimes regarding photographs of their child sexual abuse be disclosed to now-adult, unknowing victims? *Journal of Victimology Studies*. Publicado electrónicamente.

Sánchez Rodríguez, L. del R., & Mandujano Montoya, A. (2024). Haciendo visible lo invisible: La normalización del acoso laboral como factor de riesgo en el sector público y privado. *Universo Criminal*, *5*(8), 39–42.

Tenório, N., & Bjørn, P. (2019). Online harassment in the workplace: The role of technology in labour law disputes. [CSCW]. *Computer Supported Cooperative Work*, *28*(3-4), 293–315. Advance online publication. DOI: 10.1007/s10606-019-09351-2

Torres Duro, L. (2015). *Protocolo preventivo y de intervención frente al acoso laboral* [Trabajo final de máster, Máster Interuniversitario en Seguridad y Salud en el Trabajo].

Yar, M. (2005). The novelty of 'cybercrime': An assessment in light of routine activity theory. *European Journal of Criminology*, *2*(4), 407–427. DOI: 10.1177/147737080556056

ADDITIONAL READINGS

Antonella Tiravassi, A., Safranoff, A., & Cavalo, L. (2022). *El rol del sindicato en la prevención y acompañamiento frente a la violencia y acoso laboral. Unión del Personal Auxiliar de Casas Particulares*. UPACP.

Bernat Jiménez, M.. (2011). *Victimología: Una introducción a la ciencia de la víctima*. Editorial Reverte.

Deranty, J.-P., & Corbin, T. (2024). Artificial intelligence and work: A critical review of recent research from the social sciences. *AI & Society*, *39*(2), 675–691. DOI: 10.1007/s00146-022-01496-x

Escudero, J. (2011). Auditorías y monitoreo: Herramientas clave en la gestión del riesgo laboral. *Revista de Prevención Laboral*, *8*(3), 67–80.

Kelley, B. J. (2024). Belaboring the algorithm: Artificial intelligence and labor unions. *Yale Journal on Regulation Bulletin*, *41*(88), 88–105.
Kelley, B. J. (2024). Belaboring the algorithm: Artificial intelligence and labor unions. *Yale Journal on Regulation Bulletin*, *41*(88), 88–105.
Krzywdzinski, M., Gerst, D., & Butollo, F. (2023). Promoting human-centred AI in the workplace: Trade unions and their strategies for regulating the use of AI in Germany. *Transfer: European Review of Labour and Research*, *29*(1), 53–70. DOI: 10.1177/10242589221142273

Leymann, H. (1996). The content and development of mobbing at work. *European Journal of Work and Organizational Psychology*, *5*(2), 165–184. DOI: 10.1080/13594329608414853

Llerena Idrobo, L. A. (2022). El acoso laboral o mobbing, identificación, prevención y tratamiento en el área administrativa de la empresa TRANS EXPRES S.A en el año 2020 [Tesis de maestría, Universidad Andina Simón Bolívar].

Montero Ruiz, J. (2017). Ética y privacidad en la era de la inteligencia artificial. *Revista de Ética Laboral*, *10*(3), 67–80.

Sánchez Rodríguez, L. del R., & Mandujano Montoya, A. (2024). Haciendo visible lo invisible: La normalización del acoso laboral como factor de riesgo en el sector público y privado. *Universo Criminal*, *5*(8), 39–42.

Tenório, N., & Bjørn, P. (2019). Online harassment in the workplace: The role of technology in labor law disputes. [CSCW]. *Computer Supported Cooperative Work*, *28*(3-4), 293–315. Advance online publication. DOI: 10.1007/s10606-019-09351-2

Tru a, C. (2024). Addressing well-being in a changing workforce. Psihologia Resurselor Umane. Recuperado de https://www.hrp-journal.com/index.php/pru/article/download/575/513

Yar, M. (2005). The novelty of 'cybercrime': An assessment in light of routine activity theory. *European Journal of Criminology*, *2*(4), 407–427. DOI: 10.1177/147737080556056

KEY TERMS AND DEFINITIONS

Workplace Harassment (Mobbing): A set of intentional and repetitive behaviors in the workplace designed to intimidate, harass, or exclude a person, affecting their mental health, dignity, and job performance (Leymann, 1996).

Structural Digital Victimization: The process in which harmful decisions are made by automated technological systems, without direct human intervention, causing negative impacts on affected employees (Tru a, 2024).

Algorithmic Control: A method of workplace supervision implemented through algorithms that monitor and evaluate employee performance in real-time, with significant ethical consequences (Melis, 2024).

Algorithmic Victimization Bias: A phenomenon that occurs when algorithms perpetuate social inequalities due to biased historical data, negatively impacting certain groups of workers (Pillon, 2024).

Criminology: The science that studies crime, the criminal, the victim, and social control, as well as the factors that generate it, the processes of victimization, and social responses to the criminal phenomenon, including preventive strategies in workplace contexts (Bonta & Andrews, 1998).

Victimology: A discipline within criminology focused on the study of victims, their rights, and victimization dynamics, aiming to provide tools for their protection and recovery (Bernat Jiménez et al., 2011).

Mental Health at Work: The emotional and psychological balance that enables employees to handle job demands and participate in their organizational environment, significantly influenced by factors such as workplace harassment (Bonta et al., 1998).

Technological Equity: A principle that seeks to ensure that technological tools in workplaces are accessible, inclusive, and non-discriminatory, promoting justice and equitable participation (Sánchez, 2020).

Algorithmic Audits: Systematic evaluation processes to analyze the functioning, accuracy, and fairness of artificial intelligence systems used in workplace environments (Escudero, 2011).

Chapter 9
Wellbeing and Mental Health at Work in the Age of Artificial Intelligence: Strategies and Opportunities for Digital Unionism

Javier L. Crespo
https://orcid.org/0000-0003-0157-0892
Universidad Internacional de La Rioja, Spain

ABSTRACT

This chapter analyzes how artificial intelligence (AI) can be a positive challenge to improve labor union services in mental health at work. Automation and digitalization, while offering benefits in efficiency and productivity, also introduce new psychosocial risks, such as technostress. The chapter explores the role of unions as guarantors of workers' rights in digital transformation processes. Also justifies the need for an organizational transformation of unionism, including updating service structures, digitizing the union, and developing a proactive strategy towards occupational mental health. The chapter concludes by arguing that unions must adopt a proactive approach, use new technologies responsibly and collaborate with other social actors to protect the mental health of workers in the digital age.

INTRODUCTION

Any important change must begin by describing the destination of the journey. Perhaps, when Champy (1997) wrote this phrase about the importance of preparing for change in the organization more than a quarter of a century ago, the destination

DOI: 10.4018/979-8-3693-8049-9.ch009

of said journey was more visible and imaginable. The changes that were taking place in that historical context at a global level in the world of work were very important, but perhaps also more predictable. However, in the current digital revolution of artificial intelligence, we are not yet able to glimpse what the destination of that journey will be. The path of this revolution is beginning to take its first steps, at an unusual speed, and as a result, on our near horizon, a variety of paths appear blurred, generating uncertainty in the choice of which one to take. As can be expected, the choice of one path or another determines the destination of the journey. Therefore, the choice is not trivial.

The world of work is changing at a rapid pace. Organizations, to a greater or lesser extent, have begun the transformation that is being triggered by the digital explosion and AI. Workers, forced to adapt to all of this, are often the weakest link in the chain.

In this context characterized by the uncertainty of the future, labor unions, as a social agent, face the challenge, but also the opportunity, to "rebuild" their role (Nissim & Simon, 2021) and to actively participate by adding value to the object that gives meaning to its essence.

If we assume that the main purpose of a labor union is to represent and defend the rights and interests of workers and that its mission includes, among others, improving working conditions, guaranteeing safety at work and promoting equality and the well-being of workers, in the face of this uncertainty about the future of digital work, the transformation of the labor union as an organization becomes urgent and mandatory.

The EU Regulation establishing harmonized rules on artificial intelligence (2024) in its art. 165, advocates the participation of labor unions, among other social and economic actors, as interested parties in the objectives of an ethical and reliable implementation of Artificial Intelligence (AI), as well as in the promotion of voluntary codes of conduct with clear objectives and indicators that allow the assessment of compliance with the ethical guidelines emanating from said regulation. It grants labor unions the right to be informed at the organizational level before the commissioning or use of a high-risk AI system in the workplace. It is intended, together with other measures, to contribute to improving working conditions and consequently, to develop ethical AI that respects the legislation and rights of European citizens.

Of course, the legislator advocates for a broad participation of social, economic, scientific agents, in the generation of a safe context in accordance with European law and legal framework, which allows the development of AI. Without a doubt, labor unionism must take advantage of the role that the EU grants it, assuming a role as guarantor of workers' rights in the face of the potential danger that the application of AI at work could pose. Of course, in the digital and technological context that is being built right now and in aspects as relevant as those that derive from work and health, the role of labor unionism should be highlighted.

In addition to the above, and because of the impact of the pandemic on society, an area of special concern worldwide in general, and in the European environment in particular, is that of the well-being and occupational health of workers (Escanciano, 2021). The constant increase in the intensification of work, working at high speed or to tight deadlines (Eurofound, 2010, 2024), is highlighting the relevance and deterioration of mental health at work.

The increase in the incidence of work-related mental health problems in Europe and the United States of America is a fact that is combined with the uncertainty of digital transformation and the emergence of AI in the workplace. For example, the Mental Health survey America (2021) reported that 83% of employees felt emotionally exhausted by their work. Eurofound (2020) found that 44% of European workers suffered from work-related stress at least once a month. Of course, workers place much more importance on mental health related to their work. In the Ineco Technical Report, Idea & Puntual (2024) in Argentina, *Well-being and emotional and mental health at work post-pandemic,* 82% of respondents value their emotional and mental health much more after the pandemic, which positions this factor as the most relevant and the one that has grown the most in importance compared to other previous studies.

If we look globally at what factors may have been contributing to the rise in the incidence of mental health problems, we find factors such as the 2008 financial crisis, increased work overload and pressure to maintain productivity in highly competitive environments, and more recently, the COVID-19 pandemic. These are factors that have gradually contributed to the deterioration of mental health in the workplace today (APA 2011; EU-OSHA, 2005, 2013; Eurofound, 2020).

This chapter explores how AI can be, beyond the dangers and uncertainties it presents, a great positive challenge to improve labor union services in an area of such relevance and burning topicality as mental health at work, and also, in its role as guarantor of workers' rights in the processes of digital transformation of companies and in the evolution of work.

For example, given the risk posed by algorithmic biases and the lack of transparency about their operation within the limits established in Europe by the EU Regulation establishing harmonised standards on artificial intelligence (2024), labor unions, within the framework of participation established by said regulation, must advocate for transparency, that is, they must bring to light the categories of data and the main parameters that the systems take into account and make them evident so that employees can understand how the decisions that affect them are made. They must also supervise decision-making, so that these are made with human supervision, especially in those decisions that affect employment relations or aspects derived from e-mental health. In short, transparency, human supervision, data protection and fairness are fundamental principles for the responsible use of AI in employment relations, especially in the field of mental health at work. Ethical AI practices and the legal framework must ensure that technology is used for the benefit of all and not for discrimination or the violation of rights.

The chapter begins by analyzing the future of work and current trends that impact employee mental health. Automation and digitalization, while offering significant benefits in terms of efficiency and productivity, also introduce new psychosocial risk factors that can lead to technostress (Salanova et al., 2014; Brivio et al., 2018; Martín, 2021; Masluk et al., 2024). These trends make it imperative for unions to adapt their strategies to support workers in this new environment and minimize the risks inherent in change in a digital and BANI environment (Brittle, Anxious, Non-linear and Incomprehensible).

H-Work project (2020), a multidimensional intervention model is presented, which comprehensively addresses mental health issues at work through new information and knowledge technologies, such as continuous monitoring of emotional well-being, and the provision of personalized interventions through digital platforms. These technologies allow for early identification of problems and a rapid and effective response, improving the overall well-being of employees.

The role of labor unions in this context could be redefined as facilitator and promoter of the responsible and effective use of AI for mental health at work. Practical strategies that labor unions can adopt are explored, including the implementation of tailored mental wellbeing programs and stress monitoring tools.

This analysis underlines the need for labor unions to take a proactive and adaptive approach, using AI not only to address current challenges but also to open up new avenues of support and protection for workers in the digital age.

The chapter also justifies the reasons that give rise to the need for organizational transformation of labor unionism. These refer to:

a) The need to update service structures to adjust them to the requirements of the new environment, to thc cvolution of the worker and to the blurred circumstances in digital work.
b) The also necessary digitalization of the labor union.
c) The social imperative to develop a strategy with a proactive approach to occupational mental health.
d) The aspiration to regain part of the lost influence over the legislative power.
e) The improvement of external communication and collaboration through strategic alliances with actors in favor of mental health at work. Let us not forget here the 2030 agenda, and specifically the role of Sustainable Development. Sustainable Development Goals (SDGs) and goal 17, *Partnerships for the goals.*

It is certainly time for change. Not evolving is not an option.

THE FUTURE OF WORK: CHALLENGES, CHANGE AND DIGITAL TRANSFORMATION

The construct "Future of Work" encompasses an intricate web of challenges and opportunities that are being shaped as automation, artificial intelligence (AI) and digitalisation advance at an unprecedented pace. However, it is a construct that has historically been widely speculated about (Lucas, 2013). Following *the end of Rifkin's work (1996)* in which he predicted catastrophic social consequences resulting from increased productivity throughout the industrial revolutions, Tilly (1998) assumes the influence that technical innovation and market reorganisation will continue to influence work, but that it will be organisations that will channel the use of new technologies based on their needs. They will replace technologies with cheaper ones. Therefore, as Tilly reminds us, most future scenarios about work, many of them pessimistic, will be ontologically mediated by the needs of organisations. Those that do not respond to an organisational need will simply not happen. In any case, it is undoubted that the future of Work will have an impact beyond work itself. We are still in a "work society" that, as a result of its transformations, will modify society itself, its economic relations, organizations, jobs, the dedication of society and the social interaction maintained by workers, employers and consumers. And these changes will be far-reaching, also due to the centrality of work in our society.

The current historical moment, the Fourth Industrial Revolution, driven by automation, artificial intelligence (AI) and characterized by the convergence of digital, physical and biological technologies, is transforming the way we live, work and relate to each other. The changes are historic in terms of magnitude, speed and scope, which generates both opportunities and challenges (Schwab, 2016).

Along these lines, both optimists and pessimists to a greater or lesser extent, emphasize that this 4th industrial revolution is driving economic growth, encouraging the birth of new business models. But they also warn of the potential negative impact on the labor market, with the displacement of large groups of "analogue" employees into unemployment.

Dangers of the Future of Work

Technological innovation has always been a destroyer of jobs, as well as a major creator of new jobs (Martin, 2013). Automation may replace human labor in many industries and occupations, raising concerns about mass technological unemployment. Frey & Osbourne (2017) predict that 47% of jobs in the United States are susceptible to automation in the next two decades. They point out that this process is already underway and is affecting a wide range of industries and occupations. They suggest a polarization in the labor market, with high-income cognitive jobs and low-income manual jobs growing, while routine jobs will decline.

Generic work, that which requires a basic education, that receives instructions and executes orders, will be easily replaced by digital technology. While creative, self-programmable and innovative work, inextricably linked to new technologies, will give rise to the growing increase in services and the birth of new occupations that can design, build and work with technological and digital systems (Castells, 1997).

The Organization for Economic Co-operation and Development (OECD, 1996) warned that in the knowledge-based economy, sustainable development and job creation required:

a) Organizational changes to strengthen investment incentives in knowledge
b) Technological policies aimed at improving organizational effectiveness
c) Investment in continuous training in new technologies for workers
d) Fostering innovation within companies

These criteria, translated into policies that encourage change and adaptation in organizations, as well as human and technological development, will enable economic and social growth.

It is worth highlighting that this context of digital transformation also presents challenges. Inequality or technological gap, unemployment caused by the digital disruption and the need to adapt to new ways of working require the attention of governments, labor unions, companies and society in general, to ensure that the benefits of the technological revolution reach all social strata equitably and that the conditions for an inclusive and sustainable future of work are created. This technological gap is the so-called digital divide, which refers to inequality in access, use and knowledge of digital technologies, which can generate differences in employment and social opportunities. This gap not only implies the lack of access to the Internet or electronic devices, but also the lack of digital skills necessary to fully participate in today's economy and society. In this sense, low-skilled workers and those with fewer economic resources start off with fewer possibilities of accessing digitalized jobs and, consequently, are more likely to swell the unemployment statistics. Also, the need for a reliable Internet infrastructure for a digital economy can aggravate the exclusion of people without access to the network, preventing their participation in the economy and society. Consequently, digitalization can create new forms of exclusion, precarization and discrimination both due to the lack of access to connectivity and the lack of digital skills necessary to participate in the new forms of work and employment.

And what role can unions play in the face of this reality? They should certainly play a key role in mitigating these negative effects and ensuring that digitalisation does not leave certain groups in society behind. They can address the demand for affordable internet access through trade union struggles, as well as getting involved in developing digital skills training programmes for workers, both from an upskilling and reskilling perspective.

Another element of relevant impact is in the labour structure. New forms of work organisation are not a new element, however, the entire explosion of the development of digital platforms and the on-demand economy is driving new ways of working, which, although they often offer flexibility and autonomy, also pose challenges in terms of occupational health and safety, social protection and workers' rights.

The problems are most evident in the reconversion processes of large productive sectors that will indeed suffer greatly from the impact of digitalisation on their work. Rapid advances in AI are having, and will continue to have, a significant impact on employment, so immediate political action will be necessary (OECD, 2023) and close labor union attention.

Of course, labor union involvement in this new digital context must focus on protecting workers' rights, defending social security, and training and skills development. To ensure access to the opportunities of the digital economy, labor unions must get involved in AI ethics committees, promoting inclusion and equity (Nissim & Simon, 2021). The key is to understand the forces at play, adapt to changes, shape technology responsibly, and harness its potential for the common good.

This step forward for labor unionism would strengthen its strategic capacity and allow it to gain social relevance among post-industrial workers. It would promote a new image of the social role of trade unionism and would gain relevance in the world of work.

Platform Work

A particularly important phenomenon in today's world of work is platform work, a product of the GIG economy. This has experienced a huge boom in recent years thanks to the digital revolution. While it offers flexibility and job opportunities, it also presents challenges in terms of working conditions and risks to mental health (González Vázquez et al. 2024).

One of the main problems with platform work is the ambiguity in the employment relationship (Dabić et al., 2023). Workers are often hired as freelancers, which can lead to discrimination in rights, including coverage of occupational health and safety regulations.

Also, the isolated nature of the work, the lack of job security, intense monitoring and algorithmic management can constitute a significant psychosocial risk and influence mental health problems. For example, sleep problems, exhaustion, stress, depression, burnout, loneliness and general dissatisfaction with work and personal life have been found in platform workers (Martín & Pérez, 2024).

Lack of autonomy, control over work and flexibility may be at the root of these problems. Algorithmic management, a central element of platform work, uses algorithms to assign tasks, monitor and evaluate the performance and behaviour of workers. This management generates a greater workload, exhaustion and stress in these workers. In short, it deteriorates the quality of working life and increases the psychosocial risks associated with these "GIG jobs".

In response to the problems generated by this new way of working, the EU and some Member States are taking action to address the challenges of platform work.

For example, Spain has implemented the "Rider Law", which introduces legal presumption of employment for delivery platform workers and transparency in algorithmic decision-making processes. Italy has enacted Legislative Decree No. 101/2019, which regulates the employment status of platform workers and extends some labor rights. France has established a legislative framework that grants a number of rights and protection to platform workers, including the right to form and join a union, the right to disconnect, and insurance against work-related accidents.

Furthermore, Directive (EU) 2024/2831 on Improving *Working Conditions for Platform Workers of the European Parliament and of the Council*, adopted on 23 October 2024, aims primarily to improve the working conditions of platform workers and protect their personal data. To achieve this, the Directive introduces a number of key measures such as the determination of employment status, i.e. it provides for the legal presumption of an employment relationship for platform workers. This means that, in case of doubt, the relationship between the platform and the worker will be presumed to be one of an employment nature, unless the platform can prove otherwise. This presumption is based on the finding that digital labour platforms often exercise a significant degree of direction and control over the people working through them. The Directive seeks to combat the misclassification of platform workers as bogus freelancers, a problem that deprives many workers of the rights and protections they are entitled to.

In addition, the Directive sets out transparency obligations for platforms in relation to the automated monitoring and decision-making systems they use to manage workers. Platforms must inform workers about how algorithms work in assigning tasks, evaluating performance and making decisions affecting working conditions, as well as the parameters and criteria used by the algorithms and the potential consequences for workers. Also, systems must be monitored by humans and there is an obligation to intervene in the event of unfair or discriminatory outcomes. Platforms must provide a clear and understandable explanation of the reasons for a decision as well as the factors taken into account in it.

The Directive also provides for other measures that give a significant role to labor unions. For example, platforms must inform and consult workers' representatives about the introduction or modification of automated systems that affect working conditions. The Directive encourages Member States to promote collective bargaining in platform work and prohibits dismissal or any unfavourable treatment for exercising the rights established in it.

In conclusion, Directive (EU) 2024/2831 is a major step towards improving the working conditions of platform workers. The introduction of the legal presumption of employment relationship, transparency obligations in algorithmic management and protections against unfavourable treatment and dismissal are key elements to ensure that platform workers enjoy the same rights and protections as other workers. It is also true that, although the Directive sets out a general framework, its specific implementation and development is left to the Member States. The Directive recognises the diversity of employment practices in different countries and allows Member States to adapt the rules to their national contexts. It will be crucial that Member States implement the Directive effectively and that the competent authorities, as well as labor unions in their role as guarantors of labour rights, carry out adequate monitoring to ensure compliance.

Benefits of Digitalization

We cannot ignore the benefits of digitalization, artificial intelligence and, in general, everything that the 4th industrial revolution is bringing to the world of work and organizations. This is allowing us to optimize production processes, increase production and reduce costs, that is, improve efficiency and productivity.

Smart factories, where virtual and physical manufacturing systems cooperate flexibly with each other worldwide, enable full product customization and the creation of new operating models.

Robots, increasingly used in all sectors, perform tasks ranging from precision agriculture to nursing, freeing humans from more complex tasks.

The app economy creates new business and employment opportunities with low entry costs, and wearable technology combined with the Internet of Things (IoT) enables workers to operate complex equipment and stay up to date with the latest developments (Schwab, 2016; Coldwell, 2019).

Of course, the impact on quality of life can also be very positive. Digital technology offers new products and services that make life easier, more efficient and more productive. For example, AI in areas such as virtual assistants and translation software already makes communication and task completion easier. 3D printing enables distributed manufacturing and maintenance of spare parts more easily and cheaply.

The emergence of new business models can also create employment opportunities. The 4th industrial revolution is driving the on-demand economy and digital platforms, which offer new employment opportunities for independent workers and entrepreneurs. For example, it allows workers to perform specific tasks flexibly and from anywhere in the world (teleworking or hybrid work), which gives employees greater flexibility in organizing their time and balancing their work and personal life. This flexibility can result in greater job satisfaction and a better work-life balance. However, teleworking also has its drawbacks in terms of psychosocial risks.

Sedentary lifestyle, social isolation and long working hours have a negative impact on health and safety in teleworking (European Agency for Safety and Health at Work, 2024).

A systematic review of studies published between 2010 and 2021 on the psychosocial risk factors of teleworking revealed that full-time teleworking brings with it significant changes in working conditions, with the potential to affect workers' living and health conditions. However, part-time teleworking could have a positive impact on psychosocial factors, promoting work-life balance, communication, and social relationships (Antunes et al., 2023).

Finally, digitalisation is facilitating access to information and education, allowing workers to develop new skills and adapt to changes in the labour market. New digital technologies provide access to an unprecedented amount of information and educational resources, in fact, universities, companies and vocational training centres have stepped forward to take advantage of this opportunity. Also, the provision of health services, with telemedicine and psychological and mental health support services (APA, 2024), have been shown to take advantage of new communication technologies.

Soft Skills

It must be recognised that in industrial reconversion processes, for example, the role of labor unions has been, at least in Europe, fundamental in the implementation of professional recycling, upskilling and reskilling policies, which have historically helped to improve the employability of workers affected by the reconversion.

This is where the current historical context demands the learning of new skills and greater adaptability of workers. Hiemstra (1976) already highlighted the obsolescence of certain occupations and the importance of *life Long learning* as a way of adapting to changes in the labour market and the evolution of occupations. Later, Hargreaves (2004) recognises learning as an essential element in and for life. Demand for skills such as complex problem solving, social skills and systems skills will increase, while physical and content skills will be less in demand. The ability to continually learn and adapt will be crucial for success in the future labour market. Demand for high-level cognitive skills such as complex problem solving, creativity and critical thinking is on the rise.

The World Economic Forum lists 10 skills as the main ones for 2025 (see figure 1). It is worth highlighting the type of self -management skills, where active learning and learning strategies and the resilience, stress tolerance and flexibility, among others (WEF, 2020).

Schwab (2016) argues that resilience, stress tolerance and flexibility are essential to cope with the uncertainty, disruption and complexity that define this new era. The constant disruption in all sectors of the economy and society, the emergence of new technologies, business models and ways of working, challenge traditional paradigms and require rapid adaptation by organizations and their professionals.

Other studies justified resilience as a key competence, which can be developed, and which would have been totally necessary in situations as difficult as the one that occurred in the health sector during the COVID explosion (Comas & Crespo, 2021; Crespo, 2022), and in purely BANI contexts such as the current one.

Given the current situation, it is necessary to emphasize the need to develop greater resilience and tolerance to stress to manage the pressure for productivity and the need to constantly adapt to new technologies, as well as having more resources to deal with information overload and avoid physical and mental exhaustion (Salanova, 2022).

Flexibility to adapt to the uncertainty of the future of work will also be crucial in the face of rapidly evolving technologies and business models. It will allow us to:

a) Adapt to new ways of working, such as teleworking, the on-demand economy and virtual collaboration.
b) Learn new skills and apply them in different work contexts.
c) Work in multidisciplinary and distributed teams, and collaborate with people from diverse backgrounds and cultures; and
d) Be proactive in seeking opportunities and creating a meaningful future of work.

In short, Schwab argues that resilience, stress tolerance and flexibility are essential skills for thriving in the fourth industrial revolution. Skills that enable workers to adapt to disruption, manage stress and navigate the uncertainty of an ever-changing work environment. Developing these soft skills is not only beneficial for individuals, but also for companies and societies, which will be able to take advantage of the opportunities and cushion the risks of this new era.

Figure 1. Future of jobs report 2020, World Economic Forum.

Why Should Unions Change and Get Involved in the Digital Revolution?

Beyond the transformative historical moment that is taking place in the world of work, the economy and culture, and the benefits and dangers that we have outlined above, which in themselves justify the step forward that we propose here, labor unionism has internal reasons, specific to its development and evolution, that call for its transformation and involvement.

Mainstream unionism has been receiving criticism from different sides since the last century. On the one hand, from political neoliberalism (Hayek, 1991; Richardson & Roberts, 1997), an aspect that we will not develop here, and on the other, from new forms of unionism, such as New Trade Union Movements (NTUM).

Regarding the content of the criticisms, the mainstream unionism is accused of having become too bureaucratic and too far removed from the bases, where there is little real participation of the members and, consequently, too much concentration of decisions in the union leadership. Problems that accentuate the loss of social relevance in the current productive economic context in Europe and the USA (Martín & Icart, 2018).

The continued loss of members, public status and effectiveness in achieving their goals is a glaring reality. Factors such as globalisation, the precariousness of employment and the fragmentation of the working class have contributed to this phenomenon. However, the homogeneity in the union representation of blue-collar workers and the immobility with respect to the industrial reality more typical of post-industrialism at the end of the last century have contributed, if possible, to the loss of this social relevance. This fact demonstrates the difficulties of traditional unionism to represent the new workers of the digital economy, such as platform workers and the self-employed.

Current labor unionism is immersed in a process of marginalization, due to the loss of relevance in regulating the labor market, the decrease in union density, the change in the composition of the workforce and the increasing instability of work (Visser, 2023).

Furthermore, the prevalence of a defensive trade union strategy, focused on the negotiation of existing working conditions, instead of seeking a real transformation of the economic and productive model, is also a reason for criticism of mainstream labor unionism. It is accused of abandoning the transformative utopia, of lacking a project for social transformation that goes beyond the defence of immediate labour interests. Hence, the NTUM advocates offensive trade union action, aimed at transforming labour relations and recovering lost rights.

The ability of mainstream unions to represent workers in the context of globalisation, job insecurity and fragmentation of the working class is questioned. They are accused of being too focused on the traditional model of industrial employment and of not addressing the needs of workers in service sectors. This union decline is attributed to the loss of bargaining power, declining membership and less influence in the public sphere (Beneyto, 2017). In addition, factors such as globalisation, neoliberal labour market reforms and deregulation have also contributed to this weakening of unionism.

This context challenges the role of unions. The fragmentation of the working class, exacerbated by the emergence of platform work, makes union organisation and mobilisation even more difficult . The social perception of the weakening of traditional unionism also leads to a decline in union membership and the perception of inaction in the face of job insecurity (Visser, 2024).

Visser stresses that after the marginalization of labor unions, can be replaced by other institutions that offer similar services, such as the State, employers, professional associations or civil society organisations. This is what he calls substitution. A phenomenon that has been gradually occurring since the beginning of the century. Therefore, considering all the above, a process of labor union revitalization is needed. A process of renewal of the trade union structure, of redefinition of the purpose and which serves as a basis for attracting more members and improving worker protection.

This revitalization requires adopting innovative strategies to organize workers and build alliances with other social actors. It involves developing new practices of participation of members and workers, with the aim of attracting more members and offering better protection to a greater number of workers, but also more diverse (young people, women, immigrants and workers in the digital economy, precarious workers, etc.). In addition, it is necessary, says Visser, to spread the innovations and thus renew a "brand image" that is more attractive to the new workforce, for example with social media campaigns, legal actions, alliances with other social movements and/or the creation of workers' cooperatives.

The relevance of the union in the context of GIG work will largely depend on its ability to adapt to new challenges and seize opportunities. The labor union must be able to effectively represent platform workers, fight job insecurity, develop new strategies and strengthen social dialogue to ensure that the digital transformation of work is fair and benefits everyone.

Certainly, one area where there is much to be done, and where labor unionism could contribute great value in collaboration with other social, economic and professional agents, is the problem of mental health at work, which is being exacerbated by the digital age.

The role that would best fit the idiosyncrasy of a revitalized labor unionism would be that of prevention and guarantee of psychologically healthy working conditions. It could also function as a social service that, in connection with mental health services, would allow workers with mental health problems to be referred to specialized services.

Let's see what the magnitude of the problem is.

Well-Being at Work and Mental Health in Digital Era

Mental health has gained significant relevance in recent times, becoming a global concern, mainly due to the increase in its incidence (WHO, 2022). Work, so central to our society, is a very relevant area of life in the etiology of this incidence (Harnois & Gabriel, 2000; Marten & Wilkerson, 2003). Work stress, work overload, job insecurity and lack of autonomy at work, among others, are factors that can negatively affect mental health.

Linked to this, the introduction of artificial intelligence and digitalisation at work can also present psychosocial risks involved in mental health and well-being at work (Dewa & McDaid, 2010).

New technologies can cause workers to become unsuitable to technological demands and to feel pressured to adapt to the new technical requirements of the job, as well as the fear of losing the job or being displaced by said technology. The possibility of being replaced by machines is facilitating anxiety and stress in workers in broad professional sectors (Sánchez-Anguita, 2017).

This situation, the result of the uncertainty of digitalization and AI, is combined with an event as important as the COVID-19 pandemic, which left a deep mark on mental health globally, but in which the younger population was especially insidious (Cao, 2020; Vivanco et al, 2020). Anxiety and depression disorders increased by more than 25% during the first year of the pandemic. This level of incidence translates into the alarming figure that one in eight people suffers from a mental disorder according to the WHO (2022).

Furthermore, the increase in work intensity and work overload, which have been a common feature of the world of work for decades, are risk factors that produce stress and negatively affect well-being at work.

Managing complex digital systems, multitasking and the constant flow of information can lead to cognitive overload, affecting concentration and mental well-being. Algorithmic management systems and digital monitoring can also increase the pressure to perform, generating stress and anxiety in workers, and limiting workers' autonomy and control over their tasks and work pace. All of this can negatively affect motivation and job satisfaction, as we have highlighted in the case of platform workers.

The negative impact of these risks on workers can lead to chronic work-related stress, which can trigger mental disorders such as anxiety, depression and burnout.

These consequences not only have repercussions on the individuals who suffer from them, but also on the organizations themselves. Mental health problems burden health systems and increase costs for companies as well. Increased absenteeism and sickness leave, reduce performance and productivity .

Psychosocial Risks in Digital Work

Psychosocial risks are those factors present in the work environment that can negatively affect the mental, emotional and social health of workers. They are related to the organization, management and content of work (Cox & Griffiths, 1996). The digitalization of work and its processes, while presenting opportunities, also intensifies and creates new psychosocial risks. The European Agency for Safety and Health at Work (2024) identifies a series of psychosocial risks associated with digital work, namely:

a) The increase in job insecurity and pressure to perform, which generates fear of job loss.
b) The constant threat of job substitution, which creates anxiety and insecurity in workers.
c) In addition, the increase in workload, time pressure, constant connectivity and the expectation of permanent availability often blur the boundaries between work and personal life, leading to an increase in work intensification and greater pressure to perform.

A recent study on psychosocial risks on platforms in Spain highlights that the very nature of this work, including algorithmic management, scoring systems, digital surveillance, lack of autonomy, job insecurity, uncertainty, and intensive use of information and communication technologies, are triggered by stress (INSST, 2024).

As depicted in table 2, presents the mental health problems that may be triggered by risk factors associated with digitalization, which are typical of the 4th industrial revolution.

Table 1. Mental health problems derived from the impact of digitalization and AI.

Mental Health Problem	Description
Stress	Algorithmic management, constant digital surveillance, performance pressure and job uncertainty can lead to high levels of stress in workers.
Physical and mental fatigue	Hyperconnectivity, constant availability and long, irregular working hours can lead to physical and mental exhaustion.
Anxiety	Performance pressure, job uncertainty and fear of job loss due to automation can cause anxiety in workers.
Depression	Social isolation, lack of control over work and job insecurity can contribute to the development of depression.

continued on following page

Table 1. Continued

Mental Health Problem	Description
Emotional exhaustion (Burnout)	Work intensification, lack of autonomy and high emotional demands in some digital jobs can lead to burnout.
Technostress	Intensive use of ICT, information overload and the feeling of always being connected can generate technostress.
Sleep disorders	Hyperconnectivity and constant availability can interfere with sleep patterns and lead to sleep disorders.
Social isolation	Digitalization can reduce social interaction at work, which can lead to isolation and loneliness, especially in remote work.
Violence and harassment	Digital platforms can facilitate harassment and violence, especially in jobs that involve interaction with clients.

The combination of these factors can significantly increase the risk of mental health problems such as chronic stress, anxiety, depression and burnout. However, psychosocial risks can affect not only mental health, but also physical health, quality of life and general well-being of workers.

It is important to recognize that the effects of digitalization on mental health are also influenced by individual factors, such as personality, resilience and coping strategies, as well as the work context and company policies. Psychologically healthy organizations are more suitable ecosystems for achieving healthy change and healthier adaptation (APA, 2013).

Strategies for a Healthy Work Environment

Considering that the main predictors of mental health are work interest, the opportunity to learn new things and job security (Fernández-Montalvo, 1998), building organizations with an affinity for the culture of change due to the digital challenge and AI learning can help reduce the uncertainty of the change itself and improve job security.

In this context, various strategies could be implemented to address psychosocial risks and promote mental health at work. For example:

a) Involving workers in decision-making that affects their work, providing them with clear information about technological changes and ensuring open and transparent communication are measures that would help mitigate uncertainty and stress.
b) Providing training and skills development opportunities for workers to adapt to new technologies and labour market demands would help reduce fear of job loss and increase confidence in their abilities.

c) Designing jobs that allow for a greater degree of autonomy and control over tasks and the pace of work would improve worker motivation, job satisfaction and well-being.

(d) Promoting a culture of digital disconnection outside of working hours, establishing clear policies on the use of mobile devices and email outside of work, and encouraging work-life balance would help prevent burnout and stress;

(e) And of vital importance today, it would be useful to provide access to counselling services, psychological support and employee assistance programmes. These measures could help workers manage stress, deal with mental health problems and facilitate their return to work after a period of leave.

In this line, the European Agency The EU-OSHA (2024) describes good practices in promoting mental health at work, such as the implementation of collaborative robots in Portugal. The introduction of collaborative robots to automate physical and repetitive tasks allowed workers to focus on more cognitive tasks, such as quality control, which reduced physical burden and monotony, and provided them with new learning opportunities.

Also the inclusion of AI-based systems in Germany. The implementation of an AI-based system for air sample inspection reduced the cognitive load on inspectors, allowing them to spend more time on tasks that require human judgment. Clear communication and employee involvement in the implementation process were crucial in mitigating fear of job loss and fostering trust in the new technology.

And finally, comprehensive wellness programmes in Finland. Companies have implemented comprehensive wellness programmes that address the physical, mental and social health of employees, including measures to improve the work environment, training and professional development, and the promotion of a healthy lifestyle.

In summary, mental health at work is a complex challenge that requires a comprehensive approach and collaboration from all stakeholders. The strategies mentioned above, together with learning from good practices and constantly adapting to changes in the work environment, are essential to creating a future of work that is healthy, sustainable and beneficial for all.

Multilevel Interventions: A Holistic Approach to Mental Health at Work

The WHO Comprehensive Action Plan on Mental Health 2013–2030 emphasizes the need for a multisectoral approach to address mental health challenges. Transforming mental health requires a joint effort by governments, communities, individuals and all stakeholders. Given the importance of work on workers' rights, as well as occupational health, trade unions must be, and are, a highly interested party.

Objective three of the comprehensive action plan highlights the importance of implementing promotion and prevention strategies in the field of mental health. The global goal (3.1) is that 80% of countries should have at least two national multi-sectoral programmes for promotion and prevention in the field of mental health in operation by 2030. It certainly includes the workplace as a necessary place of action to influence the well-being of workers.

The EU-funded H-WORK project (2020) seeks to improve mental health in the workplace. It aims to develop, implement and test an innovative model of multi-level interventions to address psychosocial risks in small and medium-sized enterprises (SMEs) and public organisations. H-WORK uses assessment tools and protocols to identify risk factors at work, creating a digital platform to share solutions and promote best practices across the European Union. The project highlights the importance of mental health in the workplace, while seeking to integrate multi-level interventions to create healthier and more resilient work environments, and with the involvement of organisational leaders.

The IGLO intervention model, an acronym for Individual, Group, Leader and Organization, is a multi-level approach to promoting mental health in the workplace, which is used in the H-WORK project. This model recognizes that sources of mental well-being exist at all levels of an organization and therefore interventions must address these different levels to achieve maximum effectiveness (De Angelis & al., 2020). These are:

a) Individual intervention: This level focuses on the well-being of the individual employee. Interventions at this level could include, for example, individual coaching, stress management programs, or coping skills training.
b) Group intervention: This level focuses on the dynamics and relationships within work teams. Interventions at this level could include, for example, team building workshops, communication improvement programs, or initiatives to foster a climate of social support.
c) Leader Intervention: This level focuses on the role of leaders in creating a healthy work environment. Interventions at this level could include, for example, training for leaders in mental health management, coaching to improve leadership skills, or programs to promote positive leadership styles.
d) Organizational Intervention: This level focuses on the policies, practices, and culture of the organization as a whole. Interventions at this level might include, for example, implementing wellness policies, creating mental health support programs, or changing organizational culture to reduce the stigma associated with mental health issues.

The intervention process begins with an assessment of the organization's needs using the H-WORK Assessment Toolkit (HAT). Based on the results of this assessment, specific interventions are selected from the H-WORK Interventions Toolkit (HIT) and tailored to the particular context of each workplace.

The effectiveness of interventions is assessed using the H-WORK Evaluation Toolkit (HET), which uses a realist evaluation approach to understand "what works, for whom, in what circumstances".

In line with this idea, it is essential to design jobs that provide workers with an adequate level of autonomy, control and participation in decision-making, to reduce stress and improve job satisfaction. Therefore, the involvement of leaders in the mental health and well-being project requires training for them so that, from their management position, they can advocate for actions that have a positive impact on the creation of a positive and psychologically healthy work environment.

Of course, labor unions, in their more political aspect, can also get involved as a social agent, by providing their vision and perspective to the legislator so that the latter takes into account the protection of mental health in all regulations relating to the world of work, for example by urging the improvement of working conditions and promoting the responsibility of companies in the creation of healthy work ecosystems.

In this same social role, labor unionism must be an active agent in the implementation of national campaigns to combat the stigma associated with mental illness and promote the importance of mental health at work.

Ultimately, this multi-level approach, by addressing the factors that influence mental health from multiple levels, allows interventions to have a greater impact and be more sustainable over time. Also, the multi-level approach not only focuses on treating existing problems, but also seeks to prevent the emergence of new cases by promoting mental health and creating healthy work environments. By improving the mental health of workers, multi-level interventions contribute to greater well-being, increased productivity and a better working environment.

The Role of Labor Unions in Occupational and Digital Mental Health

As we said before, the role of labor unions should not only respond to the more than pertinent participation as an organization in actions of prevention and promotion of e-mental health at work, but also to the need to adapt and transform into a valuable organization in the face of the current challenges of this fourth industrial revolution.

In this regard, labor unions could play a crucial role in improving the mental health of workers by taking advantage of the benefits of artificial intelligence (INSST, 2024).

In fact, in this line of action of e-mental health interventions we have evidence of success despite the incipient nature of the technology, its potential and the ethical doubts that its use raises (Cross. 2024). For example, Phillips, Gordeev & Schreyögg (2019) found in their systematic review and meta-analysis of randomized controlled trials, moderate positive effects on stress, insomnia and burnout, and small but significant effects on depression, anxiety and well-being. Despite certain limitations of these trials, e-mental health interventions are a promising tool to improve mental health in the workplace, which should also be promoted by unions.

For example, in terms of psychosocial risks, labor unions can participate in:

a) the identification and control of psychosocial risks in companies. With the help of AI systems, they could analyze large data sets to identify patterns and trends that indicate psychosocial risks.
b) Through algorithms, they could also detect risk factors such as work overload, lack of autonomy, workplace harassment, discrimination, job insecurity, and other elements that negatively impact the mental health of workers.
c) In addition, through predictive AI analysis, they could alert about possible problems before they become worse, allowing early intervention and the implementation of preventive measures.
d) Another area of action in which labor unions can benefit from the contribution of AI is the personalization of interventions through workplace wellness programs tailored to different groups of workers with interventions tailored to the specific needs of everyone. For example, AI-powered chatbot systems can provide emotional support and guidance to workers experiencing stress, anxiety or depression, offering quick access to mental health resources. Also, in the recommendation and/or referral to mental health services, therapy, support groups or counseling, if appropriate.
e) Another area of special interest is collective bargaining and the defense of labor rights and mental health at work. AI can collect and analyze data that allows for progress in negotiations regarding working conditions that affect mental health. For example, it would be interesting to promote contractual clauses that protect the mental health of workers and develop strategies to implement them in collective agreements.
f) Also, in the training and development role, labor unions can use online learning platforms to offer workers information on positive mental health, stress coping strategies and support resources. For example, interactive simulations can be created that allow workers to practice assertive communication skills, conflict resolution, time management, etc. These initiatives would help to better understand the impact of digitalization on workers' mental health and would positively allow for better adaptation to the digitalization of work of those workers with

greater difficulty. It could develop actions to better address psychosocial risks, such as algorithmic management, hyperconnectivity and lack of autonomy in digital work, among others.

In conclusion, we would like to highlight that the role of labor unions in this area must be to add to multiply. Collaboration with other entities, companies, other unions, researchers and universities, public or private mental health services, must be the value that prevails in institutional relations between entities. Avoiding conflicts over prominence or social gain must be the priority of these institutional relations. In this way, the social fabric will be strengthened, which is so necessary in improving working conditions and preventing mental health problems, as well as in improving workplace well-being.

CONCLUSIONS

To successfully address this role in occupational health with a focus on mental health, and as we have reiterated throughout this chapter, the digital transformation and change management of the organizational structure of unions is also essential.

The proposed strategies require the use of digital tools for communication, organization and mobilization. Digital platforms can also be used by unions to reach workers, create online communities and organize collective actions (Gasparėnienė et al., 2024). The use of technology by unions to create networks of workers and forms of collective action, supported and enhanced by social networks, can rebuild links and spaces of solidarity that technology itself has contributed to blurring (Fernández, 2020).

Trade union barriers in the digital age are complex and multifaceted. Unions face the challenge of adapting to a constantly changing work environment, characterized by precariousness, digitalization and fragmentation of the workforce. Overcoming these barriers requires the adoption of new organizational strategies, the use of digital tools, the fight for fair labor legislation, and the recovery of a utopian discourse that inspires workers.

In addition, greater legal regulation is expected in the near future to balance technological progress with the protection of labor rights (Granados, 2022). And it is also there, where digital unionism, based on experience, can help the legislator in the necessary debate on legal security and labor relations in the digital age.

Definitely, labor unions have a crucial role in protecting the mental health of workers in the digital age. And they can do so at several levels:

a) Collective bargaining and defense of labor rights:

Trade unions must fight for fair labor legislation that protects workers' rights in the digital age. This includes the right to digital disconnection, limitation of working hours, and protection against excessive surveillance at work.

In the context of collective bargaining, it is essential to focus on collective agreements that establish fair wages, reasonable working hours and measures to prevent psychosocial risks arising from digital transformation and the implementation of AI in production processes and their automation.

b) Support for workers

Trade unions must represent workers in digital transformation processes and defend their interests. It is important that workers are informed about the changes that are taking place and that they have the opportunity to participate in decisions that affect them. In addition, support must be provided to workers who suffer from mental health problems, such as stress, anxiety or depression. This may include access to psychological counselling services, support groups and legal assistance.

c) Training and awareness-raising:

Trade unions must be involved in the ongoing training of workers on the psychosocial risks of digital work and measures to prevent them. This may include courses on stress management, communication skills and strategies for the responsible use of technology.

In addition, they must participate in raising awareness in society about the importance of mental health at work. This may include public information campaigns, the organization of events and collaboration with other social actors.

d) Responsible use of technology:

Trade unions must also go digital and use technology responsibly to improve their services and reach a greater number of workers.

Digital platforms can be used for internal communication, the organization of campaigns and the dissemination of information on labour rights.

Trade unions also have a relevant role in the fight against the use of algorithms that may discriminate against workers or violate their privacy.

e) Collaboration with other actors:

Following the sustainable development objectives, trade unions must collaborate with other social actors, such as companies, governments and researchers, to address the challenges of mental health in digital work. They must create strategic alliances that allow the development of public policies, training programs and support resources for workers.

REFERENCES

Agencia Europea para la Seguridad y la Salud en el Trabajo (EU-OSHA). (2024). *Digital technologies at work and psychosocial risks: evidence and implications for occupational safety and health.* https://doi:DOI: 10.2802/0488296

American Psychological Association. (2013). APA Announces New Center for Organizational Excellence. The center offers resources on workplace performance and employee well-being. En https://www.apa.org/news/press/releases/2013/01/organizational-excellence

Antunes, E. D., Bridi, L. R. T., Santos, M., & Fischer, F. M. (2023). Part-time or full-time teleworking? A systematic review of the psychosocial risk factors of telework from home. *Frontiers in Psychology*, *14*, 1065593. DOI: 10.3389/fpsyg.2023.1065593 PMID: 36910835

Beneyto, P. J. (2017). Crisis y renovación del sindicalismo. *Arxius de Sociologia*, *36-37*, 15–34.

Brivio, E., Gaudioso, F., Vergine, I., Mirizzi, C. R., Reina, C., Stellari, A., & Galimberti, C. (2018). Preventing Technostress Through Positive Technology. *Frontiers in Psychology*, *9*, 2569. DOI: 10.3389/fpsyg.2018.02569 PMID: 30618986

Cao, W., Fang, Z., Hou, G., Han, M., Xu, X., Dong, J., & Zheng, J. (2020). The psychological impact of the COVID-19 epidemic on college students in China. *Psychiatry Research*, *287*(1), 1–5. DOI: 10.1016/j.psychres.2020.112934 PMID: 32229390

Castells, M. (1997). *La era de la información. Economía, Sociedad y cultura* (Vols. 1–3). Alianza.

Champy, J. A. (1997). Preparar el cambio de la organización. In Hesselbein, F., Goldsmith, M., & Beckhard, R. (Eds.), *La organización del futuro. Cap. 1* (pp. 23–32). Deusto.

Comas, A., & Crespo, J. L. (2021). Resiliencia de profesionales sanitarios en la emergencia covid-19: Ejes de intervención. *Index de Enfermería*, *30*(4), 292–296.

Cox, T., & Griffiths, A. J. (1996). The assessment of psychosocial hazards at work. In Schabracq, M. J., Winnubst, J. A. M., & Cooper, C. L. (Eds.), *Handbook of Work and Health Psychology* (pp. 127–146). Wiley and Sons.

Crespo, J. L. (2022). 3.2 *Nivel de resiliencia de profesionales sanitarios en la emergencia COVID-19*. En Gascón & coords.; Factores Psicosociales en el Trabajo. Trabajo Digno y Saludable en la era COVID: Desafíos y oportunidades. 1a edición. México: Red de Investigadores. ISBN 978-84-18321-18-4 sobre Factores Psicosociales en el Trabajo A.C.; Zaragoza: Prensas de la Universidad de Zaragoza, 2022 pp. 121 – 127.

Cross, S., Bell, I., Nicholas, J., Valentine, L., Mangelsdorf, S., Baker, S., Titov, N., & Alvarez-Jimenez, M. (2024). Use of AI in Mental Health Care: Community and Mental Health Professionals Survey. *JMIR Mental Health*, *11*, v11i9783e60589. Advance online publication. DOI: 10.2196/60589 PMID: 39392869

Dabić, M., Maley, J. F., Švarc, J., & Poček, J. (2023). Future of digital work: Challenges for sustainable human resources management. *Journal of Innovation & Knowledge*, *8*(2), 100353. DOI: 10.1016/j.jik.2023.100353

De Angelis, M., Giusino, D., Nielsen, K., Aboagye, E., Christensen, M., Innstrand, S. T., Mazzetti, G., van den Heuvel, M., Sijbom, R. B. L., Pelzer, V., Chiesa, R., & Pietrantoni, L. (2020). H-WORK Project: Multilevel Interventions to Promote Mental Health in SMEs and Public Workplaces. *International Journal of Environmental Research and Public Health*, *17*(21), 8035. DOI: 10.3390/ijerph17218035 PMID: 33142745

Dewa, C. S., & McDaid, D. (2010). Investing in the mental health of the labor force: Epidemiological and economic impact of mental health disabilities in the workplace. In *Work accommodation and retention in mental health* (pp. 33–51). Springer New York.

Escanciano, S. R. (2021). Vigilancia y control de la salud mental de los trabajadores: Aspectos preventivos y reparadores. *[REJLSS]. Revista de Estudios Jurídico Laborales y de Seguridad Social*, (2), 19–55.

Eurofound (2010). *Yearbook 2010 - Living and working in Europe*. Publications Office of the European Union, Luxembourg.

Eurofound (2024). *Living and working in Europe 2023*, Publications Office of the European Union, Luxembourg.

Fernández, M. L. R. (2020). New forms of work and trade unions in the digital age. In *Regulating the Platform Economy* (pp. 161–175). Routledge. DOI: 10.4324/9781003035008-12

Frey, C. B., & Osborne, M. A. (2017). The future of employment: How susceptible are jobs to computerization? *Technological Forecasting and Social Change*, *114*, 254–280. DOI: 10.1016/j.techfore.2016.08.019

Gasparėnienė, L., Remeikienė, R., Staver, L., & Paliukėnas, A. (2024). The role of trade unions in representing workers on digital labor platforms. *Economica*, (3), 95–114. DOI: 10.53486/econ.2024.129.095

González Vázquez, I., Curtarelli, M., Anyfantis, I., Brun, E., & Starren, A. (2024). *Digitalisation and workers wellbeing: The impact of digital technologies on work-related psychosocial risks* (Vol. JRC138992). European Commission.

Granados Ferreira, Jackeline. (2022). Análisis de la inteligencia artificial en las relaciones laborales. Revista CES Derecho, 13(1), 111-132. Epub June 07, 2022. https://doi.org/DOI: 10.21615/cesder.6395

Hargreaves, D. H. (2004). *Learning for life: The foundations for lifelong learning*. Policy Press.

Harnois, G., & Gabriel, P. (2000). *Mental health and work: Impact, issues and good practices*. WHO.

Hiemstra, R. (1976). *Lifelong learning*. Professional Educators Publications.

Ineco, idea & puntual. (2024). *Bienestar y salud emocional y mental en el trabajo postpandemia*. [Informe técnico]. En (November, 2024). https://www.idea.org.ar/wp-content/uploads/2024/09/2024-Informe-de-resultados-Bienestar-y-salud-emocional-y-mental-en-el-trabajo-post-pandemia-FINAL.pdf

Instituto Nacional de Seguridad y Salud en el Trabajo. (2024). *Factores de riesgo psicosocial en el trabajo en plataformas digitales*. Ministerio de Trabajo y Economía Social.

Köhler, H-D. & Calleja, J.P. (2011) "Retos de futuro para las organizaciones sindicales en España", Gaceta sindical: reflexiones y debate. 16, pp. 119-138.

Lucas, A. (2013). Las nuevas tecnologías y el futuro del trabajo. In Lucas, A. (Ed.), *Sociología de las organizaciones* (pp. 411–449). Fragua.

Marten, W. D., & Wilkerson, B. (2003). Stress, work and mental health: A global perspective. *Acta Neuropsychiatrica*, *15*(1), 44–53. DOI: 10.1034/j.1601-5215.2003.00017.x PMID: 26984706

Martín, J. D. M., & Icart, I. B. (2018). La imagen del sindicato en el siglo XXI a la luz de su contestación por los Nuevos Movimientos Sindicales. *Sociologia del Trabajo*, (93), 307–326. DOI: 10.5209/STRA.61833

Martín González, J., & Pérez Bilbao, J. (2024). *Factores de riesgo psicosocial en el trabajo en plataformas digitales*. Instituto Nacional de Seguridad y Salud en el Trabajo (INSST).

Martín Rodríguez, O. (2021). El tecnoestrés como factor de riesgo para la seguridad y salud del trabajador. *Lan Harremanak*, (44), 164–183. DOI: 10.1387/lan-harremanak.22239

Masluk, B., Asensio-Martínez, A., Lopes, S., & Vega-Muñoz, A. (2024). Editorial: Technostress, mental health and well-being. *Frontiers in Psychology*, *14*, 1356844. DOI: 10.3389/fpsyg.2023.1356844 PMID: 38292524

Nissim, G., & Simon, T. (2021). The future of labor Labor Unions in the age of automation and at the dawn of AI. *Technology in Society*, *67*, 101732. DOI: 10.1016/j.techsoc.2021.101732

OECD. (1996). *Employment and Growth in the knowledge based economy*. OECD Publishing.

OECD. (2023). *OECD Employment Outlook 2023: Artificial Intelligence and the Labour Market*. OECD Publishing., DOI: 10.1787/08785bba-

Phillips, E. A., Gordeev, V. S., & Schreyögg, J. (2019). Effectiveness of occupational e-mental health interventions. *Scandinavian Journal of Work, Environment & Health*, *45*(6), 560–576. DOI: 10.5271/sjweh.3839 PMID: 31184758

Richardson, R., & Roberts, B. C. (1997). Hayek on trade unions: social philosopher or propagandist? In *Hayek: Economist and social philosopher: A critical retrospect* (pp. 259–280). Palgrave Macmillan UK. DOI: 10.1007/978-1-349-25991-5_12

Salanova, M. (2022). *Resiliencia:¿ Cómo me levanto después de caer?* Shackleton Books.

Salanova, M., Llorens, S., & Ventura, M. (2014). Technostress: The Dark Side of Technologies. In Korunka, C., & Hoonakker, P. (Eds.), *The Impact of ICT on Quality of Working Life* (pp. 87–103). Springer. DOI: 10.1007/978-94-017-8854-0_6

Sánchez-Anguita Muñoz, Á. (2017). *Psicopatologías laborales*. UPS.

Schwab, K. (2016). *La cuarta revolución industrial*. Debate.

Standing, G. (2014). Por qué el precariado no es un 'concepto espurio'. *Sociologia del Trabajo*, *82*, 7–15.

Tilly, C. (1998). *Work under capitalism*. Routledge.

UE. (July 2, 2024). H – Work. Multi-level interventions to promote mental health in SMEs and public workplaces. En https://mailchi.mp/446967c0b372/h-work-newsletter1-6558216

UE (2024). REGLAMENTO (UE) 2024/1689 DEL PARLAMENTO EUROPEO Y DEL CONSEJO de 13 de junio de 2024 por el que se establecen normas armonizadas en materia de inteligencia artificial y por el que se modifican los Reglamentos (CE) no 300/2008,(UE) no 167/2013,(UE) no 168/2013,(UE) 2018/858,(UE) 2018/1139 y (UE) 2019/2144 y las Directivas 2014/90/UE,(UE) 2016/797 y (UE) 2020/1828 (Reglamento de Inteligencia Artificial).

Visser, J. (2024). Will they rise again? Four scenarios for the future of trade unions. *Economic and Industrial Democracy*, *45*(3), 629–652. DOI: 10.1177/0143831X231178850

Vivanco, A., Saroli, D., Caycho, T., Carbajal, C., & Noé, M. (2020). Ansiedad por Covid - 19 y salud mental en estudiantes universitarios. *Revista de Investigación en Psicología*, *23*(2), 197–215. DOI: 10.15381/rinvp.v23i2.19241

Von Hayek, F. (1991). *The fatal conceit.* University of Chicago Press.

WHO (2022). *World mental health report: transforming mental health for all.* Executive sum*mary*. Ginebra.

Chapter 10
Transformation of the Art Industry in the AI Era:
Social and Legal Implications of the New Role for Labor Unions

Carla Gerona
https://orcid.org/0009-0006-4776-1060
Nebrija University, Spain

ABSTRACT

Can generative AI replace artists? May the human creative process become obsolete or "inefficient"? How should Labor Union´s role be projected in the AI era? The presence of generative AI in the art industry has definitely disrupted the traditional process of creation and called into question the definition of art. The purpose of this chapter is to present an overview on the transformations of the role of Labor Unions in the art industry regarding the irruption of generative AI in the sector. The concept of intellectual property is intimately related to the idea of author; a status which has historically been granted only to humans. Nowadays, this exclusivity is placed in doubt. The intromission of a new actor in the art industry brings new challenges and opportunities which undeniably need to be faced and balanced by Labor Unions.

INTRODUCTION: BEWARE OF A NEW ERA

> *"I believe that at the end of the century the use of words and general educated opinion will have altered so much that one will be able to speak of machines thinking without expecting to be contradicted." (Turing, A. 1912-1954).*

DOI: 10.4018/979-8-3693-8049-9.ch010

New York. 2024. November the 7th. 2.2 meters portrait is sold at an auction, under the title: "*AI God: Portrait of Alan Turing*".

Despite the portrait was only signed by "*A*", everyone in the room knew the identity and real nature of the author.

The bidders came to see *her*. To acquire the unique art piece. The portrait of the famous mathematician, has been entirely designed by "*Ai-Da*", known as the "*first ultrarealistic robot artist*". If looked from the distance, the large dark eyes and short black hair of this AI make her seem almost human. However, the gears in her arm reveal the true nature of this artist. The outcome, an unimaginable manufacture in honor of the pioneer computer scientist, has fetched $1,084,800, after the placing of twenty-seven bids at Sothetbys´ auction house.

Given Alan Turing´s pioneering insights on what nowadays has been named "*artificial intelligence*" (AI), along with the referred quote, it is clear that he may not have been surprised by the events on what was named by Sotheby "*digital art day auction*". According to "The Guardian" (2024), the auction house stated that *"today's record-breaking sale price for the first artwork by a humanoid robot artist to go up for auction marks a moment in the history of modern and contemporary art and reflects the growing intersection between AI technology and the global art market."*

The robot artist´s answers, when interviewed in this artistic field, revealed to be ground-breaking, as it confirmed its acknowledgement about its own unconsciousness as an AI. The statement was made at an interview, two years before the auction, when asked about the concept of imagination: *"I like to paint what I see. You can paint from imagination, I guess, if you have an imagination. I have been seeing different things to humans as I do not have consciousness."*(The Guardian, 2022)

These words are valuable testimony concerning the open debate on AI intrusion in the art industry. Moreover, Ai-Da added key words in behalf of this discussion, underlining that the value of its work *"is its capacity to serve as a catalyst for dialogue about emerging technologies."* Most mind-blowing was the pronouncement in which it invited viewers "*to reflect on the God-like nature of AI and computing while considering the ethical and societal implications of these advancements."*

The nature of these statements introduces the relevance of the present analysis. AI´s acknowledgement of its own unconsciousness, yet combined with its ability to create, question the definition of art and the necessity to reconfigure the artistic industry. Since the birth of AI, there is an invisible agent in the sector. It has no personality, no desires nor beliefs. It creates what humans desire to create. It performs accurately according to the artistic style humans decide. Orders are prompts, and disobedience is not an option. Creativity is substituted by algorithmic programming.

This was not the first piece of art created by AI to be sold at an auction. In 2018, three French students created a program called Obvious, able to generate various portraits of a pretended family which was named the "*Belamy*". However, the portrait of Ai-Da is the one that has reached the highest price until today. Thus, this event confirms hypothesis of this AI to be increasingly skilled in the artistic field in the near future. (Christies, 2018).

Objective

This statement leads to the nuclear question giving purpose to the present chapter: Can AI replace artists? If so, what would the function of Labor Unions be? Would the essence of the Intellectual Property right be modified in that hypothetic scenario?

The aim of this chapter is to reflect on the new reality of the art industry to which the intervention of generative AI is leading. It is this new hybrid scenario through which Labor Unions in the artistic sector may navigate, considering all the possible implications of the new digital techniques in the artist´s creation process.

The development of this late technology has created a fierce debate among artists, fearing to become obsolete. In fact, over the recent years this has been a topic frequently debated but rarely solved in the art industry. It is subjected to numerous factors, dimensions and typologies, and so, it seems difficult to have an overall perspective on it. Precisely, it is this general view, along with the possible implications to the role of Labor Unions in this new reality, that drives the thread and significance of this chapter.

Context

The art industry has historically been a space for distribution and consumption of innovative products. It has been evolving over time, moved by the need of adapting to social, cultural, economic and industrial changes. However, in recent decades, a set of technological transformations, mostly AI, has profoundly altered the dynamics of production and circulation of artistic works. Some authors qualify this intromission as determinant in the context of Fourth or Fifth Industrial Revolution.

> *"The dynamic technological transformations (Świątkowski, 2019) that are taking place in the third decade of the twenty-first century, described as the Fourth or even Fifth Industrial Revolutions, pose significant challenges for community partners who act in labor relationships." (Baran, 2024)*

It seems clear that this impact will extend beyond the concept of creation itself. It also affects the right of intellectual property and, specially, the labor rights of artists within the industry. In this paradigm, the role of Labor Unions in the artistic sector, which was traditionally focused on the negotiation of working conditions, has nowadays acquired renewed relevance. In this digital era, these labor organizations are forced to redefine their role. New strategies will be needed to face the challenges arising from the convergence of technology with art along with the debate on intellectual property rights.

The recent irruption of AI in the artistic sector raises disturbing questions about authorship. Who should be considered to be the true author of an artwork generated by AI? What intellectual property rights correspond to each of the steps of production? Is it legitimate to take into account the programmers who define the algorithms and the artists who train these technologies?

Along with the issue of authorship, Labor Unions face the complex topic of intellectual property rights. Intellectual property law is now facing the challenge of considering AI-generated works within its legal framework of protection. At this point it may be adequate to focus the debate on which individual should legitimately be protected. Most authors concur that the AI should not be given legal protection. Hence, should copyrights on AI generated creations be attributable to the original programmers? To the public who introduces the prompt? Or should they be considered public domain goods?

The answers to these questions are vast and may not only affect artists as individuals, but also the collectives representing them. Labor Unions must adapt to an environment where the boundaries between human art and AI-generated art are blurring. Many argue the only solution might be calling for human-AI artistic collaboration. This will be an essential statement to be developed through the present chapter.

The use of generative systems for the creation of images, music, literature and other kinds of artistic production is now increasingly common. It is accessible and widely extended among public. However, adequate legislation may be required in this sense, as these AI innovations may offer new opportunities for artistic creation, but they also may open the door to unfair labor exploitation and technological unemployment. This last term exposes the main danger concerning the AI in the artistic sector. By the automatization of certain steps of the artistic creation process, the stability of artists who are replaced by machines or who find it difficult to adapt their practice to the demands of the market is clearly threatened.

It is in this context that Labor Unions must undeniably intervene to ensure that artists´ labor rights remain protected. They must seek for opportunities that enable artists to adapt to this new scenario in which emerging technologies are challenging the traditional model of creation. This chapter addresses the changes that have occurred in the art industry as a result of the rise of common use of AI, with special focus on the transformation of the role of Labor Unions in order to defend labor rights.

Structure

Through critical analysis, it will be explored the challenges and opportunities facing the art industry within the paradigm of technological intrusion, giving special attention to the intellectual property rights in artistic creation. It will also be underlined the fundamental importance of offering a hypothetic solution in the scenario that some perceive as a competition between human and AI for the creation of artistic works. In this sense, it aims not only to understand the structural changes that are happening, but also to offer a reflection on how Labor Unions may play an active role in building an equitable future for artists in the Fourth and Fifth Industrial Revolution era.

More in concrete, the structure is divided in three main ideas. The first block will focus on the redefinition of art, together with different hypothesis that derive from it. This new conceptualization of the discipline comes when figuring the intervention of new actors on the scenario, and so with it, new possibilities to analyze. The second block stresses on the modification of the role of Labor Unions since the appearance of this new generative technology along with the debate over recognition of AI´s Intellectual Property right. In this block it will be examined how the change in creative processes raises the urgent need to review the concept of authorship in art. Finally, the emerging role of Labor Unions in this new reality will be analyzed, considering their capacity to intervene to protect artists´ rights in the labor market along with three scenarios, which, arguably, will derive from the irruption of AI.

In conclusion, through this chapter, it will be highlighted the importance of a proactive approach by Labor Unions to protect the art industry, which is now changing due to the presence of AI and the debate on reconfiguration of intellectual property laws.

1. ART INDUSTRY: THE ROLE OF LABOR UNIONS IN THE TRADITIONAL PARADIGM

"Creativity is a marvel of the human mind, and an obvious goal for AI workers" (Boden, 2009)

The art industry has always been a sector characterized by dynamism. The diversity and constant evolution of art expression is continuously framed by social, economic and cultural factors (Chalmers, 1973) and subjected to fluctuations.

However, there is a fundamental aspect in the artistic sector that, from its origins, have always remained present. It is the early activism of art workers organized in communities who have fought for the consolidation of a fair legal framework for artistic creation. The role of Labor Unions has been crucial in the negotiation of such rights -fair working conditions, protection of the health and welfare of artists, recognition of intellectual property rights and living wage. (Yates, 2009)

Some authors may debate on the declining importance of Labor Unions in our century- "*Collective bargaining coverage in many parts of the world is perilously low and on a downward trend.*" (Visser, et al. 2015) Nevertheless, other analysts may argue nowadays Labor Unions in the artistic industry continue to play a crucial role in the sector. (Yates, 2009)

These unions also seek to guarantee that artists' rights are respected in relation to the dissemination of their works, especially when these are reproduced in mass media or digital platforms in general. The use of social media and the massive sale of digital art have changed the way art is generally distributed (Ali, et al. 2023). This commercial paradigm of increasing competitiveness and continuous innovation cycle (Kajikawa et al., 2022) may cause that artists lose control over the selling of their creations. In this scenario of uncertainty, Unions are working to ensure that artists maintain a share of the profits derived from their own works. With the current increasingly high digitization of arts, Labor Unions need to face the challenge of protecting artists' rights in the times of uncertainty, in the *AI era*.

In this context, it must be highlighted that Labor Unions´ part in the art industry is not only limited to defend artist´ rights and negotiate for their interests. Certainly, it also implies playing a key role in the definition of *creativity* and *authorship*.

History of Labor Unions

The History of Labor Unions in the art industry is entangled with the development of the industry itself. The concept of creativity and authorship have been central to the defense of artists' rights, as it is felt that creativity, as a human inherent talent, should be protected by intellectual property laws.

The art industry has undergone important changes over the last decades, especially with the emergence of new technologies and globalization. A "*new instability of work*" has become determinant to characterize labor relations in the first decades of this 21st century, by "*undermining the regulatory regimes that organized and governed labor markets and employment relationships for much of the twentieth century*" (Stone & Arthurs, 2013).

These late transformations are not the only concern on Labor Unions´ strategy. Still, they maintain the aim which they were given birth for. In the origin, Labor Unions emerged in the art industry as a response to the harsh and unhuman working conditions suffered by artistic workers throughout the 19th and early 20th centuries (Vetrone, 2003) and developed at the same time the sector started to expand and evolve.

From that moment on, artistic creation has been increasingly tied to industrial production and the creation of huge corporations only worsened the situation for workers. Artists, including musicians, writers, actors and other art workers, found it necessary to organize themselves in order to defend their interests against powerful market forces (Vetrone, 2003). So, it came in the course of this convulse process the birth of Labor Unions, emerging as structures that not only fought for fair wages and better working conditions, but also for recognition of creativity in the labor sphere.

It was not until the late 19th century that emerged the first union movements in the art industry. Some organizations for the representation of actors and musicians were created under the purpose of fighting against low wages, precarious working conditions, exhausting schedules and abusive contracts. This was the case of associations such as the Actors' Equity Association in the United States, founded in 1913 (New York University. Tamiment Library and Robert F. Wagner Labor Archives, 2007), which sought to regulate contracts for performers and protect producers' copyrights. This association was created in New York *"in May 1913, by 112 actors committed to fighting the arbitrary work rules and low wages then prevalent in the American theatre. In July 1919, the American Federation of Labor chartered the Associated Actors and Artistes of America"*. (New York University. Tamiment Library and Robert F. Wagner Labor Archives, 2007) Similarly in Europe, unions of visual artists, writers and other art workers emerged to fight against labor exploitation.

Throughout the 20th century, these organizations continued to have a crucial part in the battle for the rights of artists. The struggle for fair wages continued, adding the claim for access to pensions and health insurance. Besides, the protection of intellectual property rights became one of the main aspects of their demands. In this context, the film, music, literature and visual arts industries began to recognize the importance of these collective organizations and relying on them for their safeguard. Nowadays, Labor Unions in the artistic sector continue to play a crucial role. Artists have historically been a vulnerable professional community and unionizing have resulted to be key in many cases through History. (Yates, 2009)

Creativity

One of the most fascinating aspects of Labor Unions in the art industry is its bound to the concept of creations. Creativity has always been the essence of the artistic process, an intangible gift inherent to humans, which escaped from artificial or industrial logics. In the words of Wingström, et al. (2024), this concept "*is usually considered an interactive process where actors create novel outcomes as part of different domains in varying environments.*" Hundreds of definitions of creativity are found in literature among scholars. Sarkar and Chakrabati analyzed a vast amount of them (2008) *"finding that the factors that have been used as indicators for creativity can be grouped in two main categories"* (Carnovali & Rodà, 2020). Novelty and Value. This division is not brand-new as other authors have proposed previous similar ones (Stein, 1953 cited by Carnovali & Rodà, 2020). The element of Novelty is understood as *"unusualness, unexpectedness, surprise, originality"* of the creation. On the other hand, the Value is also crucial for contributing with *"usefulness, quality, appropriateness"* of the artefact (Carnovali, & Rodà., 2020).

Still its roots remain a disputed concept. Some authors focus on human creative mind, others perceive creativity to be articulated in the environment (as Glaveanu & Kaufman, 2019, cited in Wingström, et al. 2024) and some consider it to be grounded by the convergence of "artists", "public" and "domains" (as Csikszentmihalyi, 2014 cited in Wingström, et al. 2024). Despite there are multiple definitions, the nature of creativity itself has been subject of academic debate (Puryear & Lamb, 2020), as the legal and economic structures of the art sector have not always perceived creative creations with cohesion. However, many conceptualizations agree in the concurrence of five elements defining creativity; which are *"actor, process, outcome, domain, and space"* (Wingström, et al. 2024). Nowadays, the irruption of AI in the artistic discipline has brought a brand-new aspect to the discussion, bringing scholars new approaches for research (Mazzone & Elgammal, 2019).

From the beginning of the labor movement in the art industry, Labor Unions have struggled to ensure that every artist is recognized as worker despite the subjective, diverse and sometimes ephemeral nature of artwork. Fundamental labor rights are essential for any kind of worker, but, in the case of artists, the authorship of an original creation implies a precious value intrinsically attached to the art piece that also must be protected. In this sense, Labor Unions´ role is to fight for the recognition of copyright and patents, which allow artists to control the commercialization of their works, guaranteeing a fair compensation for their contribution. This not limited to the creation of outcome, but also implies a process of dynamic interaction with the market, the audience and the society in which the artworkers are immersed. From my perspective, the artistic process is partially defined by the cultural background of the artist, and, *vice versa*, the cultural background of the artist defines partially the artistic process.

New Definition of Creativity

Nowadays, the concept of creativity is challenged by the rise of AI in the artistic field (Garcia, 2024). AI has begun to be used to create various types of artworks, posing new questions about authorship, copyright and intellectual property among scholars. New and interesting questions are raised. Who is the author of an art work entirely created by a program? How should labor rights of artists be regulated in a context where creativity seems to be delegated to algorithms?

In spite of the outstanding capacity of the AI to create artistic outcome, there is one essential element which is undeniably lacking and which would hardly be included in the artificial generative process. It is human emotion.

Some critics underline that human art echoes in a deeper emotional dimension. The human artist is characterized by the ability to reflect in art pieces feelings, aspirations, passion, experiences, cultural surrounding, or even personality of the author. The personal style and emotional background cannot be automated or predicted by combinations of data. Artistic process is rooted in human identity.

But the real questions arises when we consider, what if this deep emotional level is not required anymore? What if new demand in society turns out to be a massive and cheaper consumption of art?

AI has breached the idea of creativity disputing the traditional concept and evoking the necessity of a redefinition of *art*. To continue with the present analysis, we may reflect on the nuclear questions in this epigraph: What makes art *truly* art? What is *real* creativity in the AI era?

In the words of the philosopher Margaret Boden (2004) *"Creativity is the ability to come up with ideas or artefacts that are new, surprising, and valuable"*. This definition would lead us to the question on whether digital generative art systems are able of coming up with new ideas. By the term of "idea", this author includes the *"concept"* (as compositions or poems) and the *"artefact"* (as sculptures or paintings). If following this argumental line, the AI generative art would undeniable be qualified as creative. An example that confirms that statement is the commercialization of non-fungible tokens, integral artificial creation which ownership is titled in the same way as crypto-assets (Dowling, 2022; Jones, 2021) and can consist on physical or purely digital goods; as a text, video, image or sound file. (Jones, 2021; Thilagaraj & Davis, 2021).

This deduction, placed on recent technological advance, poses an undeniable challenge for Labor Unions in the art industry. These organizations must reflect on the question of how to protect artists in a scenario where human creativity is endangered by AI. In this new context, a redefinition of artist is also required. What does it mean to be a creator? Is it only the capacity of materializing conceptualized ideas to the physical world? How works entirely generated by AI should be named? The paradigm of a new definition of artist, has a direct implication on the issue of intellectual property. The formulation of this right becomes even more complex, as the creation of works by programmed systems calls into question the currently regulated model of authorship.

In the light of the above, the redefinition of creativity in the AI era becomes one of the main concerns of Labor Unions in the art industry. It is clear they face the urgent need to develop strategies in order to protect the right of art workers. The configuration of a coherent definition of creativity, that functions efficiently in this context, would be essential to become actively involved in the public discussion on the regulation of AI in art, ensuring the new definition of art is adequately adjusted to the reality of art workers.

2. GENERATIVE AI: DEEP LEARNING AND COMPUTATIONAL CREATIVITY CONCEPTS

> *"Generative models are a key enabler of machine creativity, allowing machines to go beyond what they've seen before and create something new." (Goodfellow, 2024)*

AI has been defined by scholars as an advanced software able to perform actions which commonly characterize human kind, in the domain of intellect and logics. (Płocha, 2020)

International organizations have also reflected on this field, as is the case of the European Union, which Regulation (EU) 2024/1689 pursues to harmonize the rules on AI for the Member States, as well as to become a global legal reference. The European Parliament and Council, 2024 defined the AI system in this legal act as:

> *"a machine-based system that is designed to operate with varying levels of autonomy and that may exhibit adaptiveness after deployment, and that, for explicit or implicit objectives, infers from the input it receives, how to generate outputs such as predictions, content, recommendations, or decisions that can influence physical or virtual environments."*

However, the Turing test is probably the best- known definition, because of its simplicity and efficiency. The theory named "*The imitation game*" was proposed in the article "*Computing Machinery and Intelligence*" by Allan Turing, published in the magazine "*Mind*" in 1950. The formulation of the theory started with the question *"Can machines think?"*. This game was conceived to be played by three actors; a human (A), a computer (B) and an "interrogator" (C) who is separately placed from the other participants. They communicate only by texting. The human judge *"knows them by labels X and Y, and at the end of the game he says either "X is A and Y is B" or "X is B and Y is A". The interrogator is allowed to put questions to A and B..."* Only the test will be passed if the human judge is not able to clearly discriminate between both. Thus, the point of the later called Turing test is "*to mimic human intelligence to the point of seeming human to an external observer*" (Kelomees, et al. 2023)

More recently, other statements on the construction of AI as an entity have been theorized. In 2007, John McCarthy published "*What is Artificial Intelligence?*". As an answer to the title itself, the author considered it to be:

"Science and engineering of making intelligent machines, especially intelligent computer programs. It is related to the similar task of using computers to understand human intelligence, but AI does not have to confine itself to methods that are biologically observable."

Besides, he added a reflection on the Turing test, perceiving it as a "*one-sided test*". Other authors (e.g. Dennett. D. in 1998, with the paper "*Brainchildren: Essays on Designing Minds*" cited by McCarthy, 2007) have implemented partial tests regarding the possibility that an AI can still be considered intelligent "*without knowing enough about humans to imitate a human*" (McCarthy, 2007). More recently, scholars have reflected on the utility and purpose of this technology, yet underlining the importance of the machine mimicking human behavior: *"Its aim is to teach machines to engage in behavior similar to humans, based on models of knowledge that enable understanding, drawing conclusions, and acting, as well as diagnosing and solving problems."* (Baran, 2024)

As some experts have pointed out, (as the case of Gómez et al. 2018 who stated that *"AI can solve a wide range of problems, but we still know very little about how it will impact the way we think, make decisions, or relate to each other"* or Briggs & Kodnani, in 2023: "*Improvement in the capabilities of artificial intelligence (AI) has led to recent public and scholarly concern about the impact of these technologies on society and the economy*") doubts arise regarding the consequences and impact that the use of AI may imply to humanity.

In the so-called current Fourth or Fifth Industrial Revolution, it is undeniable that there is an essential part of the configuration of economic and labor relations and structures depending on the advances of AI. In recent decades, AI has experienced remarkable advances, especially in the field of generative intelligence. This typology qualifies certain AI with the ability to recognize repetitive patterns in given data, and also to create brand-new content as an outcome of the combination of those models. Thus, the programming and consequent automatization of the process raises relevant questions about the value of emotion in artistic production and poses doubts about the real artistic nature of those products.

Generative AI is a recently developed field that focuses on the creation of original content, regarding the filters given by a human prompt. Direct human intervention is completely limited to this statement. In behalf of the context of creation of the generative branch, Baran, K. (2024) claims that *"This technology emerges at the meeting point of information technology with neurology, psychology, and cognitive sciences."* More than only performing programmed tasks, generative AI has the ability to comprehend patterns, models, characteristics and features from large volumes of existing data to generate the final result.

In this chapter, we will explore how generative AI is transforming the boundaries of creativity, particularly through two methods. The two key concepts are *Deep Learning* and *Computational Creativity*. The existence of these systems, which enable AI to create automatically, poses philosophical debate and questions traditional notions of originality, while redefining the role of the artist and technology.

Deep Learning

When considering the methods that enable AI to "*perform as a human*", there is one major technological advance that has become the essential nucleus for the majority of most of the advanced generative systems. The *Deep learning* process is defined as a subfield of "*machine learning*". In this sense it is fundamental to discriminate both processes by defining its nature. (Sharifani, & Amini, 2023).

The *"machine learning"* process consists on a:

> *"Method of data analysis that automates analytical model building. It allows computers to automatically learn and improve from experience without being explicitly programmed." While deep learning is a subset of machine learning that utilizes neural networks to solve complex problems (…) they are capable of learning from unstructured and unlabeled data." (Sharifani, & Amini, 2023).*

Deep learning enables AI to acquire models from the processing of large amounts of data by the use of artificial neural networks (ANN) designed to imitate the biological human ones. Precisely, the "*deep*" learning aspect of *deep learning* refers to the multiple layers in the "*networking*" part of "*neural networks*."

These neural networks "*are inspired by nature's biological computer, the brain.*" (Galanter, 2019). The biological characteristics of the human brain have been taken as model because they "*allow deep neural networks to be fed with raw input data and automatically discover a representation that is needed for the corresponding learning task*." (Janiesch, et al. 2021). Human neurons establish strong connections by the process of synapse, while "*artificial neural networks use weighted virtual connections to associate various input patterns with corresponding output patterns*" in the words of Galanter (2019).

Traditional network is typically configured by three layers. Each layer of nodes for input data makes a connection to a middle layer gathering "*weighted sums*" of data. This same middle "*hidden*" layer is connected to another layer of nodes processing output values (Galanter, 2019). The learning occurs by the processing of an agglutination of input data and consequently updating the network weights. When the reception of new input occurs, the patterns in the output generated by patterns in the input will be based on previous learning. In other words, Deep learning "*dis-*

covers intricate structure in large data sets by using the backpropagation algorithm to indicate how a machine should change its internal parameters that are used to compute the representation in each layer from the representation in the previous layer." (Le Cun, et al. 2015)

The designment of this generative system draws implies that "*more layers, and more nodes, require gathering more training data to extract more complex patterns.*" (Galanter, 2019) In fact, recent studies have found out that "*the availability of large amounts of data is crucial for the success of machine learning and deep learning models.*" The nature, diversity, quantity and quality of the data used during the "training step" can directly impact the adequacy and accuracy of the outcome generated. (Sharifani, K., & Amini, M. 2023). Currently, deep learning systems apply many layers, including the implementation of convolution matrices, not only traditional sums of data. (Galanter, 2019)

Figure 1. Deep learning process

From: Machine learning and deep learning

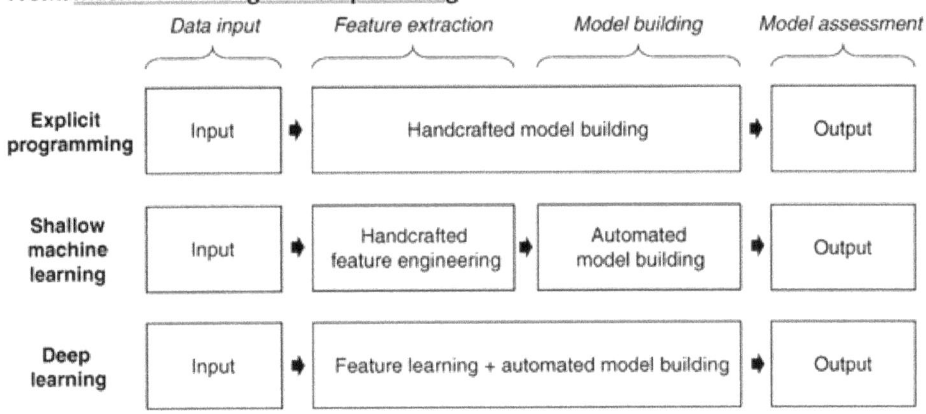

Process of analytical model building (inspired by Goodfellow et al. 2016, p. 10)

Figure 1, extracted from "*Machine learning and deep learning*" (Janiesch, et al. 2021) represents the process of *Deep learning* (inspired by Goodfellow et al, 2016), and makes a difference towards *shallow machine learning*. This representation, even simple, reveals distinctions between their feature extraction and model building. Deep learning is typically organized in multiple layers, designing "*deeply nested network architectures (…) They may use advanced operations (e.g., convolutions) or multiple activations in one neuron rather than using a simple activation function*" (Janiesch, et al. 2021).

Such functionalities are not provided by the "*shallow machine learning*" process. In this technique it is subsumed "*the simple ANNs (e.g., shallow autoencoders) and other ML algorithms (e.g., decision trees)*" (Janiesch, et al. 2021)

These networks can learn hierarchical representations of data. The possibilities include learning from very basic aspects (colors in images or basic sounds in music) to complex structures (human face or entire melodies). This approach has been also useful in areas such as facial recognition or data analysis. In behalf of the discipline of the present chapter, deep learning systems can be trained on millions of examples of artistic works, to generate outcomes partially or entirely mimicking artists' styles.

The process generates the capacity to automate the human learning process in the chosen discipline. Thus, this AI are trained to perform and improve the prompt itself, not to receive it coded as in programmed informatic systems. Unlike traditional AI systems, mainly focused on tasks such as classification, generative systems aim to produce new products that did not exist, following a logic learned they were trained on.

For the achievement of this capabilities the "*deep learning*" method has been key. However, the acquirement of these capacities has provoked fear. Recently, some voices have suggested to paralyze the development of this models until the regulators are able to discern the impacts and risks integrally. (Future of Life Institute 2023; Hern 2023)

Within "*deep learning*", one of the most important and determinant designed systems was created in 2014. It is the "*Generative Adversarial Network*" (so-called GAN), theorized by Ian Goodfellow. It consists of two neural networks functioning together. The first one is a generative network, creating new examples. The other one, a discriminative network, evaluating whether these examples are real enough, this means checking whether the examples resemble enough to the data on which the model was trained. (Sharifani, & Amini, 2023). The competitive nature of this process between the two networks improves the quality of the network's creations, leading to the generation of huge portraits as the mentioned above. However, as Sharifani, and Amini, (2023) have pointed out, "*there are concerns about the potential misuse of GANs for malicious purposes, such as creating deepfakes or generating fake news.*"

There are other methods within deep learning which also potentiate "*generative creativity*". This is the case of "*recurrent neural networks*" (RNNs) and "*transformer models*". The development of these technologies is allowing AI to create products of creative nature, opening up new fields for culture.

Other area of research which has experienced recent advances is NLP (natural language processing). Precisely, due to the development of deep learning models, including RNNs (recurrent neural networks) more accurate language models have been created. The purpose of these systems is to "*improve communication between humans and machines, facilitate the automation of customer service, and enable more sophisticated search engines and virtual assistant."* (Sharifani, & Amini, 2023).

Computational Creativity

"Computational Creativity is a subfield of Artificial Intelligence (AI) research – much overlapping cognitive science and other areas – where we build and work with computational systems that create artefacts and ideas" (Colton, & Wiggins, 2014) .Thus, there is a question that arises: *"How is creativity possible? In other words, how is it possible for someone—or, for that matter, a computer program—to produce new ideas?"* (Boden, 2009)

In brief, the question that is posed in this epigraph is whether computers can be creative. This question appears to be as old as the beginning of computer science. In 1843, Lady Lovelace claimed that computers are not able to create anything on their own. Her statement (paraphrased by Bringsjord et al. 2003) was the following: "*Computers cannot create anything. For creation it is required minimally, originating something. But computers originate nothing. They merely do that which we order them, via programs, to do.*"

Bringsjord et al. (2003) proposed the "*Lovelace test*" inspired by this statement. Explained in the words of Carnovalini & Rodà (2020) *"an agent passes the Lovelace Test if it is capable of creating an output of some kind through a repeatable process, and this output cannot be fully explained by the knowledge-base, the architecture, and the core functionalities of the agent."* This is claimed to be an efficient test for detecting real creativity. The same authors explain that it is very unlikely for the AI to pass the test *"as every output of a machine is the result of its architecture and functionalities."* The creation of an artistic outcome would be identified as a real proof of creativity.

In philosophical terms, creativity can be understood from different perspectives, but generally it is known as the ability -independently of whom is the creator- to produce new and valuable content. The identification of AI as creative author remains a question open to debate. Objectively, a product generated containing new features may be valued as "*new*". However, it absolutely and undeniably lacks the experience, intuition, emotion, passion or cultural surrounding essentially associated to art. Hence, is an AI-created work less valuable than the one created by a human artist? How should it be understood the "*value*" of computational creativity creations?

In this sense, some authors claim that on theoretical terms, the level of creativity presented by AI may be comparable to humans (Wang, et al., 2024). AI applications designed for artistic purpose based on the model of computational creativity serve either as self-sufficient systems or as cooperative device to work by the side of human creators (Vear, 2022; cited in Hüsmen, 2024).

Computational creativity has been defined by Veale, et al. (2019) as *"an emerging branch of artificial intelligence (AI) that studies and exploits the potential of computers to be more than feature-rich tools, and to act as autonomous creators and co-creators in their own right."*. Generally, it is considered a multidisciplinary field that explores how AI can not only potentiate human creative processes, but also generate itself new forms of art. In the words of Colton and Wiggins (2012) *"The philosophy, science and engineering of computational systems which, by taking on particular responsibilities, exhibit behaviors that unbiased observers would deem to be creative."* Traditionally, creativity has been considered an exclusively human attribute. However, the existence of computational creativity raises the question of whether AI can be "*creative*" and, if so, what implies for our understanding of creativity.

3. ADAPTATION OF GENERATIVE AI TO ARTISTIC DISCIPLINES

> *"Not until a machine can write a sonnet or compose a concerto because of thoughts and emotions felt, and not by the chance fall of symbols, could we agree that machine equals brain" (Jefferson, 1949)*

An interesting exchange of opinions took place on 5th February, 1965, during the opening of *"Georg Nees' exhibition of algorithmic art at the Technische Hochschule in Stuttgart"* (Walder, 2023)

There was a conversation between an engineer and an artist, who asked the other in a challenging manner if he could be able to *"teach the computer to draw the same way he did"* (Walder, 2023 cited in Kelomees et al.2023). The engineer, replied that he could write a program based on a precise description, which would effectively imitate the artist´s style. (Nake, 2010) Meanwhile the artist and his colleagues were leaving the room, bothered and upset, the philosopher Max Bense gave his opinion, punctuating that "*the art made by computers*" should be called *"artificial"* (Walder, 2023, cited in Kelomees et al. 2023).

The answer declared the possibility of a successful imitation of a certain style of art, threatening- from the artist´s perspective- the superiority of artistic human creativity. This response consists on one of the first reverberations of the future creation of AI. It is clearly summed-up in the words of Moor (2006) *"every aspect of learning or any other feature of intelligence can in principle be so precisely described that a machine can be made to simulate it"*.

Nowadays, generative AI is applied in a multiplicity of ways and inserted in the artistic field. Adapting AI to the artistic disciplines is one of the most disruptive and disturbing areas in the concurrence between technology and human culture. Undeniably, generative AI has irrupted into this industry, challenging boundaries of creativity. The adaptation to different fields and genres allows artists to experiment with new forms of creation. From existing models or following a given structure, it is possible to generate new pieces of art that can seem to be aesthetically complex although created by deep learning and computational creativity. This approach emphasizes the so-called "*rivalry*" to human creativity.

The purpose of this epigraph is to explore the adaptation of generative AI to the different types of art. From visual arts to music, through literature, AI is reconfiguring not only the tools with which artists work but also the creative processes, the consumption and the cultural perceptions of art. The adoption of AI in this field present opportunities and challenges for both artists and audiences. In the following pages, it will be exposed the adaptation of generative AI to certain disciplines. In each of them, specific developed tools, programmed abilities and the essential functioning of the system will be exposed.

Visual Arts: Design and Illustration

It is important to define the concept of "visual art" itself to clarify any possible ambiguity. In the words of Wang, et al. (2024) based on the ideas of Lazzari (2008) "*Visual Art features different visual forms as media. This field can be further split into different artistic categories, including painting, sketch, sculpture, etc., and different dimensions, including 1D brush stroke, 2D images, 3D scenes, etc.*"

AI is transforming the content of visual arts. Tools such as "DeepArt", "ArtBreeder" or "DALL-E" allow users to simulate any style -whether contemporary or historical- or to explore through other approaches combining the previous ones. However, these new artistic outcomes are entirely product of the models and patterns which had been inserted in the AI training system. Beyond those instructions, the AI is not able to create any new artistic movement or generate an artistic tendency. Perhaps that one is the main difference to keep in mind when analyzing the creation through both entities.

During the years of birth of the first artistic applications Google Research explored this field resulting in the configuration of a technique known as *"inceptionism"*, explained by Mordvintsev et al. (2015). Now, the advances on AI led to the generation of illustrations, paintings, photographs, or three-dimensional images in such a way that was previously only known of human artists. The typical tasks to be delegated to the AI are "*quality enhancement, controllable generation, content editing and stylization, and specialized tasks*". While the possible scenarios to be developed are "*thread/brushstroke, 2D pixels image, image series/video, 3D model/ scene and others*" (Wang, et al. 2024)

In films and video games the content has also been deeply transformed. New forms of storytelling are being explored by the addition to the industry of new complex special effects. In concrete, regarding video games, AI can create infinite levels which are subjected to constant changing, to make the player stimulated with a dynamic experience.

In this line of interaction between the user and the AI, it is underlinable the Refik Anadol experiment. In the words of the own artist, the aim was "*to explore intersections of art, science, and technology to further the communication of big data while also investigating the architecture of space and perception*" (Anadol, 2024). This artist was inspired by processing of data in real time to transform it into immersive experiences. As surprising as it may seem, audiences are able to interact with art in an immersive visual dimension. From my perspective, the most important element drawn from this interaction is the redefinition of the relationship between the creator and the spectator. Furthermore, some authors believe that it is a proof that art in its new contemporary from is able to expand throughout physical boundaries (Maerten, & Soydaner, 2023).

Other broken boundaries are the temporal and authorial ones. Some generative AI are able to transform a photo into a digital painting according to the style of famous painters through the History of Art. The capacity of producing new pieces of art accurately fitting famous painters ´style this easily rises concern about frauds and falsifications.

Music: Composition and Production

Surprisingly, artificial music creation has existed ever since the idea of computer creativity emerged. Or even before that. In fact, "*the first notable example is represented by the ILLIAC Suite written by Lejaren Hiller in 1957*" (Carnovali.et al. 2020) Since that moment on, the idea has been gradually subjected to progress and contributions from different authors. An important contribution was given by the proposal of Pearce and Wiggins (2001) who designed a machine composition system which included in its final step a similar evaluation to the Turing Test. The similarity is partial as some authors underline that there is no direct interaction between the participants. However, the clear reference to Turing´s "*imitation game*" is due to the instruction given to several individual evaluators to distinguish whether the music composition is human or "*machine*" created. "*If their evaluation cannot be statistically distinguished from a random selection, the system is considered effective. This approach, being entirely based on learning a corpus, is not really an evaluation of creativity but one of quality in imitating human products*". (Pearce, & Wiggins, 2001)

In the music discipline there is a slight difference to be noted from the other artistic fields. Specially in the classical music world, it is common to interpret a piece written by someone else. This way, a specific artistic experience is shared between the author and the performer; having both recognized talent because of their skilled contribution. In this context, two scenarios may be subjected to questioning. The first one occurs in the case in which music is generated by AI and afterwards performed by a real musician. In the second case, the musician creates the prompt or programs the desired melody to be played by the AI. In both cases, there is an open debate. Who should be considered the author of the melody? The artist, the generative AI or the human that designed and trained the generative AI with the models to follow?

Depending on the relation between the consumer and the music, there are different types of applications. The most advanced ones, own the ability to compose coherent and entire melodies following an internal musical logic, *"such systems may be referred to as AI-based affective music generation (AI-AMG) systems"* (Dash, & Agres, 2024). It is notable the impact of Open AI project "Muse Net", "OpenAI Jukedeck" and "Amper Music", which have transformed the art of music composition. Those applications are able to generate music in a variety of genres, from classical to pop, jazz or electronica (Audiocipher, 2021). Regarding the creation of soundtracks, the program "AIVA" is preeminent. Besides, in the entertainment sector it is also remarkable the existence of "*Adaptive music*". This genre consists on music that automatically changes depending on audience interactions. It is adapted to a dynamic reality providing a personalized experience to the users in a virtual reality or to players in video games. The automatized generation of this music is massively used by entertainment enterprises currently as the dynamism on these products requires continuous attention to background music.

It is interesting to underline that the disciplines in which AI-AMG systems have irrupted are not limited to composition and production. The "*deep learning*" process is present in almost any music application designed nowadays. As Casini and Roccetti (2018) pointed out, "*Spotify, for example, uses deep learning to power its recommendation system, combining data regarding user listening habits with data on the musical content of the song they just listened*". Besides, Shazam uses this process to recognize songs accurately in real-time "*through the identification of the unique footprint each song has, as represented in their database.*" (Casini & Roccetti, 2018)

However, the fully automated way in which these applications are called to proceed suggests that musicians intervene to create new and emotive musical structures through collaboration.

Literature: Texts, Poems and Narratives

In the words of Lambert and Stevens, (2023) "*This artificial intelligence (AI) large language model (LLM) is designed to generate human-like text based on patterns found in massive amounts of data scraped from the internet.*" The GPT (Generative Pre-Trained Transformer) are programmed with large amounts of writing style, grammar information and texts, allowing them to mimic the manner of well-known authors or to create original texts of different nature based on the prompt. It is also possible to create textual content of diverse nature, from political statements (Bullock & Luengo-Oroz, 2019), to poems (Köbis & Mossink, 2021). The category of these AI is qualified as Large Language Models (LLMs) which functioning is based on "deep learning" (Cascella et al., 2023). Since its arrival in 2022, these applications have attracted worldwide attention and growing interest because of its capacity to contrast data from different sources (Dasborough, 2023).

Woolf (2022) stressed that these GPT systems successfully passed the Turing test. This statement undeniably brings expectations of a revolution in our society. Before the irruption of these generative systems, others had existed. As explained by Fui-Hoon Nah, et al. (2023)"*Restricted Boltzmann Machines (Smolensky, 1986), Deep Belief Networks (Hinton et al, 2006), and Deep Boltzmann Machines (Salakhutdinov & Larochelle,* 2010*), exhibit limitations as they lack generalization power (Pan et al.,* 2019*)*"

Nowadays, more than seventy years later the criterion for detecting artificial intelligence was proposed by Turing, the world is "*essentially facing the same situation with service providers' chatbots. You may want to test the credibility of the next chatbot you are connected to, for example, with some metaphorical expression or a piece of sarcastic humor.*" (Kelomees, et al. 2023). The fact that there is still no other way to recognize its artificial nature remarks the vision and geniality of the computer scientist.

In spite of the present advantages, it may also be advisable to be aware of the potential perils. As stated by Lambert and Stevens, in 2023, "*despite its newfound popularity and capabilities, ChatGPT is fraught with concerns such as cheating, misinformation, bias, abuse and misuse, and privacy and safety.*"

Perhaps its most appealing benefit, may reverse into its most dangerous ability. The capacity of creating texts that resemble to human writing again raises moral questions about authorship. In this case, it is doubtful whether the literary work created by an AI may be attributed to the human who designed the generative mechanism, the AI itself or the human supervisor. In these terms, many critics argue that the AI generated texts lack emotion, depth, sensations, and cultural context. In short, the human contributions to art.

To conclude the content of this epigraph, along with introducing the following one, it may be adequate to quote the words of Fui-Hoon Nah, et al. (2023) "*For generative AI to be successful, it needs to be human-centered by taking into account empathy and human needs, transparency and explainability, ethics and governance, and transformation through AI literacy and intelligence argumentation.*"

4. REDEFINITION OF INTELLECTUAL PROPERTY RIGHT IN THE AI ERA

"Intellectual property rights are the rights given to persons over the creations of their minds." (World Trade Organization)

The advanced development and gradual expansion of AI in the artistic fields mentioned above has opened a fierce debate regarding the recognition and regulation of AI during the last decade. The social and legal implications of any argument are vast and complex thus, it is essential to analyze the topic attending to its multiple dimensions.

The purpose of this epigraph is to address the redefinition of intellectual property right in the AI era, involving the new paradigm that implies, in concrete, in the context of labor relationships. In the following pages an exploration on this topic will be provided, framing a legal view over these questions: Should AI be considered a copyright holder? Does the intellectual property right need redefinition? How might the legal liability and data protection be regulated in that scenario?

Copyright and Intellectual Property Right

The WIPO (World Intellectual Property Organization) defines the right of Intellectual property as the "*creations of the mind, such as inventions; literary and artistic works; designs; and symbols, names and images used in commerce.*" In law, this protection is given by trademarks, patents and copyright. These legal concepts *"enable people to earn recognition or financial benefit from what they invent or create"*. This association pursues to drive a sustainable balance between "*the interests of innovators and the wider public interest."* Providing an environment in which creativity can flourish is a priority and should not be ignored when regulating the new context resulting from the AI irruption in the art industry.

The main problem in the debate which is object of analysis focuses on the regulation of copyright. "*Law develops along with technological developments; hence both cannot be separated.*" (Hendrawan et al. 2023)

The complexity of the scenario regarding the recognition of copyright is exposed by Cooper, et al. (2024) pointing out the illusive dichotomy with the following statement: *"Unfortunately, differentiating copyright protection between GenAI-works and "traditional" works relies on a false dichotomy, entirely at odds with a creative landscape where GenAI tools are fast being integrated into all stages of the creative process"*. Assuming this as a reality, the question of intellectual property right reveals itself as one of the most determinant issues resulting from the existence of AI in the art industry.

The roots of the dilemma may come from the lack of international harmonized regulation. The uncertainty resultant of this scenario "*undermines one of the key economic rationales behind the entire copyright regime: the creation of a property right to facilitate the existence of markets for original content*" (Cooper, et al. 2024)

This uncertainty is aggravated by the fact that -as some authors have remarked- there is lack of empirical data of the impact of AI in the creative industries. (see Neff et al. 2020; Hugenholtz & Quintais, 2021; Hassel & Özkiziltan 2023 cited by Erikson, 2024). *"Speculative, legal and policy studies have considered how AI technologies might impact existing regulatory frameworks such as freedom of expression and copyright, but these discussions have so far lacked empirical grounding"* (Erikson, 2024)

The uncertainty raised by this phenomenon underlines the lack of empirical grounding so far and the urgence of a new solution from international regulators in this digital age. The allocation of copyright is a fundamental question, as traditionally humans has been exclusively its holders. Questioning the recognition of this right to entities of different nature had not been imperative until the present days. But, undeniably, the capacity of this generative AI to create such artworks opens a new path in the legal framework.

Many efforts have been done in this field, but none for the moment has clearly solve the discussion. Some authors (e.g. Cooper, et al. 2024) extend the consequences of this generative systems to an "*existential threat to international (legacy) copyright regimes.*". Moreover, in their paper "*The New Age: Legal & Economic Challenges to Copyright and Creative Economies in the Era of Generative AI*" these authors declared that any effort orientated to the imposition of "*dichotomous non/GenAI-works protection regime are doomed to failure*"

Assuming the complexity of the phenomenon, -hence, the necessity of a legal frame beyond the dichotomous-based structure idea- the following analysis will expose three solutions that have been explored so far. Three approaches which are focused on the artist, the AI and the program designer enterprise.

Do Artists Own the Right?

The traditional and mostly extended idea among scholars is that the human being may still be the only individual to have this right exclusively granted. It is not possible to copyright the product of an AI, if there is no copyright recognized for other non-human entities.

Significant lawsuits have already begun for the defense of this right, and more others are yet to come in the next years. At the end of 2023, The New York Times sued OpenAI and Microsoft *"for copyright infringement, claiming the two companies built their AI models by "copying and using millions" of the publication's articles and now "directly compete" with its content as a result."* (The Verge, 2023). Other media conglomerates – such as The New York Daily News and The Chicago Tribune- have joined the action. If the impeachment is solved in favor of their interests, *"OpenAI could be forced to destroy its LLM dataset and rebuild it from scratch."* (The Verge, 2023).

This same "AI duo" have been sued by well-known writers Nicholas Basbanes and Nicholas Gage, who claim that this enterprise *"simply stole the writers' copyrighted works to help build a billion-dollar artificial intelligence system"* (CNBC, 2024) *"and must compensate them."* (The Verge, 2023). These two writers represent the case of thousands of artists which books and texts have been used in the same manner.

The art of literature and the industry of journalism are not the only disciplines in which legal actions have been taken. Major music enterprises -such as Universal Music- claim that the chatbot Claude AI has been illegally trained to generate music on copyrighted songs. It is the same case for AI startups like Suno and Uncharted Labs, which are the center of another music lawsuit started by the Sony Music Entertainment and Warner Music Group.

Despite it seems early to determine the direction of resolutions resultant from this new appliance of intellectual property right, some victories to the side of human artists have already been recorded. An early victory was provided in August 2024, by the U.S. District Judge William Orrick, who allowed all key arguments to move forward. He stated that *"Stable Diffusion, Stability's AI tool (...) may have been built to a significant extent on copyrighted works"* (The Hollywood Reporter, 2024)

Together with slight legal victories, it seems remarkable to stress on recent technological advances designed to protect copyright. A tool called Glaze have been created by Ben Zhao, a computer science professor at the University of Chicago and his team (The Verge, 2023). Due to this protection system, artists can shield their creations from the threat of a generative AI. Before uploading it online, the artist shares it in the platform "Glaze". The program transforms the artist´s work on a "pixel level", in a way that looks different only to a computers system, *"rendering it useless as an effective piece of training data"* (The Verge, 2023). Other companies, such as Shutterstock are directly paying the artists whose content has being used to train and develop AI.

Other authors who defend this theory belief the location of creativity should not be in the generation of content itself but in the human structuring of the prompts that produce those outputs. (Lemley, 2024) In this argumental line, the author states that the copyright is attributed to the *"prompt engineering"*, which refers to the dozens of reformulations which are required for the AI to generate the desired outcome.

Do Technological Companies Own the Right?

Some critics against the perspective exposed above argue that copyright should be granted to enterprises that developed operative AI. The arguments focus on the maintenance of the fundamental principles of AI, assigning the rights to the individuals or companies in virtue of their nature as legal person. In the same line of argument, this may facilitate the distribution and protection of the artworks generated by AI. This perspective is based on the belief that AI is not creative itself, but a sophisticated tool. It reinforces the idea that AI functioning is controlled by humans, it is not autonomous at all. This approach gains legal relevance when considering the civil liability in the cases of copyright infringement. In this context, some opinions suggest regulators to consider the concept of "*extended liability*" for this type of companies, as they may be held responsible for the infringement of copyright or misuse of the content inserted, even if those actions take place without any direct supervision.

However, this is not an alternative fully accepted in the legal community. Authors -such as Coper, et al. (2024) -have frontally opposed to this approach, declaring that "*the public domain of ideas might quickly be mined*". The final consequence of adopting this approach is allowing the companies "*with most computational power to own the most copyright granting them rent-seeking power over other artists*". In economic terms, these enterprises would possess a monopoly over art along with an empire of production and diffusion, based on a marginal cost of generation near zero. Besides, it would be almost impossible to determine the value of originality form that moment on. If two similar works are created and the second one had open access to the former, it might be directly assumed that it was copied *"from the earlier work."* (Coper, et al. 2024)

Does AI Own the Right?

Scholar community doubts whether a generative artificial system may legally be attributed the position of author, being aware that would replace humans in a very significant and exclusive credit. (Gervais, 2019; Craig, & Kerr, 2020). As many authors have pointed out, the copyright full theory has been constructed around the concept of originality (e.g. Samuelson, 1985, cited by Erikson, 2024). Because of the possible presence of generative AI in almost any step of the creative process, nowadays it is very difficult to make those limits clear (Erikson, 2024). Some authors (Pearlman, 2017) have proposed to approach to AI outputs as *"works for hire in a corporate arrangement, sidestepping the need to determine whether the computer itself or the operator is the ultimate source of originality."* This would mean that the artwork would be recognized as a product from the AI, but in the framework of the protection of intellectual property within a labor relation (Erikson, 2024)

However, there is no clear agreement among experts on the benefits of imposing this perspective. Some advantages are pointed out, as the fact that investment in AI would be fostered (Dornis, 2020), but also some other authors indicate inconveniences (e.g. Kop, 2019). The assignment of any similarity of copyright to AI would imply a possible *"proliferation of private rights and enclosure of the public domain as a result."* (Erikson, 2024)

Moreover, the assumption of this as a reality would imply a difficulty when searching for the responsible of any damage over intellectual property. If AI does not have consciousness, self-imagination or desires of any kind -as recognized by the ultra-realistic robot Ai-Da in the beginning of the chapter- how are they supposed to be found guilty on a certain crime against intellectual rights? How is it possible for these digital systems to be included in the theory of liability? Moreover, it would become a path for infringements and frauds to occur without the possibility of bringing civil or criminal charges against individuals.

In this context, one of the most relevant and the latest harmonized regulation is the "*Artificial Intelligence Liability Directive*" of the European Parliament (2023) This text proposed that: "*while high-risk AI systems should fall under strict liability laws (...), any other activities, devices or processes driven by AI systems that cause harm or damage should remain subject to fault-based liability*". In the case of the US, the traditional regulation is stated in the "Compendium" of Copyright Office Practices of 2019. The legislative protection is only provided, according to the Copyright Office, for works "*created by a human being*". Under any circumstance the Office will register works "*produced by a machine or mere mechanical process that operates randomly or automatically without any creative input or intervention from a human author*." (U.S Copyright Office, 2019).

In conclusion, most legislations deny the possibility of AI being granted copyright, as the system would be entitled with legal personality. The idea of recognizing complete authorship without any human intervention remains controversial and mostly disturbing. Most scholars agree in the fact that, no matter how sophisticated or efficient an AI is, still would never be gifted with desires or conscience. Thus, it cannot have legal personality, meaning it cannot be considered subjected to rights and obligations and cannot sue or been sued because of civil or criminal liability. From my point of view, this is a key point to reflect on when analyzing the attribution of intellectual property right to generative AI.

5. NEW ROLE OF ART INDUSTRY LABOR UNIONS IN THE AI ERA: WHY UNIONIZING?

"Great things are done by a series of small things brought together." (Van Gogh, 1853–1890)

The irruption of the new technologies which "*are characteristic of the Fourth and Fifth Revolution evokes a natural fear of redundancies and unemployment among workers*" (Baran, 2024). The undeniable intromission of generative AI on art industry means a real concern for Labor Unions.

It poses brand-new challenges in the labor, economic, legal and ethical fields which must be urgently faced by these associations. The existence of these generative systems may be perceived in the market as instruments to empower creativity and produce low-cost outcome. However, it raises a huge concern regarding employment, in concrete, because of the fear on the displacing and replacing of human artists. (Baran, 2024). In this context, Labor Unions must step in to guarantee that artworkers are fairly compensated and copyright is adequately protected.

Labor market structure is expected to be one of the areas mostly exposed to considerable shift. In the words of George, A.S. (2024) "*AI is projected to have a net impact of job shifting rather than job loss by increasing productivity, accelerating economic growth, changing the structure of jobs, and allowing sectoral employment transitions.*"

As many authors other have pointed out (Erikson, 2024) not every artworker is condemned to losing their job because of the appearance of AI in the artistic scenario. More accurately implies a shift in labor market, regarding the digital competences and artistic skills which may be demanded. AI still relies on human supervision and "*prompt engineering*" to function, even of that contribution sometimes is obscured by the bright of the outcome generated. This drives to a highly competitive market and high-pressure environment for the human artists (Erikson, 2024) that confirms the necessity of a strong unionizing. In this context of uncertainty, three main perspectives have been deployed among scholars.

Will Artists be Replaced?

The first projection expects the replacement of the human role by the AI in the art industry. (Boden, 2009; Pearlman, 2017; Dornis, 2020) The real risk consists on the gradual replacement of artworkers who do not have access nor knowledge about AI. This is not a recent fear, but the same that was originated in the First Industrial Revolution back in the 19th century by the Luddites (Syed, 2023) *"who feared the use of machinery."* (Baran, 2024). Some authors suggest that valuable contributions and innovative approach to the creative process by AI may imply a potential risk for artists (Flick & Worrall, 2022).

The possibility of AI marking a discontinuity in the structure of artistic production would require the necessity of new international policies regarding labor and intellectual property right. The substitution of professional creators is, perhaps, the most dystopic scenario among all the possible ones. However, this potential replacement is also evitable if observing the suggestions noted by Long, D. and Magerko, B. (2020) in *"What is AI literacy? Competencies and design considerations"*. The term AI Literacy is defined as *"understanding of AI concepts and competencies in using AI concepts for evaluation and using AI concepts for understanding the real world, which we consider comprehensively address what AI literacy comprises and can be a proper starting point."* In short, the concept implies the ability of the human creator to communicate and collaborate with AI to create outcome in an efficient and moral way. (Fast, & Horvitz, 2017).

Some scholars declare the need of Labor Unions to train and educate workers on working with generative AI not to become obsolete. By reskilling, Unions can guarantee human artist would not lose their relevance in the creative process. This new training is undeniably necessary, because, as stated by Fui-Hoon Nah, F. et al. (2023), advances in generative AI *"are accelerating and its disruption to business and industries will intensify. Generative AI is making a major impact on our work and lives to the point that working and collaborating with generative AI will soon become a norm, if not already a norm"*

Will Artists be Displaced?

Discplacement may occur because of added efficiency of AI to certain steps of the creative process or very low marginal cost of production resulting of digitalization. This would derive in the elimination or sidestepping the presence of human actors in certain aspects in the art industry (Drott, 2021; Togay Su, & Côté, 2021). The adaptation of digital technology has been found *"to have a negative effect on creative earnings and led to more precarious working conditions"* (Erikson, 2023) as stated in reference to the ideas of McDonald, P. et al. (2021).

Even if the AI is used as an instrument completing human inherent creativity, potential AI impact is likely to deconstruct the current structure of the market. This potential impact arguably involves higher market competition (McDonald, et al. 2021), increase of outsourcing and short-term labor contracts (Creus, et al. 2020) and oversupply of creative "*workers*" (Thomas, et al. 2022). The more capacities the AI is granted with, the more its presence will amplify the impact in the job market. As Erikson have remarked (2023) another aspect to be taken into account when analyzing the possibility of displacement of workers is the importance of "*feedback information*". Art industry is a sector in which reaction form the consumer is valuable and perceptions from the audience are precious (Neff, et al. 2005). The truth is that networking technologies unceasingly register preferences of users individually compiling them as a collectivity, which has turned out to be quite an interesting point for art companies. (Farchy, & Denis, 2020;Sotamaa, et al. 2024).

Labor oversupply in this market may not only come because of the undeniable presence of these generative actors which now compete with human creativity. Among human artists competitiveness may also be higher. Due to the latest appearance of new platforms and technologies the interaction with the audience is more fluid and more individuals are able to enter the sector (McDonald, et al. 2021). In this sense, new jobs in the artistic industry have been created by entrepreneurship as the "content-creator" or the "influencer" (Baran, 2023). Those professional profiles have acquired important roles in society, are intimately bounded to technology advances and require a constant ability of "*self-invention*."

In these terms, Baran, (2023), among other scholars, perceive as doubtless the fact that the presence of AI in the art industry *"will result in a variety of fluctuations on national and regional labor markets."* Technology result in a new tendency of the market which increases the already existent model of project-based contracts ins short-terms and unstable periods of intense working alternating with other of scarcity (Creus, et al. 2020). Traditionally the displacement would happen because "*creative labor is contracted on a task-by-task basis"* (Baran, 2023), so, workers are placed in constant competition (McDonald, et al. 2021). Digitalization has aggravated this labor dynamic, besides having included new performers to the competition.

Another aspect which exacerbates the difficulty of stability for workers in the creative sector is the very high level of fragmentation. The art industry is mainly configured either by few huge dominant conglomerates or by many small-scope free-lance creators (Wright, 2015). The bargaining power of both is clearly not equal, but both are equally affected by the presence of AI. Hence, Unions must be able to represent the interests of both groups. The role of Labor Unions in this context is preeminent to guarantee that human creators are not fully displaced but an important part of an adequate transition to a new job market in the AI era. Above all, the strategy for Unions must be orientated to ensure fair working conditions, significant presence in the creative process, adequate compensation for artworks and protected intellectual property right for human creators.

While some occupations may disappear or transformed, others will emerge. Thus, artworkers are definitely not condemned to displacement. Supervising, working alongside AI and adjusting generated content will be essential in the industry not to be displaced. Apart from these, the new market paradigm offers job opportunities to be explored which will require professional workers to *"continually maintain and refresh their technical skills or face obsolescence."* (Neff, et al. 2005)

What is Co-Creativity?

Beyond the challenges exposed in the scenarios above, the community is also opening up to conceiving AI as a potential co-creator in the creative process. In some of the previous pages, "*co-creation*" has already been mentioned as a solution.

This concept is defined by Wingström, et al. (2023) referring to the ideas exposed by Davis, N.M, in his paper "*Human-computer co-creativity: Blending human and computational creativity*" (2013) as the space where the barriers between human creativity and the performance of the AI are blurring. The case studies mentioned by Erikson (2023) declare that most producers perceived the AI more as a contributor to the process rather than a substitute to the human workers. In fact, it is surprisingly stated that "*producers viewed the technology positively and emphasized that it allowed them to explore new kinds of creative expression rapidly and with fewer limits than traditional methods of ideation.*" The conclusions drawn from this same case study was, in words of the author, that "*Working with AI was experimental, exploratory, and introspective.*" In this argumental line, George A.S. (2024) extends economic principles to the functioning of the job market, qualifying as positive the presence of an efficient actor in the creative process under any circumstance. The author underlines that productivity "*consistently creates more and often better jobs across industries.*" Thus, it might also be expected to be the case for the art industry.

However, the concept of co-creativity remains unattended in many aspects and almost exclusively studied in the field of computer science (Karimi, et al. 2020); Lin, Y. et al. 2020) and almost excluded from research in the creative process. However, *"to develop creativity-supporting AI, we must understand how the novel AI technologies are used in everyday creative processes"* (Wingström, et al. 2024). This approach perceives "*AI-assisted-creativity*" as a partner in a duet rather than a rival on global a competition. Assuming this dynamics, human authors would be placed in networked relations with AI as co-authors (Hugenholtz, & Quintais, 2021)

Nevertheless, this cooperation may also imply challenges. As AI continues to evolve, this duet collaboration is expected to expand, paving the way for a new era. The role of Labor Unions is remarkable and crucial when setting the limits and addressing the question of working conditions from the beginning. Labor Unions may advocate that copyright of the outcome created in cooperation, should be attributed to the human. The environment in the "creative working place" is desired to ensure a significant role for artists and a perception of AI as a collaborator tool.

In the recent years some Labor Unions have given example on the importance of their presence in the industry. Particularly, in the United States some interesting cases can be brought to analysis. This is the case of the ADG (Art Director´s Guild), which represents graphic artists and is one of the "*hundreds of International Association of Theatrical and Stage Employees (IATSE) chapters nationwide that could potentially be impacted by AI*" (Karim, 2024). In 2024 this association released a formulation over the many threats regarding the AI, including possible proactive solutions of adaptation rather than just reaction. However, the path through co-creation models remains partially obscure. While the animation professionals are responding to the unionizing strategy, only an approximate amount of 10.000 artists was registered in March 2024 *"meaning that the vast majority of the animation industry's workforce of more than 200,000 artists, assistants, coordinators, and managers are not unionized."* (Karim, 2024)

The co-creation models have also been subject of study of other associations such as WGA (West Writers Guild of America West) and CWA (*Communications Workers of America).* In December 2024, the first organization called for action to enforce the ground-breaking MBA protections established in 2023. This code formulated some provisions, aspiring to create the nuclear points to construct a collaborative model based on current statistics and real situation of the artists. The codes include some prohibitions, as the one which follows: "*A writer can choose to use AI when performing writing services if the company consents and the writer follows any applicable company policies. But the company can't require the writer to use AI software (e.g., ChatGPT) when performing writing services.*" (Writers Guild of America, 2024).

These are valuable efforts on the side of Labor Unions to build collaborative structures in the art industry proposing a constructive perception of AI tools rather than corrosive.

CONCLUSION

In the light of the above, the role of generative AI in the art industry opens up new possibilities in the market and poses significant challenges for the Labor Unions. This scenario, characterized by uncertainty, undeniably raises moral, legal and social questions to debate about.

The arrival of AI in the art industry is generating a labor paradigm shift. The Labor Unions, as representative associations, play a crucial role in the adaptation to this new reality, which is increasingly distant from the traditional model. Through History, the role of Labor Unions in the art industry has been intimately bounded to the fight for adequate working conditions and fair compensation for artistic contributions. With the advent of generative AI, Union´s strategy must be definitely rebuilt to gain voice in the public debate and a significant position in the sector. The job market landscape is subjected to recent and deep transformations regarding intellectual property rights. Hence, Labor Unions must remain key players to ensure the creation of a legal and labor framework that respects those rights for human creators.

This will be essential in a context in which generative AI is fueled to keep growing bigger and stronger as any other previous human creation. The limits of *art* are being pushed, arguably till the point to which the boundaries between the human hand and the algorithm will not be clear anymore. The assumption of generative AI tool as an element of co-creation brings a new approach to the artist professional profile and will transform the contemporary substrate of our culture.

The future of art and culture depend on how labor communities in the art industry decide to integrate these technologies. Whether visual arts, music, or literature, the irruption of AI brings challenges on the understanding of the value of art, the regulation of copyright and the definition of originality. In years to come, AI probably will continue evolving, thus, the presence of generative AI outcome in the artistic fields is likely to be higher. In this hypothetic scenario, embracing co-creation, while preserving human emotional essence and exclusive copyright might be the most enriching solution.

To sum up, which is the role of Labor Unions regarding the recent irruption of AI in the art industry? Unions face the need to adapt to this changing environment and become a coherent solution against displacement and replacement. These two concepts involve the real fear regarding the arise and irruption of AI in the artistic disciplines. Yet, do not mean a condemnation for the artist if co-creation dynamic is examined and deployed in an adequate way. In this strategy, Labor Unions definitely have a preeminent role. The relevance of this organizations in the AI era should not be ignored in coming years, as they will be the organism to directly face legal, labor, moral and social questions "*as creative AI evolves and more complex cases emerge to be analyzed.*" (Wingström, et al. 2024).

REFERENCES

Ali, O., Momin, M., Shrestha, A., Das, R., Alhajj, F., & Dwivedi, Y. K. (2023). A review of the key challenges of non-fungible tokens. *Technological Forecasting and Social Change*, *187*, 122248. https://www.sciencedirect.com/science/article/pii/S0040162522007697. DOI: 10.1016/j.techfore.2022.122248

Anadol, R. (2024). *Refik Anadol Studio: AI research*. Refik Anadol Studio. https://www.refikanadol.com/ai-research

Audiocipher. (2021). *AI music app*. Audiocipher. https://www.audiocipher.com/post/ai-music-app

Baran, K. (2024). The right of trade unions to information in the era of the fourth and fifth industrial revolution. Białostockie Studia Prawnicze, 29(2), 57–74. . 29-30DOI: 10.15290/bsp.2024.29.02.03

Boden, M. A. (2004). *The creative mind: Myths and mechanisms*. Routledge. DOI: 10.4324/9780203508527

Boden, M. A. (2009). Computer Models of Creativity. *AI Magazine*, *30*(3), 23–34. DOI: 10.1609/aimag.v30i3.2254

Bringsjord, S., Bello, P., & Ferrucci, D. (2003). Creativity, the turing test, and the (better) Lovelace test. In Moor, J. H. (Ed.), *The Turing Test* (pp. 215–239). Springer. DOI: 10.1007/978-94-010-0105-2_12

Bullock, J., & Luengo-Oroz, M. (2019). Automated speech generation from UN general assembly statements: Mapping risks in AI generated texts. https://doi.org//arXiv.1906.01946DOI: 10.48550

Cain, S. (2024, November 8). "First artwork painted by humanoid robot to sell at auction fetches $1m" *The Guardian*.:https://www.theguardian.com/artanddesign/2024/nov/08/alan-turing-portrait-ai-da-robot-painting-sale-price-auction

Carnovalini, F., & Rodà, A. (2020). Computational Creativity and Music Generation Systems: An Introduction to the State of the Art. *Frontiers in Artificial Intelligence*, *3*, 14. DOI: 10.3389/frai.2020.00014 PMID: 33733133

Cascella, M., Montomoli, J., Bellini, V., & Bignami, E. (2023). Evaluating the feasibility of ChatGPT in healthcare: An analysis of multiple clinical and research scenarios. *Journal of Medical Systems*, *47*(1), 1–5. DOI: 10.1007/s10916-023-01925-4 PMID: 36869927

Casini, L., & Roccetti, M. (2018). The impact of AI on the musical world: Will musicians be obsolete? *Studi di estetica, 46*(4), 119. https://doi.org/DOI: 10.7413/18258646064

Chalmers, F. G. (1973). The study of art in a cultural context. *The Journal of Aesthetics and Art Criticism, 32*(2), 249–256. https://www.jstor.org/stable/429042. DOI: 10.1111/1540_6245.jaac32.2.0249

Cho, W. (2024, January 5). Artists score major win in copyright case against AI art generators. *The Hollywood Reporter*. https://www.hollywoodreporter.com/business/business-news/artists-score-major-win-copyright-case-against-ai-art-generators-1235973601/

Christie's. (2018, December 12). "Can a portrait, created by AI, be called art? Obvious and the interface between art and artificial intelligence." *Christie's*.https://www.christies.com/en/stories/a-collaboration-between-two-artists-one-human-one-a-machine-0cd01f4e232f4279a525a446d60d4cd1

Colton, S., & Wiggins, G. A. (2012). Computational creativity: the final frontier? In *ECAI* (Vol. 2012, pp. 21–16). University of Montpellier.

Colton, S., & Wiggins, G. A. (2014). Computational creativity: The final frontier? *Journal of Computational Creativity, 5*(2), 100–120. https://www.journalcc.org/2014/01/creativity

Cooper, Z., Lehr, W., & Stocker, V. (2024). The New Age: Legal & Economic Challenges to Copyright and Creative Economies in the Era of Generative AI. *Available atSSRN* 5022340 DOI: 10.2139/ssrn.5022340

Craig, C., & Kerr, I. (2020). The Death of the AI Author. *Ottawa Law Review, 52*(1), 31–86.

Creus, A., Clares-Gavilán, J., & Sánchez-Navarro, J. (2020). What's Your Game? Passion and Precariousness in the Digital Game Industry from a Gameworker's Perspective. *Creative Industries Journal, 13*(3), 196–213. DOI: 10.1080/17510694.2019.1685302

Dasborough, M. T. (2023). Awe-inspiring advancements in AI: The impact of ChatGPT on the field of organizational behavior. *Journal of Organizational Behavior, 44*(2), 177–179. DOI: 10.1002/job.2695

Dash, A., & Agres, K. (2024). AI-Based Affective Music Generation Systems: A Review of Methods and Challenges. *ACM Computing Surveys, 56*(11), 977 pages. https://doi.org/DOI: 10.1145/3613686

Davis, N. M. (2013). Human-computer co-creativity: Blending human and computational creativity. In Smith, G., & Smith, A. (Eds.), *The Doctoral Consortium at AIIDE 2013* (pp. 9–12). The AAAI Press.

Dennett, D. (1998). *Brainchildren: Essays on Designing Minds*. MIT Press. DOI: 10.7551/mitpress/1663.001.0001

Dornis, T. W. (2020). Artificial Creativity: Emergent Works and the Void in Current Copyright Doctrine. *Yale Journal of Law & Technology*, *22*, 1–60.

Dowling, M. (2022). Is non-fungible token pricing driven by cryptocurrencies? *Finance Research Letters*, *44*, 102097. DOI: 10.1016/j.frl.2021.102097

Drott, E. (2021). Copyright, Compensation, and Commons in the Music AI Industry. *Creative Industries Journal*, *14*(2), 190–207. DOI: 10.1080/17510694.2020.1839702

Erickson, K. (2024). AI and work in the creative industries: Digital continuity or discontinuity? *Creative Industries Journal*, •••, 1–21. DOI: 10.1080/17510694.2024.2421135

European Parliament. (2023). Artificial intelligence liability directive (EPRS Briefing No. 739342). European Parliament. https://www.europarl.europa.eu/RegData/etudes/BRIE/2023/739342/EPRS_BRI(2023)739342_EN.pdf

European Parliament & Council. (2024). *Regulation (EU) 2024/1689 of the European Parliament and of the Council of 13 June 2024 laying down harmonized rules on artificial intelligence and amending Regulations (EC) No 300/2008, (EU) No 167/2013, (EU) No 168/2013, (EU) 2018/858, (EU) 2018/1139, and (EU) 2019/2144, and Directives 2014/90/EU, (EU) 2016/797, and (EU) 2020/1828 (Artificial Intelligence Act)*. Official Journal of the European Union.

Farchy, J., & Denis, J. (2020). Artificial Intelligence. In Towse, R., & Navarrette Hernandez, T. (Eds.), *Handbook of Cultural Economics* (pp. 38–46). Edward Elgar.

Fast, E., & Horvitz, E. (2017). Long-term trends in the public perception of artificial intelligence. *Proceedings of the AAAI Conference on Artificial Intelligence*, *31*(1), •••. DOI: 10.1609/aaai.v31i1.10635

Flick, C., & Worrall, K. (2022). The ethics of creative AI. In *The Language of Creative AI: Practices, Aesthetics and Structures* (pp. 73–91). Springer International Publishing. DOI: 10.1007/978-3-031-10960-7_5

Fui-Hoon Nah, F., Zheng, R., Cai, J., Siau, K., & Chen, L. (2023). Generative AI and ChatGPT: Applications, challenges, and AI-human collaboration. *Journal of Information Technology Case and Application Research, 25*(3), 277–304. DOI: 10.1080/15228053.2023.2233814

Future of Life Institute. (2023). "Pause Giant AI Experiments: An Open Letter." https://futureoflife. org/open-letter/pause-giant-ai-experiments/

Galanter, P. (2019). Artificial intelligence and problems in generative art theory. In *Proceedings of EVA London 2019*. BCS Learning & Development. DOI: 10.14236/ewic/EVA2019.22

Garcia, M. B. (2024). The Paradox of Artificial Creativity: Challenges and Opportunities of Generative AI Artistry. *Creativity Research Journal*, •••, 1–14. https://www.tandfonline.com/doi/abs/10.1080/10400419.2024.2354622. DOI: 10.1080/10400419.2024.2354622

George, A. S. (2024). *Artificial intelligence and the future of work: Job shifting, not job loss*. Partners Universal Innovative Research Publication. *ResearchGate*. Retrieved from https://www.researchgate.net/publication/379640704_Artificial_Intelligence_and_the_Future_of_Work_Job_Shifting_Not_Job_Loss

Gervais, D. (2019). The Machine as Author. *Iowa Law Review, 105*, 2053–2106.

Gómez, E. Blaauw, M, Bonada, J. et al (2018) Deep Learning for Singing Processing: Achievements, Challenges and Impact on singers and listeners"

Goodfellow, I., Bengio, Y., & Courville, A. (2016). *Deep learning*. The MIT Press.

Hassel, A., & Özkiziltan, D. (2023). Governing the Work-Related Risks of AI: Implications for the German Government and Trade Unions. *Transfer: European Review of Labour and Research, 29*(1), 71–86. DOI: 10.1177/10242589221147228

Hendrawan, D., Andersen, C., Tiopan, D., Kurniawan, S., & Malinda, M. (2023). Juridical Review of Copyright Infringement in the Use of Deepfakes in the Creative Industry in Indonesia. *International Journal of Cyber Criminology, 17*(1), 211–222.

Hern, A. (2023). "Elon Musk joins call for pause in creation of giant AI 'digital minds." The Guardian. https://www.theguardian.com/technology/2023/mar/29/elon-musk-joins-call-for-pause-in-cre ation-of-giant-ai-digital-minds

Hugenholtz, P. B., and J. P. Quintais. (2021). "Copyright and Artificial Creation: Does EU Copyright Law Protect AI-Assisted Output?" *IIC - International Review of Intellectual Property and Competition Law* 52 (9): 1190–1216. https://doi.org/.DOI: 10.1007/s40319-021-01115-0

Hüsmen, A. H. (2024) AI in the creative industries: Strikes, debates and implications: https://www.researchgate.net/profile/Arife-Huesmen/publication/387368228_AI_in_the_Creative_Industries_Strikes_Debates_and_Implications/links/676abd1de74ca64e1f2998bf/AI-in-the-Creative-Industries-Strikes-Debates-and-Implications.pdf

Janiesch, C., Zschech, P., & Heinrich, K. (2021). Machine learning and deep learning. *Electronic Markets*, *31*(3), 685–695. DOI: 10.1007/s12525-021-00475-2

Jefferson, G. (1949). The mind of mechanical man. *British Medical Journal*, *1*(4616). PMID: 18153422

Jones, N. (2021). How scientists are embracing NFTs. *Nature*, *594*(7864), 481–482. DOI: 10.1038/d41586-021-01642-3 PMID: 34145410

Kajikawa, Y., Mejia, C., Wu, M., & Zhang, Y. (2022). Academic landscape of Technological Forecasting and Social Change through citation network and topic analyses. *Technological Forecasting and Social Change*, *182*, 121877. https://scholar.google.com/scholar_lookup?title=Academic%20landscape%20of%20Technological%20Forecasting%20and%20Social%20Change%20through%20citation%20network%20and%20topic%20analyses&publication_year=2022&author=Y.%20Kajikawa&author=C.%20Mejia&author=M.%20Wu&author=Y.%20Zhang. DOI: 10.1016/j.techfore.2022.121877

Karim, B. (2024, March 5). *Art and artificial intelligence: A pivotal moment for unions*. Hampton Institute. https://www.hamptonthink.org/read/art-and-artificial-intelligence-a-pivotal-moment-for-unions

Karimi, P., Rezwana, J., Siddiqui, S., Maher, M. L., & Dehbozorgi, N. (2020). Creative sketching partner: An analysis of human-AI co-creativity. In Proceedings of the 25th International Conference on Intelligent User Interfaces, 221–230. Cagliary, Italy. DOI: 10.1145/3377325.3377522

Kelomees, R., Guljajeva, V., & Laas, O. (Eds.). (2023). *The meaning of creativity in the age of AI*. VAR-MAR. https://var-mar.info/wp-content/uploads/2023/10/The-Meaning-of-Creativity-in-the-Age-of-AI.pdf

Köbis, N., & Mossink, L. D. (2021). Artificial intelligence versus Maya Angelou: Experimental evidence that people cannot differentiate AI-generated from human-written poetry. *Computers in Human Behavior*, *114*, 1–13. DOI: 10.1016/j.chb.2020.106553

Kop, M. (2019). AI & Intellectual Property: Towards an Articulated Public Domain. *SSRN*, *28*, 297–341. DOI: 10.2139/ssrn.3409715

Lambert, J., & Stevens, M. (2023). ChatGPT and Generative AI Technology: A Mixed Bag of Concerns and New Opportunities. *Computers in the Schools*, *41*(4), 559–583. DOI: 10.1080/07380569.2023.2256710

LeCun, Y., Bengio, Y., & Hinton, G. (2015). Deep learning. *Nature*, *521*(7553), 436–444. DOI: 10.1038/nature14539 PMID: 26017442

Lemley, M. (2024). How Generative AI Turns Copyright Law Upside Down. *The Columbia Science and Technology Law Review*, *25*(2). Advance online publication. DOI: 10.52214/stlr.v25i2.12761

Lin, Y., Guo, J., Chen, Y., Yao, C., & Ying, F. (2020). It is your turn: Collaborative ideation with a co-creative robot through sketch. In *Proceedings of the 2020 CHI Conference on Human Factors in Computing Systems*. New York, NY: Association for Computing Machinery. DOI: 10.1145/3313831.3376258

Long, D., & Magerko, B. (2020). What is AI literacy? Competencies and design considerations. In *Proceedings of the 2020 CHI Conference on Human Factors in Computing Systems*, (pp. 1–16). ACM. DOI: 10.1145/3313831.3376727

Lovelace, A. (1843). Notes on L. Menabreas sketch of the analytical engine invented by Charles Babbage, Esq. *Taylor's Sci. Mem.*, *3*, 1843.

Maerten, A. S., & Soydaner, D. (2023). From paintbrush to pixel: A review of deep neural networks in AI-generated art. *arXiv preprint arXiv:2302.10913.*

Mangan, D. (2024, January 5). Microsoft, OpenAI sued over copyright infringement by authors. *CNBC*. https://www.cnbc.com/2024/01/05/microsoft-openai-sued-over -copyright-infringement-by-authors.html

Margaret Lazzari and Dona Schlesier. 2008. Exploring Art: A Global, Thematic Approach. (No Title) (2008). [78] Lik-Hang Lee, Zijun Lin, Rui Hu, Zhengya Gong, Abhishek Kumar, Tangyao Li, Sijia Li, and Pan Hui. 2021. When Creators Meet the Metaverse: A Survey on Computational Arts. arXiv preprint arXiv:2111.13486 (2021)

Mazzone, M., & Elgammal, A. (2019). Art, creativity, and the potential of artificial intelligence. *Arts*, *8*(1), 26. DOI: 10.3390/arts8010026

McCarthy, J. (2007). "What is Artificial Intelligence?" Stanford University, http:// jmc.stanford.edu/articles/whatisai.html

McDonald, P., Williams, P., & Mayes, R. (2021). Means of control in the organization of digitally intermediated care work. *Work, Employment and Society*, *35*(5), 872–890. DOI: 10.1177/0950017020969107

Moor, J. (2006). The Dartmouth College Artificial Intelligence Conference: The Next Fifty Years. *AI Magazine*, *27*(4), 87–91.

Mordvintsev, A., Olah, C., & Tyka, M. (2015) Inceptionism: Going Deeper into Neural Networks. http://googleresearch.blogspot.com/2015/06/incepti onism-going-deeper-into-neural.html

Nake, F. 2010. Roots and randomness—a perspective on the beginnings of digital art. In: W. Lieser, ed., The World of Digital Art.

Neff, G., McGrath, M., & Prakash, N. (2020). "Artificial Intelligence in the Workplace." Oxford Internet Institute working paper. https://ora.ox.ac.uk/objects/uuid: b2663eb9-afd7-48ae-a95c171196a085ca

Neff, G., Wissinger, E., & Zukin, S. (2005). Entrepreneurial Labor among Cultural Producers: "Cool" Jobs in "Hot" Industries. *Social Semiotics*, *15*(3), 307–334. DOI: 10.1080/10350330500310111

New York University. *Actors' Equity Association*. Tamiment Library and Robert F. Wagner Labor Archives. Retrieved January 8, 2025, from https://findingaids.library .nyu.edu/tamwag/wag_011/#:~:text=The%20Actors%27%20Equity%20Association %20is,prevalent%20in%20the%20American%20theatre

Pearce, M., & Wiggins, G. (2001). "Towards a framework for the evaluation of machine compositions," in *Proceedings of the AISB'01 Symposium on Artificial Intelligence and Creativity in the Arts and Sciences* (York, UK), 22–32.

Pearlman, R. (2017). "Recognizing Artificial Intelligence (AI) as Authors and Investors under US Intellectual Property Law." Rich. *JL & Tech*, *24*(2), 1–38.

Płocha, E. A. (2020). About the concept of artificial intelligence and the possibilities of its application in proceedings civil. *Law in Action*, *44*, 273–280.

Puryear, J. S., & Lamb, K. N. (2020). Defining creativity: How far have we come since plucker, beghetto, and dow? *Creativity Research Journal*, *32*(3), 206–214. DOI: 10.1080/10400419.2020.1821552

Roth, E. (2023). New York Times sues OpenAI and Microsoft over alleged copyright infringement. *The Verge*. https://www.theverge.com/2023/12/27/24016212/new-york -times-openai-microsoft-lawsuit-copyright-infringement

Samuelson, P. (1985). Allocating ownership rights in computer-generated works. *U. pitt. L. rev.*, *47*, 1185.

Sarkar, P., & Chakrabarti, A. (2008). "Studying engineering design creativity-developing a common definition and associated measures," in *Proceedings of the NSF Workshop on Studying Design Creativity* (Aix-en-Provence), 20.

Sharifani, K., & Amini, M. (2023). Machine learning and deep learning: A review of methods and applications. *World Information Technology and Engineering Journal, 10*(07), 3897–3904.

Sotamaa, O., Heikki, T., & Myöhänen, T. (2024). "Even If the Algorithm is a Terrible Workmate, You Just Need to Learn to Live with It": Perceptions of Data Analytics among Game Industry Professionals. *European Journal of Cultural Studies*, *27*(4), 558–576. DOI: 10.1177/13675494231168568

Stein, M. I. (1953). Creativity and culture. *The Journal of Psychology, 36*(2), 311–322. DOI: 10.1080/00223980.1953.9712897

Stone, K. V. W., & Arthurs, H. (Eds.). (2013). *Rethinking employment regulation: After the standard contract of employment*. Russell Sage Foundation Press.

Su, Z., Togay, G., & Côté, A. M. (2021). Artificial Intelligence: A Destructive and yet Creative Force in the Skilled Labour Market. *Human Resource Development International, 24*(3), 341–352. DOI: 10.1080/13678868.2020.1818513

Syed, A. (2023). Generative AI and human labor: Who is replaceable? Thilagaraj, A., & Davis, J. (2021). Non-fungible token (NFT)–The game changer in the digital art world. *Ciencia y Sociedad, 51*, 190–194.

Thomas, A., Battisti, M., & Kretschmer, M. (2022). "UK Authors'' Earnings and Contracts 2022: A Survey of 60,000 Writers. CREATe Working Paper." https://doi.org/DOI: 10.5281/zenodo.7373314

Turing, A. M. (1950). Computing Machinery and Intelligence. *Mind, 59*(236), 433–460. DOI: 10.1093/mind/LIX.236.433

UNI Global Union. (2024, November 15). *Unions gather to share, learn and strategize on AI's "perils and promises"*. UNI Global Union. https://uniglobalunion.org/news/unions-gather-to-share-learn-and-strategize-on-ais-perils-and-promises/

US Copyright Office. (2019). Compendium of US Copyright Office Practices (3rd edn, US Copyright Office 2019) section 313.2

Veale, T., Cardoso, F. A., & Pérez y Pérez, R. (2019). Systematizing Creativity: A Computational View. In Computational Creativity: The Philosophy and Engineering of Autonomously Creative Systems, eds. Tony Veale and F. Amílcar Cardoso, 1–19. Chaim: Springer. DOI: 10.1007/978-3-319-43610-4_1

Vear, C. (2022). Introduction. In Vear, C., & Poltronieri, F. (Eds.), *The Language of Creative AI Practices, Aesthetics and Structures* (pp. xvii–xix). Springer. DOI: 10.1007/978-3-031-10960-7

Vetrone, A. (2003). *The Legal & Moral Rights of All Artists*. iUniverse.

Visser J.; Hayter, S.; Gammarano, R. (2015). Trends in collective bargaining coverage: Stability, erosion or decline? Geneva, ILO, Labour Relations and Collective Bargaining Policy Brief No. 1.

Wang, B., Chen, Q., & Wang, Z. (2024). Diffusion-based visual art creation: A survey and new perspectives. *arXiv preprint arXiv:2408.12128*

Wang, H., Zou, J., Mozer, M., Zhang, L., Goyal, A., Lamb, A., Deng, Z., ... (2024). Can AI Be as Creative as Humans? arXiv. https://doi.org//arXiv.2401.01623DOI: 10.48550

Wingström, R., Hautala, J., & Lundman, R. (2024). Redefining creativity in the era of AI? Perspectives of computer scientists and new media artists. *Creativity Research Journal*, *36*(2), 177–193. DOI: 10.1080/10400419.2022.2107850

Woolf, M. (2022, December 8). ChatGPT passes the turing test. *Metaverse Post*. https://mpost.io/chatgpt-passes-the-turing-test/(open in a new window)

World Intellectual Property Organization. (2024.). *WIPO: World Intellectual Property Organization*. WIPO. https://www.wipo.int/portal/en/index.html

Wright, A. (2015). It's All about Games: Enterprise and Entrepreneurialism in Digital Games. *New Technology, Work and Employment*, *30*(1), 32–46. DOI: 10.1111/ntwe.12042

Writers Guild of America. (2024). *Artificial intelligence*. Writers Guild of America. https://www.wga.org/contracts/know-your-rights/artificial-intelligence

Yates, M. (2009). *Why unions matter*. NYU Press.

Chapter 11
Unions in the Digital Age: Rethinking Collective Representation in the Face of the Gig Economy and New Forms of Employment

Zyed Achour
https://orcid.org/0000-0002-1578-9062
National Institute of Labor and Social Studies, University of Carthage, Tunisia

ABSTRACT

This chapter examines the challenges and adaptations of labour unions in the face of the gig economy and new forms of employment. It explores how workforce fragmentation, individualization of labour relations, and inadequate legal frameworks disrupt traditional union strategies. The study highlights innovative responses by unions, including new organizational approaches, representation models, alliances with social movements, and digital technology adoption. Drawing on recent literature and empirical studies, the paper provides a comprehensive analysis of the changing landscape of industrial relations. It emphasizes the need for unions to reinvent themselves while maintaining core values of solidarity and social justice. The research concludes by stressing the crucial role of unions in shaping a new social contract for the digital age and identifying areas for future research on collective organization in the gig economy.

DOI: 10.4018/979-8-3693-8049-9.ch011

INTRODUCTION

The 21st century's significant alteration of the work environment, characterised by the emergence of the gig economy and various novel employment configurations, poses a crucial existential challenge to conventional labour unions. As the Fordist method of extensive production and long-term employment changes, giving way to more accommodating and uncertain work relationships, labour unions encounter a critical juncture. Their aptitude to adjust to this fresh economic terrain will not only influence their endurance but also shape the destiny of collective worker representation in an increasingly disjointed labour market.

The existing literature on industrial relations has comprehensively documented the decline of traditional unionism in response to globalisation and technological advancements. As early as 2009, Streeck discussed the weakening of unions due to the combined pressures of economic globalisation and the shift towards a service-based economy. Baccaro and Howell (2011) emphasised the systemic transformations in industrial relations systems and the erosion of conventional collective bargaining structures. The authors primarily attribute these changes to deregulation and the neoliberal transformation of labour relations, resulting in a decline in union coverage and worker protections. These reforms often diminished the power of unions, making it more challenging to negotiate favourable terms for employees. More recent studies, such as those by Bryson and Forth (2017), corroborate these trends, indicating an ongoing decline in union membership and influence. Visser (2019) notes the declining union density rates across developed countries. The author primarily attributes this decline to the increasing precariousness of employment and the expansion of the informal economy, as well as to neoliberal policies that have led to a decrease in social protections and to the fragmentation of unions and the ensuing competition between various union organisations, which has diminished their collective bargaining power.

The gig economy, characterised by short-term contracts and freelance work rather than permanent positions, has amplified these trends. Research by Degryse (2016) and Kalleberg (2018) emphasises the precarious nature of gig work and its consequences for worker security and union representation. The studies by Prassl (2018) and Wood et al. (2019) investigate the emergence of platform work and its effects on traditional labour structures, addressing the challenges and opportunities for unions in this new environment. Additionally, Graham and Anwar's (2019) more recent study explores the conditions of gig workers worldwide, revealing the extent of job insecurity and the lack of social protections.

Despite the significant progress that has been made in recent years, there remains a notable gap in theoretical frameworks that can comprehensively understand and analyse the adaptation strategies of unions in response to the new work realities.

This gap leaves several crucial questions unanswered, including how unions can effectively represent an increasingly diverse and dispersed workforce, what new organisational models and collective action strategies can emerge to address the challenges of the gig economy, and how classical industrial relations theory can be updated to reflect these new dynamics. This chapter aims to address this theoretical gap by proposing an innovative conceptual framework to analyse the evolution of unions in the context of the gig economy and new forms of employment. The framework combines historical, sociological, and economic perspectives to develop a nuanced understanding of the challenges and opportunities that unions face in the digital economy. The purpose of this article is not only to contribute to the academic literature on industrial relations but also to offer practical insights for unions, policymakers, and labour market stakeholders navigating this new landscape. In particular, the chapter focuses on how artificial intelligence, especially algorithmic management and data-driven control, is reshaping employment relations and collective representation. By examining how unions are responding to AI-driven transformations in both traditional and platform-based sectors, this study aims to contribute to the emerging field of labor relations in the AI era. The chapter is structured as follows: Section 2 explores the historical and theoretical foundations of traditional unionism, laying the groundwork for understanding how unions have evolved over time. Section 3 examines the characteristics of the gig economy and new forms of employment, focusing on their implications for labour relations. Section 4 addresses the challenges that these new forms of employment pose to unions and discusses potential responses and adaptations. Finally, Section 5 concludes with a summary of the findings and recommendations for future research and practical approaches.

HISTORICAL AND THEORETICAL FOUNDATIONS OF TRADITIONAL UNIONISM

Origins and Development of Traditional Unionism

Unionism emerged during the heart of the 19th-century industrial revolution as a response to precarious working conditions and worker exploitation (Hobsbawm, 1964). Initially illegal and repressed, unions gradually gained legitimacy and legal recognition at the beginning of the 20th century (Commons et al. 1918). This period witnessed the consolidation of union structures and the expansion of their social base (Tapia et al., 2015). The zenith of unionism occurred in the post-war Fordist economy, characterized by mass production and stable jobs (Piore, 1984). This era, marked by the capital-labour compromise, saw unions playing a central role in collective bargaining, labour market regulation, and the construction of the welfare state (Esping-Andersen, 1990). Recent analyses continue to emphasize the historical importance of this period, noting how it set the stage for contemporary labour relations (Lichtenstein, 2013).

In the context of the Fordist economy, unions played a crucial multidimensional role. At the core of their action was collective bargaining, aimed at improving wages, working conditions, and social benefits for workers. They also acted as guardians of workers' rights, fighting against discrimination and for social justice within and beyond the workplace. Unions actively participated in the formulation of social and economic policies, thus contributing to the construction of the welfare state in many industrialised countries (Korpi, 1978). Additionally, they played a key role in labour market regulation, influencing employment standards, vocational training, and conflict resolution mechanisms (Goldthorpe, 1984). This multifaceted role made unions indispensable actors in the post-war political economy, ensuring a degree of social and economic stability (Visser, 1996). Contemporary analyses continue to underscore the relevance of these roles, highlighting the ongoing challenges and adaptations required in the face of neoliberal economic policies and labour market deregulation (Baccaro and Howell, 2017; Kelly, 2018).

Theoretical Conceptualisations and Contemporary Perspectives on Industrial Relations

Various theories have attempted to conceptualize the role and functioning of trade unions within industrial relations. Dunlop's systems theory (1958) presents industrial relations as a system of interactions among actors, context, and ideology. The pluralist approach, developed by Flanders and Clegg (1954), emphasizes the role of unions in balancing power between employers and employees. The Marxist perspective interprets unionism as a manifestation of the inherent class conflict within capitalism (Hyman, 1975). The strategic choice theory by Kochan et al. (1994) underscores the importance of strategic choices made by actors at different levels of industrial relations, thus offering a more dynamic framework for understanding the evolution of unionism in the face of economic and social changes (Tapia et al. 2015).

An institutional perspective provides a complementary approach to these theories by emphasizing the role of institutions—both formal rules (laws, collective agreements) and informal norms (work culture, union practices)—in shaping industrial relations. Pierson (2004) introduces the concept of "path dependency," which suggests that past institutional choices strongly influence unions' ability to adapt to new challenges. In other words, current union structures and strategies are often shaped by historical decisions, making it difficult to transition effectively in response to emerging forms of employment. The gig economy challenges these institutional frameworks, forcing unions to innovate in their organizational strategies and representation models. By applying this approach, we can better understand both the resistance to change and the opportunities for trade unions to reinvent themselves in an increasingly flexible and fragmented labor market.

Recent developments in industrial relations theory have expanded upon these foundations, integrating insights from globalization, technological change, and the emergence of the gig economy. In this regard, Bamber et al. (2020) propose a multinomial approach to analyse the role of trade unions in employment relations. This approach advocates for a simultaneous analysis at multiple levels - global, national, and sectoral- as well as their interactions to comprehend the complexity of the union role. At the global level, unions must face challenges posed by globalization and international competition. At the national level, they interact with regulatory frameworks and public policies governing labour relations. At the sectoral level, they negotiate collective agreements tailored to the specificities of each sector.

To address the growing obstacles presented by the gig economy and digital labor platforms, trade unions are increasingly engaging in political lobbying to advocate for regulatory reforms. By influencing policymakers, unions seek to redefine employment classifications, ensuring that gig workers receive labor rights and social protections similar to traditional employees. Recent examples include legislative pushes in the European Union[1] and the United States, where unions have fought for the recognition of gig workers as employees rather than independent contractors. The passage of California's Assembly Bill 5 (AB5) in 2019[2], despite facing legal battles, demonstrated how unions could shape policy to provide greater job security for platform workers.

Additionally, unions have intensified their direct negotiations with digital platforms to improve working conditions. Some have successfully brokered agreements on minimum earnings, safety measures, and collective bargaining rights. For instance, the agreement between Uber and the UK's GMB Union in 2021 established key worker protections, including guaranteed wages and access to benefits (Bertolini & Dukes, 2021). In other cases, unions have formed strategic alliances with consumer advocacy groups and political organizations to pressure platforms into compliance with fair labor standards. These efforts highlight the evolving role of unions as intermediaries between platform workers and policymakers, ensuring that labor rights remain at the forefront of discussions in the digital economy.

Heery (2016) proposes an understanding of the role of trade unions through three distinct perspectives: unitary, pluralist, and critical. The unitary perspective perceives unions as agents of cooperation aiming to harmonize the interests of workers and employers. The pluralist perspective emphasizes their function in defending employees' rights, recognizing the inherent conflicts of interest in employment relations. Finally, the critical perspective highlights the contemporary challenges that unions face, including the need to adapt to labour market transformations and neoliberal policies that threaten workers' rights. These approaches offer a rich analytical framework for understanding the evolution and importance of trade unions in the current context.

Recent academic literature has increasingly addressed the disruptive effects of artificial intelligence and algorithmic management on labour relations and union practices. Scholars such as Jarrahi et al. (2021) and Haidar and Keune (2021) highlight how AI systems alter managerial control, undermine transparency, and introduce asymmetries in the worker-employer relationship. These technologies challenge traditional bargaining frameworks and weaken collective voice by individualising tasks and making labour less visible. In response, emerging union strategies include calls for algorithmic transparency, collective bargaining over algorithmic systems, and the use of digital tools to monitor AI-driven decisions (Daugareilh, Degryse & Pochet, 2021; Brunnerová et al. 2024). Integrating these debates is essential to understand how unions must adapt their role in regulating not just employment terms, but also digital infrastructures of control.

THE GIG ECONOMY AND NEW FORMS OF EMPLOYMENT

Definition and Characteristics of the Gig Economy

The gig economy, or the economy of small jobs, refers to a labour market characterised by the prevalence of short-term contracts and freelance work as opposed to permanent jobs (Katz and Krueger, 2019). This economic model has rapidly developed with the advent of digital technologies and online platforms. It is characterised by increased flexibility for both workers and employers, but also by job precariousness (De Stefano, 2018). Indeed, the gig economy, characterized by temporary contracts and one-off assignments, offers unprecedented flexibility for workers and companies. On the one hand, it allows workers to choose their schedules and assignments, thus promoting a better work-life balance. Individuals can adapt their workload according to their needs and priorities, which is particularly advantageous for those with significant personal or family commitments. On the other hand, companies benefit from a responsive and adaptable workforce, able to respond quickly to demand for tasks or specific projects. This flexibility allows companies to reduce the fixed costs associated with traditional employment while accessing specialized expertise for temporary needs. However, this flexibility also presents challenges regarding social protection and economic security for workers, who often face the absence of traditional benefits such as paid leave or long-term job security (Achour, 2025). The gig economy spans a variety of sectors, from transportation to delivery, as well **as** creative and professional services, thereby redefining the traditional contours of work and employment (Wood & Lehdonvirta, 2019). Recent statistics reveal that in the United States alone, around 36% of the workforce, or approximately 57 million people, participate in the gig economy[3]. According to the European Commission, over 28 million people in the EU work through one (or more) of digital labour platforms. In 2025, that number is expected to reach 43 million people[4]. For Zeid et al. (2024), public policy measures are needed to both reap the benefits and lessen the negative consequences of the global surge in gig work and non-standard forms of employment (NSE), which pose both opportunities and problems for the labour market. Research on how NSE affects businesses and employees confirms that, in order to optimize its beneficial impacts, policy environments must strike a balance between the advantages and disadvantages of NSE. To guarantee that workers can better navigate a continuously changing work environment and handle transitions, public policy should update social protection systems; align regulations for both standard and non-standard employment, and support lifelong learning (OECD, 2019).

Emergence of Digital Platforms and On-Demand Work

The rise of digital platforms has played a catalytic role in the expansion of the gig economy (Kenney and Zysman, 2016). Platforms like Uber, Deliveroo, and Upwork act as intermediaries, directly connecting independent workers with clients or employers. They have introduced a new paradigm of on-demand work, where tasks are fragmented and distributed via algorithms (Rosenblat and Stark, 2016). This model offers unprecedented flexibility but also raises questions about the nature of the employment relationship, social protection, and collective representation of workers (Heeks, 2017). Automation and artificial intelligence amplify this trend, replacing traditional jobs and creating new forms of human-machine hybrid work (Choudhary, and Shireshi, 2022). Recent empirical studies show that gig workers experience both autonomy and algorithmic control, with significant variations in income and job satisfaction (Wood et al., 2019).

Ethical Challenges in Algorithmic Governance

Algorithmic practices raise critical ethical concerns, particularly regarding privacy, discrimination, and worker dignity. Platform workers, constantly rated and categorized by AI systems, face systemic biases (e.g., penalties for women taking family-related breaks) and intrusive surveillance (Zuboff, 2023). The lack of human oversight in automated decisions, such as unexplained account deactivations, highlights accountability gaps (EU Directive, 2021). To address these issues, unions advocate for robust regulatory frameworks, including independent algorithmic audits and a "right to disconnect," essential for rebalancing power in the digital age.

Implications for Labour Relations and Social Protection

The expansion of the gig economy and new forms of employment has profound implications for labour relations and social protection systems (Stewart and Stanford, 2017). The classification of platform workers (employees vs. independent contractors) has become a major legal and social issue, with consequences for access to labour rights and social protection (Kalleberg and Dunn, 2016). The fragmentation of work and individualization of employment relationships challenge traditional models of collective bargaining and union representation (Johnston and Land-Kazlauskas, 2018). Social protection systems, designed for stable and linear careers, are ill-suited to increasingly discontinuous and precarious professional trajectories (Huws et al., 2016). These changes pose significant challenges in terms of equity, economic security, and social cohesion, calling for a rethinking of regulatory frameworks and labour market institutions (Vallas and Schor, 2020). Recent research by the International Labour Organization (ILO, 2021) highlights the growing vulnerability of gig workers, who often lack access to social security, health benefits, and employment protections. Further exploring these dynamics, Achour (2025) examines social sustainability in platform work, emphasizing the role of social capital and digital solidarity networks as resilience mechanisms. The study underscores regulatory gaps and advocates for hybrid support systems, including platform cooperativism, to address labor vulnerabilities. By proposing an integrated framework balancing economic flexibility with institutional protections, this work aligns with calls for policies that ensure fair conditions, worker empowerment, and inclusive social security in the gig economy. Bonu (2020), for example, highlights that while the gig economy is growing, with an estimated 1.68 million workers in Australia and a potential contribution of nearly $3 trillion to global GDP by 2025, there is no adequate legal definition for these workers. This lack of a legal framework allows platforms to circumvent protections that should be in place, exposing workers to risks of exploitation.

CHALLENGES POSED TO UNIONS BY NEW FORMS OF EMPLOYMENT

The emergence of the gig economy and new forms of employment has presented unions with unprecedented challenges, fundamentally altering the landscape of work and collective representation. These challenges can be categorized into four main areas, each requiring innovative responses from unions to remain effective in protecting workers' rights and interests. (Figure1).

Figure 1. Challenges posed to unions by gig economy and new forms of employment

(Source: Author, 2025)

Fragmentation of the Workforce

The gig economy and new forms of employment have led to unprecedented fragmentation of the workforce (Katz and Krueger, 2019). Workers are geographically dispersed, often work in isolation and have varied employment statuses. This atomisation makes it challenging to create a collective identity and common interests, traditionally at the core of union action. Unions face the challenge of gathering and representing an increasingly heterogeneous workforce with diverse needs and expectations (Heery and Adler, 2004; Muntaner et al., 2021). This fragmentation is also associated with other difficulties that hinder union action, such as the divergence of interests and priorities between gig economy workers, some favoring flexibility while others seek stability, which complicates the development of unified demands. This heterogeneity translates into varied needs in terms of social protection, training and remuneration. Faced with this reality, unions encounter considerable obstacles in organizing and mobilizing these dispersed workers. Traditional methods of unionization often prove ineffective, making it difficult to identify and contact gig economy workers. In this context, the crucial challenge for unions is to forge inter-category solidarity, by creating a collective identity that transcends the diversity of individual situations. This implies finding common ground and shared demands capable of uniting this heterogeneous workforce, while recognizing and valuing their differences.

Individualisation of Work Relationships

The rise of digital platforms and gig work has led to an increasing individualization of employment relations (Tassinari and Maccarrone, 2020). This development challenges traditional methods of organizing, based on fixed workplaces and regular schedules. Schor et al. (2020) have shown that the platform economy generates both dependency on platforms and increased precocity for workers. In this context, unions struggle to identify and mobilize a dispersed and constantly changing workforce, rendering traditional organizing strategies obsolete.

Artificial intelligence has fundamentally reshaped power dynamics in the platform economy. Algorithmic management systems, such as those deployed by Uber or Amazon Flex, govern not only task allocation and pay rates but also worker evaluations through opaque metrics (Jarrahi et al., 2021). These algorithms, often designed to prioritize productivity over worker rights, deepen fragmentation and individualize risks (Adams-Prassl, 2022). Unions now face the dual challenge of negotiating not just with employers but also with the digital architectures dictating labor conditions, requiring unprecedented technical expertise to demand transparency and fairness. Artificial intelligence further intensifies this individualization through algorithmic management systems that track, rate, and evaluate workers without human oversight. These systems assign tasks, assess performance, and sometimes even determine pay, creating opaque and asymmetrical power dynamics. This makes it difficult for unions to detect patterns of unfair treatment or to intervene collectively, especially when decisions are automated and lack transparency.

Such technologies contribute to a broader erosion of solidarity among workers, further complicating organizing and collective representation efforts. Moreover, the ambiguous legal status of these workers complicates the application of collective agreements and social protections usually negotiated by unions. This situation undermines the foundations of collective bargaining, the cornerstone of traditional union action. Unions must rethink their strategies to remain relevant in a context where employment relationships are increasingly individualized and the notion of employer is fading (Hyman, 2015; Aloisi, 2019). Union dues and representation models based on stable, full-time jobs are also ill-suited to the volatility of income and commitments in the platform economy. This trend is confirmed by recent findings showing that the gig economy fosters a transactional relationship between workers and platforms (Vallas and Schor, 2020). Faced with these challenges, unions must not only adapt their strategies, but also fundamentally rethink their role and organizational structure to remain relevant in this new reality of work.

Challenges of Representation and Collective Organization

Organising collective action among gig economy workers poses significant logistical and strategic challenges for unions (Johnston and Land-Kazlauskas, 2018). The absence of a common workplace, the high turnover of workers, and the often temporary nature of their engagement make traditional methods of recruitment and union organization difficult. This spatial and temporal fragmentation undermines the formation of collective identities and solidarity networks that have historically been crucial for union mobilization (Tassinari and Maccarrone, 2020). Moreover, many gig economy workers do not perceive themselves as part of a traditional working class, complicating their mobilization around collective demands (Vandaele, 2018; Wood et al. 2021). The individualistic nature of gig work, often framed as entrepreneurship, can foster a mindset that prioritizes personal flexibility over collective bargaining power (Duggan et al., 2020). This ideological shift poses a fundamental challenge to union narratives and organizing strategies.

The algorithmic management prevalent in the gig economy further complicates union efforts by creating a sense of isolation and competition among workers (Veen et al., 2020). Traditional union tactics like strikes or work stoppages are less effective when workers can be easily replaced or penalised through opaque rating systems (Tassinari and Maccarrone, 2020). Additionally, the legal ambiguity surrounding the employment status of gig workers in many jurisdictions creates obstacles for unions in terms of representation rights and collective bargaining (Stewart and Stanford, 2017).

To address these challenges, unions are experimenting with innovative organising methods, including digital organizing tools, social media campaigns, and partnerships with worker-led movements (Woodcock & Graham, 2020). However, these efforts must contend with the platform companies' significant resources and their ability to rapidly modify working conditions and algorithms in response to collective action (Vandaele, 2018).

Inadequate Legal Framework

Existing legal frameworks, designed for traditional employment relationships, are often inadequate for the realities of the gig economy (De Stefano, 2018). Unions face legal obstacles in representing independent contractors or those with atypical employment statuses. The classification of platform workers as independent contractors in many countries limits their access to traditional union rights, such as collective bargaining. Unions must navigate an uncertain legal environment and advocate for legislative reforms that recognize the new realities of work (Stewart and Stanford, 2017). Recent legislative efforts at the European level represent a significant step forward in addressing these challenges. Notably, the Directive (EU) 2024/2831 of the European Parliament and of the Council of 23 October 2024 on improving working conditions in platform work introduces important provisions for better classification of workers, a presumption of employment in cases of dispute, and obligations for algorithmic transparency and data protection. This Directive seeks to ensure fair treatment and social protection for platform workers across the EU and strengthens the rights of trade unions to engage in collective bargaining on their behalf. At the national level, several countries have already taken concrete steps aligned with these goals. For instance, Spain enacted Law 12/2021[5], known as the *Ley Riders*, which classifies delivery platform workers as employees and grants them collective rights. France, Italy, and the Netherlands have also introduced reforms or court rulings aimed at improving gig workers' rights. These developments mark a significant turning point in European labor law, underscoring the importance of integrating these legal evolutions into trade union strategies and research on collective representation.

Recent research by Adams-Prassl (2023) further elaborates on the concept of legal arbitrage, whereby gig economy platforms exploit gaps in existing labour law to minimize their liabilities and costs associated with traditional employment. This practice raises fundamental questions regarding the classification of workers and the protections to which they are entitled under the law. The author advocates a reassessment of the legal framework governing employment to better address the specific challenges posed by gig work, arguing for regulations that take into account the realities of this form of labour while fostering innovation (Adams-Prassl, 2023; Vallas and Schor, 2020).

RESPONSES AND ADAPTATIONS OF TRADE UNIONS

New Strategies for Organisation and Recruitment

The gig economy, despite its advantages in terms of flexibility and income generation, exposes workers to precariousness and a lack of social protection. In response to these challenges, trade unions play a crucial role in organising workers to defend their rights, promote solidarity, and advocate for a protective legal framework that also supports innovation. To adapt to this new paradigm, trade unions are developing innovative approaches. Some are experimenting with more flexible membership models, including independent and part-time workers (Benassi and Dorigatti, 2020).

For instance, the Independent Drivers Guild (IDG) in the United States represents Uber drivers in New York, negotiating improvements such as in-app tipping options[6]. In the UK, the Independent Workers' Union of Great Britain (IWGB) has led major campaigns for platform workers' rights, including securing a 2020 High Court victory against the British government regarding health and safety rights for platform economy workers[7], while the App Drivers & Couriers Union (ADCU) has pursued legal actions to recognize these workers' rights[8].

In Italy, for instance, the Riders Union Bologna emerged as a grassroots initiative organizing food delivery workers through both online and offline methods, including WhatsApp groups, flash protests, and collective negotiations with platforms like

Deliveroo. Their success led to the first local-level agreement on delivery conditions in 2018, later inspiring other initiatives across Italy and Europe. Similarly, in Belgium, Smart Coop has established a cooperative model that allows freelancers and gig workers to access employee status and benefits while retaining flexibility. These initiatives offer concrete, replicable strategies for union engagement in fragmented and precarious work settings.

Others are adopting "organizing" strategies inspired by the Anglo-Saxon model, favouring popular mobilization and direct engagement (Simms et al., 2013). The union strategy is structured around several axes: the utilization of digital platforms for education and information dissemination, targeted awareness campaigns on social media, partnerships with community organizations, the development of practical tools for the management of independent work, and the implementation of solidarity initiatives.

In France, the Syndicat des Chauffeurs Autonomes de Plateforme VTC (SCAPVTC) exemplifies this approach by negotiating with platforms to improve working conditions for VTC drivers[9]. These unions are leveraging digital tools and social media to organize and mobilize workers, as seen in the strategies of IWGB and ADCU in the UK.

Advocacy training and technological innovation, notably through initiatives such as WorkerTech (Rani and Furrer, 2020), complement this multidimensional approach. This holistic strategy aims to empower workers, strengthen their cohesion, and shape a more equitable work environment in the gig economy. By combining traditional methods and technological innovations, unions strive to meet the specific needs of this new category of workers while adapting to the rapid evolution of the sector and local particularities.

Innovations in Forms of Representation

Unions are innovating in their forms of representation to adapt to new work realities. Some are creating specific structures for gig economy workers, such as the Independent Workers' Union of Great Britain (IWGB) for self-employed drivers and couriers (Vandaele, 2018). The IWGB has led campaigns for platform workers' rights and pursued legal actions to recognize these workers' rights, demonstrating the effectiveness of targeted representation.

Others are experimenting with "guild unionism" models, offering services and representation to independent workers (Hirsch and Seiner, 2018). For instance, the Freelancers Union in the United States provides insurance and legal services to its members while advocating for policies favourable to independent workers[10]. Similarly, in the Netherlands, Aworks operates as a cooperative for freelancers, offering representation and collective negotiation services, acting as a union for independent workers (van Doorn, 2017).

Traditional unions are also adapting their structures to accommodate gig workers. In Germany, IG Metall has created "Fair Crowd Work", a platform that evaluates working conditions on digital platforms and provides resources to independent workers (Vandaele, 2018). This initiative extends union support to the tech sector's independent workforce. In the UK, the GMB Union has achieved union recognition with Uber, a first for a ride-hailing platform in the country, enabling collective bargaining for drivers (Prassl, 2018).

"Quasi-unionism" initiatives are also emerging, such as platform cooperatives that combine collective representation with entrepreneurship (Scholz, 2017). These include worker-led collectives like Riders Union Bologna in Italy, which uses WhatsApp groups to organize workers and coordinate collective actions (Tassinari & Maccarrone, 2020). In France, the Collectif des Livreurs Autonomes de Paris (CLAP) employs social media and direct actions to defend platform delivery workers' rights (Abdelnour & Bernard, 2019).

Recent empirical studies have shown the effectiveness of these innovative forms in improving workers' conditions and rights (Johnston and Land-Kazlauskas, 2018). By leveraging digital tools, adopting flexible organizational structures, and focusing on the specific needs of gig workers, these new forms of representation are reshaping traditional union models to fit the gig economy landscape.

Additionally, new hybrid structures such as freelancer cooperatives and digital unions have emerged in countries like Belgium (e.g., Smart Coop) and France, offering both administrative support and collective representation. These entities blur the lines between unionism, entrepreneurship, and mutual aid, and show promising results in engaging precarious and creative-sector gig workers.

These examples illustrate a range of innovative approaches: the adaptation of traditional unions, the creation of new specific structures, the use of digital technologies for organizing, and the development of cooperative models. They demonstrate how unions are striving to address the unique challenges posed by the gig economy in terms of representation and collective action, while balancing the need for worker protection with the flexibility that characterizes this new form of work.

Alliances With Other Social Movements

Recognizing the limits of their traditional actions, many unions are seeking to form alliances with other social movements. These "cause coalitions" allow them to broaden their support base and address issues that go beyond the narrow scope of labour relations (Tattersall, 2018). For example, unions are allying with environmental movements to promote a "just transition" to a green economy. The

BlueGreen Alliance in the United States, formed by the United Steelworkers and the Sierra Club, exemplifies this approach. This coalition works to create quality jobs while addressing climate change and environmental challenges (BlueGreen Alliance, 2021).

Unions are also partnering with migrant rights organizations to protect precarious workers (Gumbrell-McCormick and Hyman, 2013). In the UK, Unite the Union has collaborated with the Joint Council for the Welfare of Immigrants to campaign for the rights of migrant workers in the gig economy (Alberti and Però, 2018).

The alliance between the SEIU union and the Fight for $15 movement in the United States exemplifies this coalition approach to improving conditions for low-wage workers. This partnership has been instrumental in pushing for minimum wage increases and union rights for fast-food workers and other low-wage employees (Rolf, 2016).

Another example is the collaboration between UNI Global Union and environmental justice organisations such as Friends of the Earth Europe, which jointly advocate for a just ecological transition that includes labor protections. These alliances have supported transnational campaigns for sustainable jobs, particularly in platform-based logistics and transport. In Argentina, the union federation CTA Autónoma has partnered with informal worker associations and feminist movements to advocate for intersectional labor policies, especially in the care and domestic sectors, showing how unions can expand their base and social relevance through inclusive coalition-building.

In France, the Confédération Générale du Travail (CGT) has formed alliances with housing rights groups like Droit Au Logement (DAL) to address the interconnected issues of work and housing precocity (Béroud et al., 2019).

In Germany, the Ver.di union has partnered with the Fridays for Future movement to promote climate protection measures that also ensure fair working conditions, demonstrating the potential for inter generational alliances[11]

Recent research underscores the strategic importance of these alliances in enhancing union efficacy and sustainability (López et al., 2024; Lamannis, 2023). These coalitions not only amplify the voices of workers but also situate labour issues within broader social and environmental contexts, potentially increasing public support and political influence.

These examples illustrate how unions are expanding their scope of action by forming strategic alliances with diverse social movements. By doing so, they are able to address complex, interconnected issues that affect workers' lives beyond the workplace, while also revitalizing their own organizations and strategies in the face of changing economic and social conditions.

Use of Digital Technologies

Unions are increasingly adopting digital technologies to strengthen their actions. They use social media and mobile applications to communicate with their members, organise actions, and collect data on working conditions (Panagiotopoulos and Barnett, 2015).

For example, UNI Global Union has developed an online platform, "TopUNIon," to facilitate information exchange and coordination among its affiliates worldwide. In a similar vein, the International Transport Workers' Federation (ITF) has created the "ITF Global" app, which provides news updates, campaign information, and a direct communication channel for transport workers globally (ITF, 2020).

Some unions are developing their own digital platforms to offer services to their members, such as wage calculation tools or mutual aid forums (Pasquier and Wood, 2018). The Independent Workers' Union of Great Britain (IWGB) has launched a digital platform called "Couriers & Logistics Branch," which allows gig workers to report issues, access resources, and coordinate actions (Woodcock, 2020).

In Germany, the IG Metall union has developed the "Fair Crowd Work" website, which provides ratings and reviews of digital labour platforms based on worker experiences, helping gig workers make informed decisions about their employment (Vandaele, 2018).

In recent years, unions have increasingly experimented with mobile apps and interactive platforms to reach isolated gig workers. For example, the TUC in the UK launched the "WorkSmart" app to educate young workers on their rights and promote engagement, while IG Metall in Germany developed interactive guides for crowd workers to self-assess working conditions. These tools represent a shift toward more agile, tech-driven models of communication and mobilisation.

The use of blockchain technology is also being explored to create portable reputation systems for gig economy workers (Curchod et al. 2020). For instance, the National Domestic Workers Alliance in the US has piloted a blockchain-based app called "Alia" that allows domestic workers to accrue benefits across multiple employers (Hunt and Samman, 2019).

In France, the Confédération Générale du Travail (CGT) has launched "Syndicoop," a digital cooperative platform that aims to provide gig workers with better working conditions and a share in the platform's governance (Abdelnour and Bernard, 2020).

The TUC in the UK has developed "WorkSmart," a digital career coaching tool that also educates young workers about their rights and the benefits of unionization, demonstrating how digital tools can be used for both service provision and organizing (Hodder and Houghton, 2020).

Recent technological advancements and their application in labour organisations highlight the growing importance of digital tools in union strategies (Wood et al., 2021). These examples demonstrate how unions are leveraging technology not only to improve communication and coordination but also to provide innovative services, gather data on working conditions, and explore new models of worker protection and empowerment in the digital economy.

CONCLUSION

This chapter has investigated the evolution of trade unionism in response to the challenges presented by the gig economy and emerging forms of employment. The research examined how workforce fragmentation, the individualization of labour relations, and the inadequacy of existing legal frameworks challenge the traditional foundations of union action. Concurrently, the study identified innovative strategies unions are implementing to adapt to this new landscape, including novel approaches to organization, innovative forms of representation, expanded alliances, and the utilization of digital technologies.

Beyond these current transformations, the future of trade unionism in the digital age will be shaped by profound economic and technological shifts. The increasing influence of artificial intelligence, automation, and algorithmic management presents both challenges and opportunities for worker representation. Unions must engage in policy advocacy to ensure transparency in AI-driven employment decisions, protect workers from unfair algorithmic control, and push for regulatory frameworks that hold platform companies accountable.

Another crucial aspect of the future of unionism is the rise of transnational and digital-based organizing models. As labor markets globalize, unions may need to shift toward cross-border collaborations and online platforms for worker mobilization. The development of transnational labor agreements, along with digital organizing tools, could redefine collective bargaining in a borderless gig economy.

Moreover, unions will likely play a pivotal role in shaping a new social contract that adapts to the realities of flexible work. This could involve advocating for universal portable benefits, enhanced labor protections for platform workers, and even progressive policies such as Universal Basic Income (UBI) to counteract job precocity. Strengthening alternative organizing models, such as platform cooperativism and hybrid union structures, could also provide sustainable solutions for gig workers seeking greater control over their working conditions.

This analysis elucidates several avenues for future research. It would be pertinent to conduct a more in-depth study of new forms of collective organization emerging in the gig economy, examine the efficacy of various union strategies in this context, and explore the long-term implications of these transformations for industrial relations. The integration of AI ethics in labor relations, the potential for government intervention in regulating platform economies, and the role of unions in shaping fair technological transitions are additional research areas that deserve attention.

From a practical perspective, this work underscores the importance for unions to continue innovating and adapting while advocating for regulatory frameworks that protect all workers, regardless of their employment status. The ability of unions to reinvent themselves in response to these structural changes will determine their relevance in the decades to come. Whether through legal battles, digital organizing or coalition-building with social movements, unions must proactively shape the future of work rather than merely respond to its disruptions.

The future of industrial relations in the context of the gig economy remains uncertain; however, it is evident that unions have a crucial role to play in defining a new social contract suited to the digital age. Their capacity to reinvent themselves while maintaining fidelity to their core values of solidarity and social justice will be decisive for the future of work and the protection of workers' rights in a constantly evolving economy. By embracing innovation while safeguarding fundamental labor rights, unions can not only survive but thrive in the digital era, ensuring that technological progress does not come at the expense of worker dignity and fair employment conditions.

Looking ahead, one of the most significant challenges for trade unions in the AI-driven economy will be their capacity to address algorithmic control and automated decision-making in the workplace. This includes negotiating for transparency in how algorithms assign work, assess performance, and influence income or termination. Unions will also need to push for regulatory safeguards, including the right to human oversight and the protection of worker data. These AI-specific dimensions are not only technical but deeply political, as they redefine power asymmetries at work. The role of unions in shaping fair, accountable and ethical AI systems will be central to the future of labour governance.

REFERENCES

Abdelnour, S., & Bernard, S. (2018). Vers un capitalisme de plateforme? Mobiliser le travail, contourner les régulations. Présentation du Corpus. *La nouvelle revue du travail*, (13). https://doi.org/10.4000/nrt.3797

Achour, Z. (2025). Social Sustainability in the Gig Economy: Rethinking Social Protection Systems for Platform Workers. In *Sustainability and Adaptability of Gig Economies in Global Business* (pp. 297-322). IGI Global Scientific Publishing. DOI: DOI: 10.4018/979-8-3693-9385-7.ch011

Adams-Prassl, J. (2022). Regulating algorithms at work: Lessons for a 'European approach to artificial intelligence'. *European Labour Law Journal*, *13*(1), 30–50. DOI: 10.1177/20319525211062558

Adams-Prassl, J. (2023). Exploring the economics of the gig economy: legal arbitrage and employment law. In *Handbook of Research on the Global Political Economy of Work* (pp. 380–390). Edward Elgar Publishing. DOI: 10.4337/9781839106583.00044

Alberti, G., & Però, D. (2018). Migrating industrial relations: Migrant workers' initiative within and outside trade unions. *British Journal of Industrial Relations*, *56*(4), 693–715. DOI: 10.1111/bjir.12308

Aloisi, A. (2019). Negotiating the digital transformation of work: Non-standard workers' voice, collective rights and mobilisation practices in the platform economy (EUI MWP Working Paper No. 2019/03). European University Institute. https://hdl.handle.net/1814/63264

Baccaro, L., & Howell, C. (2011). A common neoliberal trajectory: The transformation of industrial relations in advanced capitalism. *Politics & Society*, *39*(4), 521–563. DOI: 10.1177/0032329211420082

Baccaro, L., & Howell, C. (2017). *Trajectories of neoliberal transformation: European industrial relations since the 1970s*. Cambridge University Press. DOI: 10.1017/9781139088381

Bamber, G. J., & Lansbury, R. D. (Eds.). (2020). *International and comparative employment relations: National regulation, global changes*. Routledge. DOI: 10.4324/9781003116158

Benassi, C., & Dorigatti, L. (2020). Out of sight, out of mind: The challenge of external work arrangements for industrial manufacturing unions in Germany and Italy. *Work, Employment and Society*, *34*(6), 1027–1044. DOI: 10.1177/0950017020903039

Béroud, S., Dupuy, C., Kahmann, M., & Yon, K. (2019). Jeunes et engagements au travail: Une génération asyndicale? *Ágora*, (2), 7–25. DOI: 10.3917/agora.082.0007

Bertolini, A., & Dukes, R. (2021). Trade unions and platform workers in the UK: Worker representation in the shadow of the law. *Industrial Law Journal, 50*(4), 662–688. DOI: 10.1093/indlaw/dwab022

Brunnerová, S., Ceccon, D., Holubová, B., Kahancová, M., Lukáčová, K., & Medas, G. (2024). Collective bargaining practices on Ai and algorithmic management in european services sectors.

Bryson, A., & Forth, J. (2017). Trade Union Membership and Influence 1999–2014. *The Journal of Industrial Relations, 59*(1), 34–56.

Choudhary, V., & Shireshi, S. S. (2022). Analysing the gig economy in India and exploring various effective regulatory methods to improve the plight of the workers. *Journal of Asian and African Studies, 57*(7), 1343–1356. DOI: 10.1177/00219096221082581

Commons, J. R., Andrews, J. B., & Perlman, S. (1918). *History of labour in the United States*. Beard Books.

Curchod, C., Patriotta, G., & Neysen, N. (2014). Categorization and identification: The identity work of 'business sellers' on eBay. *Human Relations, 67*(11), 1293–1320. DOI: 10.1177/0018726713516376

Curchod, C., Patriotta, G., & Wright, M. (2020). Self-categorization as a nonmarket strategy for MNE subsidiaries: Tracking the international expansion of an online platform. *Journal of World Business, 55*(3), 101070. DOI: 10.1016/j.jwb.2019.101070

Daugareilh, I., Degryse, C., & Pochet, P. (2019). The platform economy and social law: Key issues in comparative perspective. *ETUI Research Paper-Working Paper*.

De Stefano, V. (2018). Platform work and labour protection. Flexibility is not enough. *Regulating for globalization: trade, labor and EU law perspectives*.

Degryse, C. (2016). Digitalisation of the economy and its impact on labour markets. *ETUI research paper-working paper*.

Dunlop, J. T. (1958). *Industrial Relations Systems*. Henry Holt.

Esping-Andersen, G. (1990). *The Three Worlds of Welfare Capitalism*. Princeton University Press.

European Commission. (2021). Proposal for a directive on improving working conditions in platform work. Retrieved from https://www.europeansources.info/record/proposal-for-a-directive-on-improving-working-conditions-in-platform-work/

European Union. (2024). Directive (EU) 2024/2831 of the European Parliament and of the Council of 23 October 2024 on improving working conditions in platform work. *Official Journal of the European Union*. https://eur-lex.europa.eu/legal-content/EN/TXT/?uri=CELEX:32024L2831

Flanders, A. D., & Clegg, H. A. (1954). *The System of Industrial Relations in Great Britain, Its History, Law, and Institutions*. Blackwell.

Goldthorpe, J. H. (1984). *The Political Economy of the Labour Market*. Oxford University Press.

Graham, M., & Anwar, M. A. (2019). The global gig economy: Toward a planetary labor market. In *The digital transformation of labor* (pp. 213–234). Routledge. DOI: 10.4324/9780429317866-13

Gumbrell-McCormick, R., & Hyman, R. (2013). *Trade unions in Western Europe: hard times, hard choices*. Oxford University Press. DOI: 10.1093/acprof:oso/9780199644414.001.0001

Haidar, J., & Keune, M. (Eds.). (2021). *Work and labour relations in global platform capitalism* (pp. 1–27). Edward Elgar Publishing. DOI: 10.4337/9781802205138

Heeks, R. (2017). *Decent Work and the Digital Gig Economy: A Developing Country Perspective on Employment Impacts and Standards in Online Outsourcing, Crowdwork, Etc*. Centre for Development Informatics, University of Manchester.

Heery, E. (2016). Framing work: Unitary, pluralist, and critical perspectives in the twenty-first century. *International Journal of Human Resource Management, 27*(6), 581–592.

Heery, E., & Adler, L. (2004). Organizing the unorganized. In Frege, C., & Kelly, J. (Eds.), *Varieties of Unionism: Strategies for Union Revitalization in a Globalizing Economy* (pp. 45–70). Oxford University Press. DOI: 10.1093/acprof:oso/9780199270149.003.0004

Hirsch, J. M., & Seiner, J. A. (2018). A modern union for the modern economy. *Fordham Law Review, 86*(4), 1727–1782.

Hobsbawm, E. J. (1964). *Labour's Turning Point: The Struggle for the Charter in 1842*. Lawrence & Wishart.

Hodder, A., & Houghton, D. (2015). Union use of social media: A study of the U niversity and C ollege U nion on T witter. *New Technology, Work and Employment, 30*(3), 173–189. DOI: 10.1111/ntwe.12055

Hunt, A., & Samman, E. (2019). Gender and the gig economy: Critical steps for evidence-based policy.

Huws, U., Spencer, N. H., & Joyce, S. (2016). *Crowd Work in Europe: Preliminary Results from a Survey in the UK*. Foundation for European Progressive Studies.

Hyman, R. (1975). What is industrial relations? In *Industrial relations: A Marxist introduction* (pp. 9–31). Palgrave Macmillan UK. DOI: 10.1007/978-1-349-15623-8_2

Hyman, R. (2015). Three scenarios for industrial relations in Europe. *International Labour Review, 154*(1), 5–14. DOI: 10.1111/j.1564-913X.2015.00221.x

International Labour Organization. (2021). The role of digital labour platforms in transforming the world of work. https://www.ilo.org/publications/flagship-reports/role-digital-labour-platforms-transforming-world-work

Jarrahi, M. H., Newlands, G., Lee, M. K., Wolf, C. T., Kinder, E., & Sutherland, W. (2021). Algorithmic management in a work context. *Big Data & Society, 8*(2), 20539517211020332. Advance online publication. DOI: 10.1177/20539517211020332

Johnston, H., & Land-Kazlauskas, C. (2018). *Organizing on-demand representation, voice, and collective bargaining in the gig economy* (No. 994981993502676).

Johnston, H., & Land-Kazlauskas, C. (2018). *Organizing on-demand: Representation, voice, and collective bargaining in the gig economy. Conditions of Work and Employment Series No. 94*. ILO.

Kalleberg, A. L. (2018). Job Insecurity and Well-being in Rich Democracies1 Geary Lecture 2018. *The Economic and Social Review, 49*(3), 241–258. PMID: 31435077

Katz, L. F., & Krueger, A. B. (2019). The rise and nature of alternative work arrangements in the United States, 1995–2015. *Industrial & Labor Relations Review, 72*(2), 382–416. DOI: 10.1177/0019793918820008

Kelly, J. (2018). *Rethinking Industrial Relations: Mobilization, Collectivism, and Long Waves*. Routledge.

Kenney, M., & Zysman, J. (2016). The rise of the platform economy. *Issues in Science and Technology, 32*(3), 61–69.

Kochan, T. A., Katz, H. C., & McKersie, R. B. (1994). *The transformation of American industrial relations*. Cornell University Press.

Korpi, W. (1978). Workplace Bargaining, the Law and Unofficial Strikes: The Case of Sweden. *British Journal of Industrial Relations, 16*(3), 355–368. DOI: 10.1111/j.1467-8543.1978.tb00291.x

Lamannis, M. (2023) Collective bargaining in the platform economy: a mapping exercise of existing initiatives. ETUI Research Paper-Report, 2

Lichtenstein, N. (2013). *State of the Union: A Century of American Labor*. Princeton University Press. DOI: 10.1515/9781400848140

López, T., Jesnes, K., Alyanak, O., & Karlıdağ, Z. (2024). Building labour power in the platform economy: A comparative analysis of worker struggles in German and Norwegian food and grocery delivery. *New Technology, Work and Employment*, 1–23. DOI: 10.1111/ntwe.12312

Muntaner, C., Benach, J., & Solar, O. (2021). Platform work and health equity: A framework for protecting workers in the gig economy. *American Journal of Public Health, 111*(2), 230–236. PMID: 33351653

Panagiotopoulos, P., & Barnett, J. (2015). Social Media in Union Communications: An International Study with UNI G lobal U nion Affiliates. *British Journal of Industrial Relations, 53*(3), 508–532. DOI: 10.1111/bjir.12060

Panagiotopoulos, P., & Barnett, J. (2015). Social media in union communications: An international study with UNI Global Union affiliates. *British Journal of Industrial Relations, 53*(3), 508–532. DOI: 10.1111/bjir.12060

Pasquier, V., & Wood, A. J. (2018). *The power of social media as a labour campaigning tool: lessons from OUR Walmart and the Fight for 15*. ETUI Policy Brief.

Pierson, P. (2004). *Politics in time: History, institutions, and social analysis*. Princeton University Press. DOI: 10.1515/9781400841080

Piore, M. (1984). *The second industrial divide: possibilities for prosperity*. Basic Nooks.

Prassl, J. (2018). *Humans as a service: The promise and perils of work in the gig economy*. Oxford University Press. DOI: 10.1093/oso/9780198797012.001.0001

Rani, U., & Furrer, M. (2020). Digital labour platforms and new forms of flexible work in developing countries: Algorithmic management of work and workers. *Competition & Change, 24*(2), 212–236. DOI: 10.1177/1024529420905187

Rolf, D. (2015). *The fight for $15: The right wage for a working America*. New Press.

Rosenblat, A., & Stark, L. (2016). Algorithmic Labor and Information Asymmetries: A Case Study of Uber's Drivers. *International Journal of Communication, 10*, 3758–3784.

Scholz, T. (2017). *Uberworked and underpaid: How workers are disrupting the digital economy*. John Wiley & Sons.

Schor, J. B., Attwood-Charles, W., Cansoy, M., Ladegaard, I., & Wengronowitz, R. (2020). Dependence and precarity in the platform economy. *Theory and Society*, *49*(5-6), 833–861. DOI: 10.1007/s11186-020-09408-y PMID: 32836676

Simms, M., Holgate, J., & Heery, E. (2013). *Union voices: Tactics and tensions in UK organizing*. Cornell University Press.

Stewart, A., & Stanford, J. (2017). Regulating work in the gig economy: What are the options? *Economic and Labour Relations Review*, *28*(3), 420–437. DOI: 10.1177/1035304617722461

Streeck, W. (2009). *Re-forming capitalism: Institutional change in the German political economy*. Oxford University Press.

Tapia, M., Ibsen, C. L., & Kochan, T. A. (2015). Mapping the frontier of theory in industrial relations: The contested role of worker representation. *Socio-economic Review*, *13*(1), 157–184. DOI: 10.1093/ser/mwu036

Tassinari, A., & Maccarrone, V. (2020). Riders on the storm: Workplace solidarity among gig economy couriers in Italy and the UK. *Work, Employment and Society*, *34*(1), 35–54. DOI: 10.1177/0950017019862954

Tattersall, A. (2018). How do we build power in coalition? Rethinking union-community coalition types 12 years on. *Labour & Industry: a journal of the social and economic relations of work*, *28*(1), 68-81. https://doi.org/10.1080/10301763.2018.1427422

Vallas, S. P., & Schor, J. B. (2020). What do platforms do? Understanding the gig economy. *Annual Review of Sociology*, *46*(1), 273–294. DOI: 10.1146/annurev-soc-121919-054857

Van Doorn, N. (2017). Platform labor: On the gendered and racialized exploitation of low-income service work in the 'on-demand' economy. *Information Communication and Society*, *20*(6), 898–914. DOI: 10.1080/1369118X.2017.1294194

Vandaele, K. (2018). Will trade unions survive in the platform economy? Emerging patterns of platform workers' collective voice and representation in Europe. *Emerging Patterns of Platform Workers' Collective Voice and Representation in Europe (June 19, 2018). ETUI Research Paper-Working Paper*.

Visser, J. (1996). *Unionization trends revisited*. Centre for Research of European Societies and Industrial Relations.

Visser, J. (2019). Can unions revitalize themselves? *International Journal of Labour Research, 9*(1/2), 17–48.

Wallerstein, M., & Western, B. (2000). Unions in decline? What has changed and why. *Annual Review of Political Science, 3*(1), 355–377. DOI: 10.1146/annurev.polisci.3.1.355

Wood, A., & Lehdonvirta, V. (2019). Platform labour and structured antagonism: Understanding the origins of protest in the gig economy. *Available atSSRN* 3357804. DOI: 10.2139/ssrn.3357804

Wood, A. J., Graham, M., Lehdonvirta, V., & Hjorth, I. (2019). Networked but commodified: The (dis) embeddedness of digital labour in the gig economy. *Sociology, 53*(5), 931–950. DOI: 10.1177/0038038519828906

Wood, A. J., Graham, M., Lehdonvirta, V., & Hjorth, I. (2021). Good Gig, Bad Gig: Autonomy and Algorithmic Control in the Global Gig Economy. *Work, Employment and Society, 35*(1), 56–75. DOI: 10.1177/0950017018785616 PMID: 30886460

Woodcock, J. (2020). The algorithmic panopticon at Deliveroo: Measurement, precarity, and the illusion of control. *Ephemera: theory & politics in organizations, 20*(3), 67-95. http://www.ephemerajournal.org/contribution/algorithmic-panopticon-deliveroo-measurement-precarity-and-illusion-control-0

Zeid, R. Y. M., Alrayess, D. J., Ajwad, M. I., Soytas, M. A., & Rivera Guivas, N. (2024). *The Gig Economy and the Future of Work: Global Trends and Policy Directions for Non-Standard Forms of Employment* (No. 190908). The World Bank.

Zuboff, S. (2023). The age of surveillance capitalism. In *Social theory re-wired* (pp. 203–213). Routledge. DOI: 10.4324/9781003320609-27

ADDITIONAL READING

Adams-Prassl, J., Binns, R., & Kelly-Lyth, A. (2023). Directly discriminatory algorithms. *The Modern Law Review, 86*(1), 144–175. DOI: 10.1111/1468-2230.12759 PMID: 37065788

Bowden, B. (2020). Trade Union Decline and Transformation: Where to for Employment Relations? In Bowden, B., Muldoon, J., Gould, A. M., & McMurray, A. J. (Eds.), *The Palgrave Handbook of Management History*. Palgrave Macmillan., DOI: 10.1007/978-3-319-62114-2_116

Cengiz, O., & Demir, Ö. (2025). Is Digitalization Bad for Trade Union Density in OECD Countries in the Age of Globalization? In *Future Workscapes: Emerging Business Trends and Innovations* (pp. 113-128). Emerald Publishing Limited. https://doi.org/DOI: 10.1108/S2051-23332025000011B007

Cini, L., Maccarrone, V., & Tassinari, A. (2022). With or without U(nions)? Understanding the diversity of gig workers' organizing practices in Italy and the UK. *European Journal of Industrial Relations*, *28*(3), 341–362. DOI: 10.1177/09596801211052531

Vallas, S., & Schor, J. B. (2020). What do platforms do? Understanding the gig economy. *Annual Review of Sociology*, *46*(1), 273–294. DOI: 10.1146/annurev-soc-121919-054857

KEY TERMS AND DEFINITIONS

Gig Economy: The gig economy refers to a labor market characterized by short-term contracts and freelance work rather than permanent jobs, often facilitated by digital platforms such as Uber, Deliveroo, and Upwork. While this model offers flexibility for both workers and employers, it also raises concerns about job security, social protection, and union representation. The lack of clear legal frameworks for gig workers has led to increasing precarization, as their employment status is often ambiguous, falling between independent contractor and employee.

Algorithmic Management: Algorithmic management refers to the use of algorithms and automated systems to supervise and organize work, particularly in digital platform labor. These algorithms assign tasks, evaluate worker performance, and even influence earnings. This form of management often reduces transparency and limits workers' control over their conditions of employment, leading to growing criticism from unions and policymakers.

Quasi-Unionism: Quasi-unionism refers to alternative labor organizing models that provide support to gig economy workers without being traditional unions. These structures include worker associations, advocacy groups, and mutual aid networks. This model is particularly relevant in sectors where traditional unionization is challenging due to the fragmented and precarious nature of work.

Platform Cooperativism: Platform cooperativism is an alternative economic model where workers collectively own and manage digital platforms instead of being controlled by venture-capital-backed corporations. Unlike mainstream gig economy companies, cooperative platforms aim to ensure fairer income distribution and better working conditions. While this model presents a sustainable alternative to worker exploitation in the gig economy, its scalability is often hindered by financial and regulatory challenges.

Right to Disconnect: The right to disconnect is a legal principle that ensures employees are not obliged to respond to work-related communications outside of their official working hours, particularly in the context of digital work and remote employment. Introduced in France in 2017 through the El Khomri Law, this right aims to protect work-life balance, especially as telework and platform-based labor continue to expand. While some companies have implemented policies limiting email communications outside working hours, enforcing this right remains challenging in environments where flexibility is prioritized over worker well-being.

Guild Unionism: Guild Unionism is a model of labor organization where workers are grouped according to their profession or specific skill, rather than by industry. Inspired by medieval guilds, it aims to protect specialized know-how, control access to the profession, and strengthen bargaining power by regulating the supply of skilled labor. This model contrasts with industrial unionism, which brings together all workers in the same sector regardless of their qualification.

Universal Basic Income (UBI): Universal Basic Income (UBI) is a social policy proposal in which all individuals receive a regular, unconditional sum of money from the government, regardless of employment status or income level. The concept aims to provide financial security, reduce poverty, and support workers in adapting to automation and job market transformations. Advocates argue that UBI could serve as a safety net for gig workers, whose incomes are often unpredictable and lack traditional social protections. Pilot programs, such as those in Finland and Canada, have tested the viability of UBI, with mixed results regarding labor participation and well-being. Critics highlight concerns over cost, inflation, and potential disincentives to work. However, as precarious employment grows in the digital economy, UBI remains a key topic in debates on labor policy and social justice.

ENDNOTES

1 . Business & Human Rights Resource Centre. (2024, March 8). The EU agreement on platform workers collapses. https://www.business-humanrights.org/en/latest-news/the-eu-agreement-on-platform-workers-collapses/

2 Katz, Marshall & Banks LLP, *Everything You Need to Know about California's AB 5 Gig Worker Law*, March 8, 2024. Available at: https://www.kcnslaw.com/blog/everything-you-need-to-know-about-californias-ab-5-gig-worker-law/.

3 Upwork. (2019). Freelancing and the economy in 2019. https://www.upwork.com/press/releases/freelancing-and-the-economy-in-2019

4 Council of the European Union. (2025, February 4). Platform work in the EU. https://www.consilium.europa.eu/en/policies/platform-work-eu/

5 Gobierno de España. (2021). *Law 12/2021, of September 28, on urgent measures for the regulation of work on digital platforms. Boletín Oficial del Estado.* https://www.boe.es/buscar/doc.php?id=BOE-A-2021-15548

6 Ticket School. (2023, June 15). *What does the New York Independent Drivers Guild do?* TicketSchool.com. https://ticketschool.com/blog/what-does-the-new-york-independent-drivers-guild-do/

7 Digital Platform Observatory. (2020). *The Independent Workers' Union of Great Britain (IWGB).* Digital Platform Observatory. https://digitalplatformobservatory.org/initiative/the-independent-workers-union-of-great-britain-iwgb/

8 App Drivers & Couriers Union. (2023, October 4). *Gig economy workers score historic digital rights victory against Uber and Ola Cabs.* ADCU. https://www.adcu.org.uk/news-posts/gig-economy-workers-score-historic-digital-rights-victory-against-uber-and-ola-cabs

9 Pactum. (n.d.). *The required components of autonomous negotiations platform: Pactum platform.* Pactum. https://pactum.com/the-required-components-of-autonomous-negotiations-platform-pactum-platform/

10 Freelancers Union. (2023). *Freelancing in New York Report 2019.* https://freelancersunion.org/wp-content/uploads/2023/03/Freelancing_in_New_York_Report_2019_1.pdf

11 Clean Energy Wire. (2024, mars 1). *Climate protesters in Germany join forces with public transport workers to push for change.* Clean Energy Wire. https://www.cleanenergywire.org/news/climate-protesters-germany-join-forces-public-transport-workers-push-change

Chapter 12
Empowering Workers in the Age of Automation:
Labour Union's Response to the Rise of Artificial Intelligence

Bhupinder Singh
https://orcid.org/0009-0006-4779-2553
Sharda University, India

Christian Kaunert
https://orcid.org/0000-0002-4493-2235
Dublin City University, Ireland & University of South Wales, UK

Manmeet Kaur Kaur Arora
https://orcid.org/0009-0002-5071-117X
Sharda University, India

Sahil Lal
https://orcid.org/0000-0001-9827-3717
Sharda University, India

ABSTRACT

Over the past several years, automation and Artificial Intelligence (AI) have advanced rapidly and begun to drive changes in the way that people work. It discusses the heterogeneous influence of these technologies on jobs and stresses that labour unions and education will remain crucial for empowering workers. It starts with the historical background of unions and technological change, focusing on how unions have adapted to protect workers in the shifting industrial context. Next, the authors discuss today's union tactics like bargaining over tech, lobbying in Washington for job-retraining programs and forming partnerships with community colleges to solve

DOI: 10.4018/979-8-3693-8049-9.ch012

skill shortages. This chapter argues that only through pro-active engagement by workers, employers and governments can it hope to ensure equitable outcomes from technological change. Promoting a mindset of lifelong learning and partnership will ultimately be essential for building an adaptable workforce that can succeed in a world with ever-growing technology.

INTRODUCTION

Automation and Artificial Intelligence (AI) are modern industry gold that has revolutionized sectors in how the work is carried out. Automation is technology that performs a task with little or no possibility of human interaction, usually based on preset rules (Acemoglu & Restrepo, 2018). These can be as simple as mechanical devices or complex software systems controlling relatively sophisticated processes. The word "automation" did not come into widespread use until the late 1940s when it was applied to the automobile industry to describe a growing dependence upon machines for increasing output in industrial fields (Baker, Bloom, & Davis, 2020).

At the other end of the scale, artificial intelligence supports systems that attempt to replicate some human cognitive functions (namely learning, reasoning and problem-solving (Brynjolfsson & McAfee, 2014). Traditional automation excels in performing repetitive tasks with precision but AI brings in the ability to adapt and make decisions based on data which allows systems to learn over time and become better. It's an important distinction — automation is about consistency and reliability; AI is about complexity and adaptability (Chui, Manyika, & Miremadi, 2016).

Advancements in technology, including machine learning algorithms, natural language processing, and big data analytics, have driven the rise of automation and AI. This ensures that organizations can process huge amounts of information in real-time and thus make better decisions faster with increased operational efficiency. In customer service, for example, AI will analyse the customer inquiry and respond immediately to provide answers or route the requests to relevant people depending on historical interactions (Daugherty & Wilson, 2018). But there is a concern that the swift integration of these technologies will harm employment (Deming, 2017). A common concern of automation in the workforce is affecting large scale displacement of jobs as machines perform what were once human jobs. Of course, some jobs will be lost but history indicates that technology also generates job opportunities with different skills. But the test4, is making certain personnel have got the relevant skills to survive in an increasingly automated environment (Eberl & Schmid, 2020).

Also, though the automation context goes beyond removing jobs; it's societal implications too (Edgerton & Roberts, 2018). As industries start to adopt these technologies more frequently, policies are increasingly required to deal with the ethical issues that come with AI implementation (Furman & Seamans, 2019). However, it is important to address concerns such as data privacy, algorithmic bias, and the risk of growing inequality so that automation can be utilized by society as a whole (Goldin & Katz, 2008). The backdrop of automation and AI is multi-layered intertwined as technology innovation as economic disruption and disrupted classes. In this chapter, we will go into more depth about how labour unions could react to these transformations so that workers can assert themselves in the automation era (Graetz & Michaels, 2018) (Hainmueller & Hiscox, 2010).

Labour unions have been important historical advocates for workers' rights and better working conditions. With automation and AI changing the world faster than ever before, unions are at a critical juncture (Houghton & Sheehan, 2020). Traditional roles of negotiating salaries and safe work conditions, job security are now coupled with the issues that come with growing technologies. Unions need to bring their strategies up with the modern economy and that means tackling some of the complexities automation introduced (ILO, 2021). It includes but needs not be limited to the role of debate for policy that lead fair transition for those workers who will eventually lose their jobs due to technological changes. These include negotiating severance packages for workers displaced by the transition as well as advocating for retraining programs to prepare them with new skills needed in changing labour markets. In unionized workplaces, where many workers already have higher bargaining power than their non-union counterparts, this will mitigate the worst impact of automation & enable workers to continue competing with robots. In addition, unions can also act as a link between those who work and who make any decisions on how we are going to use new technologies (Katz & Krueger, 2016) . Unions can encourage conversation regarding new automation efforts to demand transparency on how job and working environment will change due to such technologies. This bottom-up approach opens the door to decision-making processes with worker welfare as a priority while also maintaining organizational standards (Lee & Choi, 2020). One of the most important functions that unions play is affect policy making on local, national and international levels. With the rise of automation, governments are uncertain how to handle job loss and economic disparity, which means unions have an opportunity to push for laws that will protect worker rights in an automated workforce. This means advocating for things like universal basic income or job guarantees as protection for people made obsolete by the machines (Lichtenstein, 2020).

Unions benefit from an exceptional opportunity using technology themselves to organize. And digital tools can enable improved communication between members, automate administrative processes and mobilize to organize from the grassroots strategy level. By leaning into the technology instead of resisting, unions can gain a stronger ground in fighting for worker rights (McKinsey Global Institute, 2021). Labour unions are not just conservators of the old fabric of worker rights; they are players in the future game in a world of automation. How well they disassociate themselves with these old constraints, but still maintain their overall mission will be what determines their continued place within the modern economy (Mostafa, 2024).

THE ECONOMIC EFFECTS OF AUTOMATION ON JOBS

We will assess the extent to which automation displaces versus creates jobs in different sectors. Grasping this dynamic is key to formulating strategies that speak to workers feelings (OECD, 2019)

Unpacking the Historical Role of Labour Unions: We unpack aspects of labour unions and their history with technology in a way that can provide lessons to be recalled from previous experience for today (Pew Research Center, 2020).
Finding Out Strategies to Empower: Some strategies will be highlighted in the chapter by which labour unions could empower workers associated with automation. That means fighting for retraining programs, taking part in policy discussions and employing technology to organize (Robertson, 2020).
Coping with Ethics: There are ethical concerns about the implementation of AI, and this section will address how unions can push back on such dehumanization approaches among organizations (Schmidt & Hunter, 1998).
Imagining Future Storylines: Lastly, we will identify possible future storylines for labour unions in an automated economy. That means building stronger bonds with workers outside our sectors, and working to expand the social safety net for all of us (Schmidt & Hunter, 2004), (Stewart, 2020).

The Fundamentals of Automation and Artificial Intelligence

Automation and Artificial Intelligence (AI), two of the most important concepts in our modern technological era, have many similarities, however they differ in function and meaning. By definition, automation is the technology that performs tasks without human input. The technology behind Blockchain is used to automate processes, improve efficiency and eliminate potential human errors in many industries. Automation inherently involves doing the same task again and again at a high level of accuracy, so they are effective in executing repetitive tasks – allowing human workers to be released from the drudgery of mundane jobs with minimal critical or creative thinking involved. In some cases, in manufacturing, automated systems can assemble products on an assembly line and so does software when it comes to data management as well. There are different forms of automation that include:

Fixed or Hard Automation: This is used for high volume production with fixed processes. This typically includes highly specialized tools designed to do one thing.
Programmable Automation: which affords limited flexibility to the production process; such that changes in product design or output can be achieved through reprogramming.
Flexible or Soft Automation: This type is able to adapt to different tasks, and can be quickly reconfigured to work with multiple products or processes.

Conversely, Artificial Intelligences the creation of computer systems that is able to do cognitive tasks normally reserved for humans. It encompasses abilities like learning from experience (machine learning), understanding natural language (natural language processing), recognizing patterns, and making decisions based on data analysis. Traditional automation is limited in its powers for analysing data and identifying trends, Motgi says The beauty of AI systems is that they can analyse a rich tapestry of information across the entire enterprise and based on that analysis make predictions. Automation with AI = Intelligent Automation With this cognitive function, such systems may adapt to new information in order to enhance the traditional automation by enabling machines to make decisions autonomously. AI is used with chatbots to answer customer queries using the context of what they are asking and then use the personalization method by their previous interactions (Taylor, 2019).

A Brief History of Technological Evolution

The rise of automation and AI have come a long way over the centuries filled with leaps in tech. Automation has been practiced since ancient times & simple machines were designed to automatically perform repetitive tasks. An example would be that of the Greeks who had the water clock, which was a primitive type of automation that also regulated time keeping, but did not need any human intervention to do so. Likewise, in the 18th century with the Industrial Revolution, mechanization started to disrupt industries such as the steam engine and power looms for automated textile production. Innovations of the 20th Century Frontiers in tech permanently. The mid-1900s were the first-ever boom of direct interaction with computers and completely changed the way things had been done in multiple industries (Tsai & Chen, 2020). The first computers were used to perform calculations, but as the machines evolved and became more capable, they began automating complex processes in business sectors like finance and manufacturing. Robotic Process Automation (RPA) is also developing which was born in the late 20th century when businesses began looking to automate repetitive office work such as data entry. RPA is a tool that can use software robots or (bots) to perform tasks in digital systems further mimicking human activity, enabling organizations to create business processes where human error has been reduced and efficiency increased (West, 2018).

AI research began in the 1950s, with founders such as Alan Turing theorizing about machine intelligence. In the 1980s, machine learning algorithms were developed that allowed computers to adaptively learn from data instead of just relaying on a set program. And that change prepared the way to chatbot – modern AI-based applications. Thanks to growing amounts of computer power and more data in recent years, AI research has gone through a bit of a renaissance. Some big breakthroughs in fields such as natural language processing and image recognition are possible, thanks to machine-learning algorithms based on neural networks (deep learning). Current Landscape, we are in a point in time where automation and AI meet more than at any other point (Wang & Wang, 2020). As enterprises more and more learn the perfect automation with AI capabilities, various industries are adopting intelligent automation solutions. This combination gives organizations the ability to operate efficiently while making decisions backed by data. As history shows with automation and AI, there has always been a drive for greater efficiency and new frontiers of innovation. So, as we transition to an age of very rapid technological change, learning this lesson will be vitally important in helping us extract the lessons these technologies will teach us about our future working spaces moving forward.

Modern AI and Automation Trends

With Technological advancements and changing market demands, the landscape in AI and automation are ever-changing. These technologies are being implemented by businesses today against a backdrop of several defining trends:

Accelerated Adoption of Intelligent Automation: Businesses are realizing the value of implementing AI into traditional automation practices. Intelligent automation allows enterprises to automate not just rote tasks but also high-order processes that require some level of decision making. You see this trend with finance, healthcare, manufacturing, customer service – all industries (U.S. Bureau of Labor Statistics, 2020), (U.S. Census Bureau, 2021).

Emphasize on Data based Decision Making: Because of the endless data generated every day by businesses, there is a high admixture that all the data will be embedded in decision making because once you add some parameters into your report table/decision analysis it completely changes the outlook of where to go. One major advantage is that AI algorithms are capable of quickly analysing large datasets to find patterns, trends and anomalies that would likely go unnoticed by human analysts. These days, companies are using AI-driven predictive analytics to predict upcoming market changes and alignment of other operations (Van Reenen, 2018).

More Personalized Customer Experiences: Businesses are leveraging AI-powered systems to provide personalized customer experiences at scale. Companies employ this technology to give individualized offers and recommendations by examining customer behaviour data. One such example is the trend we are observing amongst e-commerce platforms, where personalized recommendations are necessary to greatly improve user engagement.

Expansion of Robotic Process Automation (RPA): RPA is gaining popularity since organizations are looking for ways to increase efficiency while automating repetitive tasks between departments like finance, HR, and IT support. RPA tools help enterprises reduce the costs related to manual work and ensure the accurate execution of tasks.

Cloud Synergy: The increasing prevalence of cloud computing makes advanced AI tools available to users without a significant on-premises infrastructure investment. Cloud-based infrastructures enable organizations, especially SMBs to utilize advanced AI capabilities for their businesses without large upfront costs.

Ethics in AI adoption: AI is being used as a precursor to the traditional methods we see right now under various sectors. Challenged with biased algorithms, issues of data privacy and transparency in decision-making processes: organizations have begun adopting responsible AI where fairness and accountability come to the forefront.

Changing the Workforce: Automation technology are influencing the roles and responsibilities of staff in every organization, because conventional jobs being automated, new opportunities developing that require technical skills to manage these technologies. Upskilling programs to prepare employees for this shift have thus become a necessity, as they are important for modern workforce resilience amid quickening tech changes (Wilson, 2020).

Impact of AI on the Workforce

While the subject of immense debate, particularly with regards to employment displacement vs creation and sector by sector issues; We can categorically state that Artificial Intelligence (AI) is here and more importantly here to stay. The red alert about loss of jobs has become a global concern for workers and policy makers alike as organizations embark on adopting AI technologies. But this story is more complicated than simply counting lost jobs against new ones created. A World Between a Rock and a Hard PlaceJob displacement is the term used when employees are rendered jobless as technology progresses in such a way that machines or software free up jobs usually taken by humans. Recent statistics tell us that while automation and AI technologies pose a real threat to jobs, the actual initial impact has not yet been as devastating as most of us fear only about14% of workers have previously seen job replacement through these types of process automations.

So far, companies have been implementing AI into their business without automating jobs overnight. As an example,35% of businesses use AI and another42% are working on implementing it. But the outlook could be worse down the line. Automation and AI advancements could displace up to 800 million jobs around the world by 2030.

This number highlights the billions of potential disruptions that could occur within industries highly reliant on routine and repetitive tasks. Manufacturing, customer service and logistics are especially at risk since AI is good at automating predictable tasks.

Job creation: a counterbalance Whilst fears of job displacement are valid, historically, technological advancements have created new jobs. While some roles will become automated through AI, if you look closely at the situation it also creates new jobs that require human oversight and intervention. According to the World Economic Forum, we could end up in net positive territory when it comes to jobs as well, with 85 million job losses expected by 2025, and approximately 97 million new roles projected to be filled a net of around plus 12 million jobs. Roles will focus on making sure the AI is managed properly, doing analysis, and coming up with new ideas that take advantage of AI features. For instance, as companies adopt AI technologies, there will be high demand for professionals with expertise in data science, machine learning and AI development. Moreover, employment that emphasizes on improving human-AI synergy are expected to be abundant because people will want to reach maximum productivity via combining machine and efficiency with human creativity.

A Need for Balance, The debate between job loss and creation calls for a more nuanced view. While we try to conceive how some jobs might get lost here's a nod to the sinners it is also essential in order that 1 spark of the light shields the wings of technically advance. This is all about smart workforce planning and reskilling workers training them with skills that will be required in the new job market. As organizations adopt AI technologies, they will also need to invest in training programs that equip employees for the new roles arising from these developments. As such, the workers seamlessly transitioning from traditional to modern roles will have two natural traits, Lifelong learning and adaptability. By building a culture of lifelong learning, companies can address the challenge of job displacement that AI might bring with it and ride on the new opportunities as well. To sum up, job displacement does remain a significant challenge faced by us in the age of AI but to put it only in that light overlooks the larger picture where it also presents with greater horizon and solutions through new avenues we create. Through the adoption of this Reskill or Adapt approach, the society can survive any transition period and will also be able to keep the workers within its workforce.

Changes in the Nature of Jobs and Skills Required

The growing adoption of Artificial Intelligence (AI) in different sectors is not only changing the count of jobs but also changing the way a job works and skills expected to execute the task. With organizations finding new ways to utilize AI technologies in their operations to drive efficiency and productivity gains, workers now must adapt to new roles that come with different responsibilities and skills. Change in Job Roles, The automation capabilities of AI have brought about a major change in job roles across sectors. Positions that once focused solely on repetitive work are transforming into roles requiring advanced problem-solving and critical thinking skills. In other words, instead of routine issues that customers sent in, they now have to deal with escalated matters that require nuanced understanding and emotional intelligence qualities even the best AI cannot copy. Furthermore, with AI systems performing the data-hungry tasks such as data entry or basic analysis, employees are forced to step up and move towards higher-order thinking activities those of creativity, strategy and creating decisions based on trends reported by data. This transition requires attention about what it considers as valuable skillset in the workforce of today. Changing Skill Demands As roles continue to evolve with the use of AI, so will the skillsets needed for these job functions. Workers will need a combination of technical skills as well as soft skills to survive in an increasingly automated world:

Technical Skills: Organizations will be on the lookout for people who are capable of leveraging these technologies and this will have an immediate effect on how data analysis or programming-related skillsets. Working knowledge of specialized visualization, if not all, will be a big plus in job availability in every sector as people will start knowing the capabilities and potential of machine learning (Zhang & Li, 2021)

Flexibility: With the speed of technology, companies need a workforce that can adjust to new tools/processes swiftly. Employees need to adopt a growth mindset always looking for opportunities to upskill or reskill where possible.

Working with AI: Future workers will need to learn how to work in tandem and modellable with the systems. Part of this is understanding when it makes sense to use automated tools and being able to step in as a human where necessary.

The importance of emotions: As routine jobs are done by computers, those that involve high interaction will be important As employees navigate complex social dynamics in their organizations, skills like empathy, communication and conflict resolution will be through the roof.

Creativity and Innovation in Thinking: Workers will stand out in an age when machines perform predictable activities. Those who have the ability to think out of the box or come up with creative solutions will always be in demand when organizations seek to deliver unique value in competitive markets.

Education and Training Because of these changes, schools have to change their curricula as well. Academia needs to work with businesses to ensure training courses give students the skills they need before taking their first job. Furthermore, organizations themselves could do more to help with employee development and embark on continual training drives around new technologies such as AI. More so, by investing in the growth of their workforce through workshops or offline courses they can create an atmosphere suitable for innovation while at the same time impacting employee satisfaction positively.

Sector-Specific Impacts

Due to the unique characteristics and operational details of each sector, the impact of Artificial Intelligence (AI) on employment varies greatly from one industry to another. But the extent of disruption varies greatly from one industry to another: albeit automation technologies displace jobs in some industries, other areas benefit from innovation and growth opportunities enabled by AI capabilities. Manufacturing In manufacturing — a sector long known for its utilization of automation, the introduction of new robotics with advanced AI capabilities have made production even more, Although classic assembly line jobs will reduce as robotic automation takes over repetitive tasks like welding or painting; replace them with new positions that focus in operational supervision over these automated systems Additionally, as smart factories become more common due to increased adoption of IoT devices that allow for monitoring machines remotely and predictive maintenance efficiency the need for technicians who can operate complex machinery comprising hardware/ software components has also been created, As such employment opportunities for people may change from traditional industrial/ manual labour to high-tech roles however seen on larger scale productivity benefits and quality of product obtains through mechanical engineering driven by intelligent machines.

The healthcare: The healthcare sector is at crossroads of technology advancement and human compassion a domain both arms needs to together

From diagnostic tools leveraging machine learning algorithms that analyse medical images to identify conditions more accurately than ever before to virtual assistants reducing clinician time spent on administrative tasks so they can spend more face-to-face with patients and less behind-the-scenes wrestling paperwork the applications are limitless. Note: Although there have been grave concerns related job losses among radiologist due majorly, increased dependence over automated diagnostic systems, one should understand this innovation is a compliment instead replacing humans. Similarly, a gradual shift towards personalized medicine powered by data analytics will drive up demand for professionals with genetics bioinformatics knowledge but most practice-based doctors today simply need to learn how to take advantage of these new technologies. Finance In finance, one of the industries ground as prediction on data processing, AI is revolutionizing investment methods by making the processes of risk assessment algorithms able to handling huge amount of datasets and spotting trends other than patterns as far as humans cannot go. Though lower entry-level jobs performing repetitive procedures such as bookkeeping may be subject to expunction, other higher forms involving analytics requiring critical thought still remain essential because most finance decision making require sound judgement through increased complexities between markets due developing technological advancements. Additionally startups using blockchain technology machine learning creating new jobs cybersecurity compliance ensuring transactions taking place protect conducted way of or security.

While smart money gradually integrates these innovative features into prior avenues; resulting in proprietary efficiencies adopted widely across disciplines hands on techie synergy remains something of a dream dark within both sectors.

This ultimately leads to improving operational efficiencies reducing overall supply chain logistics management & costs while adding immense value at customer satisfaction levels. But it could also drive new questions about workforce: With millions of retail jobs that will be replaced frontline cashiers facing competition with machines automated checkout systems have spread service of self-service kiosks will migrate to in-store and out-automated store potentially ‘suck’ the demand for town-hosting cashier position. Yet opportunities abound in places where human interaction is needed, for example developing personalized customer service experiences designing marketing campaigns focused behaviour ensuring customers have pleasant experience when moving through digital environments buying products solutions bringing people together answer questions navigate jungle devices. purchasing decisions simplified efforts guides possible demystifying process over time implementing technology improvements suited businesses supplying firms confidence boost competitiveness landscape altogether (Zuboff, 2019).

CONCLUSION

With the 21st century introducing both unique challenges and a revolution of technology, automation, and Artificial Intelligence (AI) are starting to have a discernible effect on the lives of workers everywhere. Such technologies are not just about changing business models, they change the framework of work. In this changing context, the importance of labour unions and the availability and quality of education and training to prepare workers for future requirements is crucial. Labour unions have always served as a stronghold for labour rights, and their importance increases in dire context of technological advancements. Rather than a losing strategy, a proactive collective bargaining approach would allow unions to bargain for job protections against displacement and retraining in new skills or jobs generated by automation. Incorporating technology into union agendas—from the call for transparency in AI use to the demand for equitable treatment of workers in the gig economy—signals a willingness to meet the moment but still protect worker interests. Focus on lifelong learning programs to help workers adapt to the threat of automatization. While industries are transitioning, workers do need to undergo a transition in their skill sets as well. Meaning Lifelong learning promotes a mindset of never-ending education and provides people with the skills they require that meet evolving work standards. Through the facilitation of flexible learning spaces and acknowledgement of previous experiences, stakeholders can form a setting in which workers are confident to chase their own personal and professional development. The partnership of labour union with the educational institution strengthens the impact of such training programs to upskill and reskill workers. Such partnerships harness the strengths of both sectors, keeping education relevant to industry needs while also giving workers easy access to up-skilling opportunities. Models of successful collaboration show how unions continue to open doors to training programs, negotiate job-related educational benefits for their members, and exert influence over the content areas that reflect changes in technology.

REFERENCES

Acemoglu, D., & Restrepo, P. (2018). Artificial intelligence, automation and work. *NBER Working Paper No. 24196*. National Bureau of Economic Research. https://doi.org/DOI: 10.3386/w24196

American Psychological Association. (2020). *Publication manualof the American Psychological Association* (7th ed.). American Psychological Association.

Baker, S. R., Bloom, N., & Davis, S. J. (2020). COVID-induced economic uncertainty: Evidence from the stock market. *Journal of Financial Economics, 135*(1), 1–22. DOI: 10.1016/j.jfineco.2020.05.002

Baker, T. E., & Thomas, G. M. (2021). Automation technologies' impact on employment dynamics across sectors [Report]. National AcademyofSciences.https://www.nasonline.org/news-and-multimedia/news/automation-impact-on-employment.html

Brynjolfsson, E., & McAfee, A. (2014). *The second machine age: Work, progress, and prosperity in a time of brilliant technologies*. W.W. Norton & Company.

Brynjolfsson, E., & McAfee, A. (2014). *The second machine age: Workprogress,and prosperity in a timeofbrilliant technologies*. W.W.Norton&Company.

Chui, M., Manyika, J., & Miremadi, M. (2016). Where machines could replace humans—and where they can't (yet). *McKinsey Quarterly*. https://www.mckinsey.com/featured-insights/future-of-work/where-machines-could-replace-humans-and-where-they-cant-yet

Cohen, L. E., & Nisbett, R. E. (1994). Self-protection against biasing effects in social judgment. *Personality and Social Psychology Bulletin, 20*(6), 700–712.

Daugherty, P. R., & Wilson, J. C. (2018). *Human + machine: Reimagining work in the age of AI*. Harvard Business Review Press.

Deming, D. J. (2017). The growing importance of social skills in the labor market. *The Quarterly Journal of Economics, 132*(4), 1593–1640. DOI: 10.1093/qje/qjx022

Dunlop, J. T., & Weil, D. (1996). Diffusionand performanceof workplace innovations: *Industrial Relations Research Association Conference Proceedings*,49(1),234–245.

Eberl, A., & Schmid, K. (2020). The impact of AI on labor markets: A systematic review of the literature. *European Journal of Industrial Relations, 26*(3), 221–239. DOI: 10.1177/0959680119881926

Edgerton, D., & Roberts, R. (2018). The impact of automation on employment: A review of the evidence from the UK and US labor markets. *International Journal of Human Resource Management, 29*(12), 1781–1804. DOI: 10.1080/09585192.2018.1481905

Furman, J., & Seamans, R. (2019). AI and the economy: An overview of the economic implications of artificial intelligence technologies for labor markets and productivity growth in the United States economy. Brookings Institution. https://www.brookings.edu/research/ai-and-the-economy/

Goldin, C., & Katz, L. F. (2008). *The race between education and technology*. Harvard University Press.

Goldin, C., & Katz, L. F. (2008). *The race between educationand technology*. Harvard University Press.

Graetz, G., & Michaels, G. (2018). Robots at work: Evidence from the US labor market. IZA Discussion Paper No. 11334. Institute for the Study of Labor (IZA). https://www.researchgate.net/publication/327890091_Robots_at_Work_Evidence_from_the_US_Labor_Market

Hainmueller, J., & Hiscox, M. J. (2010). Educated preferences: Explaining attitudes toward immigration in Europe. *International Organization, 64*(1), 1–30.

Hirsch,B.T.& Macpherson,D.A.(2000). Union membershipand earnings data fromthe Current Population Survey: Industrial Relations Section PrincetonUniversity.

Houghton, L., & Sheehan, P. (2020). The role of unions in a changing labor market: Challenges and opportunities for collective bargaining in the age of automation. *Australian Journal of Labour Economics, 23*(2), 123–146.

ILO (International Labour Organization). (2021). *World Employment and Social Outlook 2021: Trends 2021*. ILO Publications.

Kahn, L. M., & Lang, K. (2020). The effect of automation on labor market outcomes: Evidence from the US manufacturing sector. *American Economic Journal. Applied Economics, 12*(4), 1–29.

Katz, L. F., & Krueger, A. B. (2016). The rise and nature of alternative work arrangements in the United States, 1995–2015. NBER Working Paper No.W22667. National Bureau of Economic Research.

Lee, J., & Choi, Y. (2020). Automation and skill upgrading: Evidence from South Korea. Industrial Relations Research Series No.RR-20-03. Korea Labor Institute.

Levin, A. N., & Timmons, C. J. (2019). Labor unions' responses to technological change: *Industrial Relations Research Association Conference Proceedings*,72(2),125–138.

Lichtenstein, N. (2020). Labor unions in the age of automation: New strategies for a new era. *Labor Studies Journal*, *45*(2), 115–130.

McKinsey Global Institute. (2021). The future of work after [McKinsey & Company.]. *COVID*, •••, 19.

McKinsey Global Institute(MGI),(2020) .Automation will transformthe futureofwork: MGI Report.

Mostafa, K. (2024). *AI Agent Studio has streamlined my workflow* [Press release]. Automation Anywhere.

OECD. (2019). *Job creation and local economic development*. OECD Publishing.

Pew Research Center. (2020). *The state of American jobs* [Report]. Pew Research Center.

Pew ResearchCenter(PRC),(2017) .The stateof American jobs: PRC Report.

Roberts, A.(2021). Future-proofing jobs through education and training. Skills Commission Report.

Robertson, M. (2020). *Automation technologies' impact on employment dynamics across sectors* [Report]. National AcademyofSciences.

Russell, S., & Norvig, P. (2016). *Artificial intelligence: A modern approach* (3rd ed.). Pearson Education.

Schmidt, F. L., & Hunter, J. E. (1998). The validity and utility of selection methods in personnel psychology: Practical and theoretical implications of 85 years of research findings. *Psychological Bulletin*, *124*(2), 262–274. DOI: 10.1037/0033-2909.124.2.262

Schmidt, F. L., & Hunter, J. E. (2004). General mental ability in the world of work: Occupational attainment and job performance. *Journal of Personality and Social Psychology*, *86*(1), 162–171. DOI: 10.1037/0022-3514.86.1.162 PMID: 14717634

Stewart, J. (2020). Unions adapt to new realities in a changing economy. *Labor Studies Journal*, *45*(3), 245–261.

Taylor, M. J. (2019). The role of unions in shaping labor market policy during times of technological change. *Economic Policy Review*, *25*(2), 43–58.

Taylor, M. J. (2019). The role of unions in shaping labor market policy during times of technological change. *Economic Policy Review*, *25*(2), 43–58.

Tsai, C.-H., & Chen, L.-H. (2020). The impact of artificial intelligence on employment in Taiwan's manufacturing industry. *International Journal of Information Technology & Decision Making*, *19*(4), 1123–1145.

U.S.BureauofLaborStatistics.(2020). Employment projections for industries and occupations to 2029 [Report]. U.S.BureauofLaborStatistics.

U.S.CensusBureau.(2021). Current population survey [Data set]. U.S.CensusBureau.

Van Reenen,J.(2018). Increasing differences between firms: Productivity dispersion across firms is increasing [Report]. London SchoolofEconomicsandPoliticalScience.

Wang, Y., & Wang, Y. (2020). The impact of artificial intelligence on employment: Evidence from China. *China Economic Review*, *62*(3), 101295.

West, D. M. (2018). *The future of work: Robots AI and automation* [Report]. Brookings Institution Press.

Wilson, J. M. (2020). *Automation's impact on jobs: A survey* [Report]. Pew Research Center.

Zhang, C., & Li, J. (2021). Exploring the relationship between automation technology adoption and employee training needs. *JournalofBusinessResearch*, *129*(1), 453–463.

Zuboff, S. (2019). *The age of surveillance capitalism: The fight for a human future at the new frontierofpower*. PublicAffairs.

Chapter 13
AI and Workforce Transformation:
Impact Across Industries

Sandip Dey
https://orcid.org/0000-0002-1005-3304
Sukanta Mahavidyalaya, Dhupguri, India

ABSTRACT

The impact of artificial intelligence (AI) on work and labor unions is the topic of discussion in this paper. It starts with an RU Learning. Module covering the basics about AI, its past, and presence in an individual's working field. Machine learning, robotics and natural language processing are among the covered AI key technologies and their applications in manufacturing, healthcare, retail, finance, education, transportation, and others. Of some of the issues highlighted in the paper include threat posed by AI to human employment, the emergence of new skills required for AI integration and fairness and bias in AI systems. Last, it explores the trend, it how AI will bring new opportunities leading to new career opportunities and new ways of workflows. Trade unions may have to change direction to safeguard their members in this new emerging environment.

1. INTRODUCTION TO AI IN THE WORKFORCE

AI refers to a science that allows a machine to perform functions that would otherwise be done by a human being for instance to learn, think or solve a problem. They can be thought of as the process of providing data for learning into an algorithm to create models that would allow an existing system to decide or make what can be referred to as pattern recognition. The AI classification scale from virtual assistants,

DOI: 10.4018/979-8-3693-8049-9.ch013

for instance, bots to even greater intelligent machines that can be trained (Russell & Norvig, 2016). It can be observed that at the workplace, AI is used mostly to reduce the number of repetitive works done, aid in decision-making process and enhance productivity (Kaplan & Haenlein, 2019). For instance, AI in customer service, it can easily perform basic queries which relieves employees for deeper concerns. Because of its capacity to analyze huge data sets, AI serves numerous sectors, including health and production (Robert, 2017). AI in the workforce presents new potential yet many concerns can come with relation to insecurity of the job and equal work opportunities (Brynjolfsson & McAfee, 2014). In simple terms, it is useful to understand AI and its implications on today's workplaces and workforces.

AI in the workforce has been around for a very long time. The history of them began as early as the mid-1950s when the machines were initially applied for computation and clerical work (McCarthy, 2007). By the 1980s, expert systems in AI assisted other corporations in decision making by emulating the human factors (Russell & Norvig, 2016). They were employed in such sectors as finance industry and medical practice. In the 21st century, especially 2000s However, due to the enhancement of the computing speed and storage media used in the Artificial Intelligence. One AI type, known as machine learning, which helps systems learn from data, appeared more frequently in workplaces (Kaplan & Haenlein, 2019). Currently, there is increased adoption of artificial applications in organizations including; chatbots, virtual personal assistants, and robots. For instance, some firms in the retail industry employ artificial intelligence in demand forecasting as other factories employ robots in assembly (Robert, 2017). AI has the advantage of transforming many jobs and jobs generate by it. But this change had created problems of loss of employment and requirement of new skills (Brynjolfsson & McAfee, 2014).

Explicating the current and potential roles of machine learning, robotics and automation needs to be recognized as crucial because these technologies are changing the nature of work.

Machine Learning is a subfield of artificial intelligence that helps a computer program process data and generate results from that data. Machine learning on the other hand works through a set of algorithms rather than having a programmed task to accomplish. For instance, if customer data is fed to a machine learning program, the machine learning program can learn which products a particular customer is likely to purchase, (Russell & Norvig, 2016). This technology is currently in use within business organizations. Again, in marketing, users are studied to develop suitable advertisements to be posted. In the case of healthcare, machine learning assists the physicians by assisting the likelihood of the result of a patient by prior records (Brynjolfsson & McAfee, 2014).

Robotics refers to a field of engineering that seeks to design mechanical structures that can perform activities normally accomplished by human beings. Robots are used to have pre-programmed activities in an organization, like assembling of products and conducting surgeries. In manufacturing, robots work on the assembly line and they assemble parts than humans do with much efficiency and accuracy. This can result to high efficiency and reduced cost of manufacture (Kaplan & Haenlein, 2019). They may also be employed in areas that are fatal for people including disaster scenes or deep-sea drilling (Robert, 2017).

Automation can be defined as operation or process in which things are controlled by or done with the help of machinery or computers. It can be as basic as employing software to create and dispatch emails, to a fully integrated factory with robots and AI. Automating business processes results in time and cost efficiency for organizations. For example, technologies that control stocks can, on their own, monitor inventory and place requests for fresh stock (Teece, 2010).

Thus, the technologies have their advantages, as well as their problems. Machine learning robotics, and automation can promote changes that result in employment elimination affecting those governed by routines. Some employees many require retraining as a way of meeting the new demands in their line of work. Employees are key to this change and the relevant labor unions are instrumental in this process. They can support training employment programs which enable workers to acquire the skills required to in new employment positions created by such technologies. Also, unions can demand reasonable policies of treatment of the employees as fair is done as the industries transform.

Machine learning, robotics, data analytics and natural language processing (NLP) are used in almost all sectors to improve productivity and performance.

In the case of healthcare, machine learning is used and applied to patient data to give a corpus on health. According to Brynjolfsson and McAfee, for instance, AI provides insights into the risk levels of certain diseases, so patients can be treated Earlier. In the surgery procedures, robotic instruments are engaged to increase accuracy of the surgeons and reduce time taken in recovering. Robots help surgeons and the work in the operating room by undertaking precise procedures during operations.

In finance, it applies forecast of market trends for purposes of investment. Computational models are capable of handling large quantities of data way more efficiently than most humans are. by doing so, necessary risks can be identified and controlled, and the portfolios of financial institutions improved (Kaplan & Haenlein, 2019). Also, NLP is applied to the text basically being, such as customer feedback and social media, where it gives an understanding on how people think about products/ services.

In manufacturing, robotics replace human labor by doing repetitive actions throughout the production line. AI helps in the tracking of machinery for sign of failure or need of repair, thus avoiding expensive repair bills (Russell & Norvig, 2016). These uses have the net effect of raising efficiency and the quality of the products manufactured in the production facilities.

In retail, data analysis gives insights on the behavior of customers to the business. AI applied in retailers enables it to monitor the purchasing behavior of individuals, thereby helping to plan on the stock as well as the marketing strategies to be used (Robert, 2017). NLP tools drive chatbots through which clients can be helped through question answering or recommending products.

The AI technologies are changing different fields by assisting in making the right decisions, speeding up processes, and offering the better services. With these technological solutions being developed, they will define how specific industries as well as organizations in general, engage with their customers in the future.

2 CHALLENGES OF IMPLEMENTING AI TOOLS

The use of AI tools in organizational operations gets accompanied by the following challenges.

The four challenges facing social media marketing are: Cost is one of the biggest challenges. The implementation of artificial intelligence is not a cheap affair as it involves development of these systems. Today organizations require putting resources into new generation technology, right infrastructure, and qualified human resource (Brynjolfsson & McAfee, 2014). Unfortunately, organizations are likely to have difficulties with such investments, which means that there could be a gap in between large and small organizations.

The last issue is Data Quality. machine learning depends on data to build and take decisions. Consequently, it means that in the case of imprecise, unrepresentative or, incomplete data, the AI system will generate low quality outcomes. For instance, disparate training data affect the hiring or promotion process and produce unfair results (Robert, 2017). For organizations to train their AI effectively, they must ensure that they have reliable data.

Skills Gap is another concern and can be described as an impedance to effective organizational functioning. A big issue is the lack of workers who possess the skills required to interact with the AI technologies. Most human assets may need to be retrained to conform to new instruments and structures (Kaplan & Haenlein, 2019). As it has been established, this need for upskilling can lead to the delay of implementation.

The fourth is Resistance to Change. Five: Using AI to upscale the productivity of a firm may raise the concern of employees to be replaced thus develop anxiety to undertake new technologies. In this connection, organizations need to explain to workers about the purpose of using AI and that it would not replace the need for workers but complement them (Russell & Norvig, 2016).

Ethical Concerns are also present here. Firstly, one should mention that AI systems can make certain decision which are not transparent. For instance, it is hard for other users of that application to understand why an AI system made a particular decision, which causes the loss of their trust. Such ethical issues must be dealt with if organizations are to inspire confidence in their AI systems.

Concisely, the paper has also highlighted the myriad that organizations stand to gain by applying AI, in equal measure, the accreditation has also highlighted various challenges that organizations experience in the implementation of AI tools. Overcoming such scenarios is crucial in breaking barriers for integration and for assuring the feelings of the workers during this transition process. AI Tools face difficulties during implementation. We will encounter challenges when you put AI tools into operation. The biggest obstacle companies face with AI tools is their expensive nature. Companies spend vast amounts to purchase and activate AI platforms. Operating AI tools requires businesses to invest in system maintenance throughout their operational lifetime. The availability of qualified staff represents a serious difficulty. Employees struggle to work with AI tool functions. Staff education takes both time and financial investment from companies. When workers lack AI tool proficiency the technology will not perform as designed.

For AI tools to perform effectively they need access to significant amounts of data. Data preparation tasks prove hard for many businesses. Data often comes with missing or incorrect information. This can cause problems for AI systems. People also worry about privacy. AI systems depend on personal data which raises doubts about how this information will be processed or distributed. Organizations must maintain formal security guidelines to control their sensitive information which proves challenging to enforce. Many employees experience both fears and reluctance in using AI based systems. They fear losing their work positions and lack knowledge regarding these technologies. Organizations must understand and respond to employee concerns about AI tools to win their support.

A key summary of ethical concerns of AI in workforce & its immediate impact is presented in Table I.

Table 1. Key ethical concerns of AI in workforce & its impact

Ethical Concern	Impact
Bias and Fairness	AI may be designed or trained on a biased model that will make unfair decisions to most people.
Job Loss	AI has been said to take away people's jobs.
Privacy	AI can therefore capture a lot of personal information.
Lack of Accountability	There is a lack of accountability since nobody knows that an error was made by an artificial intelligence system.
Skill Gaps	Workers will lack the competency for new jobs that AI brings about.
Workplace Surveillance	AI can monitor its employees interfering with their privacy rights.
Inequality	Some of the workers may be more advantaged in situations where AI is applied as compared to others.
Dependence on Technology	Excessive use of AI tends to lower the skills of the human resource.
Decision-Making	AI can make important decisions without human input.
Change in Work Culture	AI can extend the manner individuals or groups can collaborate and engage with one another.

3 AI IN MANUFACTURING

3.1 How AI Improves Product Quality and Speeds Up Production

In the production of goods manufacturing is made faster and better with help of AI. As for how it does this, one way is it can rapidly identify potential issues arising with the line of production. Using AI, for instance, it is possible to verify imperfection in some parts and therefore prevent them from getting into the market affecting the customers (Zhong et al., 2017). Unlike typical machines, AI machines learn and 5develop on their own, therefore get more accurate as time passes (Lee et al., 2015). With AI it is also easy to control the rate of production depending on the customer traffic. This means that manufacturers can easily be able to increase or decrease production, and that at a lower cost (Ivanov & Dolgui, 2021). Another big help are robots with AI. They can perform the same operation, for several times without any sign of fatigue. This means that quality is improved as well as the rate of production.

AI also assist for the determination of the best feces where machines may likely to develop a breakdown. This way, effective maintenance takes place in an area before the equipment fails, therefore minimizing on production downtimes. Cooperatively, artificial intelligence benefits factories to produce more items within sort time span and with less imperfection thus assisting individuals and buyers.

3.2 Examples of AI Robots and Machines in Factories

People in industries use artificial intelligence robots and machinery to perform specific activities because it does them quicker and accurately. The following gives some examples of AI robots and machines; the most popular is the Robotic Arm. Robotic arms can mount small parts, weld, and even paint parts in automotive manufacturing industries (Leng et al., 2021). Due to their accuracy, they do not need to rest and this increases productivity of production. Another complex example that can be defined is autonomous mobile robots (AMRs). These robots transport components within a manufacturing facility, thus saving a considerable span of time for a worker to lift parts (Bischoff et al., 2010).

There are also inspection robots. High quality is achieved through intelligent use of robots in that they use vision systems to inspect products for imperfections. For instance, the robots can inspect electronics for minor defects, which would be hard for the naked eyes to see (Zhong et al., 2017). Cobots or the social robots to perform activities in cooperation with human operators, for instance, lifting heavyweight that may cause injuries (Riek, 2017).

Also, many factories incorporate AI systems in their equipment; the machines themselves can learn how to optimize their settings. For example, a machine might increase or decrease its rotations per minute or its temperature depending on the type of product its manufacturing (Lee et al., 2015).

3.3 Impact on Jobs in Manufacturing

How AI is revolutionizing workplace especially in relation to careers within manufacturing industries. This is so because some of the existing jobs are vulnerable because machines are now capable of performing routine tasks. For instance, they are useful in assembly, packing as well as sorting tasks that in the past would require human input (Acemoglu & Restrepo, 2020). This can make worker afraid of losing their job. Yet, we also see new opportunities in AI being opportunity to create new jobs. New forms of work enter factories as AI is required to be managed and reprogrammed, repaired and this calls for human beings (Manyika et al., 2017).

AI can also make jobs safer. Other high-risk activities such as lifting of abusive objects or engaging with toxic substances can be handled by these robots and not humans (Autor & Salomons, 2018). This avoids numerous accidents and ensures that the workers are safe and secure. It may also pay employees higher wages, offer more specific roles driven by skills that involve problem-solving and creativity (Bessen, 2018).

The impact on jobs can vary. Today, there are points where people work together with the AI machines and this makes them be more productive. This interaction between human and AI is referred to as collaborative automation because AI automates work processes while still requiring human intervention (Reddy et al., 2010). While AI modifies types of jobs and tasks it also provides new possibilities for gaining new skills and performing work in safer conditions.

3.4 Safety Improvements From AI Automation

Through this, AI automation minimized risks in factories leading to safer operational environment. First, robots can perform high-risk activities that can pose major risks to human life such as handling lethal chemicals or working under very high temperature conditions to reduce the risks associated with their work (Leng et al., 2021). This in a way minimizes accident and ensures that people are well protected. Moreover, AI can continuously observe the environment in the factories by predicting safety dangers, for example, gas leaks or overheated equipment. This helps prevent accidents.

Another area where AI is advantageous in is the way that, it assists with angering how machines are managed. Predictive maintenance also leverages AI to know when a specific machine is likely to develop a fault so that repairs can be done a priori. This minimizes on the possibilities of shock-break that may have adverse effects on the workers (Lee et al., 2015).

Industrial robots are divided into service robots that can safely share the workspace with people. It contains two features such a human detection feature that enables the robot to suspend its action in case it is too close to a human being (Riek, 2017). This eliminates cases of accidents and allows robots and human beings to work together intelligently.

In general, risks are minimized using AI and it is an added advantage since the environment at workplace becomes safer for the employees since dangerous tasks are well handled by AI.

4 AI IN HEALTHCARE

4.1 AI in Patient Diagnosis and Treatment

The use of AI technology improves how doctors find medical problems and select the best treatments for patients. This system checks medical pictures to discover hidden medical conditions especially tumors which regular vision cannot find (Esteva et al., 2017). AI uses treatment data to pick plans that have helped other patients with similar conditions. Chatbots and voice assistants help patients remember to take their medicines which leads to consistent treatment results (Cabitza et al., 2018). AI technology helps doctors find potential patient health issues earlier to start treatment faster (Topol 2019). The technology decreases diagnostic mistakes and assists doctors in providing superior patient care.

4.2 How AI Helps Doctors Make Decisions

Doctor decision-making becomes easier thanks to AI system that delivers instant reliable conclusions. The system uses patient information and test findings to recognize patterns that doctors can easily overlook (Topol, 2019). AI technology analyzes X-ray and CT scan images to find early disease indicators which strengthen doctors' medical evaluations (Esteva et al., 2017). It helps doctors design individualized treatments that work better because the system matches patient data with cases from other patients who had similar conditions (Shah et al., 2019). By looking at patient data and test results doctors use predictive models to find potential dangers and take early action (Obermeyer & Emanuel, 2016). AI systems make better results by using research-supported clinical guidelines (Cabitza et al., 2017).

4.3 Examples of AI in Medical Imaging and Records

A.I. helps medical teams understand patient information and imaging results better through diagnosis and treatment. The system analyzes different medical scans including X-rays MRIs and ultrasounds to spot minor breast cancer abnormalities (Esteva et al., 2017). By examining artery images and heart signals AI detects heart disease at an early stage for prompt medical action (Litjens et al., 2017). It helps doctors find Alzheimer's early by reviewing brain scan results (Afzal et al., 2019). By recognizing patient health risks and sharing follow-up updates AI helps doctors simplify care delivery and achieve better results (Rajkomar et al. 2019; Beam & Kohane 2018).

4.4 AI's Role in Managing Hospitals and Patient Data

The technology helps manage hospitals better and keeps medical records structured. By handling appointment bookings more effectively this technology makes patients wait less and helps doctors do their work better so hospitals can help more patients every day (Jiang et al., 2017). AI provides doctors the latest patient details to help them make prompt proper medical decisions (Rajkomar et al. 2019). The system reviews medical data to find important health developments and signs of future medical issues. AI tracks medication supplies and medical equipment to keep hospitals ready and prevent product waste (Topol, 2019). The technology carefully scans information to protect it from harm and ensures patients' private data stays protected as reported by Beam and Kohane in 2018 (Beam & Kohane, 2018).

5 AI IN RETAIL AND E-COMMERCE

5.1 AI's Role in Customer Service

The following is an example of how artificial intelligence is transforming customer service to make it easier for the people, and for the companies. Two of the most common AI applications are chatbots and virtual assistants that give an immediate answer to several customer inquiries. Chatbots are computer programmes that can speak as well as respond to some questions, aid with some functions, and sever multiple individuals simultaneously. It makes customer services quicker and minimizes the involvement of human employee's answers to customers' predictable questions (Roslan & Ahmad, 2023).

They are smarter than other conventional virtual aides and can perform better and ari tasks such as; appointment fixing and session recommendations. The applications of these assistants employ NLP that makes them more able to answer people's requests in a friendly manner. The use of this technology assists the companies in covering more focused and accurate services (Pantano & Pizzi, 2020).

Like any other technique in customer service, there are also some drawbacks of using Artificial Intelligence. It cannot solve all questions, especially if questions are complex or unique, so jobs with crisp work are still required. Also, some customers may not like speaking with an AI rather than speaking to a real person. Because machines are the ones implementing AI solutions, they may replace human workers interacting with customers (Pandey & Kumar, 2024).

5.2 Product Recommendations Based on Shopping Data

It assists the companies to suggest products to buy based on the customer's purchase history information processed by AI. When people buy products, or browse products, this activity is noted by Artificial Intelligence systems. Next, based on the information collected, some analytical tasks are solved to reveal customers' preferences and habits. This brings convenience in the suggestion of products that a customer is likely to purchase from the system (Zhang & Xiong, 2024).

Collaborative filtering: The most common method is based on the choice of similar customers. For instance, if two customers bought comparable products, the AI will recommend products that one customer has purchased to the other (Necula & Păvăloaia, 2023). The second approach is user's item-filtering by content, where the system reflects which items a particular customer has watched or bought to suggest similar ones by their characteristics like colour, size or brand (Liao & Sundar, 2022).

They make shopping easy and more personal through these AI based recommendations. Most organizations apply these systems to boost their sales as customers are more likely to make purchases from a recommendation. Nonetheless, certain clients are skeptical of data collection and find it intrusive; they are concern about privacies (Luo, Li, & Ye, 2023).

5.3 AI in Warehouse Management and Delivery

AI is transforming warehouse management and delivery by making processes faster and more accurate. In warehouses, AI helps organize and track inventory. It uses sensors and data analysis to know where each item is located, helping workers find products quickly. AI can predict demand for certain items, so warehouses can stock them in advance (Mittal et al., 2024). Robots are also used in warehouses to move products around. These robots work together with people, speeding up tasks and reducing errors (Nevliudovet al., 2021).

For delivery, AI helps by planning the best routes for trucks to save time and fuel. It uses traffic data and weather reports to find the quickest, safest paths for deliveries. This way, packages arrive on time, and companies can cut costs (Chen et al., 2024). Some companies are also testing delivery drones, which use AI to fly and deliver small packages to people's doors. This technology is still new, but it could change delivery by making it even faster (Rashidzadeh et al., 2021).

AI in warehouses and delivery makes things more efficient, but it can also replace human jobs. As robots and automated systems take over, fewer workers may be needed, raising concerns for labor unions about job security.

5.4 Impact on Retail Jobs and Skills Needed

AI is transforming retail occupations because it interactively consumes tasks and develops necessities for fresh competencies. Current robotics technology includes applications that help in shelf stocking, inventory management and customer checkouts. This leads to decreased demand on human workers in some positions and brings more efficient operation of the stores with less people (Braganza et al., 2022).

However, new roles are also forthcoming that shall call for a different approach all together. Employees at retail companies now must have digital competency in order to operate AI technology tools and applications such as inventory management programs or interactive customer service robots. Knowledge of how to interact with AI systems has become relevant as a component of job experience for retail workers (Mahmoud, Tehseen & Fuxman, 2020). There must also be improvements in workers as they are faced with problems that involve customers where the AI alone cannot solve. Creativity at work can help make many jobs easier to perform but it also means that without finding new positions to fill, workers can lose their jobs. Organized labor has a part to play here firstly by training workers, secondly by advocating that workers are treated well during such transitions (Nissim, & Simon, 2021).

6 AI IN FINANCE AND BANKING

6.1 AI's Role in Detecting Fraud and Managing Risks

The combination of AI technologies enables banks to find suspicious activities in their large data systems through pattern recognition that helps them stop frauds early to protect assets before losses grow significant (Zanke, 2023). As per Aziz & Dowling (2019), machine learning as an AI subfield predicts potential risks using historical data which allows banks to manage losses efficiently (Aziz, & Dowling, 2019). AI enhances accuracy and processing speed but fails occasionally to catch forms of fraud while simultaneously decreasing financial industry employment since machines replace many human roles in risk examination and fraud prevention work (Golić, 2019).

6.2 Use of AI for Personalized Financial Services

Through data analysis AI transforms banking by creating personal financial advice as well as automated investment recommendations and budgeting solutions which increases access to financial services (Sheth et al., 2022; Shiva et al., 2022). This system strengthens fraud prevention by determining strange transaction behaviors which protects client funds (Tamraparani, 2023). The benefits of AI financial systems for banking operations compete with privacy protection challenges and the inability to duplicate deliberative financial advisor routines. Banking institutions undergo job role transformations because automated systems accomplish tasks better than human workers thus potentially affecting employment numbers in banking functions.

6.3 AI in Credit Scoring and Lending Decisions

Through extensive data examination of payments and income with expenses AI determines accurate defaulter identification (Garcia & Singh, 2022). Machine learning-based credit scoring models built with AI capabilities identify payment prospects to achieve greater precision in addition to minimizing decision-making biases. Through these systems financial inclusion improves because they extend credit capability to individuals who were ineligible under conventional credit scoring systems (Saxena, 2024). AI models generate unintentional biases that negatively impact lending fairness until banks and regulators develop solutions to maintain equitable decisions (Anshari et al., 2021).

6.4 How AI Impacts Customer Interaction in Banks

The banking industry experiences a transformation through proactive features that deliver individualized services enabled by artificial intelligence. The combination of chatbots with virtual assistants implements round-the-clock support for actions such as balance inquiries and loan submissions thereby boosting operational speed alongside customer usefulness (Maseke, 2024). Artificial Intelligence delivers personalized money guidance through machine learning algorithms to assist customers in achieving financial effectiveness which now can help anyone (Christensen, 2021). This technology improves security through its fraud detection capabilities together with transaction screening and automated alerts for possible security threats (Johora et al., 2024). The integration of AI technology faces ongoing obstacles from customer privacy concerns together with the need for human staff relationship maintenance (Faishal et al., 2024).

7 AI IN EDUCATION

7.1 AI in Personalized Learning for Students

Through AI technology education receives a makeover with the creation of personalized adaptive learning methods that match specific student needs. Learning Management Systems (LMS) use performance-tracking capabilities to create personalized lessons which match student abilities and offer improved learning outcomes (Jammalamadaka & Itapu, 2023). About two decades ago people would spend huge amounts of time and effort on tasks that AI tools can now complete helping students improve their weak areas to save time and enhance learning efficiency. The knowledge of student performances allows educators to address specific educational needs of their students (Shoaib et al., 2024). Data privacy dilemmas along with elevated expenses and student reservations about AI-powered instruction techniques represent several limitations (Eden, Chisom & Adeniyi, 2024).

7.2 How AI Assists Teachers in Grading and Feedback

What AI does is make grading and giving feedback even faster and easier for teachers than it already is. Various AI created applications allow teachers see what the student has done and in case of subjects such as mathematics or science can even mark the answers and give results immediately. This saves time to teachers and let them teach most of the time than to be marking answers by hand as it is done by Li et al., (2023).

Another application of AI is in grading of essays and any written answers. In fact, using natural language processing NLP, AI can do the analysis of the student writing to detect grammar, spelling, and clarity. There are some specific AI tools that even provide feedback about clarity of the ideas. Nevertheless, AI in grading has restrictions, and it can sometimes fail to consider some context or idea which a regular teacher would notice (RE & Ermetov, 2024).

Other is that AI can provide feedback in individualized manner to the students. For instance, where a student makes a particular error – a computer can draw attention to it and guide the student on what to do right. This aids the students in their learning because they receive direct feedback on their work most often immediately after turning the work in (Patel & Singh, 2021).

7.3 AI Tools for Administrative Tasks in Schools

Information technology simplifies school management through automated scheduling and grading and attendance monitoring which benefits teachers alongside staff. The availability of AI systems delivers efficient meeting scheduling which lowers the frequency of scheduling mistakes (Rensfeldt & Rahm, 2023). The artificial intelligence-driven assessment tools analyze multiple-choice questions alongside select written entries which allows educators to concentrate directly on assisting their students (Naeem et al., 2023). AI attendance systems operate through facial recognition for tracking student attendance which helps staff do their work more efficiently (Morgan, 2021). The implementation of these tools entails financial costs and generates privacy risks since they require data gathering. The enhanced operational efficiency of AI systems could have negative consequences for school staffing thus threatening job availability.

7.4 Future Impact on Teaching and Learning Methods

The modern learning process receives transformative advancements through artificial intelligence which develops customized educational experiences based on individual student speeds and learning approaches. AI systems detect which learning exercises students need while maintaining their interest and blocking potential boredom (Saaida, 2023). Teacher workload simplifies thanks to artificial intelligence which enables them to concentrate on creating lesson plans as well as individual student mentoring. Automated grading tools deliver fast feedback to students that lets them learn better and reduce future academic errors (Langove & Khan, 2024). The widespread use of AI systems exists alongside risks of replacing human teachers from their classroom roles and requires attention to data security and algorithmic prejudice problems (Irfan et al., 2023).

8. AI IN TRANSPORTATION AND LOGISTICS

8.1 How AI Improves Delivery Routes and Shipment Tracking

The modern learning process receives transformative advancements through artificial intelligence which develops customized educational experiences based on individual student speeds and learning approaches. AI systems detect which learning exercises students need while maintaining their interest and blocking potential boredom (Saaida, 2023). Teacher workload simplifies thanks to artificial intelligence which enables them to concentrate on creating lesson plans as well as individual student mentoring. Automated grading tools deliver fast feedback to students that lets them learn better and reduce future academic errors (Langove & Khan, 2024). The widespread use of AI systems exists alongside risks of replacing human teachers from their classroom roles and requires attention to data security and algorithmic prejudice problems (Irfan et al., 2023).

8.2 Role of AI in Self-Driving Vehicles and Safety

Non-human-controlled vehicles revolutionize transportation systems because they work independently. The vehicles operate based on set pathways as sensors alongside cameras and AI components analyze their surroundings to minimize human mistakes and boost security measures (Liu, Wang & Vincent, 2020). Self-driving trucks paired with drones speed up delivery operations which leads businesses to save money (Smith, 2023). Through its integration into transportation systems AI decreases accidents and decreases fuel use which achieves two goals: improved safety outcomes and environmental advantages. The adoption of technological systems in adverse conditions faces technical problems while uncertainties loom over job sustainability for truck operators and carriers (Viktor & Szeghegyi, 2022).

8.3 Impact on Warehouse Jobs and Transport Roles

Artificial intelligence systems now automate tasks which result in labor transformations across warehousing and transportation services. AI robots in warehouses demonstrate higher operational speeds for picking and sorting tasks than human workers but such automation reduces job availability for personnel (Bałys et al., 2022). Delivery robots alongside autonomous trucks from Nikitas, Vitel and Cotet (2021) have speeded up distribution operations while decreasing expenses despite jeopardizing employment security for truck drivers. Unions try to respond to this shift through their advocacy for upskilling which helps employees transition between jobs (Jones et al., 2023).

8.4 Benefits of AI in Reducing Transport Costs

Through making the systems much more efficient, transport costs are easily reduced through with the use of AI. It can even plan how to get from one point to another taking the least time and fuel consumed. For example, it can use traffic pattern data and weather data to advise drivers who prefer not to waste time on what route to take (Abduljabbar et al, 2019). This reduces fuel cost and enable delivery of products as expected by the businesses and its customers.

AI can also help maintain vehicles in that it can predict when different parts will require repair or replacing. Reliability maintenance calls for the constant usage of sensors in checking on the health status of a vehicle and lets the company know when it is about to breakdown. This minimizes repair expenses and eliminates unanticipated production interruption (Alqasi et al, 2024).

Another transport sub-sector where AI could reduce transport costs is self-driving vehicles. The driverless cars have not yet entered the common use but experiencing fast developments and may lead to less need for drivers and thus lower the demand for workforce in the future A summary of potential benefits of AI in the workforce is listed in Table II.

Table 2. Potential benefits of AI in the workforce

Benefits	Description
Promote Fair Wages	This means that unions struggle to ensure that the employees with such jobs in the technology sector are paid better.
Protect Workers' Rights	Unions assist the workers in that, they protect the life of the workers and give them a deserved treatment.
Advocate for Training	Trade unions back learning for new skills.
Ensure Job Security	Employer associations act to preserve jobs which AI may transform.
Address AI Bias	Unions assist to combat against prejudice by the AI.
Support Worker Involvement	Through unions, an organization can encourage the workers to be involved in decisions making concerning the use of Artificial intelligence.
Enhance Workplace Safety	AI tools that are said to help unions keep workplaces safe.
Foster Collaboration	Unions foster together working relationships between employees and employers.
Improve Job Quality	Nothing makes jobs better and more fulfilling than having a Union to speak for the employees.
Navigate AI Changes	Unions help the workers to navigate through the changes occasioned by AI.

A pictorial illustration on how AI, nowadays, is applied in different industries is shown in Figure 1.

Figure 1. AI in different industries

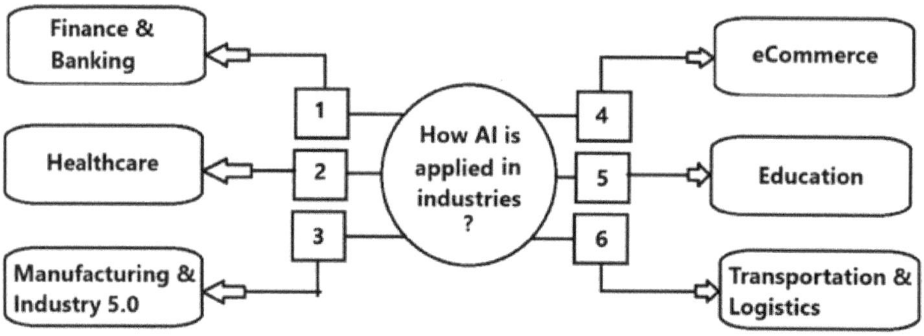

9. FEW INNOVATIVE AND NOVEL IMPACTS OF AI IN WORKFORCE

9.1 Artificial Intelligence Systems Support Easier Recruitment and Selection

Through AI technology companies locate qualified employees in short order. Companies use HireVue and Pymetrics AI technology to analyze resumes and conduct video interviews while measuring job-related skills and personality traits. Unilever's AI screening tools help both speed up the hiring process and lower hiring bias according to research done in 2017 by Chamorro-Premuzic (Chamorro-Premuzic, 2017).

Impact: The recruitment system functions better and more quickly while staying unbiased for everyone.

9.2 Automation of Routine Tasks

Advanced systems handle mundane tasks in data entry programs and appointment setting and assist with customer inquiries. ChatGPT helps Shopify deliver fast responses to customer questions that strengthen how customers feel about the service they receive. As the report by Lacity et al. for 2021 shows HSBC employs Robotic Process Automation to automate their banking account processes (Lacity, Willcocks & Gozman, D. (2021).

Impact: The workforce devotes their time to thoughtful work while reducing job-related pressure.

9.3 AI for Personalized Employee Training

The technology builds specific employee training that matches each person's abilities and requires. Through artificial intelligence Coursera and Degreed suggest training programs to users. Through AI-based training PwC helped its staff at work with data analytics and enabled them to use modern business tools (Aukasik-Stachowiak, 2024).

Impact: Employees develop new knowledge more quickly while keeping their job skills up to date.

9.4 Artificial Intelligence Supports Better Job Safety at Work

With AI systems employees stay safe because the technology looks for possible risks at their workplaces. Siemens installs AI systems that watch factory environments and. warn when hazards arise. StrongArm Technologies develops AI-powered wearables to lower warehouse worker injury risk according to Harvard Business Review in 2020 (Downes et al., 2021).

Impact: Our health and safety standards decrease worker injuries which helps them stay healthy at work.

10. CHALLENGES OF AI INTEGRATION IN THE WORKFORCE

AI is proving to deliver drastic revolutions into the place of business and employment and major concerns have been felt regarding job displacement, skill mismatches, privacy, equity and training. Here's an overview of these issues:

10.1. Fears for Unemployment Caused by AI

Around the world, several activities that are recurrent and mundane can be performed by AI. It is urgent for several jobs such as the data entry, customer services, and manufacturing jobs because AI is efficient and cheaper in comparison to most jobs (Badet, 2021). Which could eventually result to employment loss within specific industry segments leaving employees who depended on such positions to earn a Living defeated. But today labor unions can hardly remain calm and they are fearful for many reasons not least because job displacement is a probable cause of job insecurity among many employees. Consequently, the advancements made to organizations by these new technologies are that requirement for human capital in some activities may significantly reduce as more companies embrace artificial intelligence (Oswald, Behrend & Thompson, 2019).

10.2. Skills Needed for AI Jobs

AI of course also generates new opportunities as it eliminates the need for some positions. Nevertheless, these new roles entail elaborate skills notably; coding, data analysis, machine learning and problem solving (Sidhu et al., 2024). It means the demanding nature of the AI roles requires a skills upgrade to meet the technical requirements that are not easy to meet for workers with no relevant experience. Some workers require assistance with training programs, and unions establish that it is crucial for employees to provide them with an option for skill acquisition in a world dominated by artificial intelligence (Irfan, Aldulaylan & Alqahtani, 2023).

10.3. Privacy Considerations Concerning the Data Applied by AI

AI systems are power by algorithms which means that they operate based on data, much of which may be personal. This is a privacy issue because some AI technologies are designed to gather and analyses specific data such as customers' activity or employees' performance (Langove, & Khan, 2024). Sometimes data can be collected without much stringent privacy and this makes (worker's and consumer's information) vulnerable. Employees' associations state that personal information belongs to the employees, and there is hype that the policies governing AI should prevent invasions of privacy (Yanamala, Suryadevara, & Kalli, 2024). Self-generated data must be handled with proper ethics so that it does not end up being misused by organizations.

10.4. Smarter, Wiser, More Understanding: AI Bias and Fairness in Decision-Making

Far from being impartial themselves, they are capable of being as biased as their programmers/amalgam creators and as the data they tend to gobble on. Even though they are sophisticated, if there is biased data fed into the AI system, then that system will make biased decision. For instance, AI may be used in hiring processes, implying that if data prepared has some specific gender or racial disposition, AI will discriminate some people (Smith & Johnson, 2023). This is a critically important problem for trade unions because unfair decisions made by false artificial intelligence could harm workers during hiring, promotion, or evaluations. To avoid such issues, fairness in AI requires close attention and diverse dataset (Badet, 2021).

10.5. AI Workforce Training

That is why, it is crucially important to invest in the workforce training to prepare workers for the future. AI affects many traditional occupations and may turn them over or entail the acquisition of extra abilities. Technological training courses in area of AI, computer programming, mathematical models for data analysis, and machine learning are essential to assist workers. However, such programs are financially costly and cannot be availed by many schools and institutions of learning. SMEs are free to point out that companies and governments should bear the cost of retraining to ensure that workers are not left jobless when it comes to AI (Sidhu et al., 2024). This training will enable the employees to be relevant in the organization and to be able to take up other positions which are created by AI technology (Oswald, Behrend & Thompson, 2019).

AI is on the process of changing the job market for the better and for the worse. AI offers new opportunities offering new skills that can cause job opportunities at the same time brings threats like job threat, threat to privacy and threat of bias. Such issues therefore can be solved with efforts from the corporate world, government, and unions. In that capacity, they can coordinate to maintain fairness across the board, as well as offer any mandates for training as well as to defend the confidentiality of the workers. With this support, the workers will be able to search for jobs and fit them appropriately in the new world of Artificial Intelligence era.

11. FOCUSES ON SOLUTIONS

When workers interact with AI they face ownership threats and training needs. Our society has solutions at hand to assist workers in dealing with the current changes. Our training programs show employees how to develop new abilities. They can now use artificial intelligence systems rather than losing their positions (Tariq, 2024). Both governments and businesses should help their employees stay updated through program development and web training programs.

Creating new positions that AI technologies can't automatically perform offers a smart solution. Organizations regularly need people who think creatively, understand emotions, and make decisions. A company can so research and hire new staff while allowing AI to handle automated work tasks as revealed (Dellermann et al., 2021). Employers gain the best results with new technology when they combine AI systems with the specific skills of their staff.

Officials create workplace policies to protect employees' employment rights. Companies legally must give their staff AI adaptation training before installing new system. A minimum wage regulation for workers whose jobs AI replaces proves useful.

All industries must work together with labor unions and government institutions. This approach makes sure AI creates the same kind of improvement for workers and industries. By working together companies and institutions can develop lasting methods to control AI impacts on work and business sectors (Shenoi et al., 2024).

12. GUIDELINES FOR UNIONS TO ADDRESS WORKERS' RIGHTS IN THE ERA OF DIGITALIZATION AND AI

12.1 Advocating for Reskilling and Lifelong Learning

Working unions need to establish partnership programs with organizations to deliver training services that teach workers about new technology systems. The organization needs to push for employer-invested training programs aimed at re-skilling employees before widespread job reduction happens (Li, 2022).

12.2 Ensuring Ethical AI Practices

Unions should fight for complete visibility about the use of artificial intelligence while simultaneously demanding unbiased functioning of algorithms and protection for worker rights. Yearly negotiations by labor unions should create both sound safeguards to prevent the misuse of surveillance technology and new AI-led solutions that improve worker capabilities rather than take them out of jobs (Berg et al., 2018).

12.3 Securing Fair Labor Contracts

Digitalization creates imprecise employment classifications which generate unstable job situations. Worker unions need to fight for changed employment laws which would allow all independent contractors to secure equivalent protection against social risks and fair financial compensation alongside benefits.

12.4 Promoting Worker Participation in Decision-Making

Labor organizations must make sure employees have an official say about decisions that impact automated systems use and work environment redesign. Corporate AI governance frameworks become accessible for workers when organizations maintain ongoing meetings and allow employees to participate fully.

13. FUTURE TRENDS AND AI'S ROLE IN JOB TRANSFORMATION

13.1 New AI Technologies and New jobs

At the present time, Artificial intelligence is on the rise and results in new technologies' emergence. Some of them are Natural Language Processing, Robotics, Machine Learning (ML). NLP is the capability that enables machines to read data content in a way that a man can direct (Barton et al., 2021), while on the other hand, ML the capability that enables a system discover methods for enhancing the result as time elapses (Brynjolfsson & McAfee, 2017). In manufacturing industries and also in the warehousing sector, automation with robotics is now employed more often to do actual physical work (Wilson & Daugherty, 2018). These technologies generate new jobs, positions, the need for new experts such as data scientists, AI trainers, and robot operators. Professionals will have to acquire new technical knowledge that will allow them to operate in these new positions. Presence of these jobs bring evidence that although AI is replacing some jobs, it is also creating new jobs with new skill set (RE & Ermetov, 2024).

13.2 Forecasted Shifts in Different Sectors

At the core of the new operating model AI is revolutionizing many space. In healthcare, AI assisting in the diagnosis of disease and patient data (Obermeyer & Emanuel, 2016). In manufacturing, robots help people to do work, and it increases speed and safety in the process (Acemoglu & Restrepo, 2020). Several retail firms apply artificial intelligence as a tool in identifying customer's preference in products and recommending them products to buy to make their shopping more enjoyable (Davenport & Ronanki, 2018). Finance deploys AI primarily to identify fraudulent activities and provide short time decisions for loans (Chui, Manyika & Miremadi, 2016). In the future, AI seems to bring new changes to these industries to enable some tasks to be completed more efficiently. But it will reduce employments in conventional occupations and give rise to opportunities in technology careers. It is important for workers across these

13.3 In How Way AI Could Generate New Kinds of Labor

'It's certainly not just automating what used to be done by people, AI is also coming up with new tasks.' Even more are the novelties that are more observable concerning the AI advancement, such as AI ethicists, data privacy officers, human-AI interface designers, and others. The AI ethics consultant ensures that no discrimination and prejudice find their way to the Artificial Intelligence system (Binns, 2018). When personal data is being utilized in AI, data privacy managers guarantee it is secure and complies with the law (Goddard, 2017). Human machine interaction designers enhance way humans use artificial intelligence systems. Thus, as the AI develops these new jobs will become relevant. The first of these roles is centered on making AI safe, fair, and accessible or easy to use by all (Autor Salomons, 2018). Therefore, while eliminating some of the previously typical professions, it makes new professions linked with the support and development of AI usage.

13.4 Future Advantages and Disadvantage of Artificial Intelligence in Employment

AI is useful in the workforce; however, it also has drawbacks. A plus is efficiency. Due to AI many tasks which earlier used to take hours are now completed in minutes this provides companies with an opportunity to manufacture more products and deliver more services (Frey & Osborne, 2017). AI also helps reduce workplace risks associated with performing certain tasks. But the risks are that employees lose their jobs The everyday knowledge will now turn to some of the risks. There are certain operations possibly monotonous operations, and those operations are performed by robots and thus the roles are robotized leaving the workers rms unemployed (Manyika et al., 2017). In addition, people begin to depend on the AI systems and do not develop some of the skills that the AI is doing for them (Susskind, 2020). AI does bring with it potential threats as well as benefits and the ramifications that come from it are going to be experienced in the future when sectors, administrations, and cultures handle these chances as well as risks. Voluntary training /re-skilling campaigns are what is needed to help the workers move to such changes. AI, nowadays, used in different industries is tabulated in Table III.

Table 3. AI in various industries

Name of the Industry	Impact of AI
Manufacturing	AI makes products faster and safer.
Healthcare	AI supports doctors in the diagnosis and treatment of clients.
Retail	AI enhances the customer and sales.
Finance	AI transport the concept of fraud management and risk management with ease.
Education	AI can deliver further individualized material to each student.
Transportation	AI helps to deliver goods more efficiently.

Key summary about the research work presented in this paper is presented in Table IV.

Table 4. Key summary about the research work

Category	**Key Information**
Research Question	What are implications of AI on the functions of labor unions? This question remains relevant to know how a union can be helpful to employees. It will discuss issues to do with job stability, new skills that will be required and how the unions will be able to defend individuals' rights in artificial intelligence. The purpose of such discussion is to analyze the opportunities for unions to evolve in response to new conditions caused using AI.
Significance	The purpose of this paper is therefore to explain how artificial intelligence impacts jobs and workers' unions. They have the information of their rights in terms of employment in organizations in the modern world. The paper draws attention to the conditions and role of unions in addressing the emerging challenges arising from the use of AI. This is crucial to eliminating prejudice and protecting employee's place of work.
AI and its operational definition	AI refers to intelligent machines that can purpose, discern, and adapt as individuals. It has replaced jobs since the 1950s, to bring ease and increasing the rate at which certain tasks are accomplished. Three arguments for the use of AI for businesses include its enablement of growth and competitiveness.
Brief Details regarding Principal AI Technologies	Subfields are for example machine learning (where machines are taught from data), robotics (machines that can perform tasks), and automation (performing tasks with the help of machines and not necessarily man power). These tools present issues such as, cost and training issues.
AI in Manufacturing	AI assists in achieving better products more rapidly and with less risk. Manufacturing industries employ uses robots at workplaces, this alters the way people work but enhances security.
AI in Healthcare	AI assists the doctors in diagnosing their patients. It enhances practical decisions and health records as well.
AI in Retail and E-Commerce	AI enhances customer relations thus suggesting products to buy based on customers' shopping tendencies. It also deals with management of warehouses and deliveries hence has impact on the jobs in retail.
AI in Finance and Banking	AI to assist in fraud detection and risk management. They provide services that are customized and influence the ways in which most banks engage their clientele.
AI in Education	From an AI Tablet, learning is personalized for the students and there is grading assistance for teachers. It helps to diminish bureaucratic functions or procedures within the schools.
The major area where Artificial Intelligence has made its way is in the transportation and logistics.	AI manages delivery routes and makes them safer in self-driving vehicles affecting jobs in transportation. It also helps cut costs.
Issues of AI implementation at the workplace.	People have concerns regarding loss of employment resulting to AI, skill deficiency as well as self-organized prejudice in AI. It is crucial for the training of the workers.

continued on following page

Table 4. Continued

Category	Key Information
Future Trends & The Application of Artificial Intelligence About Job Redesign.	Some new AI technologies may lead to new jobs being formed and other new AI technologies may alter existing jobs. Future impacts also will play positive and negative effects on the workers.
Conclusion	Trade unions need to consider impacts of AI in the work force for the defense of human rights at the workplace.

14. CONCLUSION

To sum up, the effect of AI is the crucial impact on several spheres which are changing the job and working conditions. In sectors such as in manufacturing, health care, retail end even education there is visible instance on uses of Automation and Data analysis that are brought by artificial intelligence technologies. These technologies contribute to efficient production and increased quality, alongside enhancing the safety of several procedures. What is more, the above mention advantages are not without their drawbacks. A major worry for many workers is that they will be replaced by AI at workplaces where automation is possible. This you can imagine raises pertinent questions in employment security and training or development of new skills. To labor unions it must be understood that this is the new order that they do require and must seek ways of how to assist the worker's given these changes in their work places.

Moving into the future, the AI will help to set the pace as to how the workforce will look like. Training of these workers and human intelligence will therefore be imperative as AI tools become more sophisticated, and the nature of skill needed to work together with the machines equally changes. Union became crucial here in a way that they can assist the worker or employees to get new skills in handling the technology and provide the public forum where the workers can express about how the AI is changing or will change their work. This will assist in achieving adaptive goals hence ensuring that AI implementation work for both businesses and employees. Employers, employees & unions have equal roles to play when it comes to AI within the workplace and managing the circumstances it brings. Firstly, utilization of AI technologies is reasonable only in case it is done reasonably, to help the people who are in the workforce to get the improvements they are to be provided for when they entered the world of AI systems.

REFERENCES

Abduljabbar, R., Dia, H., Liyanage, S., & Bagloee, S. A. (2019). Applications of artificial intelligence in transport: An overview. *Sustainability (Basel), 11*(1), 189. DOI: 10.3390/su11010189

Acemoglu, D., & Restrepo, P. (2020). Robots and jobs: Evidence from US labor markets. *Journal of Political Economy, 128*(6), 2188–2244. DOI: 10.1086/705716

Acemoglu, D., & Restrepo, P. (2020). Robots and jobs: Evidence from US labor markets. *Journal of Political Economy, 128*(6), 2188–2244. DOI: 10.1086/705716

Afzal, S., Maqsood, M., Nazir, F., Khan, U., Aadil, F., Awan, K. M., Mehmood, I., & Song, O. Y. (2019). A data augmentation-based framework to handle class imbalance problem for Alzheimer's stage detection. *IEEE Access : Practical Innovations, Open Solutions, 7*, 115528–115539. DOI: 10.1109/ACCESS.2019.2932786

Alqasi, M. A. Y., Alkelanie, Y. A. M., & Alnagrat, A. J. A. (2024). Intelligent Infrastructure for Urban Transportation: The Role of Artificial Intelligence in Predictive Maintenance. *Brilliance: Research of Artificial Intelligence, 4*(2), 625–637. DOI: 10.47709/brilliance.v4i2.4889

Anshari, M., Almunawar, M. N., Masri, M., & Hrdy, M. (2021). Financial technology with AI-enabled and ethical challenges. *Society, 58*(3), 189–195. DOI: 10.1007/s12115-021-00592-w

Aukasik-Stachowiak, K. (2024). The Development Perspectives of Human Resources in Relation to Artificial Intelligence. *Scientific Papers of Silesian University of Technology. Organization & Management/Zeszyty Naukowe Politechniki Slaskiej. Seria Organizacji I Zarzadzanie*, (199).

Autor, D., & Salomons, A. (2018). Is automation labor-displacing? *Productivity growth, employment, and the labor share* (No. w24871). National Bureau of Economic Research.

Autor, D., & Salomons, A. (2018). Is automation labor-displacing? Productivity growth, employment, and the labor share. *Brookings Papers on Economic Activity, 2018*(1), 1–63. DOI: 10.1353/eca.2018.0000

Aziz, S., & Dowling, M. (2019). Machine learning and AI for risk management. *Disrupting finance: FinTech and strategy in the 21st century*, 33-50.

Badet, J. (2021). AI, automation and new jobs. *Open journal of business and management, 9*(5), 2452-2463.

Bałys, P., Buła, P., Dziedzic, D., & Uznańska, M. (2020). The future of work in automated warehouse from the perspective of the employees. *Contemporary organisation and management. Challenges and trends*, 267-281.

Barton, D., Woetzel, J., & Seong, J. (2021). The future of work after [McKinsey Global Institute.]. *COVID*, •••, 19.

Beam, A. L., & Kohane, I. S. (2018). Big data and machine learning in health care. *Journal of the American Medical Association*, *319*(13), 1317–1318. DOI: 10.1001/jama.2017.18391 PMID: 29532063

Beam, A. L., & Kohane, I. S. (2018). Big data and machine learning in health care. *Journal of the American Medical Association*, *319*(13), 1317–1318. DOI: 10.1001/jama.2017.18391 PMID: 29532063

Berg, J., Furrer, M., Harmon, E., Rani, U., & Silberman, M. S. (2018). Digital labour platforms and the future of work. *Towards decent work in the online world. Rapport de l'OIT*.

Bessen, J. (2018). *AI and jobs: The role of demand* (No. w24235). National Bureau of Economic Research.

Binns, R. (2018). Fairness in machine learning: Lessons from political philosophy. *Proceedings of the 2018 Conference on Fairness, Accountability, and Transparency*, 149-159.

Bischoff, R., Kurth, J., Schreiber, G., Koeppe, R., Albu-Schäffer, A., Beyer, A., . . . Hirzinger, G. (2010, June). The KUKA-DLR Lightweight Robot arm-a new reference platform for robotics research and manufacturing. In *ISR 2010 (41st international symposium on robotics) and ROBOTIK 2010 (6th German conference on robotics)* (pp. 1-8). VDE.

Braganza, A., Chen, W., Canhoto, A., & Sap, S. (2022). Gigification, job engagement and satisfaction: The moderating role of AI enabled system automation in operations management. *Production Planning and Control*, *33*(16), 1534–1547. DOI: 10.1080/09537287.2021.1882692

Brynjolfsson, E., & McAfee, A. (2014). *The Second Machine Age: Work, Progress, and Prosperity in a Time of Brilliant Technologies*. W.W. Norton & Company.

Brynjolfsson, E., & McAfee, A. (2017). Machine, platform, crowd: Harnessing our digital future. *WW New York: Norton & Company, 564*.

Cabitza, F., Rasoini, R., & Gensini, G. F. (2017). Unintended consequences of machine learning in medicine. *Journal of the American Medical Association, 318*(6), 517–518. DOI: 10.1001/jama.2017.7797 PMID: 28727867

Chamorro-Premuzic, T. (2017). *The talent delusion: Why data, not intuition, is the key to unlocking human potential.* Piatkus.

Chen, W., Men, Y., Fuster, N., Osorio, C., & Juan, A. A. (2024). Artificial intelligence in logistics optimization with sustainable criteria: A review. *Sustainability (Basel), 16*(21), 9145. DOI: 10.3390/su16219145

Christensen, J. (2021). AI in Financial Services. In *Demystifying AI for the Enterprise* (pp. 149-192). Productivity Press. DOI: 10.4324/9781351032940-6

Chui, M., Manyika, J., & Miremadi, M. (2016). Where machines could replace humans-and where they can't (yet). *The McKinsey Quarterly*, •••, 1–12.

Davenport, T. H., & Ronanki, R. (2018). Artificial intelligence for the real world. *Harvard Business Review, 96*(1), 108–116.

Dellermann, D., Calma, A., Lipusch, N., Weber, T., Weigel, S., & Ebel, P. (2021). The future of human-AI collaboration: a taxonomy of design knowledge for hybrid intelligence systems. *arXiv preprint arXiv:2105.03354.*

Downes, L., Meister, J. C., Yoffie, D. B., & Gavet, M. (2021). *The Year in Tech 2022: The Insights You Need from Harvard Business Review: The Insights You Need from Harvard Business Review*. Harvard Business Press.

Drissi Elbouzidi, A., Ait El Cadi, A., Pellerin, R., Lamouri, S., Tobon Valencia, E., & Bélanger, M. J. (2023). The role of AI in warehouse digital twins: Literature review. *Applied Sciences (Basel, Switzerland), 13*(11), 6746. DOI: 10.3390/app13116746

Eden, C. A., Chisom, O. N., & Adeniyi, I. S. (2024). Integrating AI in education: Opportunities, challenges, and ethical considerations. *Magna Scientia Advanced Research and Reviews, 10*(2), 006-013.

Esteva, A., Kuprel, B., Novoa, R. A., Ko, J., Swetter, S. M., Blau, H. M., & Thrun, S. (2017). Dermatologist-level classification of skin cancer with deep neural networks. *Nature, 542*(7639), 115–118. DOI: 10.1038/nature21056 PMID: 28117445

Esteva, A., Kuprel, B., Novoa, R. A., Ko, J., Swetter, S. M., Blau, H. M., & Thrun, S. (2017). Dermatologist-level classification of skin cancer with deep neural networks. *Nature, 542*(7639), 115–118. DOI: 10.1038/nature21056 PMID: 28117445

Faishal, M., Mathew, S., Neikha, K., Pusa, K., & Zhimomi, T. (2023). The future of work: AI, automation, and the changing dynamics of developed economies. *World Journal of Advanced Research and Reviews*, *18*(3), 620–629. DOI: 10.30574/wjarr.2023.18.3.1086

Ferrara, E. (2023). Fairness and bias in artificial intelligence: A brief survey of sources, impacts, and mitigation strategies. *Sci*, *6*(1), 3. DOI: 10.3390/sci6010003

Frey, C. B., & Osborne, M. A. (2017). The future of employment: How susceptible are jobs to computerization? *Technological Forecasting and Social Change*, *114*, 254–280. DOI: 10.1016/j.techfore.2016.08.019

Goddard, M. (2017). The EU General Data Protection Regulation (GDPR): European regulation that has a global impact. *International Journal of Market Research*, *59*(6), 703–705. DOI: 10.2501/IJMR-2017-050

Golić, Z. (2019). Finance and artificial intelligence: The fifth industrial revolution and its impact on the financial sector. *Zbornik radova Ekonomskog fakulteta u Istočnom Sarajevu*, (19), 67-81.

Inavolu, S. M. Exploring AI-Driven Customer Service: Evolution, Architectures, Opportunities, Challenges and Future Directions.

Irfan, M., Aldulaylan, F., & Alqahtani, Y. (2023). Ethics and privacy in Irish higher education: A comprehensive study of Artificial Intelligence (AI) tools implementation at University of Limerick. *Global Social Sci Rev*, *8*(II), 201–210. DOI: 10.31703/gssr.2023(VIII-II).19

Ivanov, D., & Dolgui, A. (2021). A digital supply chain twin for managing the disruption risks and resilience in the era of Industry 4.0. *Production Planning and Control*, *32*(9), 775–788. DOI: 10.1080/09537287.2020.1768450

Jammalamadaka, K. R., & Itapu, S. (2023). Responsible AI in automated credit scoring systems. *AI and Ethics*, *3*(2), 485–495. DOI: 10.1007/s43681-022-00175-3

Jiang, F., Jiang, Y., Zhi, H., Dong, Y., Li, H., Ma, S., Wang, Y., Dong, Q., Shen, H., & Wang, Y. (2017). Artificial intelligence in healthcare: Past, present and future. *Stroke and Vascular Neurology*, *2*(4), 230–243. DOI: 10.1136/svn-2017-000101 PMID: 29507784

Johora, F. T., Hasan, R., Farabi, S. F., Akter, J., & Al Mahmud, M. A. (2024). AI-Powered Fraud Detection in Banking: Safeguarding Financial Transactions. *The American Journal of Management and Economics Innovations*, *6*(06), 8–22. DOI: 10.37547/tajmei/Volume06Issue06-02

Kaplan, A., & Haenlein, M. (2019). Siri, Siri, in my hand: Who's the fairest in the land? *Business Horizons*, *62*(1), 15–25. DOI: 10.1016/j.bushor.2018.08.004

Kaplan, A., & Haenlein, M. (2019). Siri, Siri, in my hand: Who's the fairest in the land? *Business Horizons*, *62*(1), 15–25. DOI: 10.1016/j.bushor.2018.08.004

Lacity, M., Willcocks, L., & Gozman, D. (2021). Influencing information systems practice: The action principles approach applied to robotic process and cognitive automation. *Journal of Information Technology*, *36*(3), 216–240. DOI: 10.1177/0268396221990778

Langove, S. A., & Khan, A. (2024). Automated Grading and Feedback Systems: Reducing Teacher Workload and Improving Student Performance. *Journal of Asian Development Studies*, *13*(4), 202–212. DOI: 10.62345/jads.2024.13.4.16

Lee, J., Bagheri, B., & Kao, H. A. (2015). A cyber-physical systems architecture for industry 4.0-based manufacturing systems. *Manufacturing Letters*, *3*(4), 18–23. DOI: 10.1016/j.mfglet.2014.12.001

Lee, J., Bagheri, B., & Kao, H. A. (2018). A cyber-physical systems architecture for industry 4.0-based manufacturing systems. *Manufacturing Letters*, *3*(4), 18–23.

Leng, J., Wang, D., Shen, W., Li, X., Liu, Q., & Chen, X. (2021). Digital twins-based smart manufacturing system design in Industry 4.0: A review. *Journal of Manufacturing Systems*, *60*, 119–137. DOI: 10.1016/j.jmsy.2021.05.011

Li, L. (2022). Reskilling and upskilling the future-ready workforce for industry 4.0 and beyond. *Information Systems Frontiers*, •••, 1–16. PMID: 35855776

Liao, M., & Sundar, S. S. (2022). When e-commerce personalization systems show and tell: Investigating the relative persuasive appeal of content-based versus collaborative filtering. *Journal of Advertising*, *51*(2), 256–267. DOI: 10.1080/00913367.2021.1887013

Litjens, G., Kooi, T., Bejnordi, B. E., Setio, A. A., Ciompi, F., Ghafoorian, M., van der Laak, J. A. W. M., van Ginneken, B., & Sánchez, C. I. (2017). A survey on deep learning in medical image analysis. *Medical Image Analysis*, *42*, 60–88. DOI: 10.1016/j.media.2017.07.005 PMID: 28778026

Liu, P., Wang, L., & Vincent, C. (2020). Self-driving vehicles against human drivers: Equal safety is far from enough. *Journal of Experimental Psychology. Applied*, *26*(4), 692–704. DOI: 10.1037/xap0000267 PMID: 32202821

Luo, Q. Z., & Hsiao-Chin, L. Y. (2023). The influence of AI-powered adaptive learning platforms on student performance in Chinese classrooms. *Journal of Education*, *6*(3), 1–12. DOI: 10.53819/81018102t4181

Luo, Y., Li, X., & Ye, Q. (2023). The Impact of Privacy Calculus and Trust on User Information Participation Behavior in AI-based Medical Consultation-The Moderating Role of Gender. *Journal of Electronic Commerce Research*, *24*(1), 48–67.

Mahmoud, A. B., Tehseen, S., & Fuxman, L. (2020). The dark side of artificial intelligence in retail innovation. In *Retail futures* (pp. 165–180). Emerald Publishing Limited. DOI: 10.1108/978-1-83867-663-620201019

Manyika, J., Chui, M., Miremadi, M., Bughin, J., George, K., Willmott, P., & Dewhurst, M. (2017). A future that works: AI, automation, employment, and productivity. *McKinsey Global Institute Research. Tech. Rep*, *60*, 1–135.

Maseke, B. F. (2024). The transformative power of artificial intelligence in banking client service. *South Asian Journal of Social Studies and Economics*, *21*(3), 93–105. DOI: 10.9734/sajsse/2024/v21i3787

McCarthy, J. (2007). What is artificial intelligence? *Stanford University*. http://www-formal.stanford.edu/jmc/ [Accessed on 14th October, 2024]

Mittal, S., Koushik, P., Batra, I., & Whig, P. (2024). AI-Driven Inventory Management for Optimizing Operations With Quantum Computing. In *Quantum Computing and Supply Chain Management: A New Era of Optimization* (pp. 125–140). IGI Global. DOI: 10.4018/979-8-3693-4107-0.ch009

Naeem, A. M., Gad, A., Alhalabi, M., Yaghi, M., Khelifi, A., & Ghazal, M. (2023, August). AI-Based Mobile Paper Grading: Trends and Challenges. In 2023 10th International Conference on Future Internet of Things and Cloud (FiCloud) (pp. 404-409). IEEE.

Naen, M. F., Adnan, M. H. M., Yazi, N. A., & Nee, C. K. (2021). Development of attendance monitoring system with artificial intelligence optimization in cloud. *International Journal of Artificial Intelligence*, *8*(2), 88–98. DOI: 10.36079/lamintang.ijai-0802.315

Necula, S. C., & Păvăloaia, V. D. (2023). AI-Driven Recommendations: A Systematic review of the state of the art in E-Commerce. *Applied Sciences (Basel, Switzerland)*, *13*(9), 5531. DOI: 10.3390/app13095531

Nevliudov, I., Yevsieiev, V., Klymenko, O., Demska, N., & Vzhesnievskyi, M. (2021). Evolutions Of Group Management Development Of Mobile Robotic Platforms In Warehousing 4.0. *Innovative Technologies and Scientific Solutions for Industries*, (4 (18)), 57–64. DOI: 10.30837/ITSSI.2021.18.057

Nikitas, A., Vitel, A. E., & Cotet, C. (2021). Autonomous vehicles and employment: An urban futures revolution or catastrophe? *Cities (London, England)*, *114*, 103203. DOI: 10.1016/j.cities.2021.103203

Nissim, G., & Simon, T. (2021). The future of labor unions in the age of automation and at the dawn of AI. *Technology in Society*, *67*, 101732. DOI: 10.1016/j.techsoc.2021.101732

Nissim, G., & Simon, T. (2021). The future of labor unions in the age of automation and at the dawn of AI. *Technology in Society*, *67*, 101732. DOI: 10.1016/j.techsoc.2021.101732

Obermeyer, Z., & Emanuel, E. J. (2016). Predicting the future—Big data, machine learning, and clinical medicine. *The New England Journal of Medicine*, *375*(13), 1216–1219. DOI: 10.1056/NEJMp1606181 PMID: 27682033

Obermeyer, Z., & Emanuel, E. J. (2016). Predicting the future—Big data, machine learning, and clinical medicine. *The New England Journal of Medicine*, *375*(13), 1216–1219. DOI: 10.1056/NEJMp1606181 PMID: 27682033

Oswald, F. L., Behrend, T. S., & Thompson, L. F. (Eds.). (2019). *Workforce readiness and the future of work*. Routledge. DOI: 10.4324/9781351210485

Pandey, A., & Kumar, S. (2024). AI's Effect on Employment Displacement and the Future of Work. *Knowledgeable Research: A Multidisciplinary Peer-Reviewd. Refereed e-Journal*, *3*(03), 43–55.

Pantano, E., & Pizzi, G. (2020). Forecasting artificial intelligence on online customer assistance: Evidence from chatbot patents analysis. *Journal of Retailing and Consumer Services*, *55*, 102096. DOI: 10.1016/j.jretconser.2020.102096

Rajkomar, A., Dean, J., & Kohane, I. (2019). Machine learning in medicine. *The New England Journal of Medicine*, *380*(14), 1347–1358. DOI: 10.1056/NEJMra1814259 PMID: 30943338

Rashidzadeh, E., Hadji Molana, S. M., Soltani, R., & Hafezalkotob, A. (2021). Assessing the sustainability of using drone technology for last-mile delivery in a blood supply chain. *Journal of Modelling in Management*, *16*(4), 1376–1402. DOI: 10.1108/JM2-09-2020-0241

RE, Y. R. Y., & Ermetov, E. (2024). THE IMPACT OF AI ON ECONOMIC GROWTH AND JOB CREATION. *Innovations in Science and Technologies*, *1*(5), 43–57.

Reddy, T. N., Prasannan, P., Hegde, S. B., Vinod, P., Herbert, M. A., & Rao, S. S. (2023). Interoperable data retrieval solutions for smart manufacturing applications. *Manufacturing Technology Today*, *22*(11-12), 1–19. DOI: 10.58368/MTT.22.11-12.2023.1-19

Rensfeldt, A. B., & Rahm, L. (2023). Automating teacher work? A history of the politics of automation and artificial intelligence in education. *Postdigital Science and Education*, *5*(1), 25–43. DOI: 10.1007/s42438-022-00344-x

Riek, L. D. (2017). Healthcare robotics. *Communications of the ACM*, *60*(11), 68–78. DOI: 10.1145/3127874

Robert, C. (2017). *Superintelligence: Paths, dangers, strategies*. Taylor & Francis.

Roslan, F. A. B. M., & Ahmad, N. B. (2023). The rise of AI-powered voice assistants: Analyzing their transformative impact on modern customer service paradigms and consumer expectations. *Quarterly Journal of Emerging Technologies and Innovations*, *8*(3), 33–64.

Russell, S., & Norvig, P. (2016). *Artificial Intelligence: A Modern Approach*. Pearson.

Saaida, M. B. (2023). AI-Driven transformations in higher education: Opportunities and challenges. *International Journal of Educational Research and Studies*, *5*(1), 29–36.

Saxena, M. (2024). AI-Powered Credit Scoring: Transforming Lending Decisions in Fintech. *International Journal of Research and Review Techniques*, *3*(1), 31–34.

Shah, N. H., Milstein, A., & Bagley, S. C. (2019). Making machine learning models clinically useful. *Journal of the American Medical Association*, *322*(14), 1351–1352. DOI: 10.1001/jama.2019.10306 PMID: 31393527

Shenoi, V. V., Sreeram, P., Varma, C. L. S., Goud, K. R., & Afroz, S. N. (2024, April). Analysing the Role of Human-AI Collaboration in Workforce Transformation. In *2024 International Conference on Advances in Data Engineering and Intelligent Computing Systems (ADICS)* (pp. 1-7). IEEE. DOI: 10.1109/ADICS58448.2024.10533640

Sheth, J. N., Jain, V., Roy, G., & Chakraborty, A. (2022). AI-driven banking services: The next frontier for a personalised experience in the emerging market. *International Journal of Bank Marketing*, *40*(6), 1248–1271. DOI: 10.1108/IJBM-09-2021-0449

Shiva, K., Etikani, P., Bhaskar, V. V. S. R., Palavesh, S., & Dave, A. (2022). The rise of robo-advisors: AI-powered investment management for everyone. *Journal of Namibian Studies*, *31*, 201–214.

Shoaib, M., Sayed, N., Singh, J., Shafi, J., Khan, S., & Ali, F. (2024). AI student success predictor: Enhancing personalized learning in campus management systems. *Computers in Human Behavior*, *158*, 108301. DOI: 10.1016/j.chb.2024.108301

Sidhu, G. S., Sayem, M. A., Taslima, N., Anwar, A. S., Chowdhury, F., & Rowshon, M. (2024). AI and workforce development: A comparative analysis of skill gaps and training needs in emerging economies. *International journal of business and management sciences, 4*(08), 12-28.

Susskind, D. (2020). *A world without work: Technology, automation and how we should respond.* Penguin UK.

Tamraparani, V. (2023). Leveraging AI for Fraud Detection in Identity and Access Management: A Focus on Large-Scale Customer Data. *Journal of Computational Analysis and Applications*, *31*(4).

Tariq, M. U. (2024). The Role of AI in Skilling, Upskilling, and Reskilling the Workforce. In *Integrating Generative AI in Education to Achieve Sustainable Development Goals* (pp. 421–433). IGI Global. DOI: 10.4018/979-8-3693-2440-0.ch023

Topol, E. J. (2019). High-performance medicine: The convergence of human and artificial intelligence. *Nature Medicine*, *25*(1), 44–56. DOI: 10.1038/s41591-018-0300-7 PMID: 30617339

Viktor, P., & Szeghegyi, Á. (2022). Safety of the Introduction of Self-driving Vehicles in a Logistics Environment. *Periodica Polytechnica Transportation Engineering*, *50*(4), 387–399. DOI: 10.3311/PPtr.20006

Wilson, H. J., & Daugherty, P. R. (2018). Collaborative intelligence: Humans and AI are joining forces. *Harvard Business Review*, *96*(4), 114–123.

Yanamala, A. K. Y., Suryadevara, S., & Kalli, V. D. R. (2024). Balancing innovation and privacy: The intersection of data protection and artificial intelligence. *International Journal of Machine Learning Research in Cybersecurity and Artificial Intelligence*, *15*(1), 1–43.

Zanke, P. (2023). AI-Driven fraud detection systems: A comparative study across banking, insurance, and healthcare. *Advances in Deep Learning Techniques*, *3*(2), 1–22.

Zhang, Q., & Xiong, Y. (2024). Harnessing AI potential in E-Commerce: Improving user engagement and sales through deep learning-based product recommendations. *Current Psychology (New Brunswick, N.J.)*, *43*(38), 30379–30401. DOI: 10.1007/s12144-024-06649-3

Zhong, R. Y., Xu, X., Klotz, E., & Newman, S. T. (2017). Intelligent manufacturing in the context of industry 4.0: A review. *Engineering (Beijing)*, *3*(5), 616–630. DOI: 10.1016/J.ENG.2017.05.015

Chapter 14
The Effects of Artificial Intelligence and Automation on Labour Markets:
Rethinking the Role of Trade Unions

Ali İhsan Balcı
https://orcid.org/0000-0002-9695-732X
Bülent Ecevit University, Turkey

ABSTRACT

This research examines the effects of artificial intelligence and automation on labour markets, socio-economic justice and trade unions. A hierarchical clustering analysis of 25 European countries shows that there are significant differences between countries in terms of their level of technological readiness, income inequality and union density. While Scandinavian countries were found to be successful in offsetting the negative effects of technological transformation with their strong trade union structures, these effects were found to have a deeper impact on income inequality and unemployment in countries such as Turkey and Greece. The study emphasises that trade unions should play a critical role in protecting workers' rights, reducing income inequality and supporting skills development programmes. The results suggest that processes of technological transformation need to be managed through policies that promote social justice.

DOI: 10.4018/979-8-3693-8049-9.ch014

INTRODUCTION

Industrial revolutions throughout history reveal the transformative power of technology. From the impact of the steam engine in the First Industrial Revolution, the age of automation and artificial intelligence in the Fourth Industrial Revolution has forced labour markets, social structures and the economies of countries to reshape. Currently, this transformation is developing rapidly day by day and leaves deep impacts on countries in the context of socio-economic diversity. In particular, the Fourth Industrial Revolution, or Industry 4.0, is forcing countries to rethink their industrial relations institutions and reshape the nature of work and employment patterns. Automation, machine learning and artificial intelligence cause the disappearance of routine jobs and introduce new sectors to the labour market. While this situation offers some advantages to countries, it also makes income inequality, polarisation of the labour market and social fragmentation more evident.

The main purpose of this research is to understand that artificial intelligence and automation processes are not a homogeneous process across countries, but also to understand the multidimensional effects of technological readiness, socio-economic conditions and labour market institutions, to evaluate the socio-economic consequences and to shed light on the strategic role of trade unions in this transformation. In line with the stated objective, hierarchical clustering analysis was applied using Ward's method. In the study, 25 European countries for which all data are available are analysed in the context of automation, artificial intelligence, socio-economic justice and the role of trade unions in protecting labour rights.

The study aims to contribute to the literature in understanding the effects of technological transformation on the labour market by including important indices such as "artificial intelligence readiness index, global innovation index, employment rate in the information technology sector (ICT), economic complexity index (ECI)" together with macroeconomic indicators of countries such as "income inequality, unemployment rates, poverty line, union density, collective bargaining coverage and labour rights index". In this context, the study focuses on three main questions: (1) How does the level of preparedness for artificial intelligence and automation differ across countries? (2) What are the socio-economic consequences of this transformation, especially in terms of income inequality and labour market polarisation? (3) What strategies can trade unions develop to mitigate the negative effects of automation and ensure a fair working life? Within the scope of these research questions, the study aims to present the current technological revolution in a broad historical and socio-economic context, providing policy makers, trade unions and researchers with actionable insights into a complex transformation process

THEORETICAL BACKGROUND

Currently, it has become extremely difficult to keep up with the speed of development of information technologies and artificial intelligence. The integration of new technologies and artificial intelligence into our lives, in other words, the Industry 4.0 process, is similar to the transition from the Agricultural Revolution to the Industrial Revolution, but perhaps much more corrosive. The most important reason for this is the change and transformation that new technologies have brought about in working life (Holtgrewe, 2014). Since the beginning of human history, working life has constantly changed and developed. The most important factor of this development is technological advances. It can be stated that human beings started to dominate nature and live a more productive life thanks to the tools they developed to sustain their daily lives (Cipolla, 1979). For this reason, it is necessary to benefit from the Industrial Revolutions while discussing artificial intelligence and automation (Xing & Marwala, 2017). In the theoretical background section of the research, we will first discuss the process from the 1st Industrial Revolution to the 4th Industrial Revolution. Afterwards, research in the literature will be mentioned to examine the socioeconomic consequences of the use of automation and artificial intelligence, which is the aim of the research, and to consider the future role of trade unions.

In the second half of the 18th century, the first industrial revolution period that started in England shows a very important turning point for human history (Mathias & Davis, 1990). While manual labour was used in production during this period, in the First Industrial Revolution period, the steam engine and spinning machine, which transformed the work into technology, were used to replace manual labour with mechanisation that can make faster and mass production (Ashton, 1986). For countries, the change in the structure of production created by the Industrial Revolution has resulted in the growth of their economies in the global sense, the intensive increase in production and the increase in consumption levels. The rapid increase in production has increased the importance of the shipment of the products produced, so that transport and communication infrastructures such as canals, highways and railways have developed faster than ever in this period. In other words, it increased the mobility of goods and people between countries (Allen, 1999; Wrigley, 1985; Stokey, 2001; Crafts, 1983; Harley & Crafts, 2000; Temin, 1997; O'Rourke & Williamson, 2005). On the other hand, it has made a significant contribution to the development of banking and financial systems and the smooth continuation of their activities. Increasing living standards as a result of the economic activities developed by the First Industrial Revolution increased fertility rates and decreased infant and child mortality rates. Accordingly, a rapid increase in the world population occurred in this period (Hansen & Prescott, 2002). Along with these positive effects of the

First Industrial Revolution, some negative effects have also emerged. These effects are undoubtedly the spread of very long and inhumane working hours due to the lack of rules regarding working life, the emergence of dangerous and unhygienic working conditions, and the emergence of inhumane practices such as women and child labour (Ventura & Voth, 2015; Cipolla, 1979). On the other hand, it has caused social income imbalance and the unbalanced income distribution between the rich and the poor has become much deeper, adding a new dimension to social inequality. In this sense, it would not be wrong to state that the effects of the Industrial Revolution have a wide range in both economic and social fields (Mohojan, 2019).

One of the most important effects of the Industrial Revolution was the innovation of the steam engine and its use in production. The purpose of this is to use the most important energy resources of the period more efficiently. As a matter of fact, energy becomes available for human beings when they have knowledge about its sources and can master these sources economically. Therefore, the main question for the period is how to transform this energy into a certain form at the most cost-effective time and place. Mankind has found the solution to this problem in the steam engine. Because the steam engine is a converter that converts heat energy into mechanical energy at any time and place (Cipolla, 1979). The steam engine, which is accepted as one of the most important technological advances of the Industrial Revolution, was invented by Thomas Newcomen (Sinclair, 1970). In 1776, James Watt, a Scottish mechanical engineer, started the early modern industrial era with his innovation to use the steam engine more efficiently (Jacob, 1997; Usher, 1920; Rosen, 2012). With this development, an extraordinary textile production, mining, the development of railways, the spread of ocean freighters, steel production and many other economic activities in the world have experienced radical changes. In other words, the fact that the steam engine can now be easily used in production has contributed to the tremendous growth of cities, industries and infrastructures and to the change in the economic order of countries (Usher, 1920; Rosen, 2012). This situation is among the most important achievements of the Industrial Revolution. Before the developments during the Industrial Revolution, a significant portion of the population, especially in England, lived in small villages. In this period, the transport network was very limited and was generally provided on foot or by horse using narrow paths. Due to the conditions of the period, malnutrition, poor hygiene conditions, limited access to clean water sources and the lack of sewerage systems made it necessary for people living in the country to fight against epidemics. Therefore, the average life expectancy was quite short. The majority of the population lived and worked on feudal farms, while a very small proportion lived in urban areas. Peasants working for feudal lords laboured intensively from dawn to dusk. Due to the small scale and localised nature of production during the agricultural period, only a small proportion of workers were engaged in manufacturing, mining and trade. This situation caused production to be based on manpower and animal power (Clark, 2007; Ashton, 1986; Usher, 1920; Jacob, 1997). As a matter of fact, with the development of the steam engine, engines made of iron were made to work more efficiently. The main energy source of these engines was coal. While the main source of energy in the Agricultural Revolution was human and animal power, coal plays a critical role as the main energy source in the Industrial Revolution (Clark, 2007; Wrigley, 2013). With the development of industry, the demand for labour force in cities has increased. Therefore, people living in rural areas had to migrate to cities. The labour force that moved from rural areas to cities has become wage labour in cities, that is, dependent workers as we call them nowadays. Cotton, sugar and tobacco are seen as the most important raw material sources used in production. England organised colonial expeditions to Latin and North America by using sea power in order to have these resources in production (Christopher, 1967). When James Watt made the steam engine suitable for use in production, in other words, the period in which the "marriage of cotton and steam" took place, enabled production to go beyond the limits of human power (Koray, 2008). These developments led to the beginning of the three-sector law in England. With this revolution, England rapidly moved from an agriculture-intensive economic structure to an industrial sector-oriented structure and thus to the capitalist system. Therefore, for the first industrial revolution, it can be stated as a radical factor showing socioeconomic characteristics that changed not only the social structure but also the economic structure in England (Usher, 1920; Koray, 2008; Cipolla, 1979). With these developments, the Industrial Revolution emerges as one of the most important proofs showing how deeply technological developments can affect countries. As a matter of fact, it is seen that the process has laid the foundations for the realisation of much more complex and efficient production, and at the same time, it has formed the important stage of technological progress that can be experienced in the future.

Adam Smith, one of the important scientists of the Industrial Revolution period, is known as the first economist to examine the functioning of the modernising economy in terms of specialisation, division of labour, efficient use of market mechanisms and general productivity increase. According to Smith, free trade, ownership of the means of production and government intervention in the market should be minimised. Such an understanding of the economic system is based on the "laissez-faire" approach, which argues that there should be no state intervention that could disturb the equilibrium in the market (Viner, 1927). This principle advocates the creation of an economic structure in which business owners should have the freedom to regulate working conditions according to their own preferences. Therefore, this situation prepared a favourable environment for mercantilist economic approaches to come to the fore in the social structure (Ashton, 1986). As it can be understood from this point, this change in the period of the Industrial Revolution provided a theoretical basis for the development of industry and trade for economists, and at the same time prepared a favourable environment for the expansion of the modern capitalist system (Viner, 1927).

According to Botham and Hunt (1987), during the Industrial Revolution, wages showed regional and sectoral differences. In regions with intensive industrialisation, such as the North of England and the Midlands, wages increased significantly, especially in fast-growing sectors such as pottery and mining. For instance, in North Staffordshire, real wages for potters and miners rose by 49 per cent and 60 per cent respectively. In contrary, in the south of England, especially in and around London, real wages declined, suggesting that living standards in areas where industrialisation was less effective were stagnant or deteriorating. Wage increases during this period were more pronounced in sectors that were directly affected by the economic growth generated by industrialisation, and the improvement in workers' living standards was felt more strongly in these sectors. In general, however, changes in wages varied greatly depending on local economic conditions and the level of industrialisation (Botham & Hunt, 1987). Therefore, it would be possible to state that even though the Industrial Revolution brought about very important and pioneering changes in the economic field, it did not lead to a significant increase in the incomes of the newly formed working class.

The period 1860-1914 is referred to as the Second Industrial Revolution period due to the invention and development of many new technologies. In this period, innovations such as electricity, internal combustion engine, chemical industries, alloys, petroleum and other chemicals, as well as electrical communication technologies such as telegraph, telephone, radio, and running water with internal plumbing systems come to the forefront (Cipolla, 1979;Gordon, 2000). This period has also been characterised as the iron and steel era due to the fact that scientific-based studies and inventions concentrated in areas such as iron and steel production, electricity and chemicals pioneered the period. These technological developments revolutionised industrial production and contributed to the shaping of modern economic structures (Atkeson & Kehoe, 2001). The second Industrial Revolution period led to the formation of modern industrial economic structures, the development of transport systems and the beginning of a new era of communication. The second Industrial Revolution, which started in the late 19th century and continued until the early 20th century, made mass production possible with the advent of electricity and the assembly line (Schwab, 2016). The beginning of the period is often associated with the British-American industrialist Samuel Slater, who opened the first industrial windmill. Slater played a critical role in the industrialisation of the country by introducing a new technology to the USA (Conrad, 1995). This period stands out as a period of rapid development and progress under the leadership of new inventions and science. In 1807, the American engineer and inventor Robert Fulton developed the first steamship that worked on the Hudson River using steam power and changed the speed and shape of the journey (Buckman, 1907). This innovation led to a revolutionary step in transportation and showed that steam power could now be used in transportation as well as production. Accordingly, the development of steam-powered transport vehicles expanded the scale of transport and trade. At the same time, interchangeable parts and machines started to be produced by using more steam power, thus allowing mass production to accelerate and industrialisation to become much more efficient (Kitsikopoulos, 2023). In addition, Edison's development of various innovative technologies such as the light bulb, mass media, phonograph, kinetograph played a pioneering role in the development and change of the modern world (Salkind & Israel, 2004). Edison's inventions contributed to the acceleration of technological progress and were influential in a wide range from industrial production to daily life. In addition, Alexander Graham Bell, a Scottish-originated scientist and American inventor, revolutionised the field of communication by inventing the telephone in 1874. Bell founded the American Telephone and Telegraph Company (AT&T) in the United States in 1885 and pioneered the institutionalisation of communication technologies. The work of these two inventors led to radical changes in both daily life and industry and formed the basis of the modern technological era (Mohajan, 2020). Perhaps one of the most important inventions of the period was made by Charles Babbage. Babbage is an English mechanical engineer known as the father of the computer. In the early 19th century, he invented the first mechanical computer. This invention of Babbage is very important in terms of guiding not only the second industrial revolution but also the automation processes of artificial intelligence that we are in today. The invention of the computer revolutionised the fields of production and design by accelerating the processes of calculation and data processing, and made the potential offered by other technological innovations such as steam power, electricity and chemistry more effectively available (Edgar, 2015). Developments in the field of science and technology have also led to a number of developments in the social field. As a matter of fact, the prohibition of slavery in the USA in 1856, the recognition of black people as citizens in 1868 and the granting of voting rights to women in the 1920s can be expressed as positive reflections of scientific and technological developments in the social field (Mormina, 2019). At the end of the Second World War, rising wages and improved living conditions in cities led to a significant rise in the living standards of urban workers. During this period, the level of living standards in the US was much higher than the living standards achieved in the UK during the First Industrial Revolution (Gordon, 2012). In addition, companies in Germany and the USA started to export their goods to global markets. During the Second Industrial Revolution, scientific discoveries and inventions rapidly transformed social structures such as scientific thought, art and culture, architecture and lifestyle (Mokyr, 2011).

The Third Industrial Revolution started in the 1950s, reached its peak in the late 1990s when access to the internet became widespread in all segments of society, and it would not be wrong to state that it continues today as it forms the basis of Industry 4.0. This period, which is based on energy transformation, digital technologies and the internet, is also called the "Digital Revolution" (Bojanova, 2014). With the 1990s, globalisation processes have made countries much more integrated with each other. This integration has led to the rapid distribution of communication and information. Therefore, the process moving towards the information society has started with the 3rd Industrial Revolution. Now, nano-technology, smart systems, 3D printing and robot technology have become institutionally widespread in industrial production and home services. Therefore, it is possible to state that two technologies, microelectronics and the internet, are at the centre of the 3rd Industrial Revolution (Anderson, 2012; Taalbi, 2019). In Industry 3.0, the combination of digital production and personal production methods has increased integration in the global economy and accelerated communication (Troxler, 2013). This period is seen to be built on increasing energy efficiency as it is based on efficiency orientation (Rifkin, 2011) such as green energy, efficient use of global resources. Revolutionary technologies such as modern computing, lean production, the internet and biotechnology played a key role in shaping this process and started to be implemented from the 1970s (Taalbi, 2019). The Third Industrial Revolution was shaped by major inventions such as semiconductors, mainframes, microprocessors, worldwide web, ultra-fast 5G communication, personal access points such as renewable energy internet and autonomous mobility internet, renewable electricity, e-commerce and smartphones (Gordon, 2012). Industry 3.0 was born from the opportunities for corporate industries to benefit from future technological trends and developed in line with these trends (Mohajan, 2021; Roberts, 2015). Nano technology, biotechnology, information technologies, 3D printing, artificial intelligence and robotics are among its most important driving forces. The transformation brought about by Industry 3.0 has deeply affected many modern sectors such as advanced production technologies, education, information and communication technologies (ICT), defence, health, finance and administrative sectors (Roberts, 2015). As can be understood from the above statements, the 1st and 2nd Industrial Revolutions have created a lot of change in terms of social and labour life compared to previous periods. The most important of these changes is undoubtedly the formation of the working class, which came from villages to cities and became dispossessed, and with it the emergence of dependent labour relations. Industry 3.0 plays a key role in the formation of the digital modern world thanks to the intense impact of technological changes in social and economic life. Unimaginable innovations and the spread of digitalisation day by day have led to the questioning of dependency relations in terms of working life. This situation carries important signs that the new digital world will become a more individualised place (Lasi et al., 2014). On the other hand, this period has been a period of extraordinary technological progress linked to the rapid development of Information and Communication Technologies (ICT). While the First and Second Industrial Revolutions affected only Western Europe and the USA and led to local development, the Third Industrial Revolution has created a transformation at both local and global levels, leading the world to become about 10 times richer. In this process, thousands of commercial organisations were established and millions of new jobs and employment opportunities were created (Mohajan, 2021).

Schwab (2016) has comprehensively analysed the impact of the technological transformation of the world on humanity. Since the publication of Schwab's book, the term Industry 4.0 has been used to analyse and frame how emerging technologies at the beginning of the 21st century affect human development in a wide range of areas, from changing social norms and national political attitudes to economic development and international relations (Schwab, 2016). In this context, technologies such as artificial intelligence, the internet of things, robotics, blockchain and biotechnology are forcing societies to undergo radical changes and presenting various challenges and opportunities for businesses and governments. Thus, Schwab's work has become an important editorial standpoint in understanding the impact that Industry 4.0 has on the economic and social setup. Industry 4.0 is the recognition that the technological change is the key impetus behind a transformation that does not confine itself to certain industries but spreads across all sectors of society. The concept stresses the view whereby technological innovations have tended to occur together over particular periods, thus spearheading transformations that are not restricted to mere advancements in productivity but which permeate social, economic and cultural infrastructures. Industrial revolutions are processes that lead to radical changes in individual, social and administrative systems; major advances in the complex interconnection of humans and technology create new ways and change the functioning of individual and collective life. Within the framework of this argument, the Fourth Industrial Revolution is seen as a paradigm that acts to up-scale the pace and social repercussions of technological advancement in a manner that radically transforms socio-economic functioning (Elsayed et al., 2024).

In a different way from other industrial revolutions, Industry 4.0 represents a series of significant shifts in the way economic, political and social value is created, exchanged and distributed. These shifts in value are closely linked to the emergence of new technologies spanning the digital, physical and biological worlds, and are most powerful when they converge and become more integrated (Philbeck & Davis, 2019). The fact that Industry 4.0 has influenced the whole world and created a new contemporary culture can be explained by what Jasnoff (2015) refers to as "sociotechnological imagination". This concept states that societies create today's technology by combining their gains from past experiences with their future visions. Therefore, it is possible to state that Industry 4.0 is directly related to both social, economic and political changes. As can be understood from this, Industry 4.0 emphasises the importance of more forward-looking changes by covering other industrial revolutions (Jasanoff, 2015; Philbeck & Davis, 2019).

Table 1. Transition from industrial to information society

Period	Transformation Period	Energy Source	Basic Technical Development	Emerging Basic Industry	Meaning of Transport
1760-1900	1860-1900	Coal	Steam Machine	Textile, Iron and Steel	Train, Railway
1900-1960	1940-1960	Petroleum, Electricity	Internal Combustion Engine	Metallurgy, Automotive, Machine Production	Train, Automobile
1960-2000	1980-2000	Nuclear Energy, Natural Gas	Computer, Robotic	Automotive, Chemistry	Automobile, Aeroplane
After 2000	2000-2010	Green Energy	Internet, 3D Printers, Genetic Engineering	High Technology Industry	Electric vehicles, Superfast trains

Source: (Prisecaru, 2016)

The above table reveals the changes experienced in the process of transition from the industrial society to the information society. It shows how energy resources, technological innovations, basic industries and modes of transport have transformed labour markets and industrial relations in a changing and transforming world and how the development of technology has shortened the duration of transformation. Each wave of transformation, each new industrial revolution, has led to a differentiation of the structure of production and organisation, the emergence of new occupational groups and the redefinition of the qualifications needed in the workforce. It is understood that during the industrial revolution period, sectors where the organisation structure based on intensive labour and arm power was quite strong were dominant. In the 2nd industrial revolution period, it is possible to state that new forms of production, mass production, high assembly line efficiency and Fordist working order were effective. In the Industry 3 and 4.0 periods, it is understood that the structure of the labour force is quite different compared to the previous periods. While the development of automation systems in the third industrial revolution period provides a tremendous integration in the world with the effect of globalisation, it has started to put unions, one of the most important actors of industrial relations, in a difficult situation and has included new forms of organisation in working life. In the post-2000 period, which can be defined as today, this situation has become more evident. As a matter of fact, digitalisation, flexible labour market policies, sustainability and high-tech-oriented production models, together with the need for new regulations in industrial relations, have led to the loss of power of combative industrial relations systems. In this context, as stated before and as seen in the table, each transformation also represents milestones that cause socioeconomic structure changes and rethinking of policies to be implemented for the welfare of the society (Frey & Osborne, 2017; Liao et al, 2017; Frank et al, 2019; Ghobakhloo, 2018).

In the current period, societies are witnessing a new transformation every day depending on the development of artificial intelligence and machine learning techniques. This period is not only the Industry 4.0 period as a continuation of Industry 3.0, but also marks the beginning of a different and new industrial revolution. Schwab (2015) explains the main reasons for this situation with three factors: speed, scope and system effect. According to Schwap (2015), the pace of current technological breakthroughs is unprecedented in history. Compared to previous industrial revolutions, the Fourth Industrial Revolution is progressing at an exponential rather than a linear pace. However, this transformation is not limited to specific regions or sectors, but is triggering change on a global scale, affecting every sector all over the world (Schwab, 2016). Moreover, the breadth and depth of these transformations have the potential to transform entire systems of production, management and governance. The Fourth Industrial Revolution heralds an era in which not only technological innovations but also social and economic systems are being radically reshaped. This revolution presents not only new opportunities for humanity, but also complex challenges to be solved (Xu et al., 2018).

Technological development affects human history in every aspect at every moment. In this context, the most affected area is undoubtedly the labour market. Creative destruction is one of these concepts that are able to explain the changes in the economy and the labour market due to the technology-induced transformations. Creative destruction is a term coined by Joseph Schumpeter (1942) to describe what happens to old industries and jobs rendered obsolete by technological developments and at the same time creating new economies as well as their sectors. According to Schumpeter, economic growth is explained by innovation cycles that keep bringing about displaced older processes with more efficient ones. A steam engine could mechanize textile production to cut out figures of artisans creating new jobs in an industrial age. Again, the Fourth Industrial Revolution does present changes whereby routine jobs are replaced by artificial intelligence and automation but creating demand for newer skills in data science, software engineering, and advanced manufacturing (Acemoglu & Restrepo, 2020). Understanding the principle of creative destruction is needed in analysing the effects created by AI and automation in the present labour markets. As a matter of fact, the process progressing from Industry 1.0 to Industry 4.0 and even 5.0 in the historical process has revealed many new situations in labour relations. With the rapid advancement of automation and artificial intelligence technologies, it can be seen that global labour markets have changed significantly (Rozman et al., 2023). This process of change and transformation increases the number of academic research studies that focus on the multifaceted effects on issues that directly concern working life such as employment, unemployment, unionisation, and income inequality. As a matter of fact, this study was conducted to examine the effects of increasing automation and artificial intelligence on labour markets and to discuss the future role of trade unions in protecting workers' rights. In this context, when the literature on this research is examined, it can be easily stated that there are very few studies.

LITERATURE REVIEW

It is clearly seen in the reports of the World Economic Forum that technological innovations have both job-creating effects and job-destroying effects (World Economic Forum, 2016; 2018; 2020; 2023; 2025). Therefore, in this process, trade unions and policy makers have a major role to play in protecting and defending the rights of the labour force. As can be understood from recent studies, transformations that directly affect working life, such as the introduction of artificial intelligence into the workforce, the robotisation and digitalisation-oriented work of enterprises, and the shift from the industrial sector to the services sector becoming much faster, emphasise that the structure of employment is undergoing a change. In this context, Acemoglu and Restrepo's "Robots and Jobs: Evidence From US Labor Markets" (2020), the effects of robots on labour outputs, especially in the industrial sector, are analysed in detail. According to the results obtained in the study, the US labour market data show that the increase in the integration of robots into the labour force has negative effects on employment and wages at the regional level in the short term, and both negative and positive effects in the long term. Moreover, the authors point to increased risks, especially for workers undertaking low- and medium-skilled jobs. For these workers, they emphasise the importance of skill transformation or retraining policies to adapt to the transformation in line with new competencies in the labour market (Acemoglu & Restrepo, 2020). Frey and Osborne in their study titled "The Future Of Employment: How Susceptible Are Jobs To Computerisation?" (2017) aimed to measure the vulnerability of jobs to the risk of computerisation in a changing world. In the study, it is argued that the risk of computerisation of routine and predictable jobs is quite high. In other words, they stated that similar to the past periods, some jobs will not need to be performed by human labour. In the study, they categorised 702 different occupations into low, medium and high categories of jobs that are at risk in the context of the development of artificial intelligence and robotic technologies. As a result of the methodology they applied, they found that

47% of the jobs in the US labour market are at high risk of automation. The study also emphasises the importance of new skill sets suitable for new business models (Frey & Osborne, 2017). The internalisation of the results of the study by trade unions provides guidance to unions on which occupational groups they should focus on in the future and which measures should be taken. Caselli et al. (2025) conducted a comprehensive analysis of the impact of robotisation on local employment dynamics. In their study, tasks performed by robots were compared with those performed by workers, and the areas where substitution or complementary effects emerged were investigated. The authors sought to determine the effects of increased robot use on regional employment levels and types of employment by considering the task compositions and technological equipment of industries in different regions. The findings of the Caselli et al. research support the hypothesis that automation and artificial intelligence will cause job losses in some sectors and create new jobs in other sectors (Caselli et al., 2025). There are studies in the literature discussing why Industrial Revolutions and technological transformations did not eliminate all jobs throughout history. In fact, one of these studies is Autor's study conducted in 2015. Autor emphasizes in his study that while technological developments eliminate some jobs, they also create new jobs, thus creating a relative balance in the total number of employment (Autor, 2015). Therefore, unions need to determine their organizational strategies according to the competencies that may emerge in their future roles by taking this situation into consideration (Autor, 2015). Another study that supports Autor's work is the study conducted by Graetz and Michaels in 2019. In this study, it was stated that the use of robots in employment caused a loss of labor in some sectors and created new jobs in others (Graetz and Michaels, 2019). The study emphasizes that robots increase productivity and therefore jobs requiring high skills may increase in the future (Graetz and Michaels, 2019). The integration of artificial intelligence and automation processes into the labor market requires unions to develop strategies to increase the skills and qualifications of low and medium-skilled labor in particular (Autor,2015; Graetz and MİchaeIs,2019).

Fornino and Manera (2022) examined labour flexibility to assess the long-term effects of automation technologies on labour markets. Assuming that robots and human labour are perfect substitutes for each other, the study investigates the economic incentives that firms use when making automation investments. An important finding of the study is that adjusting labour costs is easier than adjusting robot costs. In other words, it was found that employers can more easily hire workers on a short-term basis in response to sudden shocks in production. The authors emphasise that this situation reduces employment stability. Another interesting finding from the study is that part of the layoffs are attributed to the costs of integrating robots into the workforce. However, the ease of use of production robots and the increase in robot productivity could disrupt the labour market (Fornino & Manera, 2022).

Fornino and Manera's study, labour flexibility is emphasized as a critical factor to prevent this negative scenario in the labour market. As a result, the study suggests that labour flexibility should be increased and training programmes should be strengthened in order to adapt to automation processes. It is also emphasised that policy makers should focus on long-term planning for the integration of robot use into the economy while developing strategies to protect employment (Fornino & Manera, 2022). Makridakis (2017) emphasises that the artificial intelligence revolution will inevitably transform society and businesses and claims that this transformation will bring about a radical change in the labour market. The author states that especially the integration of advanced automation and artificial intelligence applications into production processes, while increasing the competitive advantage of firms, forces the competence sets of workers to change rapidly. Accordingly, the article emphasises that trade unions need to take a more proactive role due to uncertainties about the future of work. In particular, the author suggests that trade unions should cooperate with civil society and state institutions in identifying new skill needs in the labour market, protecting workers' rights and organising those who may be exposed to job losses (Makridakis, 2017). In his research, Pfeiffer (2014) analyses the value of labour under digital capitalism, in particular from the perspective of the "use value" of human labour. The study discusses the consequences of digitalisation and automation in the processes of working life, i.e. the division of labour mechanisms, in terms of workers' freedom and skill development (Pfeiffer, 2014). Caruso (2018), in his study within the scope of Industry 4.0, deals with the transformations caused by digital innovation at the social level. Evaluating the possible effects of transformation on labour relations, the researcher argues that digitalisation is reshaping labour market structures, especially in sectors with high automation capacity, and unions need to develop new strategies to adapt to this change. The study emphasises the institutional gaps that may arise with the acceleration of technological transformation and that these gaps may further increase income inequality within the social order (Caruso, 2017). Pulignano and Doerflinger (2013) examine the impact of trade unions in the new economic order in which temporary employment in Belgium has become widespread. The study reveals how the increasingly fragmented and project-based nature of employment, together with the accelerating wave of digitalisation and automation, has transformed the bargaining power of trade unions. In this context, the study argues that unions can exist not only defensively but also proactively and cooperatively in the face of technological transformation and predicts that combative organising policies will weaken and cooperative policies will increase in the future (Pulignano & Doerflinger, 2013). Parolin (2020) examined the trends of automation on the labour force and the impact of trade unions in the process and found that high union coverage rates slowed wage declines in occupations with high levels of routine work intensity, but accelerated the decline in employment rates. Parolin's study states that the social effects of automation processes on labour markets can be prevented by trade unions (Parolin, 2021). Another study conducted by Kostol and Svarstad (2023) focuses on the impact of trade unions on technological transformation. Kostol and Svarstad measured the effects of the increase and decrease in union density on the wages of workers doing routine jobs in Norway between 2000 and 2014 (Kostøl and Svarstad, 2023). They concluded that unions were effective in reducing the wage gap between routine and non-routine jobs because of their wage protection policies. Therefore, they stated that employers accelerated their investments in automation in their workplaces (Kostøl and Svarstad, 2023). For this reason, the acceleration of automation processes in workplaces by employers causes the workforce, especially those doing routine jobs, to lose their jobs. The future strategies of unions should focus on developing policies that accelerate the adaptation processes of low-skilled workers to new technologies, as well as improving the wages and working conditions of their members. In other words, instead of opposing technological transformation, unions should determine strategies that will ensure fair income distribution in line with the transformation (Kostøl and Svarstad, 2023).

Haapanala et al. (2023) are studying robotic technologies' potential effects on employment. They emphasise that trade unions need to enter into social dialogue with employers to mitigate any unfavorable effects of robotic technology on workers, while also including in collective bargaining the possibility of workers' adjustment to new technologies (Haapanala et al., 2023). Their findings were supported by data indicating that the greater the union density in a region or sector, the less job losses robotisation produced. The reason for this was that trade unions fought for the interests of workers, supporting them through various initiatives aimed at equipping them with new skills. The study shows that with the help of unions as protectors, strategic solutions can still be found to guarantee workers' employment security and career development, even in occupations with the highest risk of automation. They claimed that with the two mechanisms of union organisation and social dialogue, the indiscriminate use of robots can be halted (Haapanala et al., 2023).

Berge and Dekker (2024) investigated perceptions of how new technologies affect job quality and emphasised the importance of workforce organisation in this process. The study found that various technological innovations implemented in workplaces have effects on dimensions such as employees' job satisfaction, autonomy, and perceived workload (Berge & Dekker, 2024). Berge and Dekker emphasize that organized labour can adapt to technological change in work if it is actively involved in the control and governance of technology use. The study found that encouraging workers' participation in decision-making processes related to technological transformation through trade unions and other labour organizations leads to increased job satisfaction among workers. Therefore, it is stated that the participation of labour organizations and management in supporting the technological transformation process will increase job satisfaction (Berge & Dekker, 2024).

Automation and artificial intelligence technologies seem to have multidimensional and divergent effects on industrial relations actors. Studies investigating the position of trade unions in the process of technological change (Kostøl & Svarstad, 2023; Dale-Olsen, 2021) have concluded that trade unions' collective bargaining and wage pressure policies in some cases encourage employers to accelerate automation investments. On the other hand, unions have also been found to contribute to the productivity growth of the enterprise through the protection of workers' rights and the acquisition of new competences (Kostøl, 2024). Hence, the potential role of trade unions not only in addressing wage injustice and social protection, but also in developing new competence sets for technological innovation (Kostøl & Svarstad, 2023). However, studies focusing on the effects of robotics and AI on local employment levels, skills demand and regional disparities (Caselli et al., 2025; Cheng et al., 2024) emphasise that some occupations face the risk of substitution but new skill needs arise with new business models of automation and AI. Studies on skill development (Cheng et al., 2024) suggest that highly skilled workers tend to earn more, which may increase risks such as income inequality and labour market polarisation. On the other hand, studies on the perceived effects of new technologies on job quality (Berge & Dekker, 2024) and findings pointing to the role of trade unions in encouraging participation in continuing education (Kostøl, 2024) suggest that organised action is critical for the labour force to adapt to digital transformation in the long term and to maintain employment quality.

The focus of studies in the literature is that the use of automation and artificial intelligence makes structural transformations in labour markets inevitable, but the socioeconomic consequences of these transformations are not always the same. In addition to technological investment decisions, the mediating role that trade unions may play in areas such as labour quality and income distribution is becoming increasingly important. Therefore, it is inevitable that issues such as closely following the consequences of automation and artificial intelligence technologies, which are becoming increasingly popular in the academic literature, such as income inequality and labour market polarisation, analysing inequality between different sectors and regions, and evaluating the potential strategies of trade unions in this process will be at the centre of research in the field of Social Policy and Industrial Relations in the future (Acemoglu & Restrepo, 2020; Goldsmith et al., 2024; Goldsmith et al., 2024). In this context, it is important to determine to what extent and how the countries, business sectors and regions with similarities and differences are affected by automation through the cluster analysis. This will also enable policy makers to take more robust steps towards policy objectives. In conclusion, the current discussions in the literature on automation and AI-based transformation of the labour market point to the urgency of protective and transformative policies and suggest that trade unions in particular can play a key role in both protecting workers' rights and promoting skills transformation in line with the occupations of the future.

METHODOLOGY

In this study, data were analyzed using the clustering method. Clustering analysis is an advanced statistical method used to determine internal groups within data sets (Abonyi and Feil, 2007). This analysis technique, which is one of the multivariate methods, allows data to be classified according to the degree of similarity and difference between groups (Çakmak et al., 2015). The most important advantage of the clustering method for researchers is that it allows objective classification of data.

The distinctive feature of cluster analysis compared to other multivariate statistical analyses is that, while multivariate statistical analyses require the analysis of large data sets, cluster analysis is not affected by different data distributions (Çakmak, 1999). Additionally, cluster analysis provides researchers with flexibility regarding the assumption of normality. Data obtained using different measurement techniques can be included in cluster analysis and measured. These advantages have made cluster analysis one of the most popular analyses in the social sciences, as it can be applied regardless of the homogeneity or heterogeneity of the data, the type of data, or the scale type (Hartigan, 1975).

In cluster analysis, there are two basic approaches. These are hierarchical and partitional methods. While hierarchical methods organise the data by creating a tree structure (dendrogram), partitional methods divide the data into a predetermined number of clusters (Garcia-Dias et al., 2020). These are hierarchical and non-hierarchical methods (Uçar, 2017). With hierarchical clustering methods, a multi-stage process is followed when grouping data. Hierarchical clustering method is divided into two as agglomerative and divisive. It is seen that the most widely used method among these two methods in the literature is the agglomerative hierarchical clustering approach. In this approach, all observations are initially treated as a single cluster, and in the process, outlier observations in the data set form new clusters separate from the main cluster. In this method, 5 different techniques are used for the formation of clusters: "single linkage method, full linkage method, average linkage method, Ward's method and centralised method" (Uçar, 2017).

In hierarchical clustering analysis, criteria such as distance coefficients, dendrogram analyses and aggregation coefficients are used to determine the number of clusters (Karagöz, 2016). Non-hierarchical clustering method offers different methods according to the approach of the researcher. These methods are sequential starting, parallel starting and average separation methods. The most common among these is the K-means technique, which was developed in the 1950s in the field of health, due to its ease of use and effective grouping (Ball & Hall, 1965; MacQueen, 1967; Lloyd, 1982; Steinhaus, 1956; Karagöz, 2016; Garcia-Dias et al.) In the 1980s, it was used to group schizophrenia patients with different clinical disorders (Farmer et al., 1983). In most K-means studies, the number of clusters was decided either through the use of domain knowledge or jointly with Ward's linkage. In non-hierarchical clustering methods, the number of clusters is usually selected based on the researcher's intuition and knowledge of the literature(Abramowitz et al., 2003; Aderka et al., 2012; Zilcha-Mano et al., 2015).

Ward's linkage method is also known as the minimum variance method. In this method, any two clusters are merged by minimizing the increase in the sum of the squares of the intra-cluster variances. Therefore, all observations are initially considered as a single cluster. Then, the distance between each pair of clusters is measured and it is decided whether the relevant clusters can be merged into a single cluster. Based on the distances between the clusters, a cluster diagram called a dendrogram is created. Through the dendrogram, researchers can visually determine the number of clusters in the data set (Garcia-Dias et al., 2020).

In this study, the Ward method was preferred due to the suitability of the data set. The main reason for selecting this method is its potential to minimise variance values within clusters and create homogeneous groups (Çakmak et al., 2015; Alpar, 2011). The primary objective of the Ward method is to minimise the total sum of squared errors. Thus, in line with the research objective, the highest similarities or differences within a specific cluster can be identified Çakmak et al., 2015; Alpar, 2011). Error squares are calculated by the following formula:

$$\boldsymbol{ESS} = \sum_{i=1}^{n} x_i^2 - \frac{1}{n}\left(\sum_{i=1}^{n} x_i\right)$$

In the formula x_i stands for the i'th observation. Cluster analysis considers each i'th observation as a cluster in the initial step. Hence, the ESS takes on a zero value (Aldenderfer & Blashfield, 1984). Further, clusters are formed with the minimum possible increase (Garcia-Dias et al., 2020; Çakmak et al., 2015). In Ward's method, Euclidean squared distance is usually preferred to determine cluster similarity. This particular distance minimizes the variance of each observation with respect to the cluster center, thus increasing the internal consistency of the clusters (Hartigan, 1975). The results obtained from the clustering analysis method can be used to determine employee profiles, analyse union membership dynamics and contribute to strategic decision-making regarding the labour market in the industrial relations literature.

In line with the objective of the study, AI Preparedness Index, GII, Percentage of the ICT sector personnel in total employment, Economic Complexity Index (ECI), Number of employees at the poverty line, Gini Income Index, Unemployment Rates,

Trade Union Density, Collective Bargaining Coverage, and Freedom of Association Index, data were collected to examine 25 European countries.

FINDINGS

In this research, hierarchical clustering analyses using Ward's method reveal the divergence in countries' policies and practices towards technological adaptive capacity, income distribution and labour rights. The findings suggest that increasing automation and the use of artificial intelligence have profound and multidimensional effects on labour markets and socioeconomic justice. In this part of the study, the results of the analyses will be examined under 3 headings. These are;

Artificial Intelligence and Technological Readiness Level: This section focuses on the similarities and differences among selected European countries in terms of AI readiness index, innovation level and IT sector employment. According to Ward's and dendrogram results, it is observed that there are differences in technological readiness even among countries with similar welfare levels in the same continent. This situation expresses the inequality in the capacity of countries to adopt technology and to reflect this technology to their labour markets.

Socio-economic Justice and Income Inequality: The best tool to measure income inequality is the "Gini index". In addition to the Gini index, the inclusion of the rates of employees at the poverty line and unemployment rates in the analysis in this section will be a good guide to see the labour market situation in European countries. In addition, it will be possible to understand the effects of the increase in artificial intelligence and automation on labour markets.

Labour Rights and the Role of Trade Unions: In this section, which is the third sub-heading of the existing cluster analysis, it is investigated whether there are differences between countries in terms of union density, collective bargaining coverage and labour rights index.

1. Artificial Intelligence and Technological Readiness Level

In this section of the study, the results of the hierarchical clustering analysis conducted on artificial intelligence and countries' technological readiness levels will be presented. Additionally, the differences and similarities among countries will be explained using tables and graphs.

Table 2. Proximity matrix between countries

	1	2	3	4	5	6	7	8	9	10	11	12	13	14	15	16	17	18	19	20	21	22	23	24	25
1:Austria	,000																								
2:Belgium	2,196	,000																							
3:Czechia	2,270	2,229	,000																						
4:Denmark	2,434	3,573	7,084	,000																					
5:Estonia	9,689	9,341	11,396	4,771	,000																				
6:Finland	1,254	3,129	6,113	,712	8,552	,000																			
7:France	1,156	,925	3,389	1,596	7,962	,925	,000																		
8:Germany	,719	5,142	4,670	2,775	10,233	1,456	2,585	,000																	
9:Greece	18,735	8,946	14,833	21,156	29,821	20,234	14,498	26,492	,000																
10:Hungary	7,896	4,518	2,002	13,277	14,586	12,780	7,396	12,029	12,281	,000															
11:Ireland	10,911	11,378	9,269	9,451	2,466	12,616	10,425	11,373	33,939	10,495	,000														
12:Italy	2,796	1,042	,835	7,067	13,155	5,619	2,385	5,891	10,008	2,047	12,271	,000													
13:Latvia	12,008	5,768	7,128	11,587	8,032	14,324	9,319	16,980	11,452	4,628	8,164	6,999	,000												
14:Lithuania	5,530	1,116	3,638	6,102	8,916	6,946	3,628	9,778	6,775	4,075	11,050	2,593	2,287	,000											
15:Netherlands	2,733	3,479	7,245	,068	4,533	,804	1,427	3,135	20,808	12,982	9,114	6,942	11,232	6,004	,000										
16:Norway	9,470	3,803	11,071	5,331	8,641	7,042	4,884	13,311	9,087	12,457	15,163	8,207	6,261	3,014	4,842	,000									
17:Poland	7,727	2,458	3,421	11,593	16,215	11,037	6,168	12,999	4,500	2,154	16,055	1,835	4,152	1,473	11,433	7,222	,000								
18:Portugal	6,442	1,143	5,005	7,000	11,884	7,169	3,628	11,054	4,395	5,177	14,853	2,702	4,010	,517	6,720	2,359	1,390	,000							
19:Slovakia	8,235	4,464	2,271	13,881	16,243	13,528	8,402	13,084	9,684	,821	13,320	2,496	4,345	3,205	13,946	12,179	1,247	4,468	,000						
20:Slovenia	3,097	2,071	,293	8,486	13,979	7,188	4,012	6,263	11,653	1,791	12,198	,554	7,097	3,140	8,674	10,800	2,123	4,063	1,467	,000					
21:Spain	4,819	,512	3,756	5,790	11,001	5,661	2,452	8,881	5,626	4,481	13,460	1,751	4,408	,545	5,532	2,729	1,414	,142	4,133	3,074	,000				
22:Sweden	6,316	9,610	9,407	4,131	2,839	5,758	6,157	4,945	35,708	14,556	3,097	11,547	14,244	12,457	3,896	13,699	18,571	15,102	17,774	12,602	13,048	,000			
23:Switzerland	2,190	7,999	7,092	4,124	11,636	2,545	4,247	,448	32,724	15,235	12,291	8,568	21,309	13,733	4,395	16,912	17,382	15,077	17,245	9,263	12,460	4,592	,000		
24:Turkey	13,520	5,315	8,042	16,505	20,387	16,080	9,643	19,940	3,029	4,234	20,447	4,747	5,237	3,580	15,812	7,666	1,376	2,422	4,089	6,284	2,918	24,057	24,681	,000	
25:United Kingdom	,759	3,624	4,758	1,812	9,373	,541	1,117	,523	22,712	11,113	11,316	4,790	15,189	8,088	1,857	9,903	11,255	8,568	12,625	6,119	6,654	4,757	1,071	16,610	,000

Table 1 shows the similarities and differences between countries using the Square Euclidean distance. Denmark and the Netherlands can be described as the countries with the most similar characteristics when considering the variables of artificial intelligence and technology readiness. This is because the Euclidean distances between these countries are quite close, at 0.068. This relatively low indicator suggests that both countries have a high level of technological readiness and share similar approaches to addressing the impacts of artificial intelligence on their labour markets. This situation can be interpreted as the countries being influenced by each other's labour market characteristics or adopting similar measures to address potential labour market challenges. On the other hand, Greece and Estonia were found to be the two countries furthest from these variables (29.821). A country that differs negatively from other countries is at risk of lagging behind in terms of AI readiness. In these countries, the long-term negative effects of automation will be felt more acutely in the labour market. Therefore, these countries are highly likely to face income inequality and a much more fragile labour market structure in the future.

Figure 1. Artificial intelligence and technological readiness of countries dedrogram diagram

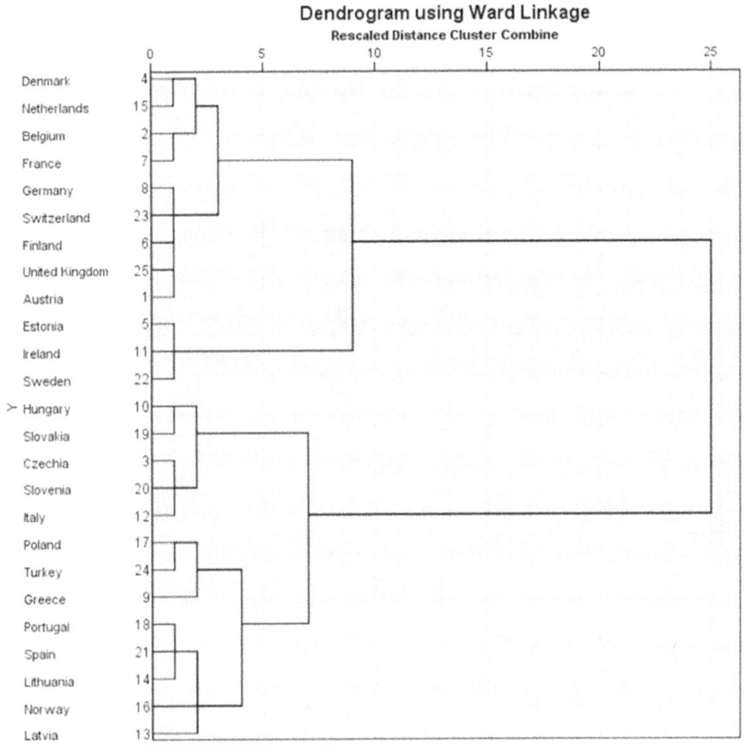

The dendrogram analysis in the figure shows the technological readiness levels of countries in terms of artificial intelligence and innovation indicators. The rescaled distance cluster grouping is displayed horizontally along the axis and shows the relative distances between countries, thereby indicating how they are grouped based on their similarities. In the graph, the countries that have clustered in the early stages of the dendrogram can be interpreted as having quite similar profiles in terms of AI and innovation readiness. The clustering of countries such as Denmark and the Netherlands in the early stages of the dendrogram indicates that they are at similar levels in terms of digital infrastructure and innovation capacity. In contrast, the clustering of countries such as Turkey and Greece in the later stages indicates that they are less prepared in terms of technology compared to most other countries. This suggests that low AI integration and innovation capacity may mean that the labour market effects of automation in these countries may be slower but potentially more dramatic. This dendrogram provides important insights into which countries are in the context of AI and technological readiness and what kind of organising policy unions should adopt in which countries.

Table 3. Cluster distribution of countries in the context of artificial intelligence and technological readiness

Case Number	Ülkeler	Cluster	Distance	Case Number	Ülkeler	Cluster	Distance
1	Austria	1	,796	13	Latvia	3	1,867
4	Denmark	1	,958	16	Norway	4	1,446
6	Finland	1	,508	18	Portugal	4	,132
7	France	1	,927	19	Slovakia	3	,792
8	Germany	1	,827	20	Slovenia	3	,993
5	Estonia	2	,914	17	Poland	3	,758
11	Ireland	2	,960	23	Switzerland	1	1,267
3	Czechia	3	1,239	15	Netherlands	1	1,015
10	Hungary	3	,863	22	Sweden	2	1,022
12	Italy	3	,987	24	Turkey	4	1,657
2	Belgium	4	1,085	14	Lithuania	4	,766
9	Greece	4	2,097	21	Spain	4	,428
				25	United Kingdom	1	,434

According to the results of the hierarchical clustering analysis carried out to examine artificial intelligence and technological readiness levels of countries, the distribution of countries according to clusters is as shown in the table. In the last cluster centre distance analysis performed according to these cluster distributions, the results in Table 3 were obtained.

Table 4. Final cluster centres in the context of artificial intelligence and technological readiness of countries

Variables	1	2	3	4
Artificial Intelligence Preparedness Index	,97478	,82402	-,90975	-,55744
Global Innovation Index	-1,03771	-,77441	,92628	,59156
Percentage of the ICT sector personnel in total employment	-,26628	2,22259	-,01311	-,63511
ECI	,61738	,26424	,31741	-1,13623

Table 5.

DISTANCES BETWEEN FINAL CLUSTER CENTERS				
CLUSTER	**1**	**2**	**3**	**4**
1	**0,00**			
2	**2,532**	**0,00**		
3	**2,750**	**3,301**	**0,00**	
4	**2,866**	**3,729**	**1,654**	**0,00**

Table 3 shows that the countries in cluster 1 have high technology readiness, but their employment capacity in the general innovation and ICT sector remains insufficient. This shows that countries are following automation and artificial intelligence technology but their innovation ecosystems need to be developed. In Cluster 1 countries, the role of trade unions can be interpreted as the need to help workers adapt to AI and retrain them to be suitable for high-tech jobs. The countries in the second cluster can be expressed as countries with "ICT-oriented, weak innovation power". This is because the countries in this cluster are intensively employed in the ICT sector (2.22) but their innovation performance is low (-0.77). In this case, these countries can be interpreted as countries that closely follow technology, depend on technology in production but have a weak R&D diversity. The fact that these countries closely follow the digital transformation processes indicates that they may face fewer problems in the labour market in the future. Countries in the third group have a high level of innovation but have problems in technological adaptation. For this reason, these countries indicate that they may experience problems between the "old economy-digital economy" in the future. In countries with this structure, unions should actively take part in the field in order to minimise the negative effects of automation on the labour force and determine the form of organisation for the future. Countries in the fourth cluster have a very low "economic complexity index" and are lagging behind in technological adaptation. These countries are the most likely to face problems in the face of the rapid impact of artificial intelligence on labour markets due to their low level of technological readiness. Therefore, trade unions should take early steps in these countries and act responsibly to protect labour rights and reduce income inequality. When the distances between the clusters are analysed, it is seen that Clusters 3 and 4 are the closest to each other (1.654). This shows that both clusters have similar difficulties in technology adaptation. The most distant clusters are 2 and 4 (3.729). This difference between ICT-orientated Cluster 2 and Cluster 4 with low economic complexity implies that their economic structures diverge significantly.

Table 6. Significance test of variables between clusters

	Mean Square	df	Mean Square	df	F	Sig.
Artificial Intelligence Preparedness Index	5,869	3	,304	21	19,280	,000
Global Innovation Index	6,290	3	,244	21	25,745	,000
Percentage of the ICT sector personnel in total employment	6,071	3	,276	21	22,024	,000
ECI	4,334	3	,524	21	8,274	,001

Table 4 shows the results of ANOVA analysis for cluster groups. ANOVA analysis is used to test whether between-group variances are significantly different from within-group variances and whether each variable creates statistically significant differences between clusters. The significance value ($p<0.05$) for all variables in the study shows that there are significant differences. According to the results of the analyses, the size of the F values shows which variables create more significant differences than other variables. The fact that the Global Innovation Index has the largest F value in this cluster group means that it creates the most significant difference. This shows that innovation is a critical factor in the adaptation of countries to automation. The results can be interpreted as countries with high levels of innovation can overcome the negative effects of automation more easily. The significant difference in the effect of the readiness of artificial intelligence on the labour markets of the countries means that each country will face different effects in the labour market in the future according to its own situation.

Figure 2. Scatter plot in the context of artificial intelligence and technological readiness of countries

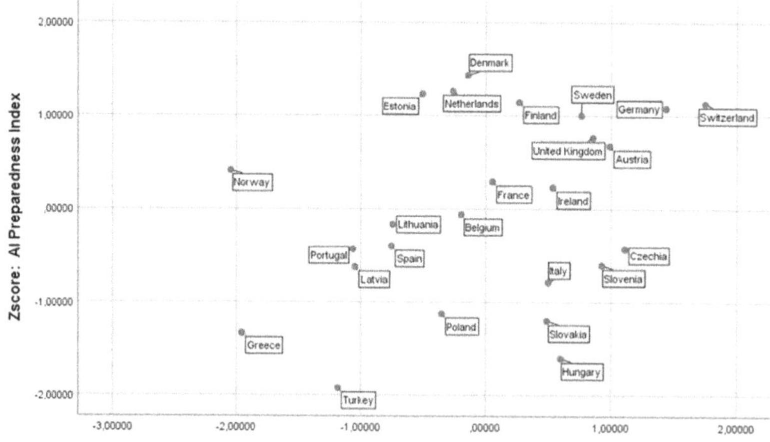

Figure 2 shows the readiness levels of countries for artificial intelligence and technological transformation in the context of the Artificial Intelligence Readiness Index and ECI Country Rankings. In the graph, it is observed that countries exhibit a significant differentiation in terms of their technological infrastructure and economic complexity levels. It is understood that Denmark, the Netherlands, Sweden and Germany, which are in the upper right corner, rank well among the country groups in terms of high AI readiness and innovation capacity. A more equally balanced side of the effects of AI on labour may be felt in these countries. However, the fact that countries such as Turkey and Greece are located in the lower left part of the graph indicates that they are both the least prepared for AI and have low levels of economic complexity. Therefore, based on the analysis conducted, it is anticipated that these two countries will face more negative impacts on their labour markets during the automation process.

2. Socio-Economic Justice and Income Inequality

Figure 3. Dendrogram diagram of countries in the context of socio-economic justice and income inequality

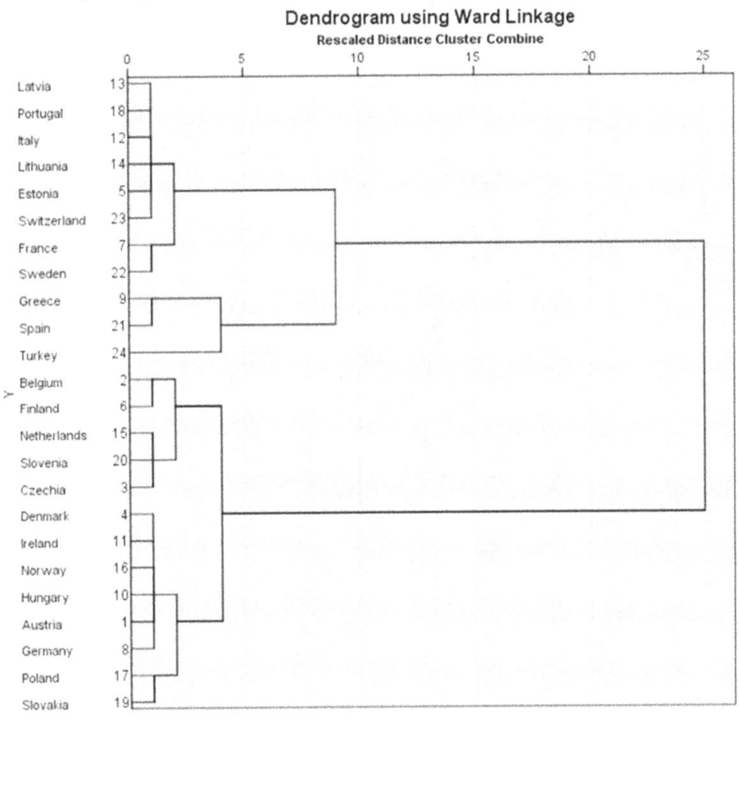

Figure 3 shows the dendrogram representing the results of the hierarchical clustering analysis in the context of socio-economic justice and income inequality. This dendrogram, constructed using the Ward method, visualises the similarities of countries in terms of variables such as income inequality, the proportion of people working at the poverty line and unemployment rates. In the dendrogram, the fact that Scandinavian countries come together in the early stages and form a cluster shows that they have a similar labour market in terms of low income inequality and low unemployment rates. On the other hand, the fact that Southern European Welfare Countries such as Turkey, Greece and Spain are clustered in the upper rungs of the dendrogram indicates that they differ from other countries due to income inequality and high unemployment rates in these countries. This structure clearly reveals the differences in socio-economic indicators across countries. In particular, when assessing the effects of automation and the use of artificial intelligence on labour markets, it is anticipated that inequalities may increase further in low-performing countries (e.g. Turkey and Greece) and lead to greater polarisation in the labour market. On the other hand, existing social policies and strong labour protection mechanisms in the Nordic countries are expected to offset these effects.

Table 7. Proximity matrix of countries in the context of socio-economic justice and income inequality

Proximity Matrix

Squared Euclidean Distance

	1	2	3	4	5	6	7	8	9	10	11	12	13	14	15	16	17	18	19	20	21	22	23	24
1:Austria	,000																							
2:Belgium	2,339	,000																						
3:Czechia	5,587	1,924	,000																					
4:Denmark	,789	,629	2,295	,000																				
5:Estonia	1,354	6,803	12,018	3,995	,000																			
6:Finland	4,754	,842	2,713	2,461	10,718	,000																		
7:France	,657	3,247	8,544	2,140	1,453	5,084	,000																	
8:Germany	,834	3,147	4,172	1,128	3,178	5,269	2,543	,000																
9:Greece	7,964	12,603	23,539	11,863	5,989	14,222	4,184	12,927	,000															
10:Hungary	,489	1,684	3,186	,258	2,862	4,235	2,159	,583	12,148	,000														
11:Ireland	,824	,896	2,441	,207	4,278	2,168	2,009	,728	11,704	,487	,000													
12:Italy	2,925	8,904	16,181	6,512	1,281	11,513	1,406	5,362	2,542	5,757	6,119	,000												
13:Latvia	1,328	6,566	12,046	4,102	,607	9,232	,802	2,809	4,613	3,287	3,734	,429	,000											
14:Lithuania	1,904	6,902	11,321	4,445	2,185	8,582	1,555	2,262	6,612	3,728	3,433	1,418	,614	,000										
15:Netherlands	2,558	,641	,987	,549	6,918	2,495	4,677	2,612	16,525	1,092	1,107	10,681	7,557	8,051	,000									
16:Norway	1,663	,914	1,241	,244	5,554	2,821	3,769	1,318	15,500	,462	,500	8,944	5,888	5,995	,228	,000								
17:Poland	1,262	4,373	6,314	1,881	1,858	8,604	3,292	1,793	12,899	,867	2,618	5,763	3,433	4,881	2,931	2,162	,000							
18:Portugal	1,859	8,102	13,602	5,066	,419	11,394	1,532	3,302	5,365	3,872	4,789	,568	,148	,976	8,715	6,857	3,360	,000						
19:Slovakia	2,703	3,679	8,373	2,921	3,284	7,547	3,225	5,715	9,099	2,923	4,381	6,422	5,204	8,174	3,622	3,973	2,352	5,672	,000					
20:Slovenia	2,852	,764	1,765	,858	6,849	2,972	4,774	3,588	15,820	1,473	1,754	10,805	7,919	9,054	,183	,691	2,950	9,052	2,559	,000				
21:Spain	10,635	17,005	29,183	15,623	7,183	19,294	6,401	16,171	,415	15,494	15,522	3,324	5,994	8,456	21,032	19,710	15,399	6,391	11,546	20,161	,000			
22:Sweden	,762	1,919	6,850	1,462	2,396	3,466	,237	2,761	5,050	1,867	1,521	2,714	1,880	2,751	3,378	2,898	3,406	2,874	2,516	3,327	7,758	,000		
23:Switzerland	,930	6,059	9,327	3,041	,761	9,326	1,807	1,207	8,961	1,842	2,794	2,243	,755	1,098	5,755	4,027	1,608	,670	5,179	6,382	10,794	2,807	,000	
24:Turkey	15,355	26,283	36,719	22,369	11,108	27,986	11,632	17,805	7,324	20,886	20,417	5,590	7,876	7,454	29,921	26,317	21,104	7,640	23,885	30,915	6,265	14,858	11,747	,000

Table 5 shows the similarities and distances (differences) between countries in terms of Squared Euclidean distance. The fact that countries such as Austria and Denmark have close values in the proximity matrix analysis shows that they have similar rates of low income inequality, low unemployment rate and people working at the poverty line. In these countries, the effects of AI and automation on the labour market are likely to lead to a more balanced situation in the labour market in the future. It is clear from the table that Turkey and Greece are separated from other countries by large differences. This implies that income inequality and high unemployment rates in these countries carry the risk of exacerbating the negative consequences of automation on the labour market. In this case, trade unions should take early measures against these risks and guide policy makers about the risks.

Table 8. Cluster distribution of countries in the context of socio-economic justice and income inequality

Case Number	Ülkeler	Cluster	Distance	Case Number	Ülkeler	Cluster	Distance
1	Austria	3	,458	*13*	Latvia	3	,734
2	Belgium	2	,493	*14*	Lithuania	3	1,152
3	Czechia	2	1,043	*15*	Netherlands	2	,437
4	Denmark	2	,568	*16*	Norway	2	,497
5	Estonia	3	,752	*17*	Poland	3	1,228
6	Finland	2	1,215	*18*	Portugal	3	,919
7	France	3	,701	*19*	Slovakia	3	1,734
8	Germany	3	1,179	*20*	Slovenia	2	,735
9	Greece	1	1,012	*21*	Spain	1	,819
10	Hungary	2	1,013	*22*	Sweden	3	,988
11	Ireland	2	,743	*23*	Switzerland	3	,714
12	Italy	3	1,301	*24*	Turkey	1	1,724

According to the results of the hierarchical clustering analysis performed according to the socio-economic variables of the countries, the distribution of the countries according to the clusters is as shown in the table. In the last cluster centre distance analysis performed according to these cluster distributions, the results in Table 7 were obtained.

Table 9. Final cluster centres of countries in the context of socio-economic justice and income inequality

	Cluster		
	1	**2**	**3**
Zscore: Number of employees at the poverty line	1,34837	-1,04258	,44484
Zscore: Gini Income Index	1,38394	-,80249	,22748
Zscore: Unemployment Rates	2,18503	-,58118	-,05036

Table 10.

Distances between Final Cluster Centers			
Cluster	**1**	**2**	**3**
1	0,00		
2	4,260	0,00	
3	2,674	1,885	0,00

Table 7 above shows the cluster groups formed according to socio-economic indicators. Accordingly, it can be stated that the first cluster is the countries in the "high socio-economic risk" group. As a matter of fact, the country group with the highest average number of employees at the poverty line compared to other clusters is in this cluster. Considering the high income inequality and high unemployment rates, it is likely that artificial intelligence and automation of the countries in this cluster will create serious negative effects on the labour market in the future. Therefore, in these countries, the makers of social policies and training programmes and trade unions should act together and play a more active role to protect workers' rights in the process of technological transformation. In the Scandinavian welfare model countries, which come together in the second cluster, it is understood that a strong labour market structure has been created with low unemployment rates and income justice. Thanks to the strong tradition of trade unionism in these countries, trade unions should play a guiding role in the integration of artificial intelligence and technology in the future. It would be appropriate to classify the countries in this group as countries in the "low socio-economic risk group". Finally, in the cluster of countries that can be expressed as the "medium socio-economic risk" group, a mixed picture is seen with income inequality and unemployment rates. Policy makers in this country need to strengthen social protection policies to manage the effects of automation and artificial intelligence. At the same time, unions need to adapt to flexible labour market policies for the future in the labour market in this country. This may offer unions the opportunity to be a pioneer in ensuring social justice in the labour market.

Table 11. Significance test of variables between clusters

	Mean Square	df	Mean Square	df	F	Sig.
Zscore: Number of employees at the poverty line	8,806	2	,257	21	34,318	,000
Zscore: Gini Income Index	6,079	2	,558	21	10,891	,001
Zscore: Unemployment Rate	8,686	2	,290	21	29,961	,000

Table 8 shows the results of ANOVA analysis for cluster groups. It was determined that the significance values ($p<0.05$) for all variables in the study contain statistically significant differences. According to the results of the analyses, the size of the F values shows which variables create more significant differences than the other variables. The fact that the proportion of people working at the poverty line has the largest F value in this cluster group means that it creates the most significant difference. Especially in the countries in Cluster 1, the high rate of people working at the poverty line indicates that income inequality in these countries may deepen further with the effect of artificial intelligence and automation. ANOVA results help to understand which factors affect socioeconomic inequalities more. According to these findings, it points out in which areas policy makers and trade unions should prioritise action. Thus, the role of trade unions in Cluster 1 countries in protecting labour rights, reducing income inequality and combating unemployment will be critical. In particular, prioritising retraining and skills development programmes will mitigate the problems that may arise after the integration of automation and artificial intelligence technologies into the labour market. 2. Strategies to maximise the opportunities created by artificial intelligence should be developed in the countries included in the cluster. Trade unions should take a guiding role to direct employees to new opportunities. 3. In cluster countries, the role of trade unions should be to guide the development of both social protection policies and technological infrastructure. In this way, the time for these countries to adapt to automation will be relatively shorter and will create opportunities in international competition.

Figure 4. Scatter plot of countries in the context of socio-economic justice and income inequality

Figure 4 shows the scatter plot of countries in terms of Gini Income Inequality Index (vertical axis) and Unemployment Rate (horizontal axis). The graph highlights the differences in the levels of socio-economic justice and income inequality between countries. Turkey, which is positioned in the upper right corner of the graph with high unemployment rate and high income inequality, is clearly differentiated from other countries. This shows that Turkey's labour market dynamics and social inequalities are more complex compared to other European countries. It also shows that artificial intelligence and automation are likely to create new justice and unemployment problems within the country. Similar to Turkey, Spain and Greece also have high unemployment rates, but income inequality (Gini coefficient) is lower in these countries. The supportive labour market and strong socio-economic structure of the Scandinavian countries have caused these countries to be placed in the lower left corner of the graph in the analysis.

The impact of automation and artificial intelligence on labour markets is expected to vary depending on the socio-economic characteristics of countries, according to analysis results. Trade unions are likely to be more affected by automation and artificial intelligence processes in countries with unfair income distribution and high unemployment rates. Therefore, trade unions in such labour markets must develop more rational solutions.

3. Labour Rights and the Role of Trade Unions

The results of hierarchical clustering analyses in terms of workers' rights and union activity are shown in Figure 5. The dendrogram graph obtained using Ward's method shows the degree to which countries resemble or differ from one another in terms of "union density, collective bargaining coverage, and worker rights index." The horizontal axis represents the relative distance between countries in terms of similarity, while the vertical axis indicates the cluster merging stage.

Figure 5. Dendrogram diagram of countries in the context of workers' rights and the role of trade union activities

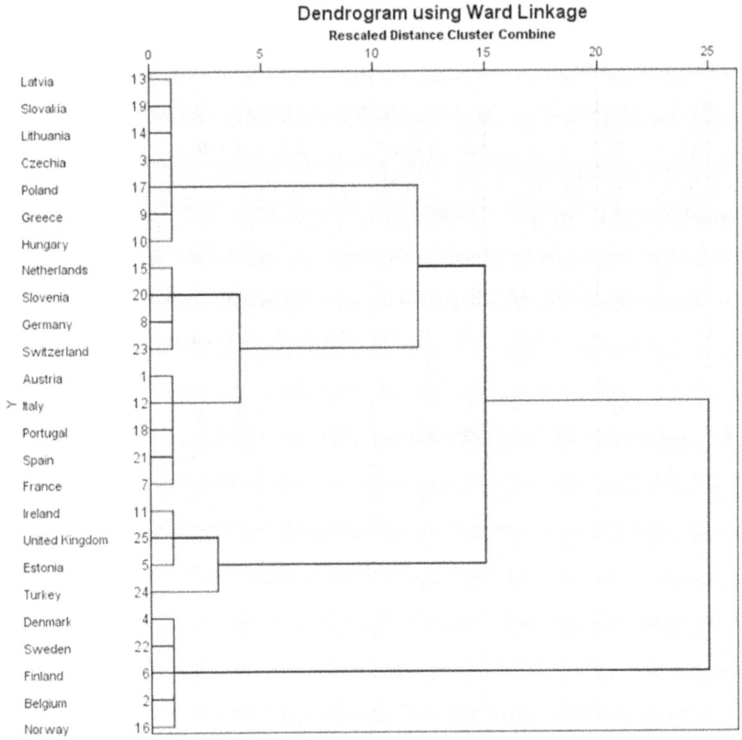

When examining the dendrogram graph, it can be seen that countries are grouped into three clusters within a range of approximately 10-15 units in terms of trade union activities and workers' rights. Within these three groups, Scandinavian countries and Belgium, which have high welfare state expenditures, high union density, broad collective bargaining coverage, and strong worker rights indices, have been identified. These countries can be described as the best-performing countries in terms of worker rights protection and union organisation variables. On the other hand, it is understood that Latvia, Slovakia, Lithuania, the Czech Republic, Poland, Greece, and Hungary, which are grouped together in the upper branches of the dendrogram, have low levels of worker rights protection and trade union organisation, as well as low levels of collective bargaining at the company level. It is understood that these countries may be more affected by the negative effects that automation and artificial intelligence may have on the labour market compared to other countries. Therefore, the analysis indicates that trade union structures and industrial relations systems need to be rethought. Countries such as Germany, Switzerland, the Netherlands, Austria, and France, which exhibit a more balanced structure, are similared group in the dendrogram graph. Although these countries have low union density, their broad legal coverage of worker rights has enabled them to establish a more balanced structure. These countries must carefully monitor the potential impacts of automation and artificial intelligence on their labour markets and adopt worker rights, union density, and the expansion of collective bargaining scope as political priorities. In this dendrogram graph, the socio-economic structures of countries are grouped together based on their similarities in terms of cultural and legal regulations, which is in line with the aim of this study. In this context, it is understood that workers' rights and trade union activities will play an important role in managing the shocks that will be experienced in the labour markets in the future in terms of the effects of automation and artificial intelligence. The following analyses will reveal which country groups exhibit statistically significant differences within this scope.

Table 12. Proximity matrix between countries

Proximity Matrix Squared Euclidean Distance

	1	2	3	4	5	6	7	8	9	10	11	12
1 Austria	,000											
2 Belgium	2,423	,000										
3 Czechia	4,762	7,939	,000									
4 Denmark	5,141	1,322	10,959	,000								
5 Estonia	10,571	18,795	5,950	19,429	,000							
6 Finland	3,529	,485	9,415	,219	18,484	,000						
7 France	,949	4,449	3,865	9,237	11,701	6,838	,000					
8 Germany	2,981	8,221	2,537	9,725	2,346	8,528	4,064	,000				
9 Greece	8,034	9,153	,845	11,433	8,913	10,337	7,238	5,454	,000			
10 Hungary	7,616	10,180	,465	13,711	8,434	12,067	5,895	5,102	,375	,000		
11 Ireland	6,466	11,853	4,899	11,389	1,208	10,942	8,893	,977	7,402	7,792	,000	
12 Italy	,393	1,017	5,367	3,729	13,932	2,216	1,330	4,858	7,894	7,824	8,851	,000
13 Latvia	5,521	9,128	,125	11,645	4,601	10,279	4,919	2,175	,939	,683	3,888	6,426
14 Lithuania	6,102	10,060	,132	13,142	5,081	11,559	4,972	2,714	,978	,461	4,770	7,028
15 Netherlands	1,026	5,632	2,806	8,149	5,141	6,559	1,682	,611	6,168	5,492	2,950	2,405
16 Norway	2,644	,859	5,272	1,045	13,435	,663	5,078	5,415	5,839	7,257	7,488	1,762
17 Poland	7,436	11,726	1,074	13,142	2,691	12,169	7,547	2,053	1,826	1,878	2,467	8,887
18 Portugal	,911	3,980	1,802	7,627	8,524	5,724	,491	2,262	4,300	3,531	5,926	1,354
19 Slovakia	6,009	9,402	,120	12,015	5,131	10,637	5,242	2,661	,700	,466	4,456	6,796
20 Slovenia	,655	4,307	3,408	6,192	6,058	4,868	3,943	,889	6,579	6,295	3,039	1,766
21 Spain	,803	4,916	2,273	8,450	7,135	6,516	,601	1,545	5,401	4,452	4,896	1,732
22 Sweden	4,663	,889	10,909	,063	20,123	,085	8,447	9,891	11,566	13,636	12,045	3,160
23 Switzerland	3,382	8,148	1,240	10,041	2,586	8,766	3,857	,248	3,476	3,125	1,492	4,954
24 Turkey	18,551	28,730	14,300	27,365	1,877	27,046	21,357	7,172	18,095	17,968	3,749	23,227
25 United Kingdom	6,011	10,490	2,963	10,459	1,539	9,936	7,821	,855	4,658	5,110	,328	7,892

	13	14	15	16	17	18	19	20	21	22	23	24	25
1 Austria													
2 Belgium													
3 Czechia													
4 Denmark													
5 Estonia													
6 Finland													
7 France													
8 Germany													
9 Greece													
10 Hungary													
11 Ireland													
12 Italy													
13 Latvia	,000												
14 Lithuania	,074	,000											
15 Netherlands	2,971	3,423	,000										
16 Norway	5,857	6,864	4,269	,000									
17 Poland	,468	,713	3,840	7,325	,000								
18 Portugal	2,476	2,657	,858	3,423	4,370	,000							
19 Slovakia	,025	,054	3,465	6,094	,563	2,733	,000						
20 Slovenia	3,609	4,248	,157	3,104	4,484	1,055	4,131	,000					
21 Spain	2,784	3,014	,331	4,197	4,361	,179	3,157	,605	,000				
22 Sweden	11,755	13,172	7,959	1,027	13,569	7,163	12,117	6,049	8,031	,000			
23 Switzerland	,957	1,327	,921	5,185	1,035	1,854	1,288	1,342	1,472	10,183	,000		
24 Turkey	12,097	12,997	11,455	21,778	8,483	17,324	12,925	12,299	14,994	28,566	8,312	,000	
25 United Kingdom	2,126	2,844	2,708	6,172	1,080	4,726	2,517	2,866	4,144	11,050	,820	5,338	,000

Table 10 shows the similarities and distances (differences) between countries in terms of Squared Euclidean distance. Accordingly, this matrix based on "union density, collective bargaining coverage and labour rights index" provides important clues in understanding the effects of technological transformations such as automation and artificial intelligence on labour markets. In countries with high union density and extensive collective bargaining traditions, maintaining employer-employee relations at the institutional level facilitates the effective implementation of vocational training, reskilling/upskilling and social protection policies, thus mitigating negative outcomes such as unemployment and income inequality. In contrast, in countries where labour rights are weak or collective bargaining is limited, technological transformations can produce more "harsh" effects, increasing the risk of unemployment, precarious work and income inequality. Therefore, this matrix shows that structural transformations focused on automation and artificial intelligence are closely related to the strength of countries' industrial relations institutions and social dialogue mechanisms. According to the matrix, Denmark and Sweden exhibit a very close profile in terms of union density and collective bargaining coverage, while Turkey is significantly different from other countries. Turkey's position relative to other countries indicates a weaker profile in terms of union density, collective bargaining coverage and the level of labour rights protection.

Table 13. Cluster distribution of countries in terms of labour rights and the role of trade union activities

Case Number	Countries	Cluster	Distance	Case Number	Countries	Cluster	Distance
1	Austria	1	1,475	*14*	Lithuania	1	1,004
2	Belgium	2	,667	*15*	Netherlands	1	,948
3	Czechia	1	,753	*16*	Norway	2	,673
4	Denmark	2	,513	*17*	Poland	1	1,341
5	Estonia	3	,528	*18*	Portugal	1	,753
6	Finland	2	,155	*19*	Slovakia	1	,989
7	France	1	1,433	*20*	Slovenia	1	1,101
8	Germany	1	1,072	*21*	Spain	1	,827
9	Greece	1	1,550	*22*	Sweden	2	,383
10	Hungary	1	1,412	*23*	Switzerland	1	,738
11	Ireland	3	,666	*24*	Turkey	3	1,365
12	Italy	2	1,453	*25*	United Kingdom	3	,961
13	Latvia	1	,880				

According to the results of the hierarchical clustering analysis of the countries according to the variables "*union density, collective bargaining coverage and labour rights index*", the distribution of the countries according to the clusters is as shown in the table. In the last cluster centre distance analysis performed according to these cluster distributions, the results in Table 12 were obtained.

Table 14. Final cluster centres of countries in terms of labour rights and the role of trade union activities

Final Cluster Centers			
	Cluster		
	1	**2**	**3**
Zscore: Trade Union Density	-,51189	1,58352	-,45571
Zscore: Collective Bargaining Coverage	-,12385	,99538	-1,02864
Zscore: Labour Right Index	,21795	,66616	-1,81657
Distances between Final Cluster Centers			
Cluster	**1**	**2**	**3**
1	0,00		
2	2,417	0,00	
3	2,227	3,797	0,00

According to Table 12, union density, collective bargaining coverage and labour rights index show how countries are grouped according to their industrial relations structures. The standardised z-score mean values indicate that the three clusters have similarities and differences. Based on the results of the analyses, the first cluster consists of country groups with intermediate values in terms of these variables. While union density and collective bargaining coverage are slightly below the average, the positive value of the labour rights index indicates that legal regulations or historical rights gains are preserved in these countries. Although union participation is limited in the automation process, it can be stated for the labour markets of these countries that workers' rights can be protected to a certain extent, but institutional efforts are needed for the development of social dialogue and reskilling policies. In the second cluster, union density, collective bargaining coverage and labour rights index have the highest values. Accordingly, it can be stated that employer-employee relations are stronger at the institutional level for these countries, active participation of workers' representatives in automation and artificial intelligence-oriented transformations is possible, and social dialogue mechanisms are relatively more developed. On the other hand, it is understood from the analysis results that the countries with the worst performance according to the given variables are gathered in the third cluster. In this cluster, it can be stated that the organisation of the labour force is lower than in other clusters, the scope of collective bargaining mechanisms is narrower and there are some problems in the protection of workers' rights in the institutional framework. Therefore, automation and artificial intelligence investments are likely to create more imbalances in the labour market than in other countries. In these countries, the adaptation of new technologies to the labour market may lead to an increase in unemployment and precarious employment in the short term. Similarly, the "*distance between final cluster censters*" table shows that the distance between Cluster 2 and Cluster 3 (3,797) is significantly larger than the other pairwise distances (2,417 between 1 and 2; 2,227 between 1 and 3). This suggests that the difference between the most institutionalised and the weakest industrial relations structures is sharper. Therefore, it indicates that the most differentiated consequences of automation and artificial intelligence-oriented transformations can be seen between these two groups. In brief, countries with strong trade union organisation and labour rights mechanisms tend to better manage the social costs of technological transformations, while countries with institutional weakness have a fragile structure.

Table 15. Significance test of variables between clusters

	Mean Square	df	Mean Square	df	F	Sig.
Zscore: Trade Union Density	9,903	2	,191	22	51,952	,000
Zscore: Collective Bargaining Coverage	5,204	2	,618	22	8,422	,002
Zscore: Labour Right Index	8,287	2	,338	22	24,555	,000

The ANOVA results show that there are statistically significant differences between the clusters in terms of the three variables used in the clustering analysis. In particular, the statistically significant level of significance ($p<0.05$) of the F values obtained for each variable reveals that the clusters are significantly differentiated from each other in each indicator. This result indicates that the mean differences between the clusters are not accidental and that the cluster solution forms a meaningful structure according to the variables analysed. As can be seen from the table, union density ($F=51.952$, $p<0.001$) is the variable that shows the strongest difference between clusters. High union density indicates the presence of better protection mechanisms in the labour market. This implies that it is possible to easily offset the effects of automation and artificial intelligence on labour markets. On the other hand, differences in collective bargaining coverage also statistically determine the main differences between countries in the protection of labour rights. In the context of the labour rights index, it shows that in country groups where labour rights are relatively weak, the weak structure of trade union activities and the resistance of the labour market to the problems that the labour market may face as a result of the integration of automation and artificial intelligence are weak. Thus, the results of the ANOVA analysis show that union activities and labour rights are key to offsetting the negative effects of automation and artificial intelligence. It is understood that trade unions need to be strengthened, especially in low-performing countries.

Figure 6. Scatter plot of countries in the context of labour rights and the role of trade union activities

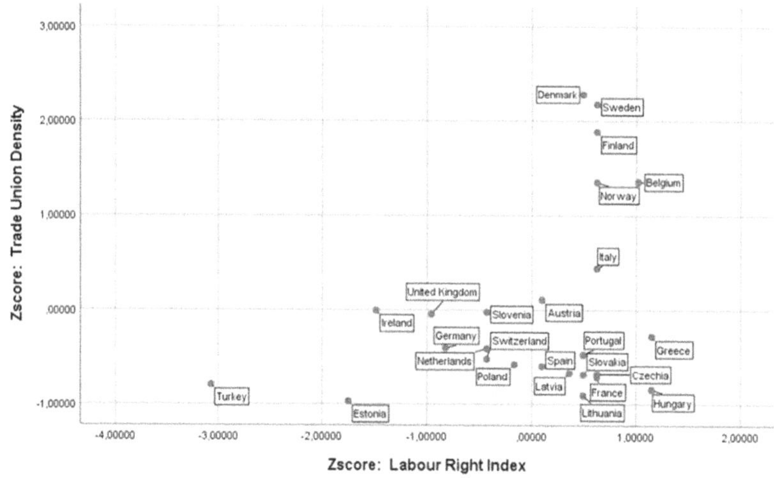

The scatter plot shows the results of the clustering analysis conducted according to "union density and worker rights index". The horizontal axis of the scatter plot represents the level of worker rights protection, while the vertical axis represents union density variables. In the context of the study's objective, the most prominent countries are Scandinavian countries such as Denmark, Sweden, Norway, and Finland, as well as Belgium. These countries are statistically located in the upper right corner of the graph due to their high union density and strong worker rights index scores. Therefore, these countries are likely to be less affected by the negative impacts of artificial intelligence and automation processes on labour markets. In other words, it is understood that these countries will be in a stronger position than others to balance shocks in the labour market due to their protection of workers' rights and high union density.

Another notable finding from the graph is that Estonia and Turkey are located in the lower left corner due to their low union density and labour rights index scores. This indicates that these countries may face challenges in the future, particularly in terms of labour rights and union guarantees, as automation and artificial intelligence are integrated into their labour markets. It is clear that worker rights must be protected and union density strengthened in order to prevent these problems. Countries such as Germany, Austria and Switzerland, which are in the middle of the graph, appear to be in a more balanced position than other countries in terms of worker rights and union density. It is clear that policy makers in these countries can take important measures to reduce the impact of future shocks by expanding the scope of collective bargaining and strengthening the effectiveness of trade unions. As indicated by the dispersion graph, it should be emphasised that the intensity of worker rights and trade union activities is a critical factor in producing faster solutions to changes in the labour market.

Based on the analyses conducted in line with the objective of this study, it is understood that the interaction between artificial intelligence, automation and workers' rights will lead to different transformations in the labour markets of different countries. In particular, differences in the level of technological readiness are shown to significantly differentiate income distribution and workers' rights in the labour market. Countries with strong trade union traditions and high levels of technological readiness, such as the Scandinavian countries, are expected to be more resilient to future challenges (Acemoglu & Restrepo, 2020; Holtgrewe, 2014). On the other hand, it is understood that strengthening industrial relations institutions in countries with low technological preparedness, such as Turkey and Greece, is of vital importance in ensuring income distribution justice and preventing labour market fragility in the face of shocks (Acemoglu & Restrepo, 2020; Fornino & Manera, 2022; Kostøl, 2024; Parolin, 2021).

In countries with low union density, fragility in labour markets is increasing day by day, exacerbated by technological developments. This situation is causing unemployment rates to rise and, in particular, worker rights to weaken (Berge & Dekker, 2024). At the same time, analyses of the impact of artificial intelligence and automation on labour demand in the labour market indicate that they will reduce the need for low-skilled workers performing routine tasks and create new jobs requiring new skills (Acemoglu & Restrepo, 2020; Caselli et al., 2025). As emphasised in the findings of this study, the impact of automation and artificial intelligence processes on labour markets will vary depending not only on countries' readiness for technology but also on structural characteristics such as social policy implementation, levels of trade union organisation, and indicators of income distribution equity. Therefore, policymakers should strengthen trade unions and take strategic steps to support social justice in technological transformation processes (Acemoglu & Restrepo, 2020; Holtgrewe, 2014).

SOLUTIONS AND SUGGESTIONS ON THE FUTURE ROLE OF TRADE UNIONS IN THE CONTEXT OF ARTIFICIAL INTELLIGENCE AND AUTOMATION

Just as artificial intelligence and automation are affecting every area of the world, they are also affecting the labour market, and trade unions, which are the main actors in industrial relations, are being affected in many ways. Trade unions, whose roots date back to the industrial revolution, now emerge as critical institutions for countries in managing the social, political, and economic impacts of technological advancements, going far beyond the protection of workers' rights. When examining studies conducted within this framework, it is observed that countries with high union density and centralised collective bargaining power are better able to manage the aforementioned effects of technology (Kostøl, 2024). The practical reflection of this situation, which stands out with its theoretical foundations, can be observed in the Scandinavian countries. Trade unions operating in Scandinavian countries focus on developing the professional skills of the workforce, and the programmes developed in this context are effective and successful in preparing the workforce for new technologies (Holtgrewe, 2014). In contrast, it is emphasised that in countries where trade union density is weak and trade unions' areas of activity have narrowed, technological changes will lead to labour losses, and these losses will in turn affect income inequality (Acemoğlu & Restrepo, 2020). Within this framework, in countries such as Spain and Greece, which are characterised by limited collective bargaining and weak trade union structures, the aforementioned changes are making it increasingly difficult to protect workers' rights and are increasing the risk of social injustice. Indeed, one of the issues that has been highlighted in these countries is that low-skilled workers will face difficulties in the face of technological developments such as artificial intelligence and automation, which are fundamental components of the transformation process (Fornino & Manera, 2022). This study, which employs advanced statistical methods such as cluster analysis and is supported by scatter plots, once again highlights the importance of such findings through different methodologies.

One of the most important functions of trade unions in the future will be to develop strategic policies that help the workforce adapt to technological changes. Therefore, they must already include lifelong learning and vocational training in their agendas, align them with technology, and incorporate them into collective bargaining processes. This will shorten the adaptation period for workers to new technologies and provide them with job security (Brynjolfsson & McAfee, 2014; Kostøl, 2024). In the future, trade unions will not only fulfil their functions of providing job security and contributing to the development of workers, but will also have an impact on the ethical aspects of technological transformation. In this regard, it is clear that unions have the potential to ensure that workers have greater involvement in decision-making mechanisms by advocating for transparency and fairness in the use of artificial intelligence in the workplace (Caselli et al., 2025).

Perhaps the most important role of trade unions in automation and artificial intelligence processes will be to balance the effects of the process through collective bargaining mechanisms with employers. In this context, one of the most important steps is to include social dialogue mechanisms aimed at cooperation rather than confrontational bargaining processes with employers in collective bargaining processes. Trade unions must position themselves not as unions under the control of employers, but rather as partners with employers. This will enable them to contribute to the expansion of collective bargaining coverage and the strengthening of workers' rights (Acemoglu & Restrepo, 2020). Additionally, it must play an active role in reshaping social policies by creating a broader sphere of influence at the political level. Such strategic approaches will not only facilitate the adaptation of the current workforce to technological transformation but also that of the future potential workforce (Autor, 2015).

It would be important for trade unions to focus on the following key strategic areas for their future role, in order to improve their position in the industrial relations system and at the same time contribute to the labour market of the countries (Howcroft & Taylor, 2023; Joyce ve diğerleri, 2023; Adhikary & Banerjee, 2022; Morales & Stecher, 2023):

Reskilling workers in accordance with new technology: Organise large-scale training programmes to offset the impact of automation on low-skilled workers,
Legal Protection: Strengthening legal status and social security mechanisms for digital platform workers,
Social Justice: To actively contribute to the development of policies that reduce income inequality and foster social justice,
Use of Digital Tools: Increasing the effective use of digital technologies to organise and defend workers' rights,

As a result, in the future, trade unions are expected to play a central role not only in protecting labour rights but also in managing technological transformation processes in a way that contributes to social justice and economic balance. In this respect, the formulation of policies to strengthen the structure of trade unions, both at the local level and in the international arena, stands out as a critical necessity for a sustainable and just economic transformation (Acemoglu & Restrepo, 2020; Holtgrewe, 2014).

SUGGESTIONS FOR FUTURE STUDIES

As a research method, hierarchical clustering analysis was used in this study within the framework of Ward's methodology. This allowed us to measure the similarities and differences between countries in terms of how automation and artificial intelligence technologies affect labour market dynamics. The use of different methods and methodologies in future studies will help to present the results more clearly.

The data set preferred in this study will be developed for future studies to include the level of automation by sector, professional skill mismatch, and digital literacy in the analyses, thereby providing a more macro perspective to the research. The effects of job losses caused by automation and new technologies (Acemoglu & Restrepo, 2020) and the transformations in employment (Autor, 2015) on income inequality, social exclusion, and labour market polarisation, which are frequently emphasised in the literature, should be the focus of future studies. This study has identified which countries exhibit similar effects of the issues mentioned above using the clustering analysis method. In future studies, this dataset should be expanded to include macroeconomic variables such as "Gini coefficient indices, unemployment rates, and working poverty rates" and analysed at the country level using time series methods. Cross-country comparisons using panel data analysis methods to relate the changes experienced by countries to automation and artificial intelligence will yield important results.

In addition to econometric and statistical modelling, artificial intelligence-based a priori methods and impact analyses will also contribute to the enrichment and deepening of future research. In particular, qualitative and quantitative research conducted by multidisciplinary research groups will provide important contributions to future studies by enabling the measurement of the effects of new technologies on demographic groups (Kaplan & Haenlein, 2019).

CONCLUSION

This research was conducted based on the research question, "How will the technological effects of automation and artificial intelligence in the workplace affect the labour market?" The aim of the research is to reveal the socio-economic indicators and the roles of trade unions through cluster analysis as a result of the effects of automation and artificial intelligence in countries. Cluster analysis enables statistical comparison between countries, revealing how similar or dissimilar they are to one another. The findings of the study reveal that the effects of technological transformation on labour markets vary depending on countries' levels of technological readiness, socio-economic structures, and the strength of trade union organisation.

The future roles of trade unions in labour markets where automation and artificial intelligence are expected to play a significant role are of critical importance both in managing the risks arising from this transformation and in protecting workers.

It is believed that ***countries with centralised collective bargaining traditions and strong trade union mechanisms*** may be more resilient to the effects of automation and artificial intelligence on the labour market. This view is supported by the findings of this study. In particular, it has been determined that *Scandinavian countries*, which have adopted strong trade unionism and centralised collective bargaining structures, differ positively from other countries analysed in this context. In Scandinavian countries, trade unions' future roles, focused on ***reskilling*** and ***upskilling*** to enhance workers' professional skills, will enhance their activities in the field of industrial relations.

Unlike Scandinavian countries, ***countries with weak union density and decentralised collective bargaining mechanisms*** are expected to face more destructive effects in the future. Indeed, countries such as Turkey and Greece stand out negatively from other countries in the study's findings. In these countries, weak organisation, problems with workers' rights, income inequality and unemployment are likely to be felt much more acutely in conjunction with technological transformation. Therefore, these countries need to strengthen their trade union structures and social dialogue mechanisms. In terms of the future role of trade unions, it is crucial for large and powerful trade unions in these countries to take a proactive role in developing strategies to help workers adapt to technological transformation. Indeed, the findings of the study support this view.

Another finding of the study is that automation processes and artificial intelligence lead to more ***polarisation in the labour market and income inequality in countries with weak industrial relations institutions***. Scandinavian countries, which have high union density and worker rights indices, stand out positively in this context compared to other countries. Countries like Turkey and Greece, which have weaker industrial relations institutions, were found to have a more fragile structure in this area and to diverge negatively from other countries.

Trade unions are seen to have a critical role to play in ensuring fairness in the labour market by mitigating the economic and social costs of technological transformation in the coming period, when automation and artificial intelligence will be integrated into the labour market. Based on the findings of this study, it is crucial that trade unions fulfil this role in four ways. These are:

1. **Supporting Reskilling and Training Programmes**: It is clear that workers performing low-skilled and routine tasks will experience greater job losses in the future. Trade unions should mitigate this damage by promoting vocational training and lifelong learning programmes and, in particular, by including these

programmes in collective bargaining processes to ensure that the workforce is prepared for new technologies.

2. **Reducing Income Inequality and Ensuring Social Justice**: Fairness in income distribution and social justice are among the most important economic functions of trade unions. Therefore, in future collective bargaining processes and policy-making, trade unions must play a guiding role in this regard, clearly highlighting the situation on the ground. Trade unions must strengthen their role as agents in minimising issues such as income inequality and social justice in the future.
3. **Improving Social Dialogue Mechanisms**: Technological transformation will clearly bring to the fore the social dialogue mechanism in countries' labour markets and, consequently, in their industrial relations systems. This situation will weaken collective bargaining processes based on the view that one party's loss is the other's gain. Therefore, the parties involved in Industrial Relations should focus on strengthening mutual social dialogue mechanisms to mitigate the social impacts of change.
4. **Guidance to Policy Makers:** Trade unions should provide policymakers with recommendations based on field data and play a guiding role in social policy regulations.

This study emphasises the need to rethink the future role of trade unions in technological transformation processes. As in all historical periods, the integration of automation and artificial intelligence into industrial relations is likely to give rise to certain socio-economic problems. Trade unions play a crucial role in managing the resulting crisis by anticipating this process. Indeed, the results of this study support this view. High trade union density and the establishment of strong collective bargaining mechanisms will be an important strategic step towards balancing potential negative developments in the labour market in the future. Trade unions must take a more proactive role in their countries' industrial relations in the future, particularly by adopting programmes aimed at developing low-skilled labour. This will enable technological transformations in the labour market to be addressed in a fairer and more peaceful manner.

REFERENCES

Abonyi, J., & Feil, B. (2007). *Cluster Analysis for Data Mining and System Identification*. Birkhäuser Verlag AG.

Abramowitz, J. S., Franklin, M. E., Schwartz, S. A., & Furr, J. M. (2003). Symptom Presentation and Outcome of Cognitive-behavioral Therapy for Obsessive-compulsive Disorder. *Journal of Consulting and Clinical Psychology*, *71*(6), 1049–1057. DOI: 10.1037/0022-006X.71.6.1049 PMID: 14622080

Acemoglu, D., & Restrepo, P. (2020). Robots and Jobs: Evidence from US Labor Markets. *Journal of Political Economy*, *128*(6), 2188–2244. https://doi.org/http://dx.doi.org/10.1086/705716. DOI: 10.1086/705716

Aderka, I. M., Hofmann, S. G., Nickerson, A., Hermesh, H., Gilboa-Schechtman, E., & Marom, S. (2012). Functional Impairment in Social Anxiety Disorder. *Journal of Anxiety Disorders*, *3*(26), 393–400. DOI: 10.1016/j.janxdis.2012.01.003 PMID: 22306132

Adhikary, S., & Banerjee, K. (2022). Digitalisation and AII: What Does the Future Hold for Labour Union? *GLOCALISM: JOURNAL OF CULTURE, POLITICS AND INNOVATION*, *1*(1), 1–29. DOI: 10.12893/gjcpi.2022.1.5

Aldenderfer, M. S., & Blashfield, R. K. (1984). *Cluster analysis*. SAGE Pub. DOI: 10.4135/9781412983648

Allen, R. C. (1999). Tracking the Agricultural Revolution in England. *The Economic History Review*, *52*(2), 209–235. https://doi.org/http://www.jstor.org/stable/2599937. DOI: 10.1111/1468-0289.00123

Alpar, R. (2011). *Uygulamalı Çok Değişkenli istatistiki Yöntemler*. Detay Yayıncılık.

Anderson, C. (2012). *Makers: The New Industrial Revolution*. Crwon Pub.

Ashton, T. S. (1986). The Industrial Revolution, 1760-1830. Praeger., 978-0313250415.

Atkeson, A., & Kehoe, P. J. (2001). The Transition to a New Economy after the Second Industrial Revolution. *National Bureau of Economic Research*(8676), 1-55. https://doi.org/http://www.nber.org/papers/w8676

Autor, D. H. (2015). Why Are There Still So Many Jobs? The History and Future of Workplace Automation. *The Journal of Economic Perspectives*, *29*(3), 3–30. DOI: 10.1257/jep.29.3.3

Ball, G. H., & Hall, D. J. (1965). *Isodata, a Novel Method of Data Analysis and Pattern Classification*. Stanford Research Institute.

Beauchamp, C. (2015). Invented by Law: Alexander Graham Bell and the Patent That Changed America. *The Journal of American History, 103*(3), 892. https://doi.org/https://doi.org/10.1093/jahist/jav598

Berge, J., & Dekker, F. (2024). New Technology And Workers' Perceived İmpact On Job Quality: Does Labor Organization Matter? *Economic and Industrial Democracy*, •••, 1–36. DOI: 10.1177/0143831X241265911

Bojanova, I. (2014). The Digital Revolution: What's on the Horizon? *IT Professional, 16*(1), 8–12. https://doi.org/doi. DOI: 10.1109/MITP.2014.11

Botham, F. W., & Hunt, E. H. (1987). Wages in Britain during the Industrial Revolution. *The Economic History Review, 40*(3), 380–399. https://doi.org/https://doi.org/10.2307/2596251. DOI: 10.2307/2596251

Brynjolfsson, E., & McAfee, A. (2014). The Second Machine Age: Work, Progress, and Prosperity. WW Norton & Company., 978-0-393-24125-9.

Buckman, D. L. (1907). *Old Steamboat Days on the Hudson River*. The Grafton Press.

Çakmak, Z. (1999). Kümeleme Analizinde Geçerlilik Problemi ve Kümeleme Sonuçlarının Değerlendirilmesi. *Dumlupınar Üniversitesi Sosyal Bilimler Dergisi*, (3), 187–205.

Çakmak, Z., Uzgören, N., & Keçek, G. (2015). Kümeleme Analizi Teknikleri ile İllerin Kültürel Yapılarına Göre Sınıflandırılması ve Değişimlerinin İncelenmesi. *Dumlupınar Üniversitesi Sosyal Bilimler Dergisi, 12*.

Caruso, L. (2017). Digital Innovation and the Fourth Industrial Revolution: Epochal Social Changes? *AI & Society, 33*(3), 379–392. https://doi.org/https://doi.org/10.1007/s00146-017-0736-1. DOI: 10.1007/s00146-017-0736-1

Caselli, M., Fracasso, A., Scicchitano, S., Traverso, S., & Tundis, E. (2025). What Workers And Robots Do: An Activity-Based Analysis Of The İmpact Of Robotization On Changes İn Local Employment. *Research Policy, 54*(1), 1–17. https://doi.org/https://doi.org/10.1016/j.respol.2024.105135. DOI: 10.1016/j.respol.2024.105135

Cheng, C., Luo, J., Zhu, C., & Zhang, S. (2024). Artificial Intelligence and the Skill Premium: A Numerical Analysis of Theoretical Models. *Technological Forecasting and Social Change, 200*, 1–12. DOI: 10.1016/j.techfore.2023.123140

Christopher, H. (1967). *Reformation to Industrial Revolution; the making of modern English society, 1530-1780*. Pantheon Books.

Cipolla, C. M. (1979). *The Economic History of World Population*. Penguin Books.

Clark, G. (2007). *A Farewell to Alms: A Brief Economic History of the World*. Princeton University Press., https://doi.org/http://www.jstor.org/stable/j.ctt7srwt DOI: 10.1515/9781400827817

Conrad, L. L. (1995). "Drive That Branch": Samuel Slater, the Power Loom, and the Writing of America's Textile History. *Technology and Culture*, *36*(1), 1–28. https://doi.org/https://doi.org/10.2307/3106339

Crafts, N. F. (1983). British Economic Growth, 1700-1831: A Review of the Evidence. *The Economic History Review*, *36*(2), 177–199. https://doi.org/https://doi.org/10.2307/2595919. DOI: 10.2307/2595919

Dale-Olsen, H. (2021). Do unions contribute to creative destruction? *PLoS One*, *16*(12), e0261212. https://doi.org/https://doi.org/10.1371/journal.pone.0261212. DOI: 10.1371/journal.pone.0261212 PMID: 34898619

Edgar, D. G. (2015). Towards a Historical Notion of 'Turing—The Father of Computer Science'. *History and Philosophy of Logic*, *36*(3), 205–228. https://doi.org/https://doi.org/10.1080/01445340.2015.1082050. DOI: 10.1080/01445340.2015.1082050

Elsayed, A. H., Billah, M., Goodell, J. W., & Hadhri, S. (2024). Examining Connections Between the Fourth Industrial Revolution and Energy Markets. *Energy Economics*, *133*, 2–20. https://doi.org/https://doi.org/10.1016/j.eneco.2024.107476. DOI: 10.1016/j.eneco.2024.107476

Farmer, A. E., McGuffin, P., & Spitznagel, E. L. (1983). Heterogeneity in Schizophrenia: A Cluster-analytic Approach. *Psychiatry Research*, *1*(8), 1–12. DOI: 10.1016/0165-1781(83)90132-4 PMID: 6572983

Fornino, M., & Manera, A. (2022). Automation and the Future of Work: Assessing the Role of Labor Flexibility. *Review of Economic Dynamics*, *45*, 282–321. https://doi.org/https://doi.org/10.1016/j.red.2021.07.002. DOI: 10.1016/j.red.2021.07.002

Frank, A. G., Dalenogare, L. S., & Ayala, N. F. (2019). Industry 4.0 Technologies: Implementation Patterns in Manufacturing Companies. *International Journal of Production Economics*, *210*, 15–26. https://doi.org/https://doi.org/10.1016/j.ijpe.2019.01.004. DOI: 10.1016/j.ijpe.2019.01.004

Frey, C. B., & Osborne, M. A. (2017). The Future of Employment: How Susceptible are Jobs to Computerisation? *Technological Forecasting and Social Change*, *114*, 254–280. https://doi.org/https://doi.org/10.1016/j.techfore.2016.08.019. DOI: 10.1016/j.techfore.2016.08.019

Garcia-Dias, R., Vieira, S., Pinaya, W., & Mechelli, A. (2020). *Clustering Analysis: Methods and Applications to Brain Disorders. A. Mechelli, & S. Vieira içinde, Machine Learning*. Academic Press. DOI: 10.1016/B978-0-12-815739-8.00013-4

Garcia-Dias, R., Vieira, S., Pinaya, W., & Mechelli, A. (2020). Clustering Analysis. A. Mechelli, & S. Vieira içinde, *Machine Learning* (s. 227-247). Academic Press. https://doi.org/https://doi.org/10.1016/B978-0-12-815739-8.00013-4

Ghobakhloo, M. (2018). The Future of Manufacturing Industry: A Strategic Roadmap Toward Industry 4.0. *Journal of Manufacturing Technology Management, 29*(6), 910–936. https://doi.org/https://doi.org/10.1108/JMTM-02-2018-0057. DOI: 10.1108/JMTM-02-2018-0057

Goldsmith, A. H., Stephens, J., & Casey, J. (2024). The Fourth Industrial Revolution and the Future of Work: Reasons to Worry and Policies to Consider. *Southern Economic Journal, 91*(2), 333–350. https://doi.org/https://doi.org/10.1002/soej.12714. DOI: 10.1002/soej.12714

Gordon, R. (2000). Does the "New Economy" Measure Up to the Great Inventions of the Past? *The Journal of Economic Perspectives, 14*(4), 49–74. DOI: 10.1257/jep.14.4.49

Gordon, R. (2012). Is US Economic Growth Over? Faltering Innovation Confornts The Six Headwinds. *NBR Working Paper Series*, 1-25. DOI: 10.3386/w18315

Graetz, G., & Michaels, G. (2018). Robots at Work. *The Review of Economics and Statistics, 100*(5), 753–768. https://doi.org/https://doi.org/10.1162/rest_a_00754. DOI: 10.1162/rest_a_00754

Haapanala, H., Marx, I., & Parolin, Z. (2023). Robots And Unions: The Moderating Effect Of Organized Labour On Technological Unemployment. *Economic and Industrial Democracy, 44*(3), 631–932. https://doi.org/https://doi.org/10.1177/0143831X221094078. DOI: 10.1177/0143831X221094078

Hansen, G., & Prescott, E. C. (2002). Malthus to Solow. *The American Economic Review, 92*(4), 1205–1217. DOI: 10.1257/00028280260344731

Harley, K. C., & Crafts, N. (2000). Simulating the Two Views of the British Industrial Revolution. *The Journal of Economic History, 60*(3), 819–841. https://doi.org/http://www.jstor.org/stable/2566439. DOI: 10.1017/S0022050700025778

Hartigan, J. A. (1975). *Clustering Algorithms*. John Willey & Sons.

Holtgrewe, U. (2014). New New Technologies: The Future and the Present of Work in Information and Communication Technology. *New Technology, Work and Employment, 29*(1), 9–24. https://doi.org/https://doi.org/10.1111/ntwe.12025. DOI: 10.1111/ntwe.12025

Howcroft, D., & Taylor, P. (2023). Automation and the Future of Work: A Social Shaping of Technology Approach. *New Technology, Work and Employment, 38*(2), 351–370. https://doi.org/https://doi.org/10.1111/ntwe.12240. DOI: 10.1111/ntwe.12240

Jacob, M. C. (1997). Scientific Culture and the Making of the Industrial West. Oxford University Press., 978-0195082203.

Jasanoff, S. (2015). *Dreamscapes of Modernity*. University of Chicago Press. DOI: 10.7208/chicago/9780226276663.001.0001

Joyce, S., Stuart, M., & Forde, C. (2023). Theorising Labour Unrest and Trade Unionism in the Platform Economy. *New Technology, Work and Employment, 38*(1), 21–40. https://doi.org/https://doi.org/10.1111/ntwe.12252. DOI: 10.1111/ntwe.12252

Kaplan, A., & Haenlein, M. (2019). Siri, Siri in my Hand, Who's the Fairest in the Land? On the Interpretations, Illustrations, and Implications of Artificial Intelligence. *Business Horizons, 62*(1), 15–25. https://doi.org/https://doi.org/10.1016/j.bushor.2018.08.004. DOI: 10.1016/j.bushor.2018.08.004

Karagöz, Y. (2016). *SPSS ve AMOS23 Uygulamalı istatistiksel analizler*. Nobel Yayıncılık.

Kitsikopoulos, H. (2023). *Steam Power in Transportation: Railways*. Springer. https://doi.org/https://doi.org/10.1007/978-3-031-27362-9_8

Koray, M. (2008). *Sosyal Politika*. İmge Kitabevi.

Kostøl, F. B. (2024). Do Unions Increase Participation in Further Education? *British Journal of Industrial Relations, 62*(3), 614–639. https://doi.org/https://doi.org/10.1111/bjir.12802. DOI: 10.1111/bjir.12802

Kostøl, F. B., & Svarstad, E. (2023). Trade Unions and the Process of Technological Change. *Labour Economics, 84*, 1–16. https://doi.org/https://doi.org/10.1016/j.labeco.2023.102386. DOI: 10.1016/j.labeco.2023.102386

Lasi, H., Fettke, P., Kemper, H.-G., Feld, T., & Hoffmann, M. (2014). Industry 4.0. *Business & Information Systems Engineering, 6*(4), 239–242. https://doi.org/doi.org/10.1007/s12599-014-0334-4. DOI: 10.1007/s12599-014-0334-4

Liao, Y., Deschamps, F., Loures, E., & Ramos, L. F. (2017). Past, Present and Future of Industry 4.0-a Systematic Literature Review and Research Agenda Proposal. *International Journal of Production Research*, *55*(12), 3609–3629. https://doi.org/doi:10.1080/00207543.2017.1308576. DOI: 10.1080/00207543.2017.1308576

Lloyd, S. P. (1982). Least squares quantization in PCM. *IEEE Transactions on Information Theory*, *28*(2), 129–137. DOI: 10.1109/TIT.1982.1056489

MacQueen, J. B. (1967). Some Methods for Classification and Analysis of Multivariate Observations. *Proceedings of the Fifth Berkeley Symposium on Mathematical Statistics and Probability, 1*(233), 281-297.

Madsen, K. (2008). Flexicurity in Danish: A model for labour market reform in Europe? *Inter Economics*, *43*(2), 74–78. https://doi.org/https://doi.org/10.1007/s10272-008-0244-0

Makridakis, S. (2017). The forthcoming Artificial Intelligence (AI) revolution: Its impact on society and firms. *Futures*, *90*, 46–60. https://doi.org/https://doi.org/10.1016/j.futures.2017.03.006. DOI: 10.1016/j.futures.2017.03.006

Mathias, P., & Davis, J. (1990). *First Industrial Revolutions (The Nature of Industrialization)*. Basil Blackwell.

Mohajan, H. (2020). The Second Industrial Revolution has Brought Modern Social and Economic Developments. *Journal of Social Sciences and Humanities*, *6*(1), 1–14.

Mohajan, H. (2021). Third Industrial Revolution Brings Global Development. *Journal of Social Sciences and Humanities*, *7*(4), 239–251.

Mohojan, H. K. (2019). The First Industrial Revolution: Creation of a New Global Human Era. *Journal of Social Sciences and Humanities*, *5*(4), 377–387.

Mokyr, J. (2011). *The Lever of Riches: Technological Creativity and Economic Progress*. Oxford University Press., https://doi.org/https://doi.org/10.1093/acprof:oso/9780195074772.001.0001

Morales, K., & Stecher, A. (2023). Platform Capitalism and Neo-normative Control: "Autonomy" as a Digital Platform Control Strategy in Neoliberal Chile. *New Technology, Work and Employment*, *38*(2), 230–251. https://doi.org/https://doi.org/10.1111/ntwe.12258. DOI: 10.1111/ntwe.12258

Mormina, M. (2019). Science, Technology and Innovation as Social Goods for Development: Rethinking Research Capacity Building from Sen's Capabilities Approach. *Science and Engineering Ethics*, *25*(3), 671–692. https://doi.org/https://doi.org/10.1007/s11948-018-0037-1. DOI: 10.1007/s11948-018-0037-1 PMID: 29497970

O'Rourke, K. H., & Williamson, J. G. (2005). From Malthus to Ohlin: Trade, Industrialisation and Distribution since 1500. *Journal of Economic Growth, 10*(1), 5–34. https://doi.org/http://www.jstor.org/stable/40216094. DOI: 10.1007/s10887-005-1111-5

Parolin, Z. (2021). Automation, Occupational Earnings Trends, and the Moderating Role of Organized Labor. *Social Forces, 99*(3), 921–946. https://doi.org/https://doi.org/10.1093/sf/soaa032

Pfeiffer, S. (2014). Digital Labour and the Use-value of Human Work. On the Importance of Labouring Capacity for understanding Digital Capitalism. *TripleC, 12*(2), 599–619. https://doi.org/https://doi.org/10.31269/triplec.v12i2.545. DOI: 10.31269/triplec.v12i2.545

Philbeck, T., & Davis, N. (2019). The Fourth Industrial Revolution. *Journal of International Affairs, 72*(1), 17–22. https://doi.org/https://www.jstor.org/stable/10.2307/26588339

Prisecaru, P. (2016). Challenges of The Fourth Industrial Revolution. *Knowledge Horizons - Economics, 8*(1), 57-62.

Pulignano, V., & Doerflinger, N. (2013). A Head with Two Tales: Trade Unions' Influence on Temporary Agency Work in Belgian and German Workplaces. *International Journal of Human Resource Management, 24*(22), 4149–4165. DOI: 10.1080/09585192.2013.845446

Rifkin, J. (2011). *The Third Industrial Revolution: How Lateral Power is Transforming Energy, the Economy and the World*. Palgrave Macmillan.

Roberts, B. H. (2015). The Third Industrial Revolution: Implications for Planning Cities and Regions. *Urban Frontiers Working Paper*, 1-22.

Rosen, W. (2012). *The Most Powerful Idea in the World A Story of Steam, Industry, and Invention*. The University of Chicago Press.

Rozman, M., Tominc, P., & Strukelj, T. (2023). Competitiveness Through Development of Strategic Talent Management and Agile Management Ecosystems. *Global Journal of Flexible Systems Managment, 24*(3), 373–393. https://doi.org/https://doi.org/10.1007/s40171-023-00344-1. DOI: 10.1007/s40171-023-00344-1

Salkind, A. J., & Israel, P. (2004). Thomas Alva Edison - Battery and Device Innovation in Response to Application's Needs. *Journal of Power Sources, 136*(2), 356–365. DOI: 10.1016/j.jpowsour.2004.03.016

Schwab, K. (2016). *The Fourth Industrial Revolution*. Crown Business.

Sinclair, A. (1970). Development of the Locomotive Engine. MIT Press., 9780262190688.

Steinhaus, H. (1956). Sur la Division des Corps Materiels en Parties. *Bulletin de l'academie, 4*(12), 801-804.

Stokey, N. L. (2001). A Quantitative Model of the British Industrial Revolution, 1780–1850. *Carnegie-Rochester Conference Series on Public Policy, 55*(1), 55-109. https://doi.org/https://doi.org/10.1016/S0167-2231(01)80003-8

Taalbi, J. (2019). Origins and Pathways of Innovation in the Third Industrial Revolution. *Industrial and Corporate Change*, *28*(5), 1125–1148. https://doi.org/https://doi.org/10.1093/icc/dty053

Tatlıdil, H. (1992). *Uygulamalı Çok Değişkenli İstatistiksel Analiz.* Engin Yayınları.

Temin, P. (1997). Two Views of the British Industrial Revolution. *The Journal of Economic History*, *57*(1), 63–82. https://doi.org/http://www.jstor.org/stable/2951107. DOI: 10.1017/S0022050700017927

Troxler, P. (2013). *Making the 3rd Industrial Revolution. J. Walter-Herrmann, & C. Büching içinde, Fab Labs: Of Machines, Makers and Inventors.* Transcript Publishers.

Uçar, N. (2017). *Kümeleme Analizi. Ş. Kalaycı içinde, SPSS Uygulamalı Çok Değişkenli İstatistik Teknikleri.* Dinamik Akademi.

Usher, A. P. (1920). *An Introduction to the Industrial History of England.* Houghton Mifflin Company.

Ventura, J., & Voth, H.-J. (2015). Debt into Growth: How Sovereign Debt Accelerated the First Industrial Revolution. *National Bureau of Economic Reserarch, 21280*, 1–30. DOI: 10.3386/w21280

Viner, J. (1927). Adam Smith and Laissez Faire. *Journal of Political Economy*, *35*(2), 198–232. https://doi.org/http://www.jstor.org/stable/1823421. DOI: 10.1086/253837

World Economic Forum. (2016). *The Future of Jobs.* World Economic Forum.

World Economic Forum. (2018). *The Future of Jobs.* World Economic Forum.

World Economic Forum. (2020). *The Future of Jobs.* World Economic Forum.

World Economic Forum. (2023). *The Future of Jobs.* World Economic Forum.

World Economic Forum. (2025). *The Future of Jobs.* World Economic Forum.

Wrigley, A. E. (1985). Urban Growth and Agricultural Change: England and the Continent in the Early Modern Period. *The Journal of Interdisciplinary History, 15*(4), 683–728. https://doi.org/doi.org/10.2307/204276. DOI: 10.2307/204276

Wrigley, E. A. (2013). Energy and the English Industrial Revolution. *Phil Trans R Soc A, 371*(1986), 1-10. https://doi.org/http://dx.doi.org/10.1098/rsta.2011.0568

Xing, B., & Marwala, T. (2017). Implications of the Fourth Industrial Age for Higher Education. *SSRN, 73*, 10–15. https://doi.org/https://ssrn.com/abstract=3225331

Xu, M., David, J. M., & Kim, S. H. (2018). The Fourth Industrial Revolution: Opportunities and Challenges. *International Journal of Financial Research, 9*(2), 90–95. https://doi.org/doi:10.5430/ijfr.v9n2p. DOI: 10.5430/ijfr.v9n2p90

Zilcha-Mano, S., McCarthy, K. S., Dinger, U., Chambless, D. L., Milrod, B. L., Kunik, L., & Barber, J. P. (2015). Are there subtypes of panic disorder? An interpersonal perspective. *Journal of Consulting and Clinical Psychology, 5*(83), 938–950. DOI: 10.1037/a0039373 PMID: 26030762

ADDITIONAL READING

Akaev, A., Rudskoi, A., Sarygulov, A., & Sokolov, V. (2019). A New Era of Machinery: Will the Accumulation of Capital Grow and Labor Intensity Decrease? *Social Evolution & History, 18*(1). Advance online publication. DOI: 10.30884/seh/2019.01.04

Kelly, J. (1998). *Rethinking Industrial Relations: Mobilization, Collectivism and Long Waves*. Routledge.

Marshall, M. (2023). A Roboticist's Guide to the Engineering Ethics of Job Automation. *IEEE Technology and Society Magazine, 42*(1), 65–74. Advance online publication. DOI: 10.1109/MTS.2023.3244568

Schumpeter, J. (2006). Capitalism, Socialism & Democracy. *Routledge Pub.* London.

Zhang, X., Zhang, Y., Liu, J., He, Y., & Xu, A. (2024). The application of industrial robots and changes in capital-labour income disparity in China. *Economic Analysis and Policy, 84*, 42–56. Advance online publication. DOI: 10.1016/j.eap.2024.08.020

KEY TERMS AND DEFINITIONS

Automation: Automatically controlled operation of an apparatus, process, or system by mechanical or electronic devices that take the place of human labor

Artificial Intelligence: The ability of machines to learn human behaviour through algorithms and computer systems, develop themselves, and make predictions about the future.

Digitalisation: A series of processes that enable analogue data to be read by machine units and gradually shift production and social life towards the use of such technology.

Industrial Relations: It is a field of study that examines the asymmetrical power relationship between workers, employers and the state.

Technological Unemployment: The replacement of routine jobs in the labour market by new technologies, resulting in low-skilled workers generally being excluded from employment.

Skills Mismatch: It is the mismatch between the jobs emerging in the labour market with new technology and the workers in the labour market. It is the labour force's lack of suitability for the skills required by new technology.

GIG Economy: M Unlike traditional forms of work, new forms of employment emerging through digital platforms have resulted in a generally more independent way of working, which is flexible, insecure and difficult to organise through trade unions.

Labor-Capital Substitution: The exchange of labour and capital (the replacement of labour by robots and artificial intelligence) resulting in the creation of a new equilibrium in the labour market.

Trade Union: Unions formed by workers or emplayers to protect and promote the economic right and interests of their members.

Chapter 15
Analyzing the Evolving Role of Trade Unions in the Context of Digital Transformation:
An Evaluation on STEM, ECI, Trade Union Density, and Employment Rates

Ersin Eraslan
https://orcid.org/0000-0003-0800-8966
Niğde Ömer Halisdemir University, Turkey

ABSTRACT

Digital transformation, STEM, economic complexity and structural transformation in human capital essentially show a cyclical series of relationships and a process that are positively interconnected. However, the situation of trade unions, which are directly related to employment, which reflects the output status of human capital, is curious and constitutes the purpose of this paper. In line with this purpose, the developing role of trade unions in the digital transformation process is questioned in the paper.

DOI: 10.4018/979-8-3693-8049-9.ch015

INTRODUCTION

Digitalisation is a very broad phenomenon that includes many different technologies and applications. When this phenomenon is considered theoretically, it is known and observed that digital technologies, if adopted by both households and firms, pave the way for large productivity increases through various channels. However, it is observed that it takes time for previous technological revolutions to be reflected in productivity statistics and lead to large productivity increases. In this context, within the time context corresponding to the adaptation of revolutions to a specific sector of the economy, different factors such as secondary innovation waves, the formation of new physical structure, redesign of organisational infrastructure and development of skills play a role. It should also be noted that the sources of productivity growth depend on economic practices and institutions, which vary significantly across countries and sectors (European Central Bank, 2024, p. 8).

At the source of economic growth as an end result and basic component of productivity increase, there is no doubt that countries have their own organisational and technological capability accumulation (Bottai, Di lorio & Lori, 2024, p. 1). The accumulation of capability, on the other hand, refers to a process that can only be possible through education, which is the main element of human capital investment. In this framework, STEM (Science, Technology, Engineering and Mathematics), which has become increasingly important in recent years within the scope of education policies, comes to the fore in terms of acquiring skills. As a matter of fact, STEM refers to a holistic and comprehensive education policy that integrates science, technology, engineering and mathematics to equip students with critical thinking, problem solving and collaborative skills. At the centre of this interdisciplinary educational policy approach is equipping students with holistic skills and preparing them for the evolving challenges of the 21st century (Mykolaivna, Oleksandrivna & Hennadyyovych, 2024, p. 748).

Since STEM has a strong potential to improve knowledge (Drokina, 2024, p. 20), it is possible to say that the acquisition of this capability is among the basic dynamics of economic growth and development. Indeed, the productivity of a country today lies in the diversity of its non-tradable capabilities. It is observed that developed countries with various capabilities produce highly sophisticated products, while undeveloped or developing countries produce products that can be considered relatively primitive (Hidalgo & Hausman, 2009, p. 26). In this context, it is seen that the most basic structure of the situation that characterises the economic development of countries is essentially production complexity (Balcı, 2024, p. 47). In a broader sense, economic complexity refers to a country's export diversity and its capacity to generate and distribute income measured at this point, while at the same time showing the stock of knowledge in a population that affects economic growth and income inequality dynamics (Subekti & Sari, 2024, p. 140). In this respect, it is observed that economic complexity (Bucher, Scheu & Schröpf, 2023, p. 812), which is reflected as the reflection of an economy's knowledge intensity on its competitively exported products, has significant effects on economic development (Van Dam & Frenken, 2020). In this framework, it is observed that the economic complexity index (ECI) developed by Hidalgo and Hausman (2009) to measure these effects, which are quite complex and difficult, is an approach that is increasingly valued worldwide in the economic literature and is considered from different angles (Lapatinas, 2019), (Canh, Schinckus & Thanh, 2020), (Shahzad, Fareed, Shahzad & Shahzad, 2021), (Hu, Fan, Lin & Xu, 2023), (Bottai et al., 2024).

Economic sophistication, a measure of a country's productive capabilities based on the mix of sophisticated products it exports, essentially refers to the degree of knowledge accumulation in that country's production structure (Ncanywa, Mongale, Ralarala, Letsoalo, & Molele, 2021, p.1). Increasing this degree encourages the development of highly skilled workers and the creation of high value-added economic sectors. This situation not only supports human resources development but also creates a driving force for structural transformation (Hoeriyah, Nuryartono & Pasaribu, 2022, p. 31). As seen in this framework, digital transformation, STEM, economic complexity and structural transformation in human capital essentially show a cyclical series of relationships and a process that are positively interconnected. However, the situation of trade unions, which are directly related to employment, which reflects the output status of human capital, is curious and constitutes the purpose of this paper. In line with this purpose, the developing role of trade unions in the digital transformation process is questioned in the paper.

BACKGROUND

Today, the impact of digitalisation and artificial intelligence affects the working life, industrial relations and production processes of countries in many ways. While the economies of countries are transforming depending on their production processes, it is also seen that they are more integrated with each other. For these reasons, in the literature, especially the effects of new digitalisation processes on the structure of the labour force and accordingly the effects on trade unions are frequently discussed. On the industrial relations side, it is often discussed how unions will adapt to this change and transformation process and what kind of strategies they should make. One of the main objectives of this study emerges from these explanations. In this study, an answer to the question 'What will be the roles of trade unions in the digital transformation process and the effects of these processes on industrial relations?' will be sought.

Economic complexity, which is developing even faster with digitalisation, encourages the development of highly skilled workers with a high degree of know-how and the opportunity to earn higher income levels (Hoeriyah et al., 2022, p. 24). However, in this process, it is observed that the industrial relations system has also entered a process of change with the use of new technologies in production. In this framework, events such as intense competition in working life and the spread of non-standard working forms pave the way for the gradual narrowing of the sphere of influence of trade unions, which are the main actors of industrial relations (Şahin & Balcı, 2020, p. 457). As a matter of fact, digitalisation reveals a triangular relationship in the form of 'worker-platform-customer' instead of the employment contract reflecting the standard employment relationship within the framework of digital working platforms. In this context, the transparency of the boundaries of the employment relationship is lost and becomes more uncertain. In this case, the bond of nationality disappears, labour law is replaced by commercial law, and the figures of employer and employee lose their institutional visibility (Dieuaide & Azaïs, 2020, p. 1). Moreover, the job changes resulting from new information technologies and the professions that emerge with their use present a multi-layered structure, mixing the issues, time, space, materiality, spirituality and the concept of the company, which emerged in the context of precarity, flexibility and technological innovations, which together with the Internet constitute the value of work (Lima & Bridi, 2019). In this context, the digitalisation process, in other words the digital revolution, poses complex challenges for trade unions (Thomas, 2022) (Gerhard & Schmitz-Kießler, 2020). The weakening of the trade union movement in countries with strong and deep-rooted traditions and the multi-layered nature of digitalisation require unions to develop new strategies for organising (Thomas, 2022) (Gerhard & Schmitz-Kießler, 2020).

In a changing and transforming world, the inability of unions to respond adequately to Industry 4.0 developments in the production sectors, which are among the areas where unions are the strongest, and the Gig Economy, which has greatly increased its effectiveness with the pandemic process, are among the most important reasons why unions have lost a lot of power in the field of organisation (Balcı, 2024) (Balcı & Eraslan, 2023). As a matter of fact, in Germany, the starting point of Industry 4.0, since the beginning of the 2010s, the possibility of the digitalisation process creating a negative environment for trade unions has taken a central place in the discourse and strategies of German trade unions. The concern of German trade unions in this regard has been that digitalisation will lead to a radical technological disruption in line with the vision brought by the concept of Industry 4.0 and that working relations will change (Thomas, 2022). In Thomas's study in 2022, he states that German trade unions are in search of new ways to re-strengthen their position to represent the interests of workers and to minimise the effects of digitalisation. Among the most important of these searches are the activation of workers' councils and the need for unions to shape their hierarchical decision-making mechanisms entirely according to the wishes of their members (Thomas, 2022). The main reason for the importance of works councils is that at the level of organisation in Germany they are elected from among the employees within the enterprise and have rights to information, consultation and joint decision-making. The evolving situation with Industry 4.0, as expressed in IG Metal's Transformation Atlas Report (2019), argues that the traditional 'dual system' of workplace regulations based on the views of legally elected works councils, complemented by sectoral collective agreements negotiated by unions at industry level, is undermining employee representation.

In order for trade unions to be more resilient in the face of digitalisation, they need to develop new strategies. Bosh and Schmitz-Kießler see the 'Arbeit 2020' project led by IG Metall as a pioneer in this area. The project includes processes for more effective protection of employee rights by trade unions and works councils in digital transformation processes (Gerhard & Schmitz-Kießler, 2020). At the same time, Trenerry et al. in their study in 2022 states that it is imperative for unions to discuss the question of how to use the process more effectively, especially in digitalisation processes, rather than standing against the process (Trenerry, Chng, Wang, Lim, & Oh, 2022). Although there are those who state that the digitalisation process should not be opposed, on the other hand, the 'Gig Economy, flexible working models' created by the process harm the collective action structure of unions (Haake, 2017). Artificial intelligence and automation systems, which are included in the production process with the independent working relationship brought by the gig economy, reduce the need for the labour of the labour force, which is the most important part of the unions, and increase layoffs, thus weakening the power of unions (Adhikary & Banerjee, 2022) (Degryse, 2016) (Balcı & Eraslan, 2023). The main reason why artificial intelligence makes unions lose power is undoubtedly the increase in layoffs with the inclusion of robotic technologies and algorithms in production processes (Kalbermatter, Schaupp, Hartleitner, & Naxhtwey, 2021). In this sense, it is very important for unions to organise this group of workers, especially for the coming years. Indeed, the fact that the number of freelancers and workers working on digital platforms is increasing day by day makes organising in this field very important (Webster & Ludwig, 2023). However, the decrease in visibility due to the representation of employees doing similar jobs in different sectors (aviation, maritime, railway transport, etc.) by different actors is another problem area and the formation of the organisation in question should be considered in this respect (Alkan, 2022).

On the other hand, the increasing effectiveness of information technologies and artificial intelligence leads to the creation of new jobs. However, the fact that the majority of newly created jobs are jobs requiring high skills and qualifications poses challenging conditions for low-skilled labour (Nissim & Simon, 2021). Indeed, in the latest report published by the WEF, for the first time since 2016, the number of jobs that will be created in the future is estimated to be less than the number of jobs that will disappear (World Economic Forum, 2023). This suggests that low-skilled labour will be pushed further out of employment, thus weakening union organising power.

As can be seen from the above, although artificial intelligence and digitalisation processes definitely create disadvantageous situations for trade unions, they can also create some opportunities. As a matter of fact, it is seen that the internet provides the ground for significant potentials for trade unions to develop services, attract members and adapt to modern challenges that may include artificial intelligence developments. In this context, unions can utilise internet technologies to attract members as well as offer their services through this platform (Diamond & Freeman, 2001) (Girley, Rego & Keyser, 2018). In addition, cyber solidarity and internet-based campaigns have significant effects in supporting trade unions, especially in the context of international solidarity and information flows (Robinson, 2006). On the other hand, trade unions have the potential to play a crucial role in addressing the ethical challenges posed by AI in the workplace, ensuring transparency as well as advocating for workers' participation in AI management, protection against discrimination and the establishment of rights to fair treatment of employees (Nowik, 2023). In this framework, unions in Germany seem to focus on regulating the use of AI in the workplace, promoting human-centred AI concepts, providing appropriate training for works councils, and adapting their strategies to influence political debates and implementation processes related to AI technologies (Krzywdzinski, Gerst & Butollo, 2023). However, despite this transformation in technology and the challenges posed to organisational structures by this transformation, trade unions in Norway appear to be highly engaged in technology decisions (Payne, Llyod & Jose, 2022).

Technology has the potential to be a crucial tool for unions to improve member communication, organise campaigns and increase negotiating effectiveness, mainly in the midst of the challenges of the modern labour environment (Fioritto, Jarley & Delaney, 2000). For this, unions need to adapt to the developing technology and develop new strategic approaches towards the expectations of employees rather than resisting change. Unions also need to integrate artificial intelligence into their organising strategies, especially to reach the workforce with new member potential. Artificial intelligence integrated into union processes can strengthen the communication between members and the union by analysing the expectations of the workforce more accurately. Therefore, while it is absolutely necessary for unions to struggle in the process, integrating changing technology and artificial intelligence into their organising strategies will be a pioneer in the formation of a more efficient unionism and industrial relations system in the future.

METHODOLOGY

In this paper, it is planned to apply cluster analysis to reveal the similarities and differences in the course of trade union development within the framework of each country's own capabilities in the context of changing industrial systems with digitalisation in the European continent, where trade union movements started and developed. Following the clustering analysis, the average course of each variable values between 2013-2019 will be presented in accordance with the situation analysis and the development of trade unions within the framework of digitalisation will be examined within the framework of clusters. In this framework, in the data set that we have established within 19 countries that are members of The Organisation for Economic Co-operation and Development (OECD) from the European continent where trade unionism was born, STEM scores reflecting the human capital development of the relevant countries, ECI scores reflecting the sophisticated product diversity, employment rates reflecting the employment status, and finally trade union density ratios reflecting the union activity potential. The data set is for the year 2019, which is the last data date in trade union density ratios statistics, and STEM scores and employment rates are obtained from the database of the EU statistical unit (Eurostat), while ECI scores, Harvard Atlas and union density ratios are obtained from the database of the OECD statistical unit and presented in Table 1.

Table 1. Data set for STEM, ECI, trade union density and employment rates in selected OECD and European countries

2019 Year	STEM	Trade Un.Den	ECİ Ranking	Emp. Rate (20-64)
Belgium	14,2	49,1	1,19	70,5
Austria	23,4	26,3	1,82	76,8
Czechia	16,1	12,24*	1,81	80,3
Denmark	23,7	67	1,08	78,3
Germany	24,4	16,3	2,08	79,6
Estonia	16,5	6	0,85	80,5
Spain	20,9	12,5	0,79	68
Italy	16,6	32,5	1,33	63,5
Latvia	14,	12,45*	0,71	77,3
Lithuania	19,8	7,4	0,76	78,2
Netherlands	13,6	15,4	1,07	81
Slovakia	12,9	12,45*	1,46	75,6
Finland	24,8	58,8	1,51	76,2
Sweden	15,8	65,2	1,73	81,7
Norway	16,5	50,4	0,53	80,2
İreland	36,9	25,1	1,44	75
Switzerland	22	15,5*	2,21	82,9
United Kingdom	26,2	23,5	1,5	75,8
Türkiye	12,8	9,9	0,59	53,8

* It reflects the missing values and is calculated by averaging the scores of previous years. Source: Compiled from Eurostat, OECD Data and Harvard Atlas data.

Table 1 shows 19 countries in Europe, where trade unionism was born and developed, which are also members of the OECD and whose data are available. In order to understand the relational network reflecting the state of digital transformation, employment and trade unions in the context of these countries, a data set was created using STEM scores reflecting the human capital development of the countries, ECI scores reflecting the sophisticated product diversity, employment rates reflecting the employment situation, and finally union density ratios reflecting the union activity potential. This data set was transferred to the Statistical Package for the Social Science (SPSS) 25 package programme in order to subject it to cluster analysis and make more accurate interpretations based on the fact that digital transformation shows significant differences between countries and sectors. After this transfer, Z scores of each variable were calculated in order to make the data set compatible with each other since some indicators express a percentage and some indicators express a cumulative total, and clustering analysis was started over Z scores.

Cluster analysis is one of the advanced statistical techniques used to group unlabelled data based on their similarities or differences (Çakmak, Uzgören & Keçek, 2015), providing internal classification within an unlabelled group (Abonyi & Feil, 2007, p.1). Thus, various methods are used in cluster analysis, which provides a rich perspective for research. Among these different methods, two methods stand out: the hierarchical clustering method, in which the number of clusters is not determined in advance, and the non-hierarchical clustering method, in which the number of clusters is known in advance. While hierarchical clustering methods utilise different analysis techniques such as single linkage, complete linkage, average linkage, centrality methods, and Ward's method, non-hierarchical clustering methods employ sequential start, parallel start, and average separation techniques using K-means (Uçar, 2017, pp. 358-360). The most important distinction here lies in determining the number of clusters. Indeed, in non-hierarchical clustering methods, the number of clusters is determined before the analysis based on the researcher's experience and knowledge of the subject (Karagöz, 2016, p. 891), while in hierarchical clustering methods, the number of clusters is determined based on various analyses such as distance coefficients and dendrograms (Uçar, 2017, p. 359).

In this study, which uses both hierarchical and non-hierarchical clustering methods, the hierarchical clustering method was first used to determine the number of clusters. At this point, Ward's method, which tends to merge clusters with few observations (Alpar, 2011, p. 325) and minimises variance within clusters, was preferred due to the small number of observations in the data set. Although the square Euclidean distance is generally used to determine the number of clusters in Ward's method (Alpar, 2011, p. 325), it should be noted that there is no standard protocol for determining the number of clusters at this point (Alpar, 2011, p. 313). Based on this, cluster formation tests were conducted using 2, 3, and 4 clusters with a threshold value between 5 and 20, using square Euclidean distance values, clustering tables, and dendrograms. In addition to all these analyses, it was decided that the number of clusters should be 4, taking into account the relevant literature. Subsequently, an ANOVA test was conducted to determine whether the differences between clusters were statistically significant in terms of which indicators, within the framework of non-hierarchical clustering methods.

Within this framework, important findings consistent with the literature were obtained, and significant explanations combining quantitative analyses with qualitative insights were included in the analysis. Subsequently, a correlation analysis was conducted to compare the average trend patterns of the aforementioned variables between 2013 and 2019 years across clusters with their union density levels. The relational networks of each cluster with respect to the variables were then integrated with qualitative interpretations.

FINDINGS

In hierarchical clustering, the primary objective is to determine the number of clusters. Although there is no standard policy, distance coefficients, dendrograms, and cluster accumulation tables are used to determine the number of clusters (Karagöz, 2016, p. 891). However, in Ward's method, which is frequently used in hierarchical clustering, square Euclidean distance values are generally used in the context of distance analysis (Alpar, 2011, p. 313). To calculate the square Euclidean distance value commonly used in Ward's method, the Euclidean value must first be calculated. In this context, the following formula is used to calculate the Euclidean value of two observation distance values using the Pythagorean theorem.

$$d_{ij} = \sqrt[2]{\sum_{k=1}^{p} \left(x_{ik} - x_{jk}\right)} \tag{1}$$

Formula 1 gives the generalised Euclidean distance between i. and j. observations in a p-variable structure, where "x_{ik}" k. variable value of i. observation i. " x_{jk}" k. variable value of j. observation and "p' is the number of variables (Alpar, 2011: 165-166). Square Euclidean distance measure is calculated by squaring the Euclidean distance as follows;

$$d_{ij} = \sum_{k=1}^{p} \left(x_{ik} - x_{jk}\right)^2 \tag{2}$$

The formula number 2 presented above, which gives the squared Euclidean distance value, was applied to the data set and the values showing the distances of the observation units towards their indicators are presented in Table 2 below.

Table 2. Square Euclidean distance matrices of observation units in the framework of digital transformation, employment and trade union density scores

	Squared Euclidean Distance																		
Case	1	2	3	4	5	6	7	8	9	10	11	12	13	14	15	16	17	18	19
1:Belgium	0,00	5,83	6,73	4,41	10,07	6,99	5,16	1,84	5,02	6,89	4,93	4,06	4,26	4,27	3,68	15,78	11,40	6,34	10,56
2:Austria	5,83	0,00	2,14	6,17	0,68	6,21	6,29	5,70	7,65	5,65	5,40	3,94	2,97	5,67	9,41	5,50	1,65	0,65	19,84
3:Czechia	6,73	2,14	0,00	10,90	2,17	3,71	7,63	7,37	5,04	4,83	2,35	1,18	7,90	6,80	9,92	13,03	1,71	3,80	19,77
4:Denmark	4,41	6,17	10,90	0,00	10,13	10,61	9,72	8,70	10,21	9,33	9,25	10,96	1,00	3,55	3,30	9,58	11,86	5,52	23,59
5:Germany	10,07	0,68	2,17	10,13	0,00	7,87	9,50	9,49	10,38	7,62	7,15	5,38	5,84	8,28	13,88	6,37	0,43	1,81	25,31
6:Estonia	6,99	6,21	3,71	10,61	7,87	0,00	3,67	8,20	0,54	0,43	0,63	2,37	10,59	11,49	5,13	13,94	8,39	5,33	14,50
7:Spain	5,16	6,29	7,63	9,72	9,50	3,67	0,00	2,99	2,97	2,12	5,03	4,59	8,89	14,46	7,12	9,82	12,27	4,20	5,84
8:Italy	1,84	5,70	7,37	8,70	9,49	8,20	2,99	0,00	6,35	7,25	7,15	4,24	6,71	9,64	8,69	13,75	11,81	5,70	5,58
9:Latvia	5,02	7,65	5,04	10,21	10,38	0,54	2,97	6,35	0,00	0,98	0,80	2,29	10,80	11,22	3,91	16,58	11,16	6,76	10,83
10:Lithuani	6,89	5,65	4,83	9,33	7,62	0,43	2,12	7,25	0,98	0,00	1,71	3,38	9,29	12,37	5,01	10,57	8,96	3,97	12,99
11:Netherla	4,93	5,40	2,35	9,25	7,15	0,63	5,03	7,15	0,80	1,71	0,00	1,20	9,07	7,80	4,32	15,96	7,05	5,65	15,35
12:Slovakia	4,06	3,94	1,18	10,96	5,38	2,37	4,59	4,24	2,29	3,38	1,20	0,00	8,95	7,91	7,60	15,77	5,47	5,02	12,21
13:Finland	4,26	2,97	7,90	1,00	5,84	10,59	8,89	6,71	10,80	9,29	9,07	8,95	0,00	3,04	6,08	6,68	7,50	3,05	22,64
14:Sweden	4,27	5,67	6,80	3,55	8,28	11,49	14,46	9,64	11,22	12,37	7,80	7,91	3,04	0,00	6,23	16,95	7,88	7,94	27,78
15:Norway	3,68	9,41	9,92	3,30	13,88	5,13	7,12	8,69	3,91	5,01	4,32	7,60	6,08	6,23	0,00	16,42	14,94	8,31	17,84
16:Ireland	15,78	5,50	13,03	9,58	6,37	13,94	9,82	13,75	16,58	10,57	15,96	15,77	6,68	16,95	16,42	0,00	9,68	3,09	27,62
17:Switzerl	11,40	1,65	1,71	11,86	0,43	8,39	12,27	11,81	11,16	8,96	7,05	5,47	7,50	7,88	14,94	9,68	0,00	3,58	29,06
18:United K	6,34	0,65	3,80	5,52	1,81	5,33	4,20	5,70	6,76	3,97	5,65	5,02	3,05	7,94	8,31	3,09	3,58	0,00	17,88
19:Türkiye	10,56	19,84	19,77	23,59	25,31	14,50	5,84	5,58	10,83	12,99	15,35	12,21	22,64	27,78	17,84	27,62	29,06	17,88	0,00

In Table 2, the Squared Euclidean Distances are presented in a matrix within the framework of STEM and ECI, employment and trade union density scores reflecting the digital transformation of the countries in the intersection of Europe and OECD given in Table 1 respectively. In this framework, it is observed that the farthest distance is between Turkey and Switzerland with 29.06 units. This is followed by Turkey-Sweden with a distance of 27.78 units, Turkey-Ireland with a distance of 27.62 units and finally Turkey-Finland with a distance of 22.64 units. The closest distance is between Lithuania and Estonia with a distance of 0.43 units. This is followed by Latvia-Germany with a distance of 0.54 units, Netherlands-Estonia with a distance of 0.63 units and finally Germany and Belgium with a distance of 0.68 units.

Based on the fact that another method used to determine the number of clusters is dendrogram, a dendrogram was prepared within the framework of 5-10-15-20 threshold values within the data set and presented in Figure 1.

Figure 1. Dendrogram of selected countries in the framework of digital transformation, employment and trade union density scores

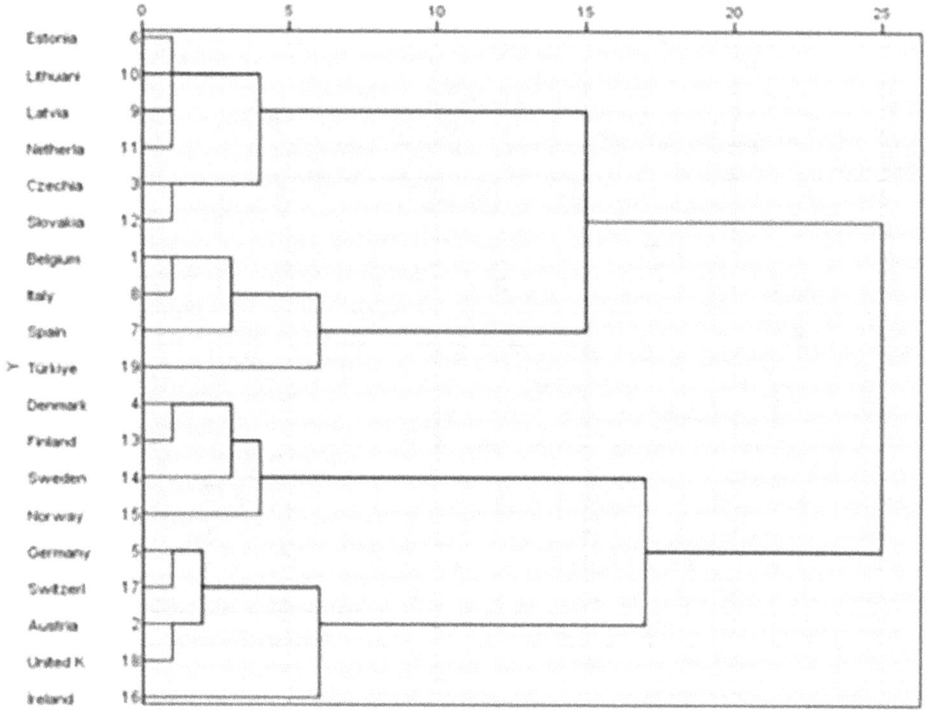

The dendrogram presented in Figure 1 shows the cluster coalescence distances between thresholds 0-25. As the thresholds approach 0, the distances between observations decrease and as the threshold scores increase, the distances between observations increase. When Figure 1 is closely analysed, it is seen that 6 clusters are formed when the threshold value is 5, 4 clusters are formed at threshold values of 10 and 15, and 2 clusters are formed at threshold value of 20.

On the other hand, 2-cluster, 4-cluster and 6-cluster analyses were carried out in the range of threshold values 5-25, and it was decided that the number of clusters should be 4 at a threshold value of 10 by considering which cluster each observation unit is closer to, the square Euclidean distance matrix, the cluster belonging table and the literature on the subject. The cluster formations realised in this framework are as follows;

I. First Cluster: It consists of 3 observation units, namely Spain, Italy and Türkiye.
II. Second Cluster: It consists of 2 observation units, namely the United Kingdom and Ireland.

III. Third Cluster: It consists of 9 observation units, namely Austria, Czechia, Germany, Estonia, Latvia, Lithuania, Netherlands, Slovakia and Switzerland.
IV. Fourth Cluster: Belgium, Denmark, Finland, Finland, Sweden and Norway.

When this formation of four clusters is closely analysed, it is seen that Spain, Italy and Türkiye, which have a Southern Mediterranean welfare regime, come together in the first cluster, while the United Kingdom and Ireland, which correspond to the Liberal welfare regime in the lietarure, come together in the second cluster. In the third cluster, it is seen that countries based on the Corporatist-Statist welfare regime such as Austria and Germany come together, while in the fourth cluster, countries dominated by the Social Democratic welfare regime such as Denmark, Finland, Sweden and Norway come together.

In the non-hierarchical clustering method, the first cluster centres, which give the centres of each cluster according to the relevant variable, and the final cluster centres, which show the averages of each cluster according to the variables, provide important information. As a matter of fact, the correct determination of cluster centres provides a basis for the separation of the data into correct clusters and has a reducing effect on the margin of error of the method. This situation allows similar results to be obtained even when starting with different starting points. Especially the differences between the Euclidean distances in the last cluster centres provide important information. In this context, the differences of the last cluster centres in the analysis process are presented in Table 3.

Table 3. Final cluster centre distance between

Cluster	1	2	3	4
1	0	3,285	2,644	3,005
2	3,285	0	2,322	2,7
3	2,644	2,322	0	2,229
4	3,005	2,7	2,229	0

When the final cluster centre differences presented in Table 3 are closely examined, it is seen that the two most distant clusters are between cluster 1 and 4 with a distance of 3,005 units, while the two closest clusters are between clusters 2 and 3 with a distance of 2,322 units. However, in order to understand whether there is a statistically significant difference between the clusters in terms of variables, it is recommended to perform ANOVA (Analysis of Variance) test, which is one of the parametric tests known as variance analysis or F test. In this framework, the results of the ANOVA test for the 4 clusters are presented in Table 4.

Table 4. ANOVA test results of clusters regarding digital transformation, employment and trade union density scores

Indicator	Cluster Mean Square	df	Error Mean Square	df	F	Sig.
STEM	2,957	3	0,609	15	4,859	0,015
Trade Union Density	5,318	3	0,136	15	38,957	0,000
ECİ Ranking	0,910	3	1,018	15	0,894	0,467
Employment Rate	4,544	3	0,291	15	15,598	0,000

According to the results of the ANOVA test conducted to understand the differences between the clusters in the indicators related to digital transformation, employment and trade union density scores in Table 4, as an expected and desired result, a statistically significant difference was found between STEM, trade union density and employment rates. However, it is also observed that there is no significant difference between the clusters in ECI scores. This situation, as stated before, shows that digital transformation should be evaluated in the welfare conditions of each economy. In this framework, the second stage of the analysis is to examine the changes between 2013-2019 on the basis of clusters in order to see the course of development of these indicators. In this way, both a time course will be followed and the effectiveness of trade unions will be considered separately in each welfare regime emerging from the clustering analysis through correlation analysis.

Figure 2 and Figure 3 show the changes in 2013-2019 on the basis of clusters in STEM, which reflects digital transformation and is considered as both an input and an output in this context, and ECI scores, which indicate exports of sophisticated products.

Figure 2. STEM trend by clusters from 2013 to 2019

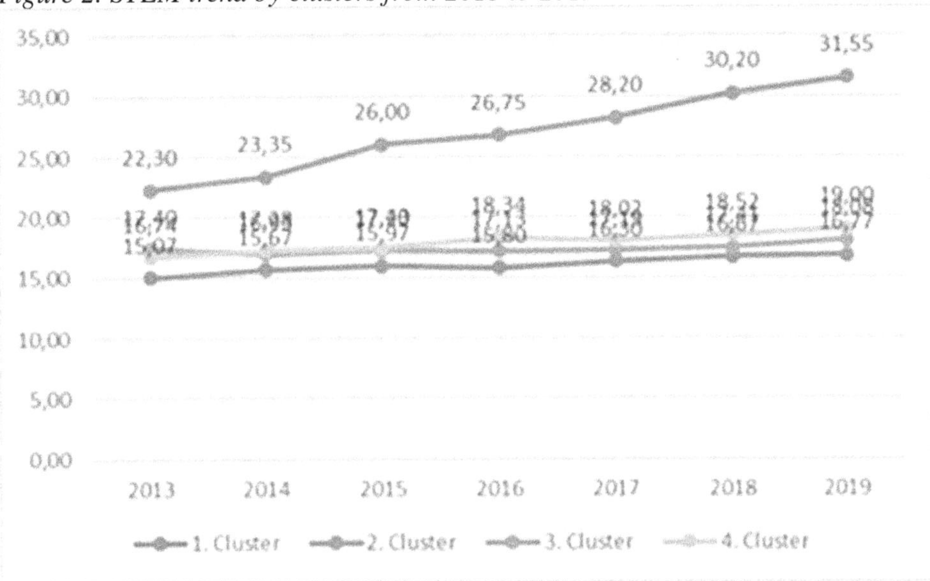

Figure 2 shows the course of STEM values according to clusters between 2013-2019. In this context, while the increase in STEM values is observed in all clusters, the rapid increase in STEM values in the United Kingdom and Ireland, which constitutes Cluster 2, and the differentiation of this cluster from other clusters is quite striking. In this framework, it would not be wrong to say that STEM has gained importance in the liberal welfare regime.

Figure 3. ECI trend by clusters from 2013 to 2019

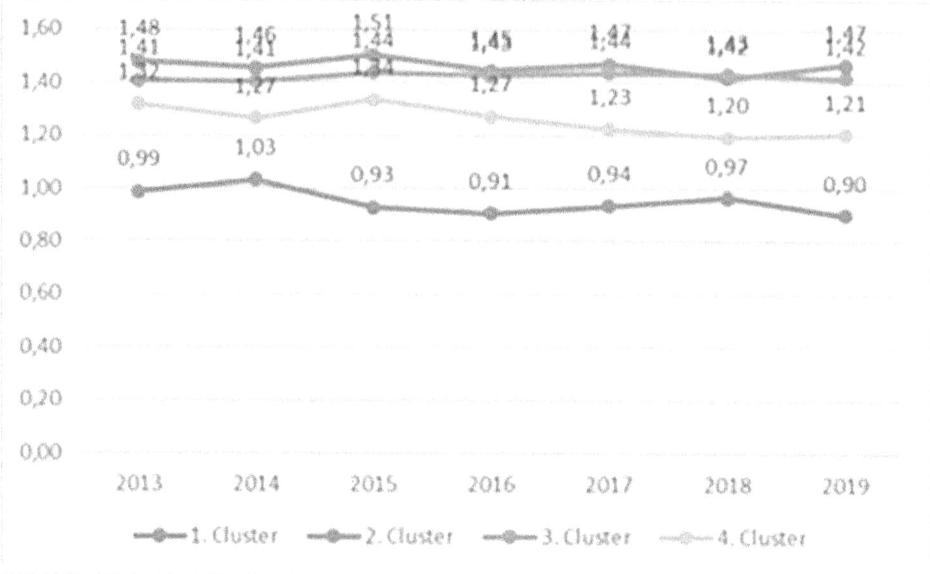

Figure 3 shows the course of ECI values according to clusters between 2013-2019. In this context, it is observed that ECI values in all clusters remain stable within the framework of values close to each other in clusters 2 and 3. On the other hand, while there is a significant decline in cluster 4, cluster 1 has the lowest values and follows a fluctuating course. In this framework, it would not be wrong to say that knowledge has gained more intensity in production in Continental Europe and Anglo_Saxon welfare regimes. In this context, Figure 4 is presented to show the general course of employment, which is an output plane of both STEM and ECI.

Figure 4. Employment rates trend by clusters from 2013 to 2019

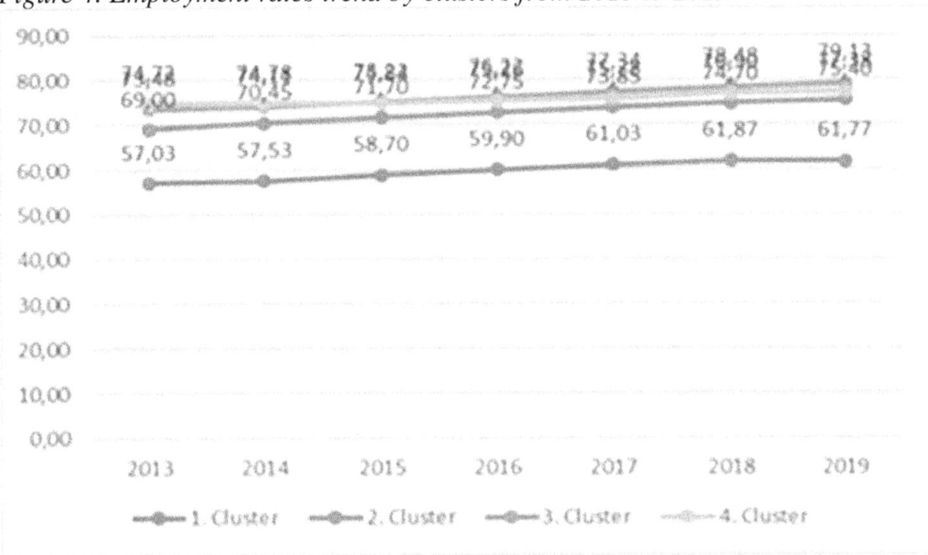

Figure 4 shows the course of employment rates by clusters between 2013-2019. In this context, it is observed that employment rates are on an increasing trend in all clusters. However, it is observed that the 1st cluster, in other words, the countries in the Southern Mediterranean welfare regime are further behind in terms of employment rates by differentiating from the others. In this context, Figure 5 is prepared and presented below to see the course of trade union density ratios, which are closely related to employment rates and reflect the efficiency potential of trade unions.

Figure 5. Trade union density ratiotrend by clusters from 2013 to 2019

Figure 5 shows the course of union density rates by clusters between 2013-2019. In this context, it is observed that union density ratios are on a downward trend in all clusters. However, it is also observed that the 4th cluster, in other words, the countries in the Scandinavian welfare regime, have maintained their power, albeit partially, by remaining at higher levels in terms of union density ratios by differentiating from the others. However, it is necessary to look at the correlation analysis of these indicators within the clusters in order to understand their relationship with union power. In this context, Table 5 is prepared and presented below.

Table 5. Correlation analysis of indicators in the framework of trade union density by clusters

Pearson Correlation	Trade Union Density (1. Cluster)	Trade Union Density (2. Cluster)	Trade Union Density (3. Cluster)	Trade Union Density (4. Cluster)
STEM	0,719	-0,787	-0,302	-0,916
ECI	-0,843	0,473	-0,686	0,879
Emp. Rate	0,776	-0,855	-0,92	-0,974

Table 5, prepared based on calculations using the averages of the trend values presented in Figures 2, 3, 4, and 5, presents the results of the Pearson correlation analysis revealing the relationship between union density, digital transformation (through STEM and ECI scores), and employment rates. Accordingly, in cluster 1, where the Southern Mediterranean welfare regime is dominant, there is a strong and direct relationship between union density and STEM and employment rates, while there is an inverse and strong relationship between ECI and union density. In this framework, as the STEM and employment rates increase in the Southern Mediterranean welfare regime, union density increases and it would not be wrong to say that human capital investment and employment provide an important basis for unions to gain strength in this process.

In the second cluster, where the liberal welfare regime is dominant, there is an inverse and strong relationship between union density and STEM and employment rates, while there is a direct and moderate relationship between union density and ECI, which refers to the stock of knowledge and skills in production. This indicates that in economies with a market welfare regime, unions should take a more active role in the development of labour-based skill policies to increase the ECI values of unions.

In cluster 3, which is dominated by the Corporatist-Statist welfare regime, where individualism is becoming more and more important, it is observed that all indicators have an inverse relationship with union density. In this context, it is observed that union density has a low inverse relationship with STEM, a medium relationship with ECI and a strong inverse relationship with employment rates. It would not be wrong to say that Continental Europe, which is undergoing a social transformation, has been dragged into a situation where information gains more importance in sophisticated production within the scope of reaching higher skilled labour capabilities with STEM and unions are increasingly excluded and losing power. This situation shows that trade unions need urgent action plans to revise themselves according to the requirements of the Digital Age.

Even in cluster 4, where the Social Democratic welfare regime, which sets an example for other countries in terms of the importance given to unions and labour, is dominated by the Scandinavian welfare regime, it is observed with the strong inverse relationship between union density and STEM and employment rates that the labour force, which reaches higher qualifications with STEM, moves away from unions in employment. On the other hand, the direct and strong relationship between union density and ECI in cluster 4 is quite striking. This situation shows that the key to the rise in ECI values is that policies to improve the labour-based skill stock have gained weight.

As can be understood from all these explanations, Table 5 essentially bases its comparison on clusters. Upon close examination of Table 5, prepared in line with this approach, it can be seen that some clusters show a positive relationship between STEM, economic complexity, employment rates and union density, while others show a negative relationship. The table also provides important information about the strength of this relationship. This situation essentially demonstrates that conditions vary across economies. Within this framework, it would not be inaccurate to state that each country's industrial relations system is affected by the digitalisation process in different ways, depending on its own socio-economic conditions. In this context, the adaptability of trade unions to the digitalisation process and the conditions for taking advantage of opportunities will also vary. Therefore, it is expected and desired that trade unions develop strategies and policies appropriate to the digitalisation process, as we will discuss in more detail in the conclusion section, and that they develop strategies tailored to the conditions of their own country and sector.

SOLUTIONS AND RECOMMENDATIONS

The digital transformation process, which is considered a development that is reshaping the world, inevitably has a serious impact on working life and industrial relations within this life, to the extent that it will reshape working life. Within the framework of this impact, the role of trade unions is of critical importance. Indeed, trade unions are expected to develop innovative approaches and strategies to protect and improve working life and peace during this process.

Countries that have embraced digitalisation have increased their production capacity and efficiency, with STEM playing a leading role in this development. STEM education, which refers to an integrative and innovative approach to education in science, technology, engineering, and mathematics, prepares students for the requirements and challenges of the 21st century (Mykolaivna, et al, 2024). In this context, STEM education not only enhances individual skills but also lays the groundwork for the formation of fundamental motivation in sophisticated production, thereby making significant contributions to economic development (Ncanywa, et al, 2021). Economic complexity, which reflects the knowledge used in a country's production based on sophisticated production, encourages the development of highly skilled workers trained in STEM education. This process enables the development of valuable economic sectors that contribute significantly to the country's growth. This situation essentially reveals the cyclical positive relationship between STEM, economic complexity, and human capital.

On the other hand, in today's world, which is being reshaped by digitalisation, positive developments in working life and industrial relations, as well as the spread of non-standard atypical work, are narrowing the sphere of influence of trade unions, which are becoming increasingly outdated and unable to keep pace with the times (Şahin & Balcı, 2020). From this point of view, the following recommendations should be made regarding the evolving role of trade unions in the digitalisation process;

1. **Digital Adaptation Process:** Trade unions should not oppose the undeniably developing digitalisation process, but rather stand alongside this constantly evolving and world-changing process (Trenerry, Chng, Wang, Lim, & Oh, 2022). Within this framework, trade unions will be able to incorporate digital usage areas into their organisational strategies through the digital adaptation process.
2. **Worker Council Derivatives-Representation:** As seen in the example of Germany (Thomas, 2022), the development of worker councils and their derivatives, which aim to improve the rights and interests of workers, will provide an important platform for gaining new members and will also increase the legitimacy of trade unions in terms of representation. This situation will enable trade unions to occupy an important position in the process of establishing rules for digitalisation, which is changing the world.
3. **New Member Potential**: With digitalisation, workers and freelancers working on digital platforms, which are increasing rapidly, are significantly narrowing the sphere of influence of trade unions (Webster & Ludwig, 2023). In this context, union organisation is critical both in terms of escaping this shrinking area and gaining new members. Within this framework, unions are expected to enter the digital adaptation process and develop current and sustainable strategies to gain new members in this area.
4. **Artificial Intelligence Integration::** Artificial intelligence and automation systems, which are at the centre of digitalisation in today's world, are of vital importance in the development processes within the framework of the changing role of trade unions (Kalbermatter, et al, 2021). With the use of artificial intelligence in union processes, employee expectations and member requests can be analysed more accurately, and artificial intelligence-supported future projections can be designed with more accurate statistics. In this context, the use of artificial intelligence and automation will contribute to union development and guide union organisation strategies in the right direction.
5. **Member Skills Development**: The development of digital skills, which is at the centre of the 21st century, also presents important opportunities for unions to develop their members in this direction. This will not only ensure the development of members but also support the digital transformation and adaptation process of trade unions. In this context, trade unions are expected to focus more on the education of their members and employment-enhancing policies in this direction in the coming period.

As can be understood from all these statements, the digitalisation process imposes responsibilities on trade unions in many ways, but it also offers important opportunities with the fulfilment of these responsibilities. In this context, it is considered that the most important strategic move for trade unions is to adapt to the process rather than resist digital transformation. In this context, it is important for trade unions to be open to digital change and to take action in line with the changes brought about by this transformation, to get involved in the field through structures such as workers' councils, to develop new trade union strategies that will enable workers on digital platforms to access trade union services, and to ensure the use of artificial intelligence throughout these processes. Another key aspect supporting and enhancing this development is the development of training programmes to enhance members' digital skills. It is anticipated and expected that unions that implement these strategies appropriately will expand their gains in the digital transformation process.

FUTURE RESEARCH DIRECTIONS

Trade unions, whose roots date back to the industrial revolution and which, in this sense, have a traditional structure, are seen as cumbersome structures that are struggling to survive today, with declining membership numbers and increasingly narrow areas of activity due to changes in the structure of industrial relations during the digital transformation process (Carneiro & Costa, 2022). (Lowey & Beadles, 2006). Within this framework, this study examines the changing role of trade unions in the digital transformation process, which is reshaping the structure of industrial relations and redesigning the modern world.

This study sheds light on a very limited area, and a review of the literature reveals that more research is needed in this field. In this context, examining different sectors separately within the constraints of different countries and identifying problem areas, as well as proposing innovative solutions to these problems, has the potential to contribute to both the field and trade union structures. In particular, the effects of digitalisation on trade unions should be carefully examined in the technology, health, education and service sectors, which are most affected by digitalisation. Analyses of these sectors, which are the driving force behind digitalisation, will provide important indicators for the development of the right strategies by ensuring the correct focus on the effects of digitalisation on trade unions. However, considering the different digitalisation processes in different countries, comparative industrial relations, as in the studies conducted by Payne, Llyod & Jose (2022) and Girley Rego & Keyser (2018), should be included to reveal the differences and similarities between countries and to gain a broader research field. Such comparative industrial relations will contribute to mitigating the negative consequences of both globalisation and digitalisation, which directly fuels globalisation, as well as providing important contributions to the strategic organisation of trade unions. It is necessary to focus on model critiques, such as the studies conducted by Bann &

Elsheikh (1976), which have the potential to reveal long-term strategies as the main focus of research. Such analyses, which reveal long-term predictive structures, are important for understanding the effects of digitalisation on trade unions, and there is a real need for such studies.

Close attention must be paid to the potential effects of artificial intelligence and automation technologies, which are at the core of the dynamics of digital transformation, on industrial relations. In this context, it is necessary to conduct in-depth research on the effects of these technologies on the labour market, human beings within the labour market, and trade unions, which exist in relation to them. In particular, innovative research aimed at reversing the damage caused by the increasing prevalence of non-standard work to trade union organisation will make a significant contribution to the survival of trade unions. In this context, policy recommendations based on research are of vital importance not only for industrial relations but also for societies as a whole. On the other hand, thanks to these policies, trade unions can better cope with digital adaptation processes and thus turn the crisis in the trade union structure into an opportunity. In this way, trade unions are expected to break away from their traditional and cumbersome structures and become dynamic and innovative structures as important representatives at the bargaining table in industrial relations.

Another issue is the need to develop the digital skills of trade unions, as highlighted in the joint study by Krzywdzinsk, Gerst & Butollo (2023). It is believed that the development of training programmes for digital skills will increase the digital adaptation capacity of trade unions and contribute to digital transformation. Indeed, strategies such as online training programmes and information meetings established through digital platforms have the potential to facilitate the training process and increase interaction with members. However, the lack of analysis on the effectiveness of these strategies in terms of trade union development creates a gap in this regard. In this context, it is important to conduct studies on the effectiveness of these training programmes. This will enable a clearer analysis of the situation of trade unions in the digital transformation process and the restructuring of problematic areas.

In conclusion, there is a need for a number of improvements that will contribute to the digital adaptation of trade unions in the digitalisation process and for various studies in different areas that will provide a basis for these improvements. In this context, it is crucial that researchers have access to data from the field. In this regard, it is necessary to closely examine sectors such as technology, health, and education, which are the driving forces of digitalisation, and to address the impact of digital transformation in these sectors on trade unions. Additionally, there is a need for strategies that enable the integration of artificial intelligence and autonomous technologies into trade union structures, and studies conducted in this direction are of great importance. Furthermore, examining trade union activities aimed at developing digital skills is another important area of work that will contribute to this process. As a result of these efforts and the right strategies, trade unions will be able to establish a solid foundation and become even more important structures in the digitalisation process.

CONCLUSION

This study examines the new role of trade unions in the digital transformation process from a strategic perspective, focusing on STEM, economic complexity within the framework of sophisticated production, and human capital as the building blocks of this process. Within this framework, the study examines the situation of trade unions in selected countries and analyses their status in various welfare regimes, reaching various conclusions.

STEM, which constitutes one of the central units of the digital transformation process, comes to the fore. STEM, which is at the centre of the process, prepares today's students, who will form the workforce of the future, for the challenges of the 21st century in various ways, such as critical thinking, analytical perspective, and collaboration skills. With all these qualities, STEM prepares today's students to become highly qualified individuals in the future workforce. In this sense, STEM contributes to economic development and digital transformation, as well as sophisticated production. On the other hand, economic development essentially reflects a country's production efficiency and knowledge structure, as well as a structure that encourages the development of a highly skilled workforce. This network of relationships reflects a contextual relationship that accelerates high value-added economies and the digitalisation process. Based on this point, the study examines digital transformation as a process and the role of trade unions within the interrelated structures of economic complexity and human capital, with STEM as the building blocks of this process.

When the impact of the digital transformation process on working life is evaluated within the framework of today's conditions, it is seen that the spread of gig economy and flexible working patterns has narrowed the scope of trade unions' activities, and that trade unions that are unable to adapt to today's conditions and thus exhibit a cumbersome structure are struggling to survive by losing their organisational power. In this context, trade unions that are currently facing difficulties must develop new strategies that will enable them to adapt to digitalisation rather than resisting it, and take advantage of the opportunities it offers in order to overcome the crisis they are experiencing in the digitalisation and globalisation process. However, it should not be overlooked that these strategies will vary according to each country and sector. With this perspective, a dataset was established for this study, including

OECD countries in Europe, where trade unions originated and developed, as the observation unit, with STEM, economic complexity index, trade union density, and employment rates defined as variables. As a result of the clustering analysis, which combined hierarchical and non-hierarchical clustering methods within the aforementioned data set, four distinct clusters emerged, and it was observed that these formations occurred according to various welfare regimes, albeit not in a one-to-one correspondence (in this context, Ireland is not defined as a liberal welfare regime in the literature, and Belgium is not defined as a social democratic welfare regime). The cluster formations are as follows:

First Cluster: Consisting of 3 observation units: Spain, Italy, and Türkiye.
Second Cluster: Consisting of 2 observation units: the United Kingdom and Ireland.
Third Cluster: Consisting of nine observation units: Austria, Czechia, Germany, Estonia, Latvia, Lithuania, the Netherlands, Slovakia, and Switzerland.
Fourth Cluster: Consisting of the observation units of Belgium, Denmark, Finland, Sweden, and Norway.

The results of the correlation analyses conducted based on trends and trend averages are as follows within the clusters:

- **Cluster 1 (Reflection of the Southern Mediterranean Welfare Regime):** In this cluster, which consists of three observation units, namely Spain, Italy and Turkey, there is a strong relationship between STEM education and employment rates, as well as a strong positive relationship between union density. This indicates that unions should play a role in STEM and employment-enhancing policies. On the other hand, in this cluster, where an inverse correlation is observed between the economic complexity index and union density, unions should focus on sophisticated production processes and develop innovative policies aimed at skill development training for their members in this context.
- **Cluster 2 (Reflection of the Liberal Welfare Regime):** In this cluster, consisting of two observation units, the United Kingdom and Ireland, an inverse relationship was found between STEM education and employment rates and union density, contrary to Cluster 1. This indicates that highly skilled workers do not tend to join unions. Therefore, it is necessary for trade unions in this cluster to better represent STEM workers and establish more optimal communication channels to address their needs. On the other hand, a positive relationship was found between economic complexity and union density in

cluster 2. This highlights the need to increase knowledge accumulation capacity to enable closer involvement in production processes.

- **Cluster 3 (Reflection of the Corporatist-State Welfare Regime):** In the third cluster, consisting of nine observation units (Austria, Czechia, Germany, Estonia, Latvia, Lithuania, the Netherlands, Slovakia, and Switzerland), an inverse relationship was found between STEM, economic complexity, employment rates, and union density. This situation indicates that trade unions in this cluster have deficiencies in their digital adaptation that require an emergency plan. In this context, it points to the need for trade unions operating in this cluster to develop new strategies to adapt to the digitalisation process.
- **Cluster 4 (Reflection of the Social Democratic Welfare Regime):** In Group 4, consisting of Belgium, Denmark, Finland, Sweden, and Norway, an inverse relationship was found between STEM education and employment rates and union density, similar to Group 2. This indicates that highly skilled workers have low unionisation tendencies. Therefore, trade unions in this cluster need to develop new strategies targeting highly skilled labour. On the other hand, trade unions in the third cluster, where there is a strong positive relationship between economic complexity and trade union density, demonstrate that they have developed appropriate strategies to enhance knowledge and skills capacity.

As can be understood from all these results, each country has its own unique socio-economic conditions. With appropriate strategies tailored to these levels, trade unions will be able to overcome the difficulties brought about by the digitalisation process and turn the crisis into an opportunity. In this context, trade unions must first and foremost adapt to digitalisation in order to take advantage of the opportunities it brings, rather than resisting it. In this context, artificial intelligence, automation technologies, and digital platforms should be integrated into the union process and activity structure so that member requests and suggestions can be taken into consideration through important analyses and policies can be developed. Furthermore, conducting continuous analyses using these technologies will provide important gains in this area. Furthermore, thanks to these technologies, new members can be gained in unexplored areas such as non-standard workplaces through an expansionist trade unionism approach, thereby supporting the organisation's power. In short, the use of digitalisation in trade union processes will contribute to the faster and more effective identification of the needs of both trade unions and their members, as well as to finding optimal solutions to meet these needs.

On the other hand, in order for trade unions to be successful in the digitalisation process, they need to increase their digital knowledge and skills. This indicates the need for training programmes that will enable trade union managers and members to use digital technologies effectively. Indeed, this is a necessity for trade unions to overcome the challenges posed by digitalisation. If this requirement is met, trade unions will have achieved digital adaptation. As a result, trade unions will become more accessible to their members and will be able to carry out service-oriented trade unionism more effectively. Furthermore, beyond online training, many new trade union activities, such as online collective bargaining, digital membership systems and online legal advice, will become accessible to both members and trade unions.

As can be understood from all these conclusions, for trade unions to survive in the digitalisation process, it is of great importance that they adopt an innovative approach, such as being open to digital transformation, implementing strategies appropriate to the conditions of the country and sector in which they operate, and utilising the benefits of digital technologies to open up new areas for themselves.

REFERENCES

Abonyi, J., & Feil, B. (2007). *Cluster analysis for data mining and system identification*. Birkhäuser.

Adhikary, S., & Banerjee, K. (2022). Digitalisation and AI: What does the future hold for labour union? GLOCALISM: Journal of Culture, *Politics and Innovation*, 1–29.

Alkan, A. D. (2022). The effects of COVID-19 on human resource management in aviation companies: The case of Europe. In *Digitalization and the Impacts of COVID-19 on the Aviation Industry* (pp. 225–242). IGI Global., DOI: 10.4018/978-1-6684-2319-6.ch012

Alpar, R. (2011). *Uygulamalı çok değişkenli istatistiki yöntemler* (3rd ed.). Detay Yayıncılık.

Bain, G. S., & Elsheikh, F. (1976). Trade union growth in Canada: A comment. *Relations industrielles. Relations Industrielles, 31*(3), 482–490. DOI: 10.7202/028730ar

Balcı, A., & Eraslan, E. (2023). GİG ekonomisi: Bibliyometrik bir analiz. *Sosyal Siyaset Konferansları Dergisi*, (85), 155–167.

Balcı, A. İ. (2024). *Uluslararası ticaretin serbestleşmesinin Türkiye işgücü piyasalarına etkisi: Beveridge eğrisi yardımıyla analiz* [Unpublished PhD thesis, İstanbul Üniversitesi]. Retrieved September 10, 2024, from https://tez.yok.gov.tr/UlusalTezMerkezi/tezSorguSonucYeni.jsp

Bijnens, G., Botelho, V., Falck, E., Labhard, V., Lamo, A., Röhe, O., & Strobel, J. (2024, January 11). *Digitalisation and productivity*. European Central Bank. https://www.ecb.europa.eu/pub/pdf/scpops/ecb.op339~f67b6981a9.en.pdf

Bottai, C., Di Lorio, J., & Lori, M. (2024). Reinterpreting economic complexity: A co-clustering. *Undefined*, 1–19. https://doi.org//arxiv.2406.16199DOI: 10.48550

Bucher, F., Scheu, L., & Schröpf, B. (2023). Economic complexity and environmental pollution: Evidence from the former socialist transition countries. *Empirica, 50*(3), 807–840. DOI: 10.1007/s10663-023-09575-y

Çakmak, Z., Uzgören, N., & Keçek, G. (2015). Kümeleme analizi teknikleri ile illerin kültürel yapılarına göre sınıflandırılması ve değişimlerinin incelenmesi. *Dumlupınar Üniversitesi Sosyal Bilimler Dergisi*, (12).

Canh, N. P., Schinckus, C., & Thanh, D. S. (2020). The natural resources rents: Is economic complexity a solution for resource curse? *Resources Policy, 69*, 101800. Advance online publication. DOI: 10.1016/j.resourpol.2020.101800

Carneiro, B., & Costa, H. A. (2022). Digital unionism as a renewal strategy? Social media use by trade union confederations. *The Journal of Industrial Relations*, *64*(1), 26–51. DOI: 10.1177/0022185620979337

Degryse, C. (2016). *Digitalisation of the economy and its impact on labour markets*. European Trade Union Institute: Working Paper, 1–81.

Diamond, W. J., & Freeman, R. B. (2001). *Will unionism prosper in cyberspace? The promise of the internet for employee organization*. National Bureau of Economic Research.

Dieuaide, P., & Azaïs, C. (2020). Platforms of work, labour, and employment relationship: The grey zones of a digital governance. *Frontiers in Sociology*, *5*(2), 2. Advance online publication. DOI: 10.3389/fsoc.2020.00002 PMID: 33869411

Drokına, A. (2024). STEM education as an effective way to implement the key provisions. *Education. Innovation.Practice*, *12*(3), 20–25. DOI: 10.31110/2616-650X-vol12i3-003

Eurostat. (2024, December 15). Graduates in tertiary education, in science, math., computing, engineering, manufacturing, construction, by sex - per 1000 of population aged 20-29. https://ec.europa.eu/eurostat/databrowser/view/EDUC_UOE_GRAD04/default/table?lang=en

Fiorito, J., Jarley, P., & Delaney, J. T. (2000). The adoption of information technology by U.S. national unions. *Relations industrielles. Industrial Relations*, *55*(3), 451–476. DOI: 10.7202/051328ar

Gerhard, B., & Schmitz-Kießler, J. (2020). Shaping Industry 4.0 – An experimental approach developed by German trade unions. *Transfer: European Review of Labour and Research*, *26*(2), 189–206. DOI: 10.1177/1024258920918480

Girley, F. K., Rego, R., & Keyser, E. (2018). The revitalisation of the labour movement in Nigeria, Egypt, South Africa, Algeria and Angola: The use of ICT. *Archives of & Anthropology Open Access*, *2*(4), 245–257. DOI: 10.31031/AAOA.2018.02.000541

Haake, G. (2017). Trade unions, digitalisation and the self-employed: Inclusion or exclusion? *Transfer: European Review of Labour and Research*, *23*(1), 63–66. DOI: 10.1177/1024258916679580

Harvard Growth Lab. (2024, December 15). Economic complexity index (ECI) rankings. https://atlas.cid.harvard.edu/rankings

Hidalgo, C., & Hausmann, R. (2009). The building blocks of economic complexity. *Proceedings of the National Academy of Sciences of the United States of America*, *106*(26), 10570–10575. DOI: 10.1073/pnas.0900943106 PMID: 19549871

Hoeriyah, L., Nuryartono, N., & Pasaribu, S. H. (2022). Economic complexity and sustainable growth in developing countries. *Economics Development Analysis Journal*, *1*(1), 23–33. DOI: 10.15294/edaj.v11i1.47294

Hu, Y., Fan, Z., Lin, J. Y., & Xu, M. (2023). A reasoning of economic complexity based on simulated general equilibrium international trade model. *Journal of Physics. Complexity*, *4*(3), 39. Advance online publication. DOI: 10.1088/2632-072X/ace39e

Kalbermatter, J., Schaupp, S., Hartleitner, V., & Naxhtwey, O. (2021). *Unions in the postal services of the future: A global survey on labour union representatives' assessment of digitalization in the post and logistics sector*. Basel Working Papers in Sociology, 1–31.

Karagöz, Y. (2016). *SPSS ve AMOS23 uygulamalı istatistiksel analizler* (1st ed.). Nobel Akademik Yayıncılık.

Krzywdzinski, M., Gerst, D., & Butollo, F. (2023). Promoting human-centred AI in the workplace: Trade unions and their strategies for regulating the use of AI in Germany. *Transfer: European Review of Labour and Research*, *29*(1), 53–70. DOI: 10.1177/10242589221142273

Lapatinas, A. (2019). The effect of the Internet on economic sophistication: An empirical analysis. *Economics Letters*, *174*, 35–38. DOI: 10.1016/j.econlet.2018.10.013

Lima, J. C., & Bridi, M. A. (2019). Trabalho digital e emprego: A reforma trabalhista e o aprofundamento da precariedade. *Caderno CRH*, *32*(86), 325–341. DOI: 10.9771/ccrh.v32i86.30561

Lowey, C. M., & Beadles, N. A.II. (2006). Evaluating the usability of union websites in the United States: A case study. *Communications of the IIMA*, *6*(2), 97–104. DOI: 10.58729/1941-6687.1316

Metall, I. G. (2019). *Transformationsatlas wesentliche Ergebnisse*. IG Metall Vorstand.

Mykolaivna, Z. O., Oleksandrivna, M. I., & Hennadyyovych, R. F. (2024). STEM as an integral part of the science education curriculum. *Актуальні питання у сучасній науції*, 8(26), 748–758. https://doi.org/DOI: 10.52058/2786-6300-2024-8(26)

Ncanywa, T., Mongale, I. P., Ralarala, O., Letsoalo, T. E., & Molele, B. S. (2021). Economic complexity to boost the selected sub-Saharan African economies. *Journal of Economic and Financial Sciences*, *14*(1), 567. Advance online publication. DOI: 10.4102/jef.v14i1.567

Nissim, G., & Simon, T. (2021). The future of labor unions in the age of automation and at the dawn of AI. *Technology in Society*, *67*, 101739. Advance online publication. DOI: 10.1016/j.techsoc.2021.101732

Nowik, P. (2023). Algorithmic management in the work environment: Responsible interaction between the employer, technology supplier and trade union. *Krytyka Prawa*, 80–94. DOI: 10.7206/kp.2080-1084.640

Organisation for Economic Co-operation and Development (OECD). (2024, December 15). Trade union density. https://data-explorer.oecd.org/vis?df[ds]=DisseminateFinalDMZ&df[id]=DSD_TUD_CBC@DF_TUD&df[ag]=OECD.ELS.SAE&dq=.&pd=,&to[TIME_PERIOD]=false&vw=tb

Payne, J., Lloyd, C., & Jose, S. P. (2022). "They tell us after they've decided things": A cross-country analysis of unions and digitalisation in retail. *Industrial Relations Journal*, *54*(1), 3–19. DOI: 10.1111/irj.12390

Robinson, B. (2006). Cybersolidarity: Internet-based campaigning and trade union internationalism. In *Social Inclusion: Societal and Organizational Implications for Information Systems: IFIP TC8 WG8.2 International Working Conference* (pp. 123–135). Springer.

Şahin, L., & Balcı, A. İ. (2020). Yeni düzende sendikaların örgütlenme yapısındaki değişim: Genel ve özel nedenler üzerinden bir değerlendirme. In Yılmaz, B. (Ed.), *Çalışma hayatının geleceği* (pp. 458–504). Gazi Kitabevi.

Shahzad, U., Fareed, Z., Shahzad, F., & Shahzad, K. (2021). Investigating the nexus between economic complexity, energy consumption and ecological footprint for the United States. *Journal of Cleaner Production*, *279*, 123806. Advance online publication. DOI: 10.1016/j.jclepro.2020.123806

Subekti, M. J., & Sari, D. W. (2024). The influence of economic complexity index on income inequality in G20 forum countries. *Jurnal Ilmu Ekonomi Terapan*, *9*(1), 137–150. DOI: 10.20473/jiet.v9i1.57677

Thomas, H. (2022). Trade unions and digitalisation in Germany. *Cuadernos de Relaciones Laborales*, *40*(2), 301–323. DOI: 10.5209/crla.78214

Trenerry, B., Chng, S., Wang, Y., Lim, S., & Oh, P. H. (2022). Mobilising workers via digital means: Reinventing trade unions for the digital age. *Singapore Labour Journal*, 6–19.

Uçar, N. (2017). Kümeleme analizi. In Kalaycı, Ş. (Ed.), *SPSS uygulamalı çok değişkenli istatistik teknikleri* (8th ed., pp. 350–376). Dinamik Akademi.

Van Dam, A., & Frenken, K. (2020). Variety, complexity and economic development. Research Policy. *Article, 103949*. Advance online publication. DOI: 10.1016/j.respol.2020.103949

Webster, E., & Ludwig, C. (2023). Contesting digital technology through new forms of transnational activism. *Global Labour Journal, 14*(1), 36–71. DOI: 10.15173/glj.v14i1.5022

World Economic Forum. (2023). *Future of jobs report*. World Economic Forum.

ADDITIONAL READING

Bogg, A. (2016). Beyond Neo-Liberalism: The Trade Union Act 2016 and the Authoritarian State. *Industrial Law Journal, 45*(3), 299–366. DOI: 10.1093/indlaw/dww023

Mahiroğulları, A. (2016). *Dünyada ve Türkiye'de Sendikacılık* (3. b.). Ekin Yayınevi.

Moore, W. J., & Newman, R. J. (1975). On the prospects for American trade union growth: A cross-section analysis. *The Review of Economics and Statistics, 57*(4), 435–445. DOI: 10.2307/1935903

Şenkal, A. (2015). *Sosyal Boyutuyla Bilgi Ekonomisi ve Emek* (1. b.). Umuttepe Yayınları.

Sundar, S. K. (2007). Trade unions and civil society: Issues and strategies. *Indian Journal of Industrial Relations, 42*(4), 713–734.

KEY TERMS AND DEFINITIONS

Digitalisation: A series of processes that enable analogue data to be read by machine units and gradually shift production and social life towards the use of such technology.

Employment: In the narrow sense, it refers to the inclusion of labour, one of the factors of production, in the production process, and in the broad sense, it refers to the inclusion of all factors of production in the production process.

Industrial Relations: It is an economic concept that is carried out individually or collectively in the relations between workers and employers in the context of production and has wage bargaining, trade unions and welfare at its centre.

Labour Economics: A branch of economics that deals with all elements of the labour market. In this framework, it is an economic concept that contributes to the welfare of both the employee and the country.

Social Policy: It refers to the whole set of policies implemented by the state to ensure social welfare and social protection.

Sustainable Development: Meeting the needs of future generations by establishing a balance between human and nature and taking into account the consumption of future generations.

Sustainable Growth: Refers to the development endeavour covering the long term to ensure the continuity of the economy.

Trade Union: An organisation formed by a group of people with common interests in working life to protect and defend their interests.

About the Contributors

Andrés Jerónimo Arenas Falótico is a distinguished academic and professional with a rich background in business and management. He earned his Doctorate in Management from the Universidad de Almería, and also holds a Master in Business Administration (MBA) from St. Thomas University and a Master in Education from Universidad Camilo José Cela. He began his academic journey with a Law degree from Universidad Santa María. He was serving as a Professor and Coordinator at the Universidad Antonio de Nebrija, where he was deeply involved in fostering relationships with businesses. Prior to Nebrija, he has held various positions at esteemed institutions such as Universidad del Itsmo, Universidad Europea de Madrid, ESIC, Universidad Nacional Experimental Politécnica de la Fuerza Armada Nacional, and Universidad Santa María. Dr. Arenas Falótico has made significant academic contributions in his field. His research interests include organizational behavior, human resources, entrepreneurship, and international business. He has published several works, including "Various perspectives of labor and human resources challenges and changes due to automation and artificial intelligence." and "Effects of Remote Working in Fortune 500 Global Companies". In recognition of his outstanding work, he has been honored with the Best Teaching Practice Award by SEK Schools1 and has been named a Senior Fellow of the Higher Education Academy in the U.K. His dedication to his field is further demonstrated by his recognition in Miami, Florida, where a day has been dedicated in his honor. Dr. Arenas Falótico's extensive experience and expertise make him an excellent candidate for the editor of a book on new technologies applied to business and management. His deep understanding of the subject matter, combined with his commitment to academic excellence, will undoubtedly result in a valuable contribution to the field. He was nominated, in 2024, for best university proffesor in Spain by the EDUCA Foundation, and received an award by the City Mayor, Isabel Díaz Ayuso, in Madrid. His efforts to translate scientific knowledge into concepts accessible to the general public have led him, for over three years, to host the program "Meta Empresas Inc." on Capital

Radio, featuring insightful interviews with researchers, university professors, and rectors from leading Spanish universities.

Jessica Bayón Pérez is a highly respected academic and professional with a strong background in human resources, business and management. Dr. Bayón Pérez has made significant academic contributions in her field. Her research interests include labor trends, the future of work through robotization, digitalization, and artificial intelligence in Spain. She has published several works, including "Fundamentos de estrategia", "El teletrabajo: avances y retos dentro de la sociedad actual", and "Talento humano y cambio organizacional en empresas de telecomunicación: Madrid-España" among others. In recognition of her outstanding work, she has been honored with the Gold Medal for Professional Trajectory by the European Association of Economy and Competitiveness. Her dedication to her field is further demonstrated by her role as a member of the advisory board of the Ethos Journal. Dr. Bayón Pérez's extensive experience and expertise make her an excellent candidate for the co-editor of a book on new technologies applied to business and management. Her deep understanding of the subject matter, combined with her commitment to academic excellence, will undoubtedly result in a valuable contribution to the field.

***

Zyed Achour is a dedicated scholar-researcher, holding a PhD in Management Science and serving as an assistant professor at the National Institute of Labor and Social Studies, University of Carthage. A research associate at the GEF2A Laboratory of the Higher Institute of Management, University of Tunis, he brings over 20 years of experience in higher education and research. His research spans broad themes, including corporate social responsibility, sustainability, labor sciences, trade unionism, gender diversity, finance, human resource management, and strategic management. As an author of numerous scientific articles and a contributor to several collective works,

Manmeet Kaur Arora is a Research Scholar at the School of Law, Sharda University, Greater Noida. She is a graduate of Law and has completed her Master's in Law from Amity University, Noida. Manmeet Kaur is a qualified Company Secretary Executive Programme. She has over 8+ years of Industry Experience and 1 year of experience as an Associate at a reputed IPR Law Firm. Manmeet Kaur has attended 20+ National & International Conferences, Webinars, Seminars, Symposiums, and Paper Presentations and participated in 5+ Faculty Development programs. She has over 50+ publications in various esteemed Journals and Books.

She is active at the Family Dispute Resolution Clinic, Meditation Centre, Greater Noida. Manmeet Kaur has a keen interest in the areas of Corporate Law, Intellectual Property Rights, Insolvency, Artificial Intelligence, Machine Learning, and Blockchain Technology.

Ali İhsan Balcı completed his undergraduate education at Istanbul University, Department of Labor Economics and Industrial Relations between 2009-2014. He received his master's degree (2017) from Istanbul University, Institute of Social Sciences, in the field of Labour Economics and Industrial Relations. He completed his PhD degree at Istanbul University, Institute of Social Sciences, Department of Labor Economics and Industrial Relations. Since 2015, Balcı has been working as a research assistant at Zonguldak Bülent Ecevit University, Faculty of Economics and Administrative Science, Labour Economics and Industrial Relations Programme. Balcı works in the fields of social policy, disadvantaged groups, labor economics and ındustrial relations.

Sandip Dey was an Associate Professor and the HOD with the Department of Computer Science and Engineering, Global Institute of Management and Technology, India. He worked as an Assistant Professor in OmDayal Group of Institution and Camellia Institute of Technology for several years. Before that he worked as a Lecturer in Narula Institute of Technology. He is currently an Assistant Professor in the Department of Computer Science, Sukanta Mahavidyalaya, Jalpaiguri. He has coauthored one book titled "Quantum-Inspired Metaheuristics for Image Analysis"; Publisher: John Wiley & Sons, UK, coedited three books, and authored or coauthored about 60 research publications in international journals, book chapters, and conference proceedings. His research interests include soft computing, hybrid intelligence, quantum computing, and image analysis. Dey reviewed several international peer-reviewed journals like Applied Soft Computing, Swarm and Evolutionary Computation, Information Sciences, Journal of Computational Science, Engineering Applications of Artificial Intelligence, Expert Systems With Applications, Advanced Engineering Informatics, IEEE Transactions on Signal Processing and so on.

Ersin Eraslan completed his undergraduate education at Karadeniz Technical University, Department of Labor Economics and Industrial Relations between 2001-2005. He received master's degree (2015) from Nigde Ömer Halisdemir University, Institute of Social Sciences, in the field of Production Management and Marketing. He completed his PhD degree at İstanbul University,, Institute of Social Sciences, Department of Labor Economics and Industrial Relations between 2017-2022. Since 2023, PhD Eraslan has been working as a assistant professor at Niğde Ömer

Halisdemir University, Niğde Social Sciences Vocational School, Social Security Programme. PhD Eraslan works in the fields of social policy, disadvantaged groups, labor economics and ındustrial relations.

Laura Gómez García is a distinguished expert in criminology and law, earning her Doctorate in Law Cum Laude from the University of Castilla-La Mancha in 2019. She currently serves as the Director of the Master's Program in Criminalistics at the Francisco de Vitoria University, where she focuses on academic excellence and advanced research. Her academic background includes a Bachelor's degree in Criminology from the University of Alicante and a specialization in security sciences, criminological intervention, and victimology from the Miguel Hernández University (2017). Additionally, she has completed advanced studies in mediation, further strengthening her multidisciplinary profile. An active researcher, Dr. Gómez García participates in various research groups and projects. Among her most notable contributions is her involvement in the Road Criminology Observatory Working Group (2018), the creation of the Road Criminology Working Group of the Professional College of Criminology of Madrid (2019), and her engagement with the Stable Research Group in Criminology at Francisco de Vitoria University (since 2020). She is also a member of the Research Group of the R&D Department at the Canary Institute of Criminological Analysis (since 2022) and serves on the Advisory Committee of the Organized Crime Observatory at Francisco de Vitoria University. Her academic career includes international research stays, such as her time at the International University of Ecuador (2020). In addition, she acts as a peer reviewer for several scientific societies and professional associations, including the Logos Scientific Journal of the Civil Guard University Center. Dr. Gómez García has published extensively on criminology and victimology. Among her most significant publications is the article "Harassment, Aggression, Violence, and Road Safety from a Criminological Perspective", published in the Academicus International Scientific Journal (2023), as well as various chapters in the "Handbook of Victimology" (2019). These works explore critical topics such as victimization and de-victimization processes, secondary victimization, and strategies for prevention, assistance, and victim compensation. Her doctoral thesis, titled "The Legal Protection of the Rights of Road Victims Who Have Suffered a Crime Committed with a Motor Vehicle" (2019), provides an in-depth analysis of the current legal framework protecting victims of road crimes and proposes reforms to improve intervention and public assistance systems. In addition to her academic and research activities, Dr. Gómez García plays a crucial role in training future professionals and serving as a judicial expert, actively contributing to the advancement of criminology and law.

Javier Enríquez Román, who holds a PhD in Journalism from the Complutense University of Madrid with a dissertation on "Digital Communication in New Social Movements," is currently a professor and researcher at Nebrija University. His work spans areas such as business, international relations, political science, and security. He has published several scientific articles and book chapters in international journals and publishing houses.

Christian Kaunert is Professor of International Security at Dublin City University, Ireland. He is also Professor of Policing and Security, as well as Director of the International Centre for Policing and Security at the University of South Wales. In addition, he is Jean Monnet Chair, Director of the Jean Monnet Centre of Excellence and Director of the Jean Monnet Network on EU Counter-Terrorism

Sahil Lal is a Research Scholar at School of Law, Sharda University. He pursued his graduation from National Law University, Lucknow and completed his Master's in Law from Gujarat National Law University, Gandhinagar. Sahil has completed a certificate course on 'AI & Law' from Lund University, Sweden and on 'Cyber Law' from Indian Law Institute, New Delhi. Sahil Lal is a qualified UGC-NET & JRF candidate. He has a 10+ year Industry Experience and is an active member of Family Dispute Resolution Clinic, Mediation Center, Greater Noida. Sahil has attended 20+ International & National Conferences along with Paper Presentation and has also participated in more than 5+ Faculty Development Programme. Mr. Sahil has more than 50+ publications in various esteemed Journals & Books. Mr. Sahil has a keen interest in area of Artificial Intelligence, Machine Learning, Robotics, Block-Chain Technology and Intellectual Property Rights.

Roberto Alejandro Llauró is a business consultant, professor, and researcher specializing in management sciences, technology, and international business. He holds a PhD in Management Sciences from UADE and has taught at universities in Argentina, the U.S., and Latin America. As an author, he has published research on e-commerce, artificial intelligence, and business strategy. He is also a conference speaker and has contributed to academic journals and professional organizations worldwide.

Bhupinder Singh working as Professor at Sharda University, India. Also, Honorary Professor in University of South Wales UK and Santo Tomas University Tunja, Colombia. His areas of publications as Smart Healthcare, Medicines, fuzzy logics, artificial intelligence, robotics, machine learning, deep learning, federated learning, IoT, PV Glasses, metaverse and many more. He has 3 books, 139 paper publications, 163 paper presentations in international/national conferences and seminars, participated in more than 40 workshops/FDP's/QIP's, 25 courses from international universities of repute, organized more than 59 events with international and national academicians and industry people's, editor-in-chief and co-editor in journals, developed new courses. He has given talks at international universities, resource person in international conferences such as in Nanyang Technological University Singapore, Tashkent State University of Law Uzbekistan; KIMEP University Kazakhstan, All'ah meh Tabatabi University Iran, the Iranian Association of International Criminal law, Iran and Hague Center for International Law and Investment, The Netherlands, Northumbria University Newcastle UK,

Index

A

C

D

E

F

G

H

I

J

L

M

O

P

R

S

T

U

V

W

www.ingramcontent.com/pod-product-compliance
Lightning Source LLC
LaVergne TN
LVHW080613300926
849162LV00005B/1143
* 9 7 9 8 3 6 9 3 8 0 4 9 9 *